C0-BPX-494

JERUSALEM AND BABYLON

SUPPLEMENTS TO
VIGILIAE CHRISTIANAE

Formerly Philosophia Patrum

TEXTS AND STUDIES OF EARLY CHRISTIAN LIFE AND LANGUAGE

VOLUME 14

Woodcut from: Augustinus De Civitate Dei cum commento [Thomae Valois et Nicolai Trivet], Basel, Johann Amerbach, 1489.

JERUSALEM AND BABYLON

A STUDY INTO AUGUSTINE'S *CITY OF GOD* AND THE SOURCES OF HIS DOCTRINE OF THE TWO CITIES

BY

JOHANNES VAN OORT

E.J. BRILL
LEIDEN · NEW YORK · KØBENHAVN · KÖLN
1991

Library of Congress Cataloging-in-Publication Data

Oort, J. van (Johannes)
Jerusalem and Babylon: a study into Augustine's City of God and the sources of his doctrine of the two cities / by Johannes van Oort.
p. cm.—(Supplements to Vigiliae Christianae, ISSN 0920-623X; v. 14)
Originally presented in Dutch as the author's thesis (doctoral)—University of Utrecht, 1986.
Includes bibliographical references and indexes.
ISBN 90-04-09323-0
1. Augustine, Saint, Bishop of Hippo. De civitate Dei.
2. Kingdom of God. 3. Apologetics—Early church, ca. 30-600.
4. Philosophy, Ancient. 5. Theology—Early church, ca. 30-600.
I. Title. II. Series.
BR65.A65052 1990
239'.3—dc20 90-24319
CIP

ISSN 0920-623X
ISBN 90 04 09323 0

PRINTED IN THE NETHERLANDS

To Ineke
To Gerdiene and Hans-Willem

CONTENTS

CHAPTER THREE

THE *CITY OF GOD* AS AN APOLOGY AND A CATECHETICAL WORK

CHAPTER FOUR

SOURCES OF AUGUSTINE'S DOCTRINE OF THE TWO CITIES

PREFACE

This book is the English version of my doctoral thesis, which was originally submitted to the Theological Faculty of the University of Utrecht in September 1986 and published in Dutch ('s-Gravenhage 1986, second and third impressions 1987). Although new studies important to this subject have appeared since the completion of my research in January 1986—such as Samuel N.C. Lieu's book on Manichaeism, Kenneth B. Steinhauser's dissertation on Tyconius' *Apocalypse Commentary* and the first fascicles of the *Augustinus-Lexikon* —I decided after due consideration to leave the text virtually unchanged. Revision would have mainly meant a supplementation of the material, but no essential change in the conclusions.

It gives me pleasure to thank my 'Doktorvater' Prof. Gilles Quispel again for his constant interest and assistance. In the course of a number of years I have gained very much from his stimulating scholarship.

Now that, over four years later, I am again writing a preface to this study, I think back with gratitude to the valuable suggestions made by Prof. T.J. van Bavel OSA, pre-eminent authority in the field of Augustine research, and to the advice and constructive criticism given by Prof. R. van den Broek, Prof. C. Graafland, Prof. J.H. Waszink and Prof. J.C.M. van Winden.

That the preparation of this English edition would require a number of years was something I did not anticipate. For seeing the work through to its completion, my thanks are above all due to Mrs. Caroline Bor-Brentlinger. It was she who persevered with me until a result was achieved that was satisfactory to both of us. Thanks are also due to Dr. A. Bor, who did substantial groundwork, and to Mr. Aart van den End, who assisted during Mrs. Bor's stay in the U.S. The entire undertaking was made possible by the financial support of the Netherlands Organization for Scientific Research (NWO).

My gratitude also goes to Mrs. Corry Blijleven for her diligence in reproducing the text and notes on her word processor. For the final processing I am indebted to the office staff of the University of Utrecht Faculty of Theology, especially Marc Rietveld, Martin Hollander, Winfried Keydener, and to Ing. Hans Zimmer.

Finally, it is a pleasure for me to dedicate the English edition as well to my wife Ineke, and to our daughter and son.

Utrecht/Zeist, Summer 1990

CHAPTER ONE

INTRODUCTION

1. Importance of Augustine

Augustine is a Father of the Church who has exerted an unparallelled influence. Sixteen centuries separate him from us, but that long period is not an empty space. The illustrious bishop from Roman Africa has become an inspiration to nearly every subsequent generation.

Already in his lifetime Augustine's spiritual leadership was recognized. Evidence of this can be found, for example, in his extensive and largely preserved correspondence. Jerome, the other great Father of the Church at the end of the fourth and the beginning of the fifth century, referred in this correspondence to Augustine's world-wide fame and even stated that he was honoured and accepted as the second founder of the ancient faith[1]. Augustine's authority is not less clearly illustrated by the large number of his major and minor works, nearly all of which were composed in reaction to actual problems. Also his great work the *City of God* was in the first instance a response to a far-reaching event and to the questions that arose in its wake.

In the following centuries as well, the bishop of Hippo was referred to approvingly again and again as *Augustinus magister*[2]. His influence, from the early Middle Ages, through Scholasticism, Humanistic and Reformational traditions and the heightened attention in the seventeenth century, has extended to the present[3]. Today he

---

[1] *Ep.* 195: 'Macte virtute in orbe celebraris. Catholici te conditorem antiquae rursum fidei venerantur atque suscipiunt ...'.

[2] G. Bardy, 'Post Apostolos Ecclesiarum Magister', *RMAL* 6 (1950) 313-316; P. Courcelle, 'A propos du titre «Augustinus Magister». Le «maître» Augustin', *AM*, III, 9-11. G. Folliet provided three more examples in 'Pour le dossier «Augustinus Magister»', *REA* 3 (1957) 67-68.

[3] For a description of his influence, see the sketch in H.-I. Marrou (avec la collaboration de A.-M. La Bonnardière), *St Augustin et l'augustinisme*, Paris 1955,

still fascinates Christians and non-Christians, philosophers and theologians, men of letters and other artists. His significance to the Church and through it to our culture cannot be easily overestimated. There is much truth in Harnack's lyrical statement: 'Er war ein Baum, gepflanzt an den Wasserbächen, dessen Blätter nicht verwelken und auf dessen Zweigen die Vögel des Himmels wohnen'[4].

In Augustine Western patristic theology, and possibly even the whole of the patristic period, reaches its undisputed zenith[5]. He also bestrides the boundary between Antiquity and the Middle Ages[6], bringing the tradition of Christian doctrine to a provisional close. It is understandable, therefore, that in books describing the history of Christian dogma *this* Father of the Church is depicted as a pivotal figure: there has been a pre-[7] and a post-Augustinian development. It is in this way that Harnack in his *Lehrbuch* assigns Augustine a central position, that Loofs' *Leitfaden* devotes a considerable number of paragraphs to Augustine and Augustinianism[8] and

147-180. It is regrettable that in his portrayal of 'Augustinianism' Marrou devoted little attention to the relationship between A. and the Reformation in the 16th century; see also the criticism by H. von Campenhausen, *Lateinische Kirchenväter*, Stuttgart 1978[4], 222.

[4] A. von Harnack, *Lehrbuch der Dogmengeschichte*, III, Tübingen 1910[4] (repr. Darmstadt 1964), 65.

[5] His counterpart for the East was Origen, whose writings were even more extensive. But A.'s influence on Church and world history is generally considered more profound. In *Augustins Konfessionen*, Giessen 1888, and *Reden und Aufsätze*, I, Giessen 1906[2], 53, Harnack was of the opinion that except for Paul and Luther there had been no figure in the Christian Church of Augustine's stature. Harnack went a step further in his *Aus Wissenschaft und Leben*, II, Giessen 1911, 20: '... der Mann, der überhaupt in der Antike und in der Kirchengeschichte nicht seinesgleichen gehabt hat ...'.

[6] In *Augustin, die christliche Antike und das Mittelalter* ..., München-Berlin 1915, E. Troeltsch saw him especially as the one who had brought the preceding period to completion: 'Er ist in Wahrheit Abschluss und Vollendung der christlichen Antike, ihr letzter und grösster Denker, ihr geistlicher Praktiker und Volkstribun' (6-7). From *DCD* Troeltsch took his evidence for A.'s being part of Christian antiquity (7), but he also saw the strong influence that A. exerted on later centuries. Particular attention was paid to A.'s place in history by R. Reitzenstein, 'Augustin als antiker und als mittelalterlicher Mensch', *Vorträge der Bibliothek Warburg*, II, 1, Leipzig-Berlin 1924, 28-65. See also A. Sizoo, 'Augustinus op de grens der oude en der nieuwe wereld', in: A. Sizoo and D. Nauta, *Augustinus. Redevoeringen (...) 1954*, Kampen 1954, 5-21.

[7] Particularly Harnack, *Lehrbuch*, III, 12-59, described preceding Western theology as a 'Vorstufe' of A.: Tertullian was little more than a precursor, Jerome and especially Ambrose served as links between the Greek fathers and A., Marius Victorinus was important for having brought A. into direct contact with Neoplatonism.

[8] F. Loofs, *Leitfaden zum Studium der Dogmengeschichte*, Tübingen 1968[7] (hrsg. von K. Aland), 265-363.

that elsewhere, too, this church father is given a prominent place. He resembles a lens that on the one side collects the rays of light and on the other side sends them out in all directions[9].

Thus Augustine is a point of reference for his own era and for the centuries following him. At the same time he constitutes a link that naturally connects the traditions of Roman Catholicism and the Reformation. To this very day he has remained a spiritual power[10]. No wonder, then, that in the course of the centuries a truly immense flood of writings has appeared on his person, his thinking and his influence. In particular, the last few decades have witnessed a rapid increase in the number of publications. Special periodicals, series and bibliographies have become necessary to record the material[11]. And above all there has been an increase in publications on specific aspects[12].

---

9 See also C. Andresen (Hrsg.), *Zum Augustin-Gespräch der Gegenwart*, I, Darmstadt 1975², 6.

10 Cf. O.J. de Jong, *Geschiedenis der Kerk*, Nijkerk 1980¹⁰, 69: 'His influence on theological thinking has remained so strong that he is only comparable to the apostle Paul'.

11 The following publications are indispensable for conducting scholarly research on A. Journals: *Ciudad*, El Escorial-Madrid 1881 ff.; *Aug. (L)*, Heverlee-Louvain 1951 ff.; *Aug.*, Roma 1961 ff. and especially *REA*, Paris 1955 ff., the continuation of *L'Année théologique (augustinienne)*, Paris 1940-1954. Series: *RA*, Paris 1958 ff., supplements to *REA*. Bibliographies: T. van Bavel – F. van der Zande, *Répertoire bibliographique de saint Augustin 1950-1960*, Steenbrugge-Den Haag 1963 (an outstanding survey of c. 4000 publications from that decade); C. Andresen, *Bibliographia Augustiniana*, Darmstadt 1973²; W. Schneemelcher, *Bibliographia Patristica*, Berlin 1959 ff., and the *Bulletin Augustinien*, which appears annually in the *REA* and is almost complete. Of particular importance for *DCD* is also J.M. del Estal, 'Historiografía de la «Ciudad de Dios». De 1928 a 1954', *Ciudad*, II, 647-774. The work by E. Nebreda, *Bibliographia Augustiniana*, Roma 1928, is, to quote its own assessment of Alfaric, 'cum magna ... cautela legendum' (215): there are many inaccuracies in the titles, some dates are incorrect, there are omissions, and several evaluations are one-sided. T.L. Miethe, *Augustinian Bibliography 1970-1980*, Westport, Conn.—London 1982, is absolutely inadequate; see my review in *NTT* 38 (1984) 239-240.

12 Cf. Andresen, *Augustin-Gespräch*, I, esp. 2 ff., where he refers to the 'Augustindarstellungen' of Harnack, Holl and Seeberg. Current research concentrates on details, and confessional interpretation is less and less frequent. Andresen also states (*Zum Augustin-Gespräch der Gegenwart*, II, Darmstadt 1981, 8 ff.) that the era of 'Augustinus Magister' seems to be over. He means the years around 1954 in particular, when the important A.-conference took place in Paris and Marrou propagated an Augustinian humanism as 'Gebot der Stunde' for a spiritual renewal of Europe. 'Nach Jahrzehnten des Höhenfluges (1950-1970), die aus der damaligen «Geistessituation» ihre Erklärung finden, muss die Augustinforschung sich damit abfinden, dass ihr Gegenstand nicht mehr so stark als Gesprächspartner in den Gegenwartsproblemen gefragt is' (33). But also in this less eventful period, research continues and a new discussion can be expected (33-34).

2. Survey of research and unresolved questions

When reading the bibliographies and other publications devoted to Augustine, one notices immediately that a vast amount of attention has been given to his *City of God*. This major work, which was to have a great influence on the structuring of the medieval world[13], this 'Bible of the European Church'[14], after the Holy Scriptures the most important book for the understanding of Western Christendom[15], has never ceased to have its readers, researchers and commentators.

Today, too, this is very much the case. For decades, it is true, many were especially captivated by Augustine's *Confessions*. This interest was notably inspired by the questions raised by Harnack[16] and Gaston Boissier[17], and later by Pierre Courcelle's impressive investigations[18]. However, interest in the *City of God* has not diminished.

It must be admitted that, especially on this work, research has focussed on details. It is not so much the *City of God* in its entirety or its main theme that has been the centre of attention, but a specific part of it. Up to now much has been written on the relationship between *civitas Dei* and Church, between *terrena civitas* and State, on certain words and concepts, questions of composition and style, the handing down of the manuscripts, etc.[19]. And no publication has appeared on (aspects of) Augustine's teachings about God, Christology, soteriology, eschatology, ethics or, for example, subsequent influence, that does not pay some attention to his extensive compendium the *City of God*. For in this work the bishop summarizes in a

---

[13] J.N. Bakhuizen van den Brink, 'Geschiedenis van het christendom tot het grote schisma van 1054', in: G. van der Leeuw (ed.), *De godsdiensten der wereld*, II, Amsterdam 1941², 261.

[14] O. Noordmans, *Augustinus* (1933/1952²), *Verzamelde werken*, 3, Kampen 1981, 149.

[15] J. O'Meara, *Charter of Christendom: The Significance of the 'City of God'*, New York 1961, VII.

[16] Harnack, *Konfessionen* (1888), *Reden und Aufsätze*, I, 49-79.

[17] G. Boissier, 'La conversion de saint Augustin' (1888), *La fin du paganisme*, I, Paris 1891¹, 339-379.

[18] In particular his *Recherches sur les Confessions de saint Augustin*, Paris 1950 (1968²) became widely known and also his *Les 'Confessions' de saint Augustin dans la tradition littéraire. Antécédents et postérité*, Paris 1963.

[19] Many of the most important studies, including those on the various books of *DCD*, are listed in *BA* 33-37. In this publication, in which the edition by Dombart and Kalb is reprinted, see also the numerous 'Notes complémentaires', most of

grand vision what he also wrote elsewhere and pronounced in his sermons, but here everything is 'like polished building stones systematically joined together'[20].

Although fewer in number, the studies in which the most important theme of the *City of God* is explicitly discussed are very substantial. However, it is especially on the origin of this central theme, viz. the contrast between the *civitas diaboli* and the *civitas Dei*, that no consensus has been reached. For where are the veritable sources of this doctrine of the two cities to be found? And is there possibly a connection between this doctrine and the structure and aim of his 'gigantic work'[21]?

Provisionally I will first enumerate, without full details of references, the principal results of investigations on the central theme and aim of Augustine's main work. It will be seen that, particularly on the question concerning the origins of the doctrine of the two cities, they are highly divergent. It is especially here that further research is necessary.

In the text editions and translations prior to 1900[22], the *City of God* was generally considered to be an apology. These editions were often provided with extensive scholia. Influential commentaries were those by the English Dominicans Thomas Waleys and Nicolaus Treveth[23], the Spanish Humanist Joannes Ludovicus Vives, the French scholar Leonardus Coquaeus and the Swiss-Dutch theologian Johannes Clericus. The Maurists included a selection of the elucidations of Vives and Coquaeus in their famous edition; Migne also reprinted comments by Clericus[24]. However, little was said in these editions about the sources of the doctrine of the two cities. The commentators limited themselves to pointing out some parallels with Plato, Philo, Cicero or Ambrose, but they did not elaborate on the question of the sources systematically.

---

which are supplied by G. Bardy and F.-J. Thonnard. The translation is by G. Combès.

20 Noordmans, *Augustinus, VW* 3, 57, after C. Bindemann (*Der heilige Augustinus*, 3, Greifswald 1869, 836).

21 *DCD* 22, 30: '... ingentis huius operis ...'.

22 Cf. A. Schröder, *Des heiligen Kirchenvaters Aurelius Augustinus zweiundzwanzig Bücher über den Gottesstaat*, I, Kempten-München 1911², LXI-LXIII; Nebreda, *Bibliographia*, 14-16, 19-20, 25-33; Bardy, *BA* 33, 137-143 and *BA* 37, 22.

23 Also Trivet or Triveth. Cf. A. Duval, *DS* XI (1982) 302-304. For Waleys or Valois, see pp. 89–90 n. 398.

24 *MPL* 41, 458-506.

Nor has this been the case in the studies which have been devoted entirely or largely to Augustine's principal work since the beginning of the nineteenth century. These publications are concerned mainly with Augustine's views on history. Notable among these studies are F.C.J. van Goens' doctoral thesis[25], J.H. Reinkens' rectorial address[26], investigations by F. Thomas[27] and G.J. Seyrich[28], and the survey composed by J. Biegler[29]. These scholars all characterized the *City of God* as an apologetic work. Not one of them, however, carried out fundamental research into the origin of the doctrine of the two cities.

Neither did Frédéric de Rougemont. Although the title of his voluminous work is promising, its subtitle already makes it clear that this, too, is a philosophy of history[30]. The writer claimed to have been guided by Augustine's plan and even wanted to create a counterpart of the *City of God*[31]. But in his ambitiously planned work he paid relatively little attention to Augustine. According to him the *City of God* has an apologetic aim[32]; concerning the doctrine of the two cities he mentioned in passing that Plato—as well as Isaiah—could have been its source[33].

Hermann Reuter, in his authoritative work[34], also paid little attention to the question of the sources of the two cities doctrine. He especially investigated Augustine's ecclesiology and doctrines concerning the State. Towards the end of 1909 Harnack was justified in writing: 'Ueber das grosse Werk Aug.'s De civitate Dei giebt es bisher nur ganz ungenügende Untersuchungen'[35].

Since 1900, however, a study had been available that opened up

---

25 F.C.J. van Goens, *De Aurelio Augustino Apologeta secundum libros De Civitate Dei*, Amstelodami-Lugduni Batavorum 1838.

26 J.H. Reinkens, *Die Geschichtsphilosophie des hl. Augustinus*, Schaffhausen 1866.

27 F. Thomas, *St. Augustin, La Cité de Dieu*, Genève 1886.

28 G.J. Seyrich, *Die Geschichtsphilosophie Augustins nach seiner Schrift 'De Civitate Dei'*, Chemnitz 1891.

29 J. Biegler, *Die Civitas Dei des heiligen Augustinus*, Paderborn 1894.

30 F. de Rougemont, *Les deux cités. La philosophie de l'histoire aux différents âges de l'humanité*, I-II, Paris 1874.

31 De Rougemont, *Deux cités*, I, 1.

32 De Rougemont, *Deux cités*, I, 386.

33 De Rougemont, *Deux cités*, II, 251.

34 H. Reuter, *Augustinische Studien*, Gotha 1887 (repr. Aalen 1967). The work consists of seven studies, most of which were published earlier and revised for this edition.

35 Harnack, *Lehrbuch*, III, 61.

new perspectives. In that year Traugott Hahn's *Tyconius-Studien* appeared[36]. Hahn called attention to important fragments from Tyconius' commentary on the *Apocalypse of John*, handed down by Beatus of Liebana, an eighth-century Spanish presbyter. In these fragments the two *civitates* are clearly mentioned, and consequently the source of Augustine's doctrine seemed evident: the Donatist Tyconius, whom Augustine held in such high esteem.

In particular Heinrich Scholz, in his *Glaube und Unglaube in der Weltgeschichte*[37], regarded the texts which Hahn had brought to the fore to be of decisive importance. Although Scholz saw traces of the Augustinian antithesis already present in, among others, Plato, Plotinus, the Stoa and Origen, he considered the influence of Tyconius to be decisive. For in Tyconius' work the contrast between two cities is apparent.

Scholz' book, and subsequently the study by Hahn too, have exerted considerable influence. Of the authors who thereafter referred to a direct influence by Tyconius, sometimes excluding all other possibilities, a small, chronologically arranged selection is given here: H.T. Karsten[38], Paul Monceaux[39], H.A. van Bakel[40], Oepke Noordmans[41], Norman Baynes[42], William Frend[43], Antoine Lauras and Henri Rondet[44], J. Wytzes[45], Antonio Quacquarelli[46],

---

36 T. Hahn, *Tyconius-Studien. Ein Beitrag zur Kirchen- und Dogmengeschichte des vierten Jahrhunderts*, Leipzig 1900 (repr. Aalen 1971).

37 H. Scholz, *Glaube und Unglaube in der Weltgeschichte. Ein Kommentar zu Augustins De civitate Dei*, Leipzig 1911 (repr. 1967).

38 H.T. Karsten, *Augustinus over het Godsrijk. Beschrijving van den inhoud der twee en twintig boeken. Met inleiding en aanteekeningen*, Haarlem 1914.

39 P. Monceaux, *Histoire littéraire de l'Afrique chrétienne depuis les origines jusqu'à l'invasion arabe*, V, Paris 1920 (repr. Bruxelles 1963).

40 H.A. van Bakel, 'Tyconius, Augustinus ante Augustinum' (1930), *Circa Sacra. Historische Studiën*, Haarlem 1935, 114-135.

41 Noordmans, *Augustinus, VW* 3, 32-192.

42 N.H. Baynes, *The Political Ideas of St Augustine's De Civitate Dei* (1936), *Byzantine Studies and other Essays*, London 1955, 288-306.

43 E.g. in W.H.C. Frend, *The Donatist Church. A Movement of Protest in Roman North Africa*, Oxford 1952.

44 A. Lauras – H. Rondet, 'Le thème des deux cités dans l'oeuvre de Saint Augustin', in: H. Rondet – M. Le Landais – A. Lauras – O. Couturier, *Études Augustiniennes*, Paris 1953, 97-160.

45 J. Wytzes, 'Augustinus en Rome', *Hermeneus* 26 (1954) 41-50, 68-73.

46 A. Quacquarelli, *La concezione della Storia nei Padri prima di S. Agostino*, I, Roma 1955.

Gerhart Ladner[47], Rinaldo Cordovani[48], Robert Markus[49], Ulrich Duchrow[50], Alfred Schindler[51] and James Dougherty[52].

At this point it should also be mentioned that, although for some scholars Tyconius was the actual source of Augustine's doctrine of the two cities, this was due not so much to Tyconius' commentary on the *Apocalypse of John*, but in particular to his influential *Liber regularum*, quoted by Augustine expressis verbis. Among others Étienne Gilson[53], Joseph Christopher[54] and Arnold Ehrhardt[55] were adherents of this view.

Arnold Ehrhardt also pointed in another direction. In his opinion Tyconius was influenced by Manichaeism. Augustine did not use Manichaean doctrines about the two kingdoms directly, but in the form in which he encountered them in Tyconius. Jakob Obersteiner[56] and Johannes Spörl[57] also mentioned both Tyconius and Manichaeism as possible sources.

After the Donatist Tyconius, it is Manichaeism that has been named most frequently as the source of Augustine's doctrine of the two *civitates*. In particular, the scholars who have made a profound study of this gnostic world religion have drawn attention to some influence of, or at any rate striking parallels with the Manichaean concept of the two kingdoms. The following can especially be named: Prosper Alfaric[58], Richard Reitzenstein[59], Ernesto Buonaiuti[60],

---

47 G.B. Ladner, *The Idea of Reform. Its Impact on Christian Thought and Action in the Age of the Fathers*, Cambridge, Mass. 1959.

48 R. Cordovani, 'Le due città nel «De catechizandis rudibus» di S. Agostino', *Aug* 7 (1967) 419-447.

49 R.A. Markus, *Saeculum: History and Society in the Theology of St Augustine*, Cambridge 1970.

50 U. Duchrow, *Christenheit und Weltverantwortung. Traditionsgeschichte und systematische Struktur der Zweireichelehre*, Stuttgart 1970.

51 A. Schindler, 'Augustin/Augustinismus I', *TRE* 4 (1979) 645-698.

52 J. Dougherty, *The Fivesquare City. The City in the Religious Imagination*, Notre Dame-London 1980.

53 É. Gilson, *Introduction à l'étude de saint Augustin*, Paris 1929[1].

54 J.P. Christopher, *St Augustine, The First Catechetical Instruction*, Westminster, Md.-London 1955[2] (*ACW* 2).

55 A.A.T. Ehrhardt, *Politische Metaphysik von Solon bis Augustin*, III, Tübingen 1969.

56 J. Obersteiner, 'Augustins «Civitas Dei» und die Geschichtstheologie der Bibel', *Ciudad*, I, 313-350.

57 J. Spörl, 'Augustinus, Schöpfer einer Staatslehre?', *HJ* 74 (1955) 62-78.

58 P. Alfaric, *L'Évolution intellectuelle de saint Augustin*, I, Paris 1918.

59 Reitzenstein, 'Augustin' (1924).

60 E. Buonaiuti, *Geschichte des Christentums*, I, Bern 1948.

Alfred Adam[61] and Alexander Böhlig[62]. Besides these, others have made references to the doctrine of Mani and his adherents, sometimes on the authority of the authors just mentioned, for instance Gustav Combès[63], Hans Eger[64] and Lope Cilleruelo[65]. Also Carsten Colpe has not excluded the possibility of Manichaean influence on Augustine's doctrine of the two kingdoms[66]. Carl Andresen saw in Augustine the influence of both Manichaeism and Neoplatonism[67].

Before naming researchers who have pointed to Plato or his adherents, it is necessary to dwell a moment on the striking fact that so many scholars have referred to a Manichaean origin of Augustine's doctrine of the two cities. Is this justified? Was Buonaiuti right in asking: 'Was ist das [Werk] *De civitate Dei* anderes als der auf die Geschichte angewandte manichäische Dualismus?'[68]. The extent to which reference to Manichaeism has been expressed to a large public may also be illustrated by a passage from Wilhelm Windelband's widely read *Lehrbuch der Geschichte der Philosophie*: '... so ist doch unverkennbar für Augustin der Dualismus des Guten und des Bösen das Endergebnis der Weltgeschichte. Der von so vielen gewaltigen Denkmotiven bestürmte Mann hat den Manichäismus seiner Jugendüberzeugung nicht überwunden,—er hat ihn in die Christenlehre aufgenommen. Bei den Manichäern gilt der Gegensatz des Guten und des Bösen als ursprünglich und unvertilgbar: bei Augustin gilt dieser Gegensatz zwar als geworden, aber doch als unausrottbar. Der allmächtige, allwissende, allgütige Gott hat eine Welt geschaffen, welche in sein Reich und in das des Satan für ewig auseinanderfällt'[69].

---

61 A. Adam in, e.g., 'Der manichäische Ursprung der Lehre von den zwei Reichen bei Augustin' (1952), repr. in H.-H. Schrey (Hrsg.), *Reich Gottes und Welt. Die Lehre Luthers von den zwei Reichen*, Darmstadt 1969 (*WdF* CVII), 30-39 and in A. Adam, *Sprache und Dogma. Untersuchungen zu Grundproblemen der Kirchengeschichte*, hrsg. von G. Ruhbach, Gütersloh 1969, 133-140.

62 A. Böhlig, 'Zu gnostischen Grundlagen der Civitas-Dei-Vorstellung bei Augustin', *ZNW* 60 (1969) 291-295.

63 G. Combès, *La doctrine politique de Saint Augustin*, Paris 1927.

64 H. Eger, *Die Eschatologie Augustins*, Greifswald 1933.

65 L. Cilleruelo, 'La oculta presencia del maniqueísmo en la «Ciudad de Dios»', *Ciudad*, I, 475-509.

66 C. Colpe, 'Gnosis II (Gnostizismus)', *RAC* 11 (1981) 538-659.

67 C. Andresen, 'Erlösung', *RAC* 6 (1966) 54-219.

68 Buonaiuti, *Geschichte*, I, 284.

69 W. Windelband, *Lehrbuch der Geschichte der Philosophie*, hrsg. von H. Heimsoeth, Tübingen 1957[15], 245.

But there is more. Some scholars have also referred to Plato, Philo, Neoplatonism and the Stoa, and not surprisingly so. Augustine—especially in the years immediately following his conversion, but also in his work the *City of God*—often mentioned 'the Platonists' in a positive way. In particular he meant the Neoplatonists Plotinus and Porphyry. Christian Parma[70], among others, saw the originator of the Neoplatonic system as an important figure for the understanding of Augustine's two cities doctrine. Arguments have also been put forward for the influence of Plato himself, for instance by Edgar Salin[71]. John Burleigh[72] devoted rather much attention to Plato, Aristotle, the Stoics and the Neoplatonists, but he did not consider them to have exerted a decisive influence on Augustine's concept. Domenico Pesce[73] and Lidia Storoni Mazzolani[74] also referred in general terms to various, especially non-Christian, Greek and Latin authors, but did not investigate thoroughly the question of the predecessors of Augustine's doctrine. Hans Leisegang[75], on the other hand, perceived clear parallels with Philo, who influenced Augustine through Ambrose.

The fact that not only Leisegang, but others also, have referred to Ambrose is understandable. Substantial influence by this spiritual father of Augustine is to be expected. Did he not receive from him, to quote Possidius, Augustine's first biographer, 'the doctrine and the sacraments'[76]?

Nevertheless, an important influence exerted by this church father on Augustine's doctrine of the two cities has been pointed out by only a few. Besides Scholz, Leisegang, and Lauras and Rondet, Robert Frick[77] suggested some parallels. Viktor Stegemann[78] even put considerable emphasis on Ambrose as the source of Augustine's

70 C. Parma, 'Plotinische Motive in Augustins Begriff der Civitas Dei', *VC* 22 (1968) 45-48.

71 E. Salin, *Civitas Dei*, Tübingen 1926.

72 J.H.S. Burleigh, *The City of God. A Study of St. Augustine's Philosophy*, London 1949.

73 D. Pesce, *Città terrena e città celeste nel pensiero antico (Platone, Cicerone, S. Agostino)*, Firenze 1957.

74 L.S. Mazzolani, *The Idea of the City in Roman Thought. From walled City to spiritual Commonwealth*, London-Sidney-Toronto 1970.

75 H. Leisegang, 'Der Ursprung der Lehre Augustins von der civitas Dei', *AKG* 16 (1926) 127-158.

76 Possidius, *Vita*, 1.

77 R. Frick, *Die Geschichte des Reich-Gottes-Gedankens in der alten Kirche bis zu Origenes und Augustin*, Giessen 1928.

78 V. Stegemann, *Augustins Gottesstaat*, Tübingen 1928.

doctrine, but eventually showed him to be mainly the conveyor of Philo's ideas and of Platonic influence. Leo Ferrari[79] considered the circumstances of Augustine's life important as a background to the *City of God*. The contrast between Milan and Rome, Ambrose and Symmachus, was experienced personally by Augustine and, in combination with Manichaeism, may have given rise to his view of *civitas Dei* versus *civitas diaboli*. This interest in Ambrose's person and work reminds us of Harnack's view: 'An dem königlichen Priester ist dem Augustin die Autorität und Majestät der katholischen Kirche aufgegangen. Nur ein *römischer* Bischof—sass er auch nicht auf dem römischen Stuhl—konnte ihn die lehren, und vielleicht wäre das grosse Werk de civitate dei nie geschrieben worden, ohne den Eindruck, den Augustin von Ambrosius davongetragen hat ...'[80]. Reuter had also expressed himself in this vein[81]. And yet it must be concluded that these general remarks contain little proof of the origin of Augustine's doctrine of the *civitas Dei* versus the *civitas diaboli*. The problem has been most thoroughly discussed by Émilien Lamirande in a recent article on the heavenly Jerusalem in the theology of the bishop of Milan, but his conclusion is a negative one: '... ses exposés ne préfigurent en rien la synthèse augustinienne où, notamment, l'univers angélique et l'opposition des deux cités tiennent une place centrale'[82].

What is important, however, is the fact that reference to Ambrose draws attention to the pre-Augustinian *Christian* tradition. For is it not advisable to seek the sources of Augustine's doctrine of the two cities particularly here? The frequent references to Tyconius have already been noted. But in the Christian tradition preceding Augustine, Ambrose and Tyconius there were so many other writers and writings! Should they not be investigated for elements that may have been essential to Augustine's concept?

It is remarkable that, until now, research in this direction has been very limited. There has been no systematic, comprehensive investigation into the possible early-Christian sources of Augustine's

---

79 L.C. Ferrari, 'Background to Augustine's «City of God»', *CJ* 67 (1972) 198-208.

80 Harnack, *Lehrbuch*, III, 47.

81 Reuter, *Studien*, 150: '... die Vermutung (...) dass Augustins Ideen über Staat und Kirche in der Anschauung der praktischen Erfolge des Kirchenfürsten in Mailand ihre *sekundäre* Quelle haben'.

82 É. Lamirande, 'Le thème de la Jérusalem céleste chez saint Ambrose', *REA* 29 (1983) 209-232; quotation 232.

idea. Occasionally observations have been made, it is true, and they have significant value. The most important ones will be mentioned here, but it should be kept in mind that it was only in retrospect that the real value of their indicative character became clear.

The first scholar to be named is Scholz. In addition to the sources already mentioned, he drew attention to Holy Scripture (the Psalms), to a Jewish saying in the *Oracula Sibyllina*, to Hermas, Origen and Lactantius[83]. Salin referred particularly to Plato, but he also indicated a concept of two kingdoms in the *Pseudo-Clementines*[84]. Frick considered the first parable in the *Pastor Hermae* to be an antecedent: '... die Vorstellung von der civitas dei im Gegensatz zur civitas terrena bereitet sich hier deutlich vor'[85]. Hans Lietzmann commented in a similar way on this passage: 'Die Kirche hat ihren eigenen Organismus und ihre eigenen Gesetze, die Welt hat andere Gesetze: beide Grössen stehen sich gegenüber wie zwei grundverschiedene Staatswesen. Der Gedanke vom Gegensatz zwischen Gottesstaat und irdischem Staat, dem Augustins gewaltigstes Werk die klassische Form gegeben hat, gehört zum ursprünglichen Wesen des christlich-kirchlichen Selbstbewusstseins'[86]. In a discussion during the conference on Augustine in Paris (1954), after an overview of 'La théologie de l'histoire' by Marrou, Gilles Quispel remarked: 'L'idée de l'opposition entre la Cité de Dieu et la cité du diable se trouve déjà ... dans le *Pasteur d'Hermas*: elle est née, évidemment, de l'eschatologie de l'Église primitive'[87]. In this context mention can again be made of Ladner, who wrote: 'The special characteristic of this chapter [i.e. Hermas, *Sim.* I] is the antithetical juxtaposition of the *polis hèmōn* [sic], that is to say, the «world» and the *polis tautè* [sic!], whose Lord is God. The antithesis is almost Augustinian in its strength and precision and it is perhaps not altogether impossible that Augustine knew it'[88].

Other scholars also have referred to the previous Christian tradition. Bakhuizen van den Brink remarked on the alienation of the

---

83 Scholz, *Glaube und Unglaube*, 71 and 76-77.

84 Salin, *Civitas Dei*, 176.

85 Frick, *Reich Gottes*, 32.

86 H. Lietzmann, *Geschichte der Alten Kirche*, II, Berlin 1961^3, 43.

87 *AM*, III (Actes), 204.

88 Ladner, *Idea*, 244. Ladner's intention is clear, but he makes some mistakes. In *Hermas* there is an antithesis between 'your city' (hè polis h*y*mōn), i.e. the city of the servants of God, and 'this city' (hè polis *h*autè), i.e. the place where they sojourn as aliens. See below pp. 301-311.

Christian as it appears in the New Testament and in Hermas, *Sim.* I: 'Basically Augustine's concept of the civitas Dei and the civitas terrena can be found here ...'[89]. Frend pointed to Hermas and Tertullian and saw the doctrine of the two cities since Tertullian as 'part and parcel of Western theological thought'[90]. Karl Ludwig Schmidt noted: 'Darnach wäre in der Situation von Phil. 3, 20 der spätere weltgeschichtliche Gegensatz von civitas dei und civitas terrena (imperium Romanum) vorgebildet'[91]. And, after citing several New Testament texts, Wilhelm Kamlah asserted: 'Angesichts dieser seit dem Ursprung unangetastet geltenden, von Augustin nur in ein neues Licht gehobenen christlichen Tradition ist es abwegig, bei Plato und bei Philo und wer weiss noch in der Geistesgeschichte nach den Vorbildern des «Gottesstaates» herumzusuchen'[92].

Among others who have drawn attention to relevant data in pre-Augustinian Christian writings, finally Bardy[93], Lauras and Rondet[94], Franz Georg Maier[95] and Pierre de Labriolle[96] can be enumerated. But it must be repeated that these authors as well as those mentioned earlier provide only a few fragmentary, often incidental comments. On no account can it be said that their research was comprehensive and systematic.

This also applies to Joseph Ratzinger's article 'Herkunft und Sinn der Civitas-Lehre Augustins'[97]. Ratzinger discusses Kamlah's impressive book at length, refers for the concept *civitas Dei* especially to the early-Christian allegorical interpretation of the Old Testament (particularly the Psalms) and then concludes, in agreement with Kamlah: 'Die Civitas-Lehre Augustins ist nicht eine um-

---

89 J.N. Bakhuizen van den Brink, *Handboek der Kerkgeschiedenis*, I, Den Haag 1965, 73.

90 W.H.C. Frend, *Martyrdom and Persecution in the Early Church*, Oxford 1965, 373.

91 K.L. Schmidt, *Die Polis in Kirche und Welt. Eine lexikographische und exegetische Studie*, Zürich 1940, 23.

92 W. Kamlah, *Christentum und Geschichtlichkeit. Untersuchungen des Christentums und zu Augustins 'Bürgerschaft Gottes'*, Stuttgart-Köln 1951, 161.

93 G. Bardy, 'La formation du concept de «Cité de Dieu» dans l'oeuvre de Saint Augustin', *ATA* 12 (1952) 5-19, esp. 9-12; see also 'Les origines de la notion de «Cité»', *BA* 33, 52-74.

94 Lauras and Rondet, 'Thème', 152-153.

95 F.G. Maier, *Augustin und das antike Rom*, Stuttgart-Köln 1955, 150-152.

96 P. de Labriolle, *Saint Augustin: La Cité de Dieu, I: livres I-V*, Paris 1941 (repr. 1957), VIII-IX.

97 J. Ratzinger, 'Herkunft und Sinn der Civitas-Lehre Augustins. Begegnung und Auseinandersetzung mit Wilhelm Kamlah', *AM*, II, 965-979.

wälzende Konstruktion, sie wächst aus dem alten Kerygma, das eine neue Lage neu verstehen lehrt'[98]. In view of such an allegation, as well as Kamlah's strong assertion quoted above, further substantiation is required.

The authors named so far have all referred to the *City of God*, some more emphatically than others, as an apologetic work. This view was emphasized in the studies by, among others, John Figgis[99] and Eduard Stakemeier[100]. Another author who considered the *City of God* to be a great apology was Leonardo González, who justified this by pointing out the apologetic way in which Augustine valued miracles[101]. Ursicinio Domínguez del Val came to the same conclusion on the basis of Augustine's attitude towards martyrdom[102]. Ulpiano Álvarez Díez also described Augustine's main work as an apology, with an 'unidad perfecta'[103].

The structure of Augustine's voluminous work has been studied not only by Álvarez, but by many others as well. Did the church father, prompted by the fall of Rome, only intend to write a topical book in defence of the Christian faith and did this develop into a gigantic apology in the course of the years? Or did his goal lie on a higher plane right from the start and did he operate according to a structured design?

For a long time there has been a diversity of opinion on the composition of the *City of God*. Only two extremes which make this sufficiently clear are given here. Otto Seeck stated: 'So bietet denn auch sein Gottesstaat nicht nur in der Komposition ein gestaltloses Durcheinander, sondern mehr noch im Gedankeninhalt'[104]. A few years earlier, however, Alfred Schröder, translator of *De civitate Dei* in the *Bibliothek der Kirchenväter*, had stated that in spite of its many elaborations the work can be considered 'ein geschlossenes

---

98 Ratzinger, 'Herkunft', 979.

99 J.N. Figgis, *The Political Aspects of St. Augustine's 'City of God'*, London 1921 (repr. Gloucester, Mass. 1963).

100 E. Stakemeier, *Civitas Dei. Die Geschichtstheologie des hl. Augustinus als Apologie der Kirche*, Paderborn 1955.

101 L. González, 'Valor apologético del milagro en la «Ciudad de Dios»', *Ciudad*, I, 543-570.

102 U. Domínguez del Val, 'El martirio, argumento apologético en la «Ciudad de Dios»', *Ciudad*, I, 527-542.

103 U. Álvarez Díez, 'La «Ciudad de Dios» y su arquitectura interna', *Ciudad*, I, 65-116.

104 O. Seeck, *Geschichte des Untergangs der antiken Welt*, VI, Stuttgart 1920 (repr. Darmstadt 1966), 22.

Ganze'[105]. And especially since Jean-Claude Guy's study[106], preceded by Agnes Dicker's important article [107], nearly every Augustinian scholar is convinced of a structured composition.

In spite of this agreement, however, a number of major problems are still unsolved. For even though a logical arrangement has been demonstrated, up to now no inherent motive for it has been established. Why did Augustine structure his work into a first part in which apologetic and even polemic elements dominate, and then in a second part give a detailed exposition of beginning, progress and ultimate goal of the *civitates*? And why did he organize his argument in that second part in a 'heilsgeschichtliche' order, and describe history in terms of the contrast between two cities?

So far these questions have not been answered satisfactorily. Might it be possible that no answer is feasible until closer attention has been paid to the specific aim that Augustine had in mind with his *City of God*? Are not the structure and the content of this work inextricably entwined? And is it possible, from the internal structure of the work, to shed new light on the question of the sources of the two cities doctrine?

3. Composition, title and method of this study

After the Introduction, the main purpose of which is to give a survey of research to date, Chapter II deals with Augustine and his *City of God*. It opens with a description of Augustine's evolution along with the influences he underwent. Next structure and content of the *City of God* are studied, as well as Augustine's motive for writing, the origin and history of the two cities, the concept of *civitas*, a possible development in Augustine's works towards this concept, and his description of both *civitas Dei* and *terrena civitas*. Moreover, Chapter II deals with such matters as the peregrination of the city of God, the typically Augustinian concepts of 'use' and 'enjoyment', and the contrasts between Eusebian political theology and Augustine's view.

Chapter III describes the *City of God* as an apology and a catechetical work. Catechetical elements from Augustine's other writings are

105 Schröder, *Gottesstaat*, I, LX.

106 J.-C. Guy, *Unité et structure logique de la 'Cité de Dieu' de saint Augustin*, Paris 1961.

107 Soeur Agnes (Dicker), 'De eenheid van S. Augustinus' De civitate Dei', *StC* 6 (1929-1930) 110-126, 164-181.

also discussed. When and in what context did he mention his doctrine of the two cities? In particular the structure and the content of the first catechesis in *The Catechizing of the Uninstructed* are compared with the structure and the content of the *City of God*.

While in the third chapter important new evidence could be used, made available through one of the recently discovered letters of Augustine, Chapter IV also benefits from a new discovery: the *Cologne Mani-Codex*. This chapter gives an investigation of the sources. Was Augustine in his doctrine of the two cities influenced by Manichaeism, Neoplatonism, Philo, the Stoa, or the Donatist Tyconius? In this chapter the pre-Augustinian Jewish, Christian and typically Jewish-Christian traditions are examined too.

In the fifth and final chapter the most important results of the research are summarized and final conclusions are drawn.

The title of this study is derived from Augustine himself. Especially in *his* writings the two antithetical *civitates* are designated as Jerusalem and Babylon, the heavenly city and the city of this world. In *The Catechizing of the Uninstructed* (usually dated c. 400) and in other works from that time such as the *Confessions* and *Against Faustus*, the two cities already bear these names. And particularly in the *Enarrationes in Psalmos* Augustine points out how in this world the two cities of Jerusalem and Babylon are present[108]. As he indicates in his *Retractationes*, the *City of God* also deals with both cities, but he prefers to name the twenty-two books after the better one[109].

This study of *De civitate Dei* and the origins of Augustine's doctrine of the two cities (kingdoms, *civitates*[110]) is a historical-genetical one. Of particular concern are the possible sources of Augustine's concept, and not so much the content of the doctrine itself. For the sake of clarity some remarks are made about essential elements of Augustine's view, mainly in Chapter II. But even there the main purpose is to acquire a better insight into the possible sources. In this way I hope to avoid the peril evident in some studies, namely that Augustine's thoughts are detached from their historical context and

---

108 See below, pp. 118-123.

109 *Retract.* II, 43, 2: 'Ita omnes viginti et duo libri cum sint de utraque civitate conscripti, titulum tamen a meliore acceperunt ut De civitate Dei potius vocarentur'.

110 Sometimes the meaningful word *civitas* is left untranslated. When it is translated, preference has been given to *city*; see pp. 102-108.

serve as *dicta probantia* in a more or less systematic-dogmatic exposition.

Notwithstanding, it is hoped that as a result of this investigation into the origins of Augustine's doctrine more light will be shed on this theory itself. And, moreover, that in this way the true background will be revealed of later concepts of the two cities or kingdoms, often largely influenced by Augustine.

The text editions from which the material for this study has been drawn need no detailed description here. Invariably the best ones were utilized: the authoritative fourth edition of *De civitate Dei* by B. Dombart and A. Kalb, reprinted virtually unchanged in both the *Corpus Christianorum* and the *Bibliothèque Augustinienne*; the *Enarrationes in Psalmos* after the edition by E. Dekkers and J. Fraipont in *CC*; the *Epistulae* after the editions by A. Goldbacher and J. Divjak in the Corpus of Vienna (*CSEL*), etc. When editions of Augustine's works were available in neither *CC*, *CSEL* nor *BA*, usually Migne was quoted. Any significant differences between the text editions have been indicated in the footnotes.

This study is not only meant for specialists in Augustinian research. I have aimed at writing a usable and clear book for a wider circle of readers. Therefore the quotations from Latin have almost all been consigned to the footnotes and appear in the text in translation. In translating them I have tried—in accordance with Augustine's preference[111]—to render their substance lucidly and transparently, retaining as far as possible the original word order and sentence structure. The fact that this aim could not always be realized, and actually sometimes turned out to be undesirable, will be understood especially by those familiar with the long sentences in *De civitate Dei*.

Greek, Hebrew and other texts such as Coptic are rendered in transcription. Italics in the text or footnotes are generally mine; those of others were maintained when I found them useful. The lists of text editions and secondary literature contain the complete titles of the works to which I have referred or from which I have quoted. In the footnotes these titles appear in full the first time, and thereafter in an abbreviated form.

---

[111] Cf. *De doctr. chr.* II, 15, 22.

CHAPTER TWO

AUGUSTINE AND HIS 'CITY OF GOD'

A. The author

A few essential details of Augustine's life and spiritual development should be presented at this point, for an adequate understanding can only be gained if proper attention is given to the circumstances and the spiritual currents that influenced him. Knowledge of Augustine's milieu and development appears to be particularly indispensable for an inquiry into the possible sources of his doctrine of the two *civitates*. Of course this account is confined to a few relevant main features[1].

1. The man from Africa

Augustine[2] was born on 13th November 354 in the Numidian provincial town of Thagaste[3], present-day Souk-Ahras in Algeria,

---

[1] This biographical sketch is based mainly on: F. van der Meer, *Augustinus de zielzorger. Een studie over de praktijk van een kerkvader*, Utrecht-Brussel 1947; Courcelle, *Recherches*; J.J. O'Meara, *The Young Augustine. An Introduction to the Confessions of St. Augustine* (1954), London-New York 1980; Marrou, *Augustin*; A. Sizoo, *Augustinus. Leven en werken*, Kampen 1957; R. Lorenz, 'Augustin', *RGG* I (1957), 738-748; P. Brown, *Augustine of Hippo. A biography*, London 1967; A. Mandouze, *Saint Augustin. L'aventure de la raison et de la grâce*, Paris 1968; T.J. van Bavel, *Augustinus. Van liefde en vriendschap*, Baarn 1970; E. Feldmann, *Der Einfluss des Hortensius und des Manichäismus auf das Denken des jungen Augustinus von 373*, Münster 1975 (Diss. Mschr.); Schindler, 'Augustin'.

[2] It is by no means certain that Aurelius was Augustine's *praenomen*. It was quite possibly added through the association of his name with that of Aurelius of Carthage. See Mandouze, *Augustin*, 72 n. 2; Schindler, 'Augustin', 646, and particularly A.-M. La Bonnardière, '«Aurelius Augustinus» ou «Aurelius, Augustinus?»', *RBén* 91 (1981) 231-237. L. Brix agrees with La Bonnardière in his notice (*REA* 28 (1982) 366); P. Petitmengin raises objections and supplies textual evidence in support of the opposite view (*REA* 29 (1983) 390-391). M.M. Gorman, 'Aurelius Augustinus: The Testimony of the Oldest Manuscripts of Saint Augustine's Works', *JTS* 35 (1984) 475-480 sides with Petitmengin and points out that A. was referred to in the earliest mss. of his writings as Aurelius Augustinus; J.-P. Bouhot, however, contradicts this opinion (*REA* 31 (1985) 339).

[3] A description of Thagaste at the time of A. is given, for example, in O. Perler (en collaboration avec J.-L. Maier), *Les voyages de saint Augustin*, Paris 1969, 119-125.

near the Tunesian border. He may have been of Berber extraction. Especially René Pottier[4] depicted him as a descendant of the original inhabitants of the country: a pure-bred Berber, full of hatred towards the Roman Empire[5]. There is no solid scientific foundation for this view, however[6]. William Frend also saw at least some Berber influence in Augustine: Monnica is a Berber name and the Berber element appears also in the name of Augustine's son Adeodatus[7]. John O'Meara, with reference only to Frend, went a step further: Monnica was a descendant of the original inhabitants of the country and probably her husband was too[8].

Yet all this does not tell us very much[9]. Even if Augustine's mother and perhaps also Patricius were Berbers[10], it is still true that they manifested themselves in a typically Roman fashion. They belonged to the Roman cultural elite, had ties with the Catholic Church and spoke Latin. For Augustine Latin was not only the civilized language that moulded his thinking, it was also his mother tongue[11]. He came into the world as a Roman citizen and that was what he remained. He belongs to the West European cultural sphere.

4 R. Pottier, *Saint Augustin le Berbère*, Paris 1945.

5 Pottier's view is largely based on the sharp criticism in *DCD*.

6 The tone of the book is more emotional than rational. An example of 'argumentation' is the assertion on p. 26 that besides Latin A. is supposed to have spoken the Berber language: 'Si nous n'en sommes pas absolument certain—nul part il n'y fait allusion—nous sommes en droit de le croire: il n'était pas homme à imposer à son clergé ce dont lui-même n'aurait pas été capable'.

7 W.H.C. Frend, 'A Note on the Berber Background in the Life of Augustine', *JTS* 43 (1942) 188-191 (repr. in *Religion Popular and Unpopular in the Early Christian Centuries*, London 1976, Ch. XIV) and Frend, *Donatist Church*, esp. 230: '... Monnica, a Berber name, perhaps derived from the Libyan deity Mon ... The rather odd name which he gave to his own son, «Adeodatus», is intelligible only with reference to the Berber usage of naming children with a name connected with the worship of Baal—Adeodatus = Iatanbaal'.

8 O'Meara, *Young Augustine*, 28: 'She was *certainly* Berber ... But there is no good reason for believing that her husband was not a Berber also'.

9 In *Donatist Church*, 230, Frend also refers to 'Augustine's tendency to follow Berber traditions and to attribute a nearer relationship to a brother than to a son'.

10 Marrou, *Augustin*, 11, states: 'Le calcul des probabilités permet d'inférer qu'il était de pure race berbère'. Sizoo, *Augustinus*, 20, writes that A.'s family gave the impression of being typically African; earlier he wrote of 'a different race than ours' (7). Mandouze, *Augustin*, 72 ff., makes no decision. With reference to Patricius, Schindler remarks in 'Augustin', 646: 'Der Sprache und wohl auch der Abstammung nach weder punisch noch berberisch ...'; with reference to Monnica: '... eher berberischer Abstammung ...'.

11 Cf. *Conf.* I, 14, 23.

But he evidently was a Roman from Africa. Certain statements in his writings display an unmistakably African chauvinism[12]. And although Augustine had an expert command of Latin, as a former professor of rhetoric he still complained about his African accent[13]. It might also be seriously considered whether he was familiar with the indigenous languages of Romanized Africa: 'Berber' (Libyan) and Punic[14]. To be sure, this question cannot be answered with certainty. Christian Courtois presumed that he spoke the language of the ordinary people around him, Libyan, but he could not provide adequate proof[15]. This is easier with respect to Punic, the other civilized language besides Latin, for more than once Augustine referred to certain Punic words and explained them[16]. However, these fragmentary remarks prove only that he was familiar with some elements of this language which was a close cognate of Hebrew, not that he had complete mastery of it[17].

For the time being we have the following picture of Augustine. Very probably his descent was neither purely Roman nor purely indigenous African, but a combination resulting from the living together for centuries of Berbers, Phoenicians and Romans. At the same time he had grown up in a milieu that was dominated by the

---

12 See Brown, *Augustine*, 22 ff. and, among others, E. Hendrikx, 'Augustinus en het Imperium Romanum', *AThijm* 44 (1956) 95-110, esp. 106-110.

13 *De ord.* II, 17, 45: 'Me enim ipsum, cui magna necessitas fuit ista perdiscere, adhuc in multis verborum sonis Itali exagitant ...'. This was also said of Emperor Septimius Severus (Spartianus, *Vita Severi* 19, 9).

14 For these languages that occurred in Africa alongside of Latin, see Frend, 'Note'; Ch. Courtois, 'S. Augustin et le problème de la survivance du punique', *RAfr* 94 (1950) 259-282, and in particular M. Simon, 'Punique ou berbère? Note sur la situation linguistique dans l'Afrique Romaine' (1955), repr. in *Recherches d'histoire Judéo-Chrétienne*, Paris 1962, 88-100. Whereas Frend, and more strongly Courtois, objected to the idea that Punic was in widespread use at the time of A., Simon argued forcefully that its use was spreading, along with Jewish and (Jewish-) Christian proselytizing. See also his 'Le Judaïsme berbère dans l'Afrique ancienne' (1946), repr. in *Recherches*, 30-87.

15 Courtois, 'Survivance'.

16 For passages in which A. refers to the *lingua punica*, see e.g. P. Brown, 'Christianity and Local Culture in Late Roman Africa' (1968), repr. in his *Religion and Society in the Age of Saint Augustine*, London 1972, 279-300, esp. 285-287.

17 See in particular F. Vattioni, 'Sant'Agostino e la civiltà punica', *Aug* 8 (1968) 434-467. He states on the one hand that A. probably did not know Punic (446), and on the other hand that he nevertheless made use of it (449). The difference between making use of a language and speaking or reading it readily should not be overlooked; on the basis of A.'s remarks we can only conclude that the former applied to him.

Latin language and mores. In short, he was a civilized African as we can imagine one to be in the Late Roman period[18].

This brief sketch already supplies a possibly important datum for the interpretation of the *City of God*. This work, so influential in world history, was written by a Roman from Africa. Was his attitude towards the Empire different from that of its citizens elsewhere? Could there have been in him the same permeating element of hostility towards Rome that was undeniably present among Berbers and Phoenicians[19]? These questions merit further consideration.

2. *Classical education and knowledge of Greek*

Augustine was fortunate to have been born in a cultivated environment. In the small town of Thagaste—and a town in those days and in that world was in itself a symbol of civilization[20]—his father was a member of the council. The town councillors, the *decuriones* or *curiales*, were among the most distinguished inhabitants. However, in those days of economic decline it was not an unqualified pleasure to hold this office: the honour had turned into a heavy strain, because the *decuriones* were compelled to bear the very large financial burden for the community[21]. Thus Patricius was part of a citizenry that became increasingly impoverished.

Augustine's father could just provide the means to give his son the beginnings of a classical education. After completing his primary education at Thagaste, Augustine went to nearby Madaura. The first steps on the road to a full classical education had thus been taken. With the help of Romanianus[22], who was willing to act as

---

18 Cf. Mandouze, *Augustin*, 74: '... se résoudre tout simplement à reconnaître en Augustin un Africain de son temps'.

19 Cf. Simon, 'Le Judaïsme berbère' and 'Punique ou Berbère?', in: *Recherches*, esp. 64 f., 76 f., 95.

20 Brown, *Augustine*, 20.

21 Mazzolani, *Idea*, 208, concerning the *curiales*: 'The collection of taxes, and of food for the government pool; the recruitment of soldiers; the imposition of forced loans—all this weighed on the shoulders of these officials, condemned by birth to become instruments of the imperial tyranny ...'.

22 A. Gabillon, 'Romanianus, alias Cornelius. Du nouveau sur le bienfaiteur et l'ami de saint Augustin', *REA* 24 (1978) 58-70, provides interesting details about this benefactor whose life was closely connected with A.'s: at the end of the 19th century an architrave was found at Thagaste bearing the names (Cor)nelius Romanianus; this confirmed that Romanianus was the Cornelius admonished in *Ep.* 259; like A. he became a convert to Manichaeism, like him he also became a Catholic; he was only about 10 years older than his protégé.

benefactor of the gifted young man, Augustine was able to embark upon his higher education. This he completed in Carthage, the capital of Africa, after Rome the largest city of the Latin Western world.

Thus from the age of seven to twenty or twenty-one[23], Augustine received a complete classical education. In his day this meant becoming a 'vir eloquentissimus atque doctissimus', a fully-fledged rhetor. For centuries Greeks and Romans had cultivated rhetoric and developed it into a comprehensive programme of theoretical and practical disciplines[24]. The young Catholic Augustine, too, received this completely pagan education[25].

It was especially the works of Terence, Sallust, Virgil and above all of Cicero that were studied in great detail[26]. To be sure, this was only a small number of authors, but in accordance with a fixed scheme they were commented upon word for word. This method was so thorough that Simplicius, a childhood friend of Augustine's, knew Virgil and a major portion of Cicero by heart[27]. Augustine, too, familiarized himself thoroughly with these classical writers[28]. Marrou considered him to be to the very end of his life the grammarian, rhetor and dialectician that he was at the beginning[29].

The foregoing helps to explain an important characteristic of the *City of God*. In this work Augustine frequently quotes from pagan

---

[23] C. 375 he returned to Thagaste to teach grammar and rhetoric himself: *Conf.* IV, 4, 7 and IV, 2, 2.

[24] For rhetoric and its arrangement, see in particular H.-I. Marrou, *Histoire de l'éducation dans l'antiquité*, Paris 1948, 268. Marrou describes its influence on A. at greater length in his *Saint Augustin et la fin de la culture antique*, Paris 1958[4] (1938[1], supplemented with a *Retractatio* 1949[2]); a brief summary in Marrou, *Augustin*, 13-17. O'Meara, *Young Augustine*, 39-45, also gives a clear exposition.

[25] Marrou, *Éducation*, 416-434, deals with the matter of Christians and classical education: religious instruction was given by the Church and in the family; for hundreds of years school education remained unchanged.

[26] See esp. H. Hagendahl, *Augustine and the Latin Classics*, Göteborg 1967, 384, 479, 692-693 on the *quadriga auctorum*.

[27] *De anima* IV, 7, 9. Cf. Hagendahl, *Latin Classics*, 321, 385, 479; Brown, *Augustine*, 36.

[28] Hagendahl, *Latin Classics*, 693: 'Augustine's writings are marked by the predilection for the old classics of the school: the great majority of his quotations belong to the traditional *quadriga*'.

[29] Marrou, *Augustin et la fin*, 16: 'Dans l'auteur du *de Trinitate* ou de la *Cité de Dieu* survit toujours le *grammaticus* de Madaure'; 55: '...le rhéteur de Carthage

authors: particularly Virgil, Cicero, Sallust and, above all, Varro. He did this not so much from an appreciation of pagan civilization as such, but from apologetical considerations: his opponents had to be refuted on their own ground. Harald Hagendahl[30] shows how Augustine was influenced in his early writings by the pagan classics in both form and content, and that he often quoted from them. In his theological writings dating from 391 to 413, however, there are remarkably few quotations, except in some works and letters whose subject or addressee required them. But when Augustine started his main work, there was a sudden increase in *testimonia* from pagan authors. Obviously the author of *De civitate Dei* reread his classics before commencing his work, as he would continue to do in the years to follow[31]. He wanted his work to be well-documented, and it was for this reason that he studied even new writers and writings[32]. When Othmar Perler establishes that in the winter of 412-413 Augustine sojourned at Carthage for a long time, the reason for this is clear: the author of the *City of God* was making his preparations in the libraries there[33]. It is noticeable that in this work the classical sources are quoted with exceptional care[34].

Thus the training in grammar and rhetoric exerted a profound influence on Augustine. Every word, every turn of phrase in a text had become important for him. This is particularly evident in the *City of God* with respect to the (Latin!) classical authors, but it is also apparent in the works that give an interpretation of Holy Scripture. The meaning of each and every word and phrase was closely traced. Referring to the entire *corpus augustinianum* Peter Brown states: 'Augustine will cite his new, Christian «classic» 42,816 times'[35]. Surely

survit et transparaît toujours'; 241: 'Ce ne sont pas seulement les *Dialogues* philosophiques, c'est l'oeuvre entière d'Augustin qui témoigne d'une connaissance approfondie des lois du raisonnement autant que d'une parfaite maîtrise de l'art de la discussion'. Earlier Alfaric expressed a similar view, *Évolution*, 13 ff.

30 Hagendahl, *Latin Classics*, 690-729.

31 Hagendahl, *Latin Classics*, 705, 708; similarly Marrou, *Augustin et la fin*, 19 n. 5, 129, 148 and O'Meara, *Young Augustine*, 94.

32 Hagendahl, *Latin Classics*, 705: Livy, Florus, Eutropius, Iustinus, Labeo, Cicero's *De fato*, Sallust's *Historiae, Asclepius*, Varro's *De gente populi Romani, De cultu deorum* and *De philosophia*, Cicero's *De divinatione*.

33 Perler, *Voyages*, 315 and 424.

34 Hagendahl, *Latin Classics*, esp. 697, 710 and 717.

35 Brown, *Augustine*, 37.

to make such an assertion is not without risk. For who knows exactly which writings can be safely attributed to Augustine? And what is an accurate Bible quotation, what—as is frequently found in Augustine's writings—merely a more or less clear allusion? But in any case such an assertion does give an indication: the repeated quotation of the Scriptures (often from memory) can as a method be attributed, at least to a considerable extent[36], to his classical training.

In this context special mention should be made of Augustine's knowledge of Greek[37]. Initially it must have been slight, due partly to the then current educational system, but mainly to his own lack of interest. In later years also, when he felt this deficiency especially with regard to the exposition of the Scriptures, his competence in Greek was still limited. He was capable enough of comparing an ambiguous Latin passage with the Greek text, particularly from the Septuagint and the Greek New Testament. But for the larger works he had to rely on translations. Therefore, in almost every instance his dependence on writings by Greek fathers can be assumed only when a Latin translation was available.

Admittedly, our knowledge of these translations is still fragmentary. For example, did Augustine become directly acquainted with Philo, Origen and other important Greek writers? With Altaner one is inclined to have doubts, at least as regards their complete works[38]. And as far as classical authors such as Aristotle, Homer, Herodotus and others are concerned, a negative conclusion is virtually certain[39]. Practically all the knowledge Augustine had of

---

[36] Influence of the synagogical method of exposition of the Scriptures deserves consideration in this context. Cf. J. van Oort, 'Augustinus Verbi Divini Minister', in: J. van Oort et al. (ed.), *Verbi Divini Minister* ..., Amsterdam 1983, 175.

[37] B. Altaner, 'Augustinus und die griechische Sprache' (1939); 'Die Benützung von original griechischen Vätertexten durch Augustinus' (1948) and 'Augustinus und die griechische Patristik. Eine Zusammenfassung und Nachlese zu den quellenkritischen Untersuchungen' (1952), repr. in: B. Altaner, *Kleine patristische Schriften*, Berlin 1967 (*TU* 83), 129-153, 154-163, 316-331. See also Marrou, *Augustin et la fin*, 27-46, 631-637 (*Retractatio*!); P. Courcelle, *Les lettres grecques en Occident. De Macrobe à Cassiodore*, Paris 1948², 137-194. Although O'Meara, *Young Augustine*, 45, refers to the 1948 study by Altaner, he gives Marrou's somewhat disparaging (earlier) estimation.

[38] Altaner, *Schriften*, esp. 151-152, 162, 321 ff. On the other hand it is striking that Alypius, A.'s childhood friend and future bishop of Thagaste, did have a good command of Greek. And of course this also held good for his Greek predecessor as bishop of Hippo Regius: Valerius.

[39] Altaner, *Schriften*, 148, who summarizes here the conclusions of a number of other studies.

Christian and Neoplatonic Greek authors beyond the well-known translations by Rufinus and Marius Victorinus reached him via Ambrose and his circle[40]. Thus it is evident that this church father did not have a thorough knowledge of the Greek-Christian tradition. However, it is through this deficiency that his genius becomes apparent: because he was unable to graft his theology onto previous Greek theological thinking, he was forced to resort to independent reflection and consequently he achieved great originality[41].

3. *The young Catholic*

Augustine, the man from Africa, thoroughly trained in grammar, rhetoric and dialectics, but with a limited knowledge of Greek. These are in themselves important facts for understanding the form and especially the content of the *City of God*. But there is more that merits attention in this connection. Firstly, that from his youth he had been educated in the tradition of the Catholic Church.

Usually this aspect of his development is insufficiently emphasized. The attention of writers concerned with the young Augustine is quickly focussed on his Christian mother, and this is understandable. For in his *Confessions*, when before God and man he describes in detail his inner life, Monnica occupies the central position (although her name is actually mentioned only once[42]). And with reason: behind the real mother figure Augustine discerns that other mother, the Church. Especially in his portrayal of Monnica as mother, widow and handmaiden, the *factum* points to the *mysterium*[43].

However, in a discussion of the large role assigned to Monnica, in which her steadfast Christian faith is in sharp contrast to her son's doubts and deviations, one thing must not be forgotten: Augustine

---

40 P. Agaësse and A. Solignac in *BA* 48, 628, not only refer to Ambrose, but also make special mention of Simplicianus, tutor of both church fathers: 'Mais il est également possible qu'Augustin, qui durant son séjour à Milan s'est intéressé au problème de l'image, ait reçu de Simplicianus, au cours de ses entretiens avec lui (cf. *De beata vita* 4), des explications précises inspirées des auteurs grecs et dont il s'est rappelé plus tard le contenu de façon très exacte'.

41 Cf. Marrou, *Augustin*, 14.

42 *Conf.* IX, 13, 37.

43 See in particular P.M.A. van Kempen-van Dijk, *Monnica. Augustinus' visie op zijn moeder*, Amsterdam 1978, who develops and enlarges upon the work of Chr. Mohrmann and R. Guardini. Cf. Van der Meer, *Augustinus*, 175-176.

himself had never been a pagan, nor did he become one when he was entangled in error and scepticism[44]. From his early youth he received a Christian education and grew up in the tradition of the Church of Africa.

By piecing together data from the various writings one can obtain a clear picture. In his *Confessions* Augustine mentions the fact that he had a passionate longing for baptism when as a little boy he had stomach cramps[45]; also that as a boy he began to invoke God's name and beseeched Him with great fervour that he might not be flogged at school[46]. In church, when he was an infant, the name of Christ had already been placed upon him[47]. He wanted to set his feet upon the step his parents had placed him on as a boy[48]. Further evidence of his ties with the Christian faith is provided by the information that as a student in Carthage he attended church regularly[49], that in all probability his concubine was a Christian[50], and possibly that the son born in 372 or 373 was given the name Adeodatus[51].

Other writings confirm all this. At the end of his debate with Fortunatus, Augustine says quite characteristically that he *returned* to the Catholic faith when the Manichaeans were unable to satisfy his spiritual and intellectual needs[52]. To Honoratus he declares that he, Honoratus, was converted to Manichaeism as a non-Christian,

---

[44] *Conf.* VI, 5, 8: '... semper tamen credidi et esse te et curam nostri gerere ...'; cf. the end of VI, 5, 7. Maier, *Augustin*, 18-21, is completely unjustified in referring to the years before 386 as 'Augustins *heidnische* Lebenszeit'.

[45] *Conf.* I, 11, 17.

[46] *Conf.* I, 9, 14.

[47] *Conf.* VI, 4,5: '... ecclesia unica ... in qua mihi nomen Christi infanti est inditum ...'.

[48] *Conf.* VI, 11, 18: 'Figam pedes in eo gradu, in quo puer a parentibus [!] positus eram ...'.

[49] *Conf.* III, 3, 5.

[50] *Conf.* VI, 15, 25: 'Et illa in Africam redierat *vovens tibi* alium se virum nescituram ...'.

[51] *Conf.* IX, 6, 14. Frend (cf. n. 7) does not substantiate his argument convincingly. His reference to the name Adeodatus as 'the rather odd name' is puzzling. If one consults Diehl's work (with which Frend is quite familiar) one finds many Adeodati, not only in Africa but especially in Italy (Rome); cf. E. Diehl, *Inscriptiones Latinae Christianae Veteres*, III, Dublin-Zürich 1970³.

[52] *C. Fort.* 37: '... et ad fidem catholicam me converterem vel potius *revocarem* ...'.

but he himself as a Christian[53]. Here and elsewhere he emphasizes the fact that Christianity was 'sown' in him during his childhood[54].

Still more statements can be clarified through such close reading, particularly of the *Confessions*. For example that he prayed to God with the words: 'My hope *from my youth*, where were you for me and whither had you retreated'[55]? But Augustine also stated explicitly that he was very closely associated with the Christian Church: he was, remained and became again, but then from deep conviction, a catechumen. He says this especially at the end of Book V and in Book I of the *Confessions*. After his disenchantment with the Manichaeans, and at a time when he could not commit himself fully to the Academic philosophers because the saving name of Christ was not present in their teachings[56], he decided 'to *remain* a catechumen in the Catholic Church—recommended to me by my parents [!]—until something certain should light up whither I might direct my course'[57]. That he had been a catechumen for a long time Augustine records in the description of his earliest youth: as a boy he had heard about eternal life; already from his birth he had been signed with the sign of the cross and seasoned with the salt[58].

---

53 *De ut. cred.* 2: 'Sed de me quid dicam qui iam catholicus christianus eram? (...) Tu nondum christianus'.

54 *De ut. cred.* 2: '... religione, quae mihi puerulo a parentibus [!] *insita* erat ...'; *De duab. an.* 1: 'Multa enim erant ... ne tam facile ... religionis verissimae semina mihi a pueritia *insita* ... ex animo pellerentur'; *C. Acad.* II, 2, 5: 'Respexi tamen confite(b)or quasi de itinere in illam religionem quae pueris nobis *insita* est et medullitus inplicata ...'.

55 *Conf.* VI, 1, 1: 'Spes mea *a iuventute mea* (*Ps.* 70:5 = Heb. 71:5), ubi mihi eras et quo recesseras?'

56 *Conf.* V, 14, 25: '... quibus tamen philosophis, *quod sine salutari nomine Christi essent*, curationem languoris animae meae conmittere omnino recusabam'.

57 *Ibid.* : 'Statui ergo *tamdiu esse catechumenus in catholica ecclesia* mihi a parentibus commendata, donec aliquid certi eluceret quo cursum dirigerem'. Cf. *De ut. cred.* 20: 'Decreveramque *tamdiu esse catechumenus in ecclesia* cui traditus a parentibus eram, donec aut invenirem quod vellem aut mihi persuaderem non esse quaerendum'.

58 *Conf.* I, 11, 17: 'Audieram enim ego adhuc puer de vita aeterna ... et signabar iam signo crucis eius [sc. Christi] et condiebar eius sale iam inde ab utero matris meae ...'. Cf. the commentary by B. Busch, 'De modo quo s. Augustinus descripserit initiationem christianam', *Eph.Lit.* 52 (1938) 386: 'Iam prima infantia Augustinus signum Christi acceperat simulque sacramentum salis; quos ritus saepius iteratos esse per formam grammaticam imperfecti indicatur. Cum puer ad aetatem discretionis pervenisset, primam instructionem de rudimentis fidei accepit ...'.

The foregoing information, however, presents us with a problem: were these really rites for entrance into the catechumenate, or were they only private measures on the part of the Christian mother? Franz Joseph Dölger took the latter view: 'Es handelt sich nicht um eine kirchliche rituelle Aufnahme in das Christentum, sondern um eine private Massnahme der christlichen Mutter. In jener Zeit, da die Verschiebung der Taufe auch in christlichen Familien so stark überhand genommen hatte, wird man den Wunsch, dass das Kind dem Christentum angegliedert werden möge, dadurch bekundet haben, dass man ihm ein Kreuzzeichen auf die Stirne machte und dieses Kreuzzeichen tatsächlich als eine private Aufnahme in das Christentum betrachtete'[59].

In order to defend his opinion, Dölger had to resort to some additional interpretations. To him salt represents the Christian doctrine that Augustine heard from his mother, and Monnica's making the sign of the cross is no more and no less than a blessing. Also the church, which Augustine mentions in another context[60] as the place where as a child he received the name of Christ, should be taken figuratively as the community of believers[61].

This last fact is evident from the text: *ecclesia unica* does not refer to a building. But is the rest of Dölger's exposition also true? He refers to a remark by Jerome: he was born of Christian parents, had borne the sign of the cross from his youth[62], but was not baptized until the age of twenty. Other instances of private blessing with the sign of the cross are also known[63].

But why should it be denied that the double rite mentioned here by Augustine involved the acceptance of very young children into the catechumenate, with the same ceremonial as for adults? It was precisely the receiving of *both* cross and salt that was typical of being taken into the catechumenate[64], and only the fact that he had been a cate-

---

Busch also presumes (386 n. 3), that this instruction was given by Monnica: 'Quam instructionem forsitan mater praebuit. Si tempora verborum secundum rigorem grammaticae explicantur («audieram – signabar – speravit»), possibile est ad instructionem fixam ac determinatam concludi'.—J. Mayer, *Geschichte des Katechumenats und der Katechese in den ersten sechs Jahrhunderten*, Kempten 1868, 65, also comments that A.'s use of the imperfect may at any rate point to a continual repetition.

59 F.J. Dölger, 'Beiträge zur Geschichte des Kreuzzeichens, VIII', *JbAC* 8/9 (1965-1966) 45. These 'Beiträge' were edited posthumously by Th. Klauser.

60 *Conf.* VI, 4, 5; cf. n. 47.

61 Dölger, 'Kreuzzeichen', 45.

62 Hieronymus, *In Iob, praef.*: 'Ego christianus de parentibus christianis natus et vexillum crucis in mea fronte portans'. Cf. Dölger, 'Kreuzzeichen', 42 n. 197.

63 Dölger, 'Kreuzzeichen', 42-44.

64 *De cat. rud.* 50.

chumen can explain why Augustine called himself a Christian[65]. The Council of Hippo in 393 as well as that of Carthage in 397 mentioned salt as the *sacramentum* of the catechumens[66]. It is also known that giving the sign of the cross and administering a few grains of salt during the catechumenate period—which might last a lifetime—was often repeated[67].

Dölger's interpretation of this passage is not convincing. The text offers no support for his opinion that the sign of the cross was given *by Monnica*[68], nor do the words about the administering of salt need to be explained figuratively. The *unica ecclesia* in which Augustine was given Christ's name points indeed to his induction into the Catholic Church, but does this exclude the possibility that it took place in a church building? An example like that of Jerome proves only that many years could elapse between the first acceptance as a catechumen and the actual application for baptism as a *competens*[69]. If Dölger's view were correct, one should also ask when Augustine was actually admitted as a catechumen. In Milan, after leaving the Manichaeans but still before his conversion to the Christian faith, he decided *to remain* a catechumen[70] and it was only later that he applied for baptism.[71]

On the basis of the information supplied by Augustine himself, the only possible conclusion is that he became a catechumen when still a young child[72]. It is beyond doubt that in his family also he was

---

65 See esp. n. 53. *Conf.* VI, 1, 1 ('... non me quidem iam esse manichaeum sed neque catholicum christianum ...') seems to contradict this, but here A. is describing how, in Milan, he was riddled with doubts: no longer a Manichaean, but not yet a Catholic Christian by inner conviction. That a catechumen was entitled to call himself a Christian is stated explicitly by A. in *Tract. in Ioh. Ev.* 44, 2. *Codex Theod.* 16, 7, 2 states this also; cf. H. Karpp, 'Christennahmen', *RAC* 2 (1954) 1135.

66 P. de Puniet, 'Catéchuménat', *DACL* 2 (1925) 2596.

67 See e.g. Mayer, *Katechumenat*, 60-74; Busch, 'Initiatio', 399, 412 ff., 419 ff.; Van der Meer, *Augustinus*, 312-314.

68 Dölger, 'Kreuzzeichen', 45: 'Das von der Mutter Monnica dem Knaben Augustinus gemachte Kreuzzeichen ...'.

69 For the distinctions between accedentes (= those desirous of admission to the catechumenate), catechumen (also audientes), competentes (= electi, illuminandi: those who are to receive baptism shortly, usually at Eastertime) and neophyti (the newly-baptized) see, besides De Puniet, 'Catéchuménat', for example Christopher, *Cat. Instruction*, 3 f.

70 *Conf.* V, 14, 25 (text above, n. 57). Cf. *Ep.* 36, 32: '... et nobis adhuc catechumenis ...'.

71 *Conf.* IX, 6, 14: 'Inde ubi tempus advenit quo me nomen dare [= terminus technicus for the move to the state of competens] oporteret, relicto rure Mediolanium remeavimus'.

72 Cf. Van der Meer, *Augustinus*, 309: '... he was already a catechumen ...'; Mandouze, *Augustin*, 85: 'Inscrit tout jeune sur le registre des catéchumènes ...'. But they did not substantiate this assertion.

given a Christian upbringing and that this made a deep impression on him. In the description of his earliest years he refers to himself as *believing* and in this way he depicts those around him[73]. Only his father was still a pagan then.

At this point a few comments should also be made about Patricius which will give a clearer picture of both the young Catholic Augustine and his father. It is known that in the *Confessions* Monnica occupies a central position[74]; the father, however, remains in the background and even appears in an unfavourable light[75]. But is that all that can be said about him? It must be taken into consideration again that the material in the *Confessions* was selected with a special intention[76]. Only what is significant for a delineation of his spiritual development and provides food for reflection on God's works is recorded[77]. Patricius was of little importance in this framework.

Yet Augustine makes incidental remarks about Patricius that reveal more about him. For instance, he says that his father some time before he died had become a catechumen[78] and that 'at the end of his temporal life' he was baptized[79]. These events took place when the son was about 15 and 16 years old[80]. Can it not be assumed that eventually Patricius' conversion exerted such a positive influence that in retrospect Augustine could write about 'the Catholic Church recommended to me by *my parents*', 'the Christian religion which *my parents* had sown in me when I was a young boy', and 'the step upon which I had been placed as a boy by *my parents*'[81]?

---

[73] *Conf.* I, 11, 17: 'Ita iam credebam et illa [sc. Monnica] et omnis domus, nisi pater solus, qui tamen non evicit in me ius maternae pietatis, quominus in Christum crederem, sicut ille nondum crediderat'.

[74] See p. 25.

[75] Esp. *Conf.* IX, 9, 19.

[76] Cf. Courcelle, *Recherches*, esp. 40-43, for intentional and unintentional omissions.

[77] Cf. Courcelle, *Recherches*, esp. 13-29. Feldmann shows in *Einfluss*, esp. 103-208, that the *Conf.* aim to inspire (excitare!) the spirit and mind of the reader and lead him to the meditation on the merciful acts of God.

[78] *Conf.* II, 3, 6: '... nam ille adhuc catechumenus et hoc recens erat'.

[79] *Conf.* IX, 9, 20: '... in extrema vita temporali ...'. The use of the term *fidelis* here is evidence for his having been baptized; for *fidelis* see e.g. *Conf.* VI, 1, 1 and IX, 3, 5.

[80] *Conf.* III, 4, 7; II, 3, 6.

[81] See n. 57, 54 and 48 resp. That *puer* could denote, for A., a boy of 15 or 16 is clear from *Conf.* IX, 6, 14 (Adeodatus was still a *puer* of about 15) and IX, 7, 15 (Valentinianus II is a *puer* in 387; he was 16 then).

At any rate it is clear that, in addition to a thorough classical schooling, Augustine received a Christian education that had a lasting influence upon him. He grew up in the tradition of the Church of Africa. The possible implications of this fact will certainly have to be considered in this investigation into the origins of his doctrine of the two cities.

4. *Cicero's 'Hortensius'*

One incident in the course of the young Augustine's life deserves special mention, for it further elucidates the influence of his classical schooling and that of his Christian education in particular. And what is more, it clarifies his sudden conversion to Manichaeism: in 373 he read Cicero's *Hortensius*[82].

Although the study of philosophy was not a standard part of the curriculum, Cicero's dialogue, which aimed to stimulate an interest in philosophy[83], inspired Augustine to yearn 'with an incredible ardour in my heart for the immortality of wisdom'[84]. He was required to address himself to the work in order to study its style, but it was the contents that made an indelible impression on him.

What was it that Cicero taught? As far as the dialogue can be reconstructed from Augustine's works, the aspect that moved him most must have been the view that all people wish to be happy, but that in the desire for happiness it is not wealth and honour that provide the keys, but only wisdom. Or rather: it is the very *search* for wisdom that makes man happy[86]. Not the sensually perceptible life is the true life, but the spiritual one.

This teaching was persuasive for the eighteen-year-old student.

---

[82] *Conf.* III, 4, 7.

[83] The dialogue *Hortensius* was written originally as the first part of a trilogy: *Hortensius, Catulus, Lucullus*. In this book Cicero used the *Protreptikos* by the young Aristotle, who was still close to Plato; thus A. became acquainted with Platonic philosophy at this early stage.

[84] *Conf.* III, 4, 7: '... et inmortalitatem sapientiae concupiscebam aestu cordis incredibili ...'.

[85] Cf. M. Testard, *Saint Augustin et Cicéron. I. Cicéron dans la formation et dans l'oeuvre de saint Augustin*, Paris 1958, 19 ff.; Hagendahl, *Latin Classics*, 79-94 and 486-497; Feldmann, *Einfluss*, 77-100. A reconstruction of the entire work—besides A., Lactantius and a few other Latin writers handed down fragments of it—has since been provided by L. Straume-Zimmermann, *Ciceros Hortensius*, Bern-Frankfurt 1976.

[86] Cicero, as an Academic, must have taught this; cf. Feldmann, *Einfluss*, 95.

Though all around him at Carthage 'the cauldron of ignominious loves was seething'[87], and though he met his concubine here and begot his son Adeodatus, it was also in this city that his desire for wisdom was aroused. 'A certain Cicero'[88] taught him that true happiness is spiritual and bestowed on man through *philosophia*. From then on Augustine wished to devote himself to the search for wisdom as the supreme good[89].

This turn in Augustine's life has been referred to as his first conversion[90]. And not entirely without justification. For he described the whole event unequivocally as a sudden change which aroused all the energy of his soul[91]. And what is most striking is that once again his Christian education exerted a strong influence: his disposition, his prayers to God, his wishes and desires changed[92]. The *Hortensius* was apparently able to inspire Christian consciousness powerfully and to strengthen it: 'How I was burning, my God, how I was burning to fly from earthly things back to Thee'[93]. True, the fire of his enthusiasm was tempered, because Christ's name, which he had already taken in with his mother's milk, did not occur in Cicero's work[94]. It was for this reason that he turned to the holy Scriptures[95].

The study of the Scriptures, however, resulted in profound disappointment. The young rhetor was disgusted by the poor style of the Bible translation: it appeared rough-hewn and unworthy of compar-

---

87 *Conf.* III, 1, 1: 'Veni Carthaginem, et circumstrepebat me undique sartago flagitiosorum amorum'.

88 *Conf.* III, 4, 7: '... perveneram in librum cuiusdam Ciceronis ...'.

89 There is a striking similarity here between *Conf.* III, 4, 7-8; VIII, 7, 17; *De b. vita* I, 4 and *Sol.* I, 10, 17.

90 M. Peters, 'Augustins erste Bekehrung', in *Harnack-Ehrung* ..., Leipzig 1921, 195-211. The second conversion would be that of the intellect through his becoming acquainted with Neoplatonism; the third the conversion of the will to the Church and the ascetic ideal. For criticism of her view, partly because she was supposed not to have discerned sufficiently the importance of the *Hortensius* for A., see Feldmann, *Einfluss*, 23 n. 30.

91 Cf. Peters, 'Bekehrung', 208: 'Augustin erlebt eine *subita conversio*, die alle Aktivität seiner Seele wachruft'.

92 *Conf.* III, 4, 7: 'Ille vero liber mutavit affectum meum et ad te ipsum, domine, mutavit preces meas et vota ac desideria mea fecit alia'.

93 *Conf.* III, 4, 8.

94 *Ibid.*

95 *Conf.* III, 5, 9: '*Itaque* institui animum intendere in scripturas sanctas et videre quales essent'. The *itaque* with which III, 6, 10 opens is also very significant: because A. is searching for *Christ*, he ends up among the Manichaeans.

ison with the dignity of Cicero's manner of expression[96]. For a man who had been trained to analyse a text and to pay attention to its logical structure, the diversity of the genealogies of Jesus must have been an insurmountable problem[97]. In neither style nor content could the Scriptures stand the test of comparison with Cicero's work. Augustine was in search of wisdom, he wanted knowledge, but he was unwilling to believe on authority; to him the Catholic faith seemed unworthy of an intellectual.

Thus the spiritual awakening brought about by his becoming acquainted with the *Hortensius* led at first to a quickening of the Christian impressions from his youth[98]. But a return to this former belief was an impossibility for Augustine.

Nevertheless he continued his search for Christ. Therefore it was not the Catholic Christianity of Africa that appealed to him, but a new spiritual Christianity. In it the Old Testament was pushed aside because of its unspiritual and loathsome character. Christ, however, was at the centre and was revered as the true teacher of wisdom, who enlightens man and guides him to true knowledge. Augustine, in his thirst for knowledge, joined the disciples of the 'apostle of Jesus Christ': Mani.

5. The Manichaean

Now that we have reached in this sketch of Augustine's development his years as a Manichaean, it should be noted first of all that this

---

96 *Conf.* III, 5, 9: '... sed visa est mihi indigna, quam Tullianae dignitati conpararem.' For the nature of the African Bible translations, see e.g. Monceaux, *Histoire*, I, 97-173 and J. Daniélou, *The Origins of Latin Christianity*, London-Philadelphia 1977, 6-8. The reactions of A. and others to these translations was already described by Alfaric, *Évolution*, 71-73, and particularly by Marrou, *Augustin et la fin*, 473-503.—A.'s advice to Deogratias, *De cat. rud.* 13, becomes clear in this context: the solid diction (solidum eloquium) of the Bible should not cause the candidates from grammar and rhetoric schools to shrink back, for it is not inflated (inflatum); words and deeds should not be taken literally; etc. Cf. *Conf.* IX, 5, 13: A. postpones further reading of Isaiah until he has more training 'in our Lord's manner of speech'.

97 See the closely-reasoned analysis of Courcelle, *Recherches*, 61-63; he relates *Conf.* III, 5, 9 to *s.* 51, 4. Besides, training in rhetoric included logic: Scripture appeared illogical to A. For this reason, too, he used *itaque* at the beginning of *Conf.* III, 6, 10.

98 Cf. Feldmann, *Einfluss*, 512, after a thorough analysis of both the *Hortensius* and Book III of the *Conf.*: 'Der Hortensius war geeignet, mit manchen seiner Äusserungen christliche Eindrücke in Augustinus zu wecken und zu bestätigen'.

period deserves special attention. For it was long and intensive, and, particularly as regards Augustine's later doctrine of the two cities, note should be taken of possible Manichaean reminiscences. Moreover, the origin of this gnostic world religion itself has to a large extent been placed in a new light, mainly because of the discovery of the *Cologne Mani-Codex*.

The significance of this and other discoveries for our knowledge of Mani and his teachings will be discussed later[99]. Here we shall concentrate on Augustine's conversion to Manichaeism. Why did he take that step? What exactly took place? How profound was his knowledge of the Manichaean doctrines? And how long did this period in his life last?

As to the reason for his conversion the *Confessions* do not leave us in the dark. 'Therefore I fell among arrogant fools, very carnal and garrulous, in whose mouths were the devil's snares and birdlime concocted with the addition of syllables of Your name and of the Lord Jesus Christ and of the Paraclete, our Comforter, the Holy Ghost. These names were never out of their mouths ...'[100]. Evidently Augustine, in his search for Christ, was attracted by the proclamation of a Christian message which even included a concept of trinity. It was truth that he was seeking: 'And they said «truth» and again «truth», and they spoke much about it to me ...; oh Truth, Truth, how deeply even then did my inmost soul yearn for You, while they frequently and in a multiplicity of ways expressed Your name to me, in exterior sound and by means of many thick books'[101].

We can visualize the background of Augustine's conversion as follows: disciples of Mani propagated their teachings in his environs, especially in intellectual circles and mainly in secret[102]. In contrast

---

99 See pp. 229-234.

100 *Conf.* III, 6, 10. 'Fools' (delirantes) is undoubtedly a play on words on Mani (Gr. manía = folly) and the Manichaeans. Cf. *De ut. cred.* 36 (phrenetici); *Conf.* XIII, 30, 45 (insani); et al., but also *Keph.* 225, 6-9.

101 *Conf.* III, 6, 10.

102 In 372 Valentinianus I had promulgated a law against Manichaean propaganda; see the text in A. Adam, *Texte zum Manichäismus* (*KlT* 175), Berlin 1969[2], 84. Shortly after the death of Mani (277?), missionaries arrived in Roman Africa: Diocletian's edict from Alexandria to the proconsul of Africa, dated 31 March 297, had been written on the occasion of *official* charges from Africa in the preceding year. Edicts against the 'Persian danger' were reiterated frequently. See E.H. Kaden, 'Die Edikte gegen die Manichäer von Diokletian bis Justinian', *Festschrift für Hans Lewald*, Basel 1953, 55-68. The spread of Manichaeism in the

to the mainstream of African Christianity, which was legalistic in nature and originally bore in many of its institutions and practices the hallmark of the Jewish synagogue[103], they offered a spiritual Christianity which on a first hearing satisfied the mind. As everywhere else, these missionaries gathered fellowships of hearers (*auditores*) around them, comparable to the catechumens of the official Christian Church.

Augustine, the intellectual in quest of truth, also joined them. Here he would find an answer to his burning questions. For the Manichaeans pretended to offer a rational religion that was free of offence to reason. Among them he found criticism of the Bible, particularly of the Old Testament, which they rejected almost outright[104]. Equally attractive to Augustine, who was throughout his life very receptive to instrumental and vocal music[105], were the communal worship services with their enthusiastic psalm-singing[106]. He also found among them a great appreciation of asceti-

---

Roman Empire is also described by P. Brown, 'The Diffusion of Manichaeism in the Roman Empire' (1969), repr. in Brown, *Religion and Society*, 94-118. He also mentions *public* debates with Manichaeans (112 n. 2) and gives a clear picture of the almost exclusively intellectual circles in which Mani's teaching found acceptance. Even a Manichaean auditor, General Sebastianus, almost became an emperor (109).

103 For more information on this view, developed esp. by G. Quispel, W.H.C. Frend and M. Simon, see pp. 365-371.

104 They did not reject the Old Testament totally, for some good is mixed with the bad. See esp. P. Alfaric, *Les écritures manichéennes, II: Étude analytique*, Paris 1919, 139-160. The Old Testament and the New Testament are like the good and the bad tree referred to by Jesus in *Luke* 6 and *Matt.* 7 and 12 (Alfaric, 145). Yet the Manichaeans quoted not only Jewish and Christian Apocrypha and the New Testament, but also the Old Testament on more than one occasion, interpreting the text each time in their own way.—As for the Old Testament they seemed to have a preference for the *Psalms* and *Isaiah*; see Alfaric, *Écritures*, II, 147 f.; A. Böhlig, *Die Bibel bei den Manichäern*, Münster 1947 (Diss. Mschr.), 30 f.; A. Böhlig, 'Christliche Wurzeln im Manichäismus' (1957/1960), *Mysterion und Wahrheit. Gesammelte Beiträge zur spätantiken Religionsgeschichte*, Leiden 1968, esp. 213-215.

105 See e.g. Van der Meer, *Augustinus*, esp. 294 f.; K.G. Fellerer, 'Die Musica in den Artes Liberales', in: J. Koch (Hrsg.), *Artes Liberales. Von der Antiken Bildung zur Wissenschaft des Mittelalters*, Leiden 1976^2, 33-49. With reference to *De musica* I, 6 and VI, Fellerer shows the great spiritual value A. attached to music: this art form can lead to God.

106 *Conf.* III, 7, 14; X, 33, 49. And A. joined in! We should take note of an error that occurs frequently in (English) translations: 'Et cantabam carmina ...' (*Conf.* III, 7, 14) should not be rendered 'And I composed/made verses', but translated literally: 'And I sang verses'. Cf. Alfaric, *Évolution*, 162 n. 5; E. Feldmann, 'Christus-Frömmigkeit der Mani-Jünger ...', in: E. Dassmann - K.S. Frank (Hrsg.), *Pietas. Festschrift für Bernhard Kötting* (*JbAC*, Erg. Bd. 8), Münster 1980,

cism. Moreover, the mysterious nature of Manichaeism must have fascinated him, for occultism exerted a powerful attraction on people in those days. But above all Mani's teachings answered, in an easy and fundamental way, the questions: 'Whence comes evil? Whence comes man?'[107]

Within a few days[108] Augustine joined the disciples of Mani. But how did this actually take place? And why exactly was he affected by the Manichaean teachings? A few specific comments on this topic can explain the background of some of the themes and various digressions in the *City of God*.

> Particularly in works other than the *Confessions*, Augustine describes the Manichaean methods of proselytizing. For example in *The Christian Combat*: the Manichaeans did not start by presenting their complicated and basically irrational myths, but they selected *capitula* from the Scriptures that were unintelligible to simple believers. They were put on the wrong track by the question: 'unde malum', whence comes evil?[109] The Manichaeans also carried on extensive and vehement disputations[110], thereby trying to show errors in the Catholic Christian teachings. By doing so they prepared the confused listeners for their own preaching. Especially from *De Genesi contra Manichaeos* it is clear that this was done in debates in which both parties spoke on

---

208.—That A. knew many Manichaean hymns has already been demonstrated by Alfaric, *Écritures*, II, 124, with references to *De mor.* II, 55; *En. in Ps.* 140, 11; *C. Faust.* XIII, 18 and *Conf.* III, 7, 14. Concerning these hymns, see e.g. Alfaric, *Écritures*, II, 126-134 and 206. In particular H.-Ch. Puech, 'Liturgie et pratiques rituelles dans le Manichéisme (suite)', *ACF* 59 (1959) 264-269, points to the fact that these psalms and hymns were of a devotional nature and had a redeeming effect. Cf. also Puech, 'Musique et hymnologie manichéennes', *Encyclopédie des musiques sacrées*, I, Paris 1968, 353-386, and Feldmann, 'Christus-Frömmigkeit'.

107 It is striking that the Manichaeans in A.'s day were concerned with precisely the same problems as were the Gnostics in Tertullian's day. One can compare *De duab. an.* 10 with Tertullian's *De praescr.* 7. See W.H.C. Frend, 'The Gnostic-Manichaean Tradition in Roman North Africa', *JEH* 4 (1953) 17 (repr. in W.H.C. Frend, *Religion Popular und Unpopular in the Early Centuries*, London 1976, Ch. XII).

108 *De duab. an.* 1: '... ne tam facile ac diebus paucis religionis verissimae semina ... ex animo expellerentur'. The period of time indicated as 'few days' in *Conf.* IX, 2, 2 (paucissimi dies) can be compared with IX, 2, 4 ('Nescio utrum vel viginti dies erant'). It is reasonable to suppose that his change-over also took place in c. 20 days, not long after he had read the *Hortensius*.

109 *De agone* 4: 'Sed illi quando capiunt homines non ista [sc. the mythical cosmogony] prius dicunt; quae si dicerent, ridentur, aut fugerentur ab hominibus: sed eligunt capitula de scripturis, quae simplices homines non intelligunt; et per illa decipiunt animas imperitas, quaerendo unde sit malum'.

110 *De ut. cred.* 2: 'Sed quia diu multumque de imperitorum erroribus latissime ac vehementissime disputabant ...'; cf. *De mor.* II, 16; *De Gen. c. Man.* I, 1, 2.

the same subject, after which the listener gave the verdict[111]. The charge was directed mainly against the Old Testament, but also against some portions of the New Testament. The Old Testament in particular had to be exposed as a collection of absurdities[112].

Augustine, too, was fascinated by this Manichaean criticism. In Book III of the *Confessions* he sets forth three questions which in this context also have a central place elsewhere in his writings. It is evident that they were crucial for his joining Mani's disciples. First of all the question: 'unde malum?' In the dialogue *On Free Will* he mentions it to Evodius, calling it an issue that disturbed him intensely when he was a young man[113]. He is afflicted by the problem of the origin of evil and the wickedness of creation. Also the question of whether God is enclosed in a physical shape and has hair and nails[114] appears in another passage as the great objection the Manichaeans offered to *Gen.* 1:26: if man has been created in God's image, God has to be depicted as anthropomorphous[115]. The objections to the way of life of the patriarchs: ' ... whether they are to be deemed righteous who had many wives at the same time and killed people and sacrificed animals'[116], appears clearly in other texts as Manichaean polemics against which Augustine was directing his statements[117].

In 373 Augustine must have been persuaded by these and similar polemics, directed especially against the opening chapters of *Genesis*. The exact phrasing of questions posed at that time by the Manichaeans is not recorded either in the *Confessions* or in other writings. But a particularly clear picture of Manichaean criticism emerges from *On Genesis Against the Manichaeans* and *Against Adimantus*.

From the former a long list of questions can be enumerated. In what *principium* did God create? What did He do before He created the

---

111 Feldmann, *Einfluss*, 564 f.: 'genus iudiciale'.

112 *De ut. cred.* 17: 'At *absurda* ibi dici videbantur. (...) Cum legerem, per me ipse cognovi'. From the context it appears that the Old Testament is meant here. Cf. *Conf.* VI, 5, 8: 'Iam enim *absurditatem*, quae me in illis litteris solebat offendere ...'; VI, 4, 6: 'Gaudebam etiam, quod vetera scripta legis et prophetarum iam non illo oculo mihi legenda proponerentur, quo antea videbantur *absurda* ...'; VI, 11, 18: 'Ecce iam non sunt *absurda* in libris ecclesiasticis, quae *absurda* videbantur, et possunt aliter atque honeste intellegi'.

113 *Conf.* III, 7, 12 and esp. *De lib. arb.* I, 2, 4: '... dic mihi unde male faciamus. A. Eam quaestionem moves, quae me admodum adolescentem vehementer exercuit et fatigatum in haereticos impulit atque deiẹcit'.

114 *Conf.* III, 7, 12: '... et utrum forma corporea deus finiretur et haberet capillos et ungues ...'. Cf. V, 10, 19.

115 E.g. *De Gen. c. Man.* I, 17, 27: 'Istam maxime quaestionem solent Manichaei loquaciter agitare ...'.

116 *Conf.* III, 7, 12: '... utrum iusti existimandi essent qui haberent uxores multas simul et occiderent homines et sacrificarent de animalibus'.

117 E.g. *C. Faust.* VI, 2; XXII, 24. 30. 47; *De lib. arb.* I, 6, 14-15.

world? Was God in darkness before He created light? Was water the dwelling-place of God's Spirit? The creation of water is not mentioned: where did water come from? God made fruitful plants come into existence, but who made the thorns? The sun was not created till the fourth day, what were the days like before that? Why did God create so many useless and dangerous animals? Who created the devil?, etc.[118]. *Against Adimantus* also presents a large number of antitheses[119] between the opening chapters of *Genesis* and other books of the Old Testament on the one hand and pronouncements in the New Testament on the other hand: God created through Himself (*Gen.* 1: 1-5)—God created through Christ (*John* 1:10); God rested *Gen.* 2:2)—God works all the time (*John* 5:17); God created a wife for Adam (*Gen.* 2)—marriage should be renounced (*Matt.* 19:29; *Mark* 10:29ff); man was created in God's image (*Gen.* 1:26)—man's father is the devil (*John* 8:44), etc.[120].

Thus Mani's disciples not only totally rejected the creation narratives, but also had severe criticism of, among other things, the patriarchs' way of life. Against this background it becomes clear why Augustine in the *City of God*, when giving his *narratio* of the *Heilsgeschichte*, dwells so extensively on primeval history: it is the main constituent of Books XI-XIV and, together with the narratives on well-known figures from the first book of the Bible such as Cain, Abel, Noah and the patriarchs, the main constituent of Books XI-XVI. An analogous picture is given in the long catechesis in *The Catechizing of the Uninstructed*: there the story of creation, paradise, the Fall, the rise of the two cities and the Flood, followed by that of Abraham and the other patriarchs, constitutes a sizable part[121].

It also becomes apparent why in other works, too, Augustine gives so much attention to *Genesis*. Already in 388-390 he wrote a commentary on the first few verses of this book of the Bible, directed against his former co-religionists: *De Genesi contra Manichaeos*. But because of his conviction that in this work too much space had been devoted to allegorical interpretation, he attempted from 393 to write a literal exegesis: *De Genesi ad litteram*. He soon realized, however, that his strength was not equal to the task and therefore he left the work unfinished. When he considered it again at the time of his *Retractations*, his first

---

[118] *De Gen. c. Man.* I, 2, 3 ff.

[119] This is reminiscent of Marcion's *Antitheses*. Mani must have been familiar with them, for he polemized against them in his *Treasure of Life*; see Alfaric, *Écritures*, II, 140.

[120] *C. Adim.* 1-4.

[121] *De cat. rud.* 29-33.

idea was to destroy it[122]. But in the end he decided to keep it, because it could demonstrate his first efforts at interpretation; he changed the title to *De Genesi ad litteram liber imperfectus*.

Meanwhile, around 400, he had once again discussed the story of creation in the last three books of the *Confessions*. Later he did this again in a comprehensive work, begun c. 401 and completed in twelve books c. 414[123]. This time he progressed in the text as far as Adam's expulsion from paradise. Again he did not attempt an allegorical interpretation but a literal one: *De Genesi ad litteram libri XII*. But in the end this larger work—with its numerous and profound digressions on the Trinity, time, knowledge of God, providence, the soul[124], paradise in the third heaven and the various visions[125]—was equally unsatisfactory to him. 'In this work more is sought than found, and of what is found only the smaller part is proved; the remainder, in fact, is presented in a way that makes it look as if it still has to be studied'[126].

In the foregoing we can already see how much Augustine's theology in general and his exegesis in particular reflect his Manichaean years. In his later works—and not least in the *City of God*[127]—he continually returns to the errors of the Manichaeans and tries to refute them.

A remarkable feature of the exegetical work immediately following his conversion is a predilection not only for *Genesis*, but for the Old Testament in general[128]. This has to be defended: its opening chapters are (also) literally true, as are the stories about the patriarchs; the two

122 *Retract.* I, 18.

123 For this dating, cf. P. Agaësse in *BA* 48, 25-31.

124 For example, Books VII and X deal entirely with this.

125 This is the subject of Book XII.

126 *Retract.* II, 24, 1: 'In quo opere plura quaesita quam inventa sunt; et eorum quae inventa sunt, pauciora firmata; cetera vero ita posita, velut adhuc requirenda sint'.

127 It is again striking that when A., in Books XI-XIV, writes on Creation and the origin of the two *civitates*, he directs his remarks specifically to the Manichaeans: XI, 10. 13. 21. 22; XII, 1; XIV, 5.21. The only other specific reference to the Manichaeans is in I, 20 (their 'error' and 'delusion' that the commandment not to kill also applies to plants and animals), while there is an implicit reference in X, 24 (evil is not an independent substance). In VI, 11 A. only refers to his treatises against the Manichaeans.

128 A. Allgeier, 'Der Einfluss des Manichäismus auf die exegetische Fragestellung bei Augustin. Ein Beitrag zur Geschichte von Augustins theologischer Entwicklung', in: M. Grabmann – J. Mausbach, *Aurelius Augustinus. Die Festschrift der Görres-Gesellschaft zum 1500. Todestage des heiligen Augustinus*, Köln 1930, 1-13, esp. 2-7.

testaments are in agreement[129], the Septuagint is divinely inspired and its text is reliable. Augustine, thoroughly familiar with the Manichaean way of criticizing the Bible, was very much opposed to any emendation of the Bible text that was at variance with the Septuagint. At first he considered the new translation from the Hebrew by Jerome to be not only superfluous but actually dangerous[130]. During the last decade of his life he modified somewhat his opinion on the inspiration of the LXX and could appreciate Jerome's new translation. But by then the Manichaeans had been defeated[131].

There are other aspects of Augustine's attitude towards the Scriptures that ought to be considered from the perspective of his Manichaean past. In his exegetical work, his emphasis on the harmony among the evangelists[132] and, for example, his special interest in the genealogies of Jesus in *Matthew* and *Luke* are also notable[133]. Besides, he wanted to make a sharp distinction between canonical and apocryphal writings. Among the Manichaeans it was precisely the apocryphal works that were held in high esteem[134], but they lack the authority of a completely certain and evident *successio*[135]. Catholic tradition testifies to canonicity[136]. It was no coincidence that the first

---

129 See esp. M. Pontet, *L'Exégèse de S. Augustin prédicateur*, Paris s.a. (1945?), 305-383.

130 Cf. *Epp.* 28, 71 and esp. 82. In *Ep.* 82, 35 we read: '... propterea me nolle tuam ex Hebraeo interpretationem in ecclesiis legi, ne contra septuaginta auctoritatem tamquam novum aliquid proferentes, magno scandalo perturbemus plebes Christi, quarum aures et corda illam interpretationem audire consuerunt, quae etiam ab apostolis adprobata est'. F. Cavallera, 'Les «Quaestiones hebraicae in Genesim» de Saint Jerôme et les «Quaestiones in Genesim» de Saint Augustin', *MAg*, II, 359, justly characterizes the difference between Jerome and Augustine as that between the scholar who makes a stand for a pure translation of the only inspired Hebrew text and the man of the Church who aims to avoid confusion within his congregation.

131 Allgeier, 'Einfluss', 12.

132 Particularly in *De consensu evangelistarum*, dating from c. 400. Cf. H. Merkel, *Widersprüche zwischen den Evangelien. Ihre polemische und apologetische Behandlung in der Alten Kirche bis zu Augustin*, Tübingen 1971, 218-261.

133 E.g. *De cons. ev.* II, 1 ff.

134 See esp. Alfaric, *Écritures*, II, 139-197; Böhlig, *Bibel*, 88 ff.; P. Nagel, 'Die apokryphen Apostelakten des 2. und 3. Jahrhunderts in der manichäischen Literatur', in: K.-W. Tröger (Hrsg.), *Gnosis und Neues Testament. Studien aus Religionswissenschaft und Theologie*, Berlin 1973, 149-182; J.-D. Kaestli, 'L'utilisation des Actes apocryphes des apôtres dans le manichéisme', in: M. Krause (ed.), *Gnosis and Gnosticism*, Leiden 1977, 107-116.

135 *DCD* XV, 23: 'Omittamus igitur earum scripturarum fabulas, quae apocryphae nuncupantur, eo quod earum occulta origo non claruit patribus, a quibus usque ad nos auctoritas veracium scripturarum certissima et notissima successione pervenit'.

136 *De doctr. chr.* II, 8, 12: 'Tenebit igitur hunc modum in scripturis canonicis, ut eas quae ab omnibus accipiuntur ecclesiis catholicis, praeponat eis quas quaedam non accipiunt: in eis vero quae non accipiuntur ab omnibus, praeponat eas

Western synods to deal with the establishment of the canon were held at Hippo (393) and Carthage (387 and 419)[137]. Augustine took an active part in them[138].

Augustine's emphasis on the truth of the Scriptures can also be explained as a reaction to his experience among the Manichaeans. After he had read the *Hortensius* he failed in his efforts to read Scripture, and subsequently it was Manichaean criticism that convinced him of its unreliability: 'Furthermore, what they [the Manichaeans] had rejected in Your Scriptures I considered impossible to defend ...'[139]. But in the *Confessions* it also appears that later on he regarded the Scriptures to be true, reliable and inspired: his love of God was inflamed by the Psalms[140]; he was consumed by anger towards the enemies of the Scriptures[141]; all the treasures of wisdom and knowledge hidden in Christ he now sought in the Scriptures[142]. For him the words of Scripture were God's very words: 'And I said: O Lord, is this Scripture of Yours not true since You, the Veritable One and the Truth, have revealed it? ... To this You answer me, because You are my God and You speak with a powerful voice unto the innermost being of Your servant, penetrating my deafness and crying: O man, indeed what my Scripture says, say I ...'[143].

In this way Augustine clearly contrasts in the *Confessions* his Manichaean past and his present state. Moreover, he illustrates the earlier experiences with an impressive image: 'But if any one of them, despising the so-called simplicity of Your words, tries to reach outside the warm, protective nest in presumptuous weakness, alas, the wretched one will fall, and, Lord God, have mercy, lest the passers-by trample the unfledged little bird, and send Your angel that he may put it back into the nest, that it may live until it can fly'[144].

---

quas plures gravioresque accipiunt, eis quas pauciores minorisque auctoritatis ecclesiae tenent. Si autem alias invenerit a pluribus, alias a gravioribus haberi, quanquam hoc facile invenire non possit, aequalis tamen auctoritatis eas habendas puto'. Then follows, in II, 8, 13, A.'s survey of the canon.

137 Cf. Allgeier, 'Einfluss', 9.

138 Cf. Perler, *Voyages*, 215 f.; 350 f.

139 *Conf.* V, 11, 21: 'Deinde quae illi in scripturis tuis reprehenderent defendi posse non existimabam ...'.

140 *Conf.* IX, 4, 8: 'Quas tibi, deus meus, voces dedi, cum legerem psalmos David, cantica fidelia ... Quas tibi voces dabam in psalmis illis et quomodo in te inflammabar ex eis ...'.

141 *Conf.* IX, 4, 11: '... et super inimicis scripturae huius tabescebam'.

142 *Conf.* XI, 2, 4: '... in quo sunt omnes thesauri sapientiae et scientiae absconditi. Ipsos quaero in libris tuis'.

143 *Conf.* XIII, 29, 44: '... et dixi: o domine, nonne ista scriptura tua vera est, quoniam tu verax et veritas edidisti eam? (...) Ad haec tu dicis mihi, quoniam tu es deus meus et dicis voce forti in aure interiore servo tuo perrumpens meam surditatem et clamans: o homo, nempe quod scriptura mea dicit, ego dico ...'.

144 *Conf.* XII, 27, 37: 'Quorum si quispiam quasi vilitatem dictorum aspernatus extra nutritorias cunas superba inbecillitate se extenderit, heu! cadet miser et,

Feldmann[145] points out that here Augustine is recounting an episode from his own life: he was the weak one[146] who climbed out of the protective nest of the Church and 'fell' among the Manichaeans[147], because he was offended by the simple style of writing (*vilitas*) of the Scriptures. The angel denotes Ambrose[148], who brought him back into the Church[149].

Thus the controversy about Scripture occupies a central position in Augustine's works. It provides us with one aspect of the influence of Manichaeism, but this is not the only one. For a long time Augustinian research has been addressing itself to the question of how much the greatest Father of the Western Church was influenced, not only in a negative way (as is apparent from his continual defensive reaction), but also in a positive way by this gnostic world religion. Some of his contemporaries accused the former Manichaean of not having renounced his past. And especially since in this century, as a result of various discoveries, we have become better informed about Manichaeism, there have been more and more references to Manichaean vestiges in his theology. Rightly or wrongly? This question will be dealt with here, particularly with regard to the origins of Augustine's doctrine of *civitas Dei* and *civitas diaboli*.

A more thorough knowledge of Augustine's development can provide important data for this study. He was a Manichaean for some years. But how long exactly was this period? And to what extent did the young Augustine become acquainted with the teachings of Mani's disciples? Did he read their writings?

It is certain that from his nineteenth to his twenty-eighth year—precisely the years that can be considered the period in which one develops a philosophy of life—Augustine was a Manichaean[150].

---

domine deus, miserere, ne inplumem pullum conculcent qui transeunt viam, et mitte angelum tuum, qui eum reponat in nido, ut vivat, donec volet'.

145 Feldmann, *Einfluss*, 163-164 and 522-523, where he compares *Conf.* XII, 27, 37 with *s.* 51. Earlier Courcelle, *Recherches*, 61-62, called attention to this sermon, but not to the similarities with *Conf.* XII.

146 *Conf.* III, 4, 7: 'Inter hos ego *inbecilla tunc aetate* discebam libros eloquentiae ...'.

147 *Conf.* III, 6, 10: 'Itaque *incidi* in homines superbe delirantes ...'.

148 *Conf.* VI, 1, 1: 'Dilegebat [sc. Monnica] autem illum virum [sc. Ambrosius] sicut *angelum Dei* ...'.

149 It should be observed in passing that this 'putting back' (*Conf.* XII, 27, 37: reponat) is further proof of A.'s originally belonging to the Christian Church: he was a catechumen, he became an apostate, Ambrose brought him back.

150 *Conf.* IV, 1, 1: 'Per idem tempus annorum novem, ab undevicensimo anno

That was from 373 to 382. In the summer of 382 Bishop Faustus, renowned among the Western Manichaeans, finally arrived at Carthage. Shortly thereafter a meeting must have taken place between Augustine and the man from whom he expected so much[151]. This meeting was a disappointment, however, and the doubts concerning the Manichaean doctrines increased. But in the summer of the following year, by which time Augustine was living in Rome, he was still having frequent contacts with Mani's disciples[152]. As late as the autumn of 384[153] Manichaeans acted as his mediators with Rome's city-prefect Symmachus, enabling him to receive an appointment as state professor of rhetoric in Milan[154].

It should be observed that Augustine describes his departure for Milan as follows: 'I was going away in order to disengage myself from them, but neither of us knew it'[155]. We have no reason to doubt this representation. But what emerges from this passage is that in Rome at the end of 384 Augustine still had close ties with Mani's disciples. It was probably not coincidental that Symmachus, a declared antagonist of Christianity, sent *this* rhetor to the imperial capital[156]. At any rate it is clear that the number of nine years which Augustine himself indicates as the time he spent among the Manichaeans[157] should be regarded with reservations: there were at least ten. Is this the later Catholic bishop speaking, wishing to

---

aetatis meae usque ad duodetricensimum, seducebamur et seducebamus ...'. Courcelle, *Recherches*, 78, is incorrect in stating that A.'s 19th year extended from Nov. 373 to Nov. 374. This should be Nov. 372 – Nov. 373. Several scholars have followed him in this error.

151 *Conf.* V, 6, 10 f.

152 *Conf.* V, 10, 18 and 19, inter alia: 'Amicitia tamen eorum familiarius utebar quam ceterorum hominum, qui in illa haeresi non fuissent'.

153 Courcelle, *Recherches*, 79 n. 1, gives proof for this date, with a reference to Seeck; cf. Schindler, 'Augustinus', 648.

154 *Conf.* V, 13, 23: '... ego ipse ambivi per eos ipsos manichaeis vanitatibus ebrios ...'.

155 *Conf.* V, 13, 23: '... quibus ut carerem ibam, sed utrique nesciebamus ...'.

156 Cf. Courcelle, *Recherches*, 79. For Symmachus, the reactionary-pagan prefect of the city of Rome and his attitude toward the Christian Church and the emperor, see esp. J. Wytzes, *Der Streit um den Altar der Viktoria*, Amsterdam 1936; R. Klein, *Symmachus, eine tragische Gestalt des ausgehenden Heidentums*, Darmstadt 1971; R. Klein (Hrsg.), *Der Streit um den Viktoriaaltar* ..., Darmstadt 1972. When A. arrived in Milan in the autumn of 384, the sharp controversy had been over for only a few months.

157 *Conf.* III, 11, 20; IV, 1, 1; V, 6, 10; cf. *De ut. cred.* I, 2: '... annos fere novem ...'.

minimize the number of years he had lived in error? Or does the number nine in the *Confessions* have mainly a symbolic meaning: the number of imperfection[158]? Whatever the case may be, it is certain that Augustine associated with Mani's disciples for quite a number of years.

It is also certain that the importance of his 'hearer'-status should by no means be underestimated. The position of the 'hearers' was somewhat comparable to that of the catechumens in the official Christian Church. Their catechumenate, however, did not merely consist of fasting, prayer and the giving of alms. The *auditores* were also required to look after the material well-being of the 'elect', providing them with food and shelter. Particularly in this last function they played an indispensable role, as Julien Ries has shown using evidence from Coptic texts[159]. It was by means of their participation in the everyday life of the community that they, in contrast to the *electi*, were pre-eminently able to do missionary work.

To what extent this proselytizing could bring about desired results has become especially clear through Augustine. From the first year of his belonging to the sect he persuaded many: his benefactor Romanianus, a childhood friend who died young, his friends Alypius, Nebridius, Honoratus, Fortunatus, Profuturus and another Fortunatus[160]. It is remarkable that nearly all those named here later became members of the Catholic Church of Africa. The only notable exception was one of the men called Fortunatus[161]: he remained a Manichaean and afterwards at Hippo Regius he was an adversary of his former fellow-believer[162]. But the childhood friend, whose name we do not know, died a baptized Catholic[163], and Alypius, Profuturus and Fortunatus appeared later on the scene as

---

[158] L.C. Ferrari, 'Augustine's «Nine Years» as a Manichee', *Aug(L)* 25 (1975) 210-216.

[159] J. Ries, 'Commandements de la justice et vie missionnaire dans l'église de Mani', in: Krause (ed.), *Gnosis and Gnosticism*, 93-106. With reason he refers esp. to *Keph.* 87 (Polotsky and Böhlig, 216-218) as evidence.

[160] Courcelle, *Recherches*, 68-70; W.H.C. Frend, 'Manichaeism in the Struggle between Saint Augustine and Petilian of Constantine', *AM*, II, 859-866 (*Religion*, Ch. XIII), esp. 861 and 865.

[161] It is not clear whether Honoratus, to whom *De ut. cred.* was dedicated, was the Honoratus of *Ep.* 140, a catechumen at Carthage; cf. J. Clémence in *BA* 8, 196.

[162] Cf. Possidius, *Vita*, 6, and *C. Fort.* The debate described in the latter work took place in Aug. 392; A., a presbyter of the Catholic Church, opposed Fortunatus, a presbyter of the Manichaean Church and an influential man at Hippo.

[163] *Conf.* IV, 4, 7-8.

Catholic bishops of Africa's Church, together with their most influential friend Augustine. It is not surprising that especially in the Donatist camp these former Manichaeans were regarded with great suspicion[164].

An important question is how familiar Augustine, his friends and future colleagues—all of them *auditores*—became with the doctrines of the Manichaeans. Did they read their writings? It is telling that in the account of his conversion to Manichaeism, Augustine did not report that he had been won over by reading Manichaean works. He mentions Cicero's *Hortensius*, his Bible reading, later on the Neoplatonic writings and especially the Pauline epistles. But the *Confessions* do not report this with reference to his joining Mani's followers. It can be presumed that, in view of suppression by the State, the Manichaeans did not give their literature to possible converts.

This does not alter the fact that Augustine, already as a 'hearer', became thoroughly acquainted with the teachings of the Manichaeans and that he even read their writings. He states this explicitly in the *Confessions*[165], and also professes that he fully believed in the Manichaean religion[166]. His extensive knowledge of Manichaeism is clearly demonstrated in his writings directed against Mani's *Epistula fundamenti* and against Faustus, as well as in the often closely reasoned debates with Manichaean contemporaries. He showed himself to be so well-informed on Manichaeism that for centuries he was the most important source of information on the subject. For it was not until the finds in Central Asia round the beginning of this century and those in Egypt in the 1930's that a more detailed picture could be formed. But these discoveries have not diminished the value of what Augustine handed down from Manichaean writings: he proves to be a reliable witness.

---

164 Cf. Frend, 'Manichaeism', passim. See also Frend, *Donatist Church*, 236 and 'Gnostic-Manichaean Tradition', passim.

165 *Conf.* V, 3, 6; V, 7, 12; V, 7, 13 et al. *Conf.* III, 12, 21 is esp. relevant. First of all it shows that already then a prominent Christian in Africa was thoroughly familiar with Manichaeism: the bishop to whom Monnica turned for advice had read nearly all the Manichaean books in his youth and had copied them (... et omnes paene non legisse tantum verum etiam scriptitasse libros eorum ...). What is noteworthy is that this bishop said that A. would discover the error and ungodliness of Manichaeism *legendo*.

166 E.g. *Conf.* III, 6, 11: '... volantem autem Medeam ... non credebam: illa autem credidi. vae, vae!'

Thus Augustine's involvement with Manichaeism was deep and long-lasting: a young man who had been brought up as a Catholic was an adherent of a gnostic world religion. Here the longing in his soul was stilled by Christological piety[167] and stirring psalm-singing; here his intellect was gratified by a rational-sounding world view. It is also likely that a psychological motive played an important part in his conversion: he did not want to see himself as personally responsible for his own sins[168].

But the Manichaeans did not provide a solution to his problems. His meeting with Faustus should have led to clarity, but resulted in disillusion. From that time Augustine dissociated himself more and more from Manichaeism. He came for knowledge, but he was ordered to believe[169]. In his philosophical inquiries[170] he also turned his attention to the physical universe; he saw contradictions between the views of the Manichaeans and those held by Cicero and others concerning solar eclipses and the movements of the stars. Not the Manichaean theories, but the calculations of the astrologers proved to be true.

Moreover, he recognized increasingly that the religion he had at first professed so enthusiastically was in a dilemma. On the one hand Manichaeism taught that the believer, after being aroused to knowledge, would exercise full control of his 'self' and would be able to bring about his own salvation. On the other hand the numerous myths told him how helpless and desolate goodness is in this world: it is passive and Jesus is above all the suffering Jesus, *Jesus patibilis*. In essence, Manichaeism appeared to him as a static religion: '...

---

[167] Cf. J.P. de Menasce, 'Augustin manichéen', *Freundesgabe für Ernst Robert Curtius*, Bern 1956, 79-93. De Menasce emphasizes that A. joined the Manichaeans because of the impression that their Christ-centred piety made upon him; this piety, he believed, permeated A.'s mystic terminology. K. Holl, 'Augustins innere Entwicklung', *Gesammelte Aufsätze zur Kirchengeschichte*, III, Tübingen 1928, 57, was correct when he stated: 'Augustin hatte also wohl nicht das Gefühl, vom Christentum selbst abzufallen, als er zum Manichäismus überging'. See also Feldmann, 'Christus-Frömmigkeit', passim.

[168] See esp. *Conf.* V, 10, 18.

[169] *Conf.* V, 3, 6: 'Ibi autem credere iubebar ...'.

[170] As an astronomer or astrologer, but the latter not just in the present-day sense. Cf. Marrou, *Augustin et la fin*, 196: '... en latin comme en grec *astronomia* et *astrologia* étaient des termes interchangeables, et chacun d'eux désigne tour à tour l'authentique astronomie et la superstitieuse astrologie'.

yet I already despaired of being able to make progress in that false doctrine ...'[171].

After his disillusionment with Manichaeism, Augustine wondered whether truth could actually be found. For a short time he felt attracted to the scepticism of the Academics[172]. Through Cicero he had already become acquainted with their philosophy[173]. These Academics[174] did not doubt the existence of truth, but they questioned its knowability. As a reaction to the rational certainty which Manichaeism pretended to offer, but which proved to be non-existent, his resorting to these sceptics is really no surprise. But Augustine's sceptical period was short-lived. Already in *Against the Academics* (late 386) he set forth his fundamental criticism, and no trace of their philosophy can be found in his doctrine of the two cities. It turned out, however, that the doctrinal claims of the Manichaeans could not stand up to this sceptical criticism[175].

Again there was an opening for a new development. This new and decisive turn in Augustine's life started by his returning to his old position. At Milan he decided 'to remain a catechumen in the Catholic Church, recommended to me by my parents, until something certain should light up whither I might direct my course'[176].

6. *Neoplatonic Christians*

Few events in church history are as well-known as Augustine's conversion. Few events, too, have been so much argued about and variously interpreted.

It is not necessary to present here a more or less comprehensive report of the discussions that were begun by Harnack[177] and Boissier[178] and brought to a close especially by Courcelle[179]. Main-

---

171 *Conf.* V, 10, 18: '... sed tamen iam desperans in ea falsa doctrina me posse proficere ...'.

172 *Conf.* V, 10, 19.

173 Brown, *Augustine*, 79-80.

174 Carneades et al., generally considered to belong to the Middle Academy. Cf. Windelband, *Lehrbuch*, 87 and 137; H. Dörrie, 'Akademeia', *KP* 1, 212; E.G. Schmidt, 'Karneades', *KP* 3, 124-126.

175 Brown, *Augustine*, 80.

176 *Conf.* V, 14, 25 (cf. n. 57).

177 Harnack, *Konfessionen* (1888), in: *Reden und Aufsätze*, I, 49-79.

178 Boissier, 'La conversion de saint Augustin' (1888), *Fin*, I, 339-379.

179 *Recherches* (1950, 1968^2); *Confessions* (1963).

ly because of the investigations by Courcelle it has become almost universally accepted that the *Confessions* give a reliable picture of the crucial events in Milan. The discrepancy between what is described here and what Augustine wrote immediately after his conversion[180] is not unbridgeable. Augustine's conversion was real and was the result of an inner conviction. But a close reading of the *Confessions* also reveals that he was not instantly converted to the Catholic Christian belief which he later professed: he was carried away by a strongly Neoplatonic Christianity.

His inner development in these years can be sketched as follows. In the autumn of 384 Augustine arrived in Milan as a disillusioned man. His disappointment in the doctrines of the Manichaeans made him receptive to Academic scepticism. This scepticism caused a definitive break with Manichaeism. Once again he became a catechumen in the Catholic Church. Was this for political reasons[181]? This possibility must certainly not be excluded: he wanted to make a career, the court was Christian, Ambrose ruled Milan. At any rate there was no definitive transition through baptism. As a catechumen he heard the sermons of Ambrose and they impressed him. He also became acquainted with Neoplatonic writings in which God was pictured as a spiritual Being and evil as non-existent. The presbyter Simplicianus showed him more fully how the Logos-doctrine of the *Gospel according to John* agrees with the views held by the Neoplatonists; it was he who drew Augustine's attention to the epistles of Paul. In the garden of his rented home in Milan the definitive break took place. Some three weeks later, in the autumn of 386[182], he resigned his office and retired to Cassiciacum. In the Easter night of 387, together with Adeodatus and his friend Alypius, he was baptized by Ambrose.

Thus this crucial period can be delineated. But what do the events in Milan tell us about the later author of the *City of God*? In what way and especially to what extent did he come into contact with Neoplatonism and a Christianity largely interpreted from the Neoplatonic point of view? A closer analysis of some aspects of this

---

[180] *C. acad., De b. vita, De ord., Sol.*, all written before his baptism.

[181] Cf. Courcelle, *Recherches*, 86-87 and, among others, O'Meara, *Young Augustine*, 127 ff.

[182] *Conf.* IX, 2, 4. The autumn holiday was, according to *Cod. Theod.* II, 8, 19, from Aug. 23rd to Oct. 15th; therefore the conversion must have taken place about Aug. 1st 386.

period may provide important material for our subsequent investigation.

First of all there was the influence of Ambrose. 'And I came to Milan to Bishop Ambrose ...'[183]. In retrospect these words of Augustine are significant: his going to the imperial capital and his getting acquainted with its Catholic bishop had been of great consequence to him. It was from this bishop, according to his biographer Possidius, that he received 'the doctrine' and 'the sacraments'[184]. It was this bishop whom he refers to elsewhere as his teacher, whom he respects as a father[185] and whose works he would continue to read in later years[186]. Through Ambrose's allegorical exposition of the Scriptures[187] the discrepancies and vexations stressed by the Manichaeans ceased to exist. In his sermons Ambrose also showed that God should be thought of as nonphysical. As a Manichaean, but also as a Christian from Africa, Augustine had always supposed the opposite to be true[188]. Moreover, Ambrose taught him that evil is not an autonomous entity, but comes from man's will. This view became decisive and lasting for Augustine.

Yet care should be taken not to overestimate Ambrose's influence on Augustine's conversion and definitively joining the Church. It is significant that in the *Confessions* he does not designate Ambrose as

---

183 *Conf.* V, 13, 23.

184 Possidius, *Vita*, 1.

185 Cf. E. Dassmann, 'Ambrosius', *TRE* 2 (1978) 379, who refers to *Conf.* V, 13, 23; *Sol.* II, 14, 26; *Ep.* 147, 23 and 52; *C. Iul.* I, 3, 10 ('... quem veneror ut patrem: in Christo enim Iesu per evangelium ipse me genuit et eo Christi ministro lavacrum regenerationis accepi'); *Opus imp. c. Iul.* I, 2. In this context *C. Iul.* I, 9, 44 ('doctor meus') can also be named.

186 Particularly in the anti-Pelagian writings, in which A. had to defend his doctrine of original sin and sought support for his view in earlier tradition, he referred frequently to Ambrose's works.

187 It is incorrect to follow the common practice of pointing to Ambrose and his circle as the ones who introduced A. to an allegorical exegesis of Scripture. He was already acquainted with it from the Manichaeans; cf. Alfaric, *Évolution*, 122 n. 1; Feldmann, *Einfluss*, 561. Mani's disciples generally refused to give an allegorical exposition of the Old Testament, though they made at least one exception: for them the serpent in *Gen.* 3 was Christ; cf. Feldmann, *Einfluss*, 573 and 586-587.

188 Cf. L.H. Grondijs, 'Analyse du manichéisme numidien au IVe siècle', *AM*, III, 405-406, who refers to Tertullian, Arnobius and A. prior to his conversion; A. Kehl, 'Gewand', *RAC* 10 (1978) 998; H. Crouzel, 'Geist', *RAC* 9 (1976) 529. A. states specifically in *Conf.* V, 10, 19; VII, 1, 1-2; VII, 2, 3 and VII, 5, 7 that he visualized God in a physical form (corporeus).

the one who baptized him, but complains that Ambrose was constantly occupied. Although they met a number of times, they were not on familiar terms[189]. In a piece of advice written some years after his baptism, Augustine's disappointing experience with Ambrose probably still echoes: 'And if there is somebody who is afraid to recommend himself for starting a friendship because he feels restrained by our temporary honour or dignity, we should descend to him and offer him with kindness and humbleness of spirit what he himself dares not ask for'[190].

In the aged Simplicianus Augustine found a more important spiritual counsellor and friend than in Ambrose. Mainly through him he discovered in Milan a Neoplatonism that was interpreted in a Christian manner in the circle round Ambrose (and by this bishop himself[191]). Neoplatonism was for these Christians the true philosophy, as Aristotelism was to become for medieval Scholasticism. With its help they could enunciate their faith in a theology; they were astonished at the concurrences and at the possibilities of Neoplatonism to provide a rational world view. Augustine, too, was overwhelmed by it[192]: God and His eternal Word (*verbum*) are incorporeal[193]; He is Being itself, and creation exists through Him and is good[194]; evil does not originate from God or any independent power existing alongside of Him, but from the will of man which has turned away from God[195].

It was especially Simplicianus who led the doubting catechumen further into this view and eventually prepared the way to the bap-

---

189 J.A. Davids, 'Sint Augustinus en Sint Ambrosius', *MA*, 242-255.

190 *De div. quaest. LXXXIII, qu.* 71, 6.

191 See esp. Courcelle, *Recherches*, 93-138, who points in particular to *De Isaac* and *De bono mortis*: 'Par ses sermons *De Isaac* et *De bono mortis*, Ambroise l'initiait en même temps au spiritualisme chrétien et aux doctrines plotiniennes' (138). Marrou, *Augustin*, 30, adopts this view. H. Dörrie, 'Das fünffach gestufte Mysterium. Der Aufstieg der Seele bei Prophyrios und Ambrosius', in: *Mullus. Festschrift für Theodor Klauser* (*JbAC*, Erg. Bd. 1), Münster 1964, 79-92, notes that *De Isaac* is a good example of Ambrose's positive use of Neoplatonic philosophy, in this case *Porphyry*.

192 *De b. vita* 4: 'Lectis autem Platonis [or: Plotini?] paucissimis libris ... sic *exarsi* ...'. After becoming acquainted with the *Hortensius* A. also said that he 'burned': 'Quomodo *ardebam*, deus meus, quomodo *ardebam* ...' (*Conf.* III, 4, 8); see also *De b. vita* 4 with regard to the *Hortensius*: '... *succensus sum* ...'.

193 *Conf.* VII, 9, 13-17, 23; cf. the summary in VII, 20, 26.

194 *Conf.* VII, esp. 11, 17 and 12, 18.

195 *Conf.* VII, esp. 16, 22.

tistery for him[196]. The man who had once taught Ambrose[197], and in 397 became his successor[198], also taught Augustine. He was one of the central figures of the Milanese circle of Platonizing Christians[199].

What exactly he taught is unclear, for no writings of his have been preserved. We do know that he was in close touch with the famous Roman rhetor Marius Victorinus. The latter had translated various Neoplatonic writings into Latin and after his conversion, in which Simplicianus also played an important part[200], he wrote a number of Christian treatises with a strongly Neoplatonic character[201]. Victorinus was the first to link the metaphysics of Plotinus and Christian thinking. Simplicianus must have been the one who introduced these ideas in Milan[202].

Besides Simplicianus and Ambrose—with especially Marius Victorinus in the background—others belonged to this Milanese circle which attempted to combine Christianity and Neoplatonism. During these years Augustine also came in direct contact with Flavius Mallius Theodorus. He was very likely[203] the one who lent him 'certain books of the Platonists'[204]. Pierre Courcelle called attention to the philosophical writings of this high government official and Christian, and he characterized him as 'un fervent disciple de

---

196 *Conf.* VIII, 1, 1; 2, 3-4; 5, 10; cf. *DCD* X, 29.

197 *Conf.* VIII, 2, 3: 'Perrexi ego ad Simplicianum, patrem in accipienda gratia tunc episcopi Ambrosii et quem vere ut patrem diligebat'; cf. Ambrose, *Epp.* 27, 2 and 65, 10.

198 Simplicianus must have died in 400 or shortly afterwards. A. calls him to mind once more in *DCD* X, 29, referring to him as 'the holy old man' (sanctus senex).

199 For this circle and Simplicianus, see esp. Courcelle, *Lettres grecques*, 119-129; Courcelle, *Recherches*, passim (esp. 137-138 and 168-174 for Simplicianus); A. Solignac, 'Le cercle milanais', *BA* 14, 529-536.

200 *Conf.* VIII, 2, 4; on Victorinus also *Conf.* VIII, 2, 3-5; VIII, 4, 9; VIII, 5, 10.

201 For Marius Victorinus, see e.g. P. Hadot's introduction to P. Henry – P. Hadot, *Marius Victorinus. Traités théologiques sur la Trinité*, I, Paris 1960, (*SC* 68), 7-76; R.A. Markus, 'Marius Victorinus', in: A.H. Armstrong (ed.), *The Cambridge History of Later Greek and Early Medieval Philosophy*, Cambridge 1967, 331-340; the introduction to P. Hadot – U. Brenke, *Christlicher Platonismus. Die theologischen Schriften des Marius Victorinus*, Zürich-Stuttgart 1967, 5-71; A. Solignac, 'Marius Victorinus', *DS* 10 (1978) 616-623.

202 Solignac, 'Cercle milanais', 533; cf. Solignac, 'Victorinus'.

203 Cf. Courcelle, *Recherches*, 153-156 and 281-284, who also underscores the fact that *De beata vita* was dedicated to Theodorus.

204 *Conf.* VII, 9, 13: '... quosdam platonicorum libros ...'.

Plotin'[205]. Non-Christians also, such as Celsinus and Zenobius, belonged to the Neoplatonizing circle in Milan. Augustine knew them, as appears from later writings[206]. It is not known for sure whether one Hermogenianus was a Christian, but he was certainly a follower of Plotinus.

Such was the spiritual atmosphere around Augustine immediately before and after his conversion[207]. His philosophical thinking found fulfilment in this circle; Plotinus and very probably his pupil Porphyry as well[208] were also his spiritual guides. He even attributed his becoming acquainted with the Neoplatonic writings to God's special care[209].

This is important testimony, but its value should not be overestimated. For at the time of his conversion Augustine was not merely a Platonist with a Christian veneer, as was argued by Boissier and Harnack[210] and later by Alfaric[211]. Platonism provided Augustine with a rational answer to many questions, and therefore it was a great source of spiritual liberation. But no matter how important, this philosophy was not for him an end in itself. For it did not portray Christ correctly: the philosophers mentioned the Logos, but did not acknowledge the Word Incarnate. Augustine, hungry for the truth, continued his quest, and it was not until he reached the Scriptures—especially the Pauline epistles—that he found Christ, not so much as the Man of great wisdom but as the merciful Redeemer. Both in the *Confessions*[212] and in *Against the Academics*[213] Augustine stresses the fact that after the writings of the Neoplatonists he read the Scriptures. He found them superior.

---

205 Courcelle, *Lettres grecques*, 123.

206 Evidence is given, for example, by Solignac, 'Cercle milanais', 535-536.

207 For a clear presentation of the thinking in these circles, see also Brown, *Augustine*, 91-100.

208 The question as to which writings by Plotinus and Porphyry A. was reading at the time of his conversion has been under discussion for a long time. For a survey of this controversy, see Solignac in *BA* 13, 109-112; R. Lorenz, 'Zwölf Jahre Augustinforschung (1959-1970)', *TR* 39 (1974) 124-127; Schindler, 'Augustin', 659 and 661-662. It is generally assumed that, at any rate, A. became acquainted at that time with Plotinus' treatise 'On Beauty' (*Enn.* I, 6), probably also with *Enn.* V, 1 ('On the Three Initial Hypostases') and Porphyry's *De regressu animae*.

209 *Conf.* VII, 20, 26; cf. VII, 9, 13.

210 Cf. p. 47.

211 Alfaric, *Évolution*, esp. VIII, 399, 515, 527.

212 *Conf.* VII, 9, 13-15.

213 *C. acad.* II, 2, 6.

None of this implies that Augustine's appreciation of the Platonists had only been fleeting. There is no doubt that he became more and more deeply rooted in Christian doctrine. But he continued to hold the philosophers in high esteem. In his early work *On the True Religion* (390) he wrote: 'Consequently, if those famous men could live with us again, they would undoubtedly see on whose authority people were cared for more easily, and with a change of only a few words and opinions they would become Christians, as most Platonists of the most recent past and of our time have done'[214]. In his late work the *City of God*, especially in Book VIII, he indicates precisely the points in which, according to him, Christianity and Platonism concur: the existence of an incorporeal Creator and of Providence, the immortality of the soul, virtue, patriotism, true friendship, good morals. At the end of Book I he already gives a brief summary: 'And they agree with us on many things: on the immortality of the soul, and that the true God created the world, and on His providence through which He governs the universe which He created'[215]. Far-reaching also are Augustine's assertions that Porphyry accepted the Hebrew God as the true God[216], and that the Neoplatonists in their doctrine of *hypostaseis* already knew about the Christian trinity[217]. In another place he states that God acted through the Platonists—though they did not know it—so that the truth would become universally known[218].

But besides having a great appreciation of Plato and his followers—Augustine saw them all on the same level; essential differences largely escaped him[219]—there was also clear detach-

---

214 *De vera rel.* 7. Cf. the positive statements on the Platonists by Minucius Felix, *Octavius*, 21, or Clement of Alexandria, *Strom.* I, 21. For expositions on the relationship between Christianity and Platonism, see e.g. J.H. Waszink, 'Der Platonismus und die altchristliche Gedankenwelt', *Entretiens sur l'Antiquité classique*, III, *Recherches sur la tradition platonicienne*, Genève 1955, 139-179; E. von Ivánka, *Plato Christianus. Übernahme und Umgestaltung des Platonismus durch die Väter*, Einsiedeln 1964 (esp. 189-222 for A.); C.J. de Vogel, 'Platonism and Christianity: A mere antagonism or a profound common ground?', *VC* 39 (1985) 1-62.

215 *DCD* I, 36.

216 *DCD* XIX, 23. Porphyry acquired this wisdom from an oracle of Didyma; cf. R. van den Broek, *Apollo in Asia. De orakels van Clarus en Didyma in de tweede en derde eeuw na Chr.*, Leiden 1981, 8 and n. 26.

217 As in *DCD* X, 23 and 29.

218 *De trin.* IV, 17, 23, with the warning from *Rom.* 1: 21.

219 In *DCD* VII, 9 A. states: '... Plato et qui eum bene intellexerunt ...'. Here and elsewhere (such as *C. Acad.* III, 18, 41: Plotinus as a second Plato) he sees the Neoplatonists closely connected with Plato. Moreover, he considers Neoplatonism a theistic religion.

ment. These philosophers knew where they were to go, but of Christ as the way they were ignorant[220]. They also knew about the blessed country, but their pride kept them from entering it[221]. It is notable how in his later years Augustine became more and more critical, as can already be seen in the *City of God*. At first he is full of praise for the Platonists[222], but after Book X this praise gradually diminishes[223]. Finally he even says that the philosophers are inhabitants of the ungodly city[224] and will perish with the demons: 'And it is absolutely certain that those philosophers in the impious city who have said that the gods are their friends have fallen into the power of the wicked demons to whom that whole city is subjected, and in whose company it will suffer eternal punishment'[225]. There is certainly no exception for the Platonists in this context: they are subject to the same judgement. Ultimately a Christian has to be an anti-Platonist[226]. In his *Retractations* Augustine more than once found himself obliged to temper his earlier appreciation of Plato and the Neoplatonists[227].

The foregoing demonstrates sufficiently that Neoplatonism exerted great influence on both Augustine's conversion and his later theologizing. Increasingly there were critical reservations, but at the same time a far-reaching acceptance remained. This will be even

---

220 *Conf.* VII, 20, 26; *DCD* X, 29.

221 E.g. *DCD* X, 29; *De trin.* IV, 15, 20; *Ep.* 118, 20 f. (to Dioscorus).

222 *DCD* VIII, 5: '... nulli nobis propius accesserunt ...'; VIII, 9: '... eos omnes ceteris anteponimus eosque nobis propinquiores fatemur'; X, 1: 'Eligimus enim Platonicos omnium philosophorum merito nobilissimos, propterea quia sapere potuerunt licet inmortalem ac rationalem vel intellectualem hominis animam nisi participatio lumine illius Dei, a quo et ipsa et mundus factus est, beatam esse non posse'; X, 1: '... Deo suo qui etiam noster est ...'; etc.

223 A. condemns above all the Neoplatonic doctrine of metempsychosis: *DCD* XII, 21; XIII, 16-18; XXII, 25-28.

224 *DCD* XVIII, 41: 'daemonicola civitas': XIX, 9: 'impia civitas'.

225 *DCD* XIX, 9: 'Et illos quidem philosophos in impia civitate, qui deos sibi amicos esse dixerunt, in daemones malignos incidisse certissimum est, quibus tota ipsa civitas subditur, aeternum cum eis habitura supplicium'.

226 E.g. *DCD* XXI, 7: '...cum quibus vel *contra* quos agimus ...'.

227 *Retract.* I, 1, 4: 'Laus quoque ipsa, qua Platonem vel Platonicos seu Academicos philosophos tantum extuli, quantum *impios* homines non oportuit, non immerito mihi displicuit. *Praesertim contra quorum errores magnos defendenda est christiana doctrina*'; I, 3, 2; I, 4, 3: '... cavendum fuit, ne putaremur illam Porphyrii *falsi philosophi* tenere sententiam ...'; I, 4, 4; I, 11, 4. In addition, Porphyry is named again in II, 31 as the one 'cuius celeberrima est fama', but this recognition does not imply approval.

clearer after an investigation into a possible development in Augustine's writings leading to his concept of *civitas*[228]. The question as to whether his doctrine of the two cities was derived from Platonic tradition deserves serious consideration.

7. *The Catholic bishop*

The rest of Augustine's life will be described only briefly. After his conversion and baptism, on the one hand a strong emphasis on Neoplatonism can be seen: in the Cassiciacum dialogues and in the works written in Milan, Rome and Thagaste. As has already been said, this positive attitude towards the Platonists lasted a long time. But on the other hand from 391, the year in which Augustine became a presbyter at Hippo Regius, a steady increase in his knowledge of Scripture and Church doctrine can be discerned. As is well known, in a letter to Bishop Valerius he asked for permission to study the Scriptures and ecclesiastical doctrine before assuming his office[229]. The rest of his life was occupied with study, mainly of the Scriptures, and with a variety of official duties. Rudolf Lorenz summarizes accurately: 'Die Berufung ins kirchliche Amt führt Augustin von der neuplatonischen Introspektion zu den Wirklichkeiten des kirchlichen Lebens: Kirche, Wort Gottes, Sakramente'[230].

An extensive description of Augustine's career as a leading bishop of the Catholic Church in Roman Africa is not necessary here. It should only be recalled that it was in these years that he became profoundly acquainted with Donatism and with African theology in general; what this means for our inquiry will be discussed later. In Africa he discharged his pastoral duties, made commentaries on the Scriptures, preached, maintained a correspondence and polemized. It is particularly this last aspect of his immense episcopal work, carried out from Hippo for about 35 years, that is notable. When Augustine's pupil and colleague Possidius, bishop of Calama, added to the biography of his teacher a survey (indiculum[231]) of his writings,

---

228 See pp. 108-115.
229 *Ep.* 21, esp. 3.
230 Lorenz, 'Augustin', 742.
231 A. Wilmart, 'Operum S. Augustini elenchus a Possidio eiusdem discipulo digestus. Post Maurinorum labores novis curis editus critico apparatu numeris tabellis instructus', *MAg*, II, 149-233. Wilmart points out (158) that A. himself had

he classified them according to the opponents against whom Augustine had written: the pagans, the astrologers, the Jews, the Manichaeans, the Priscillianists, the Donatists, the Pelagians, the Arians and the Apollinarians[232].

It should be noted here that this emphasis on the apologetic and polemic aspects can already be perceived in Possidius' biography, and was possibly influenced by the survey of his writings originating from Augustine himself, but which was afterwards lost[233]. Augustine may have seen his own life's work essentially in this perspective. It should also be noted that the amount of attention he paid to each of these groups was not equal: he directed only one small work against the Apollinarians, and against the astrologers only two. Summed up in a greatly simplified outline, three periods in particular in Augustine's life emerge, in which there are three kinds of opponents: from 387 to 400 he wrote mainly against the Manichaeans, from 400 to 412 the disputations with the Donatists took place, and from that time until his death in 430 there was the struggle against the Pelagians[234]. But throughout these years, from *Against the Academics* up to and including the *City of God*, he carried on very extensive polemics against the pagans. Was it accidental that the writings *contra paganos* are the ones with which Possidius' *Indiculum* begins? Does this fact not indicate that this aspect of Augustine's oeuvre should be regarded as being of special importance?

In any case there can be no doubt that the *City of God* is the most comprehensive and influential of all these polemic and apologetic writings. It is also certain that its author was a bishop of the Catholic Church of Africa. This fact, too, should be properly evaluated in an inquiry into the possible sources of the doctrine of the two *civitates*. In what way and to what extent was Augustine influenced by the earlier Christian tradition and, within this tradition, by a distinctively African theology?

---

a catalogue of his works: see *Retract.* II, 41. Cf. G. Bardy in *BA* 12, 36 ff. and B. Altaner, 'Beiträge zur Kenntnis des schriftstellerischen Schaffens Augustins', *Schriften*, 49-50.

232 Following this, the rest of the books, treatises and letters are listed, as much as possible in chronological order.

233 Wilmart, 'Elenchus', 159: 'La *Vita* reflète en effet cette préoccupation [viz. the apologetic arrangement], la carrière d'Augustin étant remplie principalement par ses luttes contre l'hérésie. Toutefois, on pourrait se demander si l'*Indiculum* de saint Augustin ne marquait pas déjà les principes de ces distinctions'. Cf. p. 166 and n. 26.

234 See e.g. Marrou, *Augustin*, 50.

As an African who was brought up as a catechumen of the Catholic Church, received a thorough training in rhetoric, lived in Manichaean circles for more than ten years, was deeply influenced by Neoplatonism and, ultimately, became one of the leading bishops of a Church with a rich tradition of its own: thus the author of the *City of God* stands before us.

B. The 'City of God'

1. *Reasons for writing*

At first sight the *City of God*, like almost all of Augustine's works, seems to have been written in response to concrete questions. In this case the immediate cause was the sacking of Rome, on 24th August 410, and the enormous reaction this event brought about[235].

Although the eternal city[236] had been threatened for a long time, it was captured unexpectedly by the Visigoths under Alaric after a short siege, and sacked for three days. The resulting shock was great. Pelagius, for example, was distressed; he wrote to a Roman lady that 'the fall of Rome, the mistress of the world, had taken place to the sound of blaring trumpets and barbaric howling'[237]. At Bethlehem Jerome, who had just finished his commentary on Isaiah and was about to start an exegesis of Ezekiel, could not work for days; for him the fall of Rome had inaugurated the end of the world. 'After the most radiant light of all the nations had been extinguished, what is more, after the head of the Roman Empire had been cut off and, to be more precise, in one city the entire world perished, I fell silent and was humiliated and unable to speak of goodness'[238]. He re-

---

235 For a detailed description of the fall of Rome, the reactions to it in pagan and Christian circles and A.'s reaction, see esp. H. von Campenhausen, 'Augustin und der Fall von Rom' (1947) in: *Tradition und Leben. Kräfte der Kirchengeschichte. Aufsätze und Vorträge*, Tübingen 1960, 253-271; P. Courcelle, *Histoire littéraire des grandes invasions germaniques*, Paris 1964[3] (1948[1]), 15-139 (119-122 concerning A.); Maier, *Augustin*; Bardy in *BA* 33, 9-22; Brown, *Augustine*, 287-329; Mazzolani, *Idea*, esp. 201-217 on the preceding disintegration of the imperium; O. Zwierlein, 'Der Fall Roms im Spiegel der Kirchenväter', *ZPE* 32 (1978) 45-80.

236 For the concept 'Roma aeterna', 'urbs aeterna', see e.g. Maier, *Augustin*, 43-46; J. Lamotte, 'Le Mythe de Rome «Ville Éternelle» et saint Augustin', *Aug(L)* 11 (1961) 225-260; Zwierlein, 'Fall Roms', 46-48.

237 *Ep. ad Demetriadem*, 30.

238 *In Ezech. I, praef.*: 'Postquam vero clarissimum terrarum omnium lumen extinctum est, immo Romani imperii truncatum caput, et, ut verius dicam, in una orbe totus orbis interiit, obmutui et humiliatus sum et silui a bonis ...'. The quotation is from *Ps.* 38 (39) : 3 (2).

sumed his work later on, it is true, but this outpouring is characteristic of the impression made by the events of 410[239].

Although Rome no longer functioned in those days as the imperial capital, the city was still felt to be the head of the Empire and the symbol of civilization. Moreover, it was the centre of the cult of the gods, and also the location of the remains of the apostles Peter and Paul[240]. Now that this holy city had perished, had the end of the world not come?[241] Not only the pagans, but the majority of the Christians as well were disillusioned[242].

At this time questions reached the bishop of Hippo concerning the how and why of the catastrophe, from his congregation, from Africa where he occupied a prominent position, and from elsewhere. As far as we know Augustine was the only one to react immediately, in sermons and letters[243], from a well thought-out Christian point of view. In his *sermones*, for example, he says that even heaven and earth will pass away and therefore man should not be surprised by the fall of Rome[244]. The suffering of the present time chastens[245]; the Christian lives here as an alien[246]; in this world there are no eternal kingdoms: only the city of God is firm and permanent[247].

This is the tone Augustine used in his response. He was concerned

---

239 For Jerome see, for example, Courcelle, *Histoire littéraire*, 49 ff., 59 f., 65 f.,; Bardy in *BA* 33, 10-11; Zwierlein, 'Fall Roms', 49-52. Particularly interesting is his report on the fall of Rome in *Ep.* 127, 12: the description of the destruction of Jerusalem in *Ps.* 78 (Heb. 79) and that of Troy by Virgil are used in his apocalyptic picture. His account of cannibalism during the siege of 410 and of mothers eating their infants should also be considered mainly as a stylistic device.

240 Cf. A.'s *s.* 296, 6 (*MAg*, I, 404-405): 'Iacet Petri corpus Romae, dicunt homines, iacet Pauli corpus Romae, Laurentii corpus Romae, aliorum martyrum sanctorum corpora iacent Romae: et misera est Roma, et vastatur Roma: affligitur, conteritur, incenditur; tot strages mortis fiunt, per famem, per pestem, per gladium. Ubi sunt memoriae apostolorum?'

241 Cf. Jerome (n. 238).

242 This disillusionment is also connected with Eusebian *Reichstheologie*; see p. 154 ff. esp. 162.

243 For a discussion of these sermons and letters, see esp. Courcelle, *Histoire littéraire*, 64-77 and Maier, *Augustin*, 55-68 (69-75 in detail on *Ep.* 138, to be seen in particular as a prelude to *DCD*). Cf. A. Wachtel, *Beiträge zur Geschichtstheologie des Aurelius Augustinus*, Bonn 1960, 87 ff.

244 Esp. *s.* 81, 9: 'Coelum et terra transibunt; quid ergo mirum, si aliquando finis est civitati?'

245 Esp. *s. Denis* 23, 2 and *s.* 105, 8.

246 It is precisely the *sermones* dating from late 410 to early 411 that contain the theme of the *peregrinatio*; see e.g. *s. Caillau* 2, 92, 1-2; *s.* 25, 3; *s.* 81, 7.

247 E.g. *s.* 105, 9.

with the meaning of history, its theodicy and its consequences for Christian life. This earthly life is above all a preparation for eternity[248] and inevitably a *malum*[249]; every affliction works for the good of the Christian[250]; the creation is good, but evil exists through man; 'we are the times'[251].

Already in these first reactions themes of the *City of God* appear. Even a considerable time before the fall of Rome, Augustine composed a short treatise in which he sought to give a theological interpretation of the terrifying events of his day: the barbarian invasions and the ensuing suffering of the children of God. When in 409 a certain Victorianus asked him to write a comprehensive work[252] on this subject, he answered in a letter in which he pointed out that such suffering had been prophesied by Christ, and was taking place in order to test the righteous and punish the wicked. 'The humble and holy servants of God, however, who suffer a double portion of temporal evil, namely *from* and *with* the wicked, have their consolations and the hope of the world to come'[253]. Augustine went on to point out Azariah's and Daniel's prayers[254], and he quoted such texts as *Heb.* 12:6 and 1 *Cor.* 11:31-32[255]. The presbyter Victorianus was called upon to teach others 'to refrain from murmuring against God in these trials and tribulations'[256].

Thus Augustine's attitude was clear, even before the news of the sacking of Rome so violently shocked people's feelings. The letter to

---

248 E.g. *s. Denis* 23, 2: '... et intellegendum nos in hac terra mortaliter vivere, et cogitandum esse de fine, ubi non erit finis'.

249 E.g. *s. Caillau* 2, 92, 1: 'Quid enim boni aliquando habuit vita ista ab ipso primo homine ex quo meruit mortem?'

250 E.g. *s.* 25, 5: 'Dies maligni piis prosunt ad inveniendos dies bonos'; *s. Denis* 24, 11: 'Nam necesse est pressurae sint'. Cf. *s.* 296, esp. 10 (complete text of *s.* 296 in *MAg*, I, 401-412).

251 *S.* 80, 8: 'Bene vivamus et bona sunt tempora. Nos sumus tempora: quales sumus, talia sunt tempora (...). Quid est autem malus mundus? Non enim malum est coelum et terra et aquae et quae sunt in eis, pisces volatilia arbores. Omnia ista bona sunt; sed malum mundi mali homines faciunt'. This sermon may have been delivered before the fall of Rome; see below.

252 *Ep.* 111, 1: 'prolixum opus'. For its date see Goldbacher, *CSEL* 58, 32: '... extremo anno 409'; for Victorianus: Mandouze et al., *PAC*, 1190.

253 *Ep.* 111, 2: 'Servi autem dei humiles et sancti, qui dupliciter mala temporalia patiuntur, quia et ab ipsis impiis, et cum ipsis patiuntur, habent consolationes suas et spem futuri saeculi'. This is followed by *Rom.* 8:18.

254 *Dan.* 3: 25-37 (LXX) in *Ep.* 11, 3; *Dan.* 9: 3-20 in 111, 4 resp.

255 *Ep.* 111, 5.

256 *Ep.* 111, 6: '...ne adversus deum in his temptationibus et tribulationibus murmuretur'.

Victorianus is firm proof of this. Contrary to what F.G. Maier tried to prove[257], however, Augustine's other utterances cannot be dated prior to the events of August 410. With reference to the sermons and epistles[258] Courcelle justly observes: 'Augustin n'a eu qu'à systématiser ses idées pour écrire les premiers livres de son grand ouvrage'[259].

But members of his congregation and fellow believers elsewhere were not the only ones to put their questions to Augustine. There was in those days a very powerful pagan faction which clung to the belief in the ancient gods; it wanted to maintain pagan customs and, in so far as these had disappeared, tried to breathe new life into them[260]. The goal of these reactionaries was a pagan revival. Symmachus, the Roman city prefect who had once recommended Augustine for the office of state rhetor in Milan, was one of the leading figures of this circle[261]. For these neo-pagans the capture of Rome was particularly painful. City and gods were to them closely related

---

257 Maier, *Augustin*, 48-55, presents a number of A.'s statements which, in his opinion, can be dated before Aug. 24th 410: *ss.* 25 and 80; *Epp.* 111 and 122; *s. Caillau* 2, 92; *ss. Denis* 21, 23 and 24. He bases his view (50 n. 39) on A. Kunzelmann, 'Die Chronologie der Sermones des hl. Augustinus', *MAg* II, 500. However, from this study it appears that all the sermons mentioned should almost certainly be dated *after* August 410: see Kunzelmann, 'Chronologie', 500-501 *and* 518. Kunzelmann places *s.* 80 (c. 410), *s. Caillau* 2, 92 (c. 410) and *s.* 25 (c. 410, winter) *after s. Denis* 23 (dated Sept. 11th 410), *s. Denis* 21 (Sept. 22nd 410) and *s. Denis* 24 (Sept. 25th 410). In any case, no proof can be drawn from this investigation in support of the idea that the relevant sermons were delivered before Aug. 24th 410. Nor does Maier provide such proof from any other source.—Similarly *Ep.* 122 is incorrectly dated by Maier as preceding the fall of Rome; cf. Goldbacher, *CSEL* 58, 34: 'In qua epistula quod Augustinus de contritione mundi huius loquitur (...) optime referri potest ad a. 410, quo urbs a Gothis occupata direptaque ...'. This leaves only *Ep.* 111 as a clear reaction by A. to the threat of the barbarians at that time; it was written at the end of 409 (cf. n. 252). Not only is Maier's error striking, but also the fact that it has never been noticed, neither by those who have referred to his detailed study, nor by those who have reviewed it.

258 In addition to *Ep.* 122 and the sermons mentioned in n. 257, *Epp.* 125 and 126 and the *ss.* 81, 105 and 296 are particularly important.

259 Courcelle, *Histoire littéraire*, 70.

260 For a brief survey of this movement, see R. Lorenz, *Das vierte bis sechste Jahrhundert (Westen)*, Göttingen 1970, 30-31, and the references given there. Particularly fundamental is H. Bloch, 'The Pagan Revival in the West at the End of the Fourth Century', in: A. Momigliano (ed.), *The Conflict between Paganism and Christianity in the Fourth Century*, Oxford 1963, 193-218.

261 Symmachus died in 402. For other persons of this circle, see e.g. Bloch, 'Pagan Revival': Praetextatus, Nicomachus Flavianus, Caecina Albinus, Decius, Rufius Albinus, Macrobius, Ammianus Marcellinus, etc.

entities[262]. Because the cult of the gods had been neglected, a catastrophe had befallen Rome; the Christians were to blame.

After the fall of Rome, many of these pagans took refuge in Carthage[263] and began to make their influence felt in Africa. They might have been deprived of their old cult, but they had brought their sources of religious inspiration, Virgil in particular[264]. He was, as it were, their Bible[265]. Though cut off from their roots, these people remained deeply religious. In this respect they were in no way inferior to the Christians.

But to them Christianity was, in fact, an uncultivated religion. Platonists like Plotinus and Porphyry were able to provide a world view that linked up naturally with ancestral religious traditions. In their opinion, Christian belief had no intellectual basis. All this becomes particularly evident from the letter which Volusianus, one of the refugees, addressed to Augustine: to accept the Incarnation was an impossibility for this young Roman aristocrat[266]. He and his pagan comrades saw themselves as wise and civilized people, pillars of the Roman Empire, which the Christians were not[267].

Augustine was the best qualified person[268] to respond to these ac-

---

262 For the polis-idea and the cult of the gods related to it, see esp. pp. 104 and 107-108.

263 *DCD* I, 32-33.

264 Virgil provided the national epos that—as A. states in *DCD* I, 3—every Roman carried in his heart from his schooldays onwards. The *Saturnalia* by Macrobius picture how Virgil was revered: the participants in the discussion are gathered around his holy works. Virgil had a religious significance not only for the pagans, but for many Christians too: the fourth *Ecloga* was given a Messianic interpretation (see Lactantius, *Div. Inst.* 7, 24, 11) and was even read out loud in a Greek translation by Emperor Constantine at the beginning of the Council of Nicaea (325). Appreciation for it in later Christian circles can be seen, for example, from the position of Virgil in the Lamb of God reredos by the Van Eyck brothers; cf. E. Dhanens, *Hubert en Jan van Eyck*, Antwerpen 1980, 100.

265 Bloch, 'Pagian Revival', 210: '... Virgil's *Aeneid*, we might be so bold as to say, as a pagan Bible'.

266 *Ep.* 135, 2. This letter was written by Volusianus to A. Cf. A.'s *Epp.* 132 and 137 to Volusianus; also 136, 2, where Marcellinus mentions Volusianus' problems to A.

267 This appears esp. from *Ep.* 138 to Marcellinus. It contains a detailed description of the problems set forth by Volusianus and his circle (138, 1; cf. 136, 2): the biblical command teaches not to return evil for evil, how is it then possible to defend the Empire against enemies? (138, 9); if one is struck on the right cheek, one has to offer the left one too, but how is this to be realized in political and military life? (138, 12); the new faith has ruined the Empire (138, 16).

268 Cf. Altaner, 'Beiträge', *Schriften*, 18: for both Christians and non-Christians A. was continually *the* authority to turn to. 'Wer dürfte es sich schliesslich zutrauen,

cusations. He, the former protégé of Symmachus, fully understood the reasoning that Rome's fall had been caused by the forsaking of the ancient gods. On hearing the reactions from these circles, he promised his friends he would reply to them. At first he hesitated to write a book on this subject, but hoped that his friend Flavius Marcellinus would see that his open letters were circulated[269]. Marcellinus[270] did so, and at the same time asked for more: a definitive answer to the questions issuing from the side of the pagans as well as from that of the Christians[271].

In 412 Augustine set himself to the task of writing his 'great and difficult work'[272]. He was engaged upon it from 412 until 426/427. Testimony from various sides, most of all from Augustine himself, provides an outline of the progress of its composition: in 413 Books I-III were completed, in 415 Books IV-V, in 417 Books VI-XI, in the next year Books XII-XIII, in 420 Books XIV-XVI, in 425 Books XVII-XVIII and, finally, the entire work was complete when in 427 the *Retractations* were edited[273]. Augustine was then an old man of seventy-two; his friend Marcellinus had died long before[274].

---

in die Diskussion einzugreifen, bevor sich nicht der Bisschof von Hippo geäussert hatte ...'.

269 *Ep.* 138, 1.

270 Marcellinus, as tribune and *notarius*, was one of the highest imperial officials. The decisive judgement against the Donatists in 411 was carried out under his supervision. He was a Catholic Christian with apparently a great interest in theological problems. A. not only directed a number of letters to him, but he also dedicated three works to Marcellinus: *De peccatorum meritis, De spiritu et littera, De civitate Dei*. For Marcellinus, see e.g. Monceaux, *Histoire*, VII, 71-74; M. Moreau, 'Le dossier Marcellinus dans la correspondance de saint Augustin', *RA* 9 (1973) 3-181; Mandouze et al., *PAC*, 671-688.

271 *Ep.* 136, 2.

272 *DCD* I, *praef.*: 'magnum opus et arduum'. It is noteworthy that A. also characterizes *De doctr. chr.* as such: *De doctr. chr.* I, 1. Cf. n. 287.

273 See esp. Bardy, 'Les étapes de la composition', *BA* 33, 22-35; also Brown, *Augustine*, 282, 284, 378, and C. Andresen in his 'Einführung' to the translation by W. Thimme, *Aurelius Augustinus. Vom Gottesstaat (De civitate dei). Buch 1 bis 10*, München 1977, XI-XII. Cf. Scholz, *Glaube und Unglaube*, 9, with a few differences, but without further argumentation. Quite different, but likewise without argumentation, is David Knowles in his introduction to the translation by Henry Bettenson, *Augustine, Concerning the City of God against the Pagans*, Penguin Books 1972, XVI. Specifically about the date of Book XI is the article by B. Lacroix, 'La date du XI[e] livre du De Civitate Dei', *VC* 5 (1951) 121-122.

274 He got caught up in the insurrection of the *comes Africae* Heraclianus and was beheaded on Sept. 413. This happened in spite of vigorous protests by the Catholics; see A.'s *Ep.* 151. Cf. Monceaux, *Histoire*, VII, 73; Frend, *Donatist Church*, 293; Moreau, 'Dossier', 93-192; Mandouze et al., *PAC*, 687-688.

2. Contents

A short survey of the comprehensive work *De civitate Dei* will be helpful in this inquiry. Only the main points will be mentioned, with some extra attention given to ideas that are of importance for this investigation. In addition to information collected in the course of extensive reading, material is sometimes presented from the summary (breviculus), which most probably originates from Augustine himself; this has been done in spite of Marrou's opinion that this *breviculus* cannot be considered a summary as the modern reader would want, but as a kind of reading guide[275]. Moreover, grateful use has been made of Guy's survey[276], the summaries accompanying Schröder's translation[277] and the abridgement by Wytzes[278]. With Marrou one can agree unreservedly: 'le texte d'Augustin est difficile à résumer'[279].

The contents can be summarized as follows:

Book I. At the time of the capture of Rome, the (Christian!) barbarians were much more lenient towards the inhabitants than has

275 H.-I. Marrou, 'La division en chapitres des livres de *La Cité de Dieu*' (1951), in: *Patristique et Humanisme. Mélanges par Henri-Irénée Marrou*, Paris 1976, 253-265. First he points out, esp. in opposition to A. Kalb and particularly making use of the well-known letter to Firmus to which the *breviculus* was added, that A. himself must have been the author. It should be taken into account that this *breviculus* appeared separately; its inclusion in the text in later manuscripts and modern editions is incorrect. But for A. *the* literary unit is the book (265); 'plutôt qu'un sommaire ce *Canon*, ce *Breviculus*, représente une série de points de repère égrenés le long du texte, un relevé de *notabilia varia* permettant au lecteur familiarisé avec l'oeuvre de retrouver *quid lib. quisq. continet* [according to one manuscript], ou *quantum collegerit XXII librorum conscriptio*' [end of letter to Firmus] (263). We are generally willing to concede to Marrou and to Bardy, *BA* 33, esp. 51-52 (see further on p. 77) that the literary unit in *DCD* is the book. And yet we wonder whether more value can be attached to his *breviculus* as a summary. Does the end of the letter to Firmus not point out that A. is aiming to indicate the contents in it? Further inquiry should be made into what the word *breviculus* signifies for A. At any rate, it appears that in his *Breviculus collationis cum Donatistis* he gives in three books a complete and clearly arranged summary of the very extensive *acta* of the conference in 411: he follows them closely, keeping the same numbering throughout (*Brev. coll.* I, *praef.*; cf. *Retract.* II, 39). Besides it appears that *breviculus* here is identical with *breviarium* (*Brev. coll.* I, *praef.*). Neither Marrou nor Bardy refers to this work, in which the concept *breviculus* is clearly defined.

276 Guy, *Unité*, 15-25.

277 Schröder, *Gottesstaat*, in the *BKV* series.

278 J. Wytzes, *Augustinus: 'De Staat Gods'*, Kampen 1947. Karsten, *Godsrijk*, 7-74, is rather obscure.

279 Marrou, 'Division', 264.

ever been recorded in history or mythology. To be sure, calamity struck the good as well as the wicked, but that is the way God ordains. All this is for the benefit of the true Christians. It is absolutely wrong to mock the Christian God: it was not the Christian religion that led to the fall of Rome, but the depravity of the pagans.

Augustine opens his work with a brilliant sentence. In it he introduces in an ingenious way first the subject of the second part, then that of the first part. The sentence also contains the dedication to Marcellinus and, moreover, five quotations from the Bible[280]:

Gloriosissimam civitatem Dei[281] sive in hoc temporum cursu, cum inter impios peregrinatur *ex fide vivens*[282], sive in illa stabilitate sedis aeternae, quam nunc *expectat per patientiam*[283] quoadusque iustitia convertatur in iudicium[284], deinceps adeptura per excellentiam victoria ultima et pace perfecta[285], hoc opere instituto et mea ad te promissione debito defendere adversus eos qui conditori eius deos suos praeferunt[286], fili carissime Marcelline, suscepi, magnum opus et arduum[287], sed *Deus adiutor noster*[288] est.

The most glorious city of God[281]—both as it exists in this course of time, an alien that sojourns among the ungodly, *living by faith*[282], and as it will be in that fixed stability of its eternal abode, which it now *awaits with patience*[283] until justice returns to judgement[284], but which it will hereafter obtain in glory through the final victory and in perfect peace[285]—to defend [this city] against those who prefer their own gods to its Founder[286] I have taken upon myself with this work which I owe you by my promise, my dearly beloved son Marcellinus, a great and arduous task[287], but *God is our helper*[288].

Book II. Christians are blamed for the fall of Rome because they do not worship the ancient gods. But history shows that the gods did not bring Rome deliverance even in its worst afflictions. They have done nothing to combat depravity, but rather they have fostered moral decay.

Book III. If the Christians were to blame for the present calamity, Rome would have been spared all catastrophes in former times when the cult of the gods was still flourishing. Nothing, however, is farther from the truth: Troy fell, and Rome was not protected by the gods

280 Cf. Marrou, *Augustin et la fin*, 669.
281 *Ps.* 86 (87):3.
282 *Hab.* 2: 4; *Rom.* 1: 17; *Gal.* 3: 11. Cf. *DCD* IV, 20.
283 *Rom.* 8: 25.
284 *Ps.* 93 (94):15. *En. in Ps.* 93,18 shows clearly how A. wants this difficult text to be understood in the light of *Matt.* 19: 28.
285 Subject of XI – XXII.
286 Subject of I - X.
287 Cf. Hagendahl, *Latin Classics*, I, 162-163 and II, 408 n. 5: the words 'magnum opus et arduum' are reminiscent of Cicero, *De or.*, 33.
288 *Ps.* 61 (62): 9 (8).

either. There were continual wars, civil strife, natural disasters.

Book IV. The growth and prosperity of the Empire must not be attributed to the gods. Polytheism, as some wise Romans have already shown, is full of contradictions. It was Christianity that first gave the freedom and power to break with polytheism. God is the only One who measures out sovereignty and worldly goods; the times of all rulers — good and evil ones—are ordained by Him.

IV, 4 opens with the famous sentences that are particularly reminiscent of Cicero[289]:

Remota itaque iustitia quid sunt regna nisi magna latrocinia? quia et latrocinia quid sunt nisi parva regna?	If then justice has been pushed aside, what are kingdoms but big gangs of robbers? For what are gangs of robbers but petty kingdoms?

Book V. Roman world domination did not come about through fate, but—with God's blessing—through the natural virtues of the Romans. Their example should inspire the citizens of the heavenly *civitas* to even greater love for their heavenly country:

... ut cives aeternae illius civitatis, quamdiu hic peregrinantur, diligenter et sobrie illa intueantur exempla et videant quanta dilectio debeatur supernae patriae propter vitam aeternam, si tantum a suis civibus terrena dilecta est propter hominum gloriam (16).	... so that the citizens of that eternal city, as long as they are on their pilgrimage here, might contemplate those examples diligently and soberly, and see how much love they should have for the heavenly city in view of life eternal, if the earthly city is so much beloved by its citizens on account of human glory (16).

War and peace are in God's hands; He grants them to both pagan and Christian rulers. The Christian ideal of happy rulers rests on grounds different from outward ones: they are called happy if they rule justly (iuste), fear, love and honour God (si Deum timent diligunt colunt, 24). Constantine and Theodosius are examples of such rulers. V, 24 presents the famous and very influential 'mirror' for rulers[290]. V, 26 depicts Theodosius as a model Christian ruler.

Book VI. One need not worship the gods any more for eternal life

---

[289] See R.H. Barrow, 'Remota ... iustitia', *VC* 15 (1961) 116, who particularly enumerates parallels with Cicero. Cf. Barrow, *Introduction to St Augustine 'The City of God', being selections from the De Civitate Dei including most of the XIXth book* ..., London 1950, 254-257 and 282. The ablative absolute is conditional: 'if you think away ... for the moment'. A. does not say that all wordly empires, in which there is no true (= Christian) justice, are gangs of robbers. Cf. Salin, *Civitas Dei*, 188 and 243.

[290] Cf. P. Hadot, 'Fürstenspiegel', *RAC* 8 (1972) 618.

than for earthly happiness. Varro[291] gave a survey and classification of the gods according to their activities. He distinguished a mythical theology, a physical theology and a civil theology. From neither mythical theology—which furnishes poets with material for their plays—nor civil theology is eternal life to be expected.

Book VII. The absurdities of civil theology are further expounded. The 'select gods' (dii selecti) do not grant eternal life either: they are unclean demons. Only God Everlasting grants redemption and eternal life.

Book VIII. More attention must be given to physical theology, represented by the philosophers and propounded best by Plato and his followers. They see demons as mediators, which should be worshipped for the attainment of the blessed life. The Platonists' absolutely transcendent image of God is striking: God does not enter directly into fellowship with humans, but through intermediaries. The demons are situated between gods and man: they have eternal life like the gods, passions like men. It is repulsive to venerate them, however, in view of their morals; they are unfit to be mediators. Essentially the entire pagan religion is nothing but a veneration of the deceased.

Book IX. There are no good demons as mediators; in fact they are eternally wretched themselves. The true Mediator between God and men is Jesus Christ.

Book X. The demons deserve no divine worship (latreia); to God alone should offerings be made. The true sacrifice is the dedication of the congregation to God through the one Mediator, Jesus Christ. The good angels are in the service of divine providence. True purification (purgatio) through Christ enables us to triumph over the de-

---

291 For Varro (116-28/27), see esp. H. Dahlmann in *PRE, Suppl* 6 (1935) 1172-1177 or K. Sallmann in *KP* 5 (1979) 1131-1140; for the Varro-A. relationship, see esp. Hagendahl, *Latin Classics*, 265-316 (the fragments of Varro that A. included in his works, collected by B. Cardauns) and 589-630. The most important fragments of the *Antiquitates* are to be found in *DCD* VI and VII; here and elsewhere A. appears to be the main source for many of Varro's works. From his earliest writings he demonstrates his familiarity with the greatest scholar that Rome produced, but in view of the many quotations in *DCD* he must have made special preparations for this work by means of a thorough rereading of Varro and the making of abstracts (Hagendahl, 628; likewise Marrou, *Augustin et la fin*, 129). A. considers Varro the greatest pagan scholar (*De doctr. chr.* II, 17, 27); he also gives high praise to him in *DCD* (e.g. in IV, 1 and 31; VI, 2) and even calls him 'Varro noster' (VII, 25).

mons. Porphyry had many good thoughts; he knew that the soul is not purified by magic rites. But he and the others were too proud to acknowledge Christ as their Mediator: 'Christ is humble, you are proud?'[292]

Book XI. This is the beginning of the second part of the work. It deals with the origin, course and destined ends (... de ...exortu et excursu et debitis finibus ..., 1) of the two cities. From the Scriptures comes the information. The narrative of the Creation discloses the origin of the *civitas Dei*: in the world of angels. The *terrena civitas* comes into being through the Fall of angels. The two societies are opposed to each other as light and darkness. The *civitas diaboli* originates from aversion to God; this aversion exists through the will, not through the nature of the fallen angels, for that was good.

This central book contains extensive excursus on Creation and the days of Creation (4-10), the sin of the angels (11-15), the Trinity (10 and 24-29), the beauty of the universe and the antitheses (18), etc. In XI, 17 Augustine says that God makes use of the wickedness of the devil and that the devil's temptations are for the benefit of the saints. In XI, 26 he proves to be a precursor of Descartes:

Si enim fallor, sum. Nam qui non est, utique nec falli potest; ac per hoc sum, si fallor. Quia ego sum si fallor, quo modo esse me fallor, quando certum est me esse, si fallor?[293]

If I am mistaken, I am. For he who is not, cannot be mistaken. Therefore I am, if I am mistaken. So seeing that I am if I am mistaken, how can I be mistaken concerning my existence since it is certain that I am if I am mistaken?[293].

Book XII. The *civitas Dei* of the good angels and the good men is a distinct entity, as is the *civitas* of the demons and the wicked men. The Scriptures teach us that mankind was created by God: it has not existed for all eternity and it does not follow a circular course as some philosophers contend. God created man in His image, without assistance from angels or lower gods. With the first man the whole of

292 *DCD* X, 29: 'Christus est humilis, vos superbi?'. Cf. *s*. 142, 6: 'Iam humilis Deus et adhuc superbus homo' and *Conf*. I, 11, 17.

293 See e.g. Marrou, *Augustin*, 96-97, 171-172; Bardy in *BA* 35, 486-487, and esp. G. Lewis, 'Augustinisme et cartésianisme', *AM*, II, 1087-1104, also for other such texts by A. It is not known whether Descartes was acquainted with them; Lewis speaks of 'une question insoluble, puisque Descartes seul aurait pu y répondre, et ne l'a pas fait ...' (1087). J.A. Mourant, 'The «cogitos»: Augustinian and Cartesian', *AS* 10 (1979) 27-42, is of the opinion that Descartes' 'cogito must remain a symbol at least of his indebtedness to Augustine' (42).

humanity came into being. God already saw in that first man the two *societates* as two *civitates*.

Book XII is especially well-known for the masterly way in which the author speaks out against the cyclical world view.

Book XIII. The Fall brought death. This is a punishment for the righteous, too: although they have been redeemed from sin through the grace of God, the consequences of sin remain. When does death begin? At the very moment that man enters this life[294]. As regards paradise, allegorical interpretations are possible if at the same time historical reality is preserved. After the resurrection the believers are given a spiritual body, which transcends the animal body of the first humans.

Book XIV. The power of death was transmitted to all of Adam's descendants, but the grace of God rescued a number of people from the second and eternal death. Thus mankind is divided into two *civitates*: the city of those who live 'according to man' (secundum hominem) and the city of those who live 'according to God' (secundum Deum). It is not the body that causes sin, but the will; when Adam transgressed, his evil will preceded his evil deeds. How did procreation take place in paradise? Just as it does now, but without the sinful libido. From the condemned mass (massa damnata, 26) God chooses the citizens of His city according to a fixed number.

Augustine ends this book with a description of the totally opposite natures of the *civitates* (28):

Fecerunt itaque civitates duas amores duo, terrenam scilicet amor sui usque ad contemptum Dei, caelestem vero amor Dei usque ad contemptum sui. Denique illa in se ipsa, haec in Domino gloriatur[295]. Illa enim quaerit ab hominibus gloriam; huic autem Deus conscientiae testis maxima est gloria. Illa in gloria sua exaltat caput suum; haec dicit Deo suo: *Gloria mea et exaltans*

Accordingly, two kinds of love formed two cities: the earthly one is formed by self-love which extends even to contempt for God; but the heavenly one is formed by the love of God which extends even to contempt for self. The one glories in itself, the other in the Lord[295]. For the one seeks glory from men; but the greatest glory of the other is God, the witness of conscience. The

[294] Particularly clearly stated in XIII, 10. The ideas expressed here describing life as a course towards death (... ut omnino nihil sit aliud tempus vitae huius, quam cursus ad mortem ...' and the like) are most probably reminiscent of Seneca. See Bardy, *BA* 35, 13 and 271-273, and particularly Andresen in his commentary to Thimme's translation, *Aurelius Augustinus, Vom Gottesstaat. Buch 11 bis 22*, München 1978, 875. Hagendahl, *Latin Classics*, 678 n. 6, is more reserved: 'In my opinion, we find here *commonplaces* which do not prove anything'.

[295] Cf. 2 *Cor.* 10: 17.

caput meum[296]. Illi in principibus eius vel in eis quas subiugat nationibus dominandi libido dominatur; in hac serviunt invicem in caritate et praepositi consulendo et subditi obtemperando. Illa in suis potentibus diligit virtutem suam; haec dicit Deo suo: *Diligam te, Domine, virtus mea*[297]. (...)

one lifts up its head in its own glory; the other says to its God: *My glory and the One who raises my head*[296]. The one is dominated by lust for power, both in its princes and in the nations it subjugates; in the other those in authority and the subjects serve each other in love, the former in guidance, the latter in obedience. The one loves its own strength represented in its mighty ones; the other says to its God: *I will love Thee, O Lord, my strength*[297]. (...)

Book XV. The development of the city of God is described, up to and including the Flood. Cain and Abel/Seth represent the two cities: the children of the flesh and the children of the promise. Augustine goes exhaustively into the phenomenon of longevity and into all kinds of genealogical and other chronological questions concerning the first few chapters of *Genesis*. Various names give rise to allegorical speculations. The Flood is the expression of the wrath of God because of sin; the ark is a symbol of the city of God.

Also from this book a characteristic quotation. At the end of XV,1 Augustine says:

Scriptum est itaque de Cain, quod condiderit civitatem; Abel autem tamquam peregrinus non condidit. Superna est enim sanctorum civitas, quamvis hic pariat cives, in quibus peregrinatur, donec regni eius tempus adveniat, cum congregatura est omnes in suis corporibus resurgentes, quando eis promissum dabitur regnum, ubi cum suo principe rege saeculorum[298] sine ullo temporis fine regnabunt.

Accordingly, about Cain it is written that he founded a city; but Abel, as a sojourner, did not found one. For heavenly is the city of the saints, although it produces citizens here below in whom it sojourns until the coming of the time of its kingdom. At that time it will assemble all who are resurrected in their own bodies, and then the promised kingdom will be given to them, in which they with their Prince, the King of ages[298], will reign time without end.

Book XVI. On the basis of the biblical account the history of the city of God is continued. In the period from Noah until Abraham, God's city does not often come to the fore. The earthly city, however, shows itself emphatically in the building of the tower of Babel, the symbol of man's pride set against God. After the infancy and childhood of God's city its youth arrives, the period from Abra-

296 *Ps.* 3: 4 (3).
297 *Ps.* 17 (18): 2 (1).
298 *Ps.* 47 (48): 15 (14); cf. 1 *Tim.* 1:17.

ham until David. The era of the patriarchs is particularly rich in references to the Messiah and the city of God.

Book XVII. Here again the history of the *civitas Dei* is continued on the basis of the biblical account. From the days of the prophets until the end of the Babylonian captivity there are many prophecies about Christ and the city of God: those of Samuel, of Nathan, in the psalms of David and the books of Solomon. In these prophecies Christ's high-priesthood, kingship, suffering and death are foretold, and also the rejection of the Jews and the calling of the gentiles. From Solomon to the coming of Christ there are only a few prophecies concerning Christ and the city of God.

Book XVII, 3 is especially important; here Augustine deals with 'the threefold meaning of the prophecies, which refer one time to the earthly Jerusalem, another time to the heavenly Jerusalem, and yet another time to both of these'[299]:

Quocirca sicut oracula illa divina ad Abraham, Isaac et Iacob et quaecumque alia signa vel dicta prophetica in sacris litteris praecedentibus facta sunt, ita etiam ceterae ab isto regum tempore prophetiae partim pertinent ad gentem carnis Abrahae, partim vero ad illud semen eius, in quo benedicuntur omnes gentes[300] coheredes Christi[301] per testamentum novum ad possidendam vitam aeternam regnumque caelorum; partim ergo ad ancillam, quae in servitutem generat[302], id est terrenam Hierusalem, quae servit cum filiis suis, partim vero ad liberam civitatem Dei, id est veram Hierusalem aeternam in caelis, cuius filii homines secundum Deum viventes peregrinantur in terris; sed sunt in eis quaedam, quae ad utramque pertinere intelleguntur, ad ancillam proprie, ad liberam figurate.

Therefore, just like those divine oracles uttered to Abraham, Isaac and Jacob, as well as whatever other prophetic signs and words given in the earlier sacred writings, so also do the other prophecies from that time of the kings onwards refer partly to the people physically descended from Abraham and partly to those descendants of his in whom all nations are blessed[300], who are co-heirs of Christ[301] through the new covenant to obtain eternal life and the kingdom of heaven. Thus they refer in part to the handmaiden who bears children into slavery[302]; she is the earthly Jerusalem which is in slavery with her children; but in part to the free city of God, which is the true Jerusalem, eternal in heaven, whose children, the people living according to God's will, are pilgrims on earth. But there are some prophecies which are understood as referring to both: literally to the bondmaiden, figuratively to the free woman.

---

299 *Breviculus* XVII, 3: 'De tripertitis significationibus prophetarum quae nunc ad terrenam, nunc ad caelestem Hierusalem, nunc autem ad utramque referuntur'.

300 *Gen.* 12: 3.

301 *Rom.* 8: 17.

302 Here and in the following lines there are frequent allusions to *Gal.* 4: 21 ff.; cf. esp. *DCD* XV, 2.

In Book XVII Augustine dwells at length on the prophecies as they occur in the Psalms. He explains in particular Psalms 88 (Heb. 89), 44 (45), 109 (110), 21 (22), 3, 40 (41), 15 (16), 67 (68) and 68 (69). Much of what is expounded in his *Enarrationes in Psalmos* occurs here too[303]: Jerusalem and Babylon as the two antithetical cities; Christ and the devil as their two kings[304]. Also in the books 'of Solomon', for example in *Ecclesiastes*[305], he repeatedly discerns the contrast between two *civitates* and two kings.

Book XVIII. This book has no fewer than 54 chapters. First the author outlines the development of the *terrena civitas* since Abraham, so that the readers can compare the two cities[306]. He gives an overall view of world history, always chronologically related to that of Israel: Assyria (= Babylonia prima), Egypt, Greece and the rise of the Roman Empire (Roma quasi secunda Babylonia)[307]. His survey contains many attacks on paganism. An exposition is given concerning Old Testament prophets in their pronouncements about Christ and the city of God. The meaning of the Septuagint is also discussed. This translation is a work of the Holy Spirit; the translators themselves were prophets. Then there is an excursus on the Church. It suffers persecutions in this world:

Sic in hoc saeculo[308], in his diebus malis[309] non solum a tempore corporalis praesentiae Christi et apostolorum eius, sed ab ipso Abel, quem primum	Thus the Church proceeds on its pilgrimage in this world[308], in these evil days[309], not only from the time of the bodily presence of Christ and His apos-

303 Most of these *Enarrationes in psalmos* date from 412-415. See esp. H. Rondet, 'Essais sur la chronologie des *Enarrationes in psalmos*', *BLE* 61 (1960) 111-127, 258-286 and the *Tabula chronologica* in *CCL* 38, XV-XVIII. Bardy, *BA* 36, 743, is not quite accurate when he states: 'l'époque même, où il composait ce livre'.

304 See esp. XVII, 16.

305 XVII, 20: 'Sed illud magis commemorandum existimo in hoc libro, quod pertinet ad civitates duas, unam diaboli, alteram Christi, et earum reges diabolum et Christum'. Then he quotes *Eccles.* 10: 16-17 and explains it.

306 XVIII, 1: '... ut ambae inter se possint consideratione legentium comparari'.

307 XVIII, 2. Cf. XVIII, 22: '... condita est civitas Roma velut altera Babylon et velut prioris filia Babylonis ...'.

308 *Saeculum* is clearly used in a pejorative sense here, as also appears from the addition 'in his diebus malis'; cf. XVIII, 49: 'In hoc saeculo maligno, in his diebus malis ...'. For a survey (albeit incomplete) of the pejorative use of *saeculum* in *DCD*, see A.P. Orbán, 'Die Benennungen der Welt in Augustins *De civitate Dei*: eine Untersuchung über Augustins Weltanschauung', in: *Actus. Studies in Honour of H.L.W. Nelson*, ed. by J. den Boeft and A.H.M. Kessels, Utrecht 1982, 219-223.

309 Cf. *Eph.* 5:16.

iustum impius frater occidit, et deinceps usque in huius saeculi finem inter persecutiones mundi[310] et consolationes Dei peregrinando procurrit ecclesia (51).	tles, but even from that of Abel, the first righteous man, who was slain by his wicked brother, and from then to the end of this world, amid the persecutions of the world[310] and the consolations of God (51).

Book XIX. This very important book is the first of four in which the author discusses the destined ends of the two cities. What is the supreme good and what the worst evil? That is a philosophical question; Varro gave no less than 288 possible opinions on it. The wisdom of this world seeks the *summum bonum* in men themselves, but in vain. The supreme good is not here on earth, nor to be obtained from man himself: it is in God and in the hereafter. The supreme good is eternal life, eternal peace (pax). On earth, peace is the *summum bonum* that must be strived for, also by the state. But true peace is peace with God; the earthly city is unable to offer it, for it does not know true justice[311].

Book XX. The real values will be manifested at the Last Judgement. In contrast to the chiliasts, Augustine teaches that the millennium will not be a reign of Christ and His saints in the future, but that it is already present now in the Church. The first resurrection is the resurrection of the souls from spiritual death; the second will take place at the end of time. Detailed attention is given to events at the end of time: the coming of Elijah, the conversion of the Jews, the persecution by the Antichrist, the appearance of the Son of Man, the resurrection of the dead, the consummation of the world by fire and the world's renewal. This is all substantiated by testimony, first from the New and then from the Old Testament[312].

Book XXI. This book deals with the eternal punishments of the condemned. The perpetuity of these punishments is not contrary to reason, nor to what can be seen in nature. Augustine (again) writes at length about the nature of the resurrected body, about sin and punishment, and he refutes the opinion of Christians who, out of

---

310 *Mundus* here is also used pejoratively; cf. Orbán, 'Benennungen', 229-233.

311 An analysis of the argumentation in Book XIX is given esp. by Barrow, *Introduction*, 177-180. Book XIX will be discussed in detail later; it is essential for the understanding of A.'s doctrine of the *civitates*. See 'Using and enjoying' (pp. 142-145) and particularly 'Peace in earthly things' (pp. 145-150).

312 Likewise method and order are mentioned in the *Breviculus* (XX, 4): 'Quod ad disserendum de novissimo iudicio Dei novi primum testamenti ac deinde veteris testimonia prolaturus est'.

compassion, refuse to accept the idea of eternal punishment. In doing so they fall into the error of Origen, who taught that even the devils would be included among the angels again.

Book XXII. The last book deals with heavenly bliss. God will grant the righteous eternal life and, by adding the number of the chosen, complete the number of the (good) angels, perhaps even increase it:

... qui de mortali progenie merito iusteque damnata tantum populum gratia sua colligit, ut inde suppleat et instauret partem, quae lapsa est angelorum, ac sic illa dilecta et superna civitas non fraudetur suorum numerum civium, quin etiam fortassis et uberiore laetetur (1, in fine).	... and out of the mortal progeny, deservedly and justly condemned, He assembles through His grace a people so numerous that from their ranks He completes and restores the number of the angels that have fallen. And in this way that beloved and heavenly city will not be deprived of the full number of its citizens, but perhaps it may even rejoice in a still greater number (end of 1).

All this is a miracle. In our time, too, many miracles take place. The resurrected body will be perfect, spiritual and immortal. The blessed will devote themselves to beholding and praising God. That will be their life. All illness, trouble, grief and sin will have ceased to exist. The eternal sabbath will have begun.

Augustine ends his work of many years with impressive words about this rest:

Ibi vacabimus et videbimus, videbimus et amabimus, amabimus et laudabimus. Ecce quod erit in fine sine fine. Nam quis alius noster est finis nisi pervenire ad regnum, cuius nullus est finis?[313]	Then we shall rest and see, see and love, love and praise. Behold what there will be in the end without end. For what other end is there for us than to attain the kingdom which has no end[313]?

[313] In these closing sentences—as in the opening ones—the foregoing passages are summarized in an ingenious way. The combination of 'vacabimus et videbimus' comes from *Ps.* 45 (46): 11 (10): 'Vacate et videte quoniam ego sum Deus'. Cf. *Conf.* IX, 2, 4; *En. in Ps.* 45, 14; *En. in Ps.* 70, *en.* I, 18: 'Quid est: *Vacate et videte quoniam ego sum Dominus*, nisi, ut sciatis quia Deus est qui operatur in vobis, et non de vestris operibus extollamini?' and esp. *En. in Ps.* 134, 26. After A. discusses Zion and the heavenly Jerusalem 'cui *laudandae* lingua non sufficit', he writes: '... et *vacabimus* ad *videndum* Deum in pace aeterna, cives Ierusalem facti civitatis Dei'.—'Laudabimus' definitely harks back to *Ps.* 83 (84): 5: 'Beati, qui habitant in domo tua, in saecula saeculorum *laudabunt* te', possibly also to *Ps.* 47 (48): 2 (1): 'Magnus Dominus *laudabilis* valde, in civitate Dei nostri', which is often referred to in *DCD* (cf. the opening of the *Conf.*). Moreover in the exposition of *Ps.* 86 (87), the psalm that opens *DCD*, 'laudare' is referred to abundantly; see *En. in Ps.* 86, 9.

3. Composition

The *City of God* can be seen as a large compendium of Augustine's theology in which many important themes are treated. One's first impression is that the contents of the work are somewhat chaotic. And even after careful study, many scholars have criticized its structure as being poorly thought out[314].

Yet it has become increasingly clear that in its main lines the work is constructed according to a logical and clear plan. Guy, in particular, has investigated and demonstrated this unity in composition: 'Car nous pensons que la Cité de Dieu est un ouvrage magistralement composé et fortement unifié. Même si parfois tel ou tel développement a l'apparence d'une digression gratuite, il y a, du premier au vingt-deuxième livre, une unité logique, on pourrait même dire une rigueur de raisonnement qui mérite d'être soulignée'[315].

Guy's opinion is similar to that of Berthold Altaner, who stated earlier: 'Von Anfang an stand der Gesamtplan des Werkes fest. Die erstmals konzipierten grandiosen geschichtstheologischen Ideen sucht Augustin konsequent zur Darstellung zu bringen und ordnet alle seine Gedanken seinem Beweisziel unter (...). Der Leser von heute muss, um die tatsächlichen Leistung Augustins richtig einzuschätzen, nicht nur viel geschichtliches Verständnis besitzen und mit Geduld und Ausdauer gewappnet sein, sondern auch in sich die Kraft haben, auf allerlei Umwegen mit dem Verfasser immer wieder zur Hauptstrasse der dem Ganzen zugrunde liegenden Idee zurückzufinden'[316]

One can agree unreservedly with this judgement. Also with the opinion of others who have expressed themselves in positive terms

---

314 E.g. Scholz, *Glaube und Unglaube*, 12 ff., esp. 14 on XI-XXII: 'Aber die Durchbildung im einzelnen! Da stockt es an allen Ecken und Enden. Es fehlt die Einheit und Konzentration' (although he also expresses some appreciation: I-X are 'wohlgefügt und geschlossen', 14); Seeck, *Geschichte*, VI, 22: 'So bietet denn auch sein Gottesstaat nicht nur in der Komposition ein gestaltloses Durcheinander, sondern mehr noch im Gedankeninhalt'; Marrou, *Augustin et la fin*, 61: 'Saint Augustin compose mal, sa composition est beaucoup trop lâche ...', Sizoo, 'Augustinus op de grens', 10: 'The Confessiones offer a typical example of poor design, and even a work like De Civitate Dei, which has something of a sketchy organization, at least in the main lines, is in its components so lacking in form and harmony that there is a total absence of balance'; Spörl, 'Staatslehre?', 65: 'Die 22 Bücher sind ein schwerfälliges Produkt, weitschichtig und kompliziert'.

315 Guy, *Unité*, 1.

316 Altaner, 'Beiträge', 36.

about a previously determined structure[317]. Admittedly, this design is carried out in an expansive and sometimes verbose style[318]. A few circumstances, however, should be taken into account. Firstly, that Augustine dictated his works to stenographers[319]. Secondly, that an ancient writer did not use footnotes, and so further elucidations and elaborations are included in the text. Besides, that Augustine wrote[320] the *City of God* under the pressure of many official duties, and was working on a number of other writings at the same time[321].

The *City of God* is divided into two distinct parts: Books I-X and Books XI-XXII. The first part has two subdivisions. In Books I-V Augustine discusses the fall of Rome and then refutes the opinion of those who maintain that worship of the ancient gods is necessary for earthly happiness. In Books VI-X the author contests the view of those who admit that there have always been catastrophes and there always will be, but also declare that worship of the gods is nevertheless necessary for the sake of life after death. In the second part, in

---

317 E.g. Schröder, *Gottesstaat*, I, LX: 'So bildet das Werk trotz mancher Abschweifung vom Thema ein geschlossenes Ganze, das jedoch stückweise, je mehrere Bücher auf einmal, der Öffentlichkeit übergeben wurde'; Dicker, 'Eenheid', 110: 'immanent unity', 181: 'splendid unity'; Marrou, *Augustin et la fin*, 665-672 (*Retractatio*!); Álvarez Díez, 'Arquitectura', 116: 'Es posible apreciar en el todo el conjunto de la obra, con una *unidad perfecta* y cuya *arquitectura*, sólida y bien trabada, apoya en la idea-madre de defensa que le da origen y preside su construcción'; Bardy, *BA* 33, 35-52, although his remarks *BA* 34, 21 f. are less positive.

318 In *s.* 355, 7 the seventy-year-old A. admitted a certain amount of verbosity: 'Multa locutus sum, date veniam loquaci senectuti ...'. Cf. B. Legewie, 'Die körperliche Konstitution und die Krankheiten Augustin's', *MAg*, II, 13, who also remarks, '... doch können wir von einer eigentlichen *loquacitas senilis* bei ihm nicht reden, da wir keine wesentliche Aenderung gegen frühere Zeiten objektiv feststellen können'.

319 In *Retract.* II, 67 he reports that he has *dictated* (dictasse) 93 works (opera) in 232 books (libri). Cf. H. Hagendahl, 'Die Bedeutung der Stenographie für die spätlateinische christliche Literatur', *JbAC* 14 (1971) esp. 33-36. 'Ob der Autor diktiert oder mit der Hand schreibt, macht einen grossen Unterschied in stilistischer Hinsicht' (31).

320 *Scribere* also applied to works that had been dictated: Hagendahl, 'Stenographie', 30.

321 While he was engaged upon the writing of *DCD*, A. wrote—as we may in the first place conclude from *Retract.* II, 44 ff.—among others, works directed against the Pelagians (and particularly against Julian of Eclanum), the *Enchiridion*, the *Locutiones* and *Quaestiones in Heptateuchum*, and many letters. Moreover, he completed *De Trinitate*, the *Tractatus in Iohannis Evangelium, De doctrina christiana*.—Legewie, 'Konstitution', 13: 'Im Ganzen besteht unbedingt der Eindruck, dass die Produktion, rein quantitativ genommen, mit zunehmendem Alter bei Augustin erheblich steigt'.

three sets of four books, he discusses the origin (XI-XIV), the course (XV-XVIII) and the final ends (XIX-XXII) of both the city of God and the earthly city.

This division of the work is clearly indicated by Augustine in his *Retractations*[322]. Also in the *City of God* he refers repeatedly to the structure of the entire work or a major part of it[323]. This shows unmistakably that from beginning to end he had a clear vision of its composition. Moreover, in a letter to a certain Firmus he gave instructions for the arrangement of the book when copies were made: in accordance with its structure this had to be in two parts (I-X; XI-XXII) or in five (I-V; VI-X; XI-XIV; XV-XVIII; XIX-XXII)[324].

Generally speaking the first part is mainly apologetic, the second thetic. However, there are also many apologetic passages in the second part, while in the first ten books a number of thetic expositions can be indicated. Furthermore, Augustine himself writes:

Quanquam ubi opus est, et in prioribus decem quae nostra sunt asseramus, et in duodecim posterioribus redarguamus adversa[325].	Although, where necessary, in the first ten books also, we explain our view, and in the twelve subsequent ones we refute that of our opponents[325].

A greatly simplified outline of the structure of the *City of God* can be given as follows:

A. *Apologetic part* (I-X):

1. Against those who say that the gods must be worshipped for this temporal life (I-V);

2. Against those who say that the gods must be worshipped for the life to come (VI-X).

B. *Thetic part* (XI-XXII):

1. The origin of the two cities (XI-XIV)

- in the world of angels (XI-XII, 9);
- in the first human beings (XII, 10-28);
- the Fall of man and his punishment: death (XIII);

---

322 *Retract.* II, 43.

323 Particularly in I, 35; II, 2; IV, 1-2; V, 26; VI *praef.* and 1; X, 32; XI, 1; XV, 1; XVII, 1; XVIII, 1; XX, 30.

324 The letter to Firmus was discovered and published by C. Lambot, 'Lettre inédite de saint Augustin relative au *De civitate Dei'*, *RBén* 51 (1939) 109-121 (the letter itself 112-113). It has been reprinted in *CCL* 47, III-IV; *BA* 33, 168-172; *MPL,S.* II, 1373-1375. The conclusions reached by Lambot, Marrou, Bardy and others on the basis of this letter, however, are to a considerable degree incorrect. See p. 171 ff.

325 *Retract.* II, 43.

- further consequences of sin (XIV);
2. The history of the two cities (XV-XVIII)
- up to and including the Flood (XV);
- the city of God from Noah to David (XVI);
- the city of God from David to the Exile (XVII);
- the two cities from Abraham to the end of the world (XVIII);
3. The destiny of the two cities (XIX-XXII)
- the supreme good and the uttermost wretchedness (XIX);
- the Last Judgement (XX);
- eternal punishments (XXI);
- eternal bliss (XXII).

4. Why twenty-two books?

Basically, the *City of God* can be characterized as a work with a logical and lucid composition. But why is it divided into twenty-two books? Arthur Darby Nock called attention to this unusual number, all the more remarkable because Augustine generally conformed to the principles that were common in the schools of rhetoric for the composition of extensive works[326].

It is already evident from the just-given survey of XI and XII that the unity of thought does not always concur with the unity of the content of the book. Marrou and Bardy, however, have argued in favour of concurrence[327]. But in Book XVIII also the lack of concurrence is very clear. Augustine states at the beginning of this book that he is going to describe the development of the earthly city. He proceeds to do this in Chapters 1-26, but then continues with expositions of quite different matters: pronouncements by Old Testament prophets on the coming of Christ and on the city of God, the nature of canonical books and the value of the Septuagint, the time of the Church as a time of persecutions, the impossibility of calculating the time of the end of the world. Furthermore, neither Book IV nor

---

326 A.D. Nock, *JEH* 2 (1951) 225 (review of Courcelle, *Recherches*): 'The Civitas Dei consists of 22 books which is another [sc. as the *Conf.*] unconventional number; otherwise, save in collections of quaestiones and tractatus and in the Contra Faustum, Augustine follows traditional practise'.—That the *Conf.* are composed of 13 books can be accounted for through the later addition of Book X (according to E. Williger and, following him, Courcelle, *Recherches*, 25). In *C. Faustum* A. evidently followed the lead of Faustus' *capitula*; see esp. P. Monceaux, *Le Manichéen Faustus de Milev. Restitution de ses capitula*, Paris 1924.

327 See p. 63 n. 275.

Book V forms a separate unity, but on the whole they deal with the same subject: the grandeur of Rome cannot be attributed to the worship of the gods. It is characteristic that at the end of Book IV Augustine declares: the discussion has gone on long enough now; the continuation will be kept for the next book[328].

Obviously it was not the subjects for discussion themselves that led Augustine to the number of twenty-two books. Nevertheless, as has been indicated, he had a clear, fixed scheme in mind[329]. He developed this scheme through the years. But did he purposely give shape to it in twenty-two books, or was this number just accidental?

One of those who have tried to answer this question is Joseph A. McCallin. He referred to Augustine's frequent use of number speculation: human perfection is symbolized by the number ten; the universal Church by twelve. In his description of the history of the two cities, presented in three sets of four books, the Trinity (three) and the world (four) are symbolized. Moreover, twelve is the span of the outstretched arms, ten indicates the height of the human body. The entire work is an image of the crucified Christ[330].

So far McCallin has found no adherents for his view. Understandably, for it is highly speculative, and by no means substantiated by convincing arguments. The same objection must be raised to Edgar Salin's opinion[331]. He assumed that the main division of the *City of God* was chosen after the example of Plato's *Republic* and *Laws*, divided into ten and twelve books respectively. However, decisive substantiation is lacking here too.

Another view was offered by Alfred Adam. In his opinion there could be only one example for the *City of God*: Mani's *Living Gospel*. This also consisted of twenty-two books, according to the letters of the Syriac alphabet. 'Hat Augustin vielleicht daran gedacht, sein Werk dem «Grossen Evangelium» des genialen Ketzers entgegenzusetzen, ja es durch seine Leistung zu ersetzen?'[332]

---

[328] *DCD* IV, 34: 'Iam quod sequitur in volumine sequenti videndum est, et hic dandus huius prolixitatis modus'; cf. XVIII, 54: 'Sed aliquando iam concludamus hunc librum ...'.

[329] This can also be seen in his references to the 'ratio huius operis': *DCD* I, *praef.*; XIX, 1.

[330] J.A. McCallin, 'The Christological Unity of Saint Augustine's *De Civitate Dei'*, *REA* 12 (1966) 85-109.

[331] Salin, *Civitas Dei*, 174.

[332] A. Adam, 'Das Fortwirken des Manichäismus bei Augustin' (1958), *Sprache und Dogma*, 141-166 (quotation on 161); cf. Adam, *Lehrbuch der Dogmengeschichte*, I, Gütersloh 1970², 296.

In any case, this supposition seems more plausible than that of either McCallin or Salin. For not only does Augustine describe the history of the world as the struggle between *civitas Dei* and *terrena civitas*, God and Satan, but also for Mani there was a struggle: between the kingdoms of light and darkness. For that reason Adam and, among others, Böhlig[333] believed that in the arrangement of his main work Augustine was guided by a Manichaean work. They did not, however, offer further arguments.

To be sure, it is difficult to demonstrate agreement in substance between the *Living Gospel* and Augustine's *City of God*. Only small fragments of Mani's gospel have been preserved, recently augmented by the discovery of the *Cologne Mani-Codex*[334]. They are not enough to give a reliable insight into its structure and contents. What is certain about it is the arrangement into twenty-two chapters. Furthermore, it is known that in this work Mani called himself the Paraclete and the Seal of the prophets, that prayer was discussed and that the first part described the Kingdom of Light. The new discovery seems to confirm Puech's assumption that it is 'ein Werk lehrhaften und dogmatischen Charakters, das das manichäische System im Ganzen oder wenigstens einige seiner Hauptpunkte darlegte'[335].

Thus the supposition of Adam and others remains very hypothetical. A major objection is that they overlooked one important fact: Augustine never mentioned the *Living Gospel*. So one should ask whether he was acquainted with it. This question acquires more weight when we realize that others in Africa did not mention the work either.

Elsewhere, however, the *Living Gospel* was of great importance to the Manichaeans. It was often named as the foremost of Mani's writings. Can it not be supposed that in Africa this prominent posi-

---

333 Böhlig, 'Grundlagen', 292. Cf. A. Böhlig, *Die Gnosis, III, Der Manichäismus*, Zürich-München 1980, 45 and 312 n. 134; also Böhlig, 'Der Manichäismus', in: M.J. Vermaseren (Hrsg.), *Die orientalischen Religionen im Römerreich*, Leiden 1981, 445. C. Colpe also expresses himself cautiously in this vein; cf. p. 207 n. 47.

334 See e.g. Alfaric, *Écritures*, II, 34-42; Adam, *Texte*, 1-2 and 111; H.-Ch. Puech, 'Gnostische Evangelien und verwandte Dokumente', in: E. Hennecke – W. Schneemelcher, *Neutestamentliche Apokryphen*, I, Tübingen 1959^3, 261-270 (Das Evangelium des Mani); A. Böhlig, 'Zu den Synaxeis des Lebendigen Evangeliums', *Mysterion und Wahrheit*, esp. 227. For the most recently found fragments, see *CMC* 66 ff.

335 Puech, 'Gnostische Evangelien', 267.

tion was occupied by the *Epistula fundamenti*? This work above all played a central role for Augustine and his Manichaean opponents. It contains nearly everything the Manichaeans believed[336]. In addition, it was this work that—as the *Living Gospel* elsewhere—was read aloud at the religious gatherings in Africa; it brought enlightenment to those present[337]. But nothing is known about its size or structure.

There may, however, be one fact to support the hypothesis of Adam and Böhlig. If Augustine was acquainted with the whole or even with a part of a Latin translation of the *Psalm-Book* which was found in Egypt—that he was familiar with Manichaean psalms is certain—he may have heard of Mani's *Living Gospel* and its structure. A passage in one of the *Bema*-psalms states explicitly that it consisted of twenty-two parts[338]. Furthermore, this gospel is mentioned here as an antidote (antidotos).

The word *antidotos*, which occurs as far as I can see once in the Manichaean *Psalm-Book*, also occurs once in the *Confessions*[339]. There Augustine wrote that he was becoming acquainted with the biblical Psalms and he called them an antidote (antidotum). This not only sounds deliberately anti-Manichaean, but is also reminiscent of the *Bema*-psalm just mentioned[340].

Augustine may have known, in an indirect way, about the structure of the *Living Gospel*, and this might be the reason why he wrote the *City of God* in twenty-two books. To provide an antidotum to Mani's principal work? This is another possibility. In any case, the fact that in the arrangement of his works he very consciously directed himself against the Manichaeans can be proved with one clear piece of evidence.

In a letter Paulinus of Nola and his wife Therasia wrote that they

336 *C. ep. fund.* 5: '... ubi totum paene, quod creditis, continetur'.

337 *C. ep. fund.* 5: 'Ipsa enim nobis illo tempore miseris quando lecta est, illuminati dicebamur a vobis'. Cf. *C. ep. fund.* 25: '... quae fere omnibus qui apud vos illuminati vocantur solet esse notissima'.

338 *Psalm-Book* 46, 20-22: 'There are two and twenty compounds (migma) in his antidote (antidotos):/His Great Gospel (euangelion), the good tidings of all them that are/of the Light'.

339 *Conf.* IX, 4, 8.

340 There is more in this part of the *Conf.* that is reminiscent of the Manichaean psalm. We will just point to *medicamentum* (*Conf.* IX, 4, 8) and the lengthy discussion of Mani as a physician with his medicine chest and medicines (*Psalm-Book*, 46). A.'s use of the word *insani* in this context is also significant, as is e.g. *turgidus spiritus* and *tyfus*.

had a work by Augustine which consisted of five books directed against the Manichaeans. This work, which they had received through Alypius[341], is characterized explicitly as an anti-Manichaean pentateuch[342]. Apparently Augustine deliberately turned against his former fellow-believers in this small set of books. It is known that Mani's followers often combined their leader's books into a pentateuch directed against the Mosaic one. Augustine knew about this, as is evident from his debates with Felix[343].

All the same, one can ask whether the number twenty-two could not be explained in another, more convincing way. Nock could find no parallels, and my inquiries into the composition of classical Greek and Roman works led to the same negative conclusion[344]. Gnostic number speculation and two texts from *Jubilees*[345] is all that could be supplied concerning the use of the number twenty-two[346]. But Augustine seems to have had no knowledge of the magical-mystical use of the alphabet as it occurred among Gnostics in particular. And as far as I have been able to discover, the texts from the *Jubilees* played no part in his work[347].

---

341 *Ep.* 24, 2 (Paulinus and Therasia to Alypius): 'Accepimus enim insigne praecipuum dilectionis et sollicitudinis tuae *opus* sancti et perfecti domino Christo viri, fratris nostri Augustini, *libris quinque confectum* ...'.

342 *Ep.* 25, 2 (Paulinus and Therasia to A.): 'Ideoque cum *hoc Pentateucho tuo contra Manichaeos* me satis armaveris ...'. Both letters were written before the winter of 394; cf. Goldbacher, *CSEL* 58, 13.

343 *C. Fel.* I, 14: 'Felix dixit: Et ego, si mihi attuleris *scripturas Manichaei, quinque auctores* quos tibi dixi, quidquid me interrogaveris, probo tibi.

Augustinus dixit: De ipsis *quinque auctoribus* est ipsa epistula, cuius aperuimus principium ...'. This quotation shows clearly the importance of the *Ep. fund.*; shortly after this the *Thesaurus* is referred to as the *second* book.

344 Various articles (Akrostichon, Alphabet, etc.) in *KP, RAC, RGG, IDB, DACL, TRE* were consulted and, among others, O. Weinreich, *Triskaidekadische Studien. Beiträge zur Geschichte der Zahlen*, Giessen 1916 (repr. Berlin 1967). Particularly in 'Exkurs V' ('Zahl und formale Gliederung') Weinreich provides much information on symbolism and divisions of books, though nothing on the number 22.—The later speculations on numbers in, for example, the *Kabbala* are insignificant in this context.—For the following exposition C. Wendel, *Die griechisch-römische Buchbeschreibung verglichen mit der des Vorderen Orients*, Halle 1949, 120 n. 334, gave an important indication: the significance of the number 22 in the works of Origen, Athanasius and Cassiodorus.

345 *Jub.* 2: 15 mentions 22 acts of God in the creation; 2: 23 also the 22 chief men from Adam until Jacob.

346 Cf. Adam, *Sprache und Dogma*, 161 n. 78.

347 Although *Jub.* was known within the Church; see, for example, E. Schürer, *Geschichte des jüdischen Volkes* ..., III, Leipzig 1909[4], 381-382. Schürer (382) makes mention of an early Latin translation; E. Littmann in Kautzsch (Hrsg.), *APAT*,

But besides Mani's gospel, there is another notable example that may have been of importance to Augustine. It has been described especially by Theodor Zahn in his *Geschichte des Neutestamentlichen Kanons*[348]. For centuries, within the Church too, the canon of the Old Testament was ordered in twenty-two books, initially in accordance with the letters of the Hebrew alphabet. This ordering originated from Palestinian Jewry[349] and was mentioned by Josephus[350]. It is true that the later Jewish ordering of the sacred scriptures was usually in twenty-four books[351], in accordance with a tradition that probably came from Babylonia. But the other tradition was preserved, especially in the Church. The number twenty-two was named explicitly by Cyril of Jerusalem[352], Athanasius[353] and Origen[354]. Also Hilary[355], Epiphanius[356], Jerome[357] and Cassiodorus[358] gave evidence that this old numbering was still known. It is highly probable that Augustine, too,—although he mentions the number forty-four in *De doctrina christiana*[359]—was acquainted with

---

II, 36, dates it about 400. R.H. Charles in Charles (ed.), *APOT*, II, 3 and 7, mentions, referring to Rönsch, '(the middle of) the fifth century'. Therefore it is most unlikely that A. was familiar with this translation; moreover, the fragments that have been handed down do not contain the passages in question. We have found no evidence that A. was aware of the existence of other poems besides the Old Testament Psalms whose initial letters of lines or stanzas were arranged in accordance with the Hebrew alphabet and which—if complete—therefore number 22 lines or stanzas. He was aware of this only in respect to the Psalms; cf. n. 360.—The well-known *Alphabeticum Siracidis* is of a later date; see e.g. V. Ryssel in Kautzsch (Hrsg.), *APAT*, II, 240-241.

348 Th. Zahn, *Geschichte des Neutestamentlichen Kanons*, I, Erlangen 1888 (repr. Hildesheim-New York 1975), 112 and II, Erlangen-Leipzig 1890 (repr. Hildesheim-New York 1975), 1-284 and 318-343. A good survey is also given by H. Leclercq, 'Livres canoniques', *DACL* 9 (1930) 1791-1810.

349 See also G. Wanke, 'Bibel, I', *TRE* 6 (1980) 5. Wendel, *Buchbeschreibung*, 120 n. 334, is incorrect when he states that *Alexandrian* Jews counted 22 canonical books while *Palestinian* ones had 24. In making this mistake he followed the assertion of H.L. Strack, *RE*[3], IX, 757 f.; cf. Strack, *RE*[2], VII, 429 and 435 f.

350 *C. Apionem* I, 8.

351 Cf. also 4 *Ezra* 14, 44-47.

352 *Cat.* IV, 35.

353 *Ep.* 39!

354 See e.g. Eusebius, *HE* VI, 25, 2.

355 *In. Ps.* prol.

356 E.g. *De mens. et pond.* 10 and 22.

357 E.g. *Prol. gal.*

358 *Inst.* I, 12. Even Isidore of Seville, John of Damascus, Patriarch Nikephoros of Constantinople and Archbishop Agobardus of Lyon considered the OT to have 22 canonical books; see Leclercq, 'Livres canoniques', 1807-1810.

359 *De doctr. chr.* II, 8, 13, in which it is striking that he first enumerates 22

this ordering of the Old Testament. Did it contribute to his arrangement of the *City of God*, the work that describes the history of the two cities especially on the basis of the *narratio* of the Old Testament?

A few additional data can be offered that may be useful in explaining the number twenty-two. Augustine knew, as he reports at the end of his long analysis of *Psalm* 118 (Heb. 119)[360], that some psalms were originally arranged according to the twenty-two letters of the Hebrew alphabet. He was familiar with Hilary's interpretation of *Psalm* 118 in twenty-two parts[361], as well as the one by his spiritual father Ambrose in twenty-two books[362]. Whether he was also acquainted with the interpretation by Origen[363] and its arrangement according to the Hebrew alphabet is not clear. It is not

---

historical books, then 22 prophetic ones. Cassiodorus (*Inst.* I, 13) came back to this later, emphasizing the number 22.

360 *En. in Ps.* 118, *s.* 32, 8; cf. *s.* 21, 2.

361 Hilary, *In Ps.* 118, 15, 10, quoted in *De nat. et grat.* 72, 73 (c. 414-415); A. alludes to this work in *En. in Ps.* 67, 1 (also c. 414-415). Cf. C. Kannengiesser, 'Enarratio in psalmum CXVIII: Science de la révélation et progrès spirituel', *RA* 2 (1962) 365 n. 29.

362 Ambrose, *Expositio psalmi CXVIII*, by M. Petschenig (*CSEL* 62, VI) dated to 386-388. In his introduction the editor also remarks that Ambrose himself may have published these sermons as a unit (XI). Did A. already become acquainted with this work in 22 books when he was in Milan? However, according to H.J. Auf der Maur, *Das Psalmenverständnis des Ambrosius von Mailand* ..., Leiden 1977, 15 and elsewhere, the sermons date from 389-390.—Kannengiesser, 'Enarratio', 365 n. 29, is inaccurate in stating that in *C. duas ep. Pelag.* IV, 11, 30, A. was quoting Ambrose's work. In that passage A. offers a version of *Ps.* 118: 36 that also occurs in Ambrose's work ('*Declina* cor meum in testimonia tua et non in avaritiam'), but, as appears from the context, the quotation comes from Ambrose's *De fuga saeculi* I, 1 (cf. A.'s *De dono pers.* 13, 33). In his exposition of *Ps.* 118:36 (*Exp. Ps.* 118, 5, 27) Ambrose gives the text as: '*Inclina* cor meum ...'.—Although we have been unable to find a literal quotation from Ambrose's commentary on *Ps.* 118 in A.'s work, it may safely be assumed that A. was acquainted with it. Evidence can be seen in A.'s *En. in Ps.* 118, *s.* 32, 8. His reference to those who had interpreted *Ps.* 118 before him ('Quod profecto melius sapientiores doctioresque fecerunt ...') definitely applies to Hilary and Ambrose. Although his name is not mentioned, the reference is unmistakably to Ambrose because only he—unlike Hilary and Origen—gave a detailed explanation with each Hebrew letter. For that matter, A. rejects this practice: 'Quod autem de alphabeto hebraeo, ubi octoni versus singulis subiacent litteris, atque ita psalmus totus contexitur, nihil dixi, non sit mirum, quoniam nihil quod ad istum proprie pertineret inveni ...'.

363 For the problems concerning Origen's explanation of the Psalms, see e.g. Auf der Maur, *Psalmenverständnis*, esp. 243-249, 440-442, and P. Nautin, *Origène. Sa vie et son oeuvre*, Paris 1977, 261-292, esp. 275 ff. Easy access to Origen's explanation of *Ps.* 118 is now possible, thanks to the edition of the relevant *Catenae* by M. Harl: *La Chaîne palestinienne sur le psaume 118 (Origène, Eusèbe, Didyme, Apollinaire, Athanase, Théodoret)*, Paris 1972 (*SC* 189-190).

out of the question, for he knew much more of Origen's writings than was generally assumed in former times[364]. In any case, he was acquainted with Origen's interpretation of *Psalm* 118 via Hilary and Ambrose[365]. Both of them consciously preserved the old classification in twenty-two strophes, an arrangement that came from Jewish teaching[366]. That is also why both Origen and Ambrose characterized this psalm in its structure and contents as ethical-didactic[367].

With these data in mind we can once again pose the question concerning the unusual ordering of the *City of God* in twenty-two books. Did Augustine choose *this* number of books for his magnum opus, in which the psalms about the city of God occupy such an important place from beginning to end[368], according to the examples given in the works of predecessors like Hilary, Ambrose and (perhaps) Origen? Or did he possibly follow the example of the so-called alphabetical psalms themselves?

In this framework, finally, a unique example merits our attention. It involves both the number twenty-two and an alphabetical psalm of an apologetic and didactic nature.

In 393 Augustine composed his *psalmus abecedarius*, directed against the Donatists[369]. In this, his only extensive attempt at poetic art[370], he appealed to his opponents to return to the Catholic Church and expounded the background of the schism. This alphabetical psalm is a propagandistic hymn like many of this type among the Donatists[371]. It is striking that the 'refrain', the *hypopsalma*, oc-

---

364 B. Altaner, 'Augustinus und Origenes' (1951), *Schriften*, 224-252; cf. Altaner, 'Augustinus und die griechische Patristik' (1952), *Schriften*, esp. 324-325.

365 Origen's influence on Hilary is generally accepted; his influence on Ambrose is shown again by Auf der Maur, *Psalmenverständnis*, 241-309, who concludes (309): 'Das Verhältnis beider Texte ist viel enger, als bislang geglaubt wurde ...'. This certainly applies to the explanations of *Ps.* 118 of both of them.

366 Cf. H. Tur-Sinai (Torczyner), 'The Origin of the Alphabet', *JQR* 41 (1950) 277-301.

367 Auf der Maur, *Psalmenverständnis*, 271 f., esp. n. 383. Hilary also emphasized that structure and content of *Ps.* 118 point to a didactic character; he did that particularly in the introduction to his interpretation (*CSEL* 22, 355 A. Zingerle).

368 Cf. pp. 64 and 73. Here we only refer to the new start in *DCD* XI, 1: words from the Psalms are prominent.

369 Text of the *Psalmus contra partem Donati* in *BA* 28, 150-190, with an introduction by Y.M.-J. Congar; in 1935 C. Lambot provided the first complete edition.

370 Monceaux, *Histoire*, VII, 83: 'Ainsi que d'autres grands écrivains, Augustin n'était poète qu'en prose'; then he refers esp. to the *Conf.* Leclercq, *DACL*, VI, 2500, makes mention of an acrostic on the word *diaconus*, but see also *MPL*, *S.* II, 356-357.

371 For the 'new psalms' of Parmenian in particular, see Monceaux, *Histoire*,

curs twenty-two times. It is also remarkable that the hymn has a total of twenty-two stanzas[372]. Augustine composed his militant hymn according to the order of the Latin alphabet, but he used only the letters A – V. Why not X, Y and Z as well? Klaus Thraede stated: 'Im Lateinischen machten XYZ Schwierigkeiten; daher lässt Augustin diese Buchstaben fort; denn für sie liessen sich nur Fremdwörter finden'[373]. This argument is not entirely convincing[374], for words and names can be found starting with these letters that were familiar to ordinary churchgoers[375]. Could the real reason be that, in his hymn, Augustine deliberately did not want to exceed twenty-two occurrences of the *hypopsalma* and an equal number of stanzas? Is this because in his day there were also Punic alphabetical songs[376] in which, as in the Hebrew alphabetical psalms, this number was a constituent element?

In the foregoing analysis a number of possibilities have been summed up and considered. It is difficult to choose one of them.

V, 225-226, in which he makes references to A.'s *Ep.* 55, 18, 34 and Praedestinatus, *De haeresibus* 43; likewise Frend, *Donatist Church*, 193-194. These songs have all become lost; only A.'s *Psalmus* provides an idea of their structure and content.

372 In accordance with the alphabet 20 stanza's of 12 lines each, preceded by an introductory stanza of 5 lines and concluded by an epilogue of 30 lines.

373 K. Thraede, 'Abecedarius', *JbAC* 3 (1960) 159.

374 Thraede may be thinking of *Retract.* I, 20. However, A. states there that he did not write a lyrical poem (carmen) because the rules of metrics would have forced him to use words that were unfamiliar to the people: 'Ideo autem non aliquo carminis genere id fieri volui, ne me necessitas metrica ad aliqua verba, quae vulgo minus sunt usitata, compelleret'.

375 From the *sermons* of A. there is for X *xenodochium* (*Tract. in Ioh. Ev.* 97, 4); for Y possibly *Ydumea* (*En. in Ps.* 59, 1; *En. in Ps.* 69, 12) and perhaps, from *Retract.* I, 20 (according to Knöll, *CSEL* 36, 96), *ypopsalma*, used to indicate the 'refrain' of the *Psalmus* against the Donatists; for Z mention can be made of, for instance, *zelare, zelus* and *zizania*. It would also have been possible, as can be seen from Diehl's *Inscriptiones*, to make use of various names beginning with X, Y and Z which (also) occurred among African Christians.—It is striking that A. added the unusual K to his song and that this stanza opens with *Karitatem*.—We should take note of the fact that a letter like Y, according to A., creates problems; see *DCD* XVIII, 23 with reference to the ICHTHYS-acrostic: '... quia non potuerunt latina verba inveniri, quae ab eadem littera [sc. Y] inciperent et sententiae convenirent'. But this was very probably a translation that had come down to him (cf. n. 442) and the question was whether there were any words available to fit the given context.

376 A. makes note of these in *En. in Ps.* 118, *s.* 32, 8, after stating that the Hebrew psalm is arranged in accordance with the alphabet: 'Quod multo diligentius factum est, quam nostri vel latine vel *punice*, quos abecedarios vocant psalmos, facere consueverunt'.—The Punic alphabet contained 22 letters; see J. Friedrich – W. Röllig, *Phönizisch-Punische Grammatik*, Roma 1970[2], 5 (esp. the appended 'Schrifttafel').

Indeed, should and can a choice be made? Thinking along the lines of Nock, Adam, Böhlig and several others, we found some precedents. But by no means can it be claimed that they provide the true reason for the size and structure of the *City of God*. A definite answer concerning the question of the twenty-two books *could* indicate the purpose Augustine had in mind with his work. Nowhere, however, is it apparent that he had deliberately chosen this number. In a letter written c. 418, when he was working on the fourteenth book, he reported that at that moment he did not yet know how many there would ultimately be[377]. Whether he possibly endeavoured consciously after that to divide his total work into twenty-two books, one can only guess. But there is no doubt that the composition of the whole reveals a certain balance: two sets of five books in the mainly apologetic part, three sets of four books on origin, course and destiny of the two cities. It was this division into three parts that Augustine certainly had in mind from the outset (cf. I, 35 and, for example, XI, I).

5. *Not an occasional work*

The events of August 410 and their repercussions were important for the origin of the *City of God*. But it should certainly not be regarded merely as an occasional work. Nearly all recent studies correctly emphasize that even without the fall of Rome a work on the two cities would almost certainly have been written. Bardy remarked: 'Dans la réalité, il est permis de croire que saint Augustin avait depuis longtemps le désir d'écrire ce vaste ouvrage sur la cité de Dieu ou plus exactement sur les deux cités ...'[378]. Guy shares this opinion[379], as does, among others, Brown: 'The *City of God* cannot be explained in terms of its immediate origins. It is particularly superficial to regard it as a book about the sack of Rome. Augustine may well have written *a* book «On the City of God» without such an event. (...) The *City of God*, itself, is not a «tract for the times»; it is the careful and premeditated working out, by an old man, of a mounting obsession'[380].

---

[377] *Ep.* 184A, 5; cf. p. 171.

[378] In *BA* 33, 20; cf., for example, 42.

[379] Guy, *Unité*, 5-10, esp. 6: 'Ainsi, cette journée du 24 août 410 n'est nullement la cause, mais seulement l'occasion de la réflexion d'Augustin'.

[380] Brown, *Augustine*, 312.

Although Augustine, in his *Retractations*[381] and at the beginning of Book I, names the fall of Rome and the ensuing discussion as the initial impetus for his writing the *City of God*, in the remaining twenty-one books he rarely mentions this event. This is also the case with the summaries of the contents in the *City of God* itself[382] . The catastrophe of 410 is not the real reason for the genesis of the work, but only a first stimulus.

More evidence for this view can be found in a passage in *De Genesi ad litteram*. Here Augustine speaks about the two loves (duo amores) and then about the two cities (duae civitates). He finally says that he would perhaps write at greater length about these two cities elsewhere[383]. Neither in this passage nor in its context is there any allusion to the fall of Rome. But it is notable that years later, in *De civitate Dei* XIV, 28, he writes in the same way about two kinds of love and two kinds of cities. The Maurists were quite right when, in their famous edition, they pointed out the similarity between these two texts[384].

Moreover, it is significant that in many other books, sermons and letters preceding his magnum opus, Augustine also referred repeatedly to the two cities, their origin, their antithetical nature and their history. We will study this closely when we examine the possibility of a development in Augustine's treatment of the concept *civitas*[385]. The elements of the view that he expands on later in the *City of God* appear to have been present for a long time. They were waiting, as it were, for a thematic elaboration. The *City of God* is not an occasional pamphlet that developed into a comprehensive work[386], but one of Augustine's principal works, written after a long process of maturation. In a grand vision he brought together what he had written earlier and often enunciated in sermons. Only now everything is—to quote Noordmans again—'joined together systematically like polished building-stones'[387].

---

381 *Retract.* II, 43.

382 Cf. n. 323.

383 *De Gen. ad litt.* XI, 15, 20: 'De quibus duabus civitatibus latius fortasse alio loco, si dominus voluerit, disseremus'.

384 Cf. *MPL* 41, 436 n.

385 See pp. 108-115.

386 See esp. Ch. Dawson, 'St. Augustine and his Age', in: M.C. d'Arcy et al., *Saint Augustine*, New York-London 1957³, 43.

387 Noordmans, *Augustinus* (1933/1952²), in *VW* 3, 57, following C. Bindemann.

6. Characteristics

The *City of God* is a compendium of Augustine's theology, a major work in which previous thought has matured and settled down. It is a work that grew in the course of a substantial period of time, unlike the sermons intended for the congregations of Hippo or Carthage, unlike the letters written to specific people in particular circumstances. It is a work addressed to the intellectual elite of the Roman world.

In the foregoing a few important characteristics of the *City of God* have been stated. First of all, that we are dealing with a work in which thoughts that had been spoken or written earlier on various occasions were given a systematic ordering[388]. Therefore, in a discussion of Augustine's thinking, equal weight cannot be assigned to his various texts. It makes a difference whether a statement originates in a sermon, sometimes casually and without systematic reflection, or in a letter in response to a specific question. In a sermon for the common people the subtle distinction that would be appropriate elsewhere is often lacking; in a letter the addressee, his questions and his circumstances often play an important role.

For this reason, in a study of Augustine's doctrine of the two cities, the first and foremost task is investigate *De civitate Dei*. In this work Augustine gives a systematic exposition, although this does not imply that his letters to Marcellinus, Bonifatius or Macedonius are without important illustrative material to draw from. This certainly applies to the *Enarrationes in Psalmos*, rightly called the best commentary on the *City of God*[389].

Besides being a compendium of his theology, often regarded as the major work[390] of Augustine's oeuvre, the *City of God* is an apology. This is also an important characteristic. Augustine's writing opposed the pagan elite, but it was not primarily in reaction to the

---

388 To give but one example: the theme of *Ep.* 91 recurs clearly in *DCD*, particularly in II and VI; cf. H. Huisman, *Augustinus' briefwisseling met Nectarius*, Amsterdam 1956, esp. 91. *Ep.* 91 was written at the end of July 408 (according to Huisman, 30; but according to Goldbacher, *CSEL* 58, 28, it was Aug. 408 or 409); *DCD* VI was completed c. 416.

389 By, among others, Bardy, 'Définition de la Cité de Dieu', *ATA* 12 (1952) 129; Lauras and Rondet, 'Thème', 114; cf. B. Altaner – A. Stuiber, *Patrologie. Leben, Schriften und Lehre der Kirchenväter*, Freiburg-Basel-Wien 1978[8], 424.

390 See e.g. Loofs, *Leitfaden*, 331; Troeltsch, *Augustin*, 7; Noordmans, 'Augustinus' (1940), *VW* 3, 249 and 251-252; É. Lamirande, *L'Église céleste selon saint Augustin*, Paris 1963, 30.

shocking events of 410. Even if Rome had not fallen, a work like this would certainly have appeared. The view that the *City of God* is an apology was and is generally acknowledged[391]. However, the author not only *attacked* the pagans, he also *addressed* them. He defended, but he also intentionally gave a thetic exposition. It is particularly this characteristic of the *City of God* that has not received enough attention.

At this point a few more characteristics should be presented. Not only was the work the last and greatest apology of the Early Christian Church, but it was to perform another function in later centuries. It became, as Noordmans said, the Church Bible of the Middle Ages, in which emperor and pope, priest and monk found their portraits[392]. It was also Noordmans who characterized it as a book 'for the congregation', because its main emphasis is on pastoral care[393]. A work, too, in which the author dismantles twelve Roman centuries in the first ten books, and wins ten Christian centuries in the remaining twelve[394].

Still more characteristics of this immensely rich opus can be given. It has been correctly observed that, although the *City of God* finishes with the Roman past, it transmits something—and in certain respects even a good deal—of the Roman spirit and the values of the Empire to later generations[395]. It has also been observed that this work, like Plato's *Politeia* and Cicero's *De republica*, originated in a period of crisis[396]. Augustine's style of writing has been likened to Gothic architecture: intelligible in its parts and imposing as a whole[397]. An anagogic sense (sensus anagogicus) has been discerned: everything aspires to excel and seeks a higher coherence[398].

---

391 See p. 164 ff.

392 Noordmans, *Augustinus, VW* 3, 66; cf. 49 and 149. A. Wilmart, 'La tradition des grands ouvrages de saint Augustin', *MAg*, II, 279 n. 1 and 292, shows that particularly in the 12th – 15th centuries many manuscripts were made of *DCD*; this fact testifies to special interest.

393 Noordmans, 'Augustinus' (1940), *VW* 3, 250.

394 Noordmans, 'Augustinus' (1940), *VW* 3, 252; a somewhat different wording on p. 149.

395 E.g. P. Delhaye, 'S. Augustin et les valeurs humaines', *RSR* 12 (1955) 121-138, esp. 132: *DCD* 'contribuera plus que tout autre ouvrage à transmettre l'esprit romain au m.a. et à sauver quelque chose de l'empire qui s'effondre, même s'il fait maudire son passé païen'.

396 Pesce, *Città*, 169.

397 Noordmans, *Augustinus, VW* 3, 78.

398 Scholz, *Glaube und Unglaube*, 195, following Thomas Valois, a 14th-cent.

Right from the beginning the groundwork is laid for what is to come, and the themes and antitheses characteristic of the work are indicated.

Special attention should be given to a characteristic that is of importance for some interpretations which will come later. Although it is absolutely clear from Augustine's writings that the two cities exclude each other completely, in scholarly discussions this vital question appears again and again: how is his thinking on Church and State to be combined with his pronouncements on *civitas Dei* and *terrena civitas*?

Although it is not necessary to treat this question as a theme of this investigation, it occurs in the background several times. In this context one comment should be made before we proceed: Augustine was trained in rhetoric and this also found expression in the *City of God*. With stirring eloquence the earthly city of Rome is sometimes identified with the *civitas diaboli*, the empirical Catholic Church with the *civitas Dei*[399]. And yet in other passages Augustine is well aware of the limits of his rhetoric and considers such an identification to be exaggerated.

Of course, by drawing attention to the rhetorical element and thus to a predilection for the antithesis, we do not suggest that we should not be constantly on the lookout for what Augustine said about the earthly city and the city of God, the State and the Church, Babylon and Jerusalem. But we should be careful not to typify him in a distorted way. The *City of God*—as will be seen again and again—deals primarily with what could be termed 'ideal-pictures' or 'religious abstractions'; what finally matters to the author is to repeat the biblical revelation. Between belief and disbelief there is only antithesis, no synthesis.

Therefore the absolute contrast between *civitas Dei* and *terrena civitas* is indisputable. But how these entities can be applied to the Catholic Church and the earthly State is a *crux interpretum*[400].

---

commentator of *DCD*. Scholz quotes a later edition (of 1468), thereby creating the impression that Valois (also Waleys, Walleis and Guallensis) lived in the middle of the 15th cent. But Thomas Waleys died in 1349. See in particular B. Smalley, 'Thomas Waleys O.P.', who also analyses Waleys' commentary.

399 Sizoo, 'Augustinus op de grens', 9-10; H.-I. Marrou, 'Civitas Dei, civitas terrena: num tertium quid?', *SP* 2 (*TU* 64), Berlin 1957, 342-343; Markus, *Saeculum*, esp. 45 ff.

400 Cf. Brown, 'Saint Augustine' (1963), *Religion and Society*, 26: 'To try to extract from this infinitely flexible book a rigidly coherent system of political ideas is

Walther von Loewenich attributed this especially to the fact that to a certain extent Augustine remained a pupil of Plato: 'Für den Platoniker Augustin sind Urbild und Abbild nicht absolut zu trennen. Das Abbild hat seine eigentliche Wirklichkeit im Urbild, aber das Urbild verwirklicht sich nicht restlos im Abbild'[401]. Noordmans formulated the problem of interpretation as follows: 'But it is hard to say precisely what he thinks about Rome, the city of God, the State and the Church. Again and again the light shifts, and brightness and darkness are turned into each other. The figure who here represents a devil returns elsewhere in human form and the one who appears in this niche as an obdurate pagan can serve in another one as a prophet pointing to Christ'[402]. Scholz, in his commentary on the *City of God*, used the image of three-colour printing: the contrasts are sharpest on the bottom layer, while on the upper layers transitions become apparent[403]. Of particular importance, however, is what Markus shows clearly[404]: Augustine was again and again aware of the limits of his thinking and interpreting; he knew the distinction between sacred and secular history, between the inspired speech of the Scriptures and our human speech. The latter is fallible and limited; that of Scripture is normative. Through revelation the fundamental principles are unmistakably clear; the application to our earthly reality and to our history remains subject to human limitations.

Finally in this connection one more remarkable fact should be pointed out. It could be described as the great derailment in the interpretation of the *City of God*. Soon after his death and increasingly in subsequent centuries the historical Augustine became a 'churchified' and 'politicized' Augustine. His opus magnum was no longer understood in accordance with its original intention, but used as a reference book for Church and State politics. In it was sought and found a doctrine on the State as *terrena civitas*, on the Church as the representation of the heavenly *civitas* and guardian of the worldly

---

like trying to square the circle: it is a problem that has fascinated many great minds and baffled all of them'.

401 W. von Loewenich, *Augustin und das christliche Geschichtsdenken*, München 1947, 25; Marrou, 'Tertium?', 343: 'Enfin n'oublions jamais que saint Augustin pense dans une atmosphère platonicienne', and Marrou in *AM*, III (Actes), 200: '... que notre Magister Augustinus était de formation platonicienne ...'.

402 Noordmans, *Augustinus, VW* 3, 79.

403 Scholz, *Glaube und Unglaube*, 134.

404 Markus, *Saeculum*, esp. 1-21.

order. Stripped of its eschatological content, the *City of God* became a theological and political programme. Whereas Augustine saw Church and State merely as transitional phases in the divine plan of salvation, an interim during which the State is responsible for earthly peace—which is basically a Babylonian peace, to be *used* by the citizens of the heavenly City—in the Middle Ages the State was seen differently. To what extent has divine justice taken its shape in it? Only the Church can establish this norm.

In turn, popes have referred to the *City of God* for their ideal of a Church State, and emperors have done so for their State Church. But it should be borne in mind that a theocratic order in this sense was completely alien to Augustine. To him there was absolutely no form of *imperium christianum*, nor was the Church to be identified with the City of God on earth. His emphasis was on the idea of peregrination.

In this investigation no more attention will be devoted to this remarkable historical development. It has only been referred to as it is a particularly distinctive trait of this enormously influential book. Medieval life was modelled to a great extent after the *City of God*, but this occurred through a radical metamorphosis. In what, since Arquillière's studies[405], has been called the 'augustinisme politique', it is not the original Augustine speaking. True, there are passages in his works that would fit into a theocratic concept. But a theocratic vision as it existed in the Middle Ages was unknown to the bishop of Hippo. This is already evident after a brief comparison is made between his thoughts and the ideal of a Christian emperor and a Christian empire as it was held by his contemporaries and had been stated in particular by Eusebius[406].

The primary aim of the author of the *City of God* is to describe the antithesis between the two cities[407]. We will look especially at this in the course of our investigation: the heavenly city as opposed to the earthly one, the *civitas Dei* as opposed to the *civitas diaboli*, the society of the believers as opposed to the society of the wicked.

---

[405] H.-X. Arquillière, *L'Augustinisme politique. Essai sur la formation des théories politiques du Moyen Age*, Paris 1934 (1955²); idem, 'Réflexions sur l'essence de l'augustinisme politique', *AM*, II, 991-1001.

[406] See pp. 154-163.

[407] Cf. Reuter, *Studien*, 136: 'Augustin wechselt nicht selten mit den Massstäben, welche er anlegt; er gebraucht am liebsten den absoluten ...'.

C. The doctrine of the two cities

1. *Origin and history of the two cities*

Especially in the first ten books of the *City of God*, Augustine presents a grand apology. But from the outset he has a higher aim. In refuting the accusations of his opponents he shows immediately that there is a fundamental antithesis between the citizens of the city of God and those of the earthly city. He points out to his Roman opponents not only that their own history contradicts their assertions, but especially that the course of history should be judged in the light of the antithesis between *civitas Dei* and *terrena civitas*.

We will first consider the origin and the history of the two cities, particularly as Augustine expounds them in the *City of God*. In Book XI he states that the earthly city originated from the rebellion of the angels against God, before the creation of man. This is the reason for the split between the good, God-fearing angels and the evil ones who follow the devil. Besides this origin in the world of angels, there was its incipience among men. In Adam, to the foreknowledge of God, both *civitates* came into this world: a society of those desiring to live according to the flesh, to man, and a society of those desiring to live according to the spirit, according to God's will[408]. At the time of the Fall the course (excursus or procursus[409]) of the two cities or societies began, and it will continue until the Day of Judgement. This is the age we call the time of the world.

In this context mention should be made of the fact that both in the beginning of Book XI and at the end of Book X Augustine comments explicitly on three stages in the existence of the *civitates*: their origin (exortus), their course (excursus/procursus) and their destined ends (debiti fines)[410]. The same division occurs in his *Retractations*[411]. Is it possible to perceive here, as Alfred Adam

---

408 Esp. *DCD* XIV, 1 and XV, 1.

409 In *DCD* A. uses the words *excursus* and *procursus* indiscriminately: *procursus* in I, 35; X, 32; XV, 1; XVI, 12. 35. 43; XVII, 1. 4. 14; XVIII, 1. 2; *excursus* in XI, 1; XV, 1. 9. It is clear from the letter published by Lambot that he actually prefers *excursus*; see *Ep. ad Firmum* 1: '... procursum sive dicere maluimus excursum ...'. In *Retract.* II, 43 we find: 'excursum sive procursum'.

410 *DCD* XI, 1: '... de duarum civitatum ... exortu et excursu et debitis finibus ... disputare ... adgrediar ...'; X, 32: '... de duarum civitatum ... exortu et procursu et debitis finibus quod dicendum arbitror ... expediam'.

411 *Retract.* II, 43: 'Duodecim ergo librorum sequentium primi quattuor continent exortum duarum civitatum ... secundi quattuor excursum sive procursum; tertii vero ... debitos fines'.

did[412], a similarity to the Manichaean doctrine of the three epochs or three moments[413]?

The actual history of the two cities is arranged by Augustine in different ways. To begin with, there is a division into six periods: the first from Adam to the Flood (Noah), the second from Noah to Abraham, the third from Abraham to David, the fourth from David to the Babylonian captivity, the fifth from the captivity to the birth of Christ, the sixth from Christ to the end of the world. In the *City of God* this periodization does not appear in full until the end (XXII, 30), but elements of it are to be found earlier in the work[414]. Moreover, it is apparent elsewhere in Augustine's writings that he had had this arrangement in mind for a long time[415]. For example, in his work against the Manichaean Faustus, he compared the six periods to the six days of creation[416]. And especially in his *Commentary on Genesis against the Manichaeans*[417] he gave a detailed and clear exposition.

It is also in this last-named work, composed shortly after his conversion[418], that another periodization is found that runs parallel to the one according to the six days of creation. Here, as well as elsewhere[419], Augustine made a division according to man's six stages of life: *infantia, pueritia, adolescentia, iuventus, gravitas* and *senectus*. He took the dividing lines of the six periods from the genealogical register of the *Gospel according to Matthew*[420]. The first two *aetates*, the one of *infantia* beginning with Adam and the one of *pueritia*

---

412 Adam, 'Fortwirken', *Sprache und Dogma*, 159.

413 See also p. 224 ff.

414 E.g. *DCD* XVI, 24 and 43.

415 E.g. *s.* 259, 2; *De cat. rud.* 39; *De trin.* IV, 4, 7. It should be noted that sometimes it is not the birth of Christ that heralds the 6th epoch, but the appearance of John: *Tract. in Joh. Ev.* IX, 16; and XV, 9; *En. in Ps.* 92, 1. We suppose that this is connected with A.'s interpretation of *Luke* 16:16 and *Matt.* 11:12-13; cf. esp. *DCD* XVII, 24 and *C. litt. Petil.* II, 37, 87.

416 *C. Faust.*. XII, 8.

417 *De Gen. c. Man.* I, 35-41; cf. esp. K.-H. Schwarte, *Die Vorgeschichte der augustinischen Weltalterlehre*, Bonn 1966, 23-32.

418 It is generally accepted that *De Gen. c. Man.* dates from 388-390.

419 A complete enumeration in this form also occurs in *De div. quaest.* 58, 2; cf., among others, *De vera rel.* 48; *s.* 87, 5; *s.* 49, 1; *En. in Ps.* 127, 15; *DCD* XVI, 43; *Ep.* 213, 1.

420 *De div. quaest.* 58, 2: '... sic enim Matthaeus evangelista partitur'; *De cat. rud.* 39: '... reliquarum autem trium [sc. articuli aetatum] in evangelio etiam declarantur, cum carnalis origo domini Jesu Christi commemoratur'; *DCD* XVI, 43; XXII, 30. Cf. esp. *C. Adim.* 7.

from Noah, he regarded as self-evident and commonly known[421].

It is not essential for this study to investigate extensively other divisions of history[422] found in Augustine's writings or their possible origins[423]. Neither the periodization according to the story of creation nor the division according to the stages of man's life appears to have originated with him, but they seem to have been taken over from earlier traditions[424]. Augustine was probably original in his *combining* of the two systems of division, as, among others, Luneau concludes[425]. It is above all on his authority that in later centuries many scholars not only indicated the same number of periods, but also compared the six periods to the stages of human life. Medieval historiography followed Augustine almost completely, and his influence continued after that, for example in Bossuet[426].

---

421 See esp. *De div. quaest.* 58, 2: 'Prima itaque generis humani aetas est ab Adam usque ad Noe, secunda a Noe ad Abraham: qui articuli sunt evidentissimi et notissimi'; *De cat. rud.* 39: 'Isti enim articuli duarum aetatum eminent in veteribis libris ...'. A. is probably referring here to the genealogical tables in *Gen.* 5 and 10.

422 A. is familiar with, among others, Paul's division (*Rom.* 5): before the law, under the law, under grace (see e.g. Scholz, *Glaube und Unglaube*, 164) and he is acquainted with the periodization provided by Origen in connection with the parable of the vineyard (*Matt.* 20); see e.g. Schwarte, *Vorgeschichte*, 203-207.

423 See e.g. Scholz, *Glaube und Unglaube*, 154-165; Wachtel, *Beiträge*, 48-78; A. Luneau, *L'histoire du salut chez les Pères de l'Église. La doctrine des âges du monde*, Paris 1964, passim; Schwarte, *Vorgeschichte*, passim.—Less emphasis on A. himself and more on the Jewish and Christian sources is given by J. Daniélou, 'La typologie millénariste de la semaine dans le christianisme primitif', *VC* 2 (1948) 1-16 and O. Rousseau, 'Les Pères de l'Église et la théologie du temps', *MD* 30 (1952) 36-44.—For a systematic survey of the divisions of history, see J.H.J. van der Pot, *De periodisering der geschiedenis. Een overzicht der theorieën*, 's-Gravenhage 1951.

424 Cf. Scholz, *Glaube und Unglaube*, 157-162; Van der Pot, *Periodisering*, 39 ff. (days of creation) and 103 ff. (ages of the human individual); Wachtel, *Beiträge*, 571 f. (days of creation) and 60 f. (ages of human life), as well as the studies by Daniélou, Rousseau, Luneau and Schwarte.

425 Luneau, *Histoire*, 291. But see Van der Pot, *Periodisering*, 105. Also R. Schmidt, 'Aetates mundi. Die Weltalter als Gliederungsprinzip der Geschichte', *ZKG* 67 (1955-'56) 288-317, surmises that A. was the first to connect the division according to the various ages of human life with that according to the world epochs.—P. Archambault, 'The Ages of Man and the Ages of the World', *REA* 12 (1966) 193-228, offers nothing new but is elucidating. He, too, states that A. was the first to link the ages of man with the ages of the world (205). His remarks on Bacon, Pascal, Herder, Hegel, Spengler, Toynbee et al. are particularly interesting: these writers also compared the epochs of world history with the ages of man.

426 Van der Pot, *Periodisering*, esp. 41 ff. and 105. 'Almost completely', for the schemes show light variations: for example, Moses—omitted by A. because he is not mentioned in *Matt.* 1—was soon included; Origen named him, as did Jerome (cf. Scholz, *Glaube und Unglaube*, 161); see also Irenaeus (*Adv. Haer.* III, 2, 8): 4

Of special interest are some characteristic elements in Augustine's description of the history of the two cities and consequently of the history of the world[427]. First of all, it is noteworthy that he divides the latter according to the periods that emerge from the historical course of the city of God: the periodization of the history of salvation determines that of world history. Moreover, he classifies the periods on the basis of *Genesis* 1: just as man was created on the sixth day, the sixth period is heralded by the coming of the second Adam, Jesus Christ. Then the new Man makes his appearance, in the final period, which at the same time means a total renewal.

The division according to the stages of man's life, borrowed from predecessors and running parallel to the days of creation, must have appealed greatly to Augustine. This periodization, in which mankind (or a people, originally the Romans[428]) is regarded as an organism subjected to the biological laws of rise, climax and decline, fits excellently into his design, for he often refers to the city of God as Christ's body[429]. Moreover, as a man trained in rhetoric he was familiar with the scheme used by the Romans. Now he could apply it in his apology: the true city is not Rome, but the city of God. It is this city of God whose birth, development and future Augustine describes for his cultivated readers.

In yet another respect Augustine can relate directly to the thinking of his opponents. When describing the history of the earthly city—this occurs mainly in Book XVIII—he shows that the kingdom of the East is succeeded by that of the West. This is the way Varro, among others, also described it[430].

For Augustine Rome is the second Babylon, Babylon the first

---

covenants, with Adam, Noah, Moses, Christ. Schmidt, 'Aetates', 314: 'Man kann eigentlich gar nicht von *dem* Weltalterschema sprechen'.

[427] It may be noted in passing that, still in the 19th century, the influential statesman and historian Guillaume Groen van Prinsterer (1801-1876) described world history as the 'victory of the kingdom of Christ over the one founded by Satan'. What is also striking about him — as about A.—is his 'deuteronomic' view of history; cf. H. Smitskamp, *Groen van Prinsterer als historicus*, Amsterdam 1940, 35 f. and 144.

[428] As by Cicero, Seneca (the Elder), Julius Florus, Ammianus Marcellinus; cf. Scholz, *Glaube und Unglaube*, 160-161; Van der Pot, *Periodisering*, 103-105; Luneau, *Histoire*, 51-52 (he also names Varro); Schwarte, *Vorgeschichte*, 42 ff. (who also points to Prudentius, Ambrose, then [45-52] to the classifications in Roman law).

[429] See for instance p. 123 ff.

[430] Cf. Scholz, *Glaube und Unglaube*, 175 n. 2; Wachtel, *Beiträge*, 66.

Rome[431]. One empire took the place of the other. Thus a caesura in the history of the earthly city is indicated. But can the history of the other *civitas* be synchronized with this? Although Augustine's basic starting-point is the course of the city of God as described in Scripture, he sees clear parallels. For the two instances in the history of the city of God in which its worldwide diffusion is prophesied, namely in the days of Abraham and those of the Old Testament prophets, coincide with the beginning of Assur-Babylon and of Rome respectively[432].

The worldwide diffusion of the city of God was proclaimed especially to Abraham, and after that mainly during and after the Babylonian captivity. But its presence is not clearly discernible in all of the six periods. At the beginning of Book XVIII Augustine remarks that the city of God went its way in the shadows until the revelation of the New Covenant[433]. The full light broke through with the coming of Christ. Until the days of Heber, Abraham's ancestor, there was little differentiation between the development of the two cities in the world of man. At the time of Heber, however, Babylon arose, the pre-eminent symbol of the earthly city. After the confusion of tongues it was only in Heber's lineage that the universal language of mankind, Hebrew, was preserved; his descendants in particular were the citizens of the *civitas Dei*[434]. The city of God revealed itself even more clearly in Abraham; his lineage was, as it were, the *plantatio civitatis Dei*[435].

From then onward the history of the city of God was for a long time identical to that of Israel. This people received the law and the promise before all other nations. And yet Israel lost its citizenship of the city of God, especially after the Babylonian captivity. Instead of being the chosen people the Israelites increasingly became enemies; they became apostate and this apostasy was soon accompanied by the disappearance of their independent existence as a state[436]. At

---

[431] E.g. *DCD* XVI, 17: '... conditam Romam, veluti alteram in occidente Babyloniam'; XVIII, 2: '... Babylonia, quasi prima Roma ...'; XVIII, 22: '... condita est civitas Roma velut altera Babylon et velut prioris filia Babylonis ...'; XVIII, 27: '... occidentalis Babylonis exordio ...'.

[432] Esp. *DCD* XVIII, 27.

[433] *DCD* XVIII, 1: '... quamvis usque ad revelationem testamenti novi non in lumine, sed in umbra cucurrerit'.

[434] *DCD* XVI, 11.

[435] *DCD* XVI, 12.

[436] Esp. *DCD* XVIII, 45.

the birth of Christ the alienation had advanced to such an extent that Isaiah's words 'only a remnant shall be saved' applied[437]. After the hardening of the hearts of the Jewish people, the call for the citizenship of the city of God went out to all nations; what in earlier times had been promised to Abraham[438] and announced by the prophets was fulfilled. It is no accident, therefore, that in Book XVIII Augustine mentions especially the prophecies of the hardening of the hearts of the Jews and the call to the gentiles[439].

Were there before the coming of Christ already citizens of the city of God outside Israel? Augustine gives an affirmative answer: there were non-Jewish citizens of the city of God, not an entire nation, but individual persons. It is true, he says in XVIII, 47, that only one people in the proper sense of the word is allowed to call itself God's people: Israel. But it cannot be denied that from other nations there were individuals who belonged to the company of the true Israelites, the citizens of the heavenly country[440], not by virtue of the earthly, but by virtue of the heavenly fellowship. Here and elsewhere in the *City of God*[441] he names the Edomite Job as well as the Sibyl[442]. In

---

437 *Isa.* 10: 22 in *DCD* XVIII, 46.

438 *DCD* XVI, 16.

439 *DCD* XVIII, 28-35 and 45.

440 *DCD* XVIII, 47: 'Populus enim re vera, qui proprie Dei populus diceretur, nullus alius fuit; homines autem quosdam non terrena, sed caelesti societate ad veros Israelitas supernae cives patriae pertinentes etiam in aliis gentibus fuisse negare non possunt ...'.

441 *DCD* I, 24; XVIII, 23 and 47.

442 For the remarkably positive statements on the sibyls by A. and others, see H.C. Weiland, *Het Oordeel der Kerkvaders over het Orakel*, Amsterdam 1935, 65-76 (68-75 on A.); cf. B. Altaner, 'Augustinus und die neutestamentlichen Apokryphen, Sibyllinen und Sextussprüche' (1949), *Schriften*, esp. 212-215, and Altaner and Stuiber, *Patrologie*, 119-121.—The sibyls were cited, often in an apologetic framework, by Hermas, Justin Martyr, Athenagoras, Theophilus, Tertullian, et al. A. considered their gift a prophetic one and probably (fortasse) God-given (Weiland, 73); on the other hand he was also critical, esp. in *De cons. evang.* I,19 (Weiland, 75). They were rejected unequivocally by the Ambrosiaster, Paulinus of Nola, et al. (Weiland, 74).—In *DCD* the *Sibylline Books* are discussed more than once; in XVIII, 23 there is a translation of the well-known ICHTHYS acrostic. Courcelle (*Lettres grecques*, 177-178) wonders if this was not translated from the Greek by A. himself. However, Marrou (*Augustin et la fin*, 36 and 635), Altaner (*Schriften*, 213) and Bardy (*BA* 36, 757) are correct in having serious doubts about this. It *is* assumed (Altaner, 214; Marrou, 635 and also Courcelle, 178), that the lines from the *Sibylline Books* VIII and VI which were subsequently mentioned in *DCD* XVIII, 23 were translated by A. himself; he had read them in Lactantius (*Div. Inst.* IV, 18-19). This would be an example of A.'s proficiency: a simple, literal translation preserving the Greek word-order. But it may be asked how much of it

other works he also mentions Melchizedek, the inhabitants of Nineveh, and Rahab[443]. They are all prefigurations of the later clearly universal character of the city of God. Thus Augustine can, in an apologetic form, demonstrate the universality, already present before the coming of Christ, of the Christian doctrine of salvation.

As the history of salvation progresses, the contents of the message of salvation becomes clearer. But at the same time an increasing unwillingness to accept salvation manifests itself. Augustine sees this repeatedly in the behaviour of Israel, the nation in which, in the Old Testament, the city of God received its particular form on earth.

Due to this obstinacy each period in the history of the *civitas Dei* eventually experiences a decline. But again and again God makes a new start. This view of the history of salvation is reminiscent of a historiography in Israel itself, as it has been studied especially by Gerhard von Rad[444]. And Augustine's view can be better understood if it is related to his division of history by analogy with the days of creation: each time night falls, but after that God creates a new day. After the morning of Adam's creation comes the evening of the Fall, and finally the Flood. With Noah a new day dawns, but it ends in confusion with the building of the tower. Abraham is a new beginning, but his descendants go astray. With David a new day breaks, but it, too, fades. This goes on until the coming of Christ, the decisive turn. But this period, too, has its evening, on the Day of Judgement. Then, however, the seventh day dawns, without end, eternal.

Thus Augustine saw the history of salvation as a process that starts over and over again[445]. For him an immanent evolution is

---

could have been done by A.'s close associates.—A.'s authority must have contributed to the fact that in later centuries there was also room for the sibyl(s): in the well-known hymn by Thomas of Celano (?): 'Dies irae, dies illa/Solvet saeclum in favilla/Teste David cum Sibylla', and, for example, in Michelangelo's famous painting on the ceiling of the Sistine Chapel: sibyls next to the Old Testament prophets.

443 *Ep.* 177, 12; *Ep.* 164; *C. mendac.* 34, resp.

444 For the way in which the OT speaks of history and for deuteronomic historiography, see e.g. G. von Rad, 'Die deuteronomistische Geschichtstheologie in den Königsbüchern' (1947), in: *Gesammelte Studien zum Alten Testament*, München 1958, 189-204; 'Theologische Geschichtsschreibung im Alten Testament' (1948) and 'Das Wort Gottes und die Geschichte im Alten Testament' (1941), in: *Gottes Wirken in Israel. Vorträge zum Alten Testament*, Neukirchen 1974, 175-190 and 191-212. Besides Von Rad, special mention should be made of M. Noth's studies on the Deuteronomic History.

445 Wachtel, *Beiträge*, 73, properly characterizes A.'s view as 'Prozess ständiger Neuanfänge'; cf. Rousseau, 'Pères', 42 ff. and Schwarte, *Vorgeschichte*, 40-43.

out of the question, but there is a continuing plan of salvation in which God acts creatively[446]. In this context it should be noted that the period starting with Christ's coming in the flesh has a nature of its own: the time before Christ is that of promise, the final period that of fulfilment[447]. Now the body of Christ attains its full realization.

An important aspect of the aforementioned should not be neglected, however. Augustine regards the appearance of Christ as a decisive caesura in the history of the city of God. But not as an absolute one. For salvation did not begin with the coming of Christ; it had been present throughout the history of mankind. The incarnation was preceded by periods of salvation which were all determined by Christ, which all pointed to Him, all derived their meaning from Him. The patriarchs, the prophets and an individual like Job are all to be characterized as Christians 'avant la lettre'. For belief in salvation through Christ has always existed. Thus Abel was already justified, as were all the believers from the period of the Old Covenant and also those from the gentile nations like Job[448]. The Church has existed since the beginning of mankind[449]; long before the birth of Christ there was the earthly history of the city of God[450]. It is precisely by reason of a particularistic doctrine of predestination that Augustine can speak universalistically. For there is 'eine histo-

---

[446] His view—based mainly on the OT—also resembles in many aspects that of Oscar Cullmann, which is based on NT texts. See esp. his *Heil als Geschichte. Heilsgeschichtliche Existenz im Neuen Testament*, Tübingen 1965[1], particularly 106 f. on the 'Wellenlinie'; cf. O. Cullmann, 'Die Schöpfung im Neuen Testament', in: *Ex auditu verbi. Theologische opstellen aangeboden aan Prof. Dr. G.C. Berkouwer* ..., Kampen 1965, 56-72.

[447] It is not true, though, that A. explicitly divided history into one epoch before and one after Christ. This division, according to Van der Pot, *Periodisering*, 51 ff., was used for the first time in historiography c. 830, viz. in the chronicle of Freculphus, bishop of Lisieux; since the 18th cent. it has been the most commonly used one.—Nevertheless, in A.'s concept there is a clear distinction between the two main epochs. This distinction is always in the background when he gives his expositions in *DCD* and is more palpable in, e.g., *De cat. rud.* 39: first a summary on the 5 epochs before Christ as a whole, then a separate exposition on the 6th one. The sole reference by Wachtel, *Beiträge*, 53, viz. to *De vera rel.* 50, does not stand up to scrutiny.

[448] E.g. *DCD* VII, 32; X, 25; XVIII, 23. 47; *De cat.rud.* 28.

[449] E.g. *DCD* XVI, 2: '... ecclesia cuius ab initio generis humani non defuit praedicatio ...'.

[450] E.g. *DCD* XVII, 16: 'Ac per hoc Christus Deus, antequam in illa civitate per Mariam fieret homo, ipse in patriarchis et prophetis fundavit eam'. Cf. *De cat. rud.* 6 and 33; *En. in Ps.* 36, 4; 61, 4.

rische Präexistenz des historischen Christentums, des christlichen Glaubens, eine Anticipation desselben'[451].

Is there no progress then in history, and can Augustine be reproached for not having acknowledged the crucial significance of Christianity—or rather, of the coming of Christ? Scholz thought he could and spoke of a serious error: 'es ist ... ein Fehler, dass Augustin es gänzlich unterlassen hat, das Christentum als den Wendepunkt der Weltgeschichte zu würdigen'[452].

Yet Scholz exaggerated here, in my opinion. And he certainly did in his statement that 'eine einzige Ausnahme genügt, um die Notwendigkeit der Sendung Jesu in Frage zu stellen und die geschichtsbildende Kraft des Christentums in ihren Grundlagen zu erschüttern'[453]. Indeed, Augustine perceives that, prior to the incarnation, non-Jewish people shared in the salvation through Christ. However, this came about through special revelation and applied only to individuals[454]. But since the incarnation there has been a universal call to salvation, going out to all nations. This time it is clearly the *Christian* religion[455]. It was present all the time, but from now on it is evident and has as its apogee the human manifestation of Christ.

Thus there is a progression in the stages of the history of salvation and there is *one* decisive event: the incarnation of Christ. Yet this event is not the termination of history. And Christ is not its final goal, nor is the Church. The purpose of history is to complete the number of those who are predestined[456]. Then the city of God will have returned to what it was in the beginning[457]. Heaven is its origin, heaven its final destination.

On the preceding pages the main points of Augustine's view of the origin and history of the two cities have been given. Other important

---

451 Reuter, *Studien*, 93.

452 Scholz, *Glaube und Unglaube*, 174; cf. Scholz, 153, and Reuter, *Studien*, 95.

453 Scholz, *Glaube und Unglaube*, 154.

454 E.g. *DCD* XVIII, 47: '... fuisse et in aliis gentibus homines, quibus hoc mysterium revelatum est ...', etc. Mention is made of Job.

455 *Retract.* I, 13: 'Nam res ipsa, quae nunc christiana religio nuncupatur, erat apud antiquos, nec defuit ab initio generis humani, quousque ipse Christus veniret in carne, unde vera religio quae iam erat, coepit appellari christiana'.

456 *DCD* XIV, 10: '... donec ... praedestinatorum sanctorum numerus compleretur ...'; XIV, 23: '... quod sanctorum numerus quantus conplendae illi sufficit beatissimae civitati ...'; cf. *En. in Ps.* 34, 2: '... sed ut numerus omnium nostrum usque in finem possit impleri'.

457 And possibly even larger in respect to the number of its citizens; see *Ench.* 29 and *DCD* XXII, 1.

details will be examined later. We have already spoken about the division into three stages (*exortus, excursus, debiti fines*). Is this division not related to the division that was common among the Manichaeans? It is apparent that the division of history into six or seven periods is an important element in Augustine's works. It is, for example, present in his sermons, where it is considered to be a well-known element[458]. This periodization is the framework within which the history of salvation is recounted in *The Catechizing of the Uninstructed*[459]. In the same way it is present in the *City of God*.

2. *The concept 'civitas'*

Up till now the word *civitas* has sometimes been left untranslated. There is a reason for this. The Latin word *civitas*, certainly as it was used by Augustine, has several meanings which are difficult to render into our vernacular. It is apparent that in translation this word acquires additional meanings that were not present in the original and that some connotations of the original word are in danger of being lost. One should be alert to this danger.

What are the meanings of the word *civitas*? Latin dictionaries usually distinguish four:
a. the community of citizens (*cives*), citizenry (without emphasis on the political organization);
b. the city or the area where a group of citizens lives;
c. the state (with emphasis on the political organization);
d. the status of citizen (*civis*), citizenship, civil rights[460].

These were also the possible meanings in Augustine's time. But

---

458 Cf. p. 94 n. 415 and n. 419. The seventh epoch is the final one, starting with the (second) resurrection, which is followed by the judgement, and, continuing onto the eighth day, the sabbath without end. See e.g. *DCD* XXII, 30: 'Haec tamen septima erit sabbatum nostrum, cuius finis non erit vespera, sed dominicus dies velut octavus aeternus ...'. For statements on the seventh and eighth epochs (the *hebdomas* and the *ogdoas*) by A. and other early-Christian writers, see, besides Daniélou, 'Typologie', esp. F.J. Dölger, 'Zur Symbolik des altchristlichen Taufhauses. Das Oktogon und die Symbolik der Achtzahl', in: F.J. Dölger, *Antike und Christentum*, 4, Münster 1934 (repr. 1975), 153-187 and J.H. Waszink, *Q.S.F. Tertulliani De anima, edited with introduction and commentary*, Amsterdam 1947, 429-430. Here and elsewhere (such as in the article by K. Schneider, 'Achteck', *RAC* 1 (1950) 72-74) the significance of the number eight in early-Christian art and liturgy is also evident.

459 *De cat. rud.* 39.

460 E.g. *TLL*, III, 1229-1240 and Blaise, *Dictionnaire*, 156, s.v. *civitas*.

what did he himself mean by *civitas*? In *De civitate Dei* XV, 8 it is said that a *civitas* is 'nothing else but a number of people held together by some communal bond'[461]. In this case *civitas* can denote the same as *societas*. Indeed, there are various passages in the *City of God* in which Augustine uses *civitas* and *societas* synonymously[462].

From this point to our concept 'city' (*urbs*) is but a small step. It is precisely this meaning that Augustine uses frequently, for Jerusalem, the *civitas Dei*, is a city and its exact opposite Babylon is, too. When writing the first words of his work: 'Gloriosissimam civitatem Dei ...', Augustine undoubtedly has Psalm 86 (Heb. 87) in mind[463]. And in the opening passage of Book XI, where a new start is made, he sets down the literal text of this psalm: 'Gloriosa dicta sunt de te, civitas Dei'. That *civitas* can be the same as *urbs*, Augustine indicates in XIX, 17: 'After the *civitas* or *urbs* comes the world ...'[464]. This can also be seen clearly in XV, 1: Cain founded a *civitas*, that is: he built a city. A little further on Augustine says—not by chance—the same of the other well-known fratricide: Romulus founded the *civitas* of Rome[465].

Civitas can also mean state. For Augustine this is first of all the city-state, the Greek *polis*. Cain and Romulus each founded a city and this means also: a small state. Strictly speaking the word *polis*, like *civitas*, is untranslatable. It is often rendered as city-state, but a *polis* encompasses much more than we can indicate with this word combination, namely the entire communal life of a group of people, including their politics, culture, ethics and economics[466]. And a *po-*

---

461 *DCD* XV, 8: '... civitas, quae nihil est aliud quam hominum multitudo aliquo societatis vinculo conligata ...'.

462 *DCD* II, 29; X, 6; XI, 34; XII, 1. 28; XIV, 1. 9. 13, etc. See R.T. Marshall, *Studies in the political and socio-religious terminology of the De Civitate Dei*, Washington 1952, 15; cf. G. del Estal - J.J.R. Rosado, 'Equivalencia de civitas en el De civitate Dei', *Ciudad*, II, 391. In *De cat. rud.* 31, *civitas* is also synonymous with *societas*.

463 Cf. p. 64 n. 281.

464 *DCD* XIX, 7: '... post civitatem vel urbem sequitur orbis terrae ...'.

465 *DCD* XV, 5: 'Primus itaque fuit terrenae civitatis conditor fratricida [sc. Cain] ... Sic enim condita est Roma, quando occisum Remum a fratre Romulo ...'.

466 H.D.F. Kitto, *The Greeks*, Penguin Books 1951, 75. Of the extensive literature on *polis* c.a., reference may be made in this context to Schmidt, *Polis*, 1-11, and H. Strathmann, 'Polis', *TWNT*, VI, 516 ff. No new perspectives are offered by A. Mandouze, 'Saint Augustin et la cité grecque', *REL* 47 (1969) 396-417: he examines the place A. gives to ancient Greece as he sets forth the history of the *terrena civitas*, esp. in *DCD* XVIII, 2-26. Bardy, 'Formation', confines himself to a few general observations.

lis certainly need not be a city with one centre, with walls and so forth: Sparta consisted of four or five settlements, but was a *polis* nonetheless; even regions could be denoted by this name[467].

It is especially significant in this context that every *polis* had its own particular cult: religion and *polis*, *polis* and religion were inextricably bound up with each other. The *civitas* was even the central object of the Roman religion. Therefore the word *pietas* indicates not only piety towards the gods, but also what we now understand by patriotism. To see the extent to which *civitas* could be an explicitly religious concept for the Romans, one has only to look at various epithets found in non-Christian classical writings[468].

If a definitive choice must be made for a 'translation' of the comprehensive concept *civitas*, the best approximation would be *polis*[469], certainly if we remember that in Augustine's description of *civitas Dei* and *terrena civitas* the unity of culture, custom and especially religion has a prominent role. A *civitas* is not just a group of people living together, but a *community* with its own religion, legal standards, culture and moral values. Therefore, when Augustine uses the word *civitas*, we should above all think of the ancient concept *polis*, the city-state. Here the elements of community, politics and religion are inseparable.

But is 'state' also a possible translation? Particularly in earlier studies in German and Dutch, *De civitate Dei* is often rendered as *(On) the State of God*[470]. Yet this can lead to a serious distortion of what Augustine actually means. His writing does not aim to offer a detailed political theory. Only rarely does he use the word *civitas* to indicate the state as we know it today. He prefers to use words like *res publica, imperium* and *regnum*[471]. Scholz was correct in observing:

---

467 Cf. Strathmann, 'Polis', 517.

468 *TLL*, III, 1231-1232: *civitas aeterna, beata, immortalis, sancta* et al. (all in Cicero); *civitas religiosa* (Livius); *civitas sanctissima atque optima, civitas sanctissima et invictissima* (Cicero); *destinata hominum ac deorum domicilio civitas* (Florus); etc.

469 Cf. Ratzinger, 'Herkunft', esp. 972 n.1. Duchrow, *Christenheit*, 244, feels obliged to object to this back-translation, for it 'entzieht sich (...) der notwendigen Übersetzungsarbeit, ohne die ein wirkliches Verstehen nicht möglich ist'. But is such an allegation tenable? For *civitas-polis* see also Del Estal, 'Equivalencia', 377 ff., esp. 383: 'El arquetipo romano de civitas responde principal y directamente al patrón de la polis helénica ...'.

470 Such as in the translations by Schröder, C.J. Perl (1951-'53), Thimme, Wytzes (partial translation) and in the excerpts in Sizoo, *Augustinus over den Staat*.

471 *DCD* I, 15. 30. 33. 36 etc., and esp. XIX, 21. 24: *res publica*; I, 21. 23. 24 etc.: *imperium*; I, 36; II, 16. 18 and esp. IV, 2-9 and XVIII, 2 ff.: *regnum* of the Ro-

'Es ist für das Verständnis der Augustinischen Gedanken verhängnisvoll geworden, dass man civitas zu sorglos mit «Staat» übersetzt hat'[472].

Yet Scholz himself referred repeatedly to 'Weltstaat' and 'Gottesstaat', though he did not give an explicit reason for doing so. Was the translation 'city' too limited for him after all? Kamlah came to the conclusion that *civitas* can best be translated by 'Bürgerschaft', but he acknowledged that in this way the idea of 'city' was not given its due[473]. Duchrow argued in favour of 'Herrschaftsverband', but he, also, admitted that in doing so the meaning 'city' is not being taken into account[474]. Sizoo gave as meanings 'city', 'state' and 'empire'[475], but translated *De civitate Dei* nearly always as *The State of God*. Finally, L.J. van der Lof devoted a separate article to the translation of *civitas Dei*, discussed a few opinions at length and chose the word *city*[476].

As already put into practice on the preceding pages, the use of the word *city* is, in my opinion, the best way to denote the meaning of *civitas*. Thus we are in agreement with the way it is generally done in English and French publications. But we should always bear in mind the manifold senses associated with the Greek concept *polis* and the Latin *civitas*. A strong argument for the choice of 'city' is the fact that, when writing about the origin and nature of the *civitas Dei*, Augustine makes special reference to biblical passages pertaining to Jerusalem[477]. The same applies for the designation of the *terrena*

---

mans, of the Assyrians, of Alexander. See the tables by Rosado, 'Equivalencia', 420-451.—There are a few exceptions to this rule: 'res publica cuius conditor rectorque Christus est' (II, 21); 'res publica caelestis' (II, 19); cf. n. 480.

472 Scholz, *Glaube und Unglaube*, 84. See also 86: 'Es folgt, dass «Staat» eine sehr ungenügende, ja irreführende Übersetzung von civitas Dei ist, da auch in den Fällen, wo beide sich inhaltlich annähernd decken, die Klangfarbe eine verschiedene ist'.

473 Kamlah, *Christentum*, 155-158.

474 Duchrow, *Christenheit*, 243-246.

475 Sizoo, *Augustinus*, 313. Cf. Sizoo, *Augustinus over den Staat*, 10: 'God's kingdom or God's State' and Wytzes, *Staat Gods*, 24 n. 1: 'The word «civitas» as it is used by Augustine can mean city, state and kingdom. (...) We have chosen one of these three translations in accordance with the context in which the word occurs'. This context usually requires—as it did obviously for Schröder whom Wytzes was following—a translation by state, except in quotations from the Bible or when *civitas* refers directly to a city such as Babylon, Jerusalem or Rome.

476 L.J. van der Lof, 'Die Übersetzung von «civitas Dei» ins Deutsche und ins Niederländische', *Aug(L)* 13 (1963) 373-386.

477 Esp. from the Psalms. E.g. *DCD* II, 21: '... in ea ... civitate ... de qua scrip-

civitas as a city: Babylon[478]. It is only in the word 'city' that this symbolic language of Scripture, as Augustine unmistakably knew it, is preserved.

However, a slight difficulty arises when *civitas* is translated as 'city'. Del Estal considered this such a serious problem that he saw 'reino de Dios' as the 'término ideal'[479]; for a kingdom has a prince, a city has not; one society is ruled by Christ, the other by Satan.

But this problem does not seem insurmountable. Del Estal correctly pointed out that Augustine's *civitas* is inextricably bound up with a *princeps*. But it is also clear—especially from Rosado's tables—that Augustine himself did not opt for the word *regnum*, much less for *res publica* or *societas*[480]. He was familiar with the two communities and their two rulers, but he definitely preferred to call them *civitates*. This terminology is already clearly and firmly present in *The Catechizing of the Uninstructed* and in, for example, the earliest sermons on the Psalms. Augustine also uses *civitas* as a technical term in the passage in his *Retractations* that deals with the *City of God*[481]. In doing so he frequently refers to biblical texts concerning Jerusalem or Babylon. This reference and this imagery ought to be respected, in the knowledge that each of these cities is ruled by a prince[482].

---

tura sancta dicit: *Gloriosa dicta sunt de te, civitas Dei'*, and particularly XI, 1 where *Ps.* 87 (86), 48 (47) and 46 (45) are cited. Then there is a reference to other testimonies about the city of Jerusalem: 'His atque huius modi testimoniis, quae omnia commemorare nimis longum est, didicimus esse quandam civitatem Dei ...'.

478 In *DCD* XVI, 4. 10. 11 et al.; elsewhere for example *En. in Ps.* 86, 6 and *En. in Ps.* 136.

479 Del Estal, 'Equivalencia', 451-453.

480 Rosado, 'Equivalencia', 420, reports that in *DCD civitas* occurs 588 times, *regnum* 358, *res publica* 141, *societas* 112. Marshall, *Studies*, 4, gives as 'approximate frequency' 525, 250, 120 and 100 resp.—*Regnum* and *populus Dei* can occur as equivalents of *civitas Dei*, as can—see n. 462—*societas*. Yet A. prefers *civitas*, no doubt because he refers to Bible texts that deal with the *civitas* Jerusalem. Ladner's question (*Idea*, 267 ff. and elsewhere; cf. Marrou, *AM*, III, 199) as to why *DCD* was not entitled *De regno Dei* is thus answered.—*Civitas Dei* cannot be fully equated with *res publica* (notwithstanding II, 19 and 21; see n. 471). In II, 21 there is a more detailed description: '... vera autem iustitia non est nisi in ea re publica, cuius conditor rectorque Christus est, si et ipsam rem publicam placet dicere, quoniam eam rem populi esse negare non possumus. Si autem hoc nomen, quod alibi aliterque vulgatum est, ab usu nostrae locutionis est forte remotius, in ea certe civitate est vera iustitia, de qua scriptura sancta dicit: *Gloriosa dicta sunt de te, civitas Dei*'. In II, 19 only *res publica caelestis* is given as the antithesis of *res publica romana*.

481 *Retract.* II, 43.

482 E.g. *DCD* XVII, 16: 'Eius [sc. of Jerusalem] inimica est civitas diaboli

A few more remarks should be made on the meaning of the concept *civitas*. For Augustine, as for others[483], it is an equivalent of the Greek concept *polis*. In the *City of God* he gives twice what he understands to be the exact meaning of *civitas*. At the very beginning, in Book I, he states that a *civitas* is a single-minded multitude of people[484]. In Book XV he gives the previously mentioned definition: a *civitas* is a multitude of people joined together by some communal bond[485]. Such a definition can also be found elsewhere in his work[486]. One can agree with Del Estal that this testifies to the personalistic element in the ancient *polis*: people are fellow-citizens in a specific community; for Augustine it is either that of Christ or that of Satan[487].

Thus Augustine found his starting point in the manifold concept *civitas*. One final argument can be put forward for his choice of this word. The *City of God* is an apologetic work, and in his very choice of the term *civitas Dei* the author is defending himself against the pagan opposition. While his opponents argued that Christianity is not a community-building force, the name *civitas Dei* is the self-assured proclamation of the Christian idea of community: the *civitas* surpassing all *civitates* is of divine origin. While all *civitates (poleis!)* are linked to their particular cult of gods, the *civitas Dei* is united with the true God. Only the worship of *this* God can create the true *civitas*-community, the community of saints. Only here does true justice (*iustitia*) prevail and blessed life (*vita beata*) become manifest.

Once we realize the meaning of the *civitas* as a cult community,

Babylon ...; ex qua tamen Babylone regina ista [sc. the Church] in omnibus gentibus regeneratione liberatur et a pessimo rege ad optimum regem, id est a diabolo transit ad Christum' and *En. in Ps.* 61, 6: '... illa [sc. Babylonia] rege diabolo, ista [sc. Jerusalem] rege Christo'.

483 Cicero also translated *polis* as *civitas*, as was usually done in the Vulgate. For the latter cf. Strathmann, 'Polis', 533. His objections ('eine erhebliche Sinnverschiebung, weil sie den Sinn von polis ins Politische verfärbt' etc.) are based on a one-sided interpretation of *civitas*. Nor is justice done here to A.'s concept *civitas* and with it to the meaning of *DCD*, in spite of the reference to Kamlah.

484 *DCD* I, 15: '... cum aliud civitas non sit quam concors hominum multitudo'.

485 See n. 461.

486 The former occurs literally in *Ep.* 155, 3 addressed to Macedonius (c. 414), the latter in *Ep.* 138, 10 to Marcellinus (c. 411). These concurrences in themselves demonstrate the consistency in A.'s terminology.

487 Del Estal, 'Equivalencia', 388.

yet another aspect of the *City of God* becomes clear. Why does the author allow himself to digress at such length on the Roman deities? This is not due to a lack of structure, as has been contended[488]. Augustine wants to show that the existence of the earthly city is extensively interwoven with a particular cult of idols. Opposite this he places the city of God as the true cult community. For this the only valid sacrifice has been made, by Jesus Christ. Here the true God is worshipped.

3. *A development towards the concept 'civitas'?*

The word *civitas* indicates a complex mixture of ideas. What Augustine meant by the absolutely antithetical concepts *civitas Dei* and *terrena civitas* will be considered in the following sections. But first of all it should be asked whether there was anything in Augustine's earliest writings that pointed towards a concept of *civitas* or a closely related idea. In what way did this concept develop, if indeed it did, into the later view that is worked out in great detail, particularly in the *City of God*? We know from his *Retractations* that Augustine wanted the reader to study his works in their chronological order and in this way perhaps see that the author had been making progress in the course of his writing[489]. This method may also help us to arrive at a correct interpretation of the origin of the doctrine of the two cities and of this doctrine itself.

For their inquiry into 'pre-forms' within Augustine's writings, many scholars have taken *On the True Religion* as their starting point[490]. For in this work, written from 389 to 391, he mentions two kinds of people (*duo genera hominum*) which are opposites: the old, outer, earthly man contrasted to the inner, new, heavenly man[491].

---

[488] As by Scholz, *Glaube und Unglaube*, 12 ff.; cf. p. 74 ff.

[489] *Retract.*, *prol.*: 'Inveniet enim fortasse, quomodo scribendo profecerim, quisquis opuscula mea ordine, quo scripta sunt, legerit'.

[490] Such as Scholz, *Glaube und Unglaube*, 76 n. 1; Bardy, 'Formation', 13-14; Lauras and Rondet, 'Thème', 101-102; A. Lauras, 'Deux cités, Jérusalem et Babylone. Formation et évolution d'un thème central du «De Civitate Dei»', *Ciudad*, I, 118; Maier, *Augustin*, 147-148; Ladner, *Idea*, 263 f.; É. Boularand, 'Le Thème des deux Cités chez saint Augustin', *EPh* 17 (1962) 218.

[491] *De vera rel.* 50: 'Sicut autem isti ambo nullo dubitante ita sunt, ut unum eorum, id est veterem atque terrenum, possit in hac tota vita unus homo agere, novum vero et coelestem nemo in hac vita possit nisi cum vetere (...), sic proportione universum genus humanum cuius tanquam unius hominis vita est ab Adam usque ad finem huius saeculi, ita sub divinae providentiae legibus administratur, ut in duo genera distributum appareat'. Etc.

For the source of this view scholars have usually pointed to the influence of the apostle Paul (the old man contrasted to the new man) and to Tyconius (the apocalyptic antithesis between the man who will die and the one who will have eternal life in the kingdom of God).

Ulrich Duchrow, however, chose to go further back[492]. Scholars who start from *On the True Religion* do indeed have to see Paul and Tyconius as the major sources of inspiration for Augustine's doctrine of the two *civitates*. But do Augustine's earliest works—in which, after all, there is no evidence of fundamental influence by Paul or apparent acquaintance with Tyconius—show a distinction between old and new, outer and inner, earthly and heavenly man? And is there no earlier reference to a kingdom of God? The answer to each of these questions must be an affirmative one. Consequently—still according to Duchrow—one should not only be on the lookout for the passages in Augustine's works in which the notion of a *civitas* is more or less clearly present, but also give attention to the ideas associated with it as they occur in his earliest writings[493].

Duchrow's method seems quite correct. In the course of his inquiry he developed it in an impressive way[494]. I shall now outline his analysis, although in the end one must ask whether in his exposition he showed convincingly the origin of Augustine's doctrine of the two *civitates*.

First of all attention must be paid to the concept kingdom of God/kingdom of Christ. From writings composed at Cassiciacum (*On Order* and *Soliloquies*) it emerges that Augustine identified the kingdom of God with the Neoplatonic *mundus intelligibilis*, the transcendental, spiritual world that is only accessible to the intellect. In the *Soliloquies* we read, for example: 'God, whose kingdom is that whole world which the senses do not know'[495]. The *mundus intelligibilis* of the philosophers is here and elsewhere equated by the young convert with the kingdom of God or the kingdom of Christ (Christ is, as the Logos, the sum total of ideas).

How does man receive part in that kingdom? Augustine's answer

---

[492] Duchrow, *Christenheit*, 186-243: 'Herkunft und Anfänge der civitas-Lehre Augustins'.

[493] Duchrow, *Christenheit*, 185.

[494] Cf. also J. Ratzinger in *JbAC* 15 (1972) 185-189; G. Madec in *REA* 15 (1969) 346-348.

[495] *Sol.* I, 1, 3.

is: through *illuminatio* as a gift from God. He considers it possible even now to share fully in that spiritual world[496]. In his *Retractations*, however, he takes this back: the spiritual world is the one to come, with a new heaven and a new earth[497].

Now the important question is when this eschatological view of the kingdom of God, that is so clear later on, first appeared. It was in *On the True Religion*, which Augustine finished in Africa about four years after his earliest writings. But before having a closer look at this work, which many scholars consider so important for the doctrine of the two cities, let us trace the development of its other central component: the antithesis between the two kinds of people.

Basically this antithesis between the outer, old, earthly man and the inner, new, heavenly man appears to have developed in the same way. In the dialogues written at Cassiciacum (386-387) Augustine posed the question about the blessed life. We have already established that he then considered absolute *beatitudo* possible in this life. It is attainable for the wise, the inner man; not for the outer, earthly, foolish man. Here Augustine used the Stoic-Neoplatonic distinction between the wise and the foolish man, the inner and the outer man. Not long after that, in *The Catholic and the Manichaean Ways of Life*, begun in Rome (388) and completed at Thagaste (389-390), this antithesis gained in depth by the addition of Paul's distinction between the old and the new man. Here the author describes, for example, the *temperantia*, one of the four classical cardinal virtues, as a casting off of the old man and a renewal in God[498]. This work is the earliest one containing the distinction—so characteristic of Augustine—between using (*uti*) and enjoying (*frui*): the temporal is to be used, the eternal to be enjoyed[499]. He who uses the temporal practises *temperantia*. At the same time it is clear that old is equated with physical-sensual and new with spiritual-invisible[500].

Concerning the writings of this period it should also be noted that in *On Genesis against the Manichaeans* (388-390), the well-known texts *Gen.* 1:26 and 28 are interpreted as the dominion of the inner man over bestial affects[501]. In *The Free Choice of the Will* Augustine distin-

---

496 E.g. *De ord.* I, 11, 32; *Sol.* I, 1, 6.

497 *Retract.* I, 4, 2; cf. I, 3, 2.

498 *De mor.* I, 36.

499 Cf. *De mor.* I, 37 and 39.

500 According to Duchrow, *Christenheit*, 204, a 'Rehellenization' of the Pauline views. He points to the influence of Ambrose and via him to Philo.

501 *De Gen. c. Man.* I, 31.

guishes between two kinds of things (temporal and eternal), two kinds of people (those who of their own free will love either what is temporal or what is eternal) and two kinds of laws: temporal law (*lex temporalis*) and eternal law (*lex aeterna*)[502].

Having considered the preceding works we can now look at *On the True Religion*, written c. 390. Sections 48-50 are especially important in this context. What is new is an emphasis on the eschatological element: before the eschaton there can be no blessed life (*vita beata*). Augustine discusses the two kinds of people and their history. The pious will rise from the dead and live; then the remains of the old man will be changed into the new one. The godless people will also rise, but they will be precipitated into the second death.

Where did this last idea come from? Duchrow believed that after Augustine had studied Paul, he must also have made a thorough study of the *Apocalypse of John*[503]. For it is there that the second death is mentioned[504]. And it is precisely from the fragments of Tyconius' commentary on this book of the Bible that we have knowledge not only of this concept, but also of the two groups progressing towards the eschaton, described as two *civitates*. Here we find most probably the earliest traces of Tyconius' influence on Augustine! This supposition is confirmed, still according to Duchrow, by the discovery in these sections of *On the True Religion* of some other ideas that are characteristic of Tyconius and are associated with the concept of the *civitates*: the division into world periods, the notions tare and chaff (see *Matt.* 13:24-30 and 3:12) applied in an ecclesiology; the wicked, earthly people (*mali, terreni homines*) as a multitude of godless people (*turba impiorum*). Besides, Tyconius was also familiar with the antitheses—as present in *On the True Religion* — between the active and the contemplative life and between the old and the new man.

In this way we have, in Duchrow's opinion, the most important elements of Augustine's doctrine of the two *civitates*. In addition to the Stoic-Neoplatonic distinction between those who are wise and those who are foolish, inner and outer people, to the Pauline antithesis of the old and the new man that is considered especially in this light, to the distinctions between *mundus intelligibilis* and *mundus sen-*

502 *De lib. arb.* I, finished when he was still in Rome (388), II and III in Africa (391-395); cf. F.J. Thonnard in *BA* 6, 126; cf. also *Retract.* I, 9, 1.

503 Duchrow, *Christenheit*, 221-222.

504 *Apoc.* 2: 11; 20: 6; 20: 14; 21: 8.

sibilis and between contemplative life and active life, which came to Augustine mainly through Ambrose and his circle, in *On the True Religion* for the first time the apocalyptic idea is found of *two groups of people* progressing towards the Day of Judgement. It is especially in this last element that the influence of Tyconius' commentary on the *Apocalypse* is evident.

As to the subsequent development it is particularly characteristic that the eschatological dimension changed the earlier elements more and more. The completion of the new man is considered to be an eschatological event. We know that after entering ecclesiastical office, Augustine devoted himself increasingly to the study of the Scriptures. This fact is of great consequence for his concept of the *civitates*. To the existing dualistic basic design, influenced by philosophy and apocalypticism, ever more scriptural themes were added, especially from the Psalms. Increasingly Scripture and Church doctrine influenced Augustine's thinking. In later writings, for example, he no longer equates the old man and the outer one, but he is of the opinion that the outer man was created perfect in God's image and will one day be resurrected.

This is, in outline, Duchrow's view of the process of development. Although his depiction is impressive, some questions concerning his view must still be asked. For does it convincingly show the origins of Augustine's doctrine of the two cities?

Duchrow correctly pointed out that a certain development in Augustine's thinking can be discerned. This might indicate that in his doctrine of the two cities earlier philosophical traditions, among other factors, exerted their influence. These traditions were still making themselves felt in the later expositions in the *City of God*. Indeed, it is possible to speak of 'Anfänge'. But did Duchrow also explain the 'Herkunft'?

First of all it should be noted that the clearly defined term *civitas* as it manifests itself again and again in later writings does not occur in the earliest ones. It appears as a technical term that was obviously known and accepted by others in *The Catechizing of the Uninstructed* (c. 400?) and before that in some sermons[505]. Does this not point in a

---

505 For the dating of *De cat. rud.*, see p. 177 n. 72. Of the sermons *En. in Ps.* 148, 4 and *En. in Ps.* 145, 20 can be named, both dating from 395 (Eastertime), according to Zarb.

certain direction? In Africa the meaning of this terminology of the two cities was understood immediately. For the deacon Deogratias no further explanation appears to have been necessary, nor was it necessary for the common churchgoers when Augustine used the terms *civitas Dei* and *terrena civitas* in sermons at Hippo Regius or Carthage.

On the basis of his expositions Duchrow might have responded that it was through Tyconius that Augustine and others in Africa became acquainted with these ideas. It is precisely the influence of Tyconius' commentary on the *Apocalypse* that he refers to repeatedly[506]. But is this justifiable? It is true that the fragments cited by Hahn mention the two *civitates*. On the other hand, it is not certain that they originated entirely from Tyconius. The text of his commentary can only be reconstructed from later authors who were also familiar with Augustine and his *City of God*[507]. It is very possible that they had adopted the terminology of the two cities from Augustine (or from others!).

Even if it were certain that Tyconius used the concept of the two *civitates*, should it not be asked where he acquired it? Or should it be assumed that this concept originated with the 'Reform-donatist'[508], and that its influence grew so quickly in a short time that it became generally accepted in Africa[509]? This has to be regarded as improbable, certainly if it can be proved that in earlier writings, and also elsewhere, the doctrine of the two cities occurred. Moreover, nowhere is it stated by Augustine or others that they have borrowed the concept of the two cities from Tyconius[510]. Is it not necessary, in an inquiry into its origin, to search further back in the tradition preceding both Augustine and Tyconius?

There are some more aspects of Duchrow's view that need to be questioned. For example, the division into world periods was not just typical of Tyconius and his (?) doctrine of the two cities, but occurred frequently[511]. The same is true of the reference to *Matt.*

---

506 Cf. Duchrow, *Christenheit*, esp. 222 f., 232 f., 242.
507 See p. 271 f.
508 Hahn, *Tyconius-Studien*, 110 n. 1.
509 As Scholz states, *Glaube und Unglaube*, 80.
510 One might expect this in the case of such a personal idea. A. does do this for the notion of a *corpus permixtum*; cf. *De doctr. chr.* III, 32, 45, with the reference to Tyconius' *Liber regularum*.
511 Cf. p. 95 ff.

13:24-30[512]. The concept 'second death', too, need not be explained on the basis of the *Apocalypse of John* and Tyconius' commentary on it. It was already present in writings of Hippolytus, Tertullian, Commodian and extensively in Lactantius[513]. It is notable not only that this concept occurred frequently in the works of authors from Africa[514], but also that the Manichaeans were acquainted with it[515]. It may be that Augustine did not become acquainted with the term through Tyconius, but earlier, through the Manichaeans.

Finally a last critical comment must be given on Duchrow's exposition. He paid insufficient attention to possible Manichaean influence[516]. But need there be, for this possible Manichaean influence, a 'Naturen-Dualismus, also das manichäische Spezifikum' in the *origin* of Augustine's doctrine of the two *civitates*[517]?

We can agree with Duchrow that 'der civitas-Begriff überhaupt nicht der Ausgangspunkt der Entwicklung ist'[518]. Indeed, no *civitas*-concept was present in Augustine's earliest works and consequently it was not his starting point. Should it, however, be assumed that there was a *development* towards the concept *civitas* as Duchrow claimed? He was right in pointing out philosophical-theological elements adopted by Augustine. Later these would continue to play a part. But is it not more plausible that a doctrine of the two cities, already present in the preceding Christian tradition, was taken over

---

512 As early as Callistus (according to Hippolytus, *Ref.* IX, 12, 20 ff.), Cyprian, Optatus; cf. Kamlah, *Christentum*, 118; H.B. Weijland, *Augustinus en de kerkelijke tucht*, Kampen 1965, 60 f.

513 See J.C. Plumpe, 'Mors secunda', *Mélanges de Ghellinck*, I, Gembloux 1951, 387-403.

514 Esp. Lactantius, *Div. inst.* II, 12, 8 f. and VII, 10, 9-11. Cf. also H.W.A. van Rooijen-Dijkman, *De vita beata. Het zevende boek van de 'Divinae Institutiones' van Lactantius* ..., Assen 1967, 67 and 80-81.

515 See *Kephalaia* (ed. H.J. Polotsky – A. Böhlig, mit einem Beitrag von H. Ibscher), Band I, Stuttgart 1940, 103, 32; 104, 1-20; 106, 9 f.; 150, 26 f. The notion is also current among the Mandaeans; see M. Lidzbarski, *Ginzā*. Der Schatz oder das Grosse Buch der Mandäer, Göttingen-Leipzig 1925, 185, 23; 186, 3 f. and 23; 189, 2; 226, 1; 227, 5; etc.

516 Duchrow, *Christenheit*, 229: 'Nur eine [sc. Hypothese] unter ihnen kann man m. E. mit ziemlicher Gewissheit von vornherein ausschliessen, nämlich diejenige, die einen konstitutiven Einfluss des Manichäismus annimmt'. That is why Duchrow does not discuss the Manichaean texts elsewhere either; cf. e.g. U. Duchrow – H. Hoffmann (Hrsg.), *Die Vorstellung von Zwei Reichen und Regimenten bis Luther* (*TKTG* 17), Gütersloh 1972.

517 Duchrow, *Christenheit*, 229.

518 Duchrow, *Christenheit*, 229 n. 215.

by Augustine, expanded with his own thoughts and in this way developed further?

The opus magnum the *City of God* offers a comprehensive vision. Through this work the doctrine of the two cities acquired worldwide importance. But it was in the more elaborated model catechesis of *The Catechizing of the Uninstructed* that the fully developed theme of the two cities appeared for the first time. In this catechetical work we read:

Duae itaque civitates, una iniquorum, altera sanctorum, ab initio generis humani usque in finem saeculi perducuntur, nunc permixtae corporibus, sed voluntatibus separatae, in die vero iudicii etiam corpore separandae. (...) Sicut autem Ierusalem significat civitatem societatemque sanctorum, sic Babylonia significat civitatem societatemque iniquorum, quoniam dicitur interpretari confusio. De quibus duabus civitatibus, ab exordio generis humani usque in finem saeculi permixte temporum varietate currentibus, et ultimo iudicio separandis, paulo ante iam diximus[519].

So there are two cities: one of the wicked, the other of the saints. Their existence stretches from the beginning of mankind to the end of the world. Now they are joined in body, but separated by will. On the Day of Judgement, however, they will be separated in body, too. (...) Just as Jerusalem signifies the city and fellowship of the saints, so Babylon signifies the city and fellowship of the wicked. For its name is said to mean 'confusion'. About these two cities, which, intermingled, are advancing throughout the changing times from the beginning of mankind to the end of the world, and which will be separated on the Day of Judgement, we spoke a little earlier[519].

4. *The city of God opposed to the earthly city*

On the preceding pages we have seen more than once that Augustine placed the two cities opposite each other. For the difference between the two is great: the society of the believers is in opposition to that of the wicked; the two societies are allied with angels, the good ones or the evil ones[520]. And although the two cities are intermingled in this temporal existence, there is fundamentally an absolute antithesis, an unbridgeable gap.

The absolute difference in the natures of the two cities is apparent from the names Augustine uses. In the *City of God* and in his other works time and again he sees them opposite each other as:

---

519 *De cat. rud.* 31 and 37.

520 E.g. *DCD* XIV, 13: 'Profecto ista est magna differentia, qua civitas, unde loquimur, utraque discernitur, una scilicet societas piorum hominum, altera impiorum, singula quaeque cum angelis ad se pertinentibus, in quibus praecessit hac amor Dei, hac amor sui'.

city of God	- city of the devil
heavenly city	- earthly city
eternal city	- temporal city
city of the believers	- city of the wicked
immortal city	- mortal city
holy city	- wicked city[521] etc.

These names in themselves make it clear that the antithesis is absolute. This is also evident from an enumeration of some characteristics of the two cities:

supernatural birth	- natural birth
eternity	- temporality
everlastingness	- transitoriness
humility	- pride
obedience	- disobedience
love of God	- love of self
worship of the true God	- worship of idols
living according to the flesh	- living according to the Spirit, etc.

Again and again the antithesis is evident. There is nothing in between[522]. 'Whatever is not of faith is sin', Augustine often declares in his later writings[523]. Although this statement of Paul's is not quoted literally in the *City of God*, the work is, as it were, one long commentary on this text. There is only belief or unbelief; a middle course does not exist.

This last remark should not lead to any misunderstanding. In associating the antithesis between the two cities with the contradistinction between belief and unbelief, we do not go so far as to agree with the idealistic interpretation put forward by Heinrich Scholz in particular. To Scholz the two cities were allegories for belief and un-

---

521 *Civitas Dei-diaboli, civitas caelestis-terrena, civitas aeterna-temporalis, civitas piorum-impiorum, civitas immortalis-mortalis, civitas sancta-iniqua*, etc.

522 See further pp. 151-153: 'A third, neutral city?'

523 This text (*Rom.* 14:23b)) played an important role in the struggle against Pelagius and Julian; it was often combined with *Heb.* 11:6, *Rom.* 1:7, and the like. Cf. A.C. de Veer, 'Rom. 14, 23b dans l'oeuvre de saint Augustin (Omne quod non est ex fide, peccatum est)', *RA* 8 (1972) 149-185. Related to this was A.'s ultimate judgement of the virtues of the pagans as vices; this can be seen in *DCD* XIX, 25 (cf. p. 149 and n. 667). In this context it is interesting to note the official Roman Catholic condemnation of Michael Baius, who taught: 'Omnia opera infidelium sunt peccata et philosophorum virtutes sunt vitia'. See De Veer, 179 n. 88.

belief[524]. In his expositions on the two cities, however, Augustine was not concerned with mere allegories or ideas[525], nor with a myth[526], but with real entities. The city of God is the actually existing society of good angels and true believers; its antipole is the truly existing city of Satan, the fallen angels and the unbelievers[527].

But what does Augustine mean by the term *mystice*? It is not by chance that, for his allegorical interpretation, Scholz referred principally to the well-known statement in Book XV: '... these [two groups of people] we also call *mystice* two cities ...'[528]. He concluded from it: 'Hier ist deutlich ausgesprochen, dass unter dem Bilde der beiden Staaten die Mächte des Unglaubens und des Glaubens gedacht sind, die sich um den Besitz der Menschheit streiten und die Menschheit selbst in zwei feindliche Lager spalten'[529].

It must be conceded to Scholz that *mystice* can be taken to mean 'allegorically' in this context. But then it is an allegorical interpretation of an extraordinary kind! Reality does not evaporate here into an idea, a notion or merely a metaphysical concept. It is possible to point, as Joseph Ratzinger does, to the allegorical interpretation of Scripture. The term *mystice* means: 'Mit einem der Schrift entnommenen Wort von heilig-allegorischem Sinn'[530]. Augustine speaks of two cities because in his opinion the Scriptures themselves already do so. This is evident from a comparison of the quotation from Book XV with a parallel statement from XIV, 1: '... yet there are not more than two kinds of human society, which we may well denominate as two cities *in accordance with our Scriptures*'[531].

---

524 Scholz, *Glaube und Unglaube*, esp. 70.

525 Even Marrou says too little when he calls the two cities 'des notions d'ordre idéal ou mieux idéel' and 'idées' as in Platonic philosophy. See Marrou, 'Tertium?', 343; cf. Marrou in *AM*, III, 200-202. Also Pesce's interpretation (*Città*, 155-160) is too spiritual.

526 Cf. J.-M. Le Blond, *Les conversions de saint Augustin*, Paris 1950, 305.

527 Cf. Lamirande, *L'Église céleste*, 99.

528 *DCD* XV, 1: '... quas etiam mystice appellamus civitates duas ...'.

529 Scholz, *Glaube und Unglaube*, 70.

530 Ratzinger, 'Herkunft', 971 n. 3; cf. J. Ratzinger, *Volk und Haus Gottes in Augustins Lehre von der Kirche*, München 1954, 290-294. In *JbAC* 15 (1972) 188 Ratzinger answers Duchrow's criticism in *Christenheit*, 235-236.

531 *DCD* XIV, 1: '... quas civitates duas secundum scripturas nostras merito appellare possemus'. Two codices (Sangallensis 178 and Lugdunensis 606) give *possimus* instead of *possemus*; see also the editions by the Maurini and by Migne.

Augustine refers explicitly to Scripture[532]. He finds in it his justification for calling the two societies two cities. And above all he finds in Scripture that these antithetical cities can be designated by the 'mystical' names of Jerusalem and Babylon.

5. *Jerusalem and Babylon*

It is noteworthy that Augustine referred repeatedly to the two antithetical cities as Jerusalem and Babylon. Antoine Lauras made a special study of this phenomenon and concluded that it resulted from Augustine's personal interpretation[533].

My own investigation leads me to agree largely with this opinion. Very emphatically and in a distinctive way Augustine described the antithesis between the two cities as that between Jerusalem and Babylon. Yet there were probably elements in the preceding tradition which exerted considerable influence on his personal view.

Let us first look at a few texts in which Augustine mentions the theme of Jerusalem and Babylon. He did so as early as the year 395[534], in a sermon on Psalm 148 in which Jerusalem and Babylon, the life to come and the imprisonment in the present life, are placed opposite each other; a little further on Augustine admonishes his congregation not to take delight in the love of Babylon, nor to forget Jerusalem[535]. It is highly probable that the sermon on Psalm 145 (146) dates from the same time[536]; it also contains a passage in which the two cities are set opposite each other, this time under the names of Zion and Babylon[537].

In many other sermons and writings from the following years this theme is heard, and even with an increasing frequency: Jerusalem stands in opposition to Babylon. Of the many examples I shall mention only *The Catechizing of the Uninstructed* (c. 400)[538], the work

532 Cf. *DCD* V, 19: '... quae in sacris litteris nostris dicitur civitas Dei ...'; XVIII, 41 and, of course, the well-known opening passage of Book XI. For the texts involved here and the use of Scripture as evidence, see pp. 312-318.

533 Lauras, 'Deux cités', esp. 118 n. 4: 'Il semblerait donc qu'il s'agisse d'une interprétation personnelle de Saint Augustin'.

534 Cf. the 'Tabula chronologica' in *CCL* 38 (ed. E. Dekkers and J. Fraipont), XV, following S. Zarb's chronology. Lauras, 'Deux cités', 123 n. 24 dates it 395-400.

535 *En. in Ps.* 148, 4.

536 Cf. *CCL* 38, XV.

537 *En. in Ps.* 145, 20.

538 *De cat. rud.* 37.

against the Donatist Parmenianus (c. 400-405)[539] and various explanations of the Psalms[540]. In a wider context there are also references to Jerusalem and Babylon, for example in *Against Faustus*[541] and in the *Confessions*. In the latter work the author not only refers to the Eternal City Jerusalem as his native city and mother[542], but also mentions its antipole. He was wandering about the streets of Babylon with his friends and was wallowing in the mud of that city, while his mother after the flesh had already fled from the middle of Babylon[543]. In another passage of the *Confessions* he describes the *Babylonian* dignity of the idolaters[544].

In great detail, however, the theme is discussed in the *City of God*, especially in Books XVI-XVIII. Of course this is partly because Augustine describes in these books the period of the building of the tower of Babel and the confusion of tongues, then the Babylonian captivity, and finally the histories of the empires of Assyria (Babylonia prima) and Rome (Babylonia secunda). But this still does not explain why, in a characteristic manner, Jerusalem or Zion is set against Babylon (*confusio*, confusion)[545]. For example in XVII, 16:

... sicut in alio psalmo de illa (sc. regina) dicitur: *civitas regis magni*[546]. Ipsa est Sion spiritaliter; quod nomen latine interpretatum speculatio est; speculatur enim futuri saeculi magnum bonum, quoniam illuc dirigitur eius intentio. Ipsa est Hierusalem eodem modo spiritaliter, unde multa iam diximus. Eius inimica est civitas diaboli Babylon, quae confusio interpretatur; ex qua tamen Babylone regina ista in omnibus

... as that queen is named in another psalm: *the city of the great king*[546]. In a spiritual sense she is Zion. This name means 'prospect'. For she is looking forward to the great good of the life to come, because it is there that her concentrated attention is directed. In the same spiritual sense she is also Jerusalem, of which we have already said much. Her enemy is the city of the devil, Babylon, which means 'confu-

539 *C. ep. Parm.* II, 4, 9.

540 Such as *En. in Ps.* 26 *en.* II, 18; 61, 6; 64; 86; 136; 138, 18; 147; 148.

541 In *C. Faust.* XII, 36 the return from the Babylonian captivity is a symbol of the entrance of the Church of God into the heavenly Jerusalem.

542 *Conf.* IX, 13, 37; X, 35, 56; XII, 16, 23; XIII, 9, 10.

543 *Conf.* II, 3, 8. This flight from the middle of Babylon (cf. *Is.* 48:20 et al.) is interpreted in *DCD* XVIII, 18 as the flight from the city of this world, the society of fallen angels and ungodly people. It can be compared with *Ep.* 108, 32 of Jerome: Paula had fled from the middle of Babylon and had saved her soul; likewise Origen, *Hom. in Ier.* II, 2: 'Qui valde demersus in vitiis, hic medius Babylonis habitator est ...'.

544 *Conf.* VIII, 2, 4. One may well wonder whether *dignitas* is not used here in an ironic sense.

545 Such as in *DCD* XVI, 4. 10. 11. 17; XVIII, 41.

546 *Ps.* 47 (48): 3 (2).

gentibus regeneratione liberatur et a pessimo rege ad optimum regem, id est a diabolo transit ad Christum. Propter quod ei dicitur: *Obliviscere populum tuum et domum patris tui*[547].

sion'. From that Babylon, however, this queen among all nations is set free by rebirth and passes over from the worst king to the best king, that is, from the devil to Christ. Therefore it is said to her: *Forget your people and your father's house*[547].

Thus to a remarkable extent Augustine names Jerusalem/Zion and Babylon in his *Enarrationes in Psalmos* and in the *City of God* whenever the Bible text or biblical history gives him occasion to do so. It is obvious from the preceding that he does so on other occasions, too. Apparently the names of these two cities and the antithesis between them are a characteristic and essential element of his theology. But has he for his concept not adopted some elements from predecessors?

It is known that the explanation of the name Babylon as 'confusion' already occurs in Old Testament folk etymology (e.g. *Gen.* 11:9) and in later Jewish writings. The Christian Church took over this interpretation; it is to be found especially in Origen, Gregory of Nyssa, Gregory of Nazianze, Ambrose and Jerome[548]. According to Altaner, Origen was the first to give an allegorical interpretation of the biblical statements about Babylon. He regarded Babylon as the city of the devil and of all power directed against God; man has to fight against sin as the spirit of Babylon; perfection is reached in the city of God, Jerusalem (heaven, the Church)[549]. In this context Altaner states that Origen influenced Augustine directly. The latter used, though very freely, sermons of Origen which had been translated into Latin[550].

That this was a *free* use should be stressed. For often in Origen—as in the others named, including Ambrose[551] — there is a tendency to spiritualize. The antithesis Jerusalem - Babylon is particularly an antithesis within the soul of man[552]. This interpretation very proba-

---

547 *Ps.* 44 (45): 11 (10).

548 As appears from most of the texts listed by B. Altaner, 'Babylon', *RAC*, I, 1132-1133.

549 Altaner, 'Babylon', 1132.

550 Altaner, 'Babylon', 1132; cf. Altaner, *Schriften*, 244. At the same time, however, he states that it is difficult to prove that A. was citing Origen, for A. used 'literarische Anregungen' freely, independently, he recast them.

551 Cf. Ambrose, *De paen.* II, 11, 105-106; *De fide* III, 1, 4; *Expl. Ps.* 45, 16.

552 Cf. Origen, *Hom. in Ier.* III, 2: 'An figuraliter dicit omnem *animam* contrariam Hierusalem, visioni pacis, Babylonem esse?'; *Hom. in Ier.* II, 11: 'Si autem

bly influenced the young Augustine, for example when in one of his earliest *Enarrationes in Psalmos* he wrote of the *civitates* (= the souls!) in which the devil reigns[553]. Also in later writings we find interpretations that were present in Origen and in others who, in this respect, were very probably his direct followers. One example is Augustine's explanation of Psalm 136 (137):8-9: the children of the daughter of Babylon are the evil desires; the rock against which they will be dashed is Christ[554]. The same was said not only by Origen, but also by Ambrose and Jerome[555].

Thus it is clear that, in his references to the two antithetical cities as Jerusalem/Zion and Babylon, Augustine learned from predecessors. He also refers explicitly to predecessors when, in *The Catechizing of the Uninstructed*, he explains the name Babylon: 'Its name means, *as they say*, confusion'[556]. Also in the recurring depiction of Jerusalem as *visio pacis*, 'vision of peace', and Zion as *speculatio*, 'prospect' or *contemplatio*[557] he undoubtedly follows the examples of others[558].

At this point it should be noted that sometimes the etymology of Zion is given hesitantly[559]. It should also be borne in mind that in

---

in alicuius *corde* non cecidit civitas confusionis, huic necdum Christus advenit'; *Hom. in Ez.* XII, 2: 'Si vero principali cordis tranquillitas, serenitas, pax fructum fecerit, sciamus quia Hierusalem versetur in ea [sc. anima]; visio quippe pacis *intrinsecus* est'.

553 *En. in Ps.* 9, 8: 'Civitates autem in quibus diabolus regnat ...' (dated 392).

554 E.g. *En. in Ps.* 136, 21.

555 Cf. Origen, *C. Celsum* VII, 22; Ambrose, *De paen.* II, 11, 105-106; Jerome, *Ep.* 22, 6 and 130, 8.

556 *De cat. rud.* 37: '... qui dicitur interpretari confusione ...'. Elsewhere, such as in *DCD* XVI, 4. 11. 17; XVII, 16; XVIII, 41 and repeatedly in the sermons on the Psalms, we find: 'Babylon interpretatur confusio'. This can be compared with Origen, *C. Celsum* VII, 22; Ambrose, *Expl. Ps.* 1, 22; 35, 23.

557 E.g. *De cat. rud.* 36; *DCD* XVII, 16; XIX, 11; *En. in Ps.* 9, 12; 50, 22; 61, 7; 64, 3-4; etc.

558 Such as Origen, *Hom. in Ier.* III, 2; IX, 2; *Hom. in Ez.* XII, 2. Earlier Philo referred to Jerusalem as *horasis eirènès* in *De somn.* II, 250. For Zion see, among others, Jerome, *In Hier.* VI, 31, 3; Hilarius, *In Ps.* 68, 31 and esp. the treatise *De montibus Sina et Sion* (Ps. Cyprian, late 2nd cent.?). Probably Tyconius can also be mentioned in this framework. In any case Beatus of Liebana states: 'Pro peregrinatione autem praesentis saeculi ecclesia Sion dicitur, eo quod ab huius peregrinationis longitudine posita promissionem rerum caelestium speculetur. Et propterea Sion speculatio nomen accepit, quia corporaliter terrena deserens, spiritu et mente in contemplatione perseverans, semper ad superiora tendit. Hic vero Sion dicitur, et in futuro Ierusalem caelestis nuncupatur, quamvis et in hoc saeculo ecclesia Ierusalem dicatur. (...) Ierusalem vero Latine visio pacis interpretatur.' See *Beati in Apocalipsin libri duodecim*, ed. H.A. Sanders, Roma 1930, 512-513; cf. 559.

559 *En. in Ps.* 2, 5: 'Sion autem, si speculationem, ut quidem interpretantur, significat ...'.

most texts Jerusalem and Zion are equivalent concepts[560]. For some time Augustine stressed the difference between Zion as the Church in peregrination and Jerusalem as the eternal city of God[561]; later this distinction hardly ever occurs. In the *City of God* it plays no role. In this work the believers who are peregrinating on earth are designated as citizens of the heavenly city Jerusalem. Augustine even speaks of the city of God in its entirety as the *civitas Dei* on its pilgrimage[562]. The name Zion is absent in this context.

The foregoing arguments show unmistakably that Jerusalem (sometimes also Zion) and Babylon are the names with which Augustine designated the two cities. It is also clear that predecessors may have exerted an essential influence. Within this framework Tyconius can also be mentioned. In his hermeneutic work, which was highly esteemed by Augustine, he set Jerusalem and Babylon opposite each other[563]. However, the Manichaeans may also have spoken of the antithesis Jerusalem - Babylon[564].

Would it not appear that, with all this material that has been presented, the sources of Augustine's doctrine of the two cities have been found? In any case it has been established that preceding ecclesiastical writers may have provided important elements. The antithesis between Jerusalem and Babylon was definitely present in their works. Moreover, this antithesis was also evident in the *Apocalypse* and in the early Christian interpretation of this book of the Bible[565].

However, does this explain Augustine's own doctrine of the two cities? He sees the history of the world from beginning to end as the antithesis between two cities. He also presents world history in this

---

560 E.g. *En. in Ps.* 142, 3: 'Antiqua ergo ista civitas Dei ... quae etiam Ierusalem vocatur et Sion'; *En. in Ps.* 149, 5: '... sed Sion vera et Ierusalem vera (quia ipsa Sion, quae Jerusalem), aeterna est in caelis, quae est mater nostra'.

561 In considerable detail in *En. in Ps.* 9, 12.

562 *DCD* I, 35: '... Dei civitas ... quamdiu peregrinatur in mundo ...'; XIX, 17: '... caelestis civitas dum peregrinatur in terra ...', and the like. A. makes a clearer distinction in XIX, 17 when he states: 'Civitas autem caelestis vel potius pars eius, quae in hac mortalitate peregrinatur et vivit ex fide ...'.

563 *Liber regularum, reg.* IV (ed. F.C. Burkitt, *The Book of Rules of Tyconius*, Cambridge 1894, *TS* III, 1, p. 50): 'Babylon civitas adversa Hierusalem totus mundus est, qui in parte sua, quam in hac Hierusalem habet, convenitur'.

564 *Manichäische Homilien* (ed. H.J. Polotsky), Band I, Stuttgart 1934, 14.

565 It is noteworthy that in A.'s discussion of the two cities the passages on Jerusalem and Babylon in the *Apocalypse of John* do not play an important role, neither in *DCD* nor elsewhere. When there is an explicit reference to Scripture in this context, it is mainly to the *Psalms*. See further pp. 312-318.

manner in *The Catechizing of the Uninstructed*; he returns to it repeatedly in his other works and particularly in the *City of God* and the *Enarrationes in Psalmos*. Each of the two cities consists of angels and humans; in this earthly existence they are mingled, but on the Day of Judgement they will be separated. One city is ruled by Christ, the other by Satan.

Of importance is the occurrence of the 'mystical' names Jerusalem and Babylon and the antithesis between the two cities. But of particular importance is whether the just mentioned elements of Augustine's doctrine of the two *civitates* can be found in works of predecessors. And if this is the case, in what context do they occur? That will have to be examined in a wider framework.

6. The city of God and the Church

In the foregoing we have seen that Augustine's doctrine of the two cities has been interpreted in different ways. Now we will look at this more closely. In the Middle Ages a political ideal was discerned in the *City of God*, that of the Christian state closely allied to the Church. This might be termed the theocratic interpretation. From Charlemagne until well into the sixteenth century this remained the universally accepted interpretation.

Starting with Luther, however, recognition grew for a somewhat idealistic interpretation: the doctrine of the two 'regiments'[566]. But especially since c. 1900, when German liberal theology was at its zenith, an idealistic interpretation has been articulated. Besides the very authoritative Adolf von Harnack, special mention should be made of his pupil Heinrich Scholz, whose view still exerts considerable influence. The very title of his book, *Glaube und Unglaube in der Weltgeschichte*[567], shows that for Scholz the *civitas Dei* and the *terrena civitas* were spiritual entities, 'Glaubensgrössen'. Whereas for centuries the *City of God* was interpreted above all as a political work, particularly since Hermann Reuter (1887)[568], Scholz and Ernst Troeltsch (1915)[569] Augustine's *civitates* have been seen as spiritual entities. However, mainly Roman Catholics, such as Bruno Seidel

[566] See e.g. Schrey (Hrsg.), *Reich Gottes und Welt*.
[567] Leipzig 1911 (repr. 1967).
[568] Reuter, *Studien* (repr. 1967).
[569] Troeltsch, *Augustin* (repr. 1963).

(1909)[570], Otto Schilling (1910)[571], Joseph Mausbach (1909)[572], but also a scholar like Karl Holl (1922)[573], have stressed that for Augustine the *civitas Dei* was identical with the *ecclesia catholica*.

It is obvious that there is here an absolute divergence of opinion. Does this testify to a certain prejudice or could it be that Augustine's writings, particularly the *City of God*, are not consistent on this matter?

We will first examine this problem as it relates to the concept *civitas Dei*. In many passages in his writings, predominantly in the *City of God*, Augustine equates *civitas Dei* with *ecclesia*: the city of God is the Church. But what exactly did the word *ecclesia* mean for him? Especially by Hermann Reuter a fundamental discussion on this question was initiated, one that is still going on today. Reuter found, in a study in which he discussed the relationship between Augustine's doctrine of the Church and his doctrine of the 'prädestinatianische Gnade'[574], a twofold ecclesiology. In Augustine's writings he saw a sharp contrast between 'das Prädestinatianische und das vulgär Katholische'. There was the hierarchical Catholic Church, 'ein Unentbehrliches, das Urelement, in welchem er atmete'[575]. Furthermore Augustine, influenced by his doctrine of predestination, expressed his view of the Church as the community of saints (communio sanctorum)[576]. But 'Gerade weil das vulgär Katholische für Augustin das Übermächtige war, konnte das Prädestinatianische ihn nicht beirren'[577].

Reuter's view spread. Harnack, for example, was following it when he argued for the existence of a contradistinction between the hierarchical Church and the *communio sanctorum*. Harnack thought he could discern in Augustine's works even more concepts of the word Church within this distinction. Yet there is a certain unity, namely in the person of their 'Urheber', whose rich inner life was governed by different states of mind[578].

---

570 B. Seidel, *Die Lehre vom Staat beim hl. Augustinus*, Breslau 1909.

571 O. Schilling, *Die Staats- und Soziallehre des hl. Augustin*, Freiburg 1910.

572 J. Mausbach, *Die Ethik des heiligen Augustinus*, Freiburg 1909 (1929²).

573 Holl, 'Entwicklung', in: *Aufsätze*, III, esp. 100 n. 6.

574 Reuter, *Studien*, 47-100.

575 Reuter, *Studien*, 98-99.

576 See also Reuter, *Studien*, 250-251.

577 Reuter, *Studien*, 99.

578 Harnack, *Lehrbuch*, III, 165. Reuter, *Studien*, 98, already accentuated A.'s personality as the unifying element. It should be noted that those who have referred

Reinhold Seeberg also considered Augustine's doctrine of the Church complicated because it combines polemics aimed at the Donatists, popular views of the Church which were then current, the church father's doctrine of grace, and certain Donatist 'Anregungen'[579]. Therefore Seeberg, too, arrived at a twofold concept of the Church[580]. A similar opinion was held by Loofs: Augustine gave two views of the Church that are intertwined, a 'vulgar'-Catholic and an ethical-religious one, the Church as the hierarchic institution of salvation and as the congregation of the saints[581].

It is not surprising that Roman Catholic authors especially have objected to the idea of the twofold concept of the Church as defended mainly by Protestants[582]. Such a separation of *communio sacramentorum* (the empirical Catholic Church) and *communio sanctorum* is, according to them, not present in the writings of Augustine.

Fritz Hofmann in particular saw a single doctrine of the Church in Augustine's works[583]. Although Augustine's ecclesiology distinguished between the empirical and the holy Church, Hofmann did not believe it included a twofold view of the Church. For Augustine there was one *ecclesia*. True, its nature is 'mehrschichtig'. Hofmann saw a 'dreifache Tiefenschichtung', consisting of the visible Catholic Church (the communio sacramentorum), the invisible Church of the saints (communio sanctorum) and the fixed number of the predestinated (certus numerus praedestinatorum). These different groups are not separated from each other, but lie one within the other like concentric circles. 'Die Zugehörigkeit zu einer tieferen Schicht setzt jeweils die Zugehörigkeit zu der weniger tiefen Schichten voraus: niemand steht also in der ecclesia sancta, der nicht auch in der sichtbaren Kirche steht ...'[584].

Hofmann's argumentation in favour of unity in Augustine's ecclesiology and especially his large collection of references in

---

to Reuter for their distinction usually go beyond him. Reuter saw more unity in A.'s concept of Church than did other scholars; see e.g. *Studien*, 118, 122, 151.

579 R. Seeberg, *Lehrbuch der Dogmengeschichte*, II, Leipzig 1923[3] (repr. Basel 1953[4]), 445.

580 Seeberg, *Lehrbuch*, II, 446 ff., et al.

581 Loofs, *Leitfaden*, 301.

582 Besides those named above: Scholz, *Glaube und Unglaube* (1911); Troeltsch, *Augustin* (1915); Salin, *Civitas Dei* (1926); Frick, *Reich Gottes* (1928) et al.

583 F. Hofmann, *Der Kirchenbegriff des hl. Augustinus in seinen Grundlagen und in seiner Entwicklung*, München 1933.

584 Hofmann, *Kirchenbegriff*, 242-243.

support of it have not failed to influence opinion. For this church father there is the one *ecclesia*! Does this also mean he identified *ecclesia* with *civitas Dei*? Many of Augustine's pronouncements point to an equation of the two concepts. But how and in what respect can they be identified with each other?

An important contribution to this discussion—inspired in its essential elements by Hofmann—has been made by Wilhelm Kamlah. In his study *Christentum und Geschichtlichkeit* (1951)[585], which has already been quoted several times, he also brings up these questions. What did Augustine mean by *civitas Dei*? What did he mean by *ecclesia*? Should they be identified with each other? Was Augustine only referring to the predestinated when he spoke of the city or the kingdom of God?

Instead of a theocratic, an empirical or a purely idealistic interpretation, Kamlah presents an eschatological view[586]. He shows that by *civitas Dei* Augustine meant nothing other than the *ecclesia*. *Civitas Dei* and *ecclesia* are to be connected by an equals sign: *civitas Dei* = *ecclesia*. What is the *ecclesia* then? With Augustine we have to distinguish clearly between the Church as it is now (ecclesia qualis nunc est) and the eschatological Church (ecclesia qualis tunc erit). This distinction was used by Bishop Callistus of Rome against rigorists who were only willing to accept an undefiled Church; later it was used in the polemic against the Donatists. This distinction has nothing to do with a so-called twofold concept of the Church, but denotes the difference between the actual Church which is still sojourning as an alien and the perfect Church of the future. Now it is still a mixed body (corpus permixtum), but in the end it will be 'without stain or wrinkle' (sine macula nec ruga).

According to Kamlah Augustine did no more or no less than refer to the empirical congregation[587] by an appellative name: *civitas Dei*[588]. 'Freilich wenn Augustin gesagt hätte: «Die empirische

[585] This work appeared earlier as *Christentum und Selbstbehauptung. Historische und philosophische Untersuchungen zur Entstehung des Christentums und zu Augustins 'Bürgerschaft Gottes'* (1940).

[586] Kamlah, *Christentum*, esp. 133-152; 158-166.

[587] Kamlah, *Christentum*, esp. 139, prefers 'congregation' to 'Church' as the translation of *ecclesia*: 'In unserer Sprache hat das Wort «die Gemeinde» den alten eschatologischen Sinn von ekklèsia besser bewahrt als das Wort «die Kirche». (...) Übersetzen wir ecclesia mit «Kirche», so erliegen wir leicht den Druck dieses Sprachgebrauches und denken an «hierarchische Organisation»'.

[588] Ratzinger, *Volk*, 289 n. 28, agrees with Kamlah on this count. On the other

katholische Kirche ist der Staat Gottes auf Erden», so wäre das aufsehenerregend, beunruhigend, mittelalterlich. Augustin aber hat gesagt: «Die Gemeinde Christi ist Gottes Bürgerschaft auf Erden», und das ist ein alter Satz der christlichen eschatologischen Tradition, gemeinsam der ganzen alten Kirche von Paulus bis zu Augustin'[589]. When the congregation is indicated by the names *ecclesia* and *civitas Dei* or is designated house of God or temple of God[590], it is adorned with eschatological names. The congregation *is* already the kingdom of God, but it has not yet reached its fulfilment.

Although I cannot agree with all of Kamlah's assertions[591], I believe that he has performed a lasting service. He shows that ultimately *ecclesia* and *civitas Dei* have the same meaning for Augustine: both are eschatological terms. The church father sees the congregation now (nunc) from the point of view of the congregation in the end (tunc, eschatologically). This is what he calls it and how he judges it. This is also why to him *civitas Dei* and *ecclesia* are identical and interchangeable. Equating the two is not an incidental act, but a fundamental one. Augustine's designation of the empirical congregation by the names *ecclesia* or city of God implies an appeal, an eschatological summons. The historical congregation (or Church)[592] is the city of God on earth, at present in exile, in the end at home in the heavenly Jerusalem.

A few passages from Augustine's writings may illustrate the extent to which he identifies the city of God with the Church. In the *City of God*: '... the city of God is the holy Church ...' (VIII, 24); '... the city of God, which is His Church ...' (XIII, 16); '... of the city of God, which is of the Church ...' (XV, 26); '... Christ and His

---

hand, he attaches greater importance—and he is right, in our opinion—to the significance for A. of the visible Catholic Church.

589 Kamlah, *Christentum*, 159.

590 For *domus Dei* and *templum Dei*, see e.g. *DCD* XV, 19. A comprehensive study of these and similar concepts was made by Ratzinger, *Volk*, passim.

591 Not so much his historical analyses, but his interpretations are open to discussion. Kamlah proves to be greatly influenced by Heidegger. Very debatable are his statements on 'adlige Selbstbehauptung' in the first edition (1940!) and, for example, his view that 'das geschichtliche Sein' of the individual is 'zugleich wesentlich leiblich' and that therefore 'wesentlich die leibliche Gemeinschaft des Blutes' belongs to the original 'Geschichtlichkeit' (14 f.).

592 The word *Church* can certainly be used, but only in its original sense of *ekklèsia*: not a hierarchical institute of salvation, but the community of the faithful.

Church, the city of God ...' (XVI, 2)[593]. Likewise in his expositions on the Psalms, this identification occurs time and again; for example: '... about the city of God, which is about the Church ...' (*En. in Ps.* 71, 18); '... what is the city of God but the holy Church?' (*En. in Ps.* 98, 4)[594].

Obviously city of God and Church have the same meaning. But is it not advisable to state more precisely what these terms mean? Does *civitas Dei* not often seem to be a more comprehensive concept than *ecclesia*, since Augustine emphasizes that the city of God consists of angels as well[595]?

Important investigations, of great value for this facet too, were carried out by Émilien Lamirande[596]. They shed new light on Augustine's ecclesiology, this time mainly based on the latter's ideas concerning the heavenly Church. The Church on earth appears as a *heavenly* entity and represents to a certain extent the eschatological city. The heavenly Church (ecclesia caelestis) is without doubt absolutely identical with the city of God; especially in the *Enchiridion* for Laurentius the heavenly nature of the *ecclesia* is emphasized[597]. But the Church in its earthly manifestation is also identified by Augustine with the city of God. However, in this context, the two are not for him entirely equivalent concepts.

For concerning the *civitas Dei* he hardly ever states that it has reprobate people in its midst[598]; but concerning the *ecclesia* he does so on several occasions[599]. There is evidently a subtle difference in Augustine's use of the two terms. Lamirande concludes: 'Bien que les termes «cité de Dieu» et «Église» soient très souvent pris

---

593 '... civitas Dei quae est sancta ecclesia ...'; '... civitatem Dei, hoc est eius ecclesiam ...'; '... civitatis Dei, hoc est ecclesiae ...'; '... ad Christum et eius ecclesiam, quae civitas Dei est ...' resp. See also *DCD* XVII, 4. 15. 20 and XX, 11 (2 x).

594 '... de civitate Dei, hoc est, de ecclesia ...'; '... quae est civitas Dei, nisi sancta ecclesia?' resp. Cf. *s.* 341, 9: '... una ecclesia, civitas regis magni ...'.

595 Ratzinger, *Volk*, 326 et al.

596 *L'Église céleste selon saint Augustin*, Paris 1963. For the slight difference between *ecclesia* and *civitas Dei*, see also P. Borgomeo, *L'Église de ce temps dans la prédication de saint Augustin*, Paris 1972, esp. 299 ff. and T.J. van Bavel, 'Wat voor kerk kies je? De ruimheid van Augustinus' ecclesiologie', *TvT* 16 (1976) 355-375.

597 Particularly *Ench.* 61: 'Haec ergo quae in sanctis angelis et virtutibus Dei est ecclesia ...'.

598 Probably the only exception is *DCD* I, 35; cf. Marshall, *Studies*, 41 and 88.

599 As in *DCD* XX, 19; *De cat. rud.* 11 and 54-55. More examples are given in Marshall, *Studies*, 41.

comme équivalents, il ne faut pas oublier qu'ils comportent des résonances différentes et qu'ils ne sont pas toujours interchangeables. Il paraît impossible de sauvegarder l'originalité propre de la pensée augustinienne si on affirme une identité absolue entre Église et cité de Dieu'[600].

Yet the essence of Kamlah's interpretation can be accepted. For *civitas Dei* and *ecclesia* are in Augustine's theology above all eschatological concepts! Hence the frequent identification of the one with the other: the city of God is the Church. To illustrate this once more with a passage from his sermons: 'This Church/congregation (ecclesia), which is a stranger now, will be joined to that heavenly Church/congregation where we shall have the angels as fellow-citizens [...] and there will be *one Church/congregation, the city of the great King*[601]'.

7. The earthly city

Augustine opens his work with the statement that he wishes to defend 'the most glorious city of God'. Against what? It is apparent from the first part that he is directing his remarks against Rome, against those who glorify the Roman Empire and the Roman past. In scathing terms he denounces Rome's pride and thirst for power. There is a continual antithesis between: they—we, their authors—our Scripture, their fate—our Christ, their gods—our God[602]. For the last time pagan Rome is subjected to an extensive and fundamental judgement. According to Harald Fuchs[603] Augustine is the last of a long tradition. In this bishop from Africa hostility against Rome appears once more, an apocalyptically tinted enmity against the city of the devil which persecutes the city of Christ.

But later in his work Augustine's defence against Rome fades into the background. The enmity of the pagan opponents is seen in a wider perspective. A pagan Rome persecutes the *civitas Dei/ecclesia*,

---

600 Lamirande, *L'Église céleste*, 94; cf. 37 following an analysis of the descriptions in *DCD* of the heavenly Church: '... c'est seulement dans la mesure où elle cesse d'être «céleste» que l'Église risque de ne plus s'identifier pleinement à la cité de Dieu'.

601 *S.* 341, 9.

602 This antithesis is also very obvious between *your* literature—*our* Scripture, *your* native city—*our* native city, etc. in the discussion with the high-ranking Roman Nectarius. See *Ep.* 91, 2 ff. and *Ep.* 104, 3 ff. The letters were written shortly before 410 (Huisman, *Briefwisseling*, 30).

603 H. Fuchs, *Der geistige Widerstand gegen Rom in der antiken Welt*, Berlin 1938, 22-25 and 87 ff.

but is not the first or only one to do so. Rome is the embodiment of the *terrena civitas*, but throughout all the ages the city of God has been confronted by this power, even before Rome existed.

What, then, is this *terrena civitas*[604] which has existed throughout the centuries? From the beginning of time semblance has vanished into nothingness before truth, and outside *veritas* there is only *vanitas*. The city of the believers (civitas fidelium) was and still is confronted by that of the unbelievers (civitas infidelium), the city of this world (civitas huius saeculi; XVIII, 1), the wicked city (impia civitas; XVIII, 41 and 51; XX, 11), the wicked city and the unfaithful people (impia civitas et populus infidelium; XX, 9), the city of mortals (civitas mortalium; XVIII, 2), the demon-worshipping city (daemonicola civitas; XVIII, 1), the city of the devil (civitas diaboli; XVII, 16 and 20, etc.). The citizens of the *terrena civitas* are the sinners, both angels and humans (peccatores, et angeli et homines; XIV, 27), those living according to the flesh and according to man (secundum carnem et secundum hominem; XIV, 1; XV, 1 and 20; XVI, 17 et al.).

These are only a few of the terms Augustine uses to describe the *terrena civitas*[605], but they are enough to see clearly what he has in mind with this antithesis of the city of God. The earthly city knows only birth (generatio), the heavenly city rebirth (regeneratio). Ultimately both societies are founded on the predestination of God (XII, 28; XV, 1 and 17 et al.).

Thus the earthly city is the absolute antithesis of the city of God. Although here on earth, in this time of the world, the existence of the two communities is interwoven and intermingled, on the Day of Judgement the definitive separation will take place. For Augustine not only the *civitas Dei/ecclesia* is ultimately an eschatological entity, but also its antithesis is.

Is then the *terrena civitas* identical with the state, in Augustine's time Rome? It is clear that the church father considers all the states of this earth to be *earthly* states, *terrenae civitates*. Even when they are ruled by Christian emperors and have Christians as their citizens they are and remain earthly states. Thus Rome, too, is a *terrena civitas*. Pagan Rome, like a second Babylon, is even pictured as the community in which the *terrena civitas* has been pre-eminently realized as

---

604 A. nearly always used this word order!
605 See also p. 116.

the city of the devil. It is understandable that this rhetorical identification of Rome with the *civitas diaboli* serves a useful purpose for Augustine in his debates with the pagan opponents.

On the other hand it is clear that he does not stop at this identification. For Augustine *terrena civitas* is a much wider concept. The earthly city encompasses all those who live according to man, according to the flesh, and not according to God's will; basically the earthly city includes everything that does not belong to the city of God. In this way the Roman Empire is *terrena civitas*, but the *terrena civitas* does not coincide with it.

Later on in this study there will be sufficient opportunity to look more closely at the concept 'earthly city'. It will be apparent that a state—even the Roman state prior to Constantine and Theodosius—is not necessarily demonic, but that it always remains second-rate; that the city of God does make grateful use of earthly peace, but does not enjoy it as the supreme good; that—through God's *providentia*—there are indeed Christians who are called to be emperors, but that there are no Christian empires. The earthly state and its peace are only earthly, temporal, transient. Essentially the citizen of the heavenly city is a pilgrim here on earth. True, he can benefit from the goods of the earthly city, but he can *rejoice* only in God and His kingdom.

8. *The city of God as an alien*

In the foregoing it was observed more than once that the city of God sojourns as an alien in this world. This is obviously a fundamental aspect of Augustine's doctrine of the two cities. Its importance can be seen from the following passages from the *City of God*.

Our enumeration is limited to the keywords *peregrinari* (to sojourn abroad, to be absent, to be an alien, to wander, to peregrinate), *peregrinus* (adj. alien, foreign; n. alien, foreigner, non-citizen) and *peregrinatio* (journey or stay abroad, status of being an alien, pilgrimage)[606]. An inquiry into the occurrence of these words[607] suffices to reveal Augustine's view of the city of God as *civitas peregrinans*.

---

606 E.g. Blaise, *Dictionnaire*, s.v.. See also B. Kötting, *Peregrinatio religiosa. Wallfahrten in der Antike und das Pilgerwesen in der alten Kirche*, Münster 1950, 7-11.

607 Words like *alienatio, alienus, alienare* do not offer any new points of view, nor does *viator*. *Accola* and *accolere* do not occur in *DCD*.

Of course the contexts of these quotations are indicated as clearly as possible, but it did not always seem advisable to quote the often very lengthy sentences in their entirety. To facilitate looking up the passages and to see them better in their contexts, the pages of the edition by Dombart and Kalb in *CCL* 47 and 48 are added[608].

Gloriosissimam civitatem Dei sive in hoc temporum cursu, cum inter impios peregrinatur ... I, praef. (p. 1)	The most glorious city of God, both as it exists in this course of time, sojourning among the ungodly ...
... quam oportebat eos, qui in hoc mundo perigrinantur ... I, 9 (p. 9)	... as it should be for those who sojourn as aliens in this world ...
... qui supernam patriam veraci fide expectantes etiam in suis sedibus peregrinos se esse noverunt. I, 15 (p. 17)	... [the saints] who, expecting in true faith a heavenly country, know that they are aliens even in their own dwelling-places.
... bonisque terrenis tamquam peregrina utitur nec capitur ... I, 29 (p. 30)	... and she [viz. the *familia Dei*] uses the earthly goods as an alien, without being obsessed by them ...
Haec et alia ... respondeat inimicis suis redempta familia domini Christi et peregrina civitas regis Christi. I, 35 (p. 33) ...	These and similar answers ... may the redeemed family of Christ the Lord, the pilgrim city of Christ the King, deliver [them] to its enemies ...
... sicut ex illorum numero etiam Dei civitas habet secum, quamdiu peregrinatur in mundo, conexos communione sacramentorum ... I, 35 (p. 35)	... as also from their number, the city of God, while it sojourns in this world as an alien, has those in its midst who are united with it through the sharing of the sacraments ...
... inde fidei pignus accepimus, quamdiu peregrinantes eius pulchritudini suspiramus ... V, 16 (p. 149)	... from there [viz. from the eternal city] we have received the pledge of our faith, as long as we, peregrinating, long for its beauty ...
... quamdiu hic peregrinantur ... V, 16 (p. 149)	... as long as they are pilgrims here ...

608 Occasionally it turns out that *peregrinatio* etc. cannot be applied to the city of God or its citizens, for example when A. discusses foreign gods (numina peregrina; dii peregrini), the wandering (peregrinatio) of Israel in the desert, a journey (peregrinatio) of Plato's, and the like. These passages have not been included. For the sake of completeness their occurence is indicated: *DCD* I, 31; II, 14; III, 12. 14. 22 (2 x); IV, 6; V, 2. 5. 6; VI, 2; VIII, 4. 11 (2 x); X, 17; XXII, 8.

... ut in huius vitae peregrinatione expeditior ambulet viam, quae perducit ad patriam ...
V, 18 (p. 153)

... so that during the pilgrimage of this life he [i.e. the Christian] may walk more easily on the way that leads to the homeland ...

Cum ipsis enim sumus una civitas Dei, cui dicitur in psalmo: Gloriosissima dicta sunt de te, civitas Dei; cuius pars in nobis peregrinatur, pars in illis opitulatur.
X, 7 (p. 280)

For with them [i.e. the angels] we form one city of God, to which it is said in the Psalm: 'Most glorious things are spoken of you, city of God.' The part which we constitute is on pilgrimage, the part that they constitute helps.

... quae huius civitatis et magna pars est et eo beatior, quod numquam peregrinata ...
XI, 9 (p. 328)

... [the holy angels], who form the greater part of this city, and the more blessed part, since it has never been on pilgrimage.

In hoc autem libro de civitate Dei, quae non peregrinatur in huius vitae mortalitate, sed inmortalis semper in caelis est ...
XI, 28 (p. 348-349)

In this book, then, [let us speak] of the city of God, which is not sojourning as an alien in this mortal life, but is forever immortal in heaven ...

Sancti vero angeli quorum societati et congregationi in hac peregrinatione laboriosissima suspiramus ...
XI, 31 (p. 351)

The holy angels, however, for whose society and fellowship we sigh on this most laborious pilgrimage ...

... illam huic inludentem, ut nolens prosit persecutionibus suis, hanc illi invidentem, cum peregrinos colligit suos ...
XI, 33 (p. 353)

... the one [society of angels] is deriding the other, because it unwillingly benefits by its persecutions; the latter envying the former, when it gathers its pilgrims together ...

Cuius pars, quae coniungenda inmortalibus angelis ex mortalibus hominibus congregatur et nunc mutabiliter peregrinatur in terris ...
XII, 9 (p. 364)

The part of it [i.e. of the city of God] that is to be united with the immortal angels is being gathered from mortal men, and is now, under the condition of change, sojourning as an alien on earth ...

Apud nos autem iuxta scripturas sanctas sanamque doctrinam cives sanctae civitatis Dei in huius vitae peregrinatione secundum Deum viventes metuunt cupiuntque, dolent gaudentque ...
XIV, 9 (p. 426)

Among us, on the other hand, in accordance with the holy Scriptures and sound doctrine, the citizens of the holy city of God fear and desire, grieve and rejoice as they live according to the will of God in the pilgrimage of this life ...

... quales esse debeant in hac peregrinatione cives civitatis Dei, viventes secundum spiritum, non secundum carnem ...
XIV, 9 (p.429)

... how the citizens of the city of God must be during this pilgrimage, living a life according to the Spirit and not according to the flesh ...

Quapropter quod nunc in civitate Dei et civitati Dei in hoc peregrinanti saeculo maxime commendatur humilitas ...
XIV, 13 (p. 435)

That is why humility is highly recommended now in the city of God, and especially for the city of God during its pilgrimage in this world ...

... prior est natus civis huius saeculi, posterius autem isto peregrinus in saeculo et pertinens ad civitatem Dei, gratia praedestinatus gratia electus, gratia peregrinus deorsum gratia civis sursum ...

... the first to be born was a citizen of this world, and later appeared one who was an alien in this world, belonging to the city of God, predestined by grace, and chosen by grace, by grace an alien here below, and by grace a citizen above ...

Abel autem tamquam peregrinus non condidit. Superna est enim sanctorum civitas, quamvis hic pariat cives, in quibus peregrinatur, donec regni eius tempus adveniat ...
XV, 1 (p. 454)

Abel, however, as an alien, did not found a city. For the city of the saints is above, although it begets citizens here below in whom it sojourns as an alien until the time of its kingdom comes ...

Primus itaque fuit terrenae civitatis conditor fratricida; nam suum fratrem civem civitatis aeternae in hac terra peregrinantem invidentia victus occidit.
XV, 5 (p. 457)

The first founder of the earthly city was consequently a fratricide; for, overcome by envy, he killed his own brother, who was a citizen of the eternal city sojourning upon this earth.

... propter quod dicitur proficientibus bonis et ex fide in hac peregrinatione viventibus ...
XV, 6 (p. 458)

... therefore it is said to the good who are making progress and who are living by faith during this peregrination ...

Hoc modo curantur cives civitatis Dei in hac terra peregrinantes et paci supernae patriae suspirantes.
XV, 6 (p. 459)

In this way the citizens of the city of God are restored to health, as they sojourn as aliens on this earth and sigh for the peace of the heavenly homeland.

... cursum gloriosissimae civitatis in hoc mundo peregrinantis et supernam patriam requirentis ...

... the course of the most glorious city, that sojourns in this world as an alien and seeks the heavenly homeland ...

Hunc secutus Abel, quem maior frater occidit, praefigurationem quandam peregrinantis civitatis Dei ...

After him [i.e. Cain] came Abel; he was killed by his elder brother, thus being a kind of foreshadowing of the sojourning city of God ...

Cum itaque istae duae series generationum, una de Seth, altera de Cain, has duas, de quibus agimus, distinctis ordinibus insinuent civitates, unam caelestem in terris peregrinantem ...
XV, 15 (p. 475)

Thus there are these two lines of descent, one from Seth and the other from Cain, and they represent by their separate genealogies these two cities which we are discussing, one the heavenly city sojourning on earth ...

Cain quippe genuit Enoch, in cuius nomine condidit civitatem, terrenam scilicet, non peregrinantem in hoc mundo,

For Cain begot Enoch, and in his name he founded a city, namely the earthly city which does not sojourn as an

sed in eius temporali pace ac felicitate quiescentem ..
XV, 17 (p. 479)

alien in this world but is reposing in its temporal peace and happiness ...

In spe igitur vivit homo filius resurrectionis; in spe vivit, quamdiu peregrinatur hic, civitas Dei ...
XV, 18 (p. 480)

It is in hope, therefore, that man, son of the resurrection, lives; it is in hope that the city of God lives, so long as it sojourns here as an alien ...

Civitatem vero Dei peregrinantem in hoc saeculo regeneratione perducit ad alterum saeculum ...
XV, 20 (p. 482)

But the city of God, which sojourns in this world as an alien, is brought by Him through regeneration to another world ...

Hoc est quippe in hoc mundo peregrinantis civitatis Dei totum atque summum in hac mortalitate negotium ...
XV, 21 (p. 486)

For this [i.e. invoking the name of the Lord] is, in this mortal life, the whole and supreme occupation of the city of God while sojourning as an alien in this world ...

... ut ex ipsa etiam conparatione vasorum irae superna civitas discat, quae peregrinatur in terris, non fidere libertate arbitrii sui ...
XV, 21 (p. 487)

... so that the celestial city, which sojourns as an alien on earth, may learn, through this very comparison with the vessels of wrath [cf. *Rom.* 9], not to trust the freedom of its own will ...

... amatae sunt a filiis Dei, civibus scilicet peregrinantis in hoc saeculo alterius civitatis, propter pulchritudinem corporis.
XV, 22 (p. 487)

... they [i.e. the women of the earthly city] were loved for their physical beauty by the sons of God, that is, by the citizens of the other city which sojourns in this world.

... sed sicut esse possunt in hac peregrinatione perfecti ...
... procul dubio figura est peregrinantis in hoc saeculo civitatis Dei, hoc est ecclesiae ...
XV, 26 (p. 493)

... but as they can be perfect during this peregrination ...
... without doubt it [i.e. the ark] is a symbolic representation of the city of God sojourning as an alien in this world, that is, of the Church ...

... dum tamen ea ... ad hanc de qua loquimur Dei civitatem in hoc saeculo maligno tamquam in diluvio peregrinantem omnia referantur ...
XV, 26 (p. 494)

... provided that all that is said has reference to our subject, the city of God, which sojourns as an alien in this wicked world as in a deluge ...

... in quo Dei civitas et in sanctis peregrinata est et in omnibus sacramento adumbrata.
XVI, 3 (p. 503)

... in it [i.e. in the people of Israel] the city of God has sojourned, both in its saints and, mysteriously prefigured, also in all the people.

... illam in terris peregrinantem civitatem Dei ...
XVI, 9 (p. 510)

... that [famous] city of God sojourning as an alien on earth ...

Sciendo scies, quia peregrinum erit semen tuum in terra non propria ... (2 x)
XVI, 24 (p. 526)

'Thou shalt surely know that thy seed shall sojourn in a land that is not their own ...' (quotation from *Gen.* 15; 2 x)

... propter populum Christianum, in quo Dei civitas peregrinatur in terris ...
XVI, 41 (p. 546)

... in consideration of the Christian people, in whom the city of God sojourns on earth ...

... partim ergo ad ancillam, quae in servitutem generat, id est terrenam Hierusalem, quae servit cum filiis suis, partim vero ad liberam civitatem Dei, id est veram Hierusalem aeternam, in caelis, cuius filii homines secundum Deum viventes peregrinantur in terris ...
XVII, 3 (p. 553)

[the prophecies refer] in part, then, to the bondmaiden who genders to bondage, that is, the earthly Jerusalem, who with its children is in slavery; but in part to the free city of God, that is the true eternal Jerusalem in heaven, whose children are those who live according to God's will in their pilgrimage on earth ...

... supernam civitatem Dei eiusque filios in hac vita peregrinos ...
XVII, 3 (p. 554)

... the heavenly city of God and its children who are pilgrims in this life ...

Porro qui rebus ipsis, quae iam coeperunt etiam in hac terrena peregrinatione compleri, convenienter movetur ...
XVII, 4 (p. 556)

Furthermore, whoever is suitably moved by these events themselves [i.e. those foretold in the prophecies of Hannah], whose fulfilment has already begun even in this earthly pilgrimage ...

... pia per fidem vita in hac aerumnosa peregrinatione ducenda est.
XVII, 13 (p. 578)

... a devout life, guided by faith, must be lived during this arduous peregrination.

De civitatum duarum, quarum Dei una, saeculi huius altera, in qua est, quantum ad hominum genus pertinet, etiam ista peregrina, exortu et procursu et debitis finibus me scripturum esse promisi ...
XVIII, 1 (p. 592)

I promised to write about the origin, the progress and the appointed ends of the two cities, one of which is the city of God, the other the city of this world, in which the former sojourns as an alien, as far as its human element is concerned ...

... ut appareat quem ad modum Babylonia, quasi prima Roma, cum peregrina in hoc mundo Dei civitate procurrat ...
XVIII, 2 (p. 594)

... so that it may appear how Babylon, like a first Rome, proceeds on its course beside the city of God in its pilgrimage in this world ...

Ut ascendam, inquit, in populum peregrinationis meae, recedens utique a populo maligno carnalis cognationis suae, non peregrinante in hac terra nec supernam patriam requirente.
XVIII, 32 (p. 625-626)

'So that I may go up', says he [i.e. Habakkuk], 'to join the people of my pilgrimage', that is, leaving the wicked people, his own blood-relations, who were not on pilgrimage on this earth and did not seek the heavenly country.

... adversus peregrinantem in hoc mundo civitatem Dei ...
XVIII, 51 (p. 649)

... against the city of God which is sojourning as an alien in this world ...

Sic in hoc saeculo, in his diebus malis non solum a tempore corporalis praesentiae Christi et apostolorum eius, sed ab ipso Abel, quem primum iustum impius frater occidit, et deinceps usque in huius saeculi finem inter persecutiones mundi et consolationes Dei peregrinando procurrit ecclesia.
XVIII, 51 (p. 650)

In this way the Church proceeds on its pilgrimage in this world, in these evil days, not just from the time of the bodily presence of Christ and His apostles, but even from the time of Abel, the first righteous man, who was slain by his ungodly brother, and thence to the end of this world-time, amid the persecutions of the world and the consolations of God.

... illa autem, quae caelestis peregrinatur in terra, falsos deos non facit ...
XVIII, 54 (p. 656)

... that heavenly one, however, which sojourns as an alien on earth, does not create false gods ...

Et quoniam, quamdiu est in isto mortali corpore, peregrinatur a Domino: ambulat per fidem, non per speciem ...
XIX, 14 (p. 681)

And since, so long as he is in this mortal body, he sojourns as an alien far from the Lord: he walks by faith, not by sight ... [cf. 2 *Cor.* 5:6-7].

Sed in domo iusti viventis ex fide et adhuc ab illa caelesti civitatis peregrinantis ...
XIX, 14 (p. 681)

But in the house of the just man who lives by faith and who is still on pilgrimage, far from that celestial city ...

... domus autem hominum ex fide viventium expectat ea, quae in futurum aeterna promissa sunt, terrenisque rebus ac temporabilus tamquam peregrina utitur ...
XIX, 17 (p. 684)

... but the household of men who live by faith awaits the blessings which are promised as eternal in the future, and uses earthly and temporal things as an alien ...

Civitas autem caelestis vel potius pars eius, quae in hac mortalitate peregrinatur et vivit ex fide ...
... ac per hoc, dum apud terrenam civitatem velut captivam vitam suae peregrinationis agit...
XIX, 17 (p. 684)

But the heavenly city, or rather the part of it which is an alien in this mortal life and lives by faith ...
... and therefore, as long as it leads, as it were, a life of captivity as an alien in the earthly city ...

Haec ergo caelestis civitas dum peregrinatur in terra, ex omnibus gentibus cives evocat, atque in omnibus linguis peregrinam colligit societatem ...

Therefore this heavenly city, while it sojourns as an alien on earth, calls its citizens from all nations, and from all languages it gathers together its society of pilgrims ...

Utitur ergo etiam caelestis civitas in hac sua peregrinatione pace terrena ...

Thus even the heavenly city on its pilgrimage here makes use of the earthly peace ...

Hanc pacem dum peregrinatur in fide habet atque ex hac fide iuste vivit ... XIX, 17 (p. 685)	This heavenly peace it possesses in faith, while on its pilgrimage, and by this faith it lives righteously ...
... per quam sine dubitatione ambulamus, quamdiu peregrinamur a Domino ... XIX, 18 (p. 686)	... due to this [i.e. faith] we walk without doubting, for as long as we sojourn far from the Lord ... [2 *Cor.* 5:6].
Sed Deus ille, quem coluerunt sapientes Hebraeorum, etiam caelestibus sanctis angelis et virtutibus Dei, quos beatissimos tamquam cives in hac nostra peregrinatione mortali veneramur et amamus, sacrificari vetat ... XIX, 23 (p. 694)	But that God, whom the wise men of the Hebrews worshipped, forbids sacrifices to be offered even to the holy angels in heaven and the powers of God, whom we, in this mortal pilgrimage of ours, venerate and love as our most blessed fellow-citizens ...
... ex qua ita per fidem populus Dei liberatur, ut apud hanc interim peregrinetur. XIX, 26 (p. 697)	... from there [i.e. from Babylon] the people of God are set free through faith, so that in the meantime they sojourn in that city as aliens[609].
Testis est oratio totius civitatis Dei, quae peregrinatur in terris. XIX, 27 (p. 697)	The evidence for this [610] is the prayer of the whole city of God, which sojourns as an alien on earth.
Et hanc quidem in hac peregrinatione gustantes, non ad satietatem sumentes ... XXI, 24 (p. 792)	And this [i.e. the sweetness of God] we taste rather than partake of to satiety in this our pilgrimage ...
Neque tunc civitas Christi, quamvis adhuc peregrinaretur in terris et haberet tamen magnorum agmina populorum, adversos impios persecutores suos pro temporali salute pugnavit ... XXII, 6 (p. 813).	Nor did the city of Christ in those days [i.e. in the time of the persecutions] fight against its godless persecutors for a temporal salvation, although it was still sojourning on earth and was supported by a great multitude of people ...

From this and the preceding pages it can be established that for Augustine the state of being an alien is an essential characteristic of the city of God on earth. The Christian congregation is not at home here, it is far away from its mother city in heaven, it is sojourning in a foreign land.

---

609 *Ex qua* and *hanc* can also have *pax* for their antecedent. Then the translation is: '... from this [viz. from the peace of Babylon] God's people is delivered through faith, so that for the time being it sojourns in this peace as an alien'. The passage that follows could favour this translation, as could the fact that caput 27 opens by mentioning the totally different peace: 'Pax autem nostra propria et hic est cum Deo per fidem et in aeternum erit cum illo per speciem'.

610 Viz. that justice in this life consists in the forgiveness of sins rather than in the perfection of virtues.

That is why the citizen of the city of God is in this world a *peregrinus*. But what exactly does this word mean? It makes hardly any difference whether it is translated as 'alien', 'someone who sojourns (as an alien)' or as 'pilgrim'. The constant element in its meaning is that it concerns a person who has no home here, but is on his way to his native city (patria) in heaven.

Guy[611] has rightly drawn attention to the fact that the Latin noun *peregrinus* can have two meanings. The first is juridical: the state of a free man living in a Roman city, but not enjoying the usual rights of citizenship of the city, a kind of 'étranger domicilié'. The other is figurative: a believer who travels as an alien in this earthly reality, a man who is on a pilgrimage which must bring him into the heavenly city. Although Guy considers the choice difficult, he has a preference for the former meaning: *peregrinus* as an 'étranger domicilié'. In order to account for this choice he points to an idea set forth several times by Augustine:

Perplexae quippe sunt istae duae civitates in hoc saeculo invicemque permixtae, donec ultimo iudicio dirimantur[612].	Indeed, these two cities are interwoven in this world and mutually intermingled, until they are separated at the Last Judgement[612].

We will see later on in this study that the citizen of the city of God who is sojourning here does indeed participate in the life of this world: he *uses* the goods of this earthly life; they are gifts from God. But what Augustine stresses in the *City of God* is that the *peregrinus* does *not* have his real domicile in this world. His stay is only temporary, he is not a citizen here. Therefore not the 'domicilié' should be emphasized, but the idea of being an alien. Earthly goods are used, but not enjoyed; earthly peace is indeed appreciated, but it is only of this earth, temporal. If this intermingled state is emphasized too much there will be an inclination to assume that for Augustine there was a third *civitas*, a *tertium*. However, for the eschatologically thinking church father[613] there was no independent, neutral area[614]. When

611 Guy, *Unité*, 113.

612 *DCD* I, 35. Cf. X, 32. '... de duarum civitatum, quas in hoc saeculo perplexas dicimus invicemque permixtas ...' and XI, 1: '... de duarum civitatum, terrenae scilicet et caelestis, quas in hoc interim saeculo perplexas quodam modo diximus invicemque permixtas ...'.

613 E.g. Eger, *Eschatologie*, 15: 'Augustins Theologie ist eine Theologie der Sehnsucht. Sie ist es darum, weil sein Leben auf die Erfüllung in der Ewigkeit ausgerichtet ist'.

614 See further pp. 151-153.

Augustine used the term *peregrinus* he meant principally the *peregrinating* believer, who is residing now in a foreign country, not at home but living in tents[615], but who will later dwell in his proper abode, the heavenly Jerusalem.

Augustine's references to peregrination and his yearning for the heavenly city, not only in the *City of God* but in other writings as well, can only be commented on briefly here. For example in the *Confessions* we find: '... that eternal Jerusalem, for which Your people in their pilgrimage [literally: the pilgrimage of Your people] are yearning from their departure to their return'[616]; '... while I am groaning with groans too deep for words [cf. *Rom.* 8:26] during my pilgrimage, and remembering Jerusalem, towards which my heart is raised high, Jerusalem, my country, Jerusalem, my mother [*Gal.* 4:26] ...'[617]. In X, 4, 6 he speaks about 'my fellow citizens and those who are pilgrims with me' (civium meorum et mecum peregrinorum), and in XII, 15, 21 he even depicts his whole life as a pilgrimage: 'Let my wandering be a sighing for You ...' (Tibi suspiret peregrinatio mea ...). There are other passages in the *Confessions* that illustrate this point. But the concurrence between the *City of God* and this rather early work (c. 400) should be sufficiently clear: in his life on earth the Christian sojourns as an alien; his native city Jerusalem is in heaven.

Some passages from Augustine's sermons on the Psalms can also be cited in this context. In these sermons, more than anywhere else in his writings, the Christian's state of being an alien is a frequently recurring theme[619]. While especially in the *City of God* Augustine gives a systematic, apologetic exposition, here and in other sermons he expresses these thoughts in a meditative style. Two examples, which also show a similarity with other themes in the *City of God*, may serve to illustrate this:

Sed est in caelo aeterna Ierusalem, ubi sunt cives nostri angeli: ab ipsis civibus nostris peregrinamur in terra. In peregrinatione suspiramus, in civitate	But in heaven is eternal Jerusalem, where our fellow-citizens are, the angels; we are sojourning on earth far away from these fellow-citizens of ours.

615 For *domus – tabernaculum*, see Ratzinger, *Volk*, 237-240.

616 *Conf.* IX, 13, 37: '... aeterna Hierusalem, cui suspirat peregrinatio populi tui ab exitu ad reditum ...'.

617 *Conf.* XII, 16, 23: '... gemens inenarrabiles gemitus in peregrinatione mea et recordans Hierusalem extento in eam sursum corde, Hierusalem patriam meam, Hierusalem matrem meam ...'.

619 It may be noted in passing that even if there is no (unconscious) reminiscence or deliberate antithesis here, there is in any case parallelism with the Manichaean psalms of the pilgrims. For these psalms, see p. 219.

gaudebimus. Invenimus autem et socios in ista peregrinatione, qui iam viderunt ipsam civitatem, et invitant nos ut curramus ad illam[620].	On our pilgrimage we sigh, in the city we shall rejoice. But we also find companions on this pilgrimage who have already seen this city, and who summon us to hasten to it[620].
... omnis ergo numerus fidelium sanctorum, ex hominibus commutandorum ut fiant aequales angelis Dei, adiuncti etiam ipsi angelis, qui modo non peregrinantur, sed expectant nos quando a peregrinatione redeamus; omnes simul unam domum Dei faciunt, et unam civitatem. Ipsa est Ierusalem[621].	... the entire number, therefore, of the holy believers, who have to be ransomed out of mankind so that they may be the equals of God's angels, who will also be added to the angels who are not on pilgrimage now, but who await us when we return from this peregrination. All of them together form one house of God and one city. This is Jerusalem[621].

It is unmistakably clear from Augustine's writings that the pilgrimage of the city of God on earth and of its citizens is strongly emphasized[622]. This also emerges from other images often used by Augustine: this world is like Egypt[623], like a desert[624]; the seventy years of captivity in Babylon are symbolic of life at present[625]; the forty days of Lent are a symbol of earthly troubles[626]. Here below the city of God/*ecclesia* is a widow (vidua)[627]; she is destitute and suffering[628]. Present-day life and the life to come are sharply contrasted as night and day[629], hunger - satiety[630], anxiety - freedom from anxiety[631], trouble - calm[632]. The path to the paternal home

---

620 *En. in Ps.* 121, 2.

621 *En. in Ps.* 126, 3.

622 Texts in which the theme of the *peregrinatio* is heard continually are, besides the *En. in Ps.*, esp. *s. Caillau* 2, 92; *s.* 25; *s.* 80 and *s.* 81; from the letters they include *Ep.* 155 to Macedonius, in which the question of how a Christian can serve in the state is treated.

623 *En. in Ps.* 133, *s.* I, 3; cf. *Conf.* VII, 9,15. Origen in particular made use of the image, as in *Hom. in Num.* II, 1: '... populus Dei egrediens de mundi huius Aegypto ...'.

624 *En. in Ps.* 43, 15; 69, 9; 72, 5; et al.

625 E.g. *En. in Ps.* 147, 5; *De cat. rud.* 37.

626 E.g. *s.* 205, 1; *s.* 226, 3; *Ep.* 55, 29-31.

627 *En. in Ps.* 131, 23. For the position of the widow and handmaiden (ancilla) Monnica in the *Conf.* as image of the Church, see e.g. Van Kempen-van Dijk, *Monnica*, 86-87.

628 *En. in Ps.* 87, 15.

629 *En. in Ps.* 100, 13.

630 *En. in Ps.* 32 *en.* II, *s.* 2, 25.

631 *S.* 154, 7.

632 *Ep.* 55, 17.

is long and thorny[633]. A Christian's life is: being trained in yearning[634]. In one of his tractates on the *Gospel according to John*, Augustine sketches the two ways of living of the *ecclesia*: one by faith, the other by sight; one in exile, the other in the eternal abode; one in trouble, the other in calm; one *in via*, the other *in patria*, etc.[635].

But surely the city of God is in this world? Did the Catholic bishop practise some kind of gnostic contempt for the world? Did he not value the earth and its goods as gifts from God?

We will deal with these questions in the next section. First it is necessary to consider a central theme of his theology: the distinction between *uti* and *frui*, using and enjoying. These concepts in particular clarify Augustine's notion of peregrination and thus they provide a better insight into his doctrine of the two cities.

9. *'Using' and 'enjoying'*

'For the good use the world in order to rejoice in God, the wicked on the contrary want to use God in order to enjoy the world'[636]. This is one more illustration of the antithesis between the earthly city and the city of God. The children of this world are attached to worldly matters as if they were the greatest goods. The children of God, however, have their supreme good in heaven. They use this world as non-users[637].

When Augustine wants to point out an essential characteristic of the city of God, he often says that it is the *civitas* which delights in God. For example: 'God has founded her ...; God is her light ...; she delights in God ...' (XI, 24). Or: 'she is the perfectly ordered and completely harmonious fellowship (societas) in the enjoyment of God and of one another in God' (XIX, 13 and 17)[638].

Let us first see what Augustine meant by *uti* and *frui*. In Book I of *On Christian Doctrine* he explains these concepts several times. We read that *frui* is: 'love for its own sake' and *uti*: 'love for the sake of

---

633 *S. Caillau* 2, 19, 1.

634 *Tract. in Ep. Ioh.* 4, 6.

635 *Tract. in Ioh. Ev.* 124, 5.

636 *DCD* XV, 7: 'Boni quippe ad hoc utuntur mundo, ut fruantur Deo; mali autem contra, ut fruantur mundo, uti volunt Deo ...'.

637 See 1 *Cor.* 7:31 in *DCD* I, 10: '... si mundo utebantur tanquam non utentes ...'.

638 E.g. *DCD* XI, 32: '... angelica societas fruens Deo ...'.

something else'[639]. The citizen of the city of God can only rejoice in God and heavenly things[640].

The scheme 'using'- 'enjoying', so characteristic of Augustine, already occurs in his earliest writings[641]. In the dialogue *The Happy Life* the 'delight in God' (Deo frui) has a typically Neoplatonic ring[642]. But in *The Morals of the Catholic Church and the Morals of the Manichaeans*, written during his sojourn in Rome shortly after his baptism, the distinction between using and enjoying is clearly given the meaning that often recurs later: in God alone may one delight, what is visible and temporal must only be used for sustenance[643].

Rudolf Lorenz has made a convincing case for the idea that the scheme *uti - frui* probably came to Augustine via Varro and Cicero[644]. Georg Pfligersdorffer points to Varro, Horace and Seneca, and in particular to Cicero's *Hortensius*[645]. There may have been influence from Plotinus[646], possibly even from the Manichaeans[647]. But wherever this double concept may have originated[648], it is important that for Augustine the distinction between 'using' and 'enjoying' is the difference between the divine and the worldly, the eter-

---

639 *De doctr. chr.* I, 22, 20: 'diligere propter se'; 'diligere propter aliud'. Cf. I, 4, 4.

640 Cf. *De doctr. chr.* I, 5, 5; I, 10, 10; I, 33, 37. See also *De div. quaest.* 83, 30. R. Canning, 'The Augustinian uti/frui Distinction in the Relation between Love for Neighbour and Love for God', *Aug(L)* 33 (1983) 165-231, esp. 206 ff., shows—esp. with reference to *De doctr. chr.* I, 33, 36—that in this distinction A. still has positive interest in man (the neighbour): 'enjoying' is close to 'using with love' (cum dilectatione uti).

641 See e.g. Duchrow, *Christenheit*, 195 ff.

642 *De b. vita* 34.

643 E.g. *De mor.* I, 37: 'Amandus igitur solus Deus est: omnis vero iste mundus, id est omnia sensibilia contemnenda; utendum autem his ad huius vitae necessitatem.' *Frui* has just been discussed.

644 R. Lorenz, 'Die Herkunft des augustinischen Frui Deo', *ZKG* 64 (1952-'53) 34-60. He points (40) to Varro for the above-quoted definition from *De doctr. chr.* I, 22, 20. See also Lorenz, 'Fruitio Dei bei Augustin', *ZKG* 63 (1950-'51) 75-132, and for a summary on *uti-frui*: Lorenz, *Das vierte bis sechste Jahrhundert*, 56.

645 G. Pfligersdorffer, 'Zu den Grundlagen des augustinischen Begriffpaares «uti-frui»', *WSt* 84 (1971) 195-224, particularly 215-224 for the influence of the *Hortensius*.

646 Duchrow, *Christenheit*, 202, refers to the distinction made by Plotinus: *pros to chreian - pros to telos*.

647 See p. 223.

648 P. Smulders, 'De Pelgrim naar het Absolute. Eeuwigheidsverlangen en tijdelijke waarden bij Augustinus', *Bijdragen* 16 (1955) 151-152, following J. Burnaby (*Amor Dei*, 104 f.), attributes the notion of *uti* to Stoic influence via Ambrose.—But it is also possible to point to affinity with Philo; see e.g. Philo, *De cher.*, 117 ff.

nal and the temporal, the city of God and the city of this world.

There is no need to enumerate here all the passages of the *City of God* in which *uti* and *frui* occur. The quotations earlier in this chapter give a clear enough picture. It is apparent that the enemies (inimici) of the city of God have reversed the order. They have become entangled in what is temporal; their greatest enjoyment is in earthly things[649]; for these they yearn[650]. Totally different, however, are the citizens of the heavenly Jerusalem. Their true delight is in God and His kingdom. When the thought of heaven is aroused in them, they hold the earthly goods in contempt[651].

Augustine limits true and full enjoyment to eternal life and God as the supreme good (summum bonum). God Himself will be for the blessed the total of all good things[652]. Therefore, as regards earthly goods, the *bona terrena*, the citizen of the city of God is like an alien. He makes *use* of them, avails himself of them only temporally. 'Temporal goods are health, wealth, honour and esteem, friends, a house, children, a spouse and all the other things of this life through which we travel as pilgrims. So let us not, at the inn of this life, regard ourselves as owners who reside here permanently, but as pilgrims who will move on'[653]. In the misery of our exile the earthly goods are a consolation (consolatio) with which the good Lord comforts us[654]. At the same time, however, God has added a grain of bitterness 'lest the traveller, who is going to his country, become enamoured of the inn instead of his home'[655].

But is all this not a gnostic contempt for the world? Does not Augustine's emphasis on alienation point to a gnostic world-view? And, in this context, is the image of the inn not significant—even though Augustine sometimes cites *Luke* 10:25-37 explicitly[656]?

---

649 E.g. *DCD* I, 30; II, 20; XI, 25.

650 E.g. *DCD* IV, 34: '... illa terrena bona, quibus solis *inhiant*, qui meliora cogitare non possunt ...', and XV, 15: '... alteram terrenam [sc. civitatem] terrenis tanquam sola sint gaudiis *inhiantem* vel inhaerentem'.

651 *DCD* V, 18: '... qui pro inmortalis patriae legibus omnia ... bona terrena contemnunt?'

652 E.g. *DCD* XXII, 30: '... et vita et salus ... et pax et omnia bona'.

653 *S.* 80, 7.

654 E.g. *En. in Ps.* 34, *s.* I, 6.

655 *En. in Ps.* 40, 5.

656 See p. 223 and n. 120 for the metaphor of the inn in A.'s imagery, that of the Manichaeans and in the *Acta Thomae* (not gnostic). But the motif of being an alien and the metaphor of the inn also occur in the Stoa; see the collection of texts by T. Baarda, 'Jezus zeide: «Weest passanten». Over betekenis en oorsprong van

Yet there is an important and essential difference. It is true that the citizen of the city of God is a pilgrim and dwells here like a traveller at the inn. But for Augustine this does not imply an absolute rejection of what is earthly. He frequently stresses that the earthly goods (bona terrena) are good gifts from God. Gold in itself is not bad, nor is greed a fault attached to gold, but the fault lies in man who loves the gold in a wrong way[657]. The same can be said of physical beauty. It is a gift from God, but man loves in a wrong way[658]. The order of love (ordo amoris), which should concur with the true nature of things (ordo naturarum), has been distorted by man when he loves instead of using. Love of the creature, however, is subordinate to love of the Creator. 'God does not forbid you to love those things, but only to love them in order to find your salvation in them'[659]. 'That is why the *familia* of the supreme and true God uses the earthly goods as an alien (peregrina) and is not obsessed by them'[660].

The same thoughts are found time and again in the famous, already frequently quoted Book XIX of the *City of God*. For Augustine the *bona terrena* are summarized in the concept *pax terrena*, earthly peace. But also this good of the earthly city, however highly it is to be esteemed, is surpassed by far by the *pax aeterna Dei*, the eternal peace of God.

10. Peace in earthly things

Book XIX has always aroused special interest[661], for in it Augustine begins his discussion of the destined ends (debiti fines) of the two

logion 42 in het Evangelie van Thomas', in: *Ad interim. Opstellen ... R. Schippers ...*, Kampen 1975, 122-125.

657 *DCD* XII, 18.

658 *DCD* XV, 22.

659 *Tract. in Ep. Ioh.* 2, 11.

660 *DCD* I, 29: '... omnis familia summi et veri Dei ... bonis terrenis tamquam peregrina utitur nec capitur ...'.

661 The first to be named is H. Fuchs, *Augustin und der antike Friedensgedanke. Untersuchungen zum neunzehnten Buch der Civitas Dei*, Berlin 1926. Fuchs referred particularly to Varro, for XIX, 12-17 to his *Pius de pace*. But of this work only the title is known! For criticism of Fuchs, see esp. J. Laufs, *Der Friedensgedanke bei Augustinus. Untersuchungen zum XIX. Buch des Werkes 'De Civitate Dei'*, Wiesbaden 1973. He points out that for Virgil also *pax* was closely connected with *pietas*. Another who is critical of Fuchs' theses is Hagendahl, *Latin Classics*, 620-630, esp. 627 on the reference to *Pius de pace*. However, the influence of Varro's *De philosophia* on Book

cities. And most importantly: here he deals at length with the question of the supreme good (summum bonum). This question plays a central role in his doctrine of the two cities. Therefore firstly a summary of this book will be given so that the framework in which the author makes his statements on the earthly peace and its use may become clear.

Augustine opens by remarking that the philosophers have been pondering over the supreme good. According to Varro there were no fewer than 288 possible opinions. They all agreed to the extent that they were seeking the *summum bonum* in man himself and that they considered it attainable in this life on earth. Varro summarized the numerous opinions in three basic ones and chose the ancient-academic one: having virtue and the so-called first goods of nature makes man happy. Furthermore, the wise man lives in a community; he must choose between a life of scholarly reflection (otium litterarum) and a life of public activity (negotium publicum) (1-3).

The attitude of Christians towards the supreme good and the greatest evil is absolutely contrary to that of the philosophers. They proclaim the supernaturalness of the *summum bonum* and true happiness. If one considers how inconstant and imperfect the so-called first gifts of nature and human virtues are, one realizes that here on earth and by himself man is unable to attain true happiness (4).

Christians, too, choose a social life. But no matter how valuable life in marriage, family and *civitas* may be, it is a source of distress (5). As it is in one's own family and circle of relatives, so is it also in the city: there are all kinds of misery because the judge, in holding down his office, has to resort to torturing the innocent (6). In the society that has grown into a state consisting of a number of peoples there is a variety of languages, which forms a barrier; moreover, there is the misery of war, including the so-called just wars (7). Nor does friendship bring true happiness, for there is always the worry about the physical and spiritual well-being of the friends (8). We, as

---

XIX is generally recognized.—C. Cary-Elwes, 'Peace in the City of God', *Ciudad*, I, 417-430, gives a general exposition, but lacks new perspectives and research into sources. H. Rondet, 'Pax, tranquillitas ordinis', *Ciudad*, II, 343-364, besides discussing *DCD* XIX, goes further into passages from *De ord.*, *De mus.*, the *En. in Ps.* et al., and particularly the *Tract. in Ioh. Ev.*. Each time the conclusion is that earthly peace is transient and threatened time and again; only peace in the city of God is lasting. For Book XIX see also Maier, *Augustin*, 182-195; E. Dinkler, 'Friede', *RAC* 8 (1972) 478-479.

Christians, have a communal bond with the angels which is free from worry. But often the devil appears as an angel of light, and in this way we are time and again in danger of falling into his power. That is clearly the case with the *terrena civitas* (9).

True peace can be found only in heaven; this eternal peace is the supreme good. Happiness on earth will, in comparison with this heavenly bliss, turn out to be nothing but misery (10). The final end, the true perfection of the saints, is eternal life in peace (11). It is peace to which all creation, even inanimate nature, aspires. Peace is even the goal of war and revolt (12). There is a universal peace, a natural law ordained by a righteous Judge, through which everybody and everything are assigned their rightful places. God has bestowed gifts on man befitting this life, viz. temporal peace in accordance with this mortal life (... pacem temporalem pro modulo mortalis vitae ...). If one correctly *uses* these gifts that are aimed at peace among mortals, one will receive bigger and better ones, viz. the peace of immortality and the glory and honour that accompany it in a life eternal for the enjoyment of God and of one's neighbour in God (... ad fruendum Deo et proximo in Deo ..., 13).

Thus in the earthly city the *use* of temporal things is entirely aimed at *enjoying* the *earthly* peace; in the heavenly city, on the contrary, the aim is the *enjoyment* of *eternal* peace (... ad fructum pacis aeternae). The citizen of the city of God places the peace of the body and the soul, and the peace between these two at the service of his peace with God. Likewise, he orders his earthly relationships in accordance with this peace: in his household (14), in his relations with slaves (15), in the proper exercise of power in his household and towards his slaves (16).

Chapter 17 is of central importance and will be summarized in greater detail. Augustine begins by saying that unbelievers seek earthly peace in the things and advantages of this temporal life. Believers await the eternal things, *use* the earth and temporal things as aliens, and do not allow themselves to be ensnared by them or to be diverted from their aspiration to God. 'Therefore the use (usus) of the things necessary for this life on earth is common to both kinds of people (...), but their purpose in using them (finis utendi) differs enormously'. The earthly city is striving for peace on earth. The heavenly city in its pilgrimage must make *use* of the earthly peace also, until this mortal life, which needs such a peace, has passed. Therefore it now obeys the laws by means of which the earthly city regulates what is necessary for maintaining the earthly existence. May thus this harmony (concordia) remain between the two cities in the things related to this mortal life.

Earthly wise men believed in the necessity of making a multitude of gods favourably disposed towards men's lives; the heavenly city worships the one God. Therefore it could not have the same laws concerning religion. It became a burden to others and had to suffer their anger, hatred and attacks.

During its sojourn on earth the heavenly city calls its citizens from all nations and assembles the society of pilgrims (peregrina societas) from all tongues, paying no heed to differences in mores, laws or institutions by which earthly peace is established or maintained. The heavenly city does not demolish or destroy any of these. On the contrary, it preserves and follows (servans ac sequens) whatever fulfils the purpose of the one and the same goal of the earthly peace, provided this does not interfere with the religion that teaches that the one true God must be served. Thus in its pilgrimage the heavenly city *uses* the earthly peace. It relates this peace to the heavenly peace, which is the true peace for the rational creature, namely the perfectly ordered and completely harmonious society in the enjoyment of God and of one another in God (... ordinatissima scilicet et concordissima societas *fruendi* Deo et invicem in Deo).

In contrast to the Academics with their scepticism, the city of God knows the firm certainty of faith (18). The Christian way of life consists of a combination of *otium* and *actio* (19). The supreme good of the city of God is eternal peace. This is the perfectly blessed life. Who would wish to deny that, compared with this, life here on earth is most wretched (... vel in eius comparatione istam — sc. vitam— ... non miserrimam iudicet)? Life on earth without hope for eternal life is a false happiness and a great misery (beatitudo falsa et magna miseria, 20).

After discussing peace and its relation to society, Augustine considers the time ripe to fulfil a promise made earlier[663], namely to answer the question of whether Rome had ever been a *civitas*[664]. According to Scipio's definition, which Cicero cited in *De re publica*[665],

---

663 *DCD* II, 21. This fact, too, testifies to unity in the composition of *DCD*.

664 *Civitas*, here and in what follows, has particularly the meaning of our word 'state'.

665 *De rep.* I, 39: 'Est res publica res populi, populus autem ... coetus multitudinis iuris consensu et utilitatis communione sociatus'. Cf. Testard, *Augustin et Cicéron*, I, 207, and Hagendahl, *Latin Classics*, 542 ff.

Rome could never have been a *civitas*: it lacked the essential characteristic of justice (iustitia), for the Romans did not recognize the true God (21). This true God is the God of the Christians (22). When, in spite of God's prohibition, people make sacrifices to the idols, justice, which is the essential characteristic of the state, is lacking (23). If, however, we apply the following definition: 'A people is the association of a multitude of rational beings united in fellowship by their agreement about the objects they love'[666], then the Roman people is a people and its estate a state (res publica). Similarly, the other pagan societies of people are *civitates* too, but without true justice (24). Also without true virtue; their virtues are vices rather than virtues (... vitia sunt potius quam virtutes, 25)[667]. Yet this transient peace should not be rejected: it is important for us, too (etiam nostri interest). For as long as the two cities are intermingled, we also make *use* of the peace of *Babylon* (quamdiu permixtae sunt ambae civitates, utimur et nos pace Babylonis). God's people will be delivered from it, but now it is still sojourning here as an alien. That is why, as in the days of Jeremiah, man should pray for Babylon. 'For in her peace is your peace (*Jer.* 29:7), a temporal, transient peace (pax temporalis) of course, common to the good and the wicked' (26). 'However, our peace is peace with God, here by faith, in eternity by sight.' But both the common peace and our own peace are in this life on earth rather a solace in our misery than the positive enjoyment of felicity. Not before eternity will peace be perfect, the highest good (27). The wicked, on the other hand, are subjected to eternal punishment and everlasting strife (28).

It is clear from this exposition that in Book XIX also the emphasis is ultimately on alienation. A citizen of the city of God makes use of what is earthly, but does not become absorbed in it. He recognizes the transience of earthly goods, does not rely on them while using them and does not allow himself to be captivated by them (capiatur, 17). Augustine indeed regards temporal goods as *bona*, gifts from God. The citizen of the city of God may make grateful use of them. In using them well he will receive better and greater goods: eternal glory in which he delights in God, and takes delight in his neighbour in God (13).

---

666 *DCD* XIX, 24: 'Populus est coetus multitudinis rationalis rerum quas diligit concordi communione sociatus'.

667 Cf. p. 116 and n. 523.

Continually the question is stated: what is earthly happiness compared with heavenly bliss? Misery! (10) In other passages of the *City of God* also the misery of this life is emphasized, particularly in XXII, 22. There we even read that God permits baptized children to be tormented in order to show that the evil of this life should be deplored and an entirely different happiness should be sought. The good things here on earth never provide true happiness; they only give the citizen of the city of God *consolatio*[668].

Earthly peace is a good thing (bonum); earthly goods are gifts from God[669]. The Christian uses and appreciates them. Augustine even says that the heavenly *civitas* protects and strives for earthly peace (tuetur atque appetit, 17). For him this *civitas* makes not only a purely passive, but also an active use of the earthly goods and political institutions. But that is the absolute limit. Nowhere in Augustine's work do we read about a Christian political theology such as occurs explicitly in the work of Eusebius of Caesarea. The part of the heavenly city which is in exile here on earth makes use of earthly peace until mortality passes away (17). There is a common use of it, but the individual objectives are very different (17). There is *concordia* (17) in matters that are related to this mortal life. The city of God avails itself of this concord now. Earthly peace is of concern to it also. But ultimately it is said '... we use the peace *of Babylon*' (26).

This last statement should not lead us to overlook the fact that Augustine is referring not only to the peace of the pagan state, but also to that of the state ruled by Christians. Nowhere in Book XIX is a fundamental distinction made between the two. Here, as elsewhere, it appears that earthly peace is *earthly* peace[670]. Augustine never speaks about *Christian* earthly peace. Such a positive interpretation of this concept does not occur in his writing.

But if he ascribes neither a negative, nor an explicitly positive Christian meaning to earthly peace, is it possible that he recognizes a third *civitas* as a neutral area between the city of God and the city of this world? This question will be discussed next.

---

668 E.g. XXII, 21 and 24.

669 E.g. XV, 22: 'Quod *bonum* Dei quidem *donum* est'.

670 E.g. *En. in Ps.* 61, 8. A. says here that citizens of the city of God are sometimes called upon to serve in the earthly city. But he speaks about ancient Babylon and the (Christian!) Roman Empire of his day without making a fundamental distinction. Cf. *Ep.* 47, 2 on the *pax barbarica*, which is looked on favourably.

11. A third, neutral city?

As we have seen, the city of God and the earthly city are absolutely antithetical; there are no intermediate forms. Yet Augustine says: 'In this *saeculum* the two cities are intermingled and interwoven, until they are separated at the Last Judgement'[671]. The citizen of the heavenly city partakes of this earthly life; he even appreciates the earthly goods as gifts from God. Could we not speak then of a third city, a *tertium*, as an independent neutral area in which the earthly life takes form?

A number of scholars have studied this question. Indeed, many themes are connected with it: no less than Augustine's attitude towards the entire human culture, the State, politics! Charles Journet, in particular, has argued that there was such a third city, which is ethically good, but has a temporal and earthly aim: '... en dessous des cités ... il y a place pour un *tertium quid*, qui affleure constamment au cours de l'ouvrage sur la Cité de Dieu, qui n'est pas l'objet de la préoccupation directe d'Augustin, auquel il ne donne pas de nom précis ...'[672].

However, well-founded objections can be raised to Journet's view[673], and not only because he approached Augustine's concept from Thomistic premises. Thomas Aquinas saw man as a social being; the State belongs to the natural order of things and is good. And yet it must remain absolutely clear that Augustine did not see temporal goods separately as neutral goods, but according to the use man makes of them. That use is either good or evil, and in this way temporal goods belong to one of the two cities, either that of God or that of the devil. Not once did Augustine mention an independent, neutral area between the two cities, a city of man. But he did repeat emphatically that there are only two cities.

Although there is no reference anywhere in Augustine's theology to an autonomous third city, is there then nothing between the two cities, a *tertium quid*? Marrou thinks there is: 'Oui, il y a quelque chose d'autre, bien entendu d'un ordre tout différent, c'est ce que je proposais d'appeler «le donné empirique de l'histoire», ce donné

---

671 *DCD* I, 35; for the text see n. 612.

672 Ch. Journet, 'Les trois cités: celle de Dieu, celle de l'homme, celle du diable', *Nova et Vetera* 33 (1958) 25-48, quotation 29.

673 Earlier in *L'Église du Verbe incarné*, II, Paris 1951, 26-34. Cf. Marrou, 'Tertium?', 342; Guy, *Unité*, 114 n. 2; Borgomeo, *L'Église de ce temps*, 302 f.

mystérieux où bien et mal, cité de Dieu et cité du diable sont inextricablement mêlés. Si l'on veut un terme augustinien pour le désigner, je proposerai celui de *saeculum*,—un des sens que le mot *saeculum*, traduisant un des sens du grec *aiōn* dans le N.T. revêt sous la plume d'Augustin'[674].

To a considerable extent one can agree with this view. Although in an ontological sense there are only two cities, in this present age they are inextricably intermingled. This empirical, historical fact needs to be examined. It forms the core of the aforementioned study by R.A. Markus[675]; he defines *saeculum* inter alia: '... not as a no-man's land between the two cities, but as their temporal life in their interwoven, perplexed and only eschatologically separable reality'[676].

In fact, Augustine was aware of such a reality. In this present age the two cities are intermingled; it is only in the eschaton that they will be separated and thus the absolute antithesis will be fully revealed. But it should be borne in mind that there is no *neutral* area between the two cities. Markus goes too far when he asserts that ultimately Rome was seen as neutral by Augustine[677]. For was the Rome against which he defended the city of God not affiliated with paganism? And has not unambiguous judgement been passed on this Rome in 'sacred history' (historica sacra)?

Likewise one can ask whether Markus' choice of and preference for the word *saeculum* is not more reminiscent of Dietrich Bonhoeffer or Harvey Cox than of Augustine. It should be noted that the neutral meaning of *saeculum* (age, eternity,—indefinite—long time) is hardly present in Augustine[678]. But it is precisely in a pejorative sense that he used the word. This world (hoc saeculum) is antithetical to the future one[679]. The word *saeculum* has a negative ring in expressions like 'the literature of this world' (litterae huius saeculi[680]) and 'the scholars of this world' (saeculi huius

---

674 Marrou, 'Tertium?', 348. He refers to *DCD* XV, 1 '... hoc enim universum tempus sive saeculum, in quo cedunt morientes succeduntque nascentes, istarum duarum civitatum ... excursus est'.

675 *Saeculum: History and Society in the Theology of St Augustine* (1970).

676 Markus, *Saeculum*, 71; cf. esp. 133.

677 Markus, *Saeculum*, esp. 55 f.

678 Cf. Orbán, 'Benennungen', 223: 'Der neutrale Gebrauch ... von *saeculum* in Augustins *De civitate Dei* ist keineswegs relevant'.

679 For example, in *DCD* XVII, 20 and XXI, 24 the two antithetical *saecula* are spoken of in one sentence.

680 *DCD* XVIII, 37.

litterati[681]; docti huius saeculi[682]; saeculi huius doctissimi homines[683]). And the pejorative connotation of *saeculum* is very emphatic in a phrase like 'in this wicked world'[684], and in the warning not to conform to this world[685]. The meaning of *saeculum* is also very obvious when Augustine says that there are two cities, 'one is of God, the other of this world'[686]. Moreover, it is noteworthy that 'this world' (hoc saeculum) and the believer's state of being an alien are often directly connected to each other[687]. Cain is a citizen of this world (civis huius saeculi), but Abel is an alien in the world and belongs to the city of God (peregrinus in saeculo et pertinens ad civitatem Dei, XV, 1).

On the basis of these facts serious objections should be made to Markus' use of the term *saeculum*. Although he does not ascribe to Augustine a doctrine of a third *civitas* as an independent domain, he goes too far in his interpretation of 'the theologically neutral conception towards which his thought was moving'[688]. Of course one can disagree with Augustine's teaching and prefer to stress slightly different or even entirely different aspects. But this does not entitle one to interpret his doctrine of the two cities in accordance with later thinking, whether of Thomas Aquinas, Luther or Calvin, or of Bonhoeffer, Harvey Cox or Jürgen Moltmann. Augustine, in his eschatological way of thinking, is definitely concerned with the antithesis between the city of God and the earthly city, not with a neutral area between the two cities. It is the *antithesis* that is emphasized time and again, not so much the fact that the two *civitates* are intermingled in this present age.

---

681 *DCD* XIV, 9.

682 *DCD* XXII, 22.

683 *DCD* XXII, 15.

684 *DCD* XV, 26 and XVIII, 49: '... in hoc ... saeculo maligno ...'. Cf., for example, XVIII, 51: '... in hoc saeculo, in his diebus malis ...'.

685 *DCD* X, 6 and XXII, 16. Cf., for example, *Conf.* XIII, 13, 14. 21, 30. 21, 31 and 22, 32 in which *Rom.* 12:2 is also quoted.

686 *DCD* XVIII, 1: 'De civitatum duarum, quarum Dei una, saeculi huius est altera ...'.

687 *DCD* XIV, 13: '... et civitati Dei in hoc peregrinanti saeculo ...; XV, 1; XV, 20: 'Civitatem vero Dei peregrinantem in hoc saeculo ...'; XV, 22: '... civibus scilicet peregrinantis in hoc saeculo alterius civitatis ...'; XV, 26: '... figura est peregrinantis in hoc saeculo civitatis Dei ...; ... civitatem in hoc saeculo maligno tamquam in diluvio peregrinantem ...'; XVIII, 1; XVIII, 51: 'Sic in hoc saeculo ... peregrinando procurrit ecclesia'.

688 Markus, *Saeculum*, 56.

12. A Christian emperorship and a Christian imperium?

If one reads the *City of God* in search of information about the author's views on a Christian *imperium romanum* and a Christian emperorship one will be disappointed. Augustine does not consider the Roman Empire to have been Christianized, nor the emperorship, but he acknowledges that since Constantine Christians have been called to the office of emperor by the grace of God.

This is surprising in view of the prevailing thought of his day. Obviously Augustine does not recognize any definitive turn of events in the history of the Roman Empire. He only sees alterations in temporal things: the true God grants earthly kingdoms both to the good and to the evil, as it pleases Him[689]. The emperorship was granted to Augustus, but also to Nero; to the two Vespasians, but also to the cruel Domitian; to Constantine, but to Julian as well[690]. Why? To enable the Christian to learn that earthly dominion should be counted as one of the *temporal* goods in which he should not put his trust[691].

Of course Augustine, too, expresses his joy about the happy turn that events took when Constantine became emperor[692]. But he did not see it as a complete change as did Eusebius and others. The empire has not turned Christian, only an emperor. His successor may easily be wicked. According to this African bishop the kingdom of God has not been foreshadowed, let alone definitely realized, in a Christian Roman Empire.

The extent to which he differs in this view from many predecessors and contemporaries, Eusebius of Caesarea in particular, will now be sketched. It will become clear that Augustine's doctrine of the two cities also influenced his attitude towards the Roman Empire and the Roman emperorship, which differs in many respects from the evaluations of others.

Let us first consider the statements of Eusebius and others on the Roman Empire and its relation to Christianity[693]. Erik Peter-

689 *DCD* V, 21: '... regnum vero terrenum et piis et impiis, sicut ei placet ...'.
690 *DCD* V, 21.
691 E.g. *DCD* V, 24.
692 For Constantine, see esp. *DCD* V, 25; for Theodosius, see e.g. V, 26.
693 Only a few main lines can be sketched here. The scholarly—and sometimes also emotional—discussion on Constantine, Eusebius and the new era that started with Constantine is still going on. Of the more recent publications, J.N. Bakhuizen van den Brink, *Constantijn de Grote*, Amsterdam-Oxford 1975 and G.J. van der

son[694] made it clear that Eusebius' positive view of the link between *imperium* and *evangelium* was preceded by a tradition whose most important proponents were Melito of Sardes[695] and Origen. Especially through the influence of Origen, Eusebius took the coincidence of the birth of Christ and the reign of Augustus (*Luke* 2:1) as the point of departure for his observations. The peace under the Emperor Augustus laid the foundations for the Christian message and furthered its dissemination. 'God prepared the nations for the reception of His teaching (didaskalia)'[696].

Eusebius developed this idea further. Not only did he stress the fact that Christ's birth took place when, due to Augustus, peace prevailed, but he also saw in this peace the fulfilment of Old Testament prophecies. What had been established under the Emperor Augustus as peace was brought to definitive completion by Constantine, for the latter believed in the peace of Christ.

Heide, *Christendom en politiek in de tijd van keizer Constantijn de Grote*, Kampen [1979] should be named in particular. For some of my objections to the latter, see *TRef* 23 (1980) 139-143. H. Berkhof's expositions are still largely of great value; see his *Die Theologie des Eusebius von Caesarea*, Amsterdam 1939 and *De kerk en de keizer. Een studie over het ontstaan van de byzantijnse en de theocratische staatsgedachte in de vierde eeuw*, Amsterdam 1946 (German trans.: Zürich 1947). It should be noted that Eusebius' view of universal truth and the triumph of Christianity was not so much developed under the influence of the decisive turn of events that occurred under Constantine, but earlier, during the period of peace for the Church in the last decade of the third century, prior to the persecutions under Diocletian. This is shown by T.D. Barnes, *Constantine and Eusebius*, Cambridge, Mass.-London 1981, esp. 94-105; cf., for example, 164 and 186. There are important introductions to Constantine and Eusebius, their era and their theology in H. Kraft (Hrsg.), *Konstantin der Grosse*, Darmstadt 1974 (*WdF* CXXXI) and G. Ruhbach (Hrsg.), *Die Kirche angesichts der konstantinischen Wende*, Darmstadt 1976 (*WdF* CCCVI).—Special mention should be made of E. Peterson, *Der Monotheismus als politisches Problem. Ein Beitrag zur Geschichte der politischen Theologie im Imperium Romanum*, Leipzig 1935, included with only minor changes in his *Theologische Traktate*, München 1951, 45-147 (my quotations are from this more accessible edition). Although Peterson's thesis (viz. the orthodox doctrine of trinity of the 4th cent. made political theology impossible) was criticized severely right from its inception and was recently analysed and contradicted again (see A. Schindler (Hrsg.), *Monotheismus als politisches Problem? Erik Peterson und die Kritik der politischen Theologie*, Gütersloh 1978, esp. the contributions by J. Badewien and E.L. Fellechner), some evidence from his study is used here, particularly for the *pax romana – evangelium* connection, for Eusebius' view and, although Peterson used few texts to substantiate his opinion, the accurate depiction of A.'s evaluation of the Roman Empire and its peace.

694 'Monotheismus'; see esp. his 'Kaiser Augustus im Urteil des antiken Christentums', *Hochland* 30 (1932-'33) 289-299.

695 Cf. Eusebius, *HE* IV, 26, 7 ff.

696 *C. Celsum* II, 30.

In yet another way Eusebius linked *imperium* with *evangelium*. Just as a variety of rulers in separate states and polytheism go together, so do monarchy and monotheism. In the Roman Empire a development had taken place towards one ruler and the worship of the one God. Essentially monotheism had already begun at the time of Augustus. The process was completed under Constantine: *one* ruler, *one* empire, *one* God[697].

Thus for Eusebius the Roman *imperium*, the *pax romana*, monotheism and monarchy were closely connected. He gave high praise to the ruler Constantine, chosen by God to carry out the plan of salvation; now the Spirit came into the dry bones (*Ezek.* 37), now righteousness and praise sprang forth before all the nations (*Is.* 61). For Eusebius Constantine possessed Messianic traits. Through him the divine victory was realized which had essentially been granted with the coming of Christ. Though Eusebius did not mistake the emperor for Christ, nor the *imperium* for the kingdom of God, for him Constantine represented the image of the Logos and his empire the image of the kingdom of Christ[698].

Rarely in the Church have messianic qualities been deemed so applicable to the rule of an emperor. But was Eusebius, in this matter, merely a flattering Caesaropapist, to be denounced as a 'hoftheologischen Friseur der kaiserlichen Perücke' (Franz Overbeck)? We must keep in mind that Eusebius was not just concerned with the person of Constantine: he saw him as an instrument in God's hand[699]. It was not the person of the emperor that brought about salvation, but in the end God Himself; it was not so much Constantine who was praised, but the new age of salvation which especially in his reign had dawned for Church and world[700]. Eusebius never described Constantine as the ruler who owed his power to himself; dependence on God remained the real theme[701].

---

697 Cf. esp. Peterson, 'Monotheismus', 90 ff. and the textual evidence he offers there. One can agree in the main with his assertions; cf. Badewien in Schindler (Hrsg.), *Monotheismus*, 43-49. But a doctrine of trinity, too, can be of service in a political theology; cf. Badewien, 45 (who refers to Eusebius, *Vita Constantini* IV, 40, 2) and Fellechner in Schindler (Hrsg.), *Monotheismus*, 58-59.

698 Cf. esp. Berkhof, *Theologie*, 53-59 and Berkhof, *Kerk en keizer*, 76-77.

699 This is how Constantine judged himself too; see e.g. Bakhuizen van den Brink, *Constantijn*, 29.

700 See esp. *HE* X, 2, 2.

701 G. Ruhbach, 'Die politische Theologie Eusebs von Caesarea' (1974), in: Ruhbach (Hrsg.), *Konstantinische Wende*, esp. 244, 246-252; for some criticism of this view, see Badewien in Schindler (Hrsg.), *Monotheismus*, 44 n. 2.

Eusebius' view is to be understood first of all from his experience of the God-given age of salvation. In his special appreciation of the Roman peace and its providential significance for the Church he was not alone. Mention can be made, for example, of John Chrysostom and other theologians of the Antiochene school, such as Diodore and Theodoret[702]. There were also statements from the West in this spirit, made by Prudentius, Ambrose and Jerome[703].

And especially the historical work by Paulus Orosius was permeated with this view. As Augustine's close assistant, he wrote at the latter's instigation his *Seven Books of History against the Pagans*[704]. His purpose was to refute with historical evidence the allegations that the Christians were to blame for the calamities befalling the Empire. Orosius accomplished this task independently in 417-418 at the latest[705]. His apologetic chronicle of world history extended from Adam to his own day. Its aim was to demonstrate the realization of God's plan, which culminates in Christianity and finds its completion in a homogeneous, Christian Roman Empire full of peace and happiness.

Orosius wrote a comprehensive world history. His books were originally intended as an amplification and proof of one of Augustine's theses in the first part of the *City of God*, viz. that calamities have always struck mankind and thus the Roman Empire as well. So it is preposterous to blame Christianity for them. Yet his view differs greatly from Augustine's. For Orosius the conversion of the *imperium* to Christianity was the best guarantee of prosperity and happiness (felicitas). The Roman Empire was a chosen empire[706]; the Christian times (tempora christiana) were the most felicitous

---

702 Cf. Fuchs, *Friedensgedanke*, 162 f.; Peterson, 'Monotheismus', 93-94 and 138.

703 Cf. Fuchs, *Friedensgedanke*, 162 f.; Peterson, 'Monotheismus', 95-97 and 139-141.

704 *Historiae adversus paganos*. For Orosius and his theology of history, see H.-W. Goetz, *Die Geschichtstheologie des Orosius*, Darmstadt 1980 (*IdF* 32) and the studies he names (esp. A. Lippold, 1952; K.A. Schöndorf, 1952; B. Lacroix, 1965 and E. Corsini, 1968). For Orosius' attitude towards the imperium romanum, see also Peterson, 'Monotheismus', 97 ff. and Badewien in Schindler (Hrsg.), *Monotheismus*, 60 f. A good, concise introduction to Orosius' philosophy of history is provided by K. Löwith, *Weltgeschichte und Heilsgeschehen. Die theologischen Voraussetzungen der Geschichtsphilosophie*, Stuttgart 1953 (1973[6]), 160-167.

705 Cf. Goetz, *Geschichtstheologie*, 10.

706 E.g. *Hist.* VI, 1, 5: 'unus et verus Deus ... Romanumque imperium ... fundavit'. See further Peterson, 'Monotheismus', 99-100; Goetz, *Geschichtstheologie*, esp. 48 and 80-88.

ones[707]. In the same vein as Eusebius, Orosius pointed out that during the peace under Augustus Christ was born; His advent concurred with this peace. And precisely at that time God appeared in human form: it was not coincidental that Christ came into the world a *Roman* citizen[708].

In this way Empire and Christian faith were also closely related for this assistant of Augustine. And this very description of history was used in the Middle Ages as an authoritative textbook and source for chroniclers[709].

But what was the opinion of Augustine himself? Did he also picture Constantine and Theodosius as the ones who completed what God had prepared in the coming of Christ? Was the Roman *imperium* and its peace just as much for him a fact that fitted into God's history of salvation? And did the concepts *romanus* and *christianus* coincide for him too[710]?

The truth is almost the reverse. In the *City of God* no trace is to be found of a Christian Roman kingdom of God on earth, no special attention is paid to the Roman peace which smooths the way for the preaching of the Christian gospel[711], no mention is made of a con-

---

707 For Orosius' appreciation of the *tempora christiana*, see esp. the passages from the *Hist.* given by G. Madec, 'Tempora christiana. Expression du triomphalisme chrétien ou récrimination païenne?', in C.P. Mayer – W. Eckermann (Hrsg.), *Scientia Augustiniana.* (FS A. Zumkeller), Würzburg 1975, 129-132.

708 *Hist.* 6, 22, 6-8; 7, 3, 4. Orosius was the first in this context to associate *census* with citizenship and in this way he calls Christ a Roman citizen (civis Romanus); cf. Goetz, *Geschichtstheologie*, 81.

709 For example, Otto von Freising would cite the book at length in his *Chronicle, or History of the Two Cities*; King Alfred made an adaptation of it in Anglo-Saxon; etc. See Goetz, *Geschichtstheologie*, 11 and esp. 148-165. The expression 'augustinisme politique' (Arquillière) does not render Augustine's ideas accurately (cf. p. 92), and this is equally true of 'augustinisme historiographique' (Marrou). Orosius' providentialistic historiography, in which piety and prosperity, impiety and calamities are placed simplistically in a causal relationship, is different from A.'s much more careful approach, but exerted great influence. Actually on 'augustinisme politique' too: it was Orosius rather than A. who showed the way to the ideal of Charlemagne and his followers. See esp. H.-I. Marrou, 'Saint Augustin, Orose et l'augustinisme historique', *La storiografia altomedievale*, I, Spoleto 1970, 59-87.

710 Orosius even equated *romanitas, christianitas* and *humanitas* (*Hist.* 5, 2, 4-6); cf. Goetz, *Geschichtstheologie*, 115.

711 In *DCD* XVIII, 22 and 46, where there was a good opportunity to discuss in detail the *pax romana* at the time of Christ's birth, A. did not avail himself of it. In 46 he offers only a brief indication: Christ was born 'when Caesar Augustus was emperor and the world had peace through him'; in 22 we read only that Rome is the second Babylon, 'through whose agency it pleased God to conquer the whole

currence of monotheism and monarchy. Augustine did *not* subscribe to a belief in the progress of the history of salvation as contained in the Eusebian 'Reichstheologie'.

It is significant in itself that in Book XVIII Augustine calls Babylon the first Rome and Rome the first Babylon[712]. Here he uses an old apocalyptic designation for Rome. For Augustine the pagan Roman Empire, although smaller than the society of the wicked of all the ages, is in the end *the* earthly city. Rome is described as the oppressor of the small and the weak, the imperious and haughty one. He continually makes the sharp contrast between we - they: *we*, the citizens of the city of God, *they*, the enemies (inimici); *our* Scripture, *their* writers; *our* Christ, *their* fate; *our* martyrs, *their* heroes.

Yet in his attitude towards Rome and the *imperium*, Augustine is not an apocalyptic. He does not share the optimism of Eusebius and others, but he does not take a completely opposite position either. In early works and in later ones too, he even expresses himself very positively about the Roman Empire 'subjected to God's name by Christ the King'[713]; he emphasizes that times have changed since the days of the apostles: 'As then, in the days of the apostles, (the) kings did not yet serve the Lord'[714]. He even speaks of 'the Roman Empire which is Christian by the grace of God'[715].

Of course these statements should be seen in their own time and context. Bernhard Lohse comments that a difference can be perceived between the young Augustine and Augustine in later life: c. 400 he was still—in line with Eusebius, influenced by Ambrose and particularly by the North African Optatus—favourably inclined towards the Roman Empire, later unfavourably[716]. Markus, among others, shares this view[717]. But is the argumentation in sup-

---

world and impose peace everywhere, uniting it in the single society of the Roman commonwealth and its laws'.

712 *DCD* XVIII, 2 and 22.

713 *De cons. ev.* I, 14, 21: '... et Romanum imperium ... per Christum regem suo nomini subiugavit ...'.

714 *Ep.* 185, 20: 'Cum itaque nondum reges domino servient temporibus apostolorum ...'.

715 *De gratia Christi et de pecc. orig.* II, 17, 18: '... Romanumque imperium, quod Deo propitio christianum est ...'; cf. *C. Faust.* XXII, 60 and *Ep* 87, 8: *imperium christianum*.

716 B. Lohse, 'Augustins Wandlung in seiner Beurteilung des Staates', *SP* 6 (*TU* 81), Berlin 1962, 447-475.

717 Markus, *Saeculum*, esp. 38 f. His assumption, in which he partly follows Lohse, that there was such a decisive change in A.'s use of the expression *tempora*

port of a changed attitude towards the state convincing? And above all: what does Augustine mean when he calls the Empire and the emperor Christian?

From the dates of composition of the aforementioned texts it can be seen that Augustine had a favourable attitude towards the Roman Empire, not only in his early years but also later. Some of the texts were written c. 400[718], some of them, however, much later[719]. It is difficult to speak, using only these data, of a change in Augustine's attitude[720].

Certainly no less important is the question of what Augustine actually means by the expression *imperium christianum*. Does he mean 'Reichstheologie' as used by Eusebius, Optatus and later Orosius? On further reflection it becomes clear that in both the narrower and the wider context of all the statements just quoted he is referring to the Christian *imperium* in connection with the suppression of paganism or heresy[721]. Augustine does not recognize a Christian *imperium* as a new stage in the history of salvation; for him *imperium christianum* means instead a recognition of orthodox Catholic Christianity by the Christians who hold office in the state, a summons to them to serve the Church.

A Christian state as Eusebius saw it is out of the question for Augustine, as is a Christianization of the emperorship. There are Christians who are emperors and they are called upon to devote their power (potestas) to the dissemination of the true religion[722]. But then it is a question of a positive participatory *use* of the earthly

---

christiana, is out of the question; Madec demonstrates this convincingly in 'Tempora christiana', 112-136.

718 *De cons. ev.* and *C. Faust.*

719 According to Goldbacher (*CSEL* 58, 26) *Ep.* 87 dates from 404-411; *Ep.* 185 was written in 417 (Goldbacher, 47); *De gratia Christi et de pecc. orig.* is from 418 (cf. A. de Veer in *BA* 22, 9).

720 Lohse, 'Wandlung', refers to only some of the above-mentioned texts. He does mention (460) *De gratia Christi et de pecc. orig.* II, 17, 18, but gives no exact date of composition.

721 This also holds good for the texts in which A. explicitly refers to 'christiani imperatores': *DCD* V, 24; *Ep.* 138, 16; *Ep.* 185, 6.

722 See esp. *DCD* V, 24. Cf. Lohse, 'Wandlung', 466-468. Moreover, one can point to the role of the *pater familias*, who provides for *pietas*. In *Luke* 14:23 it is the *pater familias* who speaks the words A. knew so well and made so notorious: 'Compel them to come in' (Cogite intrare!). See esp. A.'s letter to the Donatist bishop Vincentius, *Ep.* 93, 5: 'Putas neminem debere cogi ad iustitiam, cum legas patrem familias dixisse servis: «Quoscumque inveneritis, cogite intrare» ...'.

political goods and institutions: they are 'consumer goods' for the citizens of the city of God. Augustine does not believe in a realization of the kingdom of God by means of Christian political action. For him earthly peace (pax) is one of the good things (bona) to be appreciated, but he never speaks of a divine or a Christian earthly peace. Earthly peace belongs to the earthly city, the *terrena civitas*. This is also true for the Roman Empire under Christian emperors. There are Christians who perform an important task in it, and in doing so they do good work. But they are like Daniel and the three young men in Babylon, like Joseph in Egypt, like Esther[723]. In one way or another they are looking after the affairs *of Babylon*[724].

Only in light of his doctrine of the two cities and the related views of 'using' and 'enjoying' and the importance of the earthly peace are Augustine's statements about *imperium* and emperorship to be understood. Thus should his special concern for the Roman governance be seen. Unlike Kamlah and Maier, Johannes Straub emphasized this appreciation Augustine had for the existing order[725]. In various letters (e.g. the famous letter 138 to Marcellinus, letter 189 to the high imperial official Boniface, letter 134 to the proconsul Apringius and also in the recently discovered letter 10*) the bishop expresses his concern for the *imperium* and its inhabitants. Augustine sees the present constellation as a gift from God, a *bonum*. He says this repeatedly in the *City of God*: earthly peace is good and a gift from God (donum Dei). The Empire may be badly shaken now, we read in IV, 7, but it also survived such blows in former times. Each time it recovered (recreatum); why then should we doubt this possibility now? Who knows God's will in this matter[726]?

---

723 *En. in Ps.* 51, 4 and 6. A. is speaking here of the Roman *imperium* of his day, i.e. after Theodosius!

724 *En. in Ps.* 51, 6: '... quando eos videmus aliqua gerere *Babyloniae* negotia ...'. Cf., for example, *En. in Ps.* 61, 8: 'Videamus si et nunc cives bonae civitatis administrent quosdam actus malae civitatis'; immediately preceding this passage the three young men in Babylon are mentioned. Zarb (see *CCL* 38, XVI-XVII) dates the sermons to 412 and 413 resp.

725 J. Straub, 'Augustins Sorge um die regeneratio imperii. Das Imperium Romanum als civitas terrena', *HJ* 73 (1954) 36-60. This article is reprinted in almost the same form in R. Klein (Hrsg.), *Das frühe Christentum im römischen Staat*, Darmstadt 1971 (*WdF* CCLXVII), 244-274, and also in J. Straub, *Regeneratio imperii. Aufsätze über Roms Kaisertum und Reich im Spiegel der heidnischen und christlichen Publizistik*, Darmstadt 1972, 271-295.

726 *DCD* IV, 7: 'Quamquam Romanum imperium adflictum est potius quam

Augustine did not write off the Empire; like others he hoped for recovery. But his positive statements should be placed in the wider framework of his doctrine of the two cities[727]. He was certainly not concerned with a holy *imperium*, but with an earthly good. Now the existing order was that of the Roman Empire. That earthly good must be appreciated, it must even be protected and sought[728]. However, it is not the final and ultimate good. True justice (vera iustitia), true happiness (vera felicitas), true piety (vera pietas) are to be found in the city of God[729].

In 410 and in the years immediately following, pagans put the blame for the fall of Rome on man's neglect of the ancient gods. Besides, large numbers of Christians who had entered the Church since Constantine's conversion were frightened. The new God had proved to be no guarantee! Like the pagans, they had doubts about the connection between Christianity and Empire as it had been laid down by the Eusebian 'Reichstheologie'. In fact, Augustine thought they were right: there are no permanent empires here on earth. Not even Christian ones, although through the mercy of God[730] there are Christian emperors.

Only the city of God is firm and permanent. On earth she sojourns under different worldly powers, always as an alien. She uses and appreciates earthly peace. In accordance with prophetic

---

mutatum, quod et aliis ante Christi nomen temporibus ei contigit et ab illa est adflictione recreatum, quod nec istis temporibus desperandum est. Quis enim de hac re novit voluntatem Dei?' Bardy's comment on this passage (*BA* 33, 550 n. 1) is incorrect: 'Saint Augustin ne peut s'empêcher de croire, comme ses contemporains, à l'éternité de l'empire'. The idea of an *eternal* Roman Empire is absolutely foreign to A.; here and in *DCD* II, 29 et al. he is only expressing his appreciation for the existing government.

727 Straub does not do this enough. And is not this the reason for his one-sided presentation of the matter? He bases his argument mainly on a few letters and sermons, and not on the overall view in the *City of God*. Straub's criticism of Kamlah and Maier is valid, but his own portrayal of A. is too much that of a Roman patriot. He gives a downright distortion of A.'s view when he states that the church father is concerned with 'die innere Durchdringung der potentiell beiden civitates zugehörigen civitas terrena mit christlichem Geist und damit ihre Einordnung in die ewige «civitas Dei» (46)'.—In this context Maier's remark (*Augustin*, 75 n. 9), that practically all of A.'s positive statements on the Christian's attitude towards the state date from the time of his dispute with the Donatists, is important. The purpose of these statements is 'durch die Betonung christlichen Wirkens im Staat die Anwendung kaiserlicher Gesetze gegen die Donatisten zu rechtfertigen'.

728 See *DCD* XIX, 17 with respect to earthly peace: 'tuetur atque appetit'.

729 E.g. *DCD* V, 16; XIX, 21 and 24; *Ep.* 155, 17 (to Macedonius).

730 *DCD* V, 19: 'Deo miserante'.

and apostolic admonition she prays for kings and those in high places, for in Babylon's peace is her peace[731]. She knows that in this world there are no eternal empires. Only the city of God is eternal. When the city that has brought us forth in a carnal way (carnaliter) no longer exists (...), *she* will remain who has brought us forth in a spiritual way (spiritualiter) (...), the holy city, the steadfast city, the city that sojourns on earth as an alien, but whose foundations are in heaven (...). Why are you frightened, because the earthly kingdoms perish? That is why you have been promised a heavenly kingdom, lest you be destroyed with the earthly one[732]'.

Augustine's attitude towards the early pagan *imperium* as well as the Christian one of his own days should be seen from the perspective of his theology of the two cities. For the author of the *City of God* there is essentially no difference between the era following Constantine and the one preceding it. Now, too, the Church is in peregrination; now, too, it is being persecuted. Being a member of the Church still means: enduring, suffering, bearing; in short: *patientia*[733]. The persecutions by Satan and the fallen world are still going on, if no longer with open violence (vis), certainly with deceit and fraud (dolus). It is only in the hope of eternal life that all this can be endured[734]. Earlier, too, the Church did not overcome persecutions by offering forceful resistance, but through enduring and suffering[735].

---

731 See 1 *Tim.* 2: 2 and *Jer.* 29: 7 combined in *DCD* XIX, 26; a similar combination in *C. Faust.* XII, 36 and *De cat. rud.* 37.

732 *S.* 105, 9.

733 *Pati, patiens, patientia* occur nearly 140 times in *DCD*, very often in connection with the attitude of the city of God/*ecclesia* towards this world, also frequently in reference to the suffering of Christ and the individual Christian.

734 E.g. *DCD* XIX, 4.

735 E.g. *DCD* XVIII, 53.

CHAPTER THREE

THE 'CITY OF GOD' AS AN APOLOGY AND A CATECHETICAL WORK

A. The 'City of God' as an Apology

1. The view of Geffcken and others

In 1907 Johannes Geffcken published his well-known study on the Greek apologists Aristides and Athenagoras[1]. This book contained a historical survey. In it Geffcken not only showed that the Christian apologists were dependent for their method on Jewish predecessors like Philo and Josephus, but he also sketched the development of the apologetic genre in the first centuries of the Christian era. Finally he came to Augustine's *De civitate Dei*, which he considered a milestone: 'Es hat etwas hoch Erhebendes, dass am Ende dieser Literatur, (. . .) dieser gewaltige Römer alles das, was das Christentum dem Heidentum zu entgegnen hatte, noch einmal in dichtgedrängter Front mit blitzenden Waffen diesem gegenüberstellte[2].

For Geffcken the *City of God* was unmistakably an apology[3]. He was not the only one to hold this view. In studies before 1900, Augustine's opus was without exception regarded primarily as an apologetic work[4]. In the subsequent years this view has persisted. It suffices to mention here the surveys of *Dogmengeschichte* by Harnack and Loofs[5], the standard work on patrology by Altaner and Stuiber[6]

---

[1] J. Geffcken, *Zwei griechische Apologeten*, Leipzig-Berlin 1907.

[2] Geffcken, *Apologeten*, 318.

[3] Geffcken, *Apologeten*, 318: '... diese gedankentiefste Apologie, die wir seit Tertullian kennen ...'; 321: '... den Gipfelpunkt der römischen Apologetik ...'; etc.

[4] For example, the Maurini, in the preface to their edition of *DCD*, as the first of the polemic writings against the pagans, strongly stressed its apologetic character; see *MPL* 51, 9-10. This was also done by Biegler, *Civitas Dei*, but in addition he stated that the second part is a 'polemisch-dogmatische Darstellung der civitas terrena und coelestis' (59; cf. esp. 8-9: 'Die Apologie geht dadurch in eine Dogmatik über', because the 'Gottesstaat' is pointed out to the pagans). Van Goens, *Apologeta*, paid special attention to *DCD* as an apology. He considered the work to be the finishing point and climax of early-Christian apologetic tradition (1-16). In his view the second part is above all an apology also: 'veri Dei cultus defensio' (54-84).

[5] Harnack, *Lehrbuch*, III, for example 124 n.; Loofs, *Leitfaden*, 331.

[6] Altaner and Stuiber, *Patrologie*, 424: 'Es enthält die wertvollste altchristliche, historisch angelegte Apologie des Christentums ...'.

and the descriptions of church history by Bakhuizen van den Brink and Kawerau[7].

Those who have devoted special attention to Augustine's *City of God* have also generally emphasized its apologetic intention. Thus Schröder described the work in the introduction to his translation as 'die grossartige Apologie des Reiches Gottes'[8], Scholz said time and again that it is primarily and originally an apology[9], and Troeltsch called it 'die letzte grosse Leistung der apologetischen Literatur[10].

A similar evaluation is to be found in other studies. J.N. Figgis referred to it as 'a «livre de circonstance» concerned with apologetic'[11]. F.G. Sihler, who devoted a separate chapter to the *City of God*, called the entire work 'a body of apologetics'[12]. Noordmans saw it as 'a Christian plea', 'an apology against paganism'[13]. Von Campenhausen spoke of 'die letzte, grösste Apologie des christlichen Altertums'[14]. Stakemeier noted throughout his study above all the apologetic intention of Augustine's great work[15]. González[16], Domínguez del Val[17], Álvarez Díez[18] and others shared these views.

In more recent publications we find the same opinion. Referring

---

[7] Bakhuizen van den Brink, *Handboek*, I, 265: 'It is first of all an apology ...'; P. Kawerau, *Geschichte der Alten Kirche*, Marburg 1967, 113-115: '... eine grosse Apologie des Christentums ...'; '... er wollte Apologie treiben ...'; De Jong, *Geschiedenis*, 75: 'Augustine wrote an apology ...'.

[8] Schröder, *Gottesstaat*, LX. See also J.N. Espenberger in his general introduction to A. in Schröder, *Gottesstaat*, IX.

[9] Scholz, *Glaube und Unglaube*, esp. IV: 'Es ergab sich, dass die Geschichtsphilosophie (...) durchaus nur Mittel zur vollständigen Grundlegung der Apologetik gewesen ist; mit andern Worten: dass die libri de civitate Dei zuerst und ursprünglich als eine Apologie des Christentums, und zwar als die letzte und grösste Apologie desselben in der alten Kirche zu würdigen sind'. Cf. esp. V and 9.

[10] Troeltsch, *Augustin*, 8. Cf., for instance, 14; 19 n. 1; 21.

[11] Figgis, *Political Aspects*, 3. Cf. esp. 5, 36, 47 and 48.

[12] F.G. Sihler, *From Augustus to Augustine* ...,, Cambridge 1923, 324.

[13] Noordmans, *Augustinus* (1933/1952[2]), *VW* 3, 57 and 73. Cf., for example, 78.

[14] Von Campenhausen, 'Fall von Rom' (1947), *Tradition und Leben*, 256. See also his *Lat. Kirchenväter*, 195-196 and 203. Cf., among others, O. Gigon, *Die antike Kultur und das Christentum*, Gütersloh 1966, 127-141, where he discusses *DCD* in the chapter entitled 'Die abschliessende Replik des Christentums'.

[15] Stakemeier, *Civitas Dei*, passim.

[16] González, 'Valor apologético', esp. 544: 'Toda la obra ... un gran tratado de Apologética'; 'En todas las páginas de la *Ciudad de Dios* palpita un fin apologético'.

[17] Domínguez del Val, 'Martirio', esp. 528: 'Tiene un carácter eminentemente apologético y es la mejor obra que de este género nos ha transmitido la antigüedad cristiana'.

[18] Álvarez Díez, 'Arquitectura', esp. 67-70.

to the accusations provoked by the fall of Rome, Knowles says: 'The *City of God* had its origin almost as an occasional essay . . .'[19]. Andresen calls *De civitate Dei* 'ein literarisches Dokument der altchristlichen Apologetik (. . .), Höhepunkt und Abschluss zugleich'[20]. Finally, to give only one more supporting reference, Eugene TeSelle investigates Augustine's strategy as an apologist, whereby the *City of God* is described as his pre-eminent apologetic work[21].

From just these few examples it may be clear that Augustine's great work has been continuously seen as an apology. This is the case in both earlier and more recent descriptions of early Christian apologetics. Some years ago Leslie William Barnard presented an excellent survey of the genre, concluding with the *City of God* as an apology[22]. Andresen also sketched the apologetics of the first centuries of the Christian era and considered Augustine's great work to be their culmination and conclusion[23]. Others before him had also given such a classification[24].

The *City of God* is an apology. This character of the work appears to be evident to everyone. In this context it is significant that in the survey of Augustine's works handed down by Possidius, the *City of God* is classified among the books *contra paganos* as the final one of a long series[25]. This fact would have even more significance if the *Indiculum* were not only dependent on a catalogue of Augustine's writings kept by the church father, but had come integrally from Augustine himself[26].

---

19 Knowles in Bettenson, *City of God*, XV; cf. XVI where special attention is given to 'defending'.

20 Andresen in Thimme, *Gottesstaat 1-10*, XVII.

21 E. TeSelle, *Augustine's Strategy as an Apologist*, Villanova 1974, e.g. 24: '... the last and greatest of his apologetic works, The City of God ...'.

22 L.W. Barnard, 'Apologetik I', *TRE* 3 (1978) 371-411, 406-408 on A.

23 C. Andresen, 'Apologetik II', *RGG* I (1957) 480-485, 482 on *DCD*. Cf. Andresen in Thimme, *Gottesstaat 1-10*, XVII and XXII ff., and particularly his introduction to Thimme, *Gottesstaat 11-22*, XVI ff.

24 E.g. L. Lemme, 'Apologetik, Apologie', *PRE*³ I (1896) 690; L. Maisonneuve, 'Apologétique III', *DThC* I^II (1931) 1535. It is remarkable that Bardy, 'Apologetik', *RAC* I (1950) 533-543, makes no mention of A. and his *DCD*. This is all the more striking as he does give attention to contemporaries of A., such as Jerome, Cyril of Alexandria and Theodoret of Cyrus.

25 See further p. 56.

26 Cf. F. Glorie, 'Das «zweite *Aenigma*» in Augustins *Opusculorum Indiculus* ...', *Corona Gratiarum. Miscellanea .. Eligio Dekkers ... oblata*, I, Brugge-'s-Gravenhage 1975, 289-309. He announces (289 n. 2) a study in which he intends to give further evidence that the survey (indiculus, indiculum?) which has come down to us was written by A. himself. This study has not (yet) appeared.

At any rate, the apologetic character of the *City of God* is also established through Augustine's description of it in his *Retractationes*[27], through the dedication to Marcellinus and through the questions from Volusianus and his circle[28]. Moreover, evidence for the apologetic character appears frequently in the work itself. Especially in the first part (Books I – X) the views of the pagans are refuted. But also in the second part (Books XI – XXII) many passages are suffused with apologetics. There is, for example, the powerful polemic in Book XII against the pagan view of history as a circular course, the recurring defence of the resurrection, and the strongly apologetic character of Book XIX in its discussion of the supreme good. Moreover, when opposing the doctrines of the chiliasts or the views of Origen, Augustine feels called upon, especially in Books XX and XXI, to defend his own views. And time and again there is his polemic against the Manichaeans, sometimes without their name being stated explicitly[29].

2. *Apology as polemics and thetic exposition*

From the foregoing it is evident that the *City of God* has always been seen as an apologetic work. It is necessary, however, to analyse this qualification. For what is an apology? It is a polemic work in which the view of the opponent is refuted, while at the same time the positive exposition of the apologist's point of view plays an important part. Geffcken showed that this was already the case with Jewish apologists like Philo and Josephus. In addition to polemics there was an exposition of the author's own views, which was intended to have a persuasive appeal to outsiders[30].

The Christian apologists, in this respect also, appear to have followed in the steps of their Jewish predecessors[31]. The apology by Aristides, for example, consists of a polemic part, aimed at the three 'races' of barbarians, Greeks and Jews (1-14), and then a mainly

---

27 *Retract.* II, 43.

28 See esp. pp. 57-62.

29 E.g. *DCD* I, 20; X, 24; XI, 10. 13 and 22 (quidam haeretici); XIV, 21 (alii).

30 Geffcken, *Apologeten*, esp. XXIV-XXXI.

31 And not just of those named. For instance, Philo passed on examples that were used by Jewish writers before him; see Geffcken, *Apologeten*, esp. XXVII, with reference to P. Wendland's view. And we need not limit ourselves to Jewish examples in this context: Socrates' apology for the people of Athens was meant to demonstrate the reasonableness of his own point of view.

thetic exposition of the doctrine and life of the fourth 'race', the Christians (15-17). This dual aim is notable in the writings of others, too. It can be found in Athanasius' *Against the Heathens* and *On the Incarnation of the Word*, originally one apologetic work[32]. It is present in Lactantius' *Divine Institutes*, the first three books of which are aimed at the pagans, and the next four mainly describe the Christian religion[33].

Yet other examples are available which illustrate how in early-Christian apologies the thetic exposition of one's own belief is placed alongside the refutation of the views of the opponents or even largely replaces it. Many of the apologies that have come down to us had the specific purpose of winning over pagans to the Christian faith. This missionary purpose preponderates clearly in, for example, the anonymous *Letter to Diognetus* and in the *Exhortation to the Greeks* by Clement of Alexandria[34]. In other works there is a close connection between defence and dogmatics. Thus the early-Christian apology is also the first Christian theology.

In the light of these facts, how is the *City of God* to be viewed? It is fully justified to characterize Augustine's work as an apology. Over and over again in these books it is apparent that the assertions of the opponents are refuted in a polemic way. The author frequently states this intention explicitly[35]. But at the same time he offers a thetic exposition. The city of God is defended against the pagans, but it is also proclaimed. This second aspect of the last great apology of the Early Church requires special attention.

---

32 Not only from the content do we know this. Jerome, *De vir. ill.* 87, mentioned it under the single title *Adversus gentes duo libri*.

33 See further pp. 290-291.

34 Cf. J. Daniélou, *Gospel Message and Hellenistic Culture*, London-Philadelphia 1973, 7-15: 'The Missionary Purpose of the Apologists'.

35 E.g. *DCD* I, 36: 'Sed adhuc mihi quaedam dicendi sunt *adversus* eos ...'; 'Postremo *adversus* eos dicitur ...'; 'Quae, nisi fallor, quaestio multo erit operiosior et subtiliore *disputatione* dignior, ut et *contra* philosophos in ea disseratur ...'; IV, 2: 'Promiseramus ergo quaedam nos esse dicturos *adversus* eos qui ...'; VI, *praef.*: 'Quinque superioribus libris satis mihi *adversus* eos videor *disputasse*...'; VI, 1: 'Nunc ergo (...) etiam hi *refellendi* et docendi sunt ...'; X, 32: '... in decem libris istis (...) satisfecimus *refutando* contradictionibus impiorum ...'; 'Quorum decem librorum quinque superiores *adversus* eos conscripti sunt ...; quinque autem posteriores *adversus* eos ...'; XVIII, 1: '... cum prius inimicos civitatis Dei (...) *refellissem*, quod voluminibus decem prioribis feci'.

B. The 'City of God' as a thetic exposition

1. *The thetic character of the 'City of God'*

Until now little attention has been given to the *City of God* as a thetic exposition. Of course many scholars have seen that, generally speaking, the character of the second part is different from that of the first. But even then the emphasis has usually been put on the apologetic-polemic nature of the work as a whole.

Yet some scholars have pointed in another direction. Karsten, for example, asserted that the *City of God* 'in the second and even more important place is meant to be a comprehensive *exposition* of the Christian doctrine (...) against pagan polytheism ...'[36]. Like Scholz[37], he distinguished two parts in Augustine's work, a polemic and a thetic one, but for him the main emphasis was obviously on the positive exposition.

The same view can be found among other scholars. Thus Welldon stated, in the introduction to his edition of *De civitate Dei*: 'It was Augustine's object in the Civitas Dei not only to condemn paganism as a religion, but to support, if not indeed to explain, Christianity'[38]. Von Campenhausen stressed that Augustine wrote his book not only for the Christians, but also—positively—for the pagans[39]. Duchrow also advances the idea that the second part, following the refutation of the pagan polemics in the first ten books, gives a thetic exposition of the nature and the history of the two cities[40]. And Guy in particular emphasizes that in the *City of God* refuting paganism and propounding the Christian religion are closely connected[41].

This matter deserves special examination. Augustine's aim in

---

[36] Karsten, *Godsrijk*, 3.

[37] Scholz, *Glaube und Unglaube*, esp. 12.

[38] J.E.C. Welldon, *S. Aurelii Augustini De Civitate Dei* ..., London 1924, 32. Cf. 22: 'It was his object to destroy the pagan religion, that he might *establish the religion of Jesus Christ*'.

[39] Von Campenhausen, 'Fall von Rom', *Tradition und Leben*, esp. 258-259: 'So wird «De civitate Dei» eine Schrift für die Christen wie für die Heiden. Sie unternimmt im Rahmen einer Apologie zugleich eine Neubegründung des christlichen Glaubens selbst in der Entfaltung einer konkreten, die aktuellen Sorgen und Nöte nennenden Theodizee'. Cf. Von Campenhausen, *Lat. Kirchenväter*, 196: 'Es geht also—im Rahmen der Apologie—um die Deutung und Begründung des christlichen Glaubens selbst ...'.

[40] Duchrow, *Christenheit*, 249.

[41] Guy, *Unité*, esp. 12 ff.

writing his apology was twofold: *refutatio* and *probatio*. He refuted the view of the pagan opponents, but in equal measure he gave a thetic exposition. To whom and for what reason? It was the author's aim to offer consolation to his fellow believers and to provide them with an answer[42]. Therefore the essence of the Christian faith was set forth in great detail. How did God act formerly, how does He act now and what will this lead to? The history of salvation is explained to inquiring fellow believers like Marcellinus.

However, there were also people like Volusianus. Like many Christians, they were deeply shocked by the occurrences that had been taking place. According to these pagans Christianity was to be held responsible. In an incisive apologetic-polemic argumentation Augustine refutes this allegation: Rome and the Empire were by no means better off under the patronage of the ancient gods. But in addition to this he has another goal. In an argument intended to win over pagans he undertakes to expound the Christian religion[43]. He wants to show the pagans that Christianity is the only and the universal way to salvation[44]. He makes a direct appeal to them to repent[45].

The extent to which this thetic, persuading element is important to Augustine is also made clear by his comments on the *City of God* in his other writings. For example in his *Retractations* he states:

Sed ne quisquam nos aliena tantum redarguisse, non autem nostra asseruisse reprehenderet, id agit pars altera operis huius, quae libris duodecim continetur. Quanquam ubi opus est, et in prioribus decem quae nostra sunt asser-	But lest someone reproach us that we have only refuted the views of others but not have expounded our own, the second part of this work, consisting of twelve books, is concerned with these, although we also expound our own

[42] *DCD* I, 16: 'Nec tantum hic curamus alienis responsionem reddere, quantum ipsis nostris consolationem'; I, 35: 'Haec et talia (...) respondeat inimicis suis redempta familia Christi et peregrina civitas regis Christi'. Cf., for example, I, 29 and II, 2.

[43] E.g. *DCD* I, 36: '... ut ... asseramus civitatem Dei veramque pietatem et Dei cultum, in quo uno veraciter sempiterna beatitudo promittitur'.

[44] *DCD* X, 22: 'Haec est religio, quae universalem continet viam animae liberandae, quoniam nulla nisi hac liberari potest'. Cf. esp. the argument of Book XIX and of Book XXII, 27 and 28.

[45] E.g. *DCD* I, 34: 'Et tamen quod vivitis Dei est, qui vobis parcendo admonet, ut corrigamini paenitendo ...' and the *cohortatio* in II, 29: 'Incomparabiliter superna est civitas clarior, ubi victoria veritas, ubi dignitas sanctitas, ubi pax felicitas, ubi vita aeternitas. (...) Proinde si ad beatam pervenire desideras civitatem, devita daemonum societatem'.

amus, et in duodecim posterioribus redarguamus adversa[46].	views in the first ten, where this is necessary, and refute opposing views in the subsequent twelve[46].

This positive intention is no less clear in a letter to two monks, Petrus and Abraham. It dates from the time when Augustine, as he reports, is working on the fourteenth book of the *City of God*. Consequently it must have been written in 418 or shortly thereafter. First he explains the object of the first five books, then that of the next five: they are refutations and are antithetical in character[47]. Then Augustine continues:

Caeteri ab undecimo quot esse potuerint, quorum iam tres absolvi, quartum in manibus habeo, ea quae nos de civitate Dei tenemus et credimus, continebunt; ne aliena tantummodo refutare, non etiam nostra in hoc opere asserere voluisse videamur[48].	The remaining books—however many there will be after the eleventh, of which three have already been completed, I am engaged on the fourth—will contain what we think and believe concerning the city of God, lest we create the impression of only wishing to reject the views of others without expounding our own as well in this work[48].

2. The letters to Firmus

The thetic character of the *City of God* appears most clearly in two letters to a certain Firmus. The first one became known in 1939 and has since then played an important role in the discussions on the classification and contents of Augustine's work. The second was discovered much later and published in 1981. This letter in particular contains data that illuminate the essence and the intention of the *City of God* in a unique way.

But let us first look at the contents of the first letter. It was published in 1939 by Cyrille Lambot after he had found it accompanying two manuscripts of *De civitate*, one from Reims (Reims 403) and the other from Paris (Paris Sainte Geneviève 2757)[49]. In it Augustine informs Firmus, to whom he has sent the twenty-two books of the *City of God*, about the division that he must make when copying and assembling the work. This compilation can scarcely be done in one volume, for the entire work is too voluminous. If it is to be

46 *Retract.* II, 43.

47 *Ep.* 184A, 5: '... redarguunt ...'; '... contra illos sunt ...'; '... refelluntur ...'.

48 *Ep.* 184A, 5.

49 Lambot, 'Lettre inédite', 109. For available text-editions of the letter, see p. 76 n. 324. The quotations here are from J. Divjak's edition of the two letters in *CSEL* 88; see below, n. 54.

assembled in two volumes, one must contain ten books and the other twelve. For in the first ten the vanities of the wicked are refuted (vanitates refutatae sunt impiorum), while in the remaining twelve our religion is expounded and defended (demonstrata atque defensa est nostra religio). Immediately following this Augustine states that in the first volume, too, there is a positive exposition, and in the second the views of the opponents are refuted. But the main parts are designated as *refutatio* of the pagans on the one hand, and *demonstratio* and *defensio* of his own religion on the other.

This is also indicated in the next part of the letter, where another possible division is discussed. In the first two groups of five books, issue is taken with those (adversus eos est disputatum) who worship the gods either for this temporal life or for life after death. The following three groups of four books explain (ostenderent) the origin, the progress and the destination of the two cities.

This is another clear indication of the polemic and thetic character of the *City of God*. But to whom is Augustine addressing himself in this letter? Lambot and, in his footsteps, Marrou and Bardy have taken the Firmus mentioned in the heading to be the same as the presbyter Firmus[50]. He is named various times in Augustine's correspondence and often served as his letter bearer[51]. He would then have also been, as can be inferred from the letter under discussion, the one who was responsible for the publication in Carthage of the *City of God*: the presbyter Firmus as Augustine's 'agent littéraire' at Carthage[52].

But was the Firmus of the letter discovered by Lambot—which will henceforth be referred to as *Epistola ad Firmum*—the same as the presbyter of that name? Closer study reveals that there is no justification for this assumption. Nowhere in this letter is there any indication that this Firmus held ecclesiastical office. Nor even that he was a baptized Christian, for the form of address generally used by Augustine in that circumstance, *frater*, is lacking[53]. Firmus was obviously neither a presbyter nor a baptized Christian.

Who this Firmus really was is clear from one of the letters recently

---

50 Lambot, 'Lettre inédite', 113-114; Marrou, 'La technique de l'édition à l'époque patristique' (1949), in: Marrou, *Patristique et Humanisme*, 247; Marrou, 'Division', *Patristique et Humanisme*, 255; Bardy, *BA* 33, 33 and 767.

51 *Epp.* 81; 82; 172; 184A; 191; 194; 200; 248.

52 Marrou, 'Technique', 247 and 249; Marrou, 'Division', 255; Bardy, *BA* 33, 33 and 767.

53 J. Divjak, 'Augustins erster Brief an Firmus und die revidierte Ausgabe der Civitas Dei', *Latinität und Alte Kirche. Festschrift für Rudolf Hanslik* ..., Wien-Köln-Graz 1977, 56-70, esp. 62-65 for the customary terms of address.

discovered and published by Johannes Divjak[54]. This letter—to be referred to as *Ep.* 2*—is closely related to the first and addressed to the same Firmus. While it appears from the first letter that Augustine had sent him the books on the city of God at his request[55] and that he had given him permission to hand them on to other people for copying[56], from the second letter we learn the reason why Augustine had handed his work to Firmus. The *City of God* was to persuade the doubting Firmus to take the final step to Christianity.

This information deserves special attention. In an unexpected way it points out an essential quality of Augustine's writing. By reading the *City of God* Firmus was to be stimulated 'to enter the city of God'. Here Augustine's work was unmistakably intended as *demonstratio*, proof of the truth of Christianity. The doubting Firmus, catechumen indeed but still not baptized, was to receive further instruction through reading the *City of God*.

A short account of the contents of the newly discovered letter may demonstrate this. Augustine wrote to Firmus that he had sent him the twenty-two books and that Firmus had replied in a letter about the first ten. But had he also read the remaining twelve? Or had he not reached that point because he had handed them all to friends for copying? Augustine wished to have a reaction on the final twelve as well[57]. When Firmus, in his letters[58], advanced arguments for not receiving the sacrament of rebirth—and consequently becoming a Christian definitively by means of baptism—he was refusing the fruit of the *City of God*[59]:

Neque enim ille fructus est eorum, quod delectant legentem, nec ille, quod multa faciunt scire nescientem, sed ille, quod civitatem dei persuadent vel incunctanter intrandam vel perseveran-	For the fruit of those books is not that they please the reader, nor that they teach the ignorant much, but that they persuade people that they should either enter the city of God without delay or

[54] *Sancti Aureli Augustini Opera. Epistolae ex duobus codicibus nuper in lucem prolatae*, rec. Johannes Divjak, Vindobonae 1981 (*CSEL* 88). See also *Les lettres de saint Augustin découvertes par Johannes Divjak. Communications présentées au colloque des 20 et 21 Septembre 1982*, Paris 1983. It contains a number of mostly plausible text emendations for *Ep.* 2* suggested by R. Braun (33-34) and particularly by A. Primmer (46-57).

[55] *Ep. ad Firmum*, 1: 'Libros de civitate dei quos a me studiosissime flagitasti (...) misi; *Ep. ad Firmum*, 2: 'Si ut fuisti diligens ad habendos hos libros ...'.

[56] *Ep. ad Firmum*, 2.

[57] *Ep.* 2*, 2: '... de duodecim posterioribus libris redde quod debes!'

[58] There were a number of them, for in *Ep.* 2* Augustine speaks of three earlier ones.

[59] *Ep.* 2*, 3: 'Nam quod in alia tua epistola te ab accipiendo sacramento regenerationis excusas, totum tot librorum quos amas fructum recusas'.

tur habitandam; quorum duorum primum regeneratione, secundum iustitiae dilectione confertur, haec in eis a quibus leguntur atque laudantur si non agunt, quid agunt? horum igitur quantum ad te ipsum attinet, quando nec illud quod prius est in te agere potuerunt, quamtumlibet eos praedices, nihil adhuc egerunt[60].

inhabit it with perseverance. The first of these comes about through rebirth, the second through love of justice. If the books do not have this effect on those by whom they are read and praised, what is their effect? Therefore, as far as you are concerned, if they have been unable to bring about in you that first effect, even though you may praise them highly, they have not yet brought about anything[60].

The letter continues with an urgent summons to Firmus Cunctator 'to enter the city of God', as his wife had done earlier[61]. Now he is still a catechumen, but through reading the books that have been sent to him he knows more about the Christian religion than his wife does[62]. Knowledge alone is not sufficient, however: the mysteries of rebirth surpass it[63]. Firmus is urged repeatedly to receive that rebirth through baptism[64].

The positive manner of expounding and, through this, the persuading character of the *City of God* is firmly corroborated by the newly discovered letter to Firmus. From this second letter also the first can be understood more clearly. There Augustine wrote that Firmus would see from his own experience how much the books on the city of God would help him[65]. This help can only mean that through the reading of the *City of God* Firmus' last doubts would vanish. This help also applied to the friends to whom Firmus could hand the work as he saw fit:

... amicis vero tuis, sive in populo christiano se desiderent instrui, sive qualibet superstitione teneantur, unde videbuntur posse per hunc laborem nostrum dei

... but you will have to see for yourself how to put them at your friends' disposal, should they either desire to receive instruction in the midst of the

60 *Ep.* 2*, 3.

61 *Ep.* 2*, 4: '... cum exemplo feminae civitatem dei te exhortor intrare'.

62 *Ep.* 2*, 4: 'Nam credo, quod etiam quamquam fideli catechumenus insinues tamen aliqua ad religionem pertinentia quae legisti et ipsa non legit'.

63 *Ep.* 2*, 4: 'Mysteria quippe regenerationis recte atque ordinate non nisi accipientibus innotescunt; ita cum tu doctrina reperiaris instructior, sacramento est illa securior'. Cf. *Ep.* 2*, 5: 'Quid prodest autem scientia etiam ipsius summi boni, si non accipitur quo solo evaditur quidquid est mali?'

64 See *Ep.* 2*, 3 and 4, and esp. *Ep.* 2*, 7: '... et suscipiendam regenerationis gratiam sine dilatione committas' and *Ep.* 2*, 11: 'Ad hanc regenerationem suscipiendam cum te exhortor ...'.

65 *Ep. ad Firmum*, 2: '... quantum adiuvent experimento potius tuo quam mea promissione cognosces'.

gratia liberari, quomodo impertias ipse videris[66].	Christian people, or be held in the possession of some superstition or other from which they can be delivered, it would seem, by the grace of God, through this work of ours[66].

Firmus was to pass on the books of the *City of God* to the Christians of Carthage, in so far as they did not yet have them, for copying. Augustine referred to this group separately as 'our brethren'[67]. In addition, he distinguished Firmus' friends as consisting on the one hand of people who wanted to be instructed[68] in Christianity—catechumens, like Firmus?—and on the other of friends who (still) lived in *superstitio*. The latter might have been pagans, but also Jews or heretics.

In any case it is clear that the *City of God* was intended for both groups, Christians and non-Christians. For the latter in particular, as for Firmus, the work had a thetic character. The *City of God* served not only as a polemic *refutatio*, but also as a *demonstratio*, proof of the truth of Christianity. For Augustine wanted to instruct, too. It is especially this fact that we now will examine from within the structure of the work itself.

C. The 'City of God' as a catechetical work

On the preceding pages we have seen that Augustine sent his complete *City of God* to a catechumen who was hesitating to take the final step towards Christianity. Firmus was to be persuaded by this writing. A letter to this catechumen precedes the text of the *City of God* in some manuscripts[69].

Of course the letter to Firmus was placed here because it contains Augustine's advice concerning the arrangement he wanted for his

---

66 *Ep. ad Firmum*, 2.

67 *Ep. ad Firmum*, 2: 'Quos tamen nostri fratres ibi apud Carthaginem ad hoc opus pertinentes quod est de civitate dei nondum habent, rogo ut petentibus ad describendum dignanter libenterque concedas'.

68 *Instruere* is used in *De cat. rud.* 3. 24. 51 et al. for catechetical instruction. Elsewhere, as in the *En. in Ps.*, it also means: to instruct in the Christian doctrine (besides 'to edify', 'to build up in faith'). *Ep.* 137, 1 offers an important parallel for the use of *instruere* in *Ep. ad Firmum*: the pagan Volusianus should be instructed in the Christian religion (doctrina instrui christiana).

69 This is the case in the earlier-mentioned manuscripts from Reims and Paris (Ste. Geneviève). In two more manuscripts this letter and *DCD* are connected directly. Cf. Divjak, 'Augustins erster Brief', 68.

comprehensive work. Another important reason may be that originally a *breviculus* accompanied this letter to clarify its contents[70]. But besides these reasons, is it not also significant that this very letter, accompanied by a summary of the contents of the *City of God*, was sent to a person who was evidently in need of further instruction? Is the work not only an apology in which the thetic element occupies an important place, but can the *City of God* not be characterized as a catechetical work as well?

Important reasons can be put forward for this view. We will discuss them separately. First, however, a few remarks should be made about the early-Christian catechesis in general and about what is known of Augustine's introductory catechesis in particular. For when the *City of God* is characterized as a catechetical work, it should be clear that we are dealing with a very special catechesis, viz. the instruction of 'novices', 'newcomers' (rudes) who want to receive an introduction into the Christian faith. We are not speaking about a dogmatic catechesis in which the essential parts of the Christian faith are expounded—mostly on the basis of the ancient credal confessions, later developed into the well-known Creeds. Nor about a mystagogic catechesis in which the meanings of the sacraments of baptism and eucharist are taught[71]. When the *City of God* is described as a catechetical work, it is especially in view of its affinity to the instruction of those who are receiving a first introduction into the elements of Christianity. The best-known work of this kind is Augustine's *De catechizandis rudibus*.

1. The introductory catechesis according to 'The Catechizing of the Uninstructed'

Augustine's *The Catechizing of the Uninstructed* is the only piece of writing that gives detailed information on early-Christian instruction to

---

[70] *Ep. ad Firmum*, 3 (in fine): 'Quantum autem collegerit viginti duorum librorum conscriptio missus breviculus indicabit'. For more on this *breviculus*, see p. 63.

[71] To a considerable degree the history of patristic catechesis and catechumenate has still to be written. Many aspects of it have been insufficiently studied. Of the earlier works we consulted in particular Mayer, *Katechumenat* (1868); A.G. Weiss, *Die altkirchliche Pädagogik dargestellt in Katechumenat und Katechese der ersten sechs Jahrhunderte*, Freiburg 1869; H.J. Holtzmann, 'Die Katechese der alten Kirche', in: *Theologische Abhandlungen Carl von Weizsäcker (...) gewidmet*, Freiburg 1892, 61-110; B. Capelle, 'L'introduction du catéchuménat à Rome', *RTAM* 5 (1933) 129-154; H. Leclercq, 'Catéchèse-Catéchisme-Catéchumène', *DACL* 2

future catechumens. Circa 400[72] the Carthaginian deacon Deogratias asked Augustine how to instruct people who want to become Christians. The bishop gave his answer in the form of a magnificent treatise. It describes the possibilities and difficulties of this specific instruction and concludes with two model catecheses. Through this piece of writing, impressive in its theology and didactic approach, Augustine became the catechetical guide for centuries: from Cassiodorus, Isidore of Seville, Bede and others down to the so-called Munich method in the twentieth century[73].

In *The Catechizing of the Uninstructed*[74] the procedure of the first instruction is set out. A *rudis*[75], a person who wants to receive instruction in the first principles of the Christian faith, presents himself. Coming from paganism or perhaps from a sect or from the Jewish

---

(1935) 2530-2579; De Puniet, 'Catéchuménat' (1935).—For the classification into dogmatical, ethical and mystagogical catecheses, see esp. J. Daniélou – R. du Charlat, *La catéchèse aux premiers siècles*, Paris 1968. This classification is clearest in the 4th cent. (Cyril of Jerusalem, Theodore of Mopsuestia, John Chrysostom, Ambrose, et al.). A. Turck, *Evangélisation et Catéchèse aux deux premiers siècles*, Paris 1962, deals with earlier centuries. Valuable material has also been collected by him in two articles: 'Catéchein et Catéchèsis chez les premiers Pères', *RSPT* 47 (1963) 361-372 and 'Aux origines du catéchuménat', *RSPT* 48 (1964) 20-31.

72 The question of the exact date of composition of *De cat. rud.* has been discussed rather extensively. The date generally given in the past was 399 or 400 (by, among others, the Maurini, Loofs, Marrou, Sciacca, Hendrikx, Cayré and Van Steenberghen, Sizoo; see the references in L.J. van der Lof, 'The Date of the De catechizandis rudibus', *VC* 16 (1962) 198-204). E.g. Combès and Farges (*BA* 11, 10) and also Christopher (*Cat. Instruction*, 5) supply arguments in favour of 405. Van der Lof, on the other hand, argues for the traditional date.—This is not the occasion for an in-depth discussion on the matter. It is not essential for this inquiry to know whether the work was composed in 399, 400 or 405. We only observe in passing that the arguments offered by Van der Lof on the basis of the various anti-Manichaean statements in *De cat. rud.* are not convincing, for in the years following 399/400 A. continued to engage in polemics with his former co-religionists. Dating the work after 400 might be advocated particularly on the grounds that in the *Retract.* the chronological order is respected as much as possible and that the debate with Felix was most probably held on the 7th and the 12th of Dec. 404 (cf. M. Jourjon, *BA* 17, 11 and 787-788). And the *Retract.* place *De cat. rud.* after *C. Fel.*; see *Retract.* II, 8 and II, 14 resp.—O. Wermelinger argues also in favour of a 'Spätdatierung', esp. with reference to *De cons. ev.* 3, 71; see his 'Erläuterungen' in: W. Steinmann – O. Wermelinger, *Aurelius Augustinus. Vom ersten katechetischen Unterricht*, München 1985, 101-102.

73 Christopher, *Cat. Instruction*, 8-10; Combès and Farges, *BA* 11, 11-12.

74 Most recent translations, with important elucidations: G. Wijdeveld: *Aurelius Augustinus, Het eerste geloofsonderricht*, Baarn 1982; W. Steinmann – O. Wermelinger (see n. 72).

75 For this term cf. Cyprian, *Ep.* 70, 2: '... qui ad ecclesiam rudis venit ...'; Ambrose, *Exp. Ps. CXVIII* 18, 26: '... rudis adhuc in fide ...'.

community, he desires to become a Christian. To that end the candidate, often accompanied by witnesses, has come to the Church's catechist. The latter asks him to give his motives. If these motives—and his conduct—appear to be honest, an exposition of the essentials of the Christian faith follows. The responsibilities one takes upon oneself as a Christian are also named. Next comes the question of whether the candidate concurs with the commitments of faith and will observe its requirements. If the answer is in the affirmative, he can be accepted as a catechumen. After an exorcism his forehead is marked with the sign of the cross; this is accompanied by a laying on of hands and the administration of consecrated salt.

From then on the candidate is considered a catechumen and thus bearer of the name Christian. The catechumenate usually lasts two or three years. In this trial period the catechumen receives additional instruction in the truths of the Christian faith and conducts himself as a Christian. As a catechumen he is admitted to the first part of the church service with its prayers, Scripture readings and sermon(s). After his trial period the catechumen applies for baptism—to that end he gives his name to the bishop, the *nomen dare*—and then a time of intensive catechesis follows. For six weeks the candidates for baptism (competentes) are prepared for the receiving of this sacrament and after that, too, the 'newly born' (neophyti; also: infantes, children) receive separate instruction.

Augustine, as he tells Deogratias, usually begins his instruction by asking the candidate why he desires to become a Christian. What is his inner condition and what motives have led him to take this step? This must all be reported by those who know the newcomer or by the candidate himself. The answer can serve as the point of departure. Even if a person has come with a hypocritical heart, through a desire for personal advantage or to escape from disadvantages, this can still serve as a point of departure[76].

The candidate may possibly relate that he was induced to become a Christian by a divine exhortation. That, too, offers a very welcome beginning to the discourse: God's great care for us. But after that the attention of the one addressed should be diverted from those miraculous events or dreams to the firmer path, that of the Scriptures and their more reliable oracles[77].

---

[76] *De cat. rud.* 9.
[77] *De cat. rud.* 10.

After the motivation of the candidate has thus been ascertained, the *narratio* is given. This narrative must begin with the creation and continue until the present time, that of the Church. Not everything in the *narratio* is equally stressed: the main points are accentuated within a perspicuous survey. The more remarkable facts (mirabiliora) that constitute the cardinal points (articuli) of history must be emphasized[78]. It should be shown how God, who works in man's personal history, acts in the same way in the history of salvation. The focal point in both is God's mercy, the story of His love that arouses love in return. Christ occupies the central position, in both the Old and the New Testament, as foreshadowing and fulfilment[79].

After the chronicle of God's love has thus been narrated—'in such a way that he to whom you speak by hearing may believe, by believing may hope, by hoping may love'[80]—the *exhortatio* is given. This *exhortatio* forms the practical application of the *narratio*. Deogratias' question is not only *how* the story should be told, but whether it should be followed immediately by an exhortation. Or does it suffice to give the *praecepta*[81]?

Augustine states that after the *narratio* the hope for the resurrection should be presented. The resurrection of the body should not only be mentioned, but also defended against derision. There must also be an exposition on the Last Judgement. After the punishments of the wicked 'mention should be made, with yearning, of the kingdom (regnum) of the just and the faithful, and of the heavenly city (civitas) and her joy'[82]. The pupil must be given courage to face trials and vexations. Short and appropriate precepts are to be given for a Christian and upright conduct (christiana atque honesta conversatio). Augustine gives a list of sinners—like the one he gave at the end of the first model catechesis[83]—and warns against sham Christiani-

---

78 *De cat. rud.* 5; cf. *De cat. rud.* 10.

79 See esp. *De cat. rud.* 6-8.

80 *De cat. rud.* 8: '... quidquid narras ita narra, ut ille cui loqueris audiendo credat, credendo speret, sperando amet'.

81 *De cat. rud.* 1: '... unde exordienda quousque sit perducenda narratio; utrum exhortationem aliquam terminata narratione adhibere debeamus, an praecepta sola, quibus observandis cui loquimur noverit christianam vitam professionemque retineri'. Cf. *De cat. rud.* 4 (in fine). It is quite possible that by these precepts Deogratias understood the ethical instruction according to the scheme of the two ways; cf. Christopher, *Cat. Instruction*, 95 n. 10.

82 *De cat. rud.* 11.

83 *De cat. rud.* 48.

ty. In closing he tells Deogratias to point out to the future catechumen 'that he will find many good Christians in the Church, most true citizens (cives) of the heavenly Jerusalem, if he begins to be one himself'[84].

These, then, are the main points of Augustine's helpful instructions for the catechesis of the *rudes*. After giving Deogratias a few more valuable pedagogical and pastoral hints[85], Augustine offers two models. It is especially the first and more comprehensive of them that requires our attention now.

2. *The model catecheses*

After what has been said about Augustine's directives for the instruction of 'newcomers', the description of the first and rather detailed model catechesis[86]—in practice this catechesis must have lasted about two hours—can be limited to the main points.

Augustine envisages a situation in which an uneducated townsman is being addressed. First he must be asked, 'whether he desires to become a Christian for the sake of some advantage in the present life, or for the rest (requies) that he hopes to receive after this life'[87]. The answer is: for future rest.

Now the catechist discourses at length on the rest which people seek but do not find in this life. 'For they wish to find rest in things that are not quiet and enduring'[88]. In riches, for example, they do not find this rest. Everything in this life is transient. 'Therefore, he who desires true rest and true felicity must withdraw his hope from mortal and transient things and place it on the word of the Lord'[89]. Likewise, those who seek their pleasure and rest in public houses and brothels, in theatrical performances or spectacles, do not find it[90].

---

84 *De cat. rud.* 11.

85 *De cat. rud.* 12-15.

86 *De cat. rud.* 24-50.

87 *De cat. rud.* 24: '... interrogatum etiam utrum propter vitae praesentis aliquod commodum, an propter requiem quae post hanc vitam speratur, christianus esse desiderat ...'.

88 *De cat. rud.* 24: 'Volunt enim requiescere in rebus inquietis et non permanentibus ...'.

89 *De cat. rud.* 24: 'Ideo qui veram requiem et veram felicitatem desiderat, debet tollere spem suam de rebus mortalibus et praetereuntibus, et eam collocare in verbo Domini ...'.

90 *De cat. rud.* 25.

Nor do they find true rest who want to become Christians in order to ingratiate themselves with people from whom they expect temporal advantages (temporalia commoda), or because they do not want to offend those whom they fear. They are in fact reprobates, unless they mend their ways and become Christians for the eternal rest to come (propter futuram sempiternam requiem). There are others for whom there is reason to hope for something better, but who nevertheless expect to find their happiness (felicitas) in this life, because they want to be happier (feliciores) in earthly things than those who do not honour God. When they see the prosperity of the wicked, they become confused and easily abandon their faith[91].

The right reasons for becoming a Christian, however, are everlasting blessedness (sempiterna beatitudo) and perpetual rest (requies perpetua). That rest is to be found in God alone[92]. True rest was foreshadowed in the seventh day, on which God rested (requievit). God made it clear that after the six ages (aetates) of this world He will rest (requieturus est) in the seventh in His saints, because they will rest (requiescent) in Him after all the good works in which they have served Him. When they rest (requiescunt) in Him, it is rightly said that He Himself rests (ipse requiescere). For God seeks no period of repose (pausatio) for Himself, because He feels no fatigue. 'He has created everything by His Word and this Word is Christ Himself, in whom the angels and all the most pure heavenly spirits rest (requiescunt) in holy silence. Man, however, in that he fell by sin, has lost the repose (requies) which he had in His divinity, and receives it again in His humanity'[93].

After the introductory discourse the *narratio* proper is given. God created all things, and also man and woman[94]. They were set in paradise, a place of perpetual blessedness (beatitudo). If they did not transgress the commandment, they would remain in that blessedness (beatitudo) of immortality forever. But man fell, led astray unto death by the devil[95].

---

91 *De cat. rud.* 26.

92 *De cat. rud.* 27. Then A. quotes 1 *Cor.* 2: 9. A. also quotes this passage in *Conf.* IX, 10, 23, when he is talking with Monnica about the future eternal life of the saints: '... qualis futura esset vita aeterna sanctorum, quam nec oculus vidit nec auris audivit nec in cor hominis ascendit'.

93 *De cat. rud.* 28.

94 *De cat. rud.* 29.

95 *De cat. rud.* 30.

Many side with the devil, few follow God. 'Therefore there are two cities (civitates), one of the wicked, the other of the saints. They extend from the beginning of mankind until the end of the world. Now they are intermingled in body, but separated in will. But on the Day of Judgement they will also be separated in body. For all men who love pride and temporal power with empty vanity and pompous arrogance, and all spirits who love such things and seek their own glory by subjecting man are bound together in one fellowship (societas) (...). But on the other hand, all men and all spirits who humbly seek the glory of God and not their own, and who follow Him in piety, also belong to one fellowship (societas)'[96].

Then the Flood is discussed and the story of the righteous Noah and his family. The wooden ark prefigures the Church; by the mystery of the cross of Christ the ark is safeguarded against sinking into the waves of this world. But also after the Flood wickedness kept springing up profusely[97].

Yet there was no lack of righteous people, 'citizens of the holy city (civitas), who were made whole by the future humiliation of Christ, their King, which was revealed to them through the Spirit'. Abraham was chosen from among these people; through his example of faith he is the father of all believers. Of him was born the people which served the one true God. Although there were many among that people who worshipped God for the sake of visible benefactions, there were also the few who thought of the rest (requies) to come and sought the heavenly fatherland (patria coelestis). To them Christ's humiliation was revealed in a prophetic way[98].

The people lived in Egypt; Moses became their deliverer. The exodus took place through the Red Sea, a prefiguration of baptism. Here, too, the sacrament of the wood was present, for Moses struck the sea with a rod. The paschal lamb foreshadowed Christ's suffering. 'With the sign of His passion and cross you will be signed today on your forehead—your doorpost as it were—and so all Christians are signed'[99].

Then Israel was led through the desert for forty years. It received the law, written by the finger of God, the Holy Spirit[100]. The peo-

96 *De cat. rud.* 31.
97 *De cat. rud.* 32.
98 *De cat. rud.* 33.
99 *De cat. rud.* 34.
100 *De cat. rud.* 35.

ple was brought to the promised land, but it practised a temporal and carnal dominion there. 'Nevertheless, that earthly kingdom (regnum terrenum) bore the image of the spiritual kingdom (regnum spirituale). There Jerusalem was founded, the most illustrious city of God (civitas Dei); it was in bondage, but served as a type of the free city (civitas) which is called the heavenly Jerusalem (*Gal.* 4:25-26). This name is Hebrew and means «vision of peace» (visio pacis). Its citizens (cives) are all the sanctified people who have been, are and will be, and all sanctified spirits (...)'. The king (rex) of this city (civitas) is Jesus Christ. David was a prefiguration of this king. Many things happened in the promised land as a foreshadowing of Christ. From the sacred books the pupil will be able to learn this gradually[101].

'Several generations later God presented another prefiguration which was particularly striking. For that city (civitas) was taken into captivity and the majority of it was led away to Babylon. Just as Jerusalem signifies the city (civitas) and fellowship (societas) of the saints, so Babylon signifies the city (civitas) and fellowship (societas) of the wicked. For its name is said to mean «confusion». About these two cities (civitates), which are having their course intermingled throughout the changes of time from the beginning of mankind to the end of the world, and which will be separated on the Day of Judgement, we have already spoken a little earlier'[102]. Then Augustine points out that during the Captivity some Babylonian kings came to know the true God. The captives prayed for the kings of Babylon and their peace (pax). They begot children in Babylon, built houses there and laid out gardens and vineyards. They received the promise that their deliverance would come at the end of seventy years. 'All this signified in a figure that the Church of Christ, in all His saints, who are citizens of the heavenly Jerusalem, was to be in bondage under the kings of this world'. According to the teaching of the Apostle, every soul should be subject to higher powers and pay tribute (cf. *Rom.* 13:1 and 7). Christ Himself set the example: He paid taxes (cf. *Matt.* 17:24 ff). 'Still all are directed to be subject to human and earthly powers, until the day when, after the foreordained time—signified by the seventy years—the Church will be delivered from the confusion of this world, as was Jerusalem

---

101 *De cat. rud.* 36.
102 Cf. *De cat. rud.* 19.

from the Captivity of Babylon.' Paul admonishes that prayers should also be made for kings (1 *Tim.* 2:1-2), even if they were persecuting the Church. 'Therefore through these kings peace (pax) was given to the Church, albeit a temporal peace, a temporal tranquillity (tranquillitas) for the spiritual building of houses and planting of gardens and vineyards'[103].

After the Captivity they returned to Jerusalem and rebuilt the temple. But the Jews were not granted lasting peace (pax) and lasting freedom: they were subjected by the Romans. In none of their kings could they find the promise of the Christ fulfilled. That is why that promise was predicted more and more clearly in many prophecies[104].

Five ages of the world (aetates saeculi)[105] had now been completed: the first from Adam to Noah, the second from Noah to Abraham, the third from Abraham to David, the fourth from David to the Captivity, the fifth from the Captivity to the coming of Christ. Since then there has been the sixth age, in which spiritual grace (spiritualis gratia) had to be made known to all nations, 'that no one would worship God for material benefit, and no one would desire from Him visible rewards for his service, nor happiness (felicitas) in this present life, but only eternal life, in which to enjoy God Himself'. 'Thus in the sixth age man is renewed after God's image, just as he was created after God's image on the sixth day'[106].

Christ revealed the new covenant, 'in which man, renewed by the grace of God, might lead a new, that is a spiritual life'. He Himself despised all earthly goods (bona terrena) in order to show that they are to be despised. And He endured all earthly ills 'so that neither happiness (felicitas) should be sought in what is good, nor unhappiness (infelicitas) be feared in what is evil'. Then follows, in a few well-chosen words, a 'life of Jesus': conception, birth from the Virgin, life in humility and poverty, flogging, crucifixion, death, resurrection[107].

The resurrection was followed by the Ascension and the descent of the Holy Spirit. It is the finger of God which once wrote the Decalogue and which now gives the power to fulfil the law as it is

---

103 *De cat. rud.* 37.
104 *De cat. rud.* 38.
105 For the *aetates* cf. p. 94 ff.
106 *De cat. rud.* 39.
107 *De cat. rud.* 40.

summarized in two commandments (*Matt.* 22:37-40). Through the Holy Spirit miracles and signs occurred. The first Christians lived harmoniously in love; they had everything in common. They were persecuted, but because of this Christ has been proclaimed everywhere. From a persecutor Paul became an apostle. Severer persecutions followed, but the vine of the Church spread its branches throughout the world and grew through the blood of the martyrs. Barren branches caused heresies and schisms in various places[108].

After this *narratio* the *exhortatio* is given. All that had been prophesied has been fulfilled. Have faith that the things which yet remain will come to pass as well. The Scriptures tell of impending tribulations. They also tell of the Day of Judgement, 'when all the citizens of both these cities (civitates) will receive again their bodies, and rise, and give account of their lives before the judgement seat of Christ, the Judge'. He shall separate the pious from the wicked. To the pious He shall give the eternal kingdom (regnum), with Himself; to the wicked eternal punishment together with the devil[109].

So you must stand firm against the mockers, particularly against those who ridicule our belief in the resurrection. Is God's omnipotence not able to bring about the resurrection[110]? Flee the torments of hell by your unwavering faith and good conduct. 'Be on fire with love and longing for the everlasting life of the saints, where work shall not be wearisome, rest (requies) not slothful'. There God will be praised forever. 'God will be the whole delight and contentment of the holy city (civitas) living in Him and by Him, in wisdom and blessedness (beate)'. We shall be the equals of the angels of God[111].

Keep all this fixed in your heart. Be on your guard against the temptations of the devil. Beware of the pagans, the Jews, the false Christians. Those who keep the right way (via recta) are put to the test. There are many sinners (Augustine gives a catalogue, as he did in *De cat. rud.* 11). 'You will also notice that the same crowds fill the churches on the feast days of the Christians as fill the theatres on the festal days of the pagans'. But do not join them; 'observe the law of God'[112]. 'Associate with the good, whom you see loving your king (rex) with you. For you will find such people in large numbers if you

---

108 *De cat. rud.* 41-44.
109 *De cat. rud.* 45.
110 *De cat. rud.* 46.
111 *De cat. rud.* 47.
112 *De cat. rud.* 48.

yourself begin to be such a person'. You must not abandon your faith because of insults or temptations, nor stray from the right way (via bona)[113].

'After these things have been said the pupil must be asked whether he believes them and desires to observe them'. This is followed by the signing with the cross and the administration of the salt[114]. The pupil should be admonished that if he hears something in Scripture that has a carnal ring, he should believe that something spiritual is signified by it that is related to holy conduct and the life to come (vita futura). By 'neighbour' he should understand everyone who can be with him in the holy city (sancta civitas)[115].

If Deogratias finds this catechesis too long, he may tell things more briefly. To this end Augustine gives a second model[116]. Basically it is the same as the first. Again it is assumed that the one who has presented himself will be asked about his motives; his answer is the point of departure. While in the first model the theme was rest (requies), in this model it is 'the great and true blessedness' (magna et vera beatitudo) which is promised to the saints in the life to come[117].

A succinct presentation of the *narratio* is followed by the *exhortatio*. What had been prophesied about Christ and the Church has been fulfilled. The rest will also come to pass, 'all the tribulations of the righteous that still remain and also the Day of Judgement'. The resurrection of the body is mentioned and defended. The faithful shall reign with Christ; they shall become the equals of the angels of God. 'Then they will love Him without falling short and without any fatigue, ever living in Him and of Him, with such joy and blessedness (beatitudo) as can be neither expressed nor conceived by man'[118].

---

113 *De cat. rud.* 49.

114 The mss. give *sane*, but we should probably read—as the Benedictines do and the context suggests—*salis*. Christopher, *Cat. Instruction*, 146 n. 315, is incorrect when he asserts that it is only a matter of the administering of the salt. For the preceding sentence indicates clearly that more is involved: 'Quod cum responderit, solemniter utique signandus est et ecclesiae more tractandus'. In any case the signing with the cross is mentioned here, and probably an exorcism and a laying on of hands too.

115 *De cat. rud.* 50.

116 *De cat. rud.* 51-55.

117 *De cat. rud.* 52.

118 *De cat. rud.* 54.

3. *The structure of the model catecheses and of the 'City of God'*

On the basis of Augustine's guidelines for the instruction of future catechumens and in particular from their application in the first, more extensive catechetical model, we can summarize the structure of his catechesis as follows:

a. The questions of those who want to become Christians constitute the point of departure. They are seeking rest (requies), happiness (felicitas), blessedness (beatitudo)[119]. These are not to be found in this life (*De cat. rud.* 24-26);

b. True rest (requies), true happiness (felicitas), true blessedness (beatitudo) are only in God, in life after this life (*De cat. rud.* 27-28);

c. Then there is a survey of the *Heilsgeschichte*, divided into six ages and narrated as the history of the two cities: creation, paradise, the Fall, Noah and the Flood, Abraham, Moses and the exodus, the Law, Israel in the promised land, captivity, return, the prophets and the expectation of the Messiah, the coming of Christ, His life, death, resurrection and Ascension, Pentecost and the descent of the Holy Ghost, the growth of the Church, its life and suffering (*De cat. rud.* 29-44);

d. The *narratio* of the history of salvation—from the creation until now—is followed by the *exhortatio*. Just as all the prophecies have been fulfilled, so will the prophecies concerning the Day of Judgement, the resurrection, eternal punishment and eternal blessedness. Belief in the resurrection of the body is specifically named and defended; we shall be the equals of the angels of God. The tribulations of the righteous are also specifically named (*De cat. rud.* 45-49).

A comparison of the structure of the catechesis to the *rudes* with the structure of the *City of God* brings to light a striking similarity. We have already discussed how the latter work, although considerable in size and composed in the course of many years, has a clear, logical construction. Augustine is constantly aware of this, as is

[119] A. used these concepts in close connection with each other. The main theme of the first catechetical model is rest (requies), of the second beatitude (beatitudo). But the concept *beatitudo* also occurs in the first model (*De cat. rud.* 27 and 30) alongside of *felicitas* (*De cat. rud.* 26 and 39). For *beatitudo/beata vita* cf., among others, Marrou, *Augustin et la fin*, 174-186; R. Holte, *Béatitude et Sagesse. Saint Augustin et le problème de la fin de l'homme dans la philosophie ancienne*, Paris 1962, passim; A. Becker, *De l'instinct du bonheur à l'extase de la béatitude. Théologie et pédagogie du bonheur dans la prédication de Saint Augustin*, Paris 1967, passim. Short surveys are given by J. Gagé, 'Felicitas', *RAC* 7 (1969) 719-721 and R. Holte, 'Glück/Glückseligkeit', *RAC* 11 (1981) 264-268. See also M. Wacht, 'Güterlehre', *RAC* 13 (Lieferung 97, 1984), 138-145.

apparent from his frequent references in the *City of God* to the plan of the entire work or a large part of it. This awareness is also evident in his descriptions of this work, for example in the *Retractations*[120].

In the first place it can be seen that in the *City of God* Augustine takes his point of departure from the questions asked by those who are to be instructed, the same method as he uses in the model catecheses. Those to be instructed seek rest (requies), happiness (felicitas), blessedness (beatitudo). In the first, mainly apologetic-polemic part of the *City of God*, the author turns against those who seek rest, happiness, blessedness in *this* life and think that the gods have to be worshipped for the sake of these temporal matters (Books I-V). Then he turns against those who assert that one must worship the gods in order to obtain these goods in the afterlife. It is stated emphatically, especially in Books IX and X, that true blessedness (beatitudo vera) is in God. The true God must be worshipped, and the true sacrifice is that of the only mediator, Jesus Christ (VI-X).

The similarities with *The Catechizing of the Uninstructed* are evident: one should begin with the questions asked by those who are to receive instruction and show them above all that true rest, happiness and blessedness are not to be found in this life (24-26; cf. 51-52); then it should be explained that perpetual rest, true happiness and eternal blessedness are only to be found in God, in the life after this life (27-28; 52).

Equally noteworthy is the similarity between the next part of the catecheses in *The Catechizing of the Uninstructed* and the *City of God*. For both give an account of the *Heilsgeschichte*, divided into six ages and presented as the history of the two cities (*DCD* XI-XVIII; *De cat. rud.* 29-45; cf. 53).

Admittedly, the length of this exposition in the two works differs considerably. But the underlying principle is the same. According to Augustine the *narratio* can be brief and sometimes, if circumstances require it, very brief. It should, however, be complete[121]. And the narrative is complete when the *rudis* has been instructed in the *Heilsgeschichte* from the creation to the present time, the time of the Church[122]. Not everything needs to be brought up for discus-

---

120 See further p. 74-77.

121 *De cat. rud.* 4: '... nec quomodo sit varianda narratio, ut aliquando brevior, aliquando longior, semper tamen plena atque perfecta sit'.

122 *De cat. rud.* 5: 'Narratio plena est, cum quisque primo catechizatur ab eo quod scriptum est, «In principio fecit Deus coelum et terram» [*Gen.* 1:1], usque ad praesentia tempora ecclesiae'.

sion. What matters are the essentials, especially certain more remarkable facts (mirabiliora) which have to do with the cardinal points (articuli) of the history of salvation[123].

In this way, then, Augustine presents his survey in the catecheses. The narrative in each is complete (narratio plena), from creation to the present time. It is very brief in the second model, considerably longer in the first. In the first model the cardinal points of the *Heilsgeschichte* are presented clearly, and accordingly the narrative is divided into six ages[124]. At the same time the metaphor of the two cities is continually present[125].

According to this catechetical scheme and using the same metaphor of the two cities, Augustine gives his account of the history of salvation in the *City of God*. We may certainly refer to it as a *narratio plena*; it might even be better to call it a '*narratio plenissima*', for in great detail and with many digressions Augustine narrates the history of salvation. These digressions are often of a strongly polemic and apologetic nature and are focussed on the questions and objections of those to be instructed. But they do not prevent the narrator from taking up, each time, the thread of his story again. He gives an account of the history of salvation according to the scheme of the six ages: the narrative of creation, paradise and the Fall, the origin of the two cities (XI-XIV); then that of the Flood and of Noah's ark, a prefiguration of the city of God (XV); then the days of Noah, Abraham, Moses, the Exodus and the giving of the Law (XVI); after that the period of David and the other kings, the Captivity and the prophets (XVII); finally the return from Babylon, the prophetic expectation of the Messiah, the coming of Christ, the growth of the Church and its suffering (XVIII, 27-54).

It must be conceded that the scheme of the six ages is not always strictly followed. Nor is it in *The Catechizing of the Uninstructed*. In neither of the two works is it specifically stated that one after the other the ages are being brought up for discussion. But it is evident that in the *City of God*, as in the catecheses, the scheme of the six ages is constantly in the background. Only at the end of his extensive

[123] *De cat. rud.* 5: '... sed cuncta summatim generatimque complecti, ita ut eligantur quaedam mirabiliora quae suavius audiuntur, atque in ipsis articulis constituta sunt ...'.

[124] *De cat. rud.* 39. For the starting point and termination of the *aetates*, see p. 184.

[125] See esp. *De cat. rud.* 31. 36. 37 and 45.

work does Augustine refer to the division into six ages[126]. However, elements of this periodization are brought to the fore in other passages as well[127].

Yet another detail should receive attention. There is not only the similarity in the *narratio plena*, the full account from the creation to the present, divided into six ages and narrated as the history of the two cities Jerusalem and Babylon. Augustine also says in his catechetical advice that the narrative should be told in such a way 'that the causes and reasons are given of all the facts and events, so that we may relate them to that ultimate goal which is love'[128]. The catechist who wants to hand down the history of salvation in an effective and convincing way should not confine himself to enumerating facts and events, but should also look for their causes and reasons (causae rationesque). The philosophy—or rather, to follow Augustine's line, the theology—of history should be stressed. It is especially in the *City of God* that this principle has been developed.

The *narratio* is followed by the *exhortatio*, the practical application of the narrative. In the catecheses the following subjects are discussed: the Day of Judgement, the resurrection of the body, eternal punishment with the devil, eternal blessedness in the city of God. It is emphasized that this has all been foretold in the Scriptures. The resurrection in particular is defended against mockery. There are many tribulations (*De cat. rud.* 45-49; cf. 54 and 11).

The same contents and order occur in the final section of the *City of God*. In Book XIX Augustine discourses at length on true blessedness (beatitudo) and true peace (pax). He repeats the questions of those who are to be persuaded of the validity of Christian truth, making explicit references to *perfect* peace and *eternal* blessedness[129]. This is followed by expositions on the Day of Judgement and the resurrection (XX), on perpetual punishment (XXI) and, finally, on eternal blessedness in the city of God (XXII). It is pointed out that the Scriptures have foretold all this[130]. More than once the author

---

126 *DCD* XXII, 30.

127 *DCD* XVI, 24: '...insignes articuli temporum ab Adam usque ad Noe et inde usque ad Abraham et inde usque ad David ...'; cf. XVI, 43 and XXI, 16 where there is a combination with the division according to the six 'ages' of man's life. For the periodizations as they occur in *DCD* and other works of A., see further p. 94 ff.

128 *De cat. rud.* 10: '... ita ut singularum rerum atque gestorum quae narramus, causae rationesque reddantur, quibus ea referamus ad illum finem dilectionis ...'.

129 Cf. p. 146 ff.

130 See particularly the extensive evidence that *DCD* XX gives for the last

defends the resurrection against attacks by unbelievers and mockers[131]. The righteous suffer persecution and are put to the test[132].

4. Further considerations

From the preceding it can be concluded that the *City of God* and the two catechetical models in *The Catechizing of the Uninstructed* show a striking similarity in content and structure. Augustine's voluminous work is an apology, but it also has the essential characteristics of a catechesis.

It should be stated that previous scholars have already made a number of conjectures in this direction, but they have never investigated systematically the catechetical nature of the *City of God*. Heinrich Scholz, for example, remarked in passing that the division of the history of the world into six ages was very probably an already existing catechetical theme: its origin predates Augustine considerably[133]. Moreover, he observed that the concept of the two kingdoms does not have a political background, but is 'eine ideale Konzeption, die im religiösen Anschauungsunterricht verwendet werden soll'[134].

Some other authors have expressed similar opinions. Oepke Noordmans most probably followed Scholz in pointing out that the scheme of ages in history and that of the two kingdoms were popular educational devices Augustine found in existing religious instruction. But at the same time he said—and one senses here some criti-

---

judgement, first from the NT, then from the OT. For the eternal punishment of the wicked, see esp. XXI, 9. 23 and 24.

[131] See esp. *DCD* XX, 5. 6. 10. 19 and XXII, 4. 11-14. 20. 25-28. But elsewhere in *DCD*, too, A. speaks emphatically about the resurrection of the body, as early as I, 13 and throughout XIII, 16-20. These are evidently the tenets that have to be inculcated and defended again and again. See also *De cat. rud.* 4. 45. 46. 54 and, for instance, the statement in *En. in Ps.* 88, 5: 'In nulla re tam vehementer, tam pertinaciter, tam obnixe et contentiose contradicitur fidei christianae sicut de carnis resurrectione'.

[132] As in the catecheses this is repeated frequently. Cf. *De cat. rud.* 48 and 54-55 with *DCD* XIX, 4; XX, 19; XXI, 21. 25 and 26. These trials and persecutions come from both outside and inside: pagans, Jews, heretics, the reprobates in the Church. It should be observed that the persecutions and trials are also discussed at length at the end of the *narratio*; cf. *De cat. rud.* 43-44 and *DCD* XVIII, 50-53.

[133] Scholz, *Glaube und Unglaube*, 158-159. To a large degree Scholz is following here F. Hipler, *Die christliche Geschichtsauffassung*, Köln 1884.

[134] Scholz, *Glaube und Unglaube*, 80.

cism of Scholz' view—that one should not attach too much significance to the philosophical nature of these schemes. The *City of God* is an *ecclesiastical* work, 'whose outlines were already indicated in the catechetical work that he wrote in 400'[135]. And of particular importance is an observation further on in his study: 'the historical mode of instruction', after the example of Augustine's catechesis, defines the entire second part of the *City of God*.

Admittedly, Noordmans was of the opinion that the narrative 'in a more proper sense' occurs in Books XV-XVIII; the preceding four he regarded more as a doctrinal exposition of faith[136]. Here one would prefer, with Augustine, to see the arrangement slightly differently: the *narratio* begins with the creation of the world and not with Cain and Abel in Book XV[137]. But right after that Noordmans demonstrated his keen insight in discerning a connection between the last four books and the end of the catechetical lesson: both deal with 'Christian conduct in view of the end of the world and of eternity'[138].

Noordmans obviously regarded the second part of the *City of God* as catechetical in nature. Thus he typified these books as 'instruction'[139]. Moreover, it is revealing that his pupil Jan Koopmans went even further in his characterization, stating that in the second part of the *City of God* the entire Christian teaching is expounded; in structure and content it corresponds with the extensive model catechesis of *The Catechizing of the Uninstructed*[140].

Thus Noordmans and Koopmans indicated important similarities between Augustine's two works. At that time no other scholars had come up with such a detailed view. Later on Lauras and Rondet saw a few parallels, for example that both works contain a narration of the beginning, the course and the destined ends of the two cities[141]. F.-J. Thonnard pointed to similarity as regards the division of history; he concluded that Augustine's work manifests itself as an

---

[135] Noordmans, *Augustinus, VW* 3, 46.

[136] Noordmans, *Augustinus, VW* 3, 160-161.

[137] Cf. *De cat. rud.* 5 and 10.

[138] Noordmans, *Augustinus, VW* 3, 161.

[139] Noordmans, *Augustinus, VW* 3, 160: 'These books contain a complete *Institutio* or Instruction, as Calvin would call it later, in the Christian religion'.

[140] J. Koopmans, *Het oudkerkelijk dogma in de reformatie, bepaaldelijk bij Calvijn*, Wageningen 1938 (repr. Amsterdam 1983), 94-95, esp. n. 5.

[141] Lauras and Rondet, 'Thème', 143; cf. 148 and 151.

immense catechetical exposition, directed at the pagans[142]. Anne-Marie La Bonnardière, in quite a different context, also drew attention to concurrence. It is noteworthy that only in the *City of God* does Augustine quote extensively from the historical books of the Old Testament. The reason is that here he gives his wide-ranging *narratio* of the Old Testament history of salvation[143].

A largely new perspective has been opened by G.H. Allard[144]. Not only does he see a concurrence between the first catechetical model of *The Catechizing of the Uninstructed* and the entire second part of the *City of God* (*including* Books XIX-XXII), but he also brings the first part into the discussion. Although he does not overlook the apologetical component, he sees Augustine's work as belonging to the catechetical genre as it is manifested in *De catechizandis rudibus*[145]. In the first ten books rest (requies) is discussed and true happiness is defended; one should note how this corresponds to the first part of the catechesis[146].

Allard has pointed out an important direction for our research. One may possibly differ with him on details, and it must be said that he has only given an initial impetus to a largely new approach. He recognizes this himself[147]. However, his view that there is more than a coincidental relationship between Augustine's catechetical models and his *City of God* is very important. The main lines of Allard's argument can be justified and this concurrence is what I have tried to show in the preceding.

But there is more. In this context it is noteworthy that the form and content of the catecheses and of the *City of God* concur not only in outline, but also in many details. Not only is history divided into

---

142 Thonnard, *BA* 37, 842-844: 'Les âges de l'homme'.

143 A.-M. La Bonnardière, *Biblia Augustiniana. A.T. Livres historiques*, Paris 1960, 3-4. Moreover, it appears that before he wrote *DCD* A. never cited the so-called minor prophets (e.g. *Obadiah*, *Nahum*), or hardly ever did; cf. A.-M. La Bonnardière, *Biblia Augustiniana. A.T. Les douze petits prophètes*, Paris 1963, 12 ff. The reason for this seems the same: he mentions them now in his very extensive *narratio*.

144 G.H. Allard, 'Pour une nouvelle interprétation de la *Civitas Dei*, *SP* IX (*TU* 94), Berlin 1966, 329-339.

145 Allard, 'Interprétation', esp. 331 and 334 ff.; cf. 339: '... la *Civitas Dei* obéit à une motivation profonde: celle d'une catéchèse du bonheur à laquelle Augustin était personnellement sensibilisé, à laquelle les esprits étaient réceptifs, vu la chute de Rome et la fragile éternité de l'empire'.

146 Allard, 'Interprétation', 336-337.

147 Allard, 'Interprétation', 339: 'Non pas que nous surestimons la preuve ici fournie, au point de la croire exhaustive et péremptoire. Loin de là'.

six ages and is the history of the two cities in this way narrated, from the creation to the present day. In what follows also, this manner of expounding the subject-matter can be seen. In a summary at the end of Book XX Augustine states that, among other things, he will discuss the following: the Scriptures have proved to be true and will come true, the Day of Judgement is coming, there will be persecutions, Christ shall be the Judge, there will be the resurrection and the separation of the good and the wicked[148]. The same disposition is present, as the first model in particular shows, in the *exhortatio* of the catecheses: so far the prophecies have been fulfilled and the remaining ones will be fulfilled, there will be tribulations, the Day of Judgement is coming, the resurrection, Christ as Judge, the separation of the pious and the impious[149].

Another point of concurrence is the considerable attention given to the apologetic element in both the introductory catecheses and in the *City of God*. Augustine mentions this element in his advice to Deogratias[150] and then applies it in his models[151]. Once again it appears that for him catechesis and apology are closely related. The Christian truth must not only be taught, but also defended. There are enemies and heretics outside the Church; there is spurious Christianity[152].

Just as instruction in—and defence of—true rest (requies) and true blessedness (beatitudo) are at the centre of the catecheses, so they are in the *City of God*. It would be too much to cite here the hundreds of texts and passages which discuss these concepts, as well as the related concept *pax*[153]. The first sentence of the work—in which, as was the custom then, the essence of the entire contents is announced—already refers to perfect peace (pax perfecta)[154]. Subsequently it is stated over and over again that what matters is true

---

148 *DCD* XX, 30.

149 *De cat. rud.* 45; cf. 54.

150 Esp. *De cat. rud.* 11.

151 Esp. *De cat. rud.* 30 and 46 ff.

152 For the latter, cf. *DCD* XX, 19 and XXI, 21. 25 with *De cat. rud.* 11. 48 and 54-55. In *DCD* I, 35 A. speaks in the same way as he does in *De cat. rud.* about the Christians who now fill the churches and now the theatres. In both passages it is emphasized that in this dispensation the two cities are *commingled*.

153 *Pax aeterna, pax caelestis, pax finalis, pax perfecta*. The close connection between this peace and eternal rest can be seen, among other places, at the end of *DCD* (XXII, 30). Cf. the end of the *Conf.* (XIII, 35, 50 f.).

154 See p. 64.

piety and worship of God[155]. True blessedness (vera beatitudo) is granted only by the one God[156]. There is a detailed discussion of God's resting on the seventh day and our rest[157], also of the blessedness (beatitudo) of the angels and of man before the Fall[158]. And to give only a few more general examples: Book XIX deals extensively with *beatitudo* and *pax*[159]; Book XXII from beginning to end is concerned with eternal happiness (aeterna felicitas) and eternal blessedness (aeterna beatitudo); the entire work closes with an exposition on eternal rest (requies).

Augustine's work can be regarded as a comprehensive exposition on true happiness and true blessedness. It is understandable that the author, when referring to his work, mentions these very concepts[160].

Finally, one more remarkable fact should be noted. The catechetical nature of the *City of God* emerges in the concurrence of its structure and content with the structure and content of the catecheses for *rudes*. And is Augustine's comprehensive work not addressed primarily to people like Volusianus, pagans who on the one hand have their critical questions, but on the other hand are eager to be (further) instructed in the Christian faith[161]?

A fine example of this last mentioned aim of the work is given in *Ep.* 137. In this letter, addressed to Volusianus and through him to his friends, we find a clear-cut presentation of the catechetical element just described. Augustine opens by saying that he is willing to

---

155 Cf. *DCD* I, 36: '... asseramus civitatem Dei veramque pietatem et Dei cultum, in quo uno veraciter sempiterna beatitudo promittitur'.

156 Esp. *DCD* X, 1 ff.

157 Esp. *DCD* XI, 8 and 31.

158 *DCD* XI, 11 f.

159 Cf. pp. 145-150.

160 E.g. *DCD* I, 36 (text n. 155); *Ep.ad Firmum*, 1: '... adversus eos est disputatum qui *felicitati* vitae huius non plane deorum sed daemoniorum cultum prodesse contendunt ...'; *Ep.* 184A, 5: 'Decem volumina non parva confeci, quorum priora quinque illos redarguunt qui propter adipiscendam vel retinendam humanarum rerum istam terrenam temporalemque *felicitatem*, non unius summi et veri, sed multorum deorum cultum necessarium esse contendunt. Posteriora vero alia quinque contra illos sunt, qui se adversus salutarem doctrinam timidius et inflatius extollentes, ad *beatitudinem* quae post hanc vitam speratur, etiam per daemonum multorumque deorum cultum existimant pervenire'.

161 Cf. pp. 61-62. In this connection it should be noted that although Volusianus was a pagan, through his Christian mother Albina and many others he was not unfamiliar with the Christian faith. See A. Chastagnol, 'Le sénateur Volusien et la conversion d'une famille de l'aristocratie romaine au Bas-Empire', *REAn* 58 (1956) 241-253.

instruct Volusianus[162]. Then he goes into the questions that are on the minds of Volusianus and the members of his circle. After discussing these at length and responding to them[163], Augustine gives a brief exposition of the *Heilsgeschichte*: creation; Abraham and his progeny; Israel in Egypt; the Exodus and the conquest of the promised land; the era of the kings; the turning away from the true God; Captivity and return; the coming of Christ, His death, resurrection and Ascension; the sending of the Holy Spirit; the first Christian congregation; the growth of the Church, its life and suffering[164]. Throughout this exposition it is emphasized that these events are the fulfilment of the prophecies. Augustine also discusses the end of the world; the tribulations of the faithful, their *patientia* and longing for eternal happiness (aeterna felicitas) in the heavenly city (civitas coelestis); the temptations caused by heresies. Up to now the prophecies of the Scriptures have been fulfilled and those still remaining will be fulfilled. How can a person who is longing for eternity and disturbed about the brevity of this life resist the light and perfection of this divine authority[165]?

The content and structure of this argument are reminiscent of Augustine's method of catechetical instruction. This impression of similarity is reinforced when further on in the epistle, just as the *rudes* being instructed in the catecheses, Volusianus attention is drawn to the two great commandments concerning love (*Matt.* 22:37-39 and par.)[166], and then to the particular style and content of Scripture[167]. Moreover, at the end of the letter Augustine writes again about the heavenly and divine city (civitas superna atque divina) and the love towards God and one's neighbour[168].

D. Conclusions

From the foregoing it can be concluded that the *City of God* is to be regarded, in structure and content, as both an apology and an exam-

---

162 *Ep.* 137, 1: 'Quis autem nostrum, qui Christi, ut possumus, gratiam ministramus, cum tua verba legerit, ita te velit doctrina instrui christiana, ut tibi tantum sufficiat ad salutem ... Parum est ergo nobis sic te instrui, ut tibi sit liberando satis'.

163 *Ep.* 137, 2-14.

164 *Ep.* 137, 15-16.

165 *Ep.* 137, 16.

166 *Ep.* 137, 17; cf. *De cat. rud.* 50 and 55.

167 *Ep.* 137, 18; cf. *De cat. rud.* 50 and 13.

168 *Ep.* 137, 20.

ple of catechetics. Evidently Augustine deems instruction the best defence. Just as in many other writings of early-Christian apologetics, positive exposition plays an important role in his main work. This thetic nature is apparent from various passages in the work itself and from what the author states about it in other writings. In particular the recently discovered letter to Firmus, in combination with the one that was already available, provides new material.

The importance of the thetic element is most apparent when a comparison is made with the catecheses for *rudes*. Structure and content of the *City of God* correspond to a great extent with what Augustine states on this type of catechesis.

This concurrence applies not only to the second part of the *City of God* (Books XI-XXII), but also to the first (I-X). In both the catecheses and the *City of God* the author starts from the questions asked by those who are to be instructed. After that comes the *narratio* of the *Heilsgeschichte*, and finally the *exhortatio*. Basically a similar structure and content are to be found in the extensive letter—which is, in fact, a complete and very carefully prepared treatise—addressed to Volusianus, a pagan who desires further instruction.

In all these works Augustine speaks about the two cities. He does so very extensively in his great work, concisely and yet completely in his introductory catecheses. Sufficiently clearly he also mentions the existence of the city of God in his exposition for Volusianus.

It is noteworthy that the doctrine of the two cities is discussed in particular in a catechetical context. Augustine presents the first complete version in his model catechesis of c. 400. He is accustomed to teaching *rudes* that there are two cities. Especially in his sermons on the Psalms Augustine repeats this theme[169]; his listeners obviously knew what he was referring to. Besides, he says in one of these sermons that everyone who has been instructed (eruditus!) in the Holy Church should be well-informed on this doctrine of the two cities[170]. He discusses it at length in his *City of God*, also in a catechetical context.

---

[169] Cf. pp. 118-123.

[170] *En.in Ps.* 136, 1: 'Oblitos vos esse non arbitror, commendasse nos vobis, immo commemorasse vos, quod omnis eruditus in sancta ecclesia nosse debet unde cives simus, et ubi peregrinemur, et peregrinationis nostrae causam esse peccatum, reversionis autem munus remissionem peccatorum et iustificationem gratiae Dei. Duas civitates permixtas sibi interim corpore, et corde separatas, currere per ista volumina saeculorum usque in finem, audistis et nostis; unam cui finis est pax

While continuing this investigation, we will search for the possible sources of Augustine's doctrine of the two cities. This search will include an inquiry into possible references to the two cities elsewhere in a catechetical context.

---

aeterna, et vocatur Ierusalem; alteram cui gaudium est pax temporalis, et vocatur Babylonia. Interpretationes etiam nominum, si non fallor, tenetis: Ierusalem interpretari visionem pacis; Babyloniam confusionem'. This sermon was delivered at Carthage (31st Dec. 412, according to Zarb; cf. *CCL* 38, XVII) as a sequel to *En. in Ps.* 64 (Carthage, 26th/28th Dec. 412).

CHAPTER FOUR

SOURCES OF AUGUSTINE'S DOCTRINE OF THE TWO CITIES

A. Manichaeism

1. 'Manichaeism' as an accusation

For Augustine world history was one uninterrupted linear process, directed towards a final destination: the total separation of the two cities. Eternal blessedness awaits the citizens of the city of God; eternal damnation those of the city of the devil. In this present age, the period between creation and the end of the world, the Church as the community of the children of God is in peregrination; she is looking forward to her definitive homecoming in the city of God, the heavenly Jerusalem.

A number of investigators have referred to Manichaeism as the source of Augustine's clear-cut duality of the two cities and of various concepts more or less related to it. This is not surprising. For nine years at least, the future bishop was an adherent of this gnostic religion, in the very period which is often regarded as being of critical importance for one's later view of life. Much of his first work seems to be imbued with Manichaean modes of thought[1]. Seeing that Augustine composed, towards the end of his life, a major work in which he placed the theme of the two kingdoms or cities in a central position and strongly emphasized the absolute antithesis between these two societies, and stressed moreover the idea of the citizen of God's city sojourning as an alien here on earth, the question of possible reminiscences of Manichaean ideas cannot be sidestepped.

Furthermore, it is known that in his lifetime Augustine was already accused more than once of being a Manichaean. Objections were made against his ordination as (Catholic) auxiliary bishop of Hippo Regius. Megalius of Calama, the primate of Numidia, refused at first to ordain him[2]. Particularly from the Donatist camp

---

[1] See *Conf.* IV, 20-27 about *De pulchro et apto*, already lost to A.; cf. esp. Alfaric, *Évolution*, 222-225.

[2] Cf. *C. litt. Petil.* III, 16, 19 and *C. Cresc.* III, 80, 92.

the accusations did not cease[3]. In the eyes of many Donatists Augustine was a crypto-Manichaean and friends of his such as Profuturus, Fortunatus and Alypius, now Catholic bishops, were also seen this way. Finally, during the last years of Augustine's life, it was Julian of Eclanum who vigorously attacked the supposed Manichaean remnants in his theology[4].

Were Julian and the other opponents right? A comprehensive answer to this question is not necessary in this framework. It suffices to indicate the extent to which his contemporaries suspected or even claimed to have evidence for Augustine's adherence to Manichaeism. It must be said that Julian turned out to be an acute critic and was able to put forward cogent reasons. Most of the others, however, could do no more than produce unfounded accusations.

In this context it should be realized that in those days 'Manichaeism' was already becoming a technical term for any form of suspected dualism and even for heresy in general. Not only was the former Manichaean Augustine charged with it, but Jerome and, for instance, Ambrose too. And for his part Ambrose accused his opponent Jovinianus of adherence to Manichaeism[5]. It was becoming customary to label others in this way for a real or supposed deviation. In later centuries, for example Patriarch Nikephoros of Constantinople considered the adversaries of the veneration of icons to be inspired by Manichaean writings[6]. It is common knowledge that in Western Europe the accusation 'Manichaeism' was heard through almost the entire medieval period[7].

This was still true at the time of the Reformation: Luther, Melanchthon and Calvin were each in turn labelled as *Manichaeus redivivus*[8]. The importance still given then to Mani's doctrine is ap-

---

3 For a discussion of the texts on this subject, see esp. Courcelle, *Recherches*, 238-245; Frend, 'Manichaeism', passim, and Lamirande, *BA* 32, 711-712.

4 E.g. *Opus imp. c. Iul.* II, 31-33; in IV, 42 the venomous remark: 'Si mutabit Aethiops pellem suam aut pardus varietatem, ita et tu a Manichaeorum mysteriis elueris'.

5 Cf. De Veer, *BA* 23, 810-811.

6 Cf. Alfaric, *Écritures*, I, 119.

7 E.g. S. Runciman, *The Medieval Manichee. A Study of the Christian Dualist Heresy*. Cambridge 1955²; H. Grundmann, *Ketzergeschichte des Mittelalters*, Göttingen 1967².

8 See J.P. Asmussen, 'Manichaeism', in: C.J. Bleeker – G. Widengren (eds.), *Historia Religionum. Handbook for the History of Religion*, I, Leiden 1969, 608. For the accusations on the part of Erasmus et al. directed at Luther, see A. Adam, 'Die Herkunft des Lutherwortes vom menschlichen Willen als Reittier Gottes', *LuJ* 29 (1962) 33-34.

parent from various statements in Calvin's *Institutes*[9]. In his *Confession de Foy* of 1561, Guido de Brès rejected 'aussi l'erreur des Manicheens, qui confessent les Diables avoir l'origine d'euxmesmes, estans mauvais de leur nature propre, sans avoir esté corrumpus'[10]. But on the other hand, the first scholarly inquiry into Manichaeism was carried out in Protestant circles. Cyriacus Spangenberg von Mansfeld wrote a *Historia Manichaeorum* in order to exonerate his friend Matthias Flacius from the blemish of Manichaeism[11]. Almost two hundred years later the Huguenot Isaac de Beausobre published two massive volumes on Mani and his doctrine[12].

Since then research has made great strides[13], in this century greatly favoured by new discoveries. Works by Manichaeans themselves have come to light, so that resorting to allegations or suppositions can increasingly be replaced by references to texts. Thus the question concerning the possible influence of Manichaeism on Augustine's doctrine of the two cities should be examined again. It is truly remarkable how little this has been done until now.

2. *Manichaeism as a source?*

A brief survey of those who have referred to Manichaeism in connection with Augustine's concept of the two cities[14] cannot begin with the study by Scholz. Although he made some general remarks on possible sources, he never mentioned Manichaeism explicitly. Yet at that time, as is apparent from the comprehensive and profound studies by Baur, Flügel and Kessler[15], much was already

---

9 E.g. *Inst.* I, 7, 3. 13, 1. 14, 3. 15, 5; II, 1, 11. 13, 1 f. 14,8; III, 11, 5. 23, 5. 23, 8. 25, 7. 33, 5; IV, 12, 19. 13, 9. 18, 25.

10 J.N. Bakhuizen van den Brink, *De Nederlandse belijdenisgeschriften*, Amsterdam 1976², 88.

11 Böhlig, *Mysterion und Wahrheit*, 219, and Böhlig, *Manichäismus*, 13.

12 *Histoire critique de Manichée et du Manichéisme*, I – II, Amsterdam 1734-1739 (repr. Leipzig 1970). On De Beausobre, see W. Delius in *RGG* I, 952 (+ lit.). L.J.R. Ort gives a short survey of the content of De Beausobre's work in his *Mani. A religio-historical description of his personality*, Leiden 1967, 3-4.

13 See H.S. Nyberg, 'Forschungen über den Manichäismus' (1935), re-issued in G. Widengren (Hrsg.), *Der Manichäismus*, Darmstadt 1977 (*WdF* 168), 3-28, for the purport of the studies by F. Chr. Baur, G. Flügel, K. Kessler, F. Cumont, W. Bousset, R. Reitzenstein, F.C. Burkitt, H.H. Schaeder et al.; cf. Ort, *Mani*, 4 ff.

14 This is the object of this enquiry; possible Manichaean influence elsewhere in A.'s theology is not within its scope.

15 F.Chr. Baur, *Das manichäische Religionssystem nach den Quellen neu untersucht und entwickelt*, Tübingen 1831 (repr. Göttingen 1928); G. Flügel, *Mani, seine Lehre und*

known about Mani and his religion. And no doubt everyone knew that the great Western church father Augustine was a follower of Mani for many years. Scholz, however, did not take this information into account. Was this perhaps because his teacher, Adolf von Harnack—following Kessler[16]—saw Mani's religious system principally in the perspective of ancient Babylonian religion and considered its Christian element to be only a separate addition[17]? In such circumstances any lasting effect on an essential doctrine like Augustine's theory of the two cities is soon outside the range of vision. This is also possibly why, in addition to the impression Hahn made with his *Tyconius-Studien*, neither Harnack nor Scholz referred to Manichaeism as a possible source[18].

Prosper Alfaric, however, was of a different opinion. Not only did this French scholar show great familiarity with the Manichaean texts available in his day[19], but he also had a thorough knowledge of Augustine's works. In a comprehensive study he traced the intellectual development of the later church father, from his childhood in Thagaste to the Neoplatonic period in Milan. In this work he also discussed Manichaeism at length. Alfaric was of the opinion that Augustine had become thoroughly acquainted with Manichaean ideas and that they had a lasting influence on him. According to the Manichaean doctrine, mankind has been divided from the beginning into two groups, one of which lives for God, the other for the devil. 'Cette conception qu'Augustin exposera plus tard très longuement dans la *Cité de Dieu* lui vient des Manichéens'[20].

This was Alfaric's only comment on the *City of God* and the source

---

seine Schriften, Leipzig 1862 (repr. Osnabrück 1969); K. Kessler, *Mani. Forschungen über die manichäische Religion, I, Voruntersuchungen und Quellen*, Berlin 1889. Moreover, in the years just before and just after 1900 important expeditions to Turfan were carried out; new Manichaean text-fragments were published by F.W.K. Müller and A. von Le Coq.

16 See esp. Kessler in Herzog-Hauck, *RE*^{3} 12 (1903) 192-228.

17 Harnack, *Lehrbuch*, II, 512-527. To be sure, he considered that Christian influence on the Babylonian sect in which Mani grew up was possible (523. 524), but at the same time he believed 'dass der Manichäismus nicht auf dem Boden des Christenthums entstanden ist' (522) and that the Western Manichaeans managed 'ihrer Lehre einen christlichen *Anstrich* zu geben' (526).

18 This had happened earlier, but in very general terms. See e.g. the work with which Scholz was familiar: Seyrich, *Geschichtsphilosophie*, 34: the dualistic element in A.'s view of history was Manichaean. Further evidence is lacking, however.

19 Alfaric, *Écritures*, I – II (Paris 1918-1919).

20 Alfaric, *Évolution*, 123 and n. 6.

of the doctrine of the two cities. He did not develop his thesis. In the framework of an exposition of Augustine's intellectual development he can hardly have been expected to do so. But references to general views held by the Manichaeans and to a passage in *Contra Faustum* can, in themselves, scarcely be regarded as substantiation[21].

Richard Reitzenstein also named Manichaeism as the source: 'Ist doch die ganze Grundvorstellung des Gottesstaates als eines Reiches, dem Gott und seine Engel, die Seligen alle und die wahrhaften Christen bei Lebzeiten angehören und das notwendig gegen das Reich dieser Welt, den Teufel, die Dämonen und die zur Verdammnis Bestimmten kämpfen muss, ohne den Manichäismus gar nicht zu erklären, sondern ist Zug für Zug ihm entnommen'[22]. He did not offer specific texts, however, to support his opinion. His view that Manichaeism had its roots in the dualistic religion of Iran in which light and darkness, good and evil were engaged in a struggle satisfied him[23]. Decisive proof from Manichaean texts is also lacking in the studies by Gustav Combès[24], Hans Eger[25] and Ernesto Buonaiuti[26].

More can be said of two fundamental articles by Alfred Adam. Thoroughly familiar with Manichaean sources and using particularly the newly discovered and (partly) published Coptic Manichaica, he entered the discussion. His first article is devoted to the question of whether Augustine's doctrine of the two kingdoms could have been derived from Manichaeism[27]. Adam answered for the most part in the affirmative. Manichaean texts often

---

21 Alfaric, *Évolution*, 123 n. 6.

22 Reitzenstein, 'Augustin', 41.

23 Reitzenstein, 'Augustin', 34-35. For Reitzenstein and his 'Paniranismus', which also determined his views on Manichaeism, see e.g. Nyberg, 'Forschungen', 17-18.

24 Combès, *Doctrine*, 36.

25 Eger, *Eschatologie*, 18: 'Die Zeichnung des schroffen in alle Ewigkeit fortdauernden Gegensatzes des Gottes- und des Teufelsreiches besonders in *De civitate Dei* gibt Anlass, nachdrücklicher als bisher geschehen ist, die äussere Verwandtschaft Augustins mit dem Manichäismus zu unterstreichen. Das dualistische Prinzip ist, so verschieden seine Motivation hier und dort ist, tief in der beiderseitigen Lehre verankert'.

26 See p. 9, also for a statement by Windelband which has been influential but lacks substantiation through source evidence. For Buonaiuti's view, see also his 'Manichaeism and Augustine's Idea of «massa perditionis»', *HTR* 20 (1927) 127: A.'s doctrine of the two kingdoms is Manichaean, too.

27 'Der manichäische Ursprung der Lehre von den zwei Reichen bei Augustin' (1952), reprinted in Adam, *Sprache und Dogma*, 133-140.

make mention of a city of God or a city of the gods, a *polis* made up of angels and humans; this city of God is also called a kingdom. The kingdom of light stands opposite that of darkness; the two kingdoms are at war; besides, a *polis* of mockery is spoken of. Moreover, one finds in Manichaeism the idea, so essential for Augustine, of a *corpus permixtum*, even in the most literal sense: all bodies consist of evil matter mixed with light. While for Augustine the history of the city of God began with Abel, for the Manichaeans it started with Seth, who for them was Adam's first-born. In conclusion the author remarks that Augustine did not adopt any one Manichaean tenet in its entirety. But, 'das heimliche Verlangen seines dualistisch fühlenden Herzens, das ihn in seiner Jugend zum Manichäismus getrieben hatte, brachte ihn im Alter dazu, auf der höheren Stufe der Vergeistigung die entscheidenden Gedanken seines ersten Aufschwungs wieder aufzunehmen. Auf dem Wege der Sublimierung kehrte er zu seinen ersten Idealen zurück, ohne sich dieses Vorganges bewusst zu werden'[28].

This article by Adam is impressive. Later we shall return to some of the texts he used as documentation. The great influence of his study can be seen from the works of nearly all subsequent scholars. The parallelism between Augustine's doctrine of the two cities and Manichaeism seemed to be clear.

In an article published a few years later, Adam saw the effect of Manichaeism elsewhere in Augustine's oeuvre, too[29]. He referred to concurrences in the concepts *concupiscentia, vocatio* and *massa* (bōlos). Are the *Confessions* and the language of the Psalms in which it was written not reminiscent of the annual confession by the Manichaean catechumens (auditores) at the Feast of the Bema? And can the arrangement of this work in 13 books (8 + 5) not be attributed to Manichaeism? We will not go into these or related questions now[30] as we are mainly concerned with possible Manichaean influence on the *City of God*. Adam substantiated this supposed impact with some more details: the division of history into three parts

---

28 Adam, 'Ursprung', *Sprache und Dogma*, 140.

29 'Das Fortwirken des Manichäismus bei Augustin' (1958), *Sprache und Dogma*, 141-166.

30 It may be noted in passing that J.P. Asmussen, *X^{u}āstvānīft. Studies in Manichaeism*, Copenhagen 1965, 124, rejects, for a variety of reasons, the idea that purport and structure of the *Confessiones* were possibly derived from Manichaeism. Earlier Alfaric, *Écritures*, II, 137, expressed himself in the same way as Adam.

(exortus, procursus, debiti fines), comparable to the three Manichaean 'Moments': the Former Time, the Present Time, the Future Time; world history as a gigantomachy; the absolutely dualistic nature of the two kingdoms; the division of the *City of God* into twenty two books, as in Mani's *Living Gospel*.

Adam referred most emphatically to Manichaean influence on Augustine in the first part of his *Lehrbuch der Dogmengeschichte*[31]. For our inquiry the following points are particularly relevant. First that the prevailing tone of the *Confessions* is gnostic: there is the duality between the transitory world of material things and the everlasting divine world; the brokenness of what is temporal and the wholeness of what is eternal; the call of the Eternal in the darkness of the temporal; the physical world as alien territory and the world of Light as the homeland of the soul[32]. Just as in the *Confessions* the solitary soul wanders about through the darkness of this world and finally arrives at the gate of the eternal homeland, so too in the *City of God* the Church since Abel has been on a pilgrimage, proceeding towards her home in heaven[33]. The source of the dualistic contrast between city of God and city of the devil can only be Manichaeism, for only here do God and devil and their respective followers oppose each other absolutely[34]. The description in the *City of God* (XI, 3) of the antithesis between the two *societates* of angels, and especially the picture given there of the *civitas diaboli* (pregnant with pride, full of dark desires and envy, etc.) point to Manichaeism[35]. And does Augustine not say elsewhere that the heavenly kingdom is still under construction? This is a remark that can best be explained with reference to Ban, the great architect of the Manichaeans, who is establishing

[31] First edition 1965. A few years earlier Adam also wrote in an assertive manner, but without offering any substantiation: 'Dass die Theologie Augustins in tiefgehender Weise durch manichäische Gedanken beeinflusst ist—ich nenne seine Lehre von den zwei Reichen, seinen Liebensbegriff, seine Seelenlehre, seine Prädestinationsauffassung und seine Lehre von der Erbsünde—...'. See Adam, 'Manichäismus', in: B. Spuler et al. (Hrsg.), *Handbuch der Orientalistik*. Erste Abteilung, Band VIII, 2, Leiden 1961, 103.

[32] Adam, *Dogmengeschichte*, I, 290.

[33] Adam, *Dogmengeschichte*, I, 292.

[34] Adam, *Dogmengeschichte*, I, 294.

[35] Adam, *Dogmengeschichte*, I, 295. This similarity was already pointed out by F.C. Burkitt, *The Religion of the Manichees*, Cambridge 1925 (repr. 1978), 103. Adam, *Texte*, 11-14, refers to a quotation in a work by Severus of Antioch which is assumed to have been taken from the *Book of the Giants*.

the new paradise[36]. The division of the *City of God* into twenty-two books may have been chosen as a reaction to Mani's principal work, the *Living Gospel*[37].

We shall take leave of Adam's opinions for now. It cannot be said that essentially new vistas have been opened up since he carried out his research or that much new evidence has been brought to light. Cilleruelo did devote an extensive article to Manichaeism in the *City of God*, stating that in Augustine's dualism there is a continuous line from *De pulchro et apto*, written during Augustine's Manichaean period, to the *City of God*[38]. Seen in this way the theme of the two *civitates* played a part in his thinking early on. But Cilleruelo showed only a sketchy line—that of 'dualism'—and referred incorrectly to the occurrence of 'dos ciudades' already in *On the True Religion*, in the work directed against Faustus, and in some early interpretations of the Psalms[39]. There is no evidence of research of his own on Manichaean texts and his knowledge of the relevant secondary sources was limited. Likewise Johannes Spörl did not contribute any new material, nor did Jakob Obersteiner[40].

Alexander Böhlig, however, endeavoured to probe deeper into the Gnostic background of Augustine's doctrine of the two cities[41]. Like Adam, he drew attention to the Manichaean contrast between the kingdom of light and that of darkness, stressing that for Augustine the kingdoms were not composed of different physical matter. The Manichaeans were most likely acquainted with books of Seth; Augustine possibly may have become familiar with them as a Manichaean. The discoveries at Nag Hammadi have made such texts accessible; they reveal that the Gnostics identified themselves with the children of Seth, who were sojourning in this world as aliens and were persecuted. In these Gnostic texts there is a contrast between the children of Seth and Adam's other offspring: two lines of descendants compete with each other in heaven as well as on earth; one should compare this especially with Book XII of the *City of God*. In the *Gospel of the Egyptians* particularly, the heavenly origin of Seth is emphasized; the supreme Father, the invisible Spirit, addresses

[36] Adam, *Dogmengeschichte*, I, 295.
[37] Adam, *Dogmengeschichte*, I, 296.
[38] Cilleruelo, 'Maniqueísmo', 476 f.
[39] Cilleruelo, 'Maniqueísmo', 482-486.
[40] Spörl, 'Staatslehre?', 66; Obersteiner, 'Civitas Dei', 333 f.
[41] Böhlig, 'Grundlagen' (1969).

Seth's family as His own. That results in a schism: God's salvation is received only by a special circle of people and spirits. 'Der Parallelismus der Gedanken bei Augustin und den Verfassern der gnostischen Sethschriften lässt sich so m. E. nicht leugnen'[42].

Meanwhile Arnold Ehrhardt had assembled some new evidence from Manichaean texts[43]. He seemed to be unaware of Adam's research, but did demonstrate knowledge of Manichaean writings, especially the Coptic ones. As the real source of Augustine's doctrine of the two cities, however, he pointed to Tyconius, though he assumed the Donatist to have been influenced by Manichaeism[44].

In the last few years no new evidence has been given. Yet it is noteworthy that some scholars accept Manichaean influence upon Augustine's doctrine of the two cities as an established fact. Kurt Rudolph believes that Augustine's Manichaean past is most palpably present in the concept of the two 'Bürgerschaften' and refers in this context to the studies by Adam[45]. In his recent publications Böhlig again observes that the twenty-two books of the *City of God* are deliberately aimed at Mani's *Living Gospel*[46]. Carsten Colpe and—in more guarded terms—Alfred Schindler do not exclude the possibility of Manichaean influence, particularly in the doctrine of the two cities[47].

---

42 Böhlig, 'Grundlagen', 295.

43 Ehrhardt, *Politische Metaphysik*, III, 34. This third volume was published posthumously in 1969 by F. Wieacker; Ehrhardt died in 1965.

44 Ehrhardt, *Politische Metaphysik*, III, 35: 'Deshalb benutzte er nicht die manichäischen Dogmen als solche, sondern nur in der Form, die sie in den Händen des grossen Ticonius erhalten hatten'.

45 K. Rudolph, *Die Gnosis. Wesen und Geschichte einer spätantiken Religion*, Göttingen 1977, 394 and 414 n. 179.

46 E.g. Böhlig, *Manichäismus*, 45 and 312 n. 134; he refers to his study just named and to the two articles by Adam.

47 Colpe, 'Gnosis', 654: 'Die Entmischung, aus der sich die Civitas Dei, auf Erden theokratisch repräsentiert, über die civitas terrena erheben wird, konnte so vielleicht nur entworfen werden, weil der manichäische Mythos von Ver- und Entmischung von Finsternis- u. Lichtwelt mit Sieg des letzteren dazu das Denkmodell geliefert hatte (wenn nicht überdies in der 22-Kapitel-Einteilung des grossen Werkes die des 'Lebendigen Evangeliums' des Mani nachklingt ...)'; Schindler, 'Augustin', 658: 'Übereinstimmungen bestehen im Grunde nur in gewissen Grundstimmungen und Grundtendenzen, die u.a. in der späteren Gnadenlehre wie im zwei-civitates-Ansatz der Geschichtsbetrachtung zur Geltung kommen. Dabei handelt es sich aber um Gemeinsamkeiten zwischen bestimmten Strömungen des katholischen und dem manichäischen Christentum, nicht um manichäische Eigentümlichkeiten'.

3. Mani and Manichaeism

Before proceeding to an investigation of the available Manichaean texts to determine whether they possibly contain views that correspond to Augustine's concept of the two cities, we will first give a sketch of Mani and Manichaeism. An analysis of Mani's descent in particular can be helpful for understanding some fundamental principles of the Manichaean system. Of course our sketch will be limited to a few distinctive characteristics; especially for expositions concerning the very complex myth, the reader must be referred to specific studies.

First of all a few historical facts[48]. Mani (Syr. Manī ḥajjā, the living Mani; Gr. Manichaios; Lat. Manichaeus), was born on 14th April 216 near the southern Mesopotamian town of Seleukia-Ktesiphon on the Tigris and grew up in a baptist sect. After two revelations he broke away from the religious milieu of his youth and, starting in 240, proclaimed a new world religion. Even before his death (276/277?)[49], his religion was being preached in the Persian Empire, in India, Syria, Armenia and Egypt. Then it spread rapidly as far as the northern part of Arabia, Roman Africa, Italy[50], Gaul and Spain; later on to the East as far as China[51]. In 763 Manichaeism even became the established religion of a Turkish kingdom in Central Asia (Turkestan).

Whereas formerly scholars had only fragmentary information on Manichaeism, found in the writings of adversaries (not the least important of whom was Augustine), since the beginning of this century works by Manichaeans themselves have been found in Turfan (East

---

48 Historical surveys and short expositions of the religious system: Polotsky, 'Manichäismus' (1935), repr. in: Widengren (Hrsg.), *Manichäismus*, 101-144; C. Colpe, 'Manichäismus', *RGG* 4 (1960) 714-722; G. Quispel, 'Manicheans', *Man, Myth & Magic* 61 (1971) 1721-1724. Among the earlier and particularly valuable studies: Burkitt, *Manichees* (1925); Puech, *Manichéisme* (1949); among the (more) recent ones: Ort, *Mani* (1967); F. Decret, *Mani et la tradition manichéenne*, Paris 1974; Rudolph, *Gnosis* (1977), 349-366; Böhlig, *Manichäismus* (1980); Böhlig, 'Manichäismus' (1981); M. Tardieu, *Le manichéisme*, Paris 1981; U. Bianchi, *Antropologia e dottrina della salvezza nella religione dei manichei*, Roma 1983.

49 For an exposition on the date of Mani's birth and of his death, see esp. Böhlig, *Manichäismus*, 309-310 n. 103 (death: 14th Feb. 276; 28th Feb. 276; 26th Feb. 277?).

50 Already contested at Rome by Bishop Miltiades shortly after 310.

51 Kawerau, *Geschichte*, 51, reports that even in the 20th century Manichaeism was forbidden by law in Vietnam. This does not necessarily mean, however, that it had followers there: laws established by foreign rulers were still in effect.

Turkestan), and especially at Medinet Madi in the Egyptian Fayum (since 1930): among them *Kephalaia*, letters, homilies and a voluminous psalter, all written in Coptic[52]. Important progress in this research has been made possible by the discovery and first publication of the *Cologne Mani-Codex* (1970). This work, which on the basis of palaeography can be dated from the fourth or the fifth century, was written in Greek, but its original language was East Aramaic. A few decades ago it was discovered near Assiut in Egypt and subsequently came into the possession of the University of Cologne. In 1969 the very small codex, measuring only 4.5 by 3.5 cm, was opened and deciphered. A. Henrichs and L. Koenen published the *editio princeps*[53]. Now there is evidence from a Manichaean work itself that Mani's roots were in a Jewish-Christian baptist sect. What this may signify for his absolutely dualistic doctrine of the two kingdoms will be examined further on in this study.

Mani taught a cosmogony of an absolutely dualistic kind: evil is an eternal cosmic force, not the result of a fall. Two kingdoms, one of light and the other of darkness, oppose each other implacably. The former is ruled by the Father of Greatness; in his fight against the kingdom of darkness he produced Primal Man by means of emanation. When this Man was in danger of perishing in the struggle, there was a new emanation: the Living Spirit came into being. He directed his Call of salvation to Primal Man and rescued him from

---

52 For surveys of discoveries and text-editions, see the references given in n. 48, particularly Ort, Rudolph and Böhlig. For Coptic Manichaica the account by C. Schmidt – H.J. Polotsky, 'Ein Mani-Fund in Ägypten. Orginalschriften des Mani und seiner Schüler', *SPAW* 1 (1933), 4-90, has kept its significance, for both the tentative description of the size and contents of the find and the valuable exposition by Polotsky accompanying it. The find consisted originally of 1200-1500 leaves (H. Ibscher in: Schmidt and Polotsky, 'Mani-Fund', 82); during and following World War II a substantial part of it was lost (see Böhlig, 'Die Arbeit an den koptischen Manichaica' (1961/1962), *Mysterion und Wahrheit*, 177-187). Not all of what remained has been published yet, but a new start was made in 1985 under the guidance of James M. Robinson (Claremont). Recently facsimile editions of the Coptic *Kephalaia* and *Homilies* have been published by Søren Giversen: *The Manichaean Coptic Papyri in the Chester Beatty Library. Vol. I: Kephalaia*, Genève 1986 and *The Manichaean Coptic Papyri in the Chester Beatty Library. Vol. II: Homilies & Varia*, Genève 1986.

53 Preliminary report: 'Ein griechischer Mani-Codex (P. Colon. inv. nr. 4780)', *ZPE* 5 (1970) 97-216. Edition of *CMC* 1 – 72, 7 in *ZPE* 19 (1975) 1-85; *CMC* 72, 8 – 99, 9 in *ZPE* 32 (1978) 87-199; *CMC* 99, 10 – 120 in *ZPE* 44 (1981) 201-318; *CMC* 121-192 in *ZPE* 48 (1982) 1-59. An English translation of *CMC* 1-99 in: R. Cameron – A.J. Dewey, *The Cologne Mani Codex (P. Colon. inv. nr. 4780) 'Concerning the Origin of his Body'*, Missoula, Mont. 1979.

matter. But the soul of the Primal Man remained behind; the world was ordered as a mixture of light and darkness, good and evil. A subsequent emanation, the Third Messenger, caused the movement towards the kingdom of light. Jesus was sent by this Messenger to Adam and Eve in order to give them knowledge (gnosis); besides there were other apostles of light: Seth(el), Enoch, Noah, Abraham, Buddha and Zoroaster. Finally came Mani, the seal of the prophets, the promised Paraclete. The goal of world history is to separate light from darkness so that the primeval state is restored. This will be the case when all the rescued particles of light have returned to the kingdom of light and the damned are locked up in the 'clod'[54] with the prince of darkness and his henchmen, together with matter and concupiscence (Pers. Āz, Gr. epithymia, Lat. concupiscentia). Then the two kingdoms will remain separated for ever.

This was a brief account of the very complicated myth[55]. A few remarks should be added concerning the internal organization of this world religion. Mani founded a community of *electi* (or perfecti) and *auditores*. The hearers had to care for the Manichaeans of the first echelon. From among the *electi* the 360 elders were chosen; above them were the seventy-two bishops, and above these the twelve teachers. The head of all of them was the leader (archègos, princeps), who was the successor of Mani. The liturgical life of this Church consisted mainly of prayer, the daily sacramental meal, the commemoration of the anniversary of Mani's death (which was described as a crucifixion), confession and stirring psalm-singing.

Mani's doctrine was typically Gnostic: the *nous* (the revelation from the other world) rescues the *psychè* (the spark of light in man) from the *hylè* (the evil matter)[56]. This doctrine—as has already been noted in connection with Augustine's biography—was presented as

[54] Besides the 'clod' (Gr. bōlos, Lat. globus) there is, for example in *Keph.* 105, 32-33, the grave (taphos) in which the female sex is stored, separate from the male sex. Other texts speak only of the *bōlos*; some name only the grave. The concept *globus* is reminiscent of A.'s *massa damnata* or *massa perditionis*; see Buonaiuti, 'Massa perditionis', 117-127.

[55] For more or less detailed expositions, see Polotsky, 'Manichäismus', 112-131; Puech, *Manichéisme*, 74-85; Colpe, 'Manichäismus', 716-718; Quispel, 'Manicheans', 1723-1724; Decret, *Mani*, 79-106; Rudolph, *Gnosis*, 359-362; M. Boyce, *A Reader in Manichaean Middle Persian and Parthian. Texts with Notes*, Leiden 1975, 4-8; Böhlig, *Manichäismus*, 27-36 and 103-188 (texts); Böhlig, 'Manichäismus', 438 ff; Tardieu, *Manichéisme*, 95-102; Bianchi, *Religione dei manichei*, 31-77.

[56] E.g. Polotsky, 'Mani-Fund', 81-82.

a rational religion. In Christian milieus the Manichaeans frequently referred to their critically expurgated New Testament, especially to the writings of Paul[57]. They almost completely rejected the Old Testament[58]. Many Christian apocryphal texts were in use among them[59].

Manichaeism was a universal, strongly missionary religion of the written word[60]. It expanded very rapidly throughout the Roman Empire[61], a fact that was furthered by government measures: the centres of Manichaeism were scattered by force, and because of this the movement spread in every direction[62]. In later times Christian bishops played an important part in the persecution through their continual insistance on the enforcement of the laws. From the middle of the fourth century especially, there was clearly no longer room for new oriental wisdom in the Christianized *imperium*: the measures taken against Mani's followers were reapplied with increasing severity[63]. Roman hatred towards the Persian world power and Christian intolerance—along with a growing theocratic ideal—were jointly responsible for this. In Diocletian's edict there was already reference to *Persian* adversaries and their doctrine[64]; the influential Eusebius expressed himself in similar terms when he wrote about the maniac (maneis) who collected false and wicked doctrines and infected the Roman Empire with a lethal poison from Persia[65]. Augustine also showed his contempt for Mani by calling him 'a certain Persian'[66].

---

57 To what extent this was the case can be seen repeatedly in the writings of A.'s Manichaean opponents. See Alfaric, *Écritures*, II, 165-169, and after him esp. F. Decret, *Aspects du manichéisme dans l'Afrique romaine. Les controverses de Fortunatus, Faustus et Felix avec saint Augustin*, Paris 1970, passim. Cf. Chr. Walter, *Der Ertrag der Auseinandersetzung mit den Manichäern für das hermeneutische Problem bei Augustin*, München 1972 (Diss. Mschr.), I, 17-80 on the Manichaean use of the Bible in general and 81-104 on their use of the Bible in the disputes with Christians.

58 See p. 35 n. 104.

59 On *acta apostolorum* esp. Nagel, 'Apostelakten' and Kaestli, 'Actes apocryphes'. Nagel assumes that a corpus of five apocryphal *acta* was in use; Kaestli disputes this. For the *Gospel according to Thomas*, see p. 234.

60 For these three characteristics (universal, missionary, book-religion), see Puech, *Manichéisme*, 61-68.

61 Brown, 'Diffusion', *Religion and Society*, 94-118.

62 Cf. Brown, *Diffusion*, 113.

63 Kaden, 'Edikte', 55-68.

64 Adam, *Texte*, 82-83.

65 Eusebius, *HE* VII, 31.

66 *De haer.* 46: 'Manichaei a quodam Persa exstiterunt, qui vocabitur Manes'; *C. Faust.* XXVIII, 4: '... et credat nescio cui ex transverso de Perside ...'.

We have already seen that a Manichaeism strongly imbued with Paulinism[67] found rapid acceptance in Roman Africa: as early as the spring of 297, twenty years after Mani's death, Diocletian was obliged to take measures in response to official complaints from Africa. We have also seen that the Manichaean way of asking questions (unde malum? unde homo?) showed a striking resemblance to that of earlier Gnostics against whom Tertullian had defended himself[68]. If one realizes that, according to Frend[69], Christianity in Africa at the beginning of the third century consisted mainly of a rigorist Montanistic movement and a Gnostic one—movements that continued to exert their influence in later times—then one can understand some of the underlying reasons for the success of the Manichaeans. Not only Augustine, but also many others in Africa were converted to Manichaeism. What the later church father was able to draw from this world religion for his concept of the two cities will be looked into now.

4. The Manichaean doctrine of the two kingdoms

Mani and his followers propagated an absolute dualism. Two kingdoms have confronted each other since eternity and each has a substance of its own: the kingdom of light opposes that of darkness, the kingdom of God opposes that of Satan. During this present age the two kingdoms are mixed together and engaged in combat with each other. At the end of time, when the separation is complete, they will confront each other again and this time eternally. But then they will be separated in such a way that no new attack by the kingdom of

---

67 See p. 34 f. Manichaeism was so much imbued with Christianity and specifically with Pauline teachings that O'Meara could write (*Young Augustine*, 79) : 'In a sense, it might seem that to become a Manichee [O'Meara was referring to the *auditor* in particular] was to depart little, if at all, from being a Christian'. In this context it should be observed that this Christian element did not apply to Manichaeism in Africa only. The earlier theory, defended in particular by L.H. Grondijs ('Numidian Manicheism in Augustinus' Time', *NTT* 9 (1954/1955) 21-42; 'Analyse du manichéisme numidien au IVe siècle', *AM*, III, 391-419), that there was a separate Numidian (Christian) Manichaeism has not held out. See e.g. L.J. van der Lof, 'Der numidische Manichäismus im vierten Jahrhundert', *SP* 8 (*TU* 93), Berlin 1966, 118-129. Cf. A. Lauras, 'Saint Léon le Grand et le Manichéisme Romain', *SP* 11 (*TU* 108), Berlin 1972, 203-209: Manichaeism at Rome as a 'Christian' sect.

68 Cf. p. 36 n. 107.

69 Frend, 'Gnostic-Manichaean Tradition', passim.

darkness upon the kingdom of light will be possible. The Coptic Psalm-Book sings of this event and this new situation in the following words:

> The Light
> shall] go to the Light, the fragrance shall go to [the fragrance], the image of the living man shall go to the living land from which it came. The Light shall return to its place, the Darkness shall fall and not rise again[70].

In Manichaeism it was taught that there are two kingdoms and three 'moments': the time before the commingling and the struggle, when the two kingdoms were still separated; the time of the commingling, being the time in which we now live; and the time in which the two kingdoms will be separated again—this time definitively.

It should be underlined that in Manichaeism this was *taught*. Besides, it is worth noting that the doctrine of the two kingdoms (or principles, 'roots') and the doctrine of the three epochs ('moments') were often taught as one unified doctrine. This, in brief, appears to have been the Manichaean creed, which very probably dated back to the founder of the religion himself. Of particular importance here is the fact that this appears to be the doctrine which was taught as a catechetical tenet to those who wanted to become Manichaeans.

We shall now illustrate with a few examples how this doctrine of the two principles and the three times formed the core of the Manichaean teaching. In the German translation of a Chinese text which, its editors assumed, goes back to Mani himself we read:

> Der König im Gesetze [= Mani]
> hat alle verborgenen Dinge verkündet.
> Die beiden Prinzipien, die drei Zeiten, den Sinn von Natur und Glorie vermochte er vollkommen klar hervortreten zu lassen, so dass keine Zweifel bleiben[71].

Another Chinese text says about Mani's mission:

> ... when explaining the two primeval (causes) perfectly just, when proclaiming the Self-Nature defining everything, when expounding the Three Epochs profoundly scholarly, when arguing the primary and secondary causes fully conclusive ...[72].

---

70 Allberry, *Psalm-Book*, 215, 2-6. Cf. 212, 4-5 and 215, 14-15.

71 E. Waldschmidt – W. Lentz, 'Manichäische Dogmatik aus chinesischen und iranischen Texten', *SPAW* 13 (1933) 491; cf. 544 for commentary.

72 G. Haloun – W.B. Henning, 'The Compendium of the Doctrines and

The Coptic Manichaean writings also refer repeatedly to both the two kingdoms and the three times. A passage in which both occur is one of the Bema-psalms. It recounts the Manichaean myth in considerable detail. A part of the beginning reads as follows:

> When the Holy Spirit came he revealed to us
> the way of Truth and taught us that there are two
> Natures, that of Light and that of Darkness, separate
> one from the other from the beginning.
> The Kingdom of Light, on the one hand, consisted in five
> Greatnesses, and they are the Father and his twelve
> Aeons and the Aeons of Aeons, the Living Air,
> the Land of Light; the great Spirit breathing in them,
> nourishing them with his Light.
> But the Kingdom of Darkness consists of five store-
> houses, which are Smoke and Fire and
> Wind and Water and Darkness; their Counsel
> creeping in them, moving them and inciting [?] them to
> make war with one another.

After the rest of the myth has been related, the psalm closes with the following lines on the three times:

> Glory and victory to our Lord Mani, the Spirit of
> Truth, that cometh from the Father, who has revealed to us
> the Beginning, the Middle and the End[73].

No further examples need be given here. The doctrine of the two kingdoms and that of the three times or 'moments' are mentioned repeatedly in the Coptic and other texts[74]. It is significant that *auditores* were also instructed in these fundamental tenets. This can be seen from a text found at Turfan, a 'Confessional' for hearers[75]:

Styles of the Teaching of Mani, the Buddha of Light', *Asia Major* 3 (1952) 191. Cf. 192 : 'I [= Mani] shall (...) explain (...) the doctrines of the three epochs and the two principles'.

[73] Allberry, *Psalm-Book*, 9, 8-9; 9, 21; 11, 29-31. A complete translation of this hymn also in R. Haardt, *Die Gnosis. Wesen und Zeugnisse*, Salzburg 1967, 224-227, and Böhlig, *Manichäismus*, 118-121.

[74] For the three 'moments' in the Coptic Manichaica, see e.g. *Keph.* 55, 17 - 57, 32 (= XVII: Das Kapitel von den drei Zeiten); *Psalm-Book* 21, 18-21; *Hom.* 7, 11-13. Other Coptic texts on the two kingdoms will be dealt with presently, as well as important data from the *Epistula fundamenti*, with which A. was certainly familiar. From a Chinese source a fragment from a hymn can be mentioned (Tsui Chi, 'Mo Ni Chiao Hsia Pu Tsan. The Lower [Second?] Section of the Manichaean Hymns', *BSOAS* 11 (1943) 191): 'On the two principles, the three moments and the meaning of the natures and forms ...'.

[75] This is the *Turkish* 'Beichtspiegel'. Besides publications by W. Radloff and

(Ever) Since we have recognized the true God (and) the pure (sacred) doctrine, we know 'The Two Principles' (roots, origins) (and) 'The Doctrine of the Three Times'. We know the light principle, the Realm of God, (and) the dark principle, the Realm of Hell. And we know what existed previously, when there was no earth and heaven, we know why God and the devil were fighting, how Light and Darkness were commingled, (and) who created earth and heaven, and finally we know why earth and heaven (once) will cease existing, how Light and Darkness will be separated, (and) what then will be (happen)[76]

The doctrine of the two principles and of the three 'moments' also appears to be of great consequence in a Manichaean text that was discovered near Tun-huang in China at the beginning of this century. The French scholar Paul Pelliot brought this text (*Fragment Pelliot*) to Paris in 1908, where it was published in 1913, together with other Chinese documents[77]. The passage in the *Fragment Pelliot* runs as follows:

VI. *Règles pour entrer en religion*
D'abord [il faut] discerner les deux principes.
Celui qui demande à entrer en religion doit savoir que les deux principes de la lumière et de l'obscurité ont des natures absolument distinctes: s'il ne discerne pas cela, comment [pourrait-il] mettre en pratique [la doctrine]?
Ensuite [il faut] comprendre les trois moments [qui sont]:
1. Le moment antérieur;
2. Le moment médian;
3. Le moment postérieur.
Dans le moment antérieur, il n'y a pas encore les cieux et les terres; il existe seulement, à part l'une de l'autre, la lumière et l'obscurité; la nature de la lumière est la sagesse; la nature de l'obscurité est la sottise; dans tout leur mouvement et dans tout leur repos, il n'est aucun cas où ces deux principes ne s'opposent.

A. von Le Coq, see the edition by W. Bang, 'Manichäische Laien-Beichtspiegel', *Le Muséon* 36 (1923) 137-242 and the new edition with an English translation and detailed commentary by Asmussen, *X^{u}āstvānīft*, 167-230. An *Iranian* 'Beichtspiegel', also from Turfan but with a different content and intended for *electi*, was edited by W.B. Henning, *Ein manichäisches Bet- und Beichtbuch (APAW* 10, 1936), Berlin 1937, 32-41.

[76] Asmussen, *X^{u}āstvānīft*, 196; vgl. Bang, 'Beichtspiegel', 157 and Böhlig, *Manichäismus*, 203.

[77] É. Chavannes – P. Pelliot, 'Un traité manichéen retrouvé en Chine', *JA* 10e sér., XVIII (1911) 499-617; *JA* 11e sér., I (1913) 99-199 (105-116: *Fragment Pelliot*) and 261-394. The beginning of the *Fragment Pelliot* did not appear until 1952:

> Dans le moment médian, l'obscurité a envahi la lumière; elle se donne libre carrière pour la chasser; la clarté vient et entre dans l'obscurité, et s'emploie tout entière pour la repousser. Par la 'grande calamité'[78], on a le dégoût [qui fait qu'on veut] se séparer du corps; dans la demeure enflammée, on fait le voeu [par lequel] on cherche à s'échapper. On fatigue le corps pour sauver la nature [lumineuse]; la sainte doctrine est fermement établie. Si on faisait du faux le vrai, qui oserait écouter les ordres [reçus]? Il faut bien discerner, et chercher les causes qui délivrent.
>
> Dans le moment postérieur, l'instruction et la conversion sont achevées; le vrai et le faux sont retournés chacun à sa racine; la lumière est retournée à la grande lumière; l'obscurité, de son côté, est retournée à l'obscurité amassée. Les deux principes sont reconstitués; tous deux se sont restitués [ce qu'ils tenaient l'un de l'autre][79].

Thus it can be concluded that all Manichaeans—not just the *electi* but, as is known from both the Turkish 'Beichtspiegel' and the *Epistula fundamenti*, also the *auditores*—were familiar with the doctrine of the two principles (kingdoms, 'roots') and that of the three times (moments)[80]. These tenets even appear to have functioned as a kind of catechesis for those who wished to become converts to Manichaeism ('the religion')[81].

It is not surprising, then, that there was frequent mention of two kingdoms in Manichaean writings. It is important to pay close attention, though, to the manner in which this took place. Did the Manichaean texts refer to these two kingdoms in general terms, or were there additional details that showed an unmistakable similarity to Augustine's doctrine of the two *civitates*?

Some of the most important texts will now be presented. In the Coptic *Kephalaia* (instructive in nature, going back largely to Mani himself[82]) it is written, for example:

Haloun and Henning, 'Compendium', 184-212. A translation of all Chinese Manichaica by H. Schmidt-Glintzer is due to appear in the *Göttinger Orientforschungen*.

78 What is meant here is man's physical existence, his being in a body.

79 Chavannes and Pelliot, 'Traité', 114-116.

80 For the two kingdoms as well as the three 'moments' in the *Ep. fund.*, see p. 224 and n. 125. A. became acquainted with this letter when he was still an *auditor*; cf. e.g. *C. ep. fund.* 6. J. Ries, 'Une version liturgique de l'*Epistola Fundamenti* de Mani réfutée par Saint Augustin?', *SP* XI (*TU* 108), Berlin 1972, 349, characterizes *Ep. fund.* as 'un exposé de catéchèse'.

81 E.g. *Fihrist* 332, 27 ff: *dīn*, the religion, is Manichaeism; only one who fulfils the requirements for the status of *electus* can be admitted to this religion.

82 See Böhlig, 'Probleme des manichäischen Lehrvortrages' (1953) and 'Eine

> ... Sie (the darkness, keke) ist in sich selber gespalten. Auch das
> Reich (mn̄tr̄ro) ist in sich selber gespalten; aber auch die Mächte, die ihren
> Abgrund verlassen haben und heraufgekommen sind, indem sie ihr [folgen], sind
> verurteilt worden wegen der Spaltung, die unter ihnen allen ist;
> die Finsternis wurde zerstört, auch ihre Mächte unterworfen. Denn
> die Kraft jenes ersten Lichtes ist wie die Art
> des Reiches (mn̄tr̄ro) dieser Welt (kosmos), denn solange seine Mysteriums-
> genossen mit ihm zusammenhalten, ... jenes Reich (mn̄tr̄ro),
> es wird bewundert und geehrt ... und übertrifft
> und überragt auch dieses Reich (mn̄tr̄ro), das ihm entgegensteht.
> Das Reich (mn̄tr̄ro) aber, dessen Mysteriumsgenossen in ihm
> [gespalten] sind, es ist notwendig, dass jenes Reich (mn̄tr̄ro) verurteilt und
> gedemütigt wird und in die Hand dieses Reiches (mn̄tr̄ro) gerät, das
> ihm entgegensteht[83].

Numerous other passages in the *Kephalaia* indicate that there are two kingdoms[84] and two kings[85].

The Coptic Psalm-Book, of which regrettably only the second part has been published, gives basically the same picture. Reference has already been made to this lengthy text, which narrates the Manichaean myth and the struggle between the two kingdoms (mn̄tr̄ro, kingdom)[86]. In other texts the word empire (kingdom) comes to the fore less often, but the concepts 'land of darkness' and 'land of light' are often mentioned[87]. The latter in particular plays

---

Bemerkung zur Beurteilung der Kephalaia' (1938), *Mysterion und Wahrheit*, 228-244, 245-251; see also Böhlig, *Manichäismus*, esp. 50.

83 *Keph.* 128, 5-17.

84 E.g. *Keph.* 25, 6 (Reich der Ewigkeit); 30, 33 (das erhabene Reich); 68, 31 (das hohe Reich); 100, 29 (das Reich der Welt); 151, 19-21 (... in gleicher Weise ist auch der Vater verborgen in seinem Reich ...); 223, 12-13 (das Reich des Lichtes). In each of these passages, as in *Keph.* 128, 5-17, the word *mn̄tr̄ro*, kingdom, occurs.

85 E.g. *Keph.* 5, 18 (König des Lichtes); 26,19 (König des Reiches der Finsternis, lit. pr̄ro n̄napkeke, the king of those who belong—or: of that which belongs—to darkness); also in 29, 18-19; 31, 2; 31, 27-28; 32, 1; 33, 2; 33, 5; 51, 23; 137, 9-10: König des Reiches der Finsternis, *pr̄ro n̄napkeke.*

86 See p. 214.

87 'Land of darkness', e.g. in *Psalm-Book* 11, 19; 96, 14; 138, 5. 20; 141, 6-7 (opposed to the land of light); 201, 12. 21-22. 23; 214, 29. 'Land of light' in 1, 10. 21; 9, 15. 23. 26; 32, 25; 69, 18-19; 95, 28; 116, 30; 135, 34; 136, 35. 38; 141, 6; 144, 13; 163, 25; 168, 25; 178, 31; 179, 13; 185, 8; 197, 18-19; 198, 29; 199, 1. 5. 22; 200, 2. 19-20. 27-28; 209, 8; 213, 13. 19; 219, 19. 24-25; 221, 9-10; 225, 15-16; 226, 13-14 (the index in Allberry s. v. Land of Light is incomplete). For land the word *kah*, land, earth, is generally used (A., *C. ep. fund.* 13 and 15, repeats from

a central role in these psalms full of fervent longing[88].

And especially striking in these psalms are the frequent references to the city of God, the city of the gods (tpolis n̄n̄noute). This city, pre-eminent quintessence and centre of the kingdom of light, is the focus of the believer's desire. She is the blessed city[89], the city of the gods, of the angels[90], the city of light[91], the city of the righteous[92], the citadel (politeuma) of the angels, habitation of the blessed[93]. The believer is on his way to this city:

> Lo, the path of Light has stretched before me unto my
> first city (polis), the place ...[94].
> I found then the Land of Light and made my way to the city (polis) of the Gods and consorted with the righteous while I was yet in the body, through my mouth which is full of praise[95].
> ... I hasten to the city of the [righteous], ...[96].
> I found the ships.
> The ships are the sun and the moon. They ferried me
> forth to my city (polis)[97].

This city is repeatedly referred to as 'our city', 'my city': here the believer is at home. Now body and world hold the soul captive, but the call of the Redeemer reminds it of its heavenly origin and it sets out for the heavenly city. For the believer this world is therefore a desert[98] in which he wanders about as an alien:

> I listened to thy words. I walked in thy laws. I
> became a stranger in the world (kosmos) for thy name's sake, my God[99].
> I became a stranger for thy name's sake.

Ep. fund. the *lucida et beata terra*, the *sancta terra* and the *terra tenebrarum* resp.; frequently *chōra* is used too.

88 Also described as: land of the immortal, of the glorious, of rest, of peace, of truth, the native country (patris).

89 *Psalm-Book* 1, 17.

90 *Psalm-Book* 50, 29. Cf. 95, 28-29 and 117, 5-6: city of the gods.

91 *Psalm-Book* 64, 13; 70, 23; 85, 12.

92 *Psalm-Book* 99, 21.

93 *Psalm-Book* 136, 42-43. Cf. 140, 17: citadel (politeuma) of the angels.

94 *Psalm-Book* 80, 29-30.

95 *Psalm-Book* 95, 28-30.

96 *Psalm-Book* 99, 21.

97 *Psalm-Book* 168, 5-8. A passage that may be compared with the preceding ones is *Psalm-Book* 50, 27-29, in which Jesus says: 'I rejoice as I ascend to my Father with whom I have conquered in / the land of the Darkness; o my great King, ferry me / to the city (polis) of the Gods, the angels'.

98 This word occurs 5 times, 3 times with the addition 'of this world' (kosmos): *Psalm-Book* 87, 17; 152, 12; 193, 26.

99 *Psalm-Book* 60, 28-29.

I took up my cross, I followed thee.
I left the things of the body for the things of the Spirit.
I despised the glory of the world (kosmos),
because of the glory that passes not away[100].
Thou art a stranger to the world (kosmos),
a sojourner on the earth for (?) men[101].

The notion of the believer sojourning as an alien is expressed in this way in almost all the psalms. One group of these psalms is explicitly entitled: *Psalmoi sarakōtōn*, psalms of the wanderers/pilgrims[102]. They are on their way to the kingdom of light, the land of light and specifically: the city of God. But where are they coming from? They are now in this world (kosmos), on earth, in the desert, in the kingdom or the land of darkness. But is this region of the demons, the antithesis of the kingdom of light, also described as a city?

Closer examination reveals that this is indeed the case. In the *Psalm-Book* we find 'the city (polis) of mockery'; Adam referred to this text[103]. This part of the *Psalms of Thomas* tells of a Messenger from the kingdom of light who goes to the city of the demons:

when they saw me, they wagged their heads ...,
they sneered (?) at me, they turned up the nose in mockery,
saying: O man, come forth from among
men (?), thou didst set fire to our city (polis)[104].

This part of the Manichaean myth can be compared with another part which is also to be found in the *Psalms of Thomas*. It also concerns a Messenger (presbeutès) from the kingdom (mn̄tr̄ro) of light who goes to the land (chōra) of the demons. When these demons of darkness see his brilliant image (eikōn), they are filled with eager longing and seductively they sing to him:

---

[100] *Psalm-book* 175, 26-30; each sentence is followed by the refrain: 'My [Saviour]'.

[101] *Psalm-Book* 181, 22-23; here the soul (psychè) is addressed. The refrain at the end of each sentence is: 'Be [mindful of thy Aeons]'..

[102] Allberry, *Psalm-Book*, XXII, had doubts about the translation of *sarakōte*; P. Nagel, 'Die Psalmoi Sarakoton des manichäischen Psalmbuches', *OLZ* 62 (1957) 123-130, demonstrates that its meaning is 'wanderer, pilgrim'. The theme of these hymns is: 'Weltverhaftung und Weltflucht, die auf der Pilgerfahrt nach der Lichtheimat begriffene Seele' (126).

[103] *Psalm-Book* 226, 1; Adam, 'Ursprung', *Sprache und Dogma*, 138.

[104] *Psalm-Book* 226, 2-5.

> Thou art come in peace, o son of the Brightnesses, son
> of the Lights and the Richnesses. Thou art come in peace,
> o son of the Brightnesses, that shalt be the illuminer of our
> worlds (kosmos). Come and rule over our land (chōra) and set peace
> in [our] city (polis)[105].

It is clear that in the land of darkness there is also a city (polis), a *civitas diaboli* as the antipole of the heavenly city. In a Chinese text found at Tun-huang and published by Chavannes and Pelliot in 1911, a *civitas diaboli* is also mentioned. In the third part of this extensive treatise—which is composed of various parts and attributed to Mani and his pupil A-t'o[106]—there is a description of the work of the great Messenger of Light. When he entered the world, he destroyed the city of the evil one:

> Vous tous, écoutez attentivement. Quand le grand Envoyé de la Lumière bienfaisante fut entré dans ce monde, il renversa les quartiers tortueux de la ville de l'hérésie, il détruisit les anciennes demeures et il pénétra jusqu'au palais du démon.
>
> Or ce démon de la convoitise, voyant que ses quartiers avaient été détruits, fit une nouvelle ville impure; à cause de la sottise qui lui appartient en propre, il y fit agir sans restrictions les cinq concupiscenses.
>
> Or il arriva que les enfants religieux vaillants du Vent pur merveilleux qui est une colombe blanche[107], et les fils[108] du grand Saint entrèrent dans cette ville; ils regardèrent des quatre côtés et ne virent que de la fumeé et des nuages qui autour protégaient les innombrables quartiers tortueux [de la ville impure]. Quand ils eurent vu cela de loin, ils continuèrent à avancer progressivement et arrivèrent au sommet du rempart [de la ville]; regardant de loin droit en bas, ils aperçurent sept perles précieuses; chacune de ces perles précieuses prise isolément a une valeur inestimable; toutes étaient recouvertes de souillures diverses qui s'enroulaient au-dessus d'elles et les recouvraient[109].

---

105 *Psalm-Book* 214, 11-15.

106 This was most likely Addas, Adda(i), a personal disciple of Mani's and known as one of his apostles.

107 This most likely refers to the Holy Ghost. The Manichaeans were familiar with the image of the Holy Ghost as a dove.

108 Or: the son (sing.), the Envoy of light, coming from the Father of Greatness?

109 Chavannes and Pelliot, 'Traité', 556-557. It is not quite certain whether this description applies to an event in the macrocosm or in the microcosm (the human body): the perspective keeps changing. If—as seems most likely—it applies to a microcosmic event, the text maintains its value in this framework: here and elsewhere in Manichaean texts parallelism between macrocosm and microcosm is to be found. Besides the explanations given by Chavannes and Pelliot, see E.

In other Manichaean texts also we find a *civitas diaboli* as a wicked city or city of sinners, but there the reference is to the city where Mani was taken prisoner and died[110]. A possible exception is a fragment from Turfan, contained in the posthumous papers of F.C. Andreas and published by Walter Henning. It reads:

> ... wir wollen hinausgehen aus [der Stadt (od. dem Reich) der] Sünder hin zur Stadt (zum Reich) der Frommen! Es spricht der kleine Schüler: 'Heil allen Menschen, die dies wünschen und erfragen!'[111]

In the last two examples (the texts published by Chavannes and Pelliot and by Henning, parts of which have been cited) the problems of translation are by no means slight and therefore great care is needed in making interpretations. But the Coptic material is quite a different matter in this respect. Here the word *polis* occurs frequently and the city of the demons is a *civitas diaboli*.

In this context still more data from Manichaean sources should be considered. In the Coptic psalms we find 'Jerusalem of the skies, the Church ...'[112]. The heavenly city is called Jerusalem and referred to as the Church (ekklèsia). Whether her counterpart is called Babylon—as in the writings of Augustine—is not quite clear[113]. It

---

Waldschmidt – W. Lentz, *Die Stellung Jesu im Manichäismus* (*APAW* 4, 1926), Berlin 1926, esp. 14 ff.

110 *Psalm-Book* 19, 29-30; 44, 18. 25. Cf. 17, 21 and also 15, 6; 22, 22-23.

111 F.C. Andreas – W. Henning, 'Mitteliranische Manichaica aus Chinesisch-Turkestan', II, *SPAW* 7 (1933) 311: *M* 219 R. It is not certain whether the word *šhr* should be translated as city or possibly as kingdom. Cf. Andreas and Henning, 'Mir. Man.', I, *SPAW* 10 (1932) 218: *šhr* als 'Welt'; Andreas and Henning, 'Mir. Man.', II, 359: *šhr* as 'Land, Reich, Welt, Stadt', Andreas and Henning, 'Mir. Man.', III, *SPAW* 27 (1934) 907; *šhr* (sogdian) als 'Land, Reich, Welt, Äon'. Cf. the glossaries in W. Sundermann, *Mitteliranische manichäischen Texte kirchengeschichtlichen Inhalts*, Berlin 1981, 171: *šhr* as 'Land, Reich, Erdteil(?), Welt'; *šhrystᵓn* as 'Stadt'; 190: *s'ryst'n* (sogdian) as 'Stadt'. M. Boyce, *A Word-List of Manichaean Middle Persian and Parthian (with a Reverse Index by R. Zwanziger)*, Leiden 1977, 84-85, translates *šhr* (ˇsahr, Middle Persian and Parthian) as: 'land, country, region; town; the world; world of the hereafter, heaven; aeon'; *ˇshrystᵓn* (ˇsahrestan, Middle Persian) as 'city, provincial capital'.

112 *Psalm-Book* 61, 2.

113 Possibly reference can be made to *Hom.* 14, 9 ff., a part of the 'Sermòn vom grossen Krieg': trial, the cup of wrath, shall come over Babylon and all its sons. But in the background there may be *Apoc.* 16:19, as may be the case in *Hom.* 8, 10. Babylon is also mentioned elsewhere, but each time in connection with Mani's mission or other events in his life. See e.g. *Hom.* 29, 10; 54, 15; 61, 17; 76, 29; *Keph.* 187, 9; *M* 566 I R ('Ein Arzt bin ich aus dem Lande Babylon'); *M* 4 ('Gegangen bin ich aus Babel, damit ich rufen sollte einen Ruf in der Welt ...').

is notable, though, that the heavenly city is a city of angels and people:

> Our resplendent city (polis).
> Town of the godly.
> Citadel (politeuma) of the Angels.
> Habitation of the blessed (makarios)[114].
>
> I have] forsaken the troubled world which [is of no] value in my eyes: I hasten to the city of the [righteous], I yearn (?) to pass from the flesh, like ...[115].

In another place we read also that the faithful are added to the numbers of the angels[116]. Moreover, a Middle Persian fragment reveals that the congregation on earth (untere Religion, Gemeinde) is united with that of the kingdom of light (obere Religion, Gemeinde)[117]. Together, according to the Chinese Hymnscroll, now in London, they form one congregation:

> Und [wir] preisen: die guthandelnde, frommen Wandel übende Schar,
> die der Vergangenheit, Zukunft und Gegenwart[118].

5. Similarities and differences

On the strength of the foregoing it can be concluded that in many respects there are similarities between the Manichaean references to the two kingdoms and those of Augustine. In both the writings of the Manichaeans and those of Augustine the heavenly kingdom and the heavenly city are named again and again. The counterpart is the kingdom of darkness as the kingdom of this world (kosmos); a *civitas diaboli* is also mentioned. The heavenly city is a city of angels and people; the faithful are on their way there and are added to the numbers of the angels. Once the heavenly city is called Jerusalem and for Mani's followers her counterpart may also be Babylon.

---

114 *Psalm-Book* 136, 40-43.

115 *Psalm-Book* 99, 20-22. By the righteous (dikaioi; cf. 99, 31: 'O virtuous assembly of the righteous ...') the deceased *electi* are meant, as they are by the *makarioi* in the preceding quotation. Elsewhere, however, *makarioi* often refers to the *electi* who are now living on earth, e.g. in *Psalm-Book* 62, 17; *Hom.* 25, 1.

116 *Psalm-Book* 213, 21.

117 *M* 738 R; Waldschmidt and Lentz, 'Dogmatik', 561 and 600 (explanation).

118 *H* 148 a-b; Waldschmidt and Lentz, 'Dogmatik', 489. Cf. e.g. *H* 136 d and 152 d.

As part of the doctrine of the two kingdoms, for the Manichaeans as well as for Augustine, great emphasis is given to the idea of the faithful sojourning as aliens. In this life the believer finds himself in strange and hostile territory, but he renounces this world[119]. His home is elsewhere. Here he finds only temporary accommodation as does a traveller at an inn[120]. In the Manichaean texts there is even a view of using and enjoying that agrees with Augustine's *uti-frui* to a considerable extent. The perfect (teleios) catechumen lives in his house as at an inn, his wife is a stranger to him and he regards gold, silver and household goods as borrowed:

> Er
> nimmt sie, bedient sich ihrer, dann gibt er sie
> ihrem Herrn. Nicht hängt er sein Herz an sie und seinen Schatz. Er hat sein Denken aus der Welt (kosmos) gerissen und sein Herz in die heilige Kirche (ekklèsia) gelegt. Zu aller Zeit ist sein Denken bei Gott[121].

There is also a similarity in the description of the kingdom of darkness as being divided in itself, swollen with pride, full of dark lusts and envy[122]. The kingdoms of this world are dominated by

---

[119] *Keph.* 36, 11. For renouncing (apotassesthai) see also *Psalm-Book* 59, 7; 77, 30; 79, 9. In this context the emphasis on fasting (nèsteia) and continence (enkrateia) should be noted, e.g. in *Keph.* 110, 4; 192, 6; 221, 26; 229, 21; etc.; *Psalm-Book*, esp. 179-181.

[120] Besides *Keph.* 228 f., see e.g. *CMC* 66, 23 – 67, 2 ('And I have shown the truth to my fellow-travellers'—tois emois xynemporois—) and *CMC* 44, 7-8 (othneiōi kai monèrei). One is reminded of the *Hymn of the Pearl* in the *Acta Thomae* (220, 19 f., ed. Bonnet; cf. G. Bornkamm in: Hennecke and Schneemelcher, *NTAp*, II, 350) with which, it is generally assumed, Mani was acquainted. But A., too, was familiar with the metaphor of the believer who sojourns temporarily in this world as an alien (peregrinus) and a traveller (viator) in the inn (stabulum); see e.g. *ss.* 14, 6; 111, 2; 177, 2 and *Tract. in Ioh. Ev.* 40, 10; 41, 13. Could we not say that he took this image from the *Acta Thomae* (along with *Luke* 10), with which he had become familiar during his Manichaean period (*C. Faust.* XXII, 79; *C. Adim.* XVII, 2; *De serm. Dom.* I, 20, 65; cf. Altaner, 'Apokryphen', 209 n. 6)? That he was very well acquainted with these *Acta* is demonstrated in *C. Faust.* XXII, 79: he quotes them from memory.

[121] *Keph.* 228, 20 ff. (quotation 229, 1-6). The words treasure and heart are reminiscent of *Matt.* 6:21 (*Luke* 12:34); cf., for example, 229, 9. After that 1 *Cor.* 7:29 ff. is brought up. For the notion *uti – frui*, see *Hom.* 14, 22-24; Mani's *Ep. fund.*, in the Latin translation that A. reproduces (*C. ep. fund.* 11), speaks literally of: '... aeterna et gloriosa vita *fruetur*'.

[122] Cf. esp. *Keph.* 128, 5-17 and a passage which has come down to us in the work of Severus of Antioch and probably originates from the *Book of the Giants* (Adam, *Texte*, esp. 13), with *DCD* XI, 33.

the *libido dominandi*, Augustine says repeatedly, and a Manichaean text concurs with this almost completely[123].

It is significant that for the Manichaeans as well as for Augustine a doctrine of the two cities is linked to a division of history into three times. We have already seen that the Manichaeans considered this a central tenet, quite probably originating with Mani himself and familiar to every Manichaean. Moreover, it evidently functioned as a catechetical tenet.

Was Augustine familiar with this doctrine? By virtue of the position it occupies in the Coptic and other Manichaean texts, it could be assumed he was: every Manichaean was familiar with it. But absolute certainty is provided by Augustine himself: he was thoroughly acquainted with Mani's *Epistula fundamenti*, which, as he declared, contains almost the entire Manichaean teaching[124]. It is precisely in this letter, with its strongly didactic character, that the two principles (substantiae) and also the three times are named[125]. And the extent of Augustine's familiarity with the three 'moments' of the Manichaeans (initium, medium, finis) is most clearly seen in his debate with Felix[126].

For the Manichaeans world history was the history of the two kingdoms: they were separate in the very beginning (initium), intermingled in the middle time (medium), separate again in the final one (finis). Similarly for Augustine, the history of the world was the history of the two cities (civitates); it has an origin (exortus), progress (procursus) and 'destined ends' (debiti fines)[127]. In accordance with these three times he divided the main part of his *City of God* into three parts of four books each.

Does this mean then that Augustine's concept of the two cities originated in Manichaeism? On the basis of the texts that have been

---

[123] Cf. esp. *DCD* XIV, 28 with *Keph.* 33, 5-8: 'Der Geist des Königs des Reiches der Finsternis ist derjenige, der herrscht heutzutage in den Regierungen und Gewalten der Erde und der ganzen Welt, ich meine diejenigen, welche herrschen über die gesammte Schöpfung, indem sie die Menschen erniedrigen in Gewaltherrschaft nach ihrem Willen.'

[124] *C. ep. fund.* 5: '... ubi totum paene, quod creditis, continetur ...'.

[125] *C. ep. fund.*, esp. 12 and 13. Evidence for the fact that the 'moments' occurred in the *Ep. fund.* is given by *C. Fel.* II, 1 where Felix says to A.: 'Ista enim epistola fundamenti est, quod et sanctitas tua bene scit, quod et ego dixi, quia ipsa continet initium, medium et finem'.

[126] *C. Fel.* I, 6; I, 10 (2x); I, 12; cf. I, 14 and II, 7. See also *C. Faust.* XIII, 6.

[127] As in *DCD* X, 32; see further pp. 93-94.

discussed, it would seem that the conjectures of numerous scholars and particularly Adam's view have been corroborated[128].

But there is more. It might first be asked whether similarity in thought and even terminology can in itself provide convincing proof of derivation[129]. Should one not speak of a direct and decisive influence only when similar ideas and terminology do not occur anywhere else? And does this apply to Augustine's doctrine of the two cities and, for example, to his views about the believer's sojourning as an alien, which are unmistakably connected with it?

The Manichaeans taught an absolute dualism: two kingdoms, quite different in their substance, have been confronting each other from eternity and will do so for ever and ever. But there is no such ontological dualism in Augustine's theology. Nowhere did he see evil, the kingdom of darkness, Satan, as an eternal power separate from God. On the contrary, Augustine repeatedly and emphatically pointed out against the Manichaeans that the devil has *forsaken* the truth: he has not had an evil nature from the beginning[130]. Satan is

---

[128] Although some elements of Adam's view can be questioned, most of his argumentation, mainly based on the Coptic texts, is correct. Incorrect is the reference to *Psalm-Book* 117, 5 ('Ursprung', *Sprache und Dogma*, 137): this passage refers to Christ. Incorrect, too, is his observation, based on *Psalm-Book* 117, 7 f., that the city of God was also called kingdom (*ibid.*). In 'Fortwirken' and in his *Dogmengeschichte* there are a number of observations which, without further elucidation from the sources, remain speculative. The statement (in 'Fortwirken', *Sprache und Dogma*, 160) that A. saw history as a 'Gigantomachie' cannot be justified: Scholz wrote this, but where did A. say it? One must also question the repeated reference (taken over by others) to Mani's *Living Gospel* as the example for the arrangement of *DCD* in 22 books: *this* work was *not* mentioned anywhere by A. Cf. pp. 78-80.—Ehrhard's references to Manichaean sources (*Metaphysik*, III, 34) give rise to many questions, such as: Did the Manichaeans prefer the idea of *polis* to that of kingdom?; is, in *Psalm-Book* 214, 11 f., the city of the demons cursed?; is in *Psalm-Book* 56, 23 the unearthly light praised?; do these psalms (214, 11 f.) make mention of a captivity of the city of God among the demons?; etc.—Alfaric's reference (*Évolution* 123 n. 6) to *C. Faust.* XX, 4 is equally unconvincing. Was he possibly referring to another text?

[129] Cf. W. Geerlings, 'Zur Frage des Nachwirkens des Manichäismus in der Theologie Augustins', *ZKTh* 93 (1971) 45-60.

[130] E.g. *DCD* XI, 13: 'Ab initio diabolus peccat [1 *John* 3:8], hoc est, ex quo creatus est, iustitiam recusavit (...). Huic sententiae quisquis adquiescit, non cum illis haereticis sapit, id est Manichaeis, et si quae aliae pestes ita sentiunt, quod suam quandam propriam tamquam ex adverso quodam principio diabolus habeat naturam mali; (...) ut ... non attendant non dixisse Dominum: A veritate alienus fuit; sed: In veritate non stetit, ubi a veritate lapsum intellegi voluit, in qua utique si stetisset, eius particeps factus beatus cum sanctis angelis permaneret'. The same line of reasoning occurs regularly in anti-Manichaean writings.

still the prince (princeps) of this world, the leader (dux) of the fallen angels[131]. But this adversary is under God's jurisdiction[132]; he is virtually vanquished and his final defeat is certain[133].

If Augustine's theology is to be characterized as dualistic, on no account should it be seen as ontologically dualistic. Yet a dualism is to be found in his work, just as it is to be found, for example, in the writings of John and Paul: a religious dualism[134]. There is the Johannine contrast between light and darkness, truth and falsehood, above and below[135]; there is the Pauline contrast between flesh and Spirit, outer and inner man, man under the power of sin and in the state of grace[136]. From Manichaean dualism Augustine, strongly influenced by Neoplatonism, moved on to a dualistically coloured phraseology as he found in the Scriptures.

This does not imply that Augustine's doctrine of the two cities could not (also) have a Manichaean origin. In more than one aspect a close affinity and even a striking similarity appears. This is not surprising for the work of a man who had lived among the Manichaeans for many years and who still remembered much from their psalms and other works[137]. It was precisely Augustine who repeatedly demonstrated his thorough familiarity with Manichaeism[138]. But in

---

131 *En. in Ps.* 90, 2, 9; *s.* 12, 7.

132 E.g. *Opus imp. c. Iul.* I, 66, where A.'s reaction to Julian's accusation that he was making two kings fight for dominion over humanity runs as follows: 'Sic sunt autem in diaboli potestate quaecumque illi, Deo iudicante, subduntur ut a Dei potestate, sub qua et ipse diabolus constitutus est, aliena esse non possint'.

133 E.g. *s.* 263, 1.

134 For this term cf. Geerlings, 'Nachwirken', 59, who follows S. Pétrement, *Le dualisme chez Platon, les gnostiques et les manichéens*, Paris 1947.

135 See, among others, R. Bultmann, *Theologie des Neuen Testaments*, Tübingen 1965[5], 367-385: 'Der johanneïsche Dualismus'.

136 E.g. Bultmann, *Theologie*, 200-203, for Paul's dualism in contrast with gnostic dualism.

137 A. sang Manichaean psalms; see p. 35. It is quite possible that their content and themes were the same as those discovered in 1931: the writings from Medinet Madi all date from the 4th century (cf. the introductions to the editions by Allberry, Polotsky and Böhlig, in collaboration with H. Ibscher); various Manichaean works had been translated into Latin. For the knowledge that A. could have had of the psalms, see esp. Schmidt and Polotsky, 'Mani-Fund', 34; T. Säve-Söderbergh, *Studies in the Coptic Manichaean Psalm-Book. Prosody and Mandaean Parallels*, Uppsala et al. 1949, 1; Feldmann, *Einfluss*, 664 (= Feldmann, 'Christus-Frömmigkeit', 208).—The Chinese, Iranian and East Turkish texts all date from later periods but often contain (very) early material.

138 He became acquainted with it in his youth; see p. 45. When he was a bishop he reread the Manichaean writings and he owned many of them. Almost all present-day investigators (with the exception of Ort, *Mani*, 40-41, but he is wrong) agree that A. was thoroughly familiar with Manichaeism. J.P. Maher, 'Saint

the foregoing an essential difference with the Manichaean doctrine of the two kingdoms has been indicated.

Yet it is a fact that Augustine's theology was determined by Manichaeism to a considerable degree. Mention has already been made of his exegesis, which reflects in many respects his Manichaean past: repeated discussion of the opening chapters of *Genesis*, the narratives about the patriarchs, the genealogies of Jesus, the concurrence of the Old and the New Testament[139]. Wilhelm Geerlings maintains that in reaction to Manichaeism Augustine particularly emphasized Christ's incarnation and not so much His crucifixion and resurrection; that would explain why he did not give sufficient attention to the cosmic significance of Christ[140]. Earlier Thomas Clarke contended that this also holds good for soteriology: in his attack on Manichaeism, Augustine regarded Paul's words in *Rom.* 8 about the groaning of creation as referring to the rational part of creation only[141]. It can be concluded that Adam was right in asserting repeatedly that Manichaean problems and 'Denkformen' are present in Augustine's works[142]; the church father could not detach himself from them, but returned to them again and again.

Augustine and Manichaean Cosmogony', *AS* 10 (1979) 91-104, stresses for example that in *C. Faust.* XV, 6 A. enumerated exactly the same five sons of the Living Spirit and in the same order as they occur in *Keph.* 91. Many more instances could be given. L. Koenen, at the end of a detailed article on 'Augustine and Manichaeism in Light of the Cologne Mani Codex', *ICS* 3 (1978) 154-195, concludes: 'The picture [viz. of Manichaeism] Augustine gives is basically correct, though he did not always understand the underlying gnostic theology' (195).

[139] Cf. p. 38 ff. For this essential aspect of A.'s theologizing see, besides Allgeier, 'Einfluss', esp. the dissertation by Walter, *Ertrag* (1972). Walter even regards A.'s abandonment of the Manichaean exegesis and his acceptance of the Catholic one as the essential element of his conversion.

[140] W. Geerlings, 'Der manichäische «Jesus patibilis» in der Theologie Augustins', *ThQ* 152 (1972) 124-131. More research is needed in this area, as Geerlings himself declares (130). For the cosmic significance of Christ, A.'s interpretation of 'In principio' in *Gen.* 1:1 as 'in verbo suo coaeterno' can be pointed to; cf. e.g. *Conf.* XII, 14, 17 ff. See further J.C.M. van Winden, *'Idee' en 'Materie' in de vroeg-christelijke uitleg van de beginwoorden van Genesis. Een hoofdstuk uit de ontmoeting tussen Griekse filosofie en christelijk denken*, Amsterdam-Oxford-New York 1985, 13 and 19 ff.

[141] T.E. Clarke, 'St. Augustine and Cosmic Redemption', *TS* 19 (1958) 133-164. Cf. T.E. Clarke, *The Eschatological Transformation of the Material World according to Saint Augustine*, Woodstock, Md. 1956. This work contains, in a slightly revised version, the sixth chapter ('The groaning of Creation') of the dissertation which Clarke defended in Rome in 1954 (Pontificia Universitas Gregoriana). In spite of repeated attempts—and with the very much appreciated assistance of Prof. Hans Quecke in Rome—I was unable to gain access to the complete dissertation.

[142] Adam, *Sprache und Dogma*, for instance 144, 161, 166; *Dogmengeschichte*, 256.

Feldmann, too, continually indicates the great importance of Manichaeism for our understanding of Augustine[143].

Did his concept of the two *civitates* then originate, partly or completely, from Manichaeism? We have pointed to many similarities and to an essential difference. Before the question can be answered, there must be an investigation into whether or not concepts of two kingdoms, concepts which might have influenced Augustine, occurred in other writings. Scholars have repeatedly referred to Tyconius, also to Neoplatonism. Justly so? A study of the preceding Jewish and Christian traditions also seems advisable: does the concept of the two kingdoms occur there—and if so, in what way? Is it possible that from these traditions the dualistic antithesis between city of God and city of the devil can be accounted for?

This brings us to a final question in this context, viz. the one concerning influences on the doctrine of the two kingdoms of Mani himself. It gradually became established that the founder of this world religion grew up in a Jewish-Christian milieu. Many typically Jewish and Christian ideas are to be found in his gnostic religion. Should it then not be possible that Mani himself found certain views of two kingdoms already present in the ideas of predecessors, and that he converted these views into his radically dualistic system?

Later we shall examine whether a doctrine of two kingdoms existed in Jewish and (Jewish-)Christian[144] milieus—and if so to what

---

[143] He concludes his book as follows (*Einfluss*, 734): 'Die Theologie wird die in erstaunlichem Masse vernachlässigten Manichäer in ihrer Forschung ernster nehmen müssen, durch deren Verkündigung Augustinus *Denkformen* kennen lernte und theologische Positionen zu beziehen sich gezwungen sah, die von folgenschwerer Bedeutung für Kirche und Theologie wurden'.

[144] In scholarly writings the terms 'Jewish-Christian' and 'Jewish Christianity' are not always synonymous. H.J. Schoeps, for example, used the term 'Judenchristentum' in a limited sense (Jewish Christianity refers particularly to heterodox Christianity as it occurs in the *Pseudo-Clementines*); J. Daniélou gave it a very wide connotation ('judéo-christianisme' is the type of Christianity that expresses itself in concepts derived from the—pluriform!—Judaism of the beginning of the Christian era) and in his description he depicts even Paul as belonging to Jewish Christianity. For an interesting discussion of Daniélou's views, see esp. the 'Diskussionsbeiträge' by B. Kötting, W. Schneemelcher, M. Noth and K.H. Rengstorf in: J. Daniélou, *Das Judenchristentum und die Anfänge der Kirche*, Köln-Opladen 1964, 25-37. Like M. Simon in particular we want to keep the term 'Jewish Christianity' and use it to denote the archaic Christianity that is strongly influenced by the synagogical and/or a more or less 'heretical' Judaism. See esp. M. Simon, 'Réflexions sur le judéo-christianisme', in: J. Neusner (ed.), *Christianity, Judaism and other Greco-Roman cults. Studies for Morton Smith at sixty*, II, Leiden 1975, 53-76.

extent. Now, finally, Mani's Jewish-Christian background will be considered.

6. Mani's Jewish-Christian background

For a long time scholars of Manichaeism have been struck by the fact that this gnostic world religion contained many elements that are reminiscent of Judaism and/or Christianity. It has often been assumed that they were the result of later modifications of Mani's religion: in a Christian environment various Christian and also Jewish ideas were adopted. These assumptions obviously applied to the Manichaeism in the Christian Roman Empire, especially in Africa. Mention has already been of an exponent of this view, the Dutch scholar L.H. Grondijs, who contended that a separate and highly assimilated 'Numidian Manichaeism' had existed[145].

Indeed, one cannot deny that Manichaeism adapted itself to its surroundings. If one studies the texts from Turfan and Tun-huang one finds, among other things, entirely different names of gods[146]. When Mani entered upon the world stage, he was already a great syncretist, incorporating religious ideas of his day and his surroundings into a gnostic system of his own. Whereas his foremost example Paul was a Jew to the Jews and a Greek to the Greeks, Mani himself went much further: he aimed to be a Christian to the Christians, a Zoroastrian to the Zoroastrians, a Buddhist to the Buddhists. And many adherents went still further, especially those who lived in Buddhist milieus in Central Asia and China.

Yet one notices again and again how ideas which accorded with Christianity, and obviously stemmed from it, occupied a special place in Manichaean writings. This applies not only to the Manichaeism in North Africa and Egypt, but also to that in Central Asia and China. Especially on the basis of the great Chinese *Hymnscroll*, Ernst Waldschmidt and Wolfgang Lentz showed the important place Jesus occupied in Eastern Manichaeism[147]. Using both Eastern and Western sources, Eugen Rose was able to write exten-

---

[145] See p. 212 n. 67.

[146] See e.g. Boyce, *Reader*, 8-10, and Tardieu, *Manichéisme*, 103-107, for parallel series of names.

[147] Waldschmidt and Lentz, *Die Stellung Jesu im Manichäismus* (1926). They also pointed (esp. 21 ff.) to the great importance of the NT for Mani and his followers, as can be seen from the Turfan fragments.

sively about Manichaean Christology[148]. Alexander Böhlig indicated convincingly the occurrence of many biblical themes, especially on the basis of the Coptic texts[149]. Apparently all these elements were integral parts of the Manichaean religion.

In this context the recent publication of the *Cologne Mani-Codex*[150] is of great consequence. It established irrefutably[151] that the young Mani grew up in a Jewish-Christian baptist milieu. Although one can have one's doubts—perhaps justly so—as to whether this was composed of (a group within) the Elchasaites[152], it certainly was a

---

148 E. Rose, *Die Christologie des Manichäismus nach den Quellen dargestellt*, Marburg 1941 (Diss. Mschr.), now available in a revised version entitled *Die manichäische Christologie*, Wiesbaden 1979.

149 Böhlig, *Die Bibel bei den Manichäern* (1947). Cf. esp. A. Böhlig, 'Christliche Wurzeln im Manichäismus' (1957/1960), *Mysterion und Wahrheit*, 202-221 and his 'The New Testament and the Concept of the Manichean Myth', in: Logan and Wedderburn (eds.), *The New Testament and Gnosis*, 90-104.

150 See p. 209 and n. 53.

151 Before 1970 the existence of a Jewish Christian (Elkesaite) influence was assumed, mostly on the basis of al-Nadīm's evidence in his *Fihrist* on the Mughtasilah, 'those who wash themselves', by, among others, Baur (*Man. Religionssystem*, esp. 486), Kessler (*Mani*, I, 8 n. 3: Elkesaitism as a 'vormanichäisches Manichäismus'), Alfaric (*Écritures*, I, esp. 18), H.J. Schoeps (*Theologie und Geschichte des Judenchristentums*, Tübingen 1949, 332) and G. Quispel (e.g. 'Der gnostische Anthropos und die jüdische Tradition' (1954), *GS*, I, 182; 'The Discussion of Judaic Christianity' (1968), *GS*, II, 156).

152 Among those who question this are A.F.J. Klijn – G.J. Reinink, 'Elchasai and Mani', *VC* 28 (1974) 277-289, and esp. G.P. Luttikhuizen, *The Revelation of Elchasai* ..., Tübingen 1985, particularly 163 ff., 220-222, 224 and 227. This is not the suitable place to discuss Luttikhuizen's learned objections, such as the fact that the name Alchasaios and not Elchasaios occurs in the *CMC*; is this the same person as the one called Elchasai by Hippolytus and Elxai by Epiphanius?; the *CMC* refers to Alchasaios as *archègos*, but does this mean 'founder'?; the baptists of the *CMC* are not called Elkesaites or Elkeseans, nor is there any reference to a book of revelations. However, Luttikhuizen too recognizes (esp. 164) that there were Jewish and Christian elements in the belief and practice of Mani's baptists. Almost all the other investigators accept the idea that the baptists of Mani's early years belonged to the Elkesaites. Besides Henrichs and Koenen, the editors of the *CMC* (although some hesitation can be discerned in Henrichs' article 'The Cologne Mani Codex Reconsidered', *HSCP* 83 (1979) 334-367, esp. 354 ff.): C. Colpe (*JbAC* 14 (1971) esp. 152); J. Daniélou (*RSR* 59 (1971) esp. 58-59 and in many publications since); G. Quispel (*VC* 26 (1972) 79-80 and in many publications since); R.N. Frye ('The Cologne Greek Codex about Mani', in: *Ex orbe religionum. Studia Geo Widengren ... oblata* ..., I, Leiden 1972, 424-429); F. Decret (*Mani*, esp. 50 ff.); K. Rudolph (e.g. 'Die Bedeutung des Kölner Mani-Codex für die Manichäismusforschung. Vorläufige Anmerkungen', in: *Mélanges d'histoire des réligions offerts à Henri-Charles Puech*, Paris 1974, 475 ff.; *Gnosis*, 351; 'Der Mandäismus in der neueren Gnosisforschung', in: B. Aland et al. (Hrsg.), *Gnosis, Festschrift für Hans Jonas*, Göttingen 1978, 272); A. Böhlig (e.g. 'Synkretismus', 154-155; *Manichäismus*, 19, 22-24, 43,

Jewish-Christian baptist sect. From the *Mani-Codex* we know that the members of this sect washed themselves daily and that they washed their food as well[153]; they referred to their religion as the law (nomos)[154], emphasized the keeping of the sabbath[155] and referred repeatedly to ancestral traditions[156]. All this points to Jewish roots. On the other hand, many Christian elements can also be perceived: these Baptists spoke of the commandments of the Saviour[157], while Mani, according to the authors of the codex, referred to the testimonies from the Gospel[158]. Just as elsewhere these Jewish Christians appear to have had an aversion to Paul[159].

It is beyond the scope of this investigation to deal with all the very complex problems concerning the sources of Mani's syncretistic religion. The discussion on this subject has been going on for a considerable time and has not diminished since the discovery of the *Cologne Mani-Codex*. How significant was the influence of Marcion—that it was present, and to an important degree, is accepted by most scholars—, of Bardesanes, of the Mandaeans, from Persia and then of Zoroastrianism in particular, possibly of Buddhism and certainly of Hellenistic philosophy[160]? These and similar questions will have to be answered in future research.

---

49); M. Tardieu (e.g. *Manichéisme*, 9-12); U. Bianchi (e.g. *Religione dei manichei*, 8 and 17) and, after all, G. Widengren ('Einleitung' in: Widengren (Hrsg.), *Manichäismus*, XXXI), although it is remarkable that in 'Der Manichäismus. Kurzgefasste Geschichte der Problemforschung', in: Aland et al. (Hrsg.), *Gnosis*, 278-315, Widengren makes no mention of the *CMC*.

153 *CMC* 80, 1-3; 80, 23 – 83, 13; 88, 13-15.

154 *CMC*, passim. See esp. 20, 9-11 ('... und zog mich aus dem Gesetz (nomos) heraus, in dem ich aufgewachsen war'); 87, 16-18 ('Andere sagten: Dieser ist der Feind unseres [Gesetzes]'); 89, 11-13 ('Dein Sohn ist von unserem Gesetz (nomos) abgefallen und will in die Welt gehen').

155 *CMC* 102, 12-16. Cf. the explanatory notes by the editors and, for example, Rudolph, 'Bedeutung', 482 n. 3, and Henrichs, 'Bab. Baptists', 48-50.

156 *CMC* 87, 2-7; 91, 4-9.

157 *CMC* 91, 9-11. Cf. 79, 20-21 and 80, 11-12 where Mani points to the commandments of the Saviour.

158 *CMC* 91, 19 - 93, 23.

159 *CMC* 80, 16-18 and 87, 18-21. See the explanatory notes by the editors, and Henrichs, 'Bab. Baptists', 51-53.

160 Besides the general works on Mani and his religion (p. 208 n. 48), see esp. Böhlig, 'Synkretismus', 144-169. He emphasizes the fact that Mani was influenced by a great diversity of religious movements (Elkesaites, Marcion, Bardesanes, other Gnostics, Mandaeans, Iran, Buddhism, etc.). It is generally accepted that the Gnostic Marcion had a great influence on Mani. This is also true for Bardesanes, but should we see him as a Gnostic (like, in particular, B. Aland[-Ehlers], e.g. 'Bardesanes von Edessa—ein syrischer Gnostiker', *ZKG* 81 (1970) 334-351 and

But from the most recently published Manichaean writing it must be concluded that from the very beginning Mani underwent a Jewish-Christian influence. He grew up within a baptist sect which adhered to certain heretical Jewish-Christian ideas. Not Iranian, but Jewish-Christian ideas basically defined primitive Manichaeism.

This may explain various views that were characteristic of Mani. He regarded himself as the true prophet and the seal of the prophets. From the *Pseudo-Clementines* we know that Jewish Christians proclaimed that the true prophet reveals himself anew in various periods of history[161]. Moreover—and this is especially important—Mani's radical dualism becomes understandable if it is considered in the light of this Jewish-Christian background. It was a reaction to the belief of his youth.

In certain Jewish circles and in Christian ones closely related to them a rigid monotheism was taught. From the *Pseudo-Clementines*—but not only there[162]—this becomes clear: evil is not an independent power detached from God, but good and evil occur because

'Mani und Bardesanes. Zur Entstehung des manichäischen Systems', in: Dietrich (Hrsg.), *Synkretismus*, 123-143) or as a typical representative of pluriform Syriac Christianity? The later view is supported by H.J.W. Drijvers with a variety of arguments. Besides his monograph *Bardaiṣan of Edessa*, Assen 1966, see esp.: 'Edessa und das jüdische Christentum', *VC* 24 (1970) 4-33; 'Mani und Bardaiṣan. Ein Beitrag zur Vorgeschichte des Manichäismus', *Mélanges Puech*, 459-469; 'Bardaiṣan von Edessa als Repräsentant des syrischen Synkretismus ...', in: Dietrich (Hrsg.), *Synkretismus*, 109-122; 'Bardesanes', *TRE* 5 (1980) 206-212, esp. 211. Drijvers, too, sees a direct influence of Bardesanes on Mani, but notes a number of differences as well. He stresses the continuity of the *problems* and *motifs* that are manifest in both Bardesanes' theology and the views of the Manichaeans. His depiction of Manichaeism against the background of the pluriform Edessene Christianity is important; much of what was latent in this Christianity was radicalized by Manichaeism, and this led to a polarization between orthodoxy and heresy. More recently ('Odes of Solomon and Psalms of Mani. Christians and Manichaeans in Third-Century Syria', in: R. van den Broek - M.J. Vermaseren (eds.), *Studies in Gnosticism and Hellenistic Religions presented to Gilles Quispel* ..., Leiden 1981, 117-130) Drijvers has also pointed out that there are similarities between Manichaean psalms and *Odes of Solomon* (esp. *Ode* 38), at the same time observing 'that Mani and Manichaeism heavily drew upon the whole of christian tradition and literature extant in that time without any restriction to a supposedly gnostic strain' (130).

161 E.g. *Ps. Clem.*, *Hom.* XVII, 4 (ed. Rehm-Irmscher-Paschke, 230) and *Rec.* II, 47 (ed. Rehm-Paschke, 80). Cf. Schoeps, *Judenchristentum*, esp. 98-116, 327 f. and 335 ff. Schoeps also points to similar representations among the Mandaeans, the Manichaeans and in Islam.

162 E.g. H.J. Schoeps, *Aus frühchristlicher Zeit. Religionsgeschichtliche Untersuchungen*, Tübingen 1950, 48 f. for details from Judaism.

God wills it; Satan is God's left hand[163]. In connection with this, these Jewish Christians, as well as Jews related to them, emphasized the existence of two kingdoms under the dominion of two spirits or kings; this will be discussed in more detail later[164]. But a kingdom of Satan as a realm or power independent of God is never mentioned. On the contrary, a rigid monotheism was taught, in which adversity and affliction were seen as also coming from God[165]. It was against this monotheism that Mani protested. He proclaimed a radical dualism: there is a kingdom of light and a kingdom of darkness, of good and of evil, and the one is completely separate from the other.

There is very probably a reflection of this protest of Mani's in later Manichaean writings, such as the Coptic *Psalm-Book*[166] and a 'Beichtspiegel' found at Turfan[167]. Also the description of the absolutely dualistic antithesis as that between God and Satan—and not only between light and darkness or good and evil—should be seen in this perspective.

Thus some characteristic traits of Mani's religion can be explained as deriving from a particular form of Jewish Christianity. Gilles Quispel and Jean Daniélou especially have welcomed the *Cologne Mani-Codex* as proof of their view that Gnosticism evolved from Judaism or Jewish Christianity as a result of a dialectic process[168]. Mani followed the path from law to evangelical freedom, from *nomos* to *gnōsis*, as Böhlig says[169].

In his youth Mani was already in contact with Christianity. This

---

163 E.g. *Hom.* XX, 3.

164 See p. 334 ff.

165 E.g. *Hom.* VII, 3: the right hand of God represents grace, his left hand judgement.

166 *Psalm-Book* 57, 3-4: 'If it was God who created the evil and the good / and Christ and Satan ...'.

167 Asmussen, *X^{u}āstvānīft*, 193-194: '... if we should have said: 'If anybody quickens, (it is) God, (who) quickens, if anybody slays, (it is) God, (who) slays', (or) if we should have said: 'God (Äzrua) has created the good and the evil entirely ...'. For this text see also Bang, 'Beichtspiegel', 147, and Böhlig, *Manichäismus*, 199.

168 E.g. Quispel, 'The Birth of the Child. Some Gnostic and Jewish Aspects' (1971/1973), *GS*, I, 223: 'The Cologne Mani Codex (...) shows how Gnosis evolved out of Judaism, or Jewish Christianity, as a result of a dialectical process'; Daniélou, review of Henrichs and Koenen, 'Ein griechischer Mani-Codex', *RSR* 59 (1971) 59: 'Il est intéressant que le passage de l'elkesaïsme au gnosticisme manichéen apporte une illustration nouvelle au fait que le gnosticisme dualiste apparaît en milieu judéo-chrétien'.

169 Böhlig, 'Synkretismus', 155.

fact provides the first explanation for the important place the figure of Christ occupies in Manichaeism. Not only within the sect of his youth, however, but also outside it Mani must have become acquainted with Christian ideas. The diversified Aramaic Christianity, whose centre was originally Edessa and in which the Jewish-Christian element carried great weight, influenced him to a great extent. In it he and his followers came in touch with various apocryphal acts of the apostles. And here Mani also became acquainted with Tatian's *Diatessaron*, the gospel of this Aramaic Christianity[170], as well as with the *Gospel according to Thomas*. Henri-Charles Puech found evidence for this last observation at the beginning of Mani's *Epistula fundamenti*[171], which was handed down by Augustine. And it may be called remarkable that, as Quispel points out, the greatest Western church father demonstrated his subconscious knowledge not only of the *Diatessaron*[172], with which he had been familiar since his Manichaean years, but possibly of the *Gospel according to Thomas* as well[173]. This, too, can indicate how much Augustine's Manichaean past had continued to influence him. When he quoted from memory, he subconsciously used the language of Tatian's harmony of the gospels and possibly even that of the *Gospel according to Thomas*.

Does this continuing subconscious influence also apply to his doctrine of the two cities? We can only look into this matter after considering other possible sources of influence. Then the often striking resemblances to the Manichean doctrine of the two kingdoms that we have just discussed can also be evaluated.

---

170 This was pointed out long ago by Schaeder ('Urform', 71-72), A. Baumstark (review of Polotsky (Hrsg.), *Hom.*, in *OrChr* 10 (1935) 257-268, esp. 264 f.) and C. Peters (*Das Diatessaron Tatians*, Rom 1939, 125-132); cf. Puech, 'Gnostische Evangelien und verwandte Dokumente', in: Hennecke and Schneemelcher, *NTAp*, I, 261 n. 3. See also G. Quispel, 'Mani the Apostle of Jesus Christ' (1972), *GS*, II, 230-237, who argues that from a variant in Tatian's *Diatessaron* ('He will *send* you another Paraclete') Mani's awareness of his mandate to evangelize becomes clear: Mani considered himself to be an apostle of Jesus Christ because Christ had sent the Paraclete to him.

171 Puech, 'Gnostische Evangelien', 203. That the Manichaeans were acquainted with the *Gospel according to Thomas* was noted earlier by Alfaric, *Écritures*, I, 67, 70; II, 185, and later esp. by E. Hammerschmidt, 'Das Thomasevangelium und die Manichäer', *OrChr* 46 (1962) 120-123.

172 G. Quispel, 'Mani et la tradition évangélique des judéo-chrétiens', *RSR* 60 (1972) 143-150; idem, *Tatian and the Gospel of Thomas. Studies in the History of the Western Diatessaron*, Leiden 1975, 59 ff.

173 G. Quispel, 'Saint Augustin et l'Évangile selon Thomas', *Mélanges Puech*, 375-378.

B. Platonism, Stoicism and Philo

1. *The significance of the Platonists, the Stoics and Philo*

Following the development in Augustine's thinking and, after Manichaeism, focussing our attention on Platonism, we are faced with similar problems. Just as many scholars see no lasting influence of Manichaean doctrines, and others perceive this influence almost everywhere, the opinions concerning the continuing influence of Platonism also vary. Admittedly, no one denies that the significance of this philosophy for Augustine's spiritual development was great. He says so himself in the account of his conversion and, moreover, almost every page of his early writings attests to it. But if and to what extent this also applies to his views when he was a Catholic bishop is still the frequent subject of scholarly debate.

Indeed, hardly anyone lives outside the culture of his time, and certainly not a man like Augustine, whose opinion on many subjects was well worth hearing. He cannot be fully understood without a thorough knowledge of the philosophy of his time: (Neo)Platonism. This philosophy provided the framework in which he set forth his ideas and others understood him. But did this philosophy determine his theology in such a decisive way that he can also be characterized in his later years as a Christian who was strongly shaped by Neoplatonism and even as a Christian Platonist[175]?

In the sketch of Augustine's development as a thinker, we have already mentioned how his becoming acquainted with Neoplatonism resulted in a spiritual deliverance[176]. It enabled him to formulate a rational explanation of the world. The importance of Platonism was also clear when the question of a possible development towards the concept *civitas* in Augustine's thinking was discussed[177]. In his earliest writings the rift between the two worlds of Neoplatonism is reflected in a series of antitheses: sensual—spiritual, outward—inward, mortal—immortal, changeable—unchangeable, temporal—eternal. The kingdom of God is identified

---

[175] Arthur Hilary Armstrong, among others, does this frequently. See e.g. his *St. Augustine and Christian Platonism*, Villanova 1967 (re-issued in A.H. Armstrong, *Plotinian and Christian Studies*, London 1979, Ch. XI) and his contribution to A.H. Armstrong and R.A. Markus, *Christian Faith and Greek Philosophy*, London 1960, 1-58.

[176] See p. 47 ff.

[177] See p. 108 ff.

with the intelligible world of the philosophers and even now a complete sharing in this spiritual world is deemed possible.

Soon, however, other views appeared and even gained the upper hand. A more thorough knowledge of Scripture, in first instance the writings especially of the apostle Paul, gave another direction to his thinking. The differences with the Platonists became more accentuated. As Augustine says in the *Confessions*[178], he was impressed at the time of his conversion with the number of aspects in which 'the books of the Platonists' already contained the essentials of Christian doctrine. From them he learned about the eternity of God and the Logos, about the divine light that shines in the darkness, about the human soul which—though not being the light itself—bears witness to the light. The Platonists, however, did not speak about the incarnation of the Word; nor did they mention the earthly life or death of Jesus. Augustine states emphatically that only when he read the Scriptures did everything become clear to him[179].

We have already noted that Augustine's attitude towards the Platonists had become increasingly critical[180]. Using incisive language he showed points of difference, and in the *City of God* it is above all Porphyry, an avowed enemy of Christianity, whom he often attacks. But on the other hand his appreciation for the Platonists was lasting, and in later years it was this same Porphyry whom he specially praised as 'the most learned of the philosophers'[181]. From the decisive years in Milan until the end of his life, Augustine had a close affinity with the Platonists. Even in his last days, when Hippo was surrounded by Vandals and barbarism was rampant, he comforted himself 'with the dictum of a certain wise man': Plotinus[182].

A few comments should be made on these facts. For when Augustine referred positively to 'the Platonists', to what extent did he really accept them? And was he truly and completely familiar with the teachings of Plato and the Platonists of his own time?

---

178 *Conf.* VII, 9, 13-15.

179 See also *C. acad.* II, 2, 6.

180 See p. 53 f.

181 *DCD* XIX, 22: 'doctissimus philosophorum'; cf. VII, 25: 'philosophus nobilis' and XXII, 3: '... teste Porphyrio, nobilissimo philosopho paganorum'.

182 Possidius, *Vita*, 28: 'Et se inter haec mala cuiusdam sapientis sententia consolabatur dicentis: non erit magnus magnum putans quod cadunt ligna et moriuntur mortales'. This is a free translation of *Enn.* I, 4, 7. Cf. P. Henry, *Plotin et l'Occident. Firmicus Maternus, Marius Victorinus, Saint Augustin et Macrobe*, Louvain 1934, 137-139 and 145.

As far as the Platonism of his day is concerned, modern research has proved conclusively that Augustine was well-informed about it. It is, however, debatable which of the well-known Neoplatonists, Plotinus or Porphyry, exerted a greater influence on him during the years of his conversion as well as afterwards. Years ago Willy Theiler made a strong case for Porphyry[183]; Paul Henry, on the other hand, argued for Plotinus[184]. Others have joined in this discussion[185], and it was especially John O'Meara who drew attention to the significance of Porphyry, not only for the years in Milan, but also, and more specifically, for the *City of God*[186]. The difficulty, though, is that only a very small part of Porphyry's work has come down to us; therefore his influence, as, after Henry, H.-R. Schwyzer stated, is often neither demonstrable nor refutable[187].

More important to us is the extent to which Augustine interpreted Neoplatonism correctly. In both his earlier and his later years he often spoke favourably about it. Limiting ourselves to a few particulars from the *City of God*, we can make the following observations. Augustine was of the opinion that Platonism contained a doctrine of trinity[188], the same view as the Christians had concerning the Word of God as the true light[189], and also a largely correct view of angels and demons[190]. The soul is immortal and man is destined for communion with God; what matters is a blessed life (vita beata)[191]. The Platonists know about the fatherland where man is to go[192]; 'you see then to some degree, though only from a distance and with clouded vision, the homeland in which we are to abide'[193]. And

---

183 See esp. W. Theiler, *Porphyrius und Augustin*, Halle 1933.

184 Henry, *Plotin*, esp. 63-145; cf. P. Henry, *La vision d'Ostie. Sa place dans la vie et l'oeuvre de saint Augustin*, Paris 1938, 15-26.

185 For surveys of research into the influence of Plotinus and/or Porphyry, concentrated particularly on the time of A.'s conversion, see: Courcelle, *Recherches*, 7-12; J.J. O'Meara, 'Augustine and Neo-platonism', *RA* I (1958) 96 ff.; R. Lorenz, 'Augustinliteratur seit dem Jubiläum von 1954', *TR* 25 (1959) esp. 17-18; Mandouze, *Augustin*, 483 f.; Lorenz, 'Augustinforschung', *TR* 39 (1974) 124 ff.; Schindler, 'Augustin', esp. 661.

186 O'Meara, *Young Augustine*, 131-155, esp. 135; 'Neo-platonism', 91-111; *Porphyry's Philosophy from Oracles in Augustine*, Paris 1959; *Charter*, esp. 74-87.

187 H.-R. Schwyzer, 'Plotinos', *PRE* 21 (1951) 586.

188 See esp. *DCD* X, 23 ff.

189 E.g. *DCD* X, 2.

190 E.g. *DCD* IX, 23.

191 See esp. *DCD* X, 1; cf., for example, VIII, 5.

192 *DCD* IX, 17 where *Enn.* I, 6, 8 and I, 2, 3 are rendered freely.

193 *DCD* X, 29: 'Itaque videtis utcumque, etsi de longinque, etsi acie caligante, patriam in qua manendum est ...'.

when, in Book VIII, he enters upon the debate with the philosophers on the question of whether the worship of the gods is required for a blessed life to come, Augustine limits himself to those who believe in one deity: the Platonists. For they are the ones who recognize a transcendent God who has created everything, and who allows the soul to partake of His own being[194]; He is the source of the light of truth and the giver of blessedness[195], the immutable being who exists in simplicity[196]. Besides, the Platonists are pre-eminent not only in physics but also in logic and ethics[197]; 'they are the nearest to us'[198].

Did Augustine judge all this correctly? It is not my intention to give here a complete description of the comprehensive philosophical movement known as Neoplatonism[199]. But a few central facts deserve mentioning. The leading figure of this philosophy, Plotinus (c. 204-270), saw all that exists as an everlasting, non-created organism, the 'emanation' of a primordial principle which is entirely transcendent, superior to thinking and being, the One, First, Good. This One has generated the world from eternity, without changing, moving or diminishing; one might compare this to the radiation of light from the sun or of heat from fire[200]. However, it is not a physical process, but a radiation of energy. This process of radiation and increasing imperfection goes through the following stages: first from

---

194 *DCD* VIII, 1.

195 *DCD* VIII, 5.

196 *DCD* VIII, 6.

197 *DCD* VIII, 6, 7 and 8. For this division of philosophy in A.'s work—'entirely in the tradition of Neoplatonism'—cf. A.C.J. Habets, *Geschiedenis van de indeling van de filosofie in de Oudheid*, Diss. Utrecht 1983, 155-156. Not only the division is of relevance, however, but also the order physics-logic-ethics. This is pointed out by P. Hadot, 'La Présentation du Platonisme par Augustin', in: A.M. Ritter (Hrsg.), *Kerygma und Logos. Beiträge zu den geistesgeschichtlichen Beziehungen zwischen Antike und Christentum. Festschrift für Carl Andresen* ..., Göttingen 1979, 273-279. In this way A. could bring together Platonism and trinitarian Christian belief and even identify them; '... les résumés du platonisme par Augustin apparaîtront comme un effort sans cesse renouvelé pour formuler en termes identiques platonisme et christianisme' (278-279).

198 *DCD* VIII, 9: '... eosque nobis propinquiores ...'. Cf., for example, VIII, 5: 'Nulli nobis quam isti propius accesserunt'.

199 Besides the surveys in the textbooks of the history of philosophy (such as Windelband and Heimsoeth, *Lehrbuch*, esp. 209-214) and of the history of dogma (such as Harnack, *Lehrbuch*, I, 808-826, particularly following E. Zeller; Adam, *Lehrbuch*, I, 202-206), especially A.H. Armstrong, 'Plotinus', in: Armstrong (ed.), *Philosophy*, 193-268 and Von Ivánka, *Plato Christianus*, 70 ff. can be named.

200 See e.g. Armstrong, 'Plotinus', 240, for more metaphors.

the One proceeds the Intellect (Nous), i.e. the World of Forms. Then from this Intellect the World-Soul (psychè) proceeds which, according to these Forms, gives shape and order to the material world—the non-being. Out of this World-Soul come the souls of the separate beings, offshoots and individualizations of the World-Soul. The physical world comes into existence because the transcendent acts upon matter as the substratum of all that will be; this world is but a shadow image of the intelligible world.

It should be evident that Augustine adopted many elements of this Neoplatonic world view, and based his views on them. Nowhere, however, did he reveal that he had examined the very essence of Neoplatonism. He depicted it as a theistic system, and said repeatedly that the Neoplatonists saw God als the Creator[201]. But he made no mention of a difference with the biblical way of referring to Creator and creation.

Of course Augustine did not have a good word to say for the worship of demons as mediators[202], and he denounced the Neoplatonists' view of history as a perpetual cycle[203], their denial of Christ's incarnation and redemption[204], and their rejection of the resurrection of the body[205]. But *in philosophicis* Augustine himself could certainly be characterized as a Platonist[206]. The impression he had at the time of his conversion of the Platonists' absolutely transcendental idea of God remained. In the *City of God*, too, God is repeatedly pictured as the absolutely transcendental One and as the supreme Good[207]. And just as, during his years in Milan, the view of

---

201 This is evidenced again and again in Books VII, X and XI. See esp. *DCD* VIII, 9; VIII, 10; X, 12 and XI, 5 (God as *conditor* and *creator*); cf. I, 36: '... nobiscum multa sentiunt, et de immortalitate animae et quod Deus verus mundum condiderit et de providentia eius, qua universum quod condidit regit'.

202 This theme occurs repeatedly in *DCD* IX and X.

203 This is described and assailed particularly in *DCD* XII, 14.

204 *DCD* X, 29 et al.

205 Esp. *DCD* XIII, 16-19.

206 A. called the teaching of Pythagoras 'illa venerabilis ac prope divina ... disciplina' (*De ord.* II, 20, 53; cf. *Retract.* I, 3, however), but he considered it of only minor importance. He did praise Aristotle highly (see esp. *DCD* VIII, 12), but otherwise the latter did not play an important role for him. He made only negative references to the Epicureans (as did the Neoplatonists). The significance of the Stoa will be discussed presently.

207 For these and other statements about God that are reminiscent of Neoplatonism, see e.g. *DCD* VIII, 6; VIII, 9 ('... lumen cognoscendarum et bonum agendarum ...'); VIII, 10 ('... qui non solum super omnia corpora est incorporeus, verum etiam super omnes animas incorruptibilis, principium nostrum, lumen

evil as being non-existent and a deprivation of what is good (privatio/amissio boni) meant the solution to a tormenting problem, in the *City of God* this view reappeared[208]. Here we also find the Neoplatonic theodicy: good and evil complement each other harmoniously, as do the light and dark colours of a painting[209].

Thus there was, besides a sharp repudiation, a grateful acceptance. From the preceding it can already be concluded that this acceptance went beyond a few purely philosophical problems. It often appears, though, that Augustine was aware of important differences with the Neoplatonists. Their significance extended to the point where, in his opinion, they contradicted the Scriptures[210]. But that borderline often remained vague. More than once he supposed, without any well-founded reason, that he had come upon thoughts of Plato or of Plato's followers which agreed with Christian belief, or he read Platonism into biblical texts. He often realized this afterwards, as appears in the *Retractations* in particular[211]. Not everything is recorded there, however.

One can disagree on the question of whether Platonism caused a substantial change in or even a transformation of Christianity. Heinrich Dörrie does not think so: 'Nie hat der Platonismus an die Substanz der christlichen Lehre gerührt'[212]. According to him the emphasis should be laid on the *use* of Neoplatonic speech and thought by 'so-called' Christian Platonists, Augustine included. It

---

nostrum, bonum nostrum ...'; '... et causa constituendae universitatis et lux percipiendae veritatis et fons bibendae felicitatis'); XI, 4 ('... a Deo ineffabiliter atque invisibiliter magno et ineffabiliter atque invisibiliter pulchro ...'); XI, 10 ('Est itaque bonum solum simplex et ob hoc solum incommutabile, quod est Deus'); XII, 1 (inmutabile bonum; unus verus beatus Deus; incummutabile bonum); XII, 2 (summa essentia).

208 *DCD* XI, 9 ('Mali enim nulla natura est; sed amissio boni mali nomen accepit'); XI, 22 (privatio boni); XII, 6 f.; XIV, 11. Cf. esp. *Enn.* III, 2, 5.

209 *DCD* XI, 23; cf. *Enn.* III, 2, 11. In this connection we should also take note of *DCD* XI, 18 in which A. speaks of the antitheses as the Neoplatonists did.

210 A. already stated in *C. acad.* III, 20, 43: '... apud platonicos me interim quod sacris litteris nostris non repugnet reperturum esse confido'. Cf., for example, *De doctr. chr.* II, 40, 60 on the philosophers, esp. the Platonists: '... si qua forte vera et fidei nostrae accommodata dixerunt (...), non solum formidanda non sunt, sed ab eis etiam tanquam iniustis possessoribus in usum nostrum vindicanda'. This is followed by the well-known story of the robbery by the Israelites of Egypt's gold and silver vessels.

211 For the works from the years prior to his episcopate, see *Retract.* I.

212 H. Dörrie, 'Die Andere Theologie. Wie stellten die frühchristlichen Theologen des 2. – 4. Jahrhunderts ihren Lesern die 'Griechische Weisheit' (= den Platonismus) dar?', *ThPh* 56 (1981) 1-46, quotation 43.

was a form of argumentation, understandable to the cultivated person of those days: Christian substance was presented in Platonist terminology, and essential differences were not mentioned.

It must be asked whether this view does justice to all the facts[213]. In this way it would have been mainly a matter of tactical adaptation, 'being a Greek to the Greeks'. But this does not take into account the fact that Augustine, and many others, also used strongly Neoplatonic language in works that were not directly aimed at the outside world—as, for instance, in Augustine's *De trinitate* and even in sermons meant for ordinary Christian people[214].

It was more than just a temporary, superficial influence that Platonism exerted on Augustine[215]. He borrowed much from it and often remoulded it into a Christian meaning. In this philosophy he found an instrument for attaining a rational understanding of revealed truth. His interest in the Neoplatonists continued to the end of his life. It can be assumed that, even though he was thoroughly familiar with their works, he reread them before writing his great work the *City of God*[216]. For nowhere else does one find so many quotations—and often passages not quoted before—from the works of Plotinus and Porphyry. To ask what the significance of the Platonists was for his concept of the two cities is completely justified.

---

213 It may be observed in passing that Dörrie, 'Theologie', 40, describes *DCD* as 'die *admonitio* an gebildete Leser, in die geistige und geistliche Ordnung des Christentums herüberzutreten'. We can subscribe to this view; see Ch. III. But Dörrie is wrong when he states that in *DCD*—unlike in *Conf.* VII, 9, 13-14—A. drew no boundary line between his views and those of the Platonists and that he was silent about essential elements; see above, pp. 54 and 240.

214 Just one example is the fact that A. repeatedly gave interpretations of the well-known text *Ex.* 3:14 in a platonic sense; see C.J. de Vogel, 'Plato in de latere en late oudheid, bij heidenen en christenen', *Lampas* 6 (1973) 249-251. See also her comprehensive, critical discussion of the views of Dörrie and others in: 'Platonism and Christianity: A mere antagonism or a profound common ground?', *VC* 39 (1985) 1-62.

215 E.P. Meijering, who has dealt with the attitude of early-Christian writers towards Platonism in many publications, correctly states: 'Der Platonismus war nicht nur eine Philosophenschule neben und gegenüber der Kirche; der Platonismus steckte als eine geistige Macht in der Brust und in den Köpfen vieler christlicher Theologen'. See E.P. Meijering, 'Wie platonisierten Christen? Zur Grenzziehung zwischen Platonismus, kirchlichem Credo und patristischer Theologie', *VC* 28 (1974) 15-28, quotation 27. That this does not mean that we can call A. a Platonist, however, is again shown by G. Madec, 'Si Plato viveret ... (Augustin, «De vera religione» 3, 3)', in: *Néoplatonisme. Mélanges offerts à Jean Trouillard*, Fontenay-aux-Roses 1981, 231-247.

216 Cf. Courcelle, *Lettres grecques*, 168. For Plotinus see also Henry, *Plotin*, esp. 121-133 and 144.

At this point some special attention should be given to Plato. Although in general Augustine saw no essential differences between the Neoplatonists and Plato himself, he often mentioned him separately. Each time he spoke of him in terms of great esteem[217]. Did this great thinker possibly exert a decisive influence on his concept of the two cities? This has been maintained by some scholars, but to do so requires establishing first how well the church father was acquainted with Plato's dialogues.

Of Plato's many works Augustine mentions only the *Timaeus*. When quoting a lengthy passage from it, he refers explicitly to Cicero's translation[218]. As Courcelle has demonstrated—and this has not been refuted—Augustine was familiar with passages from other writings by Plato also through secondary sources[219]. He read neither Plato nor any of the other Greek philosophers in the original language. What he knew of them—and that was by no means little—came via translations, compilations, and what he found in writings accessible to him in Latin: works of Varro, Apuleius and, among others, the Neoplatonists. But the principal source for his knowledge of the writings of Plato and the other Greeks remained Cicero[220].

Concerning Augustine's familiarity with one of the other great philosophical movements of antiquity, Stoicism, basically the same can be said. Here, too, Cicero seems to have been the most important intermediary. For his discussion in the *City of God* of the passions and the controversy concerning them between the Stoics and the Peripatetics, Augustine's information comes via the renowed rhetor-philosopher and statesman[221]. This holds good for other doctrines of the Stoics as well[222]. Much information must also have reached Augustine through the mediation of the Neoplatonists, for a considerable portion of the Stoic ideas had been absorbed by Neoplatonism[223]. Therefore Gérard Verbeke could point especially

---

217 E.g. *C. acad.* III, 17, 37 and III, 18, 41; *DCD* II, 7; II, 14; et al.

218 *DCD* XIII, 16; cf. Hagendahl, *Latin Classics*, 535.

219 Courcelle, *Lettres grecques*, 156-159.

220 Courcelle, *Lettres grecques*, 155: 'C'est encore Cicéron qui fournit à saint Augustin le plus clair de ses informations sur l'ancienne philosophie grecque'.

221 *DCD* IX, 4-5 and XIV, 7-9; Hagendahl, *Latin Classics*, 572 ff.

222 E.g. *DCD* V, 1-10, where A. takes issue with the Stoic views on *fatum*; cf. Hagendahl, *Latin Classics*, 526 ff.

223 Von Ivánka, *Plato Christianus*, 79-80: 'Mann kann geradezu sagen, dass der Neuplatonismus (...) eigentlich nichts anderes ist als die Ausfüllung des stoischen

to Neoplatonism as the intermediary for Augustine's knowledge of the Stoic view of the *rationes seminales* and the doctrine of the world soul[224]. Moreover, various views of the Stoics were part of the intellectual heritage of the cultivated man of those days. There is no reason to assume that Augustine was thoroughly acquainted with Stoicism[225].

The last to be considered in this framework is Philo, the Jewish thinker with whom the history of Christian philosophy began. It is no coincidence that he was known both as Philo Judaeus and as Philo Alexandrinus. With great ingenuity he related his faith, founded on divine revelation as laid down in the Torah[226], to the most important philosophical movements of his time and city. Plato in particular played a prominent role in his thinking[227], as well as the Stoics—especially Posidonius—and Neopythagorism[228].

Hans Leisegang saw this learned Alexandrian as an important source of Augustine's doctrine of the two cities. In his opinion the influence came to him through Ambrose (Philo latinus)[229]. Altaner even believed that Augustine was familiar with Latin translations of Philo's works[230]. Courcelle, however, contradicted this, and as-

---

ursprünglich materialistischen Seinsschemas mit platonischem (spiritualistischem) Inhalt'.

224 G. Verbeke, 'Augustin et le stoïcisme', *RA* 1 (1958) 67-89, esp. 68 and 84-87.

225 Verbeke, 'Stoïcisme', 88-89. More recent studies have produced hardly any essentially new points of view: Ch. Baguette, 'Une période stoïcienne dans l'évolution de saint Augustin', *REA* 16 (1970) 47-77 (a reworking of a part of an unpublished dissertation, Louvain 1968); M. Spanneut, *Permanence du stoïcisme. De Zénon à Malraux*, Gembloux 1973, esp. 145, 151, 159-160, 168-169, 172, 176, and M. Spanneut, 'Le stoïcisme et saint Augustin', in: *Forma futuri. Studi in onore del Cardinale Michele Pellegrino*, Torino 1975, 896-914. Spanneut, who in the last-named article also gives a short survey of a few other studies (such as A.J. Holloway, 1966; J. Pinborg, 1962; R.M. Bushman, 1952; P.J. Couvée, 1947), does point out a certain increase of A.'s familiarity with the Stoa. But this does not remove the difficulty in distinguishing purely Stoic ideas and pointing out their direct influence on A. A materialistic-Stoic manner of thinking on the part of A. is clearest shortly before his becoming acquainted with Neoplatonism; see *Conf.* VII, 1, 1-2.

226 Psalms and prophetic writings are seldom quoted.

227 The well-known statement found in Jerome (*De vir. ill.* 11) and various Greek Christian writers may be called to mind: 'Either Plato «philonizes» or Philo «platonizes»'.

228 E.g. H. Chadwick, 'Philo and the beginnings of Christian thought', in: Armstrong (ed.), *Philosophy*, 131-192 (137-157 on Philo); C. Colpe, 'Philo', *RGG* V (1961) 341-346.

229 Leisegang, 'Ursprung', 152.

230 Such as the *Quaestiones et solutiones in Genesin*, used in *C. Faust.* XII and *DCD*

sumed it was only through Ambrose that Augustine became acquainted with Philo[231]. P. Agaësse and A. Solignac, on the contrary, think that evidence in support of Altaner's view can be found in one of Augustine's works on *Genesis*[232].

Which of them is right is not so relevant in this framework. What is important is that Augustine was acquainted with this thinker from Alexandria who was so strongly influenced by Platonism, if not independently through Latin translations, certainly through intermediary of Ambrose. Philo, too, was significant for Augustine, and should therefore be included in the considerations about the possible origins of Augustine's doctrine of the two cities.

2. *Platonism, Stoicism or Philo as source?*

A survey of the opinions of scholars who, in discussing the sources of Augustine's concept of the two cities, have referred to Plato, Neoplatonists, Stoic influence or Philo can be brief. The reason is that there are only few of them and this is, as will be shown, no coincidence.

The first to give a rather comprehensive presentation of possible sources was Scholz. He saw traces of the Augustinian antithesis in Plato, but limited himself to noting a few superficial examples of concurrence[233]. Scholz was of the opinion that in the thinking of the Greek philosopher, as in Augustine's, the idea of Good, God himself, and not man, occupies the central position (*Leg.* 716C). Justice is the situation in which each has his due and does his share; it is the foundation of the state (*Rep.* 433A; 433E). The state is like an individual (*Rep.* 432A; 434D) and this idea also occurs in Augustine. It was Plato 'who reasoned out what a state should be like' (*DCD* II, 14); he called his state a state of God (*Leg.* 713A: polis theou). Already in his view the powers of good and evil are, together with us, engaged in a perpetual struggle (*Leg.* 906A; cf. *Theaet.* 176E). Moreover, Plato also spoke of a perpetual separation of spirits (*Rep.* 614 ff.).

XV, 26. See Altaner, 'Augustinus und Philo von Alexandrien' (1941), *Schriften*, 181-193.

231 P. Courcelle, 'Saint Augustin a-t-il lu Philon d'Alexandrie?', *REAn* 63 (1961) 78-85.

232 *BA* 49, 499-500.

233 Scholz, *Glaube und Unglaube*, 71-74.

The two worlds of the Platonic system, the realm of visible, temporary things and the realm of invisible, eternal things are central to Neoplatonism. Plotinus called for a flight to the beloved fatherland and Augustine adopted this summons approvingly (*Enn.* I, 6, 8; *DCD* IX, 17). The real road to the homeland, however, was not perceived by the Platonists (*DCD* X, 29). Yet Scholz regarded the ideal of a Platonopolis as very similar to Augustine's 'State of God'[234].

Scholz also drew attention to the Stoics[235]. The concept *polis*, Clement of Alexandria wrote (*Strom.* IV, 26, 172), was transferred by them from the earthly to the superterrestrial: the real *polis* exists only in heaven.

Even closer to Augustine was Seneca, according to Scholz[236]. Like other Stoics he distinguished two states. However, for him they did not differ in degree, but in nature: he saw the national state as being situated opposite the cosmopolitan world state which unites humans and gods in one organization (*De otio* IV, 1).

The last one named by Scholz was Philo[237]. He was the Jewish representative of the concept of the two states: from the *civitas sensibilis* one must go to the *civitas intelligibilis* (*De gig.* § 13 = *De gig.* 61). Like Augustine he distinguished two kinds of people: one living according to the divine spirit, the other caught in the life of passion (*Quis rer. div. heres* § 12 = *Quis rer. div. heres* 57).

After Scholz' exposition of the precursors of the Augustinian concept—it should be remembered that according to him the decisive influence was exerted by Tyconius—Edgar Salin was the first to call special attention to the Platonic element. Although he also believed that Augustine took over the idea of the two kingdoms from Tyconius[238], he saw in the arrangement of the *City of God* the example of Plato. For, in accordance with an old way of counting, Plato's *Republic* has ten books, his *Laws* twelve. This correspondence implies that Augustine wished to offer a political philosophy, thereby surpassing Plato[239].

It is interesting that, following this, Salin contended that the *City*

---

234 Scholz, *Glaube und Unglaube*, 74-75.
235 Scholz, *Glaube und Unglaube*, 75.
236 Scholz, *Glaube und Unglaube*, 75-76.
237 Scholz, *Glaube und Unglaube*, 76.
238 Salin, *Civitas Dei*, 175.
239 Salin, *Civitas Dei*, 174.

of God was not only an apology, but above all 'positive Setzung'[240]. However, he did not substantiate his reference to Plato[241]. His argumentation is superficial—just as too much in his book is superficial—and deserves no further comment.

In the same year Hans Leisegang presented a much more solid study[242]. Starting from *De civitate Dei* XV, 2, where Augustine discusses *Gal.* 4:21 ff. at length, Leisegang reached the conclusion that in his doctrine of the *civitates* Augustine applied a Platonic 'Stufenbau': the archetype is the city of God in heaven, its adumbration is the city of God on earth (represented by Sarah), the adumbration of this city on earth is the earthly city in a narrower sense (represented by Hagar). Thus there are three *civitates*: the *civitas caelestis spiritalis*, the *civitas terrena spiritalis* and the *civitas terrena carnalis*.

How did Augustine arrive at this view? Philo preceded him in it, according to Leisegang. For Philo, too, there were three societies: the spiritual city (noètè polis), the small group of its citizens sojourning on earth, and the large number of other people. Being in exile is characteristic for the friends of God (theophiloi) on earth; their mother city is in heaven. Through Ambrose—in whose works we find many of Philo's ideas—Augustine became acquainted with the learned Alexandrian who was such an admirer of Plato.

Of course Leisegang's argument, presented here in a highly schematic form, requires further consideration. The crux here is not only whether he interpreted Plato, Philo and Ambrose correctly, but also whether his interpretation of *De civitate Dei* XV, 2 is accurate.

A few years later Viktor Stegemann followed almost completely in Leisegang's footsteps: in his interpretation of *De civitate Dei* XV, 2[243], in his references to Philo[244] and in recognizing Ambrose as intermediary[245]. Compared with Leisegang's substantiation, however, he offered hardly any new evidence. Yet Stegemann put more emphasis on Ambrose's views[246] and he also mentioned Origen[247]. We shall come back to this later[248].

---

240 Salin, *Civitas Dei*, 175.
241 Salin, *Civitas Dei*, 241. He owes his idea to the philologist Franz Boll.
242 Leisegang, 'Ursprung' (1926), 127-158.
243 Stegemann, *Gottesstaat*, 50-52.
244 Stegemann, *Gottesstaat*, 23 f.; 26 ff.
245 Stegemann, *Gottesstaat*, 23 ff.; 28 f.
246 Stegemann, *Gottesstaat*, 23-26.
247 Stegemann, *Gottesstaat*, 29-31.
248 Zie pp. 276-284.

Neither John Burleigh[249], nor Domenico Pesce[250], nor Lidia Storoni Mazzolani[251] made a searching inquiry into the sources of Augustine's doctrine of the two cities. They are similar in that they all refer in general terms to parallels with Plato, the Stoics and the Neoplatonists. In his discourses on Augustine's philosophy, Burleigh regularly notes a concurrence and even a special relationship with Plato and the Neoplatonists, but he also remarks frequently that biblical thinking predominates[252]. Pesce sketches successively the thinking of Plato, Cicero and Augustine concerning the earthly and the heavenly city, but he does not specify any signs of influence. Mazzolani interprets Augustine's concept of the two cities in (Neo)platonic terms[253], but her exposition is superficial.

In recent years only Christian Parma[254] has made a scientific attempt to explain Augustine's concept of the two cities on the basis of prior philosophical tradition. He refers to Plotinus, who taught a twofold *polis*: the city above (hè anō polis) and the city below (hè katō polis), comparable to Augustine's supernal city (superna civitas) and earthly city (terrena civitas). He even deems it probable 'dass Augustins Konzeption der beiden civitates sowohl terminologisch wie auch in grundlegenden Motiven durch die Kenntnis plotinischer Schriften (...) entscheidend geprägt wurde'[255].

3. Views on two worlds, kingdoms and cities in Platonism, Stoicism and Philo

From the foregoing it is clear that mainly Philo and Plotinus have been pointed to as possible sources of Augustine's concept of the two cities. Analyses of other thinkers from the Greek and Latin non-Christian tradition bring to light only a few, mostly superficial, similarities. This does not prevent us from considering others beyond the ones just mentioned who may be important for Augustine's concept. Obviously we will give no more or less exhaustive sur-

---

249 Burleigh, *City* (1949).

250 Pesce, *Città* (1957).

251 Mazzolani, *Idea* (1970).

252 E.g. Burleigh, *City*, 153: 'The Platonist in St. Augustine is evident throughout, but does not subordinate the Biblicist'.

253 Mazzolani, *Idea*, esp. 257-258; cf. 255.

254 C. Parma, 'Plotinische Motive in Augustins Begriff der Civitas Dei', *VC* 22 (1968) 45-48.

255 Parma, 'Plotinische Motive', 48.

veys—such as an analysis of Plato's political philosophy or of political-ethical insights of the Stoics—but will discuss the elements contained therein which are appropriate for this research[256]. Of special importance is the question: do we find an antithesis or at least a distinction between two cities?

There is nothing in the works of Plato pointing to an antithesis between two cities; nor in those of Aristotle or any of the Greek philosophers of the period before them. As we know, the *polis*[257] played an important role in the life of the Greeks; therefore *polis* and citizenship had a central position in their thinking. According to Plato, the perfect paradigm of the *polis* is to be found in heaven[258]; in accordance with this *paradeigma* the earthly *polis*-society should be organized. So there is an archetype (eidos, paradeigma) and an image or adumbration[259], but there is no absolute antithesis between two *poleis*.

In the Neoplatonic system, which goes back to Plato, there is the difference between two worlds: the world of what is sensorially perceptible (kosmos aisthètos) and the intelligible world (kosmos noètos). Plotinus mentioned the flight from this world to the beloved homeland (patris): 'Therefore let us flee to the beloved homeland (...). The homeland for us, after all, is the place we have come from, and There is the Father'[260]. As both the *City of God* (IX, 17) and the *Confessions* (VIII, 8, 19) demonstrate, Augustine was familiar with

---

256 For classical thinking on state and politics see, besides the studies by Ehrhardt (*Politische Metaphysik*, I-III, 1959-'69) and Duchrow (*Christenheit*, 1970 [1]), e.g. F. Dvornik, *Early Christian and Byzantine Political Philosophy. Origins and Background*, Washington-New York 1966. This study also contains an abundance of texts and references. M. Hammond, *City-State and World State in Greek and Roman Political Theory until Augustus*, Cambridge, Mass. 1951, gives hardly any material relevant to our investigation.

257 Cf. p. 103 f. and the references given there. Special mention should be made of Ehrhardt, *Politische Metaphysik*, I, 4-54 ('Die rationale und die dämonische Theologie der griechischen Polis') and 55-102 ('Politische Religion').

258 As in *Rep.* 592B; cf. 500E. Plato and other classical Greek and Roman writers—including Philo—are quoted from the editions in the *Loeb Classical Library*. For Plotinus, see n. 260.

259 For *eikōn* and *skia*, see e.g. *Rep.* 510A and E.

260 *Enn.* I, 6, 8: 'Pheugōmen dè philèn ès patrida (...). Patris dè hèmin, hothen parèlthomen, kai patèr ekei'. Plotinus is quoted from the edition by P. Henry – H.-R. Schwyzer, *Plotini Opera*, I-III, Paris-Bruxelles/Leiden 1951-'73. In addition we have used the translation by S. MacKenna – B.S. Page, *Plotinus, The Enneads*, London 1969[4]. MacKenna and Page (63; cf. XXXI-II) translate *ekei* as 'There' (with a capital): *ekei* indicates the intelligible world.

this passage from the treatise 'On beauty'. He quoted from it, but only after making the alterations and transformations necessary for a Christian sense[261]. The Platonists knew what the destination was, but they did not recognize the road they had to follow[262].

Plotinus spoke not only of the beloved supernal homeland[263], but also—although he used Plato, as Theiler asserted[264], as a *Plato dimidiatus*, a Plato without politics—of the earthly city (polis) and the participation of the citizen in it. Statements on these subjects can be found throughout his treatises[265]. Plotinus argued that in man there should be harmony between the somatic needs (hai tou sōmatos chreiai) and the passions (pathè) on the one hand, and the *orthos logos* of the individual on the other hand. He compared this to the harmony that should exist in the *polis*. Supreme harmony in man is reached when the noetic principle rules alone and through it the arrangement (taxis) of the somatic needs takes place, 'analogous to a twofold city, the city above and, ordered according to the things above, the city of the things below'[266].

Thus Plotinus distinguished between the city above, the noetic city (anō always refers to the nous or the noetic) and the city below. This is perhaps comparable to Plato's views concerning the archetype and its adumbration. Whether, however, as Parma believes[267], a comparision to Augustine's concept of the two cities is possible, seems very doubtful. In any case it would be presumptuous to conclude that Plotinus influenced Augustine's concept decisively: this text, after all, is the only relevant passage to be found in the *Enneads*.

A more fruitful area of inquiry is found if we turn to Stoicism and some authors who were more or less influenced by it[268]. The most

---

261 Cf. Henry, *Plotin*, 85-89 and esp. 107-111.

262 *DCD* X, 29; for the text, see p. 237 n. 193. Cf. *Conf.* VII, 20, 26-27.

263 Cf. J.H. Sleeman - G. Pollet, *Lexicon Plotinianum*, Leiden-Louvain 1980, 829.

264 W. Theiler, 'Plotin zwischen Plato und Stoa', *Entretiens sur l'Antiquité classique*, V, *Les sources de Plotin*, Genève 1957, 67.

265 See Sleeman and Pollet, *Lexicon*, 872, for *polis, politeia*, et al.

266 *Enn.* IV, 4, 17 (in fine): '... hoion dittès poleōs ousès, tès men anō, tès de tōn katō, kata ta anō kosmoumenès'.

267 Parma, 'Plotinische Motive', 47-48.

268 For this subject, see also E. Elorduy, *Die Sozialphilosophie der Stoa*, Leipzig 1936, esp. 218-220 ('Die beiden Städte'). Cf.—for the early Stoa and its idea of the cosmic city or city of the sun (Cleanthes)—J. Bidez, *La Cité du Monde et la Cité du Soleil chez les Stoïciens*, Paris 1932.

important and essentially the only real *polis* is, according to the earliest Stoics (Zeno, Chrysippus), the heavenly one, a society of gods and (good) humans[269]. In this *kosmopolis* all creatures gifted with *logos* are assembled together; the wise man is a member of a cosmic society which stands opposite the concrete single *polis* and relativizes it.

In the Middle Stoa, with Panaetius and especially Posidonius as its principal representatives, the pivotal importance of the cosmic city was in no way denied. More attention, however, was paid to the value of the earthly *poleis*. In contrast to what Zeno and his immediate followers thought, it seems that not only the good people, but everyone was supposed to belong to this *kosmopolis*.

With the later Stoics this idea returned: there is the cosmic city (civitas, urbs, res publica, polis, politeia, patris) of gods and humans[270]. Besides, there are the earthly societies. Man is a citizen of two cities: the cosmic city and the city of his birth. This was very clearly stated by Seneca in his *De otio*[271]. Furthermore, in the early imperial period, Epictetus showed that the Platonic scheme of archetype-image can be connected with Stoic views as well: the earthly city (polis) is an adumbration of the cosmic one[272].

Definitely more Platonic elements, besides essential elements of Stoicism, can be found in the writings of Philo Alexandrinus. This is what makes this great and, for the Christian Church, influential thinker important to us, but it also creates various problems of interpretation. For what is, in fact, Philo's importance in the questions we are dealing with? He considered this world (kosmos) to be a large city (megalopolis)[273] which man enters at birth 'as an alien city'

---

269 I. ab Arnim, *Stoicorum veterum fragmenta*, I, Lipsiae 1905 (repr. 1979), 60-61 (frg. 262); *SVF*, II, Lipsiae 1903 (repr. 1979), 169 (frg. 528). Cf., for example, *SVF* II, 327-328 (frg. 1130-1131) and *SVF* III, 81-83 (frg. 333-334; 339).

270 E.g. Cicero, *De leg.* I, 23 and 61; *De nat. deor.* II, 154; Seneca, *De otio* IV, 1; Marcus Aurelius, *Medit.* II, 16; III, 11; IV, 3 and 4; et al.

271 *De otio* IV, 1: 'Duas res publicas animo complectamur, alteram magnam et vere publicam, qua dii atque homines continentur, in qua non ad hunc angulum respicimus aut ad illum, sed terminos civitatis nostrae cum sole metimur; alteram cui nos adscripsit condicio nascendi. Haec aut Atheniensium erit aut Carthaginiensium, aut alterius alicuius urbis, quae non ad omnes pertineat homines sed ad certos. Quidam eodem tempore utrique rei publicae dant operam, maiori minorique, quidam tantum minori, quidam tantum maiori'. Marcus Aurelius, *Medit.* VI, 44, also made a very clear statement on dual citizenship.

272 E.g. *Diss.* II, 6, 25.

273 For *megalopolis*, see e.g. *De opif. mundi* 19; *De Ios.* 29; *De vita Mosis* II, 51. The

(xenè polis) and in which he sojourns (paroikei) until the end of his life[274]. Philo's reference to this world as a large city is reminiscent of the Stoa. But at the same time he stressed the difference between the visible and the invisible world: the wise man goes from the visible world (kosmos aisthètos) to the spiritually perceptible, immaterial world (kosmos noètos)[275]. This corresponds clearly with the Platonic view. Moreover, Philo referred to the immaterial world as a city (noètè polis)[276], a mother city (mètropolis)[277] and a commonwealth or state (politeia)[278]. In *De gigantibus* he placed the *politeia* of this world opposite the *politeia* of ideas[279].

But did Philo subscribe to a concept of two antithetical cities? The last-named text points to a certain extent in this direction: a distinction is made between *politeia* and *politeia*. Schematizing one could emphasize that Philo referred on the one hand to this material world as a city and on the other hand to the immaterial world as a city, too. But no texts can be found in which he placed clearly one *polis* opposite the other. His reference to a 'ditton poleōs eidos'[280] should not be considered an example. This has nothing to do with a macrocosmic contradistinction between two *poleis*, but with the fact that 'of the soul-city there are two kinds, one better, the other worse'. Just as Philo called the world (kosmos) a city of God (polis theou), so did he repeatedly refer to the soul (psychè) as God's city, and even stress the latter image[281]. Finally, it is important that he distinguished between two kinds of people: 'the one of those who live according to reason (logismos), the divine spirit; the other of those who live according to the blood and the pleasure of the flesh'[282].

---

use of the term *megalopolis* in this sense seems to be characteristic of Philo; cf. F.H. Colson in his note to *De Ios.* 29 in the Loeb-edition of Philo, VI, 156.

274 This is very explicit in *De cher.* 120.

275 E.g. *De gig.* 61.

276 *De somn.* I, 46.

277 *De conf. ling.* 78.

278 *De gig.* 61; *De virt.* 219.

279 *De gig.* 61.

280 *De conf. ling.* 108.

281 E.g. *De somn.* II, 248-250: On the one hand the city of God is the whole world, on the other hand it is the soul of the wise man. Its name Jerusalem denotes 'vision of peace'; God is peace and resides in the peace-loving soul.

282 *Quis rer. div. heres* 57.

4. *Similarities and differences*

From the preceding exposition it can be seen that Greek and Latin non-Christian authors before Augustine sometimes referred to two cities. In the works of authors of the Stoic tradition this theme is heard repeatedly; thinkers influenced by Platonism made the distinction between two worlds; Philo and Plotinus in particular emphasized the supernal homeland, the yearning to return there and the state of being an alien in this world.

However, these similarities are only superficial. Further examination reveals some fundamental differences. It must even be said that in some respects a greater difference than between these views and Augustine's doctrine of the two cities is hardly conceivable.

While for (Neo)Platonists there is a distinction between two worlds, whereby the material one is a representation of the immaterial one, and the two are thus closely and positively related, Augustine lays emphasis on an absolute antithesis. Two *civitates* oppose each other from beginning to end in history; the one does not lead to the other, nor is the earthly one the adumbration of the heavenly one. The two cities are absolutely antithetical; moreover, they both have their progress (procursus) in history and are on their way to the *eschaton*. Such a historical course and final purpose does not occur in (Neo)Platonism.

Likewise, there is no more than a superficial similarity between Augustine and Stoic ways of thinking. A *kosmopolis* in which all creatures endowed with *logos* are assembled is not emphasized by Augustine. What authors who more or less followed the Stoic tradition, such as Seneca, Cicero and Marcus Aurelius, wrote about a dual citizenship of two cities—of the great cosmic city as well as of the small native city in which one has been born—does not correspond with Augustine's concept of the two cities either. One is either a citizen of the city of God, or (still) belongs to the earthly city; essentially one is not a citizen of both at the same time.

When Scholz asserted that in Plato, in Neoplatonism and in Stoicism elements of a doctrine of two cities 'in the sense of Augustine' could be found[283], he was incorrect. Also incorrect is much of what

---

283 Scholz, *Glaube und Unglaube*, 75: 'Ideen zu einer Zweistaatentheorie *im Sinne Augustins* finden sich auch [i.e. as among the Neoplatonists, esp. Plotinus] bei den Stoikern. (..). Etwas anders, noch mehr *in der Art Augustins*, hat Seneca sich ausgesprochen'. What Scholz thinks he can see in Plato's works in the way of 'preforms' is also superficially expounded.

Leisegang and Stegemann declared about Philo as a precursor of Augustine. Likewise, the passage from Plotinus put forward by Parma means no more than that Plotinus—once—mentioned a twofold city. Only by assuming that according to Augustine there is a 'gestufte Unterscheidung zweier Staaten nach ihrer Vollkommenheit'[284] could Parma point to Plotinus as a source.

Yet this assumption of a 'gestufte Unterscheidung' between two *civitates* deserves more attention. For it is an idea also expressed by Leisegang; through it he was able to refer to Philo.

It is unnecessary here to disprove again Leisegang's argumentation in its entirety. This has been done by Ferdinand Edward Cranz and especially by Erich Meuthen in a masterful and decisive manner[285]. Leisegang's main error was his opinion, based on his interpretation of the *City of God* XV, 2, that Augustine taught a Platonic hierarchy of *civitates*[286]. Just a careful reading of the passage in question reveals the incorrectness of Leisegang's view. When, in his commentary on the allegory in *Gal.* 4, Augustine speaks of the earthly city, he means in the first place the earthly Jerusalem and not—as Leisegang would have had it—the *terrena civitas* in general. From other passages it also appears that he considered the earthly city Jerusalem to be an image of the eternal heavenly city, and the earthly kingdom Israel to be a prefiguration of the heavenly kingdom[287]. It was not by way of Platonic philosophy that the church father arrived at his doctrine of the *civitates*, nor did he teach a concept of three cities.

We can only conclude that there are essential differences between Augustine and the Platonic and Stoic traditions that preceded him.

---

284 Parma, 'Plotinische Motive', 47.

285 F.E. Cranz, *'De Civitate Dei* XV, 2, et l'idée augustinienne de la société chrétienne', *REA* 3 (1957) 15-27 (this article appeared earlier as *'De Civitate Dei* XV, 2, and Augustine's Idea of the Christian Society', *Spec.* 25 (1950) 215-225 and was reprinted in R.A. Markus (ed.), *Augustine. A Collection of Critical Essays*, New York 1972, 404-421); E. Meuthen, 'Der ethische Charakter der civitates bei Augustinus und ihre platonische Fehldeutung', in: J. Engel – H.M. Klinkenberg (Hrsg.), *Aus Mittelalter und Neuzeit. Gerhard Kallen zum 70. Geburtstag* ..., Bonn 1957, 43-62.

286 See p. 246.

287 *En. in Ps.* 64, 1; 61, 9; 86, 2; 119, 7 ('... Ierusalem terrena umbra erat regni caelestis, et regnum terrenum umbra erat regni caelorum'); *De cat. rud.* 36; *DCD* XVII, 3 ('Haec enim et in terrena Hierusalem secundum historiam contingerunt, et caelestis Hierusalem figurae fuerunt'). Moreover *Gal.* 4:21 ff. is brought up again in *DCD* XVII, 3, as it is in *De cat. rud.* 36.

This does not imply that these views did not play a—sometimes important—part in the development of his thinking. It should only be remembered that the young convert identified the intelligible world of the Neoplatonists with the kingdom of God, and that in a Stoic-Platonic way he made a distinction between the wise and the foolish, the outward and the inward man[288]. There were more such elements in the preceding and contemporary philosophical movements to which Augustine's thinking shows a resemblance, for example the strong emphasis on man's state of being an alien[289].

Few relevant elements, however, are to be found in these philosophical traditions. Augustine's doctrine of the two cities involves two absolutely antithetical societies, one good and the other evil, each with its own ruler. This is not found in the thinking of the philosophers. The two cities have an origin (exortus) and a progress in time (procursus). For these, too, one searches in vain in the various philosophical schools. Lastly, there is the emphasis Augustine placed on the eschatological element: one day the two cities will have completed their course and be definitively separated. Neither in Stoic pantheism, nor among the Platonists, nor in Philo's works[290] does one find this. These elements, so essential for Augustine's doctrine of the two cities, must have come to him from another source.

C. The Donatist Tyconius

1. Tyconius, his rules for the interpretation of Scripture and his commentary on the Apocalypse

We still know little about the Donatist Tyconius. That his name and significance have not fallen into oblivion is due mainly to Augustine.

---

[288] See p. 110 f. For the distinction between two kinds of people, Philo, too, should be named (e.g. *Quis rer. div. heres* 57; cf. p. 251).

[289] This notion occupies an important place not only in the writings of the Neoplatonists and of Philo, but also among the Stoics: the gods as the true citizens of this cosmos, the people as aliens, sojourners.

[290] For Philo's eschatology—determined entirely by the Platonic view of the immortality of the soul—see, for example, the texts in (H.L. Strack-) P. Billerbeck, *Kommentar zum Neuen Testament aus Talmud und Midrasch*, IV, München 1928 (repr. 1975^6), 1020; for his concept of Hades, see 1021. A clear picture of the cycling of the souls according to Philo is given by W. Bousset – H. Gressmann, *Die Religion des Judentums im späthellenistischen Zeitalter*, Tübingen 1926^3 (repr. 1966^4, mit einem Vorwort von E. Lohse), 442.

But neither the exact dates and events of his life, nor the contents of most of his works have been passed on to us. And yet he was the very first in the Latin-speaking world to search thoroughly and systematically for the keys that would fit the mighty lock named Holy Scripture. In a number of ways he was the father of Western exegesis and hermeneutics.

The first of the many unanswered questions still concerns his name. Was it Tyconius, Ticonius or, for example, Tychonius? On the basis of the earliest manuscripts of his *Regulae* one might argue in favour of the first spelling, but the other two also have excellent credentials[291]. The dates of his birth and death are not known with certainty either. Little more can be said than that his death probably occurred around 390, and that his principal works appeared not long before that[292].

More important than exact name and dates, however, are the questions concerning his life and his thinking. What we do know is based mainly on a few rather incidental remarks made by Augustine, and on some biographical notes by the presbyter Gennadius of Marseilles[293]. The latter reported that Tyconius was born in Africa ('Tychonius natione Afer') and this referred in all probability to Africa proconsularis. That he was a 'layman', as Monceaux and Pincherle asserted[294], seems anything but certain. His very thorough knowledge of the Bible and of theology would lead us rather to presume the opposite[295]. At any rate, it is established that

---

[291] See esp. F.C. Burkitt, *The Book of Rules of Tyconius*, Cambridge 1894 (*T&S* III,1), 103. Other spellings include Thiconius, Tichonius and Thyconius. Critical editions of other texts—such as A.'s letters or *De doctr. chr.*—have not furnished any more certainty in this matter.

[292] The rather precise dates for his life and writings in Monceaux, *Histoire*, V, 170, are based mainly on suppositions. Some have followed his example, others have justly expressed their doubts. For Tyconius, his life and work, see Hahn, *Tyconius-Studien* (circumspect dating 5-6); J. Haussleiter, 'Ticonius', *RE*[3] 20 (1908) 851-855 (who only comments: 'blühte um 370-390'); Monceaux, *Histoire*, V, 165-219; A. Pincherle, 'Da Ticonio a Sant'Agostino', *RicRel* 1 (1925) 443-466; Van Bakel, 'Tyconius' (1930/1935): E.Dinkler, 'Ticonius', *PRE* 6 (1935) 849-856; G.Bardy, 'Tyconius', *DThC*15 (1950) 1932-1934; Mandouze et al, 'Tyconius', *PAC*, 1122-1127.

[293] Gennadius, *De viris inlustr.* 18 (ed. Richardson, 68-69).

[294] Monceaux, *Histoire*, V, 163; Pincherle, 'Ticonio', 450. Cf. Frend, *Donatist Church*, 201: '... he was a layman', and P. Frederiksen Landes, 'Ticonius and the End of the World', *REA* 18 (1982) 59: 'a layman'.

[295] Moreover, Dinkler, 'Ticonius', 850, suspects: 'Vielleicht darf man aus der Notiz des Gennadius (18), dass T. *ob suorum defensionem* an alte Synodalbeschlüsse

besides a profound knowledge of theology he had a thorough literary education[296]. Tyconius proves to have been an independent thinker who knew what he wanted and was therefore often obliged to go his own way.

Tyconius belonged to the Donatist movement, which was widespread in Africa. The self-confident and powerful Donatist Church regarded itself—in its confrontation with the Catholic Church which had ties with Rome—as the only legitimate continuation of ancient African Christendom. Its members still lived as they had in the days before Constantine: the Church separate from and sojourning as an alien in hostile surroundings. This Donatist element was unmistakably present in Tyconius' theology, particularly in his ecclesiology[297]. But in this matter, too, he went his own way in stressing, for instance, the universal nature of the true, persecuted Church. For this and similar reasons he was rejected in his own circle. After a bitter conflict with Bishop Parmenianus, a man of great authority among the Donatists, he was excommunicated c. 385[298]. The 'Reformdonatist'[299], however, never became a member of the Catholic Church.

Of course his writings and the ideas expressed in them are of primary interest. But here again we are confronted by the fact that much is still obscure. The earlier-named Gennadius reported that Tyconius had written the following works: *De bello intestino* and *Expositiones diversarum causarum*; also a *Liber regularum* and a commentary on the *Apocalypse of John*. The first two of these, however, seem to be definitely lost and consequently little can be said with certainty about their contents. Did *De bello intestino* deal with the struggle between Donatists and Catholics, or with controversies among the Donatists themselves? And did the *Expositiones* also concern the

---

erinnert habe, schliessen, dass er eine ihm als Priester anhängende Gemeinde um sich hatte'.

296 The main evidence for this is the only work of his that has come down to us, the *Liber regularum*. Also important is the testimony by Gennadius, *De viris inlustr.* 18: '... in divinis litteris eruditus, iuxta historiam sufficienter et in saecularibus non ignarus fuit et in ecclesiasticis quoque negotiis studiosus'. Cf. A.'s *C. ep. Parm.* I,1,1: '... Tychonium, hominis quidem et acri ingenio praeditum et uberi eloquio ...'.

297 Hahn, *Tyconius-Studien*, 99 ff.

298 A., *C. ep. Parm.* I, 1, 1: 'Et Parmenianus quidem primo eum per epistulam velut corrigendum putavit; postea vero etiam concilio eorum perhibent esse damnatum'.

299 Hahn, *Tyconius-Studien*, 110 n. 1.

Donatist problem or were they, as Pincherle suspected[300], exegetical expositions of difficult texts? Paul Monceaux seemed to give a rather detailed account[301] of the contents of each of them, but closer investigation reveals that it came to little more than general notes and a few hypotheses. The only thing beyond doubt is Gennadius' report—which there is no reason to question—that Tyconius 'in defence of his followers' appealed in these writings to the old synods and that he disclosed in them that he was a Donatist[302]. A few statements by Augustine corroborate these brief remarks[303].

As regards our knowledge of the famous *Liber regularum*, however, the situation is completely different. This work of the learned Donatist has come down to us in its entirety and since 1894 there has been, in the superb edition by F.C. Burkitt, a reliable tool for scholarly research. Augustine also referred extensively to the contents of Tyconius' book[304]. It is no doubt partly due to his recommendation[305]—and naturally to the contents of the work itself—that the *Regulae* have exerted a great influence. They were important to John Cassian, John the Deacon, Cassiodorus, Isidore of Seville, Bede and, among others, Hincmar of Rheims. Western exegesis and hermeneutics of the early Middle Ages, and even for a long time afterwards, are almost inconceivable without Tyconius.

What, then, is so interesting about his approach? Within the framework of this study only a few main points from his book can be discussed. Tyconius wanted to provide rules for a better understanding of the Scriptures. First he identified a real problem. The Church inherited the Old Testament and believes that it is Holy Writ. But what can the Church do with it? The writers of the New Testament and subsequent authors made references to many prophecies of the Old Testament. A large portion of it, however,—

---

300 Pincherle, 'Ticonio', 447.

301 Monceaux, *Histoire*, V, 171 ff. Obviously he is partially following Hahn here (*Tyconius-Studien*, 57 ff.), but in the latter's work we always find: 'vermutlich', 'dürfte', etc.!

302 Gennadius, *De viris inlustr.* 18: '... in quibus ob suorum defensionem antiquarum meminit synodorum. E quibus omnibus agnoscitur Donatianae partis fuisse'.

303 *C. ep. Parm.* I, 1, 1; *Ep.* 249; *Ep.* 93, 43-44.

304 *De doctr. chr.* III, 30, 42 – 37, 56.

305 Besides *De doctr. chr.*., see *Ep.* 41, 2 (A. and Alypius to Aurelius of Carthage) and esp. *Ep.* 249, a recommendation to the deacon Restitutus. How important the *Lib. reg.* was as an authority and guide for A. is also apparent from *Quaest. in Hept.* II, *qu.* 47, 3 and *Retract.* II, 44, 4.

Tyconius spoke literally of the 'prophetiae inmensa silva'[306]—was never quoted by an ancient writer. Did this then have no value? Tyconius believed it did, and he gave extensive quotations, accompanied by his interpretation, especially from those prophecies that had been little known until then or never touched upon.

According to Tyconius all the Scriptural prophecies can be classified into two categories: they refer either to Christ and his Church, or to the devil and his followers. Many texts in the Old Testament clearly refer to Christ. But Christ is one with his Church, his body (corpus), and therefore many prophecies refer to this body. Moreover, the body of Christ is divided into two parts: it is a *corpus bipertitum* with a right part and a left one, true and false Christians. Thus in a prophecy one verse may refer to Christ himself, and another to the false Christians.

In the first two rules (*De Domino et corpore eius; De Domini corpore bipertito*) the author illustrated this with many examples. But he went further. In the third rule (*De promissis et lege*) he indicated that no one is justified by works of the Law, but that belonging to one or the other part of the *corpus bipertitum* is dependent only on the will and the grace of God. Essentially it is a question of 'sola gratia per fidem'[307]. Rule IV is entitled *De specie et genere*: which portions of the Old Testament have specific and partial validity, which have general validity? Much of what is said *in specie* is also applicable *in genere*, and vice versa. Particularly in the prophecies of the Old Testament much must be understood *in genere*, as referring to Christ and his *corpus*, the Church. Then in Rule V, *De temporibus*, Tyconius showed in an ingenious way how indications of time, seasons and numbers in the Bible can be significant. What should be understood by recapitulation he explained in the sixth rule: *De recapitulatione*. There is *recapitulatio* when a biblical author refers to type as well as antitype, to promise as well as fulfilment. Finally, in the seventh rule (*De diabolo et corpore eius*) he taught that just as much refers to Christ and his body, so does much also refer to the devil and his body. Together they also form a unity. But there is one exception: the *corpus diaboli* is not *bipertitum*, it has no right and left, no good and evil part. It is entirely bad and even reaches into the *corpus Christi*, the Church.

With an abundance of texts, mostly from the prophets and the

---

306 *Lib. reg., prooem.*, ed. Burkitt p. 1.

307 *Lib. reg., reg.* III, p. 15.

New Testament, Tyconius elucidated his rules. In this way he attempted to explain the Scriptures and to demonstrate the unity of the Old and the New Testament. The central element in his thinking is the concept *corpus*: the *corpus Christi* is opposed to the *corpus diaboli*; the *corpus Christi* is *bipertitum*, the devil's is not. Whether this idea had any influence on Augustine's concept of the two cities—and if so to what extent—will be discussed later.

First, however, we have to turn our attention to the last work mentioned by Gennadius: the commentary on the *Apocalypse*. It is quite possible to see in this work Tyconius' own application of the exegetical principles of his *Liber regularum*. But, unfortunately, the commentary as a whole appears to be lost. Only what later interpreters of the *Apocalypse* reported about it—apart from a few fragments of a codex preserved in Turin[308]—has come down to us. Did the Donatist mention in his commentary the antithesis between two *civitates*, the city of God and the city of the devil, and in this way become the one who decisively inspired Augustine's idea? Many investigators have stated this, particularly influenced by the pioneering work of Traugott Hahn. For what Hahn rather cautiously suggested in 1900 was soon afterwards accepted as established truth.

With good reason? The very complicated problems concerning Tyconius' commentary will be discussed separately. At this point it suffices to say that his interpretation has had a great influence on Western exegesis of the last book of the Bible[309]. Jerome made use of it in his anti-chiliastic adaption of the commentary of Victorinus of Pettau; for Caesarius (bishop of Arles from 502 to 542), Primasius (bishop of Hadrumetum in Byzacena, North Africa, c. 550), (probably) Apringius (bishop of Beja in Portugal, mid-sixth century), Cassiodorus (died c. 580), Beda Venerabilis (died 735) and certainly for the Spanish presbyter Beatus of Liebana (late eighth century) the commentary played an important role. Through this work, too, the

[308] F. Lo Bue, *The Turin Fragments of Tyconius' Commentary on Revelation*, Cambridge 1963 (*T&S, NS* VII). This edition appeared posthumously and was prepared for publication by G.G. Willis (and G.D. Kilpatrick). For the significance of these fragments, see p. 266.

[309] Cf. Hahn, *Tyconius-Studien*, 3 ff. and 8 ff.; W. Bousset, *Die Offenbarung Johannis*, Göttingen 1906, 56 ff. and 65 ff. Of the numerous later studies we mention only the rather recent one by G. Maier, *Die Johannesoffenbarung und die Kirche*, Tübingen 1981 (*WUNT* 25). He gives (Teil II: 'Die Umdeutung der Apokalypse im Westen', 108-171) an interesting survey of the significance of Tyconius and A., but his interpretations are not always scientifically sound.

Donatist 'heretic'[310] made an indelible impression on the history of the Western Church. Following his example the historical-realistic exegesis of the last book of the Bible was replaced by a spiritual interpretation, and, mainly for this reason, a definitive break occurred with chiliasm[311]. A learned Donatist threw the switch for the Catholic Church, and it was in the first place through the influence of Augustine that it continued in the new direction[312].

2. *Tyconius as the source?*

Tyconius is without doubt the one who is most often mentioned as the source of Augustine's doctrine of the two cities. It has already been explained how much this was due to Traugott Hahn's pioneering work: *Tyconius-Studien. Ein Beitrag zur Kirchen- und Dogmengeschichte des vierten Jahrhunderts* (Leipzig, 1900). Hahn was particularly interested in Tyconius' theology and more specifically in his ecclesiology. In giving his exposition he referred not only to the *Liber regularum*, but also extensively to the interpretations of the *Apocalypse of John* as they appear in the works of later authors acquainted with Tyconius' commentary. Hahn even gave these later interpretations an important place in his exposition, and in his introduction he described in detail how Tyconius' lost commentary could be reconstructed from these later works[313].

An especially important aspect of Hahn's work was that he called attention to extensive passages from Beatus of Liebana. To be sure, the latter's interpretation of the *Apocalypse* could have been known through the edition by H. Florez, *S. Beati Presbyteri Hispani Liebanensis in Apocalypsin ... Commentaria*, Matriti, 1770. This edition, however, had been virtually forgotten and was, moreover, very rare. Hahn quoted at length from it, because he considered Beatus of fundamental importance for becoming acquainted with Tyconius' commentary. The simple presbyter noticed nothing of the 'heretical'

---

310 E.g. A. in *De doctr. chr.* III, 30, 43: 'Caute sane legendus est (...) maxime propter illa, quae sicut donatista *haereticus* loquitur'.

311 E.g. Gennadius, *De viris inlustr.* 18 (ed. Richardson, p. 68): 'Exposuit et Apocalipsin Iohannis ex integro, nihil in ea carnale, sed totum intelligens spiritale. (...) Mille quoque annorum regni in terra iustorum post resurrectionem futuri suspicionem tulit ...'.

312 Cf. e.g. Bousset, *Offenbarung*, 60 f.; Maier, *Johannesoffenbarung*, 108-171.

313 Hahn, *Tyconius-Studien*, 3-22.

nature of his source: he just copied. And it is precisely in Beatus that there is a striking reference to two antithetical *civitates*[314].

Thus the origin of Augustine's doctrine of the two cities seemed to be established: Tyconius, whom he esteemed highly and whose commentary on the *Apocalypse* had now come to light mainly through Beatus. Although this conclusion concerning Augustine's concept was not the central element in Hahn's study[315]—after all, his interest lay in Tyconius and particularly in the latter's ecclesiology—, for later readers of the *Tyconius-Studien* it was. It should be stressed, however, that Hahn, especially in his 'Vorwort' and 'Einleitung', displayed some hesitation and pointed repeatedly to the tentative character of his investigation[316]. Nevertheless, what was presented with circumspection by the first pioneer was taken as an established fact by later scholars. The first to do so was Scholz. Some ten years after Hahn he cited the most relevant passages from Beatus[317], and by doing so exerted great influence on later scholars. Many did not even consult Hahn's exposition—nor that of Beatus or any of the other interpreters of the *Apocalypse* who had gone back directly to Tyconius—, but confined themselves to what Scholz had stated. Scholz' somewhat cautious 'conjecture': 'Dadurch wird die Vermutung nahegelegt, dass er [Augustinus] vielleicht auch den entscheidenden Anstoss zu seiner Zweistaaten-Konzeption von Ticonius empfangen hat'[318]—it does not appear in the rest of his book that it was only a conjecture—has often been taken without

---

314 Beatus, *In Apoc.*, 506, 26-30 (ed. Florez, in Hahn, 25 n. 1): 'Ecce duas civitates, unam Dei, et unam diaboli, ...et in utrasque reges terrae ministrant'; *In Apoc.*, 507, 15-33 (ed. Florez, in Hahn, 29 n.): 'Perspicue patet duas civitates esse et duo regna, et duos reges, Christum et diabolum: et ambo super utrasque civitates regnant ... Hae duae civitates, una mundo, et una desiderat servire Christo: una in hoc mundo regnum cupit tenere, et una ab hoc mundo fugere: una tristatur, altera laetatur: una flagellat, altera flagellatur: una occidit, altera occiditur: una ut justificetur adhuc, altera ut impie agat adhuc. Hae utraeque ita laborant in unum, una ut habeat unde damnetur, altera ut habeat unde salvetur'.

315 Only at the end (*Tyconius-Studien*, 115) does he state: 'Beide stellen eine civitas Dei und civitas diaboli einander gegenüber'.

316 E.g. *Tyconius-Studien*, V: '... das Unfertige, nein auch das Mangelhafte dieser Studien'; '... nur eine Einleitung zu der Skizze (...) seiner Anschauungen'; VI: 'Nicht bei jedem Citat konnte ich den Echtheitsbeweis beibringen', etc. For the many questions surrounding the commentary by Beatus, cf. 16 ff.; we shall return to this later.

317 Scholz, *Glaube und Unglaube*, 78-79.

318 Scholz, *Glaube und Unglaube*, 79.

hesitation as an established fact. For his doctrine of the two *civitates* Augustine was dependent on Tyconius, and Beatus had provided the proof.

Of the many scholars who have followed in his footsteps, only a small selection is given here. A few years after Scholz, H.T. Karsten expressed himself in the same way[319], as did Monceaux[320], Van Bakel[321], Noordmans[322], Baynes[323], Sizoo[324], Bardy[325], Combès and Farges[326], Gilson[327], Frend[328], Lauras and Rondet[329], Wytzes[330], Quacquarelli[331], Ladner[332], Karpp[333], Bonner[334], Cordovani[335], Markus[336], Duchrow[337], Schindler[338], Quispel [339], Dougherty[340], Maier[341] and Wijdeveld[342]. Usually they stated explicitly that they meant Tyconius' commentary on the last book of the Bible; sometimes they also substantiated this with quotations

---

319 Karsten, *Godsrijk*, 1.

320 Monceaux, *Histoire*, V, 219.

321 Van Bakel, 'Tyconius', 124 ff., mainly following Hahn and Scholz. It is not clear how much value Van Bakel attaches to the *Lib. reg.* in this respect.

322 Noordmans, *Augustinus* (1933/1952²), *VW* 3, 148. Here he is obviously following Scholz. See also 137.

323 Baynes, *Political Ideas*, 291.

324 A. Sizoo, 'De geschiedbeschouwing van Augustinus', in: *De zin der geschiedenis*, Wageningen 1944, 71 (like Scholz); cf. 66. Sizoo is later more circumspect in his *Augustinus*, 313.

325 Bardy, 'Tyconius', 1934. Cf. Bardy in his *Saint Augustin. L'homme et l'oeuvre*, Paris 1946⁶, 358 and 515. He is somewhat more guarded in 'Formation', 12.

326 G. Combès and J. Farges, *BA* 11, Paris 1949, 589.

327 Gilson, *Métamorphoses*, 51 n. 3 and 39 n. 2, following Scholz.

328 Frend, *Donatist Church*, 205. Cf. 316-317 for Beatus in Hahn.

329 Lauras and Rondet, 'Thème', 153, basing their argument on Monceaux.

330 Wytzes, 'Augustinus en Rome', 71. His assertion that A. did not mention Tyconius anywhere is probably due to an inaccurate reading of Scholz, *Glaube und Unglaube*, 79 (last line).

331 Quacquarelli, *Concezione*, 131 ff.

332 Ladner, *Idea*, 259 ff., though with circumspection; see below.

333 H. Karpp, 'Ticonius (Tyconius)', *RGG* VI (1962) 885.

334 G. Bonner, *St. Augustine of Hippo. Life and Controversies*, London 1963, 289; cf. 245 with the reference to Hahn. See also G. Bonner, *Saint Bede in the Tradition of Western Apocalyptic Commentary* (Jarrow Lecture 1966), 4 and 16 n. 14.

335 Cordovani, 'Due città', 443, with an inexact reference to the quotations given by Monceaux. He also quotes Christopher, who refers to the *Lib. reg.*

336 Markus, *Saeculum*, 115 ff.

337 Duchrow, *Christenheit*, 232 ff.

338 Schindler, 'Augustin', 680.

339 G. Quispel, *The Secret Book of Revelation*, New York 1979, 121.

340 Dougherty, *City*, 154 n. 5.

341 Maier, *Johannesoffenbarung*, 116 and 161 ff.

342 Wijdeveld, *Augustinus, De stad van God*, 22.

(via Hahn/Beatus, later on also from Sanders' edition of Beatus' *In Apocalypsin*). But only a few times—Ladner is a good example[343]—has the difficult and still uncertain situation surrounding Tyconius' commentary been mentioned. The basic idea was clear for most of them, however: Tyconius, in his interpretation of the last book of the Bible, spoke of the two antithetical *civitates*; thus he became the (principal) source of inspiration for Augustine.

Others, however, have pointed in another direction. For them Tyconius' commentary on the *Apocalypse* was not—or not to such an extent—the source of Augustine's concept, but they referred especially to the *Liber regularum*. In this respect Gilson[344], Christopher[345], Bakhuizen van den Brink[346] and Ehrhardt[347] can (again) be named. Besides, Obersteiner[348] and Spörl[349] considered both the Donatist Tyconius—they probably meant his commentary on the *Apocalypse*—and Manichaeism as influential, but they did not provide any substantiation.

Which of these scholars is correct? It is not conjectures that have value as evidence, but only the extant texts by Tyconius. One work has come down to us: his *Liber regularum*. It is possible to ascertain whether any mention is made in it of two antithetical *civitates*. But it is precisely to his other influential work, the commentary on the *Apocalypse*, that most references are made. Did he (also) speak there, like Augustine, of two antithetical *civitates*, the heavenly and the earthly city, Jerusalem and Babylon? Before we look into the matter of whether Tyconius wrote about two cities—and if so, in what way—we must first go further into the problems surrounding his commentary.

3. *The problems surrounding Tyconius' commentary on the 'Apocalypse'*

The integral text of Tyconius' commentary on the last book of the Bible is not at our disposal. Although in the ninth century the library

---

343 Ladner, *Idea*, 260 ff., esp. 263.
344 Gilson, *Introduction*, 237 n. 1.
345 Christopher, *Cat. Instruction*, 128. On the preceding page, however, he draws attention to Tyconius' commentary, through quotations from Hahn.
346 Bakhuizen van den Brink, *Handboek*, I, 249.
347 Ehrhardt, *Metaphysik*, III, 35.
348 Obersteiner, 'Civitas Dei', 333-334.
349 Spörl, 'Staatslehre?', 66.

of the monastery at St. Gallen still owned a copy[350], it apparently disappeared after that. For information about the contents one has to turn to later interpreters. There were quite a number of them, for Tyconius' spiritualistic exegesis made a deep impression. But the degree to which those later commentators followed the interpretation of the illustrious Donatist literally is still a subject of scholarly debate.

It should be noted, however, that in recent years little has been contributed to this discussion. Since the studies by Haussleiter[351], Ramsay[352], Bousset[353], Hahn and later by, among others, Gómez[354] and Bonner[355], no real progress has been made. Though hypotheses have been proposed and courses laid out to arrive at a reconstruction of the lost commentary, none of this has led to definitive results.

Further consideration leads to the conclusion that this is not at all surprising. For the field of research is extensive and strewn with many obstacles. One can still understand Hahn's complaint: 'Aussichtslos erscheint mir allerdings unter den bewandten Umständen, (...) den Kommentar des Tyconius im Wortlaut zu rekonstruieren'[356]. Yet it was especially Hahn, aided substantially by earlier (but then not yet published) investigations by Wilhelm Bousset[357], who made an impressive attempt.

The basic facts concerning Tyconius' commentary are as follows. He probably wrote the work shortly before 380. With it he put an end to the historical-realistic interpretation of the last book of the Bible prevailing until then in the West. He gave a spiritualistic interpretation, and it was not in the last place this consistently sustained method that impressed later authors. Jerome made use of the

---

350 J. Haussleiter, 'Die Kommentare des Victorinus, Tichonius und Hieronymus zur Apokalypse', *ZKWL* 7 (1886) 240-241, using evidence given by G. Becker, *Catalogi bibliothecarum antiqui*, Bonn 1885. Cf. Haussleiter, 'Ticonius', 853.

351 E.g. Haussleiter, 'Kommentare' (1886) and 'Ticonius' (1908).

352 H.L. Ramsay, 'Le commentaire de l'apocalypse par Beatus de Liebana', *RHLR* 7 (1902) 419-447.

353 Bousset, *Offenbarung* (1906).

354 I.M. Gómez, 'El perdido comentario de Ticonio al Apocalipsis. Principios de crítica literaria y textual para su reconstrucción', in: *Miscellanea biblica B. Ubach*, Montisserrati 1953, 405.

355 Bonner, *Saint Bede* (1966); G. Bonner, 'Towards a Text of Tyconius', *SP* X (*TU* 107), Berlin 1970, 9-13.

356 Hahn, *Tyconius-Studien*, 18.

357 See Bousset, *Offenbarung*, 56 n. 5 and Hahn, *Tyconius-Studien*, 8 ff.

work in his adaption of Victorinus' commentary; the author of the pseudo-Augustinian homilies on the *Apocalypse*, now identified as Caesarius of Arles[358], drew on it, while concealing his dubious source. In the days of Justinianus it was the African Primasius of Hadrumetum, who—although hesitant because of its 'heretical' character—made extensive use of Tyconius' commentary. So did the Venerable Bede. In his *Explanatio Apocalypsis* he repeatedly mentioned Tyconius as one of his sources and, what is most significant, he often pointed out explicitly what he derived from the Donatist's commentary[359].

But there is more. It exerted influence on Cassiodorus, possibly on Apringius and probably on Ambrosius Autpertus[360], while its influence on Beatus of Liebana was particularly important. This Spanish presbyter, a contemporary of Charlemagne, compiled an exegesis of the last book of the Bible in twelve books. He used, as he said in his introduction, the works of a considerable number of earlier writers[361]. One of them was Tyconius. From Beatus' compilation it is clear that the Donatist predecessor was of great significance to him. Passages dealing with Africa or with the itinerant *circumcelliones* were taken over verbatim. Beatus did little more than copy and therefore his work is, as Bousset and Hahn already concluded, invaluable for the study of Tyconius' commentary[362].

But how much of Beatus' compilation was really from Tyconius? Bousset's suggestion[363] that the portion obviously originating from other sources be deleted, so that only the passages by Tyconius remain, is more easily said than done. On the basis of Bousset's suggestions and with Florez' edition as his starting-point, Hahn indeed

---

358 G. Morin, 'Le commentaire homilétique de S. Césaire sur l'Apocalypse', *RBén* 45 (1933) 43-61. Morin indicates (50-51), that he had a predecessor in the little-known abbot J.-B. Morel (died 1772). The *homiliae* (actually drafts of sermons; cf. Morin, 52) were published later by the learned Benedictine in a critical edition: G. Morin, *Sancti Caesarii Arelatensis Opera Varia* ..., Maretioli 1942, 209-277 (not reprinted in *CCL* 103-104).

359 Beda, *Explanatio Apocalypsis, MPL* 93, esp. 145D, 155D, 156A, 166C, 174B.

360 Cf. Hahn, *Tyconius-Studien*, 5 and 8 ff; Bousset, *Offenbarung*, 57 and 65 ff.

361 Beatus, *In Apoc.*, ed. Sanders pp. 1 – 2: 'quae tamen non a me, sed a sanctis patribus, quae explanata reperii, in hoc libello indita sunt et firmata his auctoribus, id est, Iheronimo, Agustino, Ambrosio, Fulgentio, Gregorio, Ticonio, Irenaeo, Apringio, et Isidoro ...'.

362 Bousset, *Offenbarung*, 55 and 68; Hahn, *Tyconius-Studien*, esp. VI and 9. Cf. Gómez, 'Comentario', 404-409.

363 Bousset, *Offenbarung*, 56 n. 5. Cf. 461 also, however.

indicated the passages that were clearly borrowed from Victorinus, Apringius, Augustine, Ambrose, Jerome, Isidore and Gregory[364]. But whether the remainder was really part of Tyconius' commentary turns out in many instances to be uncertain[365]. This, combined with the fact that the text edited by Florez is often hardly usable[366] and that Beatus by no means copied Tyconius as slavishly as would now be desired[367], does not make the matter clearer.

Nor do the Turin fragments provide conclusive evidence. Amelli presented them in 1897 as genuine Tyconian texts[368], but closer examination reveals that this is not the case. The material contained in the codex, which originally came from Bobbio, was interpolated to make it suitable for Catholic use[369]. Moreover, this material only consists of fragments, an exegesis of *Apoc.* 2:18-4:1 and 7:16-12:6. No mention is made in these fragments of an antithesis between two cities or kingdoms.

Yet there is more to be said. It should be possible to proceed further by starting from the firm basis offered by the *Liber regularum*. From this work we are acquainted with Tyconius' way of thinking, his style and concepts. In addition, each of the commentaries which depend more or less on Tyconius should be studied, particularly the one by Victorinus in Jerome's version, the pseudo-Augustinian homilies, Primasius, Bede as well as the Turin fragments. The relationships between these commentaries should be ascertained; besides, the passages containing clearly recognizable Tyconian ideas should be determined. By means of a synoptic collation and a continual comparison with the contents of the *Liber regularum*, a number of elements of the lost commentary can be reconstructed with relative certainty.

---

364 Hahn, *Tyconius-Studien*, 10-11.

365 See Hahn's enumerations, *Tyconius-Studien*, 11-12.

366 Hahn, *Tyconius-Studien*, 16; Bousset, *Offenbarung*, 68 n. 2 ('Der Text bei Florez ist noch in ausserordentlich verwildertem Zustand'); Sanders in the introduction to his edition, XVIII. Moreover, Sanders reports (XII): 'Less than a dozen copies are known today'.

367 Hahn, *Tyconius-Studien*, 16: 'B[eatus] hat vielmehr T[yconius] sicher oft gröblich missverstanden und missdeutet; 17: 'Nachweislich hat B (...) die Neigung eigne Bemerkungen einzustreuen'; 'Ferner hat B mehrfach T verfälscht ...', etc.

368 'Tyconii Afri Fragmenta Commentarii in Apocalipsin ...', *Specilegium Casinense* III,1, Montecassino 1897, 263-331. It was the fragments as they appeared in this edition that A. Hamman included in *MPL, S.*, I, Paris 1958, 622-652.

369 Such as Hahn, *Tyconius-Studien*, 15 and 16; Ramsay, 'Commentaire', 436; Gómez, 'Comentario', 410 and Lo Bue in the introduction to his edition, 35-38.

In the last few decades, however, it has been demonstrated that such a method is not very feasible. There are many snares and pitfalls[370]. It is reasonable to ask whether the commentary by Tyconius, barring a lucky find that brings the entire work to light, will ever be known in its true form. But we already possess much: the *Liber regularum*, Beatus in an accessible edition by Sanders[371], the Turin fragments in the excellent edition by Lo Bue. Furthermore, several editions of commentaries going back either directly or indirectly to Tyconius have appeared recently[372].

And above all it can be said that, in spite of the many unsolved questions surrounding the commentary by Tyconius, a number of observations can be made with a considerable degree of certainty. Later commentators referred in a special way to the antithesis between two cities, Jerusalem and Babylon. Although in many instances it is certain that they were also familiar with Augustine's *City of God*[373], again and again a typically Tyconian element is apparent.

4. *Tyconius on two 'corpora', Beatus et al. on two cities*

In the preceding we have seen that the idea of two *corpora* occupied an important place in Tyconius' thinking. Because his theology was

---

[370] To name only a few: What about the numerous concurrences (see the specification in Lo Bue's edition) between, in particular, Bede and the Turin Fragments? Did Bede have, in addition to the original commentary by Tyconius, these fragments at his disposal?—The codex from Bobbio/Turin gives, as is almost universally accepted (though Pincherle often expressed his disagreement, see 'Ticonio', esp. 456; cf. also his review of Lo Bue in *SMSR* 34 (1963) 290-296), an interpolated text, adapted for Catholic use. But was this Catholic adaption (cf. Lo Bue, 36) made very early, even before Primasius and Caesarius?—Was the *Summa dicendorum*, which Beatus placed before the actual commentary, written by Jerome (as stated by Haussleiter, 'Kommentare', 250 ff.), or by Beatus himself, or by Tyconius?—To what extent was Ramsay correct ('Commentaire') when he argued that many texts in Beatus which Hahn ascribed to Tyconius actually go back to Gregory and Isidore? Etc.

[371] It is due to Sanders that Beatus has become accessible again. But his publication cannot be recommended for the level of its scholarship; see e.g. Bonner, 'Text', 10. Furthermore, as there is no indication of the pagination of Florez' edition, studies like Hahn's are difficult to check.

[372] See R. Weber's edition of Ambrosius Autpertus' *Expositio in Apocalypsim*, Turnholti 1975 (*CCCM* 27-27A), and W. Adams' edition of Primasius, *Commentarius in Apocalypsin*, Turnholti 1985 (*CCL* 92). The long-ago announced edition of Bede's *In Apocalypsin* was not included in *CCL* 121, which appeared in 1983, nor will it be included in *CCL* 121B.

[373] See further p. 272.

above all concerned with questions of ecclesiology[374], it was in this framework that Tyconius developed his doctrine of the two bodies. The seven hermeneutic rules of the *Liber regularum* focus on this doctrine: there is the body of Christ, the Church, and there is the body of the devil; Christ and his body are one, and so is the devil and his *corpus*; the *corpus Domini* is *bipertitum*, it has a right and a left part; the devil's, however, is undivided and evil.

For this idea that the body of Christ is two-sided, Tyconius saw corroboration in many Scriptural passages. For example, he inferred it from the two kinds of children of Abraham[375]. But he found it especially in the biblical texts that speak about duality and unity at the same time. The bride in the *Song of Songs* (*Cant.* 1:5) says: *Fusca sum et decora*, 'Dark am I and comely'. That means that the one bride of Christ, the one body of the Church, has both a right and a left part, encompasses grace *and* sin[376]. In this way there are many types in Scripture symbolizing this duality: Solomon is an image (figura) of the twofold Church[377], as are the temple[378], Egypt[379], Nineveh[380], Tyre[381], and, among others, Jerusalem[382].

Besides, there are types that have a single meaning: only evil. Esau belongs to this category, as do Seir, the king of Babylon, and Babylon itself[383]. Like Christ, the devil forms a unity with his *corpus*. But it is not a *corpus bipertitum*. Only evil is symbolized in these types, and in the Church it is the left part, *pars sinistra ecclesiae*.

In his hermeneutic rules Tyconius did not picture the two *corpora* as being absolutely antithetical and separate from each other. On the contrary, he wanted to show that in the Church there are good and evil members. Christ's bride is *fusca et decora*. However, she is not entirely black, but only in her left part[384]. That left side has al-

---

374 Besides Hahn, *Tyconius-Studien*, see esp. Ratzinger, 'Beobachtungen zum Kirchenbegriff des Tyconius im *Liber regularum*', *REA* 2 (1956) 173-185 and K. Forster, 'Die ekklesiologische Bedeutung des corpus-Begriffes im Liber Regularum des Tyconius', *MThZ* 7 (1956) 173-183.

375 *Lib. reg.*, *reg.* III, ed. Burkitt pp.28-29; cf. *reg.* II, p. 11.

376 *Lib. reg.*, *reg.* II, p. 10.

377 *Lib. reg.*, *reg.* IV, pp. 38-39 and *reg.* V, p. 65.

378 *Lib. reg.*, *reg.* I, pp. 7-8.

379 *Lib. reg.*, *reg.* IV, p. 43.

380 *Lib. reg.*, *reg.* IV, pp. 41-42.

381 *Lib. reg.*, *reg.* IV, p. 46 ff.

382 *Lib. reg.*, *reg.* IV, p. 41.

383 *Lib. reg.*, *reg.* VII, p. 70 ff.

384 E.g. *Lib. reg.*, *reg.* II, p. 10: 'Iterum breviter bipertitum ostenditur Christi

ways been present, though under different names: Esau, Theman, Ishmael, the tents of Kedar or, for example, Babylon. Now the Church is suffering from false brothers, but soon, at the impending end of the world, they will be cast out[385].

In still another way it is apparent that Tyconius did not picture the two *corpora* as two absolutely antithetical entities. The *corpus diaboli* does not originate in evil nature, but in the perverted will. People are not evil 'by nature', according to their original and essential being; the good treasures of man's nature remain[386]. It is through his evil will that man follows the devil and belongs to him. The major distinction between the two *corpora* is this: the *corpus Domini* is in its essence and origin (secundum originem) of Christ, and comprises both those who willingly belong to him and those who are unwilling and have turned away from him; the *corpus diaboli* comprises only those who follow the devil through their evil will.

Thus there are two *corpora*, and in the *Liber regularum* Tyconius did not present them as being in absolute antithesis to each other. The contradistinction between two cities that is characteristic of Augustine does therefore not occur in this work. To be sure, Jerusalem is a type of the *corpus Christi*, and Babylon of the *corpus diaboli*. But Jerusalem as a *corpus bipertitum* is at the same time Babylon as well; it includes Babylon as its left part[387].

A similar view of two *corpora* occurs in the Turin fragments. Therefore it can be assumed that in these fragments Tyconius' ideas have been handed down in an authentic way. In the exegesis of *Apoc.*

---

corpus: *Fusca sum et decora* [*Cant.* 1:5]. Absit enim ut Ecclesia *quae non habet maculam aut rugam* [*Eph.* 5:27], quam Dominus suo sanguine sibi mundavit, aliqua ex parte fusca sit nisi in parte sinistra per quam *nomen Dei blasphematur in gentibus* [*Rom.* 2:24].

385 *Lib. reg., reg.* III, pp. 29-31.

386 *Lib. reg., reg.* VII, p. 82.

387 E.g. *Lib. reg., reg.* IV, p. 41: 'Ostendit in Hierusalem esse Theman, quam illic Deus interficiet et Dagon et omnia execrabilia gentium ...' [*Ezek.* 20:45 - 21:5 has just been quoted]; p. 50: 'Babylon civitas adversa Hierusalem totus mundus est, qui in parte sua, quam in hac Hierusalem habet, convenitur' [after this *Isa.* 13: 2-18 is quoted]; p. 52: '... aperte ostendit omnes gentes esse Babylonem et eas *in terra* atque *in montibus* suis, id est in Ecclesia, perdere' [this is followed by *Isa.* 14: 22-27]; p. 53: 'Item omnes gentes, quae sub caelo sunt in civitate Dei iram Dei bibere et illic percuti Hieremias testatur dicens:... [*Jer.* 32: 15-29 is quoted]; p. 54: '... Hierusalem ... in qua sunt omnes gentes terrae quas illic Deus percutiet ...'; etc. *Reg.* V, p. 63 is also important: Jerusalem is *bipertita* and has two gates, Christ and the devil.

11:8 it is stated that there are *in* the Church two *corpora*[388], in the exegesis of *Apoc.* 8:12 that there are *in* the Church two *populi*[389], and in the explanation of *Apoc.* 11:13 that there are *in* the Church two *aedificia*, one on the rock, the other on sand[390].

In the commentaries on the *Apocalypse* which depend to a greater or lesser degree on Tyconius' commentary, similar ideas are found. For example, Primasius and Beatus adhered to the idea of the two *corpora* and of the two *populi* in the Church[391]. They were also the ones who, like Caesarius, stated that there are two *aedificia* in the Church[392].

But in these later commentaries there is also an antithesis between two cities. In their explanations of the passages of the *Apocalypse* concerning Jerusalem and Babylon, the later commentators say more and different things than Tyconius' *Liber regularum* or the Turin fragments do. The first time this is apparent is in the exegesis of *Apoc.* 14:8 on the fall of Babylon: *Cecidit, cecidit Babilon illa magna*. Beatus discusses rather extensively the existence of two antithetical cities, a *civitas diaboli* and a *civitas Dei*[393]. This corresponds generally with the view of a predecessor like Caesarius[394]. Particularly interesting, however, is Beatus' interpretation of *Apoc.* 17:18 concerning the woman on the beast, who is the great city (Babylon) and has dominion over the kings of the earth. In his explanation of this text he connects *Apoc.* 21:9 about the wife of the Lamb, *Apoc.* 21:10 about the city (Jerusalem) coming down from heaven, and *Apoc.* 21:24 about the kings who bring their glory into that city. Wife, city and kings belong together, according to Beatus; they form one *corpus*, one *ecclesia*. And besides the fact that there are two antithetical *corpora* and two *ecclesiae*, he mentions the antithesis between two wives, two kings

---

388 *Turin Fragments*, ed. Lo Bue, pp. 154-155.

389 *Turin Fragments*, pp. 96-97.

390 *Turin Fragments*, pp. 168-169.

391 Primasius, *Comm. in Apoc.*, ed. Adams, *CCL* 92, p. 169 and Beatus, *In Apoc.*, ed. Sanders, p. 449; Primasius, *Comm.*, 143 and Beatus, *In Apoc.*, 419 and 580 resp.

392 Primasius, *Comm.*, 175; Beatus, *In Apoc.*, 453; Caesarius, *Exp. in Apoc.*, ed. Morin, p. 241.

393 Beatus, *In Apoc.*, 515.

394 Caesarius, *Exp.*, 248: 'Nam sicut civitas dei ecclesia est et omnis conversatio caelestis, ita e contrario civitas diaboli est Babylon in omni mundo ...'. Cf., for example, Bede, *Expl. Apoc.*, *MPL* 93, 174D and esp. 185B with reference to *Apoc.* 18:2.

(Christ and the devil), two kingdoms *and* two cities[395]. Passages from this exegesis have played—ever since Hahn and Scholz gave their fragmentary quotations—a prominent part in the discussions about the origin of Augustine's concept of the two *civitates*. It can be added that Bede also referred in a similar context to two *cities*[396].

Is it Tyconius' true voice that is heard here, or is it the interpretation of later commentators? It seems very possible and even quite probable that in his commentary Tyconius, inspired by the eschatological antithesis between Jerusalem and Babylon as mentioned in the last book of the Bible, spoke differently and more specifically than in the *Liber regularum*. Here in the commentary the emphasis was on the antithesis between two *cities*.

But none of this is absolutely certain. Supporting this supposition is the fact that the Tyconian element known from the *Liber regularum* often plays a prominent part in the works of later commentators[397]. It is present, too, in Beatus' explanation of *Apoc.* 17:18[398]. How-

---

395 Beatus, *In Apoc.*, 573-575. The entire passage is too extensive to be quoted here; so only the important passages are given *in extenso*: (573) *'Et mulier quam vidisti est civitas magna, quae habet regnum super reges terrae.* quod est mulier, hoc civitas, hoc reges terrae, omnia haec unum corpus est. sic etiam de ecclesia dictum est: *veni, ostendam tibi mulierem agni.* haec mulier ecclesia est. (574) *et ostendit mihi civitatem descendentem de caelo*; quam cum describeret, dixi *et reges terrae ferunt gloriam suam in eo.* mulier agni et civitas et reges terrae una ecclesia est, et unum corpus est. ecce duas civitates, unam Dei et unam diaboli. et illa mulier dicitur, et illa mulier, et in utrasque reges terrae ministrant. et agnus ecclesiae suae dat potestatem, qui est Christus, et virtutem suam et gloriam suam ei dat; et draco, qui est diabolus, virtutem suam et potestatem suam ecclesiae suae, id est, congregationi malignae dat. et est bestia agno semper contraria. (...) haec quae diximus, perspicue patet duae civitates esse et duo regna et duo reges, Christus et diabolus, et ambo super utrasque civitates regnant. (...) (575) hae duae civitates una mundo, et una desiderat servire Christo; una in mundo regnum cupit tenere, et una ab hoc mundo fugire; una tristatur, altera laetatur; una flagellat, altera flagellatur; una occidit, altera occiditur; una ut iustificetur adhuc, altera ut impie agat adhuc. haec utrique ita laborant in unum, una ut habeat unde coronetur, altera ut habeat unde damnetur'.

396 Bede, *Expl.*, 185A: *'Et mulier quam vidisti est civitas magna*, etc. Sic et infra sponsam Agni contemplari jussus, vidit civitatem sanctam descendentem de coelo. Quam cum describeret: *Et reges* (inquit) *terrae afferent gloriam suam in illam* [*Apoc.* XXI]. Duae sunt enim in mundo civitates: una de abysso, altera de coelestibus oriens'.

397 We only call to mind the notion of the two *corpora, populi, aedificia* in the Church; see p. 270.

398 Beatus, *In Apoc.*, 574: 'Hoc caput octavum intra ecclesiam tenet primatum, cum per pseudosacerdotes et hypocritas sub simulatione sanctitatis agnum praefert de foris quasi occisum, et intus occultat rapacem lupum'.

ever, Augustine is also quoted in his commentary[399]. And what holds for Beatus also holds for the other commentators: they were acquainted with Augustine and quoted more than once from his *City of God*[400].

5. *Similarities and differences*

It is very possible and even quite likely that Tyconius, in his commentary on the *Apocalypse*, already made mention of the two antithetical cities, Jerusalem and Babylon. Certainty can only be provided by the lost commentary itself, or possibly by a scientifically reliable reconstruction of the work.

But even if it were certain that Tyconius was speaking about the two cities in the way that is to be found in Beatus in particular, would this necessarily prove that he was the actual source of Augustine's doctrine of the two cities?

It is essential to proceed very carefully here. From the *Liber regularum* it is apparent that Tyconius found himself confronted by the mystery that two quite different notions apply to one and the same *corpus*: salvation and disaster, blessing and curse. The *corpus Domini* is both good and evil[401]. In Augustine this is different. In his discussion of the second *regula* he even stressed the fact that the *corpus Domini* is not *bipertitum*. Hypocrites are not part of it; they only seem (videantur) to be in the Church. Therefore it is better to speak of a *corpus verum* and also *permixtum* or of a *corpus verum* and *simulatum*[402].

Augustine did not use the term *civitas* in this context. But it should be noted that he did do so elsewhere. The concepts *corpus* and *civitas* are related to each other and are even equal in value. This can be seen clearly in some *Enarrationes in Psalmos*[403]. And in the first

[399] Beatus not only mentions A. as one of his sources (*In Apoc.*, *praef.*, 1), but names the work *DCD* explicitly (*In Apoc.*, 506) and subsequently quotes *DCD* XX, 19 (*In Apoc.*, 507).

[400] In the introduction to their commentaries Primasius and Ambrosius Autpertus state that their work is based on A.; Bede often refers to A. by name. They frequently quote *DCD*. Moreover, it is known that Caesarius depends on A. to a considerable extent.

[401] *Lib. reg.*, *reg.* II, p. 11: '... unum corpus et bonum esse et malum ...'.

[402] *De doctr. chr.* III, 32, 45.

[403] *En. in Ps.* 51, 3-4; *En. in Ps.* 61, 6: 'Civitas illa prior nata; civitas ista posterior nata. Illa enim incoepit a Cain; haec ab Abel. Haec duo corpora sub duobus regibus agentia, ad singulas civitates pertinentia, adversantur sibi usque in finem saeculi, donec fiat ex commixtione separatio ...'; *En. in Ps.* 90, *s.* II, 1: '... totus

model catechesis for Deogratias, Augustine stated that many consort with the devil and few follow God. That is why there are two cities (civitates), one of the wicked, the other of the just. Now they are intermingled in body (corporibus), but separate in will (voluntatibus); on the Day of Judgement, however, they will also be separate in body (corpore)[404]. In this train of thought and terminology there is a considerable similarity with Tyconius.

But there are also important differences. When later commentators of the *Apocalypse*—and probably already Tyconius himself—spoke of the two antithetical cities, they did so in the framework of their interpretation of the last book of the Bible. This is not the case with Augustine: he did not refer especially to texts from the *Apocalypse* to prove the existence of two *civitates*, neither in the *City of God*, nor elsewhere. Moreover, neither in Tyconius' *Liber regularum* nor in the later interpretations of the *Apocalypse* do we find a specific, detailed doctrine of the two cities as Augustine set out in various books, sermons, letters and especially in the *City of God*. Although Augustine was aware of their intermingling in this age of the world, he emphasized the absolute antithesis between the two cities[405]. Both in the model catecheses and in the *City of God* he narrates the history of the world from creation to end as the history of the two antithetical cities, and says that the two *civitates*, each with its king and angels, form one society. This idea is not to be found in this way in Tyconius either.

Augustine undoubtedly took over ideas from Tyconius, as he stated himself more than once. He was familiar with Tyconius' *Liber regularum*, spoke favourably of it, and recommended it to others. Besides, he was definitely acquainted with Tyconius' commentary on the last book of the Bible. He alluded to it clearly in *De doctrina christiana* for his interpretation of *Apoc.* 1:20[406].

---

populus sanctorum ad unam civitatem pertinentium; quae civitas corpus est Christi, cui caput est Christus'; *En. in Ps.* 131, 3: 'Cum autem corpus Christi est et templum, et domus, et civitas'. Comparable to this is *s.* 349, 2: '... in domo Dei, in templo Dei, in civitate Christi, in corpore Christi ...'.

404 *De cat. rud.* 31; for the complete text and a translation, see p. 115.

405 Cf. pp. 115-118.

406 *De doctr. chr.* III, 30, 42: '... sicut in Apocalypsi Iohannis quaerit, quemadmodum intelligendi sint angeli ecclesiarum septem, quibus scribere iubetur, et ratiocinatur multipliciter, et ad hoc pervenit ut ipsos angelos intelligamus ecclesias. In qua copiosissima disputatione nihil istarum est regularum, et utique res illic obscurissima quaeritur'.

There is reason, therefore, to agree with Hahn, Scholz and those who have followed in their footsteps. In all probability Tyconius exerted substantial influence on Augustine's concept of the two *civitates*. Renewed study of the *Liber regularum* and especially of the interpreters of the *Apocalypse* who were influenced by Tyconius has made this very probable. In the future other opportunities may appear that will make it possible to speak with complete certainty.

There is, however, still another aspect that deserves attention. Tyconius may have been a main source for Augustine's idea of the two *civitates*, but was he not also part of an earlier tradition? Are there no signs elsewhere of a view of two antithetical cities or kingdoms which could have led Augustine to his extensive development of this idea—an idea which through him has been so influential in world history? Nowhere did Augustine declare that the doctrine of the two antithetical cities was a speciality of Tyconius. That could well be expected if it had been a new and original concept. However, there is no mention of the learned Donatist in connection with it; his name does not even occur in the *City of God* or in the *Catechizing of the Uninstructed*.

Before we can establish the real significance of Tyconius in the given circumstances, and consider what influence should be attributed to Manichaeism, Neoplatonism et al., we must examine the tradition preceding *both* Augustine and Tyconius. Is it possible to find in it, too, views of two cities or kingdoms which are entirely or partly analogous to those of Augustine, and which may have had a direct influence on him?

D. Christian, Jewish and Jewish-Christian traditions

1. An earlier Christian tradition?

This investigation has uncovered many similarities between Augustine's doctrine of the two cities and other movements and persons. Particularly Tyconius and Manichaeism have turned out to be important. But it has also become clear that essential differences can be found. A single source that excludes other possibilities has not been discovered.

It may be that the actual source is no longer to be found. It may even be that reference can only be made to Augustine's unique personality. Did this creative genius shape the doctrine of the two cities?

In support of this view it could be argued that Augustine never mentioned predecessors. But attention should be paid especially to the opposite view, for Augustine never indicated that he was saying new and unusual things. When the theme of the two cities made its appearance in his works, it did so right from the beginning in a complete form. And at the same time Augustine expressed himself in the manner of one who is presenting something familiar. In the model catechesis for 'newcomers' he did not give the impression that he was expounding a new doctrine. On the contrary, Deogratias could obviously be expected to understand him.

There is yet another fact that shows that this concept was known in Africa. In a work directed against Parmenianus and dating, just as *De catechizandis rudibus*, from c. 400, Augustine also described the two cities in considerable detail[407]. Here again he did not give the impression of introducing a doctrine of his own. He could try to win over his Donatist opponents through a shared view. Yet in doing so he emphasized the commingling of the two peoples (populi) and cities (civitates) in the present life, until the definitive separation occurs[408].

In other works as well, such as in his sermons, Augustine never indicated he was propagating an invention of his own. He presented church doctrine and continually took the opportunity to expound it. Everyone who was instructed in the teachings of the Church should be well-informed on the doctrine of the two cities[409].

One could contend that it was through Tyconius that the idea of the two cities had become generally known in the Church of Africa[410]. But is this plausible, even if we assume for a moment that the Donatist's teachings were indeed the same as Augustine's? Neither Augustine nor anyone else ever named Tyconius as a source, which they could have been expected to do in the case of such a new and singular doctrine.

On the other hand, there is evidence that a Christian tradition existed prior to both Augustine and Tyconius which included a doc-

---

407 *C. ep. Parm.* II, 4, 9.

408 *C. ep. Parm.* II, 4, 9: 'Sed istorum populorum atque civitatum tunc erit aperta separatio, cum ista messis fuerit ventilata; quod donec fiat omnia tolerat dilectio frumentorum, ne, dum grana paleam praepropere fugiunt, a consortibus granis impie separentur'.

409 *En. in Ps.* 136, 1; see p. 197 n. 170.

410 Cf. Scholz, *Glaube und Unglaube*, 80.

trine of the two kingdoms or cities—or at least essential elements of it. As already mentioned in our introduction, it was for this reason that some investigators have pointed to earlier Christian tradition as Augustine's real source[411].

The usefulness of their fragmentary and often passing remarks will now be examined. What could Augustine have learned from predecessors in the Church for his concept of the two cities? What is important here is whether Augustine was actually acquainted with their writings, or whether it is reasonable to assume that he was.

Finally, attention should also be given to the fact that not only earlier Christian traditions, but typically Jewish and 'Jewish-Christian' ones can also be considered significant. Was the idea of two kingdoms or cities not present in certain circles in Christendom and Judaism? And furthermore, to what extent do the Old and the New Testament provide essential elements?

2. *Ambrose and Origen*

Of Augustine's immediate predecessors in the Christian Church, Ambrose should no doubt be discussed first. His influence on Augustine was great, not only during the years in Milan, but afterwards as well[412].

However, does this hold good with respect to the idea of the two cities? Some have argued it does. J.E. Niederhuber and R. Frick went furthest in their assertions: they considered Ambrose a very important source[413]. Others have limited themselves to citing a few texts in which the bishop of Milan spoke of the city of God (civitas Dei), the kingdom of sin (regnum peccati), or the antithesis between two *sectae*. In their opinion these texts can be regarded as precursors of, or at any rate as important parallels to Augustine's concept[414].

The significance of these and other points will now be investi-

---

411 See pp. 10-14.

412 Cf. p. 48 ff.

413 J.E. Niederhuber, *Die Lehre des hl. Ambrosius vom Reiche Gottes auf Erden*, Mainz 1904, esp. 49 and 236. Frick, *Reich Gottes*, 132: 'Auch er [Ambrose] sieht die Geschichte, ähnlich wie Augustin, unter dem Gesichtspunkte des Kampfes der zwei Reiche, Satans Reich und Gottes Reich ...'. Frick follows Niederhuber in nearly every respect.

414 E.g. Scholz, *Glaube und Unglaube*, 78; Leisegang, 'Ursprung', 154-157; Stegemann, *Gottesstaat*, 23 ff.; Lauras and Rondet, 'Thème', 152 and more recently Wijdeveld, *Augustinus, De stad van God*, 22.

gated[415]. Ambrose often spoke of 'this age' (hoc saeculum), equating it repeatedly with 'this world' (hic mundus). The kingdom of this world is a 'kingdom of sin' (regnum peccati); it is under the dominion of the devil, the prince of this world[416]. The unredeemed are members of the kingdom of this world[417]. In this connection Ambrose referred to the wicked as the members and the body (corpus) of the dragon, just as he referred to the saints as members of the body of Christ[418]. All who belong to Christ form together the Church (ecclesia), which is also called the kingdom (regnum) or the city of God (civitas Dei)[419]. In the future there will be one society of angels and people (angelorum atque hominum futura consortia)[420], and even now the righteous associate with these heavenly spirits[421]. The angels also belong to the mystic body of Christ, to the one temple and city of God[422].

On the basis of the preceding, one can understand why Niederhuber and several others discern a close affinity between Ambrose and Augustine. In their opinion Ambrose can definitely be regarded as a source of inspiration for Augustine's concept.

In this context several matters should be described in more detail. Ambrose repeatedly mentioned the existence of a city of God (civitas Dei)[423]. He also used such appellations as the holy city (civitas sancta)[424], the city of peace (civitas pacis)[425], the eternal city (civitas aeterna)[426], the supernal city (superna civitas)[427] and the

---

415 Of course only the main points can be named. Besides data from secondary sources—esp. Niederhuber, *Lehre* and Lamirande, 'Thème'—we made use of indices to text-editions in *CSEL, CCL* and *MPL*. For Origen the excellent registers accompanying the editions in *GCS* served as guide.

416 Niederhuber, *Lehre*, 47 ff.

417 Niederhuber, *Lehre*, 61 ff.

418 *Expl. Ps.* 37, 9: 'Sicut enim sancti corpus et membra sunt Christi, ita peccatores (...) corpus draconis et membra'.

419 Niederhuber, *Lehre*, 84, referring to *De apol. proph. David* I, 17, 82. See also G. Toscani, *Teologia della chiesa in sant'Ambrogio*, Milano 1974, 173 ff.

420 Niederhuber, *Lehre*, 234, referring to *De exc. fratris* II, 100.

421 *Ep.* 43,19: 'conversatur cum angelis'.

422 Niederhuber, *Lehre*, 235 f.

423 E.g. *Expl. Ps.* 47, 22 and 23; *De paradiso* 1, 4; *De Cain et Abel* II, 2, 7; *De virg.* 42; *De interp. Iob et David* III, 8, 24.

424 *De exc. fratris* II, 84.

425 *De fuga saeculi* 5, 31.

426 *Ep.* 15, 4; *Exp. Luc.* II, 88; *De Isaac vel anima* 7, 57.

427 *De ob. Theodosii* 56.

heavenly city Jerusalem (civitas Ierusalem caelestis)[428]. This city of God was identified with the Church[429]. One who enters the Church becomes a citizen and inhabitant of the city of God[430]. This implies, however, that he is at the same time an alien and sojourner here. Therefore the believer's state of being an alien was strongly emphasized by Ambrose[431]. It was in this framework that he referred very clearly to the existence of two antithetical cities, the *terrena civitas* and the *civitas Hierusalem*. In his letter to the clergy of Vercellae, Ambrose admonished them to leave this earthly city, the world, because their city was the heavenly Jerusalem[432].

This is the closest parallel with Augustine's idea of the two cities I have been able to find. On the strength of the text just cited and the evidence given earlier it can be said that there is a far-reaching similarity between Ambrose and his spiritual son. It is even possible that precisely through the writings of Ambrose the expression *terrena civitas*, used so often by Augustine, can be seen in its true perspective. For *terrenus* in Ambrose's parlance indicates the devil[433]. Satan and the other fallen angels have not been flung down into hell, but for the time being 'down to earth', into what is earthly and

---

428 *De sp. sancto* I, 16, 158. See also Lamirande, 'Thème', 210-211 and Lamirande, *L'Église céleste*, 73-75.

429 E.g. *De apol. proph. David* I, 17, 82 f.; *Exp. Ps. CXVIII* 15, 35: 'Civitas dei ecclesia est, ecclesia corpus est Christi. Peccat in caelum, qui caelestis civitatis iura contaminat et inmaculati corporis violat sanctitatem suorum conluvione vitiorum'.

430 *De apol. proph. David* I, 17, 83: '... quisquis bona fide atque opere ingreditur ecclesiam fit supernae illius civis et incola civitatis, quae descendit de caelo'.

431 E.g. *De Abr.* II, 4, 14: '... ut quasi *advena* ad tempus incolere, non quasi civis possidere videatur'; *De Abr.* II, 7, 41: 'Ergo non habitatores, sed *accolae* sumus terrae huius'; *De Abr.* II, 9, 62: 'Qui enim *peregrinus* hic fuerit civis in caelo est ...'. It should be realized that here and elsewhere Philo (see e.g. C. Schenkl in his explanatory remarks accompanying *De Abr., CSEL* 32/1, 615) was very influential for the notion of sojourning as an alien—as was (Neo)Platonism. But Ambrose also referred directly to the apostle Paul, e.g. *Exp. Ps. CXVIII* 7, 28: 'Unde et apostolus non vult nos in domo dei fideique vocatione advenas esse atque peregrinos, sed cives sanctorum et domesticos dei. Qui enim domesticus est dei, exul est mundo, qui conversatur in caelestibus, peregrinus est terris'.

432 *Ep.* 63, 104: 'Quod superest, charissimi, considerate quia Jesus extra portam passus est [*Heb.* 13:12], et vos egredimini de hac terrena civitate; quia civitas vestra superior est Hierusalem. Ibi conversamini, ut dicatis: 'Nostra autem conversatio in coelis est' [*Phil.* 3:20]. Ideo Iesus exivit de civitate, ut vos exeuntes de hoc mundo, supra mundum sitis'.

433 *Expl. Ps.* 48,26: 'Ergo qui non illum patrem qui in caelo est sequitur, sed illum terrena conluvione viventem, in progeniem terreni patris intrat. Qualis enim terrenus, tales et terreni [cf. 1 *Cor.* 15:48], ut sit eius vita terrena ...'.

worldly[434]. Here they form the kingdom of this world, 'the kingdom of sin, which has prevailed over all the earth for a long time'[435]. Whether Ambrose defined Augustine's terminology in this respect—and if so, to what extent—might possibly come to light through a separate investigation[436]. At any rate mention should be made here of the correspondence between Augustine's concept and Ambrose's reference to two *sectae*, represented by Cain and Abel: two groups of people opposing each other and engaged in a struggle[437].

All this testifies to an extensive parallelism. Yet one cannot speak of a doctrine of the two cities in Ambrose's writing that is identical to the one found in Augustine's. This is not just because the doctrine is much less prominent in Ambrose's writings. More significant is the fact that Ambrose spiritualized continually. There are two cities and sometimes he referred to them—as did Augustine—under the names Jerusalem and Babylon[438]. But they represented for him above all an antithesis within the soul of man.

A few of the many examples that are available should make this clear. The soul (anima) for Ambrose was a city (civitas)[439]. In this city God or Christ resides; we are God's temple, His tabernacle[440]. This soul of the believer, the peace-loving soul (anima pacifica), bears the name Jerusalem[441]. Opposing it is the soul

---

434 *Exp. Ps. CXVIII* 12,10: 'Quo cecidit [satanas] nisi in terras?'; *De paradiso* 12,54: 'Iste [homo] de terris migrabit ad caelum, cum ego de caelo lapsus in terras sim?'

435 *Expl. Ps.* 45,16: 'Regnum autem peccati mortis est regnum, quod diu toto orbe praevaluit'.

436 Already from Blaise, *Dictionnaire*, 813, it can be seen that for other Christian writers as well the word *terrenus* had a pejorative meaning, often in contrast with *caelestis*. Nevertheless, a detailed comparison of Ambrose and A. can be of great importance, esp. in view of the fact that the term *terrena civitas* was also used by the former.

437 *De Cain et Abel* I, 1, 4: 'Duae itaque sectae sunt sub duorum fratrum nomine conpugnantes invicem et contrariae sibi ...'.

438 Cf. p. 120.

439 E.g. *De Isaac vel anima* 5, 39: 'Est et anima quae dicit: ego civitas munita, ego civitas obsessa'.

440 E.g. *Expl. Ps.* 45,13: 'His igitur fluminis superni meatibus civitas illa qua deus inhabitat irrigatur et sanctificatur altissimi tabernaculum, omnis anima quae inhabitatur a Christo ...'; *De interp. Iob et David* IV, 7, 28: 'Sicut enim templum dei sumus et tabernaculum dei, in quo domini festa celebrantur'.

441 *Ep.* 20, 23: 'Intus ergo esto, intra Hierusalem, intra animam tuam pacificam, mitem atque tranquillam'; *Ep.* 70, 13: 'Omnis anima fidelis ... Jerusalem dicitur, quae pacem et tranquillitatem habet superioris Jerusalem, quae in caelo

which is carried away by physical passions: Babylon[442]

Thus there is a difference between two cities. Here, however, it is a question of internalization, of spiritualization and, at the same time, combined with it, of 'ethicalization'. To be sure, Ambrose used the word *anima* to designate the whole person[443] and constantly shifted between *anima* and *ecclesia*[444]. But he was primarily concerned with a struggle between virtues and vices in man's soul and not at all or hardly with a macrocosmic antithesis. It is also significant that what Ambrose actually meant in his exegesis by Jerusalem, the holy city, the heavenly or the eternal city, is often unclear. Was he referring to the individual soul, to the Church or to the (future) kingdom of God? Or was he referring to the one and the other?

If one rereads the texts referred to above, one notices that in Ambrose's writings the dividing lines are often vague indeed: *anima, ecclesia, civitas* and *regnum* are frequently interchangeable concepts. Therefore the antithesis between the two cities is not particularly a contradistinction which is cosmic and which, at the same time, determines the history of the world. Ambrose spiritualized and individualized. Therefore his concept, in contrast to Augustine's, does not actually include a historical development[445]. It does include the antithesis between the two cities, but this is mainly limited to the microcosmic domain of ethics and is not a constituent element of world history. In spite of their outward similarities with Augustine's, which at first sight even seem impressive, Ambrose's ideas are in fact far removed from Augustine's doctrine of the two

---

est'; *Exh. virg.* 68: '... ad Hierusalem, id est, ad animam pacificam ...'; *De ob. Valentiniani* 78: 'Si oblitus fuero te, sancta Hierusalem [*Ps.* 137:5], hoc est sancta anima, pia et pacifica germanitas ...'.

442 *De Isaac vel anima* 6, 54: 'Ergo in hoc loco exire significatur, ut dixi, anima, quando abducit se a corporis voluptatibus. Denique scriptum est: exi de Babylone fugiens a Chaldaeis [*Isa.* 48:20]. Non utique ut regiones Babylonis Hebraeus fugiat, sed ut mores, prophetico admonetur adloquio. Siquidem sint qui in Babylone sint Hebraei et de Babylone exisse moribus doceant'. Cf. *De paen.* II, 11, 106 and *Expl. Ps.* 1,22.

443 E. Dassmann, 'Ecclesia vel anima. Die Kirche und ihre Glieder in der Hoheliederklärung bei Hippolyt, Origenes und Ambrosius von Mailand', *RQ* 61 (1966) 121 n. 2: 'Mit Seele ist immer der gläubige Christ gemeint, nicht ein philosophisch-anthropologische Unterteilung'. Therefore it is better to speak of individualizing rather than spiritualizing.

444 Dassmann, 'Ecclesia vel anima', 121 f. and esp. 137-144; cf. Dassmann, 'Ambrosius', 377.

445 G.H. Kramer, *Ambrosius van Milaan en de geschiedenis*, Amsterdam [1983], 195.

civitates[446]. Von Campenhausen observed correctly that Niederhuber interpreted Ambrose too much from the viewpoint of the Augustinian concept[447].

It is in this context that Origen can be referred to. Not only was his significance in respect to Ambrose considerable, but also he exerted a *direct* influence on Augustine. The latter was acquainted with Latin translations of a number of his homilies, of his explanations of the *Song of Songs* and of *De principiis*[448]. Augustine may have made use of other (exegetical) works of the great and very influential Alexandrian[449].

It is appropriate to mention Origen at this point because the parallelism with the thinking of Ambrose that has just been sketched is striking. Origen also referred to an antithesis between two cities; he identified the Church with the city of God and, above all, he 'spiritualized'. It is through Origen that the earlier-mentioned views of Ambrose acquire a clearer perspective.

Origen spoke of 'the divine and heavenly city' of the Christians[450]. For him this city of God (polis theou) coincides with the Church (ekklèsia)[451]. The Church as the city of God is the true Jerusalem, built of living stones, the vision of peace (horasis eirènès, visio pacis)[452]. Christ is the gate of this city[453].

However, a city does not consist of stones; it is rather the inhabitants with their virtues who form the *polis*[454]. In this way Origen emphasized the individual and psychological aspects. Like Philo[455] he said that our soul is a city. She is the city of God, God is her ruler and to her it was said: 'Behold, the kingdom of God is within you' (*Luke* 17:21)[456]. The city of the great king (*Matt.* 5:35; *Ps.* 48:3) is

---

446 Cf. also—although its basis was for the most part different—the conclusion of Lamirande, 'Thème', 232.

447 H. von Campenhausen, *Ambrosius von Mailand als Kirchenpolitiker*, Berlin-Leipzig 1929, 264.

448 Altaner, 'Augustinus und Origenes' (1951), *Schriften*, 224-252.

449 Altaner, 'Gr. Patristik' (1952), *Schriften*, 324.

450 E.g. *C. Celsum* VIII, 74.

451 Besides *C. Celsum* VIII, 68-75, see e.g. *In Ier. hom.* IX, 2 ('... estin gar hè polis tou theou hè ekklèsia ...') and *In Iesu Nave hom.* VIII, 7 (the *civitas Domini* as the *ecclesia Dei viventis*).

452 E.g. *In Ier. hom.*, frgm. 48; *In Ier. hom.* IX, 2; *In Ier. hom.* XIII, 2.

453 *In Num. hom.* XXV, 6.

454 *In Ier. hom.* XIX, 14.

455 Philo, *De somniis* II, 248: 'Polin gar theou ... tèn psychèn tou sophou ...'.

456 *In Iesu Nave hom.* XIII, 1: '... ut posteaquam interemerit regem peccati de

my soul, which is under Christ's dominion[457]. Whosoever prays for the coming of the kingdom of God prays that this kingdom 'may flourish in him, bear fruit and attain its completion. For every saint is under God's dominion and obeys the spiritual laws of God, who lives in him as in a well-governed city. The Father is present in him and Christ rules with the Father in the perfect soul ...'[458].

For Origen, Jerusalem, the city and the soul were interchangeable concepts. 'For we are Jerusalem'[459]; the city of God is our soul[460]. He also stated that the city of God is *in* the soul[461]. There is no essential difference between this and the preceding, but it does clarify Origen's metaphor. He read Holy Scripture as if it were the book of the wars of the Lord[462]. Its essential element was to him the spiritual struggle in man's inner self. God may rule there, but the devil may too. If the first is the case, our soul is Jerusalem, 'the vision of peace'; however, if the devil rules, it is Babylon, 'the city of confusion'[463].

Thus for Origen the antithesis between Jerusalem and Babylon was above all an antithesis in the soul of man. Here the two cities, Christ and the devil, the virtues and the vices, are at war with each other. 'What good will it do me when Christ has subjected the whole world and occupies the cities of the adversaries if He does not conquer His adversaries *in me*, too ...?'[464] First Babylon must fall within the human heart and only then will Christ take up His abode there[465]. Whosoever is immersed in vices dwells in the middle of

---

civitate animae nostrae, fiat anima nostra civitas Dei et regnet in ea Deus et dicatur ad nos quia *ecce regnum Dei intra vos est*'.

457 *In Gen. hom.* IX, 3.

458 *De oratione* XXV, 1.

459 *In Luc. hom.* XXXVIII, 3: 'Nos enim sumus Hierusalem ...'. Cf. e.g. *In Ez. hom.* V, 4: '... sive bene sive male vivamus, Hierusalem sumus; si male vivimus, illa Hierusalem, quae cruciatibus punitur ... si bene, illa Hierusalem, quae in Dei sinu requiescit'.

460 *In Iesu Nave hom.* VIII, 7: '... sive civitatem Domini uniuscuiusque nostrum animam intelligamus, quae aedificatur a Domino ex lapidibus vivis [cf. 1 *Petr.* 3: 4], id est ex virtutibus variis et diversis ...'.

461 E.g. *De princ.* III, 1, 19: '... tèn en tèi psychèi polin ...'.

462 H. de Lubac, *Histoire et Esprit. L'intelligence de l'Écriture d'après Origène*, Paris 1950, 187.

463 E.g. *In Ier. hom.* III, 2: 'An figuraliter dicit omnem animam contrariam Hierusalem, visioni pacis, Babylonem esse?'

464 *In Gen. hom.* IX, 3: 'Quid mihi prodest quod universum mundum subiecit et adversariorum civitates possidet, si non et in me adversarios suos vincat ...?'

465 *In Ier. hom.* II, 11: '... si autem in alicuius corde non cecidit civitas confusionis, huic necdum Christus advenit'.

Babylon[466]. Each of us was once the city of King Sihon, the proud king, the devil[467].

To be sure, the antithesis between the city of God and her opposite is not always an antithesis in man's soul. Like the Stoics, Origen used the word city as a metaphor for this world (kosmos, mundus). He believed, for example, that Christ sets man free from this world[468] and that the cosmic city, the territory of evil and the *sensibilia*, must be abandoned[469]. Nor does Jerusalem as the city of God always refer to the soul. The *ekklèsia* on earth is connected with the *ekklèsia* in heaven, with the angels and the saints which have already been delivered, and together they form the heavenly *polis*[470].

But just as for his pupil Ambrose, the main emphasis for Origen was on a microcosmic antithesis between two cities rather than on a macrocosmic one[471]. In man's soul Jerusalem and Babylon confront each other. As has already been stated, Augustine, at the time of his earliest writings, also held this view[472]. In his later works, however, the emphasis is on a cosmic antithesis between two *civitates* of men and angels. This antithesis is not transformed into a spiritual event in man's soul, but is a cosmic reality that determines world history.

It cannot be concluded that Origen's views were of crucial importance for Augustine's doctrine of the two cities. There were at most a few stimuli, but they were of minor significance. Nor can any detailed doctrine of two antithetical cities be found in the writings of authors who were akin to Origen, such as his predecessor Clement[473] or his pupils Basil the Great, Gregory of Nazianzus or

---

466 *In Ier. hom.* II, 2: 'Qui valde demersus in vitiis, hic medius Babylonis habitator est ...'.

467 *In Num. hom.* XIII: 'Sed et unusquisque nostrum prius civitas fuit regis Seon, regis elati; regnabat enim in nobis stultitia, superbia, impietas et omnia, quae sunt ex parte diaboli'.

468 *In Num. hom.* XVIII, 4.

469 *Comm. in Cant.* III.

470 E.g. *De princ.* IV, 3, 8; *Comm. in Ioh.* I, 4.

471 Cf., for example, also *In Luc. hom.* XXX: the antithesis between the two kingdoms, described on the basis of *Luke* 4: 5-8 is interiorized to the spiritual struggle.

472 See p. 120-121.

473 For his statements on *polis, ekklèsia*, sojourning as an alien etc., see Schmidt, *Polis*, 57-67 and esp. W. Bieder, *Ekklesia und Polis im Neuen Testament und in der Alten Kirche*, Zürich 1941, 94-113.

Gregory of Nyssa[474]. Apparently this doctrine did not occur in the Greek theology that was sharply defined by Origen and interwoven with Platonism, any more than it did in Ambrose.

3. Lactantius, Cyprian, Tertullian

After Ambrose and Tyconius, the next Western predecessor of Augustine to be considered is Lactantius. He was not only a writer of excellent Latin (the Christian Cicero), but also, as we know, an African-born rhetor. For a long time he moved in court circles: at Nicomedia with Diocletian and the later Christian emperor Constantine, on whom he exerted much influence; later at Trier as the tutor of Constantine's son Crispus. The exact dates of his birth and death are unknown; he was probably born c. 250/260, and he died c. 325 or 330[475].

A number of important works of Lactantius have been handed down. The best-known of these is the *Divinae institutiones*, his main work in seven books, and an abridgement of it entitled *Epitome*; besides there is *De opificio Dei*, the earliest of his works that have come down to us, and *De ira Dei*. Lactantius was also very likely the author of *De mortibus persecutorum* and the poem *De ave Phoenice*. Some of the works and letters named by Jerome are lost, however[476].

It is certain that Augustine was familiar with Lactantius' main work at least. He quoted from it in the *City of God* and, moreover, it appears from the context that he expected his readers to be acquainted with it[477]. A passage from *De doctrina christiana* gives a

---

[474] Bieder, *Ekklesia*, 134 ff. We make special mention of the three Cappadocians because it is in any case clear that A. was familiar with (some of) their writings that had been translated into Latin. See the studies by Altaner, 'Augustinus und Basilius der Grosse' (1950) and 'Augustinus und Gregor von Nazianz, Gregor von Nyssa' (1951), repr. in *Schriften*, 269-276 and 277-285; cf. *Schriften*, 325-326. To be sure, Altaner states that A. was not acquainted with Gregory of Nyssa, but there is more to be said on that subject. See A. Mutzenbecher in *CCL* 35, XIII-XVII and M.-B. von Stritzky, 'Beobachtungen zur Verbindung zwischen Gregor von Nyssa und Augustin', *VC* 28 (1974) 176-185.

[475] For the different dates given by Lactantius specialists, see M. Perrin, *Lactance, L'ouvrage du Dieu créateur*, Paris 1974 (*SC* 213), I, after p. 220; for chronological matters, see Perrin's 'Introduction', 11-17. H. Kraft – A. Wlosok, *Laktanz, Vom Zorne Gottes*, Darmstadt 1983[4], XVIII, are of the opinion that he died c. 330.

[476] Jerome, *De vir. inl.* 80; see e.g. Kraft and Wlosok, *Laktanz, Vom Zorne Gottes*, VII.

[477] *DCD* XVIII, 23.

similar picture[478]. In *De natura et gratia* Augustine carried on a dispute with Pelagius about passages from the *Divine Institutes*[479]; influence from the same work can also be perceived, though less explicitly, in one of his letters[480].

Apparently Lactantius depended to a considerable degree on what Christian predecessors had passed down to him. This, along with the well-known fact that he made extensive references to pagan sources, deserves special attention. Lactantius mentioned Cyprian, Tertullian and Minucius Felix[481]; he also named Theophilus of Antioch, who wrote in Greek[482]. But most important for him, particularly since he never became fluent in Greek, were the Latin Christian writers[483]. Furthermore, Lactantius was a chiliast; he knew not only the *Apocalypse* well, but also a significant portion of Old Testament prophecy[484].

There are a number of unanswered questions surrounding his life and writings. Assuming that his conversion did indeed take place at Nicomedia, one can ask whether he had not already become well acquainted with Christianity in Africa. Does his knowledge of African Christian writers in particular, along with his avowed chiliasm, not point in this direction? Moreover, can his striking 'dualism' not be understood on the basis of ideas that were current in Africa?

Seeking solutions to these and other fundamental problems related to the study of Lactantius does not lie within the scope of this investigation, even supposing a definitive solution to be feasible on the basis of the available material. In our context it might merely be

---

478 *De doctr. chr.* II, 40, 61.

479 *De nat. et grat.* 61, 71.

480 *Ep.* 104, 3; see J. Doignon, 'Le retentissement d'un exemple de la survie de Lactance', in: J. Fontaine – M. Perrin (éds.), *Lactance et son temps*, Paris 1978, 297-306.

481 See S. Brandt's 'Prolegomena' to his edition of Lactantius in *CSEL* 19, p. XCI ff; also Brandt's 'Index auctorum' in *CSEL* 27. Cf. Monceaux, *Histoire*, III, 319; Perrin, *Lactance, L'ouvrage du Dieu créateur*, I, 61-63; P. Monat, *Lactance, Institutions divines, Livre V*, Paris 1973 (*SC* 204), I, 45-50.

482 Certainly in *Div. inst.* I, 23, 2; cf. *Epit.* 19, 5. Cf. Brandt, 'Prolegomena', XCIV and his 'Index auctorum'; also R.M. Ogilvie, *The Library of Lactantius*, Oxford 1978, 28 ff. and 92.

483 Von Campenhausen, *Lat. Kirchenväter*, 59, goes too far: '... und so hat er auch aus der christlichen Literatur später [i.e. after his study of rhetoric] nur von den lateinisch schreibenden Väter Notiz genommen'; likewise Quasten, *Patrology*, II, 398: '... without the slightest reference to any of the Greek Christian authors'.

484 V. Fàbrega, 'Die chiliastische Lehre des Laktanz', *JbAC* 17 (1974) 126-146.

noted that the so-called dualistic interpolations in *De opificio* and the *Institutiones* not only in all probability stem from Lactantius himself—that is almost generally acknowledged at the moment—but may even have been an integral element of his 'theology' from the start. True, Eberhard Heck has made an impressive case for a reverse development: from the 'Kurzfassung' of the *Institutiones* via the *Epitome* to the not quite completed 'Langfassung' of the main work in which a consistently subordinate dualism appears[485]. But whether the course of his spiritual development as described here has been proved beyond doubt is debatable. Should there be no consideration of the possibility that certain passages which were felt to be too offensive and unorthodox after Nicaea (325) were deleted by Lactantius or others, as were the eulogies for Constantine after he had had his wife Fausta and son Crispus eliminated in 326? And are there not enough reasons to support the assumption that Lactantius subscribed to the idea of subordinate dualism from the very beginning?

Lactantius taught that there are two powers, one of good and the other of evil. These confront each other and are at war. But both spirits were created by God and are subordinate to Him[486]. So this is not a case of absolute dualism as found in, for instance, Manichaeism[487], but of a consistently subordinate dualism which is in fact a consistent monotheism. Evil also comes from God and the devil is God's left hand. This is remarkably similar to ideas that have become known through such works as the *Pseudo-Clementines*[488]. Did

---

[485] E. Heck, *Die dualistischen Zusätze und die Kaiseranreden bei Lactantius. Untersuchungen zur Textgeschichte der 'Divinae institutiones' und der Schrift 'De opificio Dei'*, Heidelberg 1972.

[486] E.g. *Div. inst.* II, 8, 3-4: '... produxit [deus] similem sui spiritum, qui esset virtutibus patris dei praeditus. (...) Deinde fecit alterum, in quo indoles divinae stirpis non permansit'; *Div. inst.* II, 8, 6 *add.* 2: 'Fabricaturus hunc mundum, qui constaret ex rebus inter se contrariis atque discordibus, constituit ante diversa fecitque ante omnia duos fontes rerum sibi adversarum inter seque pugnantium, illos scilicet duos spiritus, rectum atque pravum, quorum alter est deo tamquam dextera, alter tamquam sinistra ...'. Furthermore, the two ways, the one of good and the one of evil, have been established *by God* (e.g. *Div. inst.* VI, 4, 3 ff.; VI, 4, 12) and it is *God* who makes the devil act as man's *adversarius* (e.g. *Div. inst.* VI, 4, 17).

[487] See p. 212 ff. and p. 233.

[488] For *Ps. Clem., Hom.* XX, 3 and *Hom.* VII, 3, see p. 233. We shall examine this work and its sources later; see p. 334 ff. Concurrences with the *Ps. Clem.* have already been noted; see F.W. Bussell, 'The purpose of the world-process and the problem of evil as explained in the Clementine and Lactantian writings in a system

these ideas possibly go back to certain Jewish-Christian and Jewish[489] circles, and then survive until the days of Lactantius, particularly in Africa[490]?

In order to understand Lactantius, it seems advisable to consider this approach as well. To what extent can his ideas be explained on the basis of archaic Jewish-Christian concepts? For example, the concept of Christ as an angel occurs in his writings[491]. His views on two spirits and two ways will be discussed later.

First, however, the most important question in this context should be examined. Did Lactantius, like Augustine, make use of the concept of two antithetical cities? Such a doctrine of two *civitates*, Jerusalem as opposed to Babylon, does not occur in his works. But Lactantius, when in *De opificio Dei* he reminded the Christian Demetrian of his baptism, did refer to the Church as *civitas*: 'Remember your true Parent and in what city you have given your name ...'[492]. Moreover, several times in the *Institutiones* and the *Epitome* he spoke of the *civitas sancta*, the eschatological city, as the centre of the millennium[493]. But in this context he mentioned neither the name of Jerusalem nor that of her antithesis Babylon. Lactantius passed on what he had read in the *Apocalypse* and the books of the prophets, but endued it chiefly with pagan classicism: the Sibyls, Virgil's fourth *Ecloga*, oracles of Hystaspes, Hermes Trismegistos. In this way he endeavoured to persuade his cultivated readers[494].

---

of subordinate dualism', *SBEc* 4 (1896) 133-188. Bussell gave parallels (rather superficially), but did not say that there was dependence. K. Vilhelmson, *Laktanz und die Kosmogonie des spätantiken Synkretismus*, Tartu 1940, 17, suspects that a work like the *Ps. Clem.* could have served as Lactantius' source.

489 In the case of Lactantius' doctrine of the two ways, for example, one might eventually think of Jewish influence. But this influence probably existed in another aspect also; cf., for example, the beginning of the 'addition' after *De opif.* 19, 8 with 1 *QS* III, 18 ff.

490 For some characteristic features of Christianity in Roman Africa, see p. 366 ff.

491 *Epit.* 37, 3: 'Denique ex omnibus angelis, quos idem deus de suis spiritibus figuravit, solus in consortium summae potestatis adscitus est, solus deus nuncupatus'.

492 *De opif.* 1, 9: 'Memento et veri parentis tui et in qua civitate nomen dederis ...'.

493 *Div. inst.* VII, 24, 6: ' ... civitas sancta ... in medio terrae ...'; VII, 26, 1: 'sanctae civitati'; *Epit.* 67, 3: 'sanctam civitatem'; *Epit.* 67, 6: 'sanctorum civitatum'.

494 For Lactantius' methodical point of departure, see e.g. *Div. inst.* I, 5, 1-2; V, 1, 15; VII, 13, 2. See below for the *Inst.* as an apology and a protreptical work.

But there is more to it than this. Although no doctrine of two antithetical cities or kingdoms[495] occurs explicitly in Lactantius' works, important elements of it are present. The dualism with which his views are deeply imbued has just been mentioned. Heaven as the domain of light and God is opposed to the earth as the domain of darkness[496]. The devil has dominion over the earth and the earthly things; associated with him are darkness, death, hell, the body[497], as well as the evil demons[498]. Opposing the devil are God, heaven and everything that is heavenly, perpetual light and eternal life, the soul[499]; and allied with God are the good angels[500].

In this dualistic phraseology one can discern Lactantius' close relationship to classical ways of thinking. With good reason, therefore, reference has been made to the Pythagorean doctrine of opposites[501]. Another idea connected with the dualistic antithesis between good and evil, that of the two ways, is also associated with classical views. 'There are two ways along which man's life must go; one leads to heaven, the other sinks down into hell ...'[502]. Lactantius referred first of all to the poets and philosophers[503]. He gave a detailed record of their opinions[504]. But he ended his account in sharp criticism, mainly because in pagan imagery the only choice offered was between earthly honour and earthly punishment, and because the immortality of the soul was not taken seriously[505]. Besides, it was an unchristian view, represented by the Y-sign, that

---

495 The notion 'kingdom' does occur in Lactantius' work (in such combinations as: regnum aeternum, caeleste, dei, domini, sanctum), but not as *regum diaboli* or the like. Once there is mention of two different kingdoms, but then it is a matter of Christ's *regnum terrenum* and *regnum caeleste ac sempiternum*; see *Div. inst.* IV, 7, 8.

496 E.g. *Div. inst.* II, 9, 2 and 5.

497 Esp. *Div. inst.* II, 9, passim.

498 E.g. *Div. inst.* II, 14, 3.

499 Esp. *Div. inst.* II, 9, passim.

500 E.g. *Div. inst.* I, 7, 4.

501 Cf. E. Schneweis, *Angels and Demons according to Lactantius*, Washington 1944, 112 ff. and, among others, F.-J. Dölger, *Die Sonne der Gerechtigheit und der Schwarze*, Münster 1971², 42 ff. One may also consider the possibility of Stoic influence; cf. Quasten, *Patrology*, II, 407 and Heck, *Zusätze*, 59.

502 *Div. inst.* VI, 3, 1: 'Duae sunt viae per quas humanam vitam progredi necesse est, una quae in caelum ferat, altera quae ad inferos deprimat ...'.

503 *Div. inst.* VI, 3, 1: '... quas [vias] et poetae in carminibus et philosophi in disputationibus induxerunt'. Cf. *Epit.* 54, 1: 'Duas esse humanae vitae vias nec philosophis ignotum fuit nec poetis, sed eas utrique diverso modo induxerunt'.

504 *Div. inst.* VI, 3, 2-9; cf. *Epit.* 54, 1-2.

505 *Div. Inst.* VI, 3, 5.

man was only able to choose between two variants (right or left) of the one path of life[506]. Against this Lactantius posited the Christian view: an eschatological antithesis between two ways, one leading to heaven, the other to hell[507]. Moreover, in the Christian view an immortal guide (dux inmortalis) has been appointed for each of the two ways[508]. Further on in his text Lactantius indicated that he meant God and the devil (referred to as *criminator*[509]) as guides on the way of light and the way of perdition respectively, and he gave a list of the vices and virtues belonging to the two ways[510].

Thus the idea of two antithetical ways and two spirits fighting each other was deeply rooted in Lactantius' thinking[511]. One may wonder how much influence the well-known *Didache* or the Latin *Doctrina apostolorum* exerted on him[512]. Did Lactantius himself, either in Africa or in Nicomedia, receive catechetical instruction based on a doctrine of two ways and two spirits that was present in these and similar writings? Or did he acquire such views mainly from Latin Christian writings, especially those of African predecessors with which he was apparently familiar? In any case the often

---

506 *Div. Inst.* VI, 3, 6-9.

507 *Div. inst.* VI, 3, 10: 'Nos igitur melius et verius, qui duas istas vias caeli et inferorum esse dicimus, quia iustis inmortalitas, iniustis poena aeterna proposita est'. Cf. *Epit.* 54, 3.

508 *Div. Inst.* VI, 3, 14.

509 *Div. Inst.* VI, 4, 2; cf. *Div. inst.* II, 8, 6; II, 12, 17; *Epit.* 22, 6.

510 *Div. Inst.* VI, 3, 16 – VI, 4, 7.

511 Besides the above-mentioned texts with references to two ways and two spirits, some more passages can be given in which the concept 'way' (*via*, sometimes *iter*) occupies an important place. It is worth considering whether these and other passages testify to a *Christian* doctrine of the two ways: *Div. inst.* III, 12, 35; IV, 26, 25; IV, 29, 15; IV, 30, 3; V, 1, 9; VI, 7, 1 - VI, 8, 5; VII, 1, 20-21. It should also be noted that at the beginning of his main work Lactantius describes its purpose as follows: 'ut erranti ac vago viam consequendae inmortalitatis ostenderet' (*Div. inst.* I, 1, 6). What is notable in the final chapter of his work—after a detailed discussion in Book VI on the two ways and the two spirits—are his mentioning of the straight way (recta via, VII, 27, 4), the way of justice (iustitiae via, VII, 27, 5) and the contrast between the path of virtue (iter virtutis) and the way of perdition and deceit (via perditionis et fraudis, VII, 27, 7).

512 Cf. esp. O. von Gebhardt, 'Ein übersehenes Fragment der *Didachè* in alter lateinischer Übersetzung', in: A. Harnack, *Die Lehre der zwölf Apostel*, Leipzig 1884 (*TU* II,1), 283-286; F.X. Funk, *Doctrina duodecim apostolorum*, Tubingae 1887, XV-XVI, LXIV-LXV and in particular 102-104; L. Wohleb, *Die lateinische Übersetzung der Didache kritisch und sprachlich untersucht*, Paderborn 1913, 17. New research should be carried out on the question of how much and in what version (*Doctrina apost.*, *Didache*, *Barnabas*, another?) Lactantius was acquainted with a doctrine of two ways and two spirits that went back ultimately to a Jewish source.

classical-rhetorical and gnostic-philosophical style and substance of Lactantius' work does not conceal the fact that he adopted elements of genuine Christian origin and even of tradition going back to Jewish sources[513].

Lactantius did not have a systematic or extensive doctrine of two cities or kingdoms as Augustine did. Yet one can imagine that his very elaborate antithesis of good and evil, light and darkness, God and devil, the two ways and the two warring spirits influenced the future church father. Later the possibility that there was elsewhere a doctrine of two ways and/or Spirits combined with a doctrine of two kingdoms will be investigated. If this turns out to be the case, the position of Lactantius as a possible forerunner of Augustine will, at any rate, be even more significant.

Our discussion of Lactantius will be concluded with a few comments on the purpose and structure of his main work. The *Divinae institutiones* show a similarity to *De civitate Dei* that is more than superficial. Lactantius, too, wanted to defend and instruct through his writing. He knew that 'It is one thing to reply to accusers (...), it is another thing to instruct ...'[514]. Already in *De opificio Dei* he announced his great work, one directed against the philosophers and, at the same time, a positive and persuasive exposition of the happy life[515]. The contents show this twofold purpose: the first three books are mainly polemical in their criticism of false pagan religion and philosophy[516]; the next four are mainly positive in their expounding and teaching. These four books give 'the entire substance of Christian doctrine'[517]. First Lactantius discussed salvation in Christ (IV, De vera sapientia), then Christian ethics and worship (V, De iustitia; VI, De vero cultu), and finally Christian eschatology (VII, De beata vita). He concluded with an *exhortatio*[518] in which, among other things, he admonished the reader to keep the

---

513 For the occurrence of a doctrine of two ways and two spirits in Christian and Jewish circles, see esp. p. 322 ff.

514 *Div. inst.* V, 4, 3: '... aliut est accusantibus respondere (...), aliut instituere ...'.

515 *De opif.* 15, 6: 'Sed erit nobis contra philosophos integra disputatio'; 20, 2: 'Statui enim quam multa potero litteris tradere quae ad beatae vitae statum spectent, et quidem contra philosophos ...'.

516 I, *De falsa religione*; II, *De origine erroris*; III, *De falsa sapientia*.

517 *Div. inst.* V, 4, 3: 'doctrinae totius substantiam'.

518 *Div. inst.* VII, 27, 1: 'Quoniam decursis propositi operis septem spatiis ad metam pervecti sumus, superest ut exhortemur omnes ad suscipiendam cum vera religione sapientiam ...'. Etc.

straight way, the way of righteousness, the path of virtue, and to leave the way of destruction and deceit[519].

This brief outline not only discloses Lactantius' twofold purpose, but also calls to mind the composition of Augustine's *City of God*. It is possible that further analysis and comparison of the structure and content of the two works would reveal more similarities. In any case it is certain that both works belong to the early-Christian apologetic tradition in which polemics and thetical exposition went hand in hand[520].

Before proceeding to Cyprian and Tertullian, we should make a few remarks about Arnobius, tutor of Lactantius, about Victorinus of Pettau (died 304?) and about Commodian (probably second half of the third century).

As for Arnobius and Victorinus some brief comments will suffice. Although as far as is known Augustine never named the former, he was most likely familiar with his seven books *Adversus nationes*. In any case, it would be surprising if this were not so, for the famous rhetor came from Sicca in Africa proconsularis and Augustine's contemporary Jerome was acquainted with several copies of his work[521]. Parallels of many of the themes encountered in the writing of Arnobius can be found in Augustine's works, especially in the *City of God*[522]. Arnobius did not, however, write about an antithesis between two cities or kingdoms, and the names Jerusalem/Zion and Babylon do not even occur in his work[523]. Arnobius' writing contains an abundance of rhetoric, but few signs of profound Christianity.

Victorinus of Pettau, the first great Latin exegete, was a different kind of figure. He was a prolific writer—though his style was not brilliant—and Augustine included him in a short list of Latin authors whom he esteemed[524]. Of the various exegetical works by Victorinus, however, only his *Commentary on the Apocalypse* is extant. His chiliasm is unmistakable in this work and also in the fragment that has survived on the creation, *De fabrica mundi*. But no antithesis

---

519 Cf. n. 511.

520 Cf. p. 167 ff.

521 G.E. McCracken, *Arnobius of Sicca. The Case against the Pagans*, Westminster, Md. 1949 (*ACW* 7), I, 53.

522 See e.g. the explanatory notes in *BA* 33 – 37.

523 Cf. L. Berkowitz, *Index Arnobianus*, Hildesheim 1967.

524 *De doctr. chr.* II, 40, 61.

between two cities as in the work of Augustine—and possibly in that of Tyconius, the other famous interpreter of the *Apocalypse* in the West at that time—is discernible[525]. Victorinus' statements on Jerusalem and Babylon were in keeping with the *Apocalypse*. His undisguised hatred for the Roman Empire should be mentioned specifically, though: 'the downfall of Babylon, i.e. of the Roman *civitas*'[526]. It is this attitude towards Rome, its culture and *imperium*, that can be called typical of Western Christianity of this period and the preceding one.

Within this framework, remarks on Commodian can also be brief. Much about this Christian poet—the first to write in Latin?—is still shrouded in mystery. Did he live in the third or in the fifth century and did he come from Roman Africa, Gaul or Syria? Klaus Thraede advanced an interesting argument for fixing his dates around the middle of the third century[527], but this has not gone unchallenged[528]. Joseph Martin placed him before 313[529]. If one or the other is right, Augustine could have known his writing, and this is even possible if he was living at the beginning of the fifth century[530]. But Augustine did not mention Commodian anywhere and there is no evidence of a possible influence.

Yet this poet should be mentioned here, because he may have come from Africa and possibly provides evidence for a form of Christianity in which certain archaic elements had been preserved. Commodian not only carried on a lengthy polemic with the Jews, but he also demonstrated a close affinity with their ideas[531]. Quite

---

525 See the edition by J. Haussleiter, *CSEL* 49.

526 *Comm. in Apoc.* 8, 2: ' ... ruina Babylonis, id est civitatis Romanae'.

527 K. Thraede, 'Beiträge zur Datierung Commodians', *JbAC* 2 (1959) 90-114.

528 H.A.M. Hoppenbrouwers, *Recherches sur la terminologie du martyre de Tertullien à Lactance*, Nijmegen 1961, 193 f.

529 See e.g. Martin's 'Praefatio' to his edition of Commodian in *CCL* 128, Turnholti 1960, XIII. A.F. van Katwijk, *Lexicon Commodianeum*, Amsterdam 1934, X, concludes: 'Mea quidem sententia Commodianus Diocletiano regnante vixit et paucis annis ante annum 293 scripsit'.

530 Cf. L. Herrmann, 'Commodien et Saint Augustin', *Latomus* 20 (1961) 312-321 and A. de Veer's criticism in *REA* 11 (1965) 135-136.

531 A pagan at first, he is assumed to have entered the Church via the synagogue. Monceaux, *Histoire*, III, 462, characterizes his anti-Jewish feelings as 'rancune de transfuge'. Following the opinion of H. Grégoire, F. Schmidt, 'Une source essénienne chez Commodien', in: M. Philonenko et alii, *Pseudépigraphes de l'Ancien Testament et manuscripts de la Mer Morte*, I, Paris 1967, 11-25, even maintains: 'notre poète a eu connaissance d'un certain nombre des livres d'origine essénienne' (25).

characteristically he said that God entrusted the earth to an angel, called Belial elsewhere[532], and spoke, for example, of a millennium of peace in very material terms[533]. Moreover, Commodian knew about the two ways[534], he referred to the world as *civitas*[535] and he mentioned the names Jerusalem and Babylon[536]. For him Babylon was also Rome, the harlot who will be burned to ashes[537]. However, an antithesis between two cities or kingdoms[538] that determines world history is not explicitly named in Commodian's writings.

Nor in the works of the well-known and influential Cyprian[539], bishop of Carthage from 248/49 to 258, is there any emphasis on a doctrine of two cities or kingdoms as there is in Augustine. Nowhere did Cyprian describe the history of the world as a struggle between two *civitates* or *regna*, nor did he mention an antithesis between Jerusalem and Babylon. Yet much can be found in the work of this important predecessor of Augustine—the church father knew the work of the illustrious bishop and martyr well[540]—that is of central importance in his theology of the two cities. Although one cannot speak of a word-for-word concurrence, there is definitely much agreement between the two regarding their views on this world and the Christian life.

Some of the more important aspects of this concurrence will now

---

532 *Carmen* 153-154; *Instr.* I, 35, 1-2.

533 *Instr.* I,43, 8-13. In this connection one can, with Martin, point to the influence of Jewish traditions as they are found in 1 *Henoch* and the *Orac. Sib.*

534 E.g. *Carmen* 699: 'Sunt tibi praepositae duae viae: elige quam vis'; *Instr.* I, 22, 15: 'In duas intrastis vias: condiscite rectam'.

535 *Instr.* II, 21, 3: 'Aut facite legem civitatis aux exite de illa'. There is here an unmistakable similarity with Hermas, *Sim.* I, 3.

536 *Instr.* I, 41, 12-13, but there is nothing more about the two cities than what is said in *Apoc.* 18.

537 *Instr.* I, 41, 12: 'Tunc Babylon meretrix erit incinefacta favilla'. For the fall of Rome see also *Carmen* 791-1060, esp. 813 ff., 911 f. and 923 ff.

538 *Regnum* does occur, but only in the combination *regnum Dei*, the heavenly *regnum* (e.g. *Instr.* I, 38, 7) or the millennial earthly one (e.g. *Instr.* 35, 17), never as *regnum diaboli*.

539 The quotations of Cyprian are from the editions in *CCL* 3 and 3A; those from his letters are taken from L. Bayard, *Saint Cyprien, Correspondance*, I-II, Paris 1925.

540 Cf. O. Perler, 'Le «De unitate» (chap. IV-V) de saint Cyprien interprété par saint Augustin', *AM*, II, 835-858, esp. 835 and the studies listed there. See also *CCL* 3A, 151 and M. Bévenot, 'Cyprian von Karthago', *TRE* 8 (1981) 251. Cyprian is named with notably great appreciation in *De doctr. chr.* II, 40, 61: '... Cyprianus doctor suavissimus et martyr beatissimus'.

be examined. Cyprian held a pessimistic view of this world in general and of the idolatrous Roman Empire with its persecutions in particular. World (saeculum) and devil meant for him virtually the same[541]. Egypt and the Pharaoh are images for this world and the devil[542]. To live in accordance with the world is to live as the pagans (gentiliter vivere)[543]. Not only do earthly things with their luxury, wealth, pomp and splendour belong to the world, but the flesh (caro) does, too[544]. Moreover, Cyprian saw darkness (tenebrae) and night (nox) as being closely connected with this world[545].

Almost without exception Cyprian spoke in an utterly negative way of this world and of worldly things[546]. A Christian has to renounce devil and world and he does this particularly at baptism[547]. That is why the believer's state of being an alien is stressed. 'We should consider, dearly beloved brethren, and again and again remember that we have renounced the world and are sojourning here temporarily as guests and aliens'[548]. The Christian, reborn through the Spirit, no longer lives for the world, but for God[549].

In Cyprian's negative references to the world and worldly things on the one hand, and in his emphasis on the believer's state of being an alien on the other, one can discern much similarity with Augustine[550]. But there is analogy in yet another way. Augustine

---

541 E.g. *Ad. Fort., praef.* 5: '... ne erepti de faucibus diaboli et laqueis saeculi liberati ...'; *Ad Fort.* 7: '... ne ad diabolum et ad saeculum quibus renuntiavimus et unde evasimus revertamur ...'.

542 E.g. *Ad Fort.* 7: 'In Exodo Iudaicus populus ad umbram nostri et imaginem praefiguratus, cum Deo tutore et vindice evasisset Pharaonis adque Aegypti id est diaboli et saeculi durissimam servitutem ...'.

543 E.g. *Ep.* 55, 6, 1.

544 For several examples, see Orbán, *Dénominations*, 190.

545 Cf. Orbán, *Dénominations*, 190-191.

546 This is also apparent from his generally pejorative use of *mundus* and *saecularis*; see Orbán, *Dénominations*, 221-228 and 200-203. *Mundialis* does not occur.

547 *Saeculo renuntiare* for example in *De lapsis* 2: '... sed qui saeculo renuntiasse se meminit ...'; *Ep.* 13, 5, 3: 'Saeculo renuntiaveramus cum baptizati sumus: sed nunc vero renuntiamus saeculo quando temptati et probati a Deo nostra omnia relinquentes Dominum secuti sumus et fide ac timore eius stamus et vivimus'. *Mundo renuntiare* for example in *De bono pat.* 12: 'Si autem qui diabolo et mundo renuntiavimus pressuras et infestinationes diaboli et mundi crebrius ac violentibus patimur ...'.

548 *De mort.* 26: 'Considerandum est, fratres dilectissimi, et identidem cogitandum renuntiasse nos mundo et tamquam hospites et peregrinos hic interim degere'.

549 *Ad Demetr.* 20: 'Nam qui exposita nativitate terrena spiritu recreati et renati sumus nec iam mundo sed Deo vivimus ...'.

550 For A.'s use of *saeculum* and *mundus*, see e.g. pp. 71-72 and 152-153; for the notion of sojourning as an alien, see esp. pp. 131-142.

pictures the society of God and that of the devil as engaged in a tremendous struggle: the *civitas Dei* against the *civitas diaboli*, Jerusalem against Babylon. This terminology does not occur literally in Cyprian's works. But Cyprian did emphasize that there are two army camps, the camp of God (castra Dei) and that of the devil (castra diaboli). The Christian is placed in the middle of a struggle, the *militia Christi*; he belongs to the army of Christ. Cyprian made this especially clear in his letters. He is proud of those who have remained steadfast and, bravely joining in the fight, have not deserted Christ's army camp[551]. Christ's soldiers are in His camp[552]. In *Ep.* 58, a letter full of military terminology[553], Cyprian speaks also of *God's* army camp[554], and in other passages again of Christ's army camp [555] and of the heavenly army camp[556]. Opposing this is the army camp of the devil[557].

Just as Cyprian shows in all this a considerable kinship with Augustine's doctrine of the two cities, so does his illustrious predecessor Quintus Septimius Florens Tertullianus. Not without reason has this impassioned, engaging and prolific writer been repeatedly pictured as the first important theologian of Roman Africa and even of the entire Latin Church[558].

Before Tertullian is discussed, however, a remarkable fact should be related. Augustine seldom mentioned him[559], and in the well-

---

551 *Ep.* 12, 2, 2: '... his tamen qui in fide stantes et nobiscum fortiter militantes Christi castra non reliquerunt'.

552 *Ep.* 57, 1, 2: '... milites Christi qui arma desiderant et proelium flagitant intra castra dominica colligamus'.

553 *Proelium, pugna, milites Christi, militia*, etc.

554 *Ep.* 58, 8, 2: 'Dei castra'.

555 E.g. *Ep.* 60, 2, 2: 'Christi castra'.

556 E.g. *Ep.* 74, 8, 3: 'castrorum caelestium'. Cf. *Ad Don.* 15: 'spiritalibus castris'.

557 *Ad Fort.* 10: 'Et adhuc fortius docens et ostendens Spiritus sanctus castra diaboli non timenda ...'. This is followed by a quotation from *Ps.* 26 (Heb. 27): 'Si directa fuerint in me *castra*, non timebit cor meum ...'.

558 For the most important facts concerning Tertullian's life and writings , see e.g. Altaner and Stuiber, *Patrologie*, 148 ff. and Quasten, *Patrology*, II, 246 ff; also Von Campenhausen, *Lat. Kirchenväter*, 12-36 and the introduction of Chr. Mohrmann to her translation, *Tertullianus, Apologeticum en andere geschriften uit Tertullianus' voor-montanistischen tijd*, Utrecht-Brussel 1951, esp. XXXII ff. Our quotations of Tertullian are from the editions collected in *CCL* 1 and 2.

559 *De Gen. ad litt.* X, 25, 41 and X, 26, 44; *De bono vid.* IV, 6 and V, 7; *DCD* VII, 1; *Ep.* 190, 14; *De an.* II, 5, 9; *C. adv. leg.* II, 9, 32; *De haer.* 86; *Opus imp. c. Iul.*, II, 178. Cf.—although there are differences among them—Harnack, *Literatur*, I/2, 683-685; A. d'Alès, *La théologie de Tertullien*, Paris 1905, 501 (based on an earlier

known passage from *De doctrina christiana* where he gives a short enumeration of great Latin Christian authors, Tertullian's name does not even appear[560]. Was he only slightly acquainted with Tertullian? It is much more probable that Augustine had read the writings of the man who had become a convert to Montanism (and had even formed a separate group within it), but that he refused to mention him in a favourable sense[561]. Tertullian was in disrepute, and an approving reference to a more or less sectarian theologian would have been inappropriate. Cyprian had already set the example in this respect: he borrowed much from Tertullian, but did not mention him by name[562].

The question of how much Augustine, too, borrowed from Tertullian—whether only directly or also via Cyprian, Lactantius or, among others, Hilary—has not yet been thoroughly studied. At any rate it is certain that he was acquainted with the writings of the great theologian from Carthage. And certain it is also that some scholars see the idea of the two cities already present in Tertullian's works[563].

This possibility should be examined. The first thing that strikes us in the works of Tertullian is that the word world (*saeculum*, to a lesser degree also *mundus*) took on an increasingly negative ring[564]. This was already happening in his pre-Montanistic period, and even more while he was a Montanist (first traces c. 203; not many years

study by Harnack in *SPAW*, 1895); G. Bardy, 'Saint Augustin et Tertullien', *ATA* 13 (1953) 145-150.

560 *De doctr. chr.* II, 40, 61.

561 On the basis of the just-named texts we may assume that A. was at least (somewhat) acquainted with Tertullian's *Apologeticum* (cf., moreover, Chr. Mohrmann, 'Saint Jérôme et Saint Augustin sur Tertullien', *VC* 5 (1951) 111-112; P. Courcelle, 'Propos antichrétiens rapportés par saint Augustin', *RA*, I, 184 n. 185), *De anima, Ad nationes, De carne Christi* (cf., moreover, J. Mehlmann, 'Tertulliani Liber De Carne Christi ab Augustino citatus', *SE* 13 (1966) 269-289) and *Adversus Praxean*. Might not A. have become (more) thoroughly acquainted with Tertullian when he brought 'Tertullianistae' (*De haer.* 86) into the Catholic Church?

562 Cf. Harnack, *Literatur*, I/2, 679-780; D'Alès, *Tertullien*, 499.

563 Frend, *Martyrdom*, 373; D'Alès, *Tertullien*, 423: '... Tertullien semble chercher les formules les plus absolues et les plus cassantes pour notifier la rupture entre la cité de la terre et la cité du ciel ...'.

564 Orbán, *Dénominations*, 175-185 and 214-221. Besides a development a certain modification can be discerned, for the character of the apologetic works directed towards outsiders is usually different from that in the pastoral and ascetic works intended for the inner circle. And to leave no doubt: Tertullian was not a Gnostic, he certainly considered God to be the Creator of this world (e.g. *De spect.* 2, 9: 'saeculi auctor deus'; *De spect.* 15, 8: 'saeculum dei est, saecularia autem diaboli'; *Adv. Prax.* 1,1: 'Dominum ... omnipotentem mundi conditorem'). For Tertullian's use of *saecularis* and *mundialis*, see Orbán, *Dénominations*, 193-199 and 230-231.

later came his definitive break with the Catholic Church). At baptism the Christian renounces the world[565]. Closely connected with this world and the worldly things is the devil. 'The pagans are delivered from the world by means of the water, and they leave behind their former ruler, the devil, engulfed in the water'[566]. Connected with the devil is his entire *pompa*, the whole pagan cult that pervades social life in all its manifestations[567]. This is all renounced[568]. Consequently, the renunciation means a break not only with the devil and sin, but with the entire pagan world, culture, society!

It is no wonder, therefore, that Tertullian often spoke of the world around him in extremely unfavourable terms. The demons are the magistrates of this world and the pagan state—Rome—is identical with demonic power[569]. 'Nothing is more foreign to us than the State'[570]. 'What, indeed, has Athens to do with Jerusalem? And the Academy with the Church?'[571] Hence it is not surprising that he described the Christian as an alien. 'Are not we, too, aliens in this world?'[572] 'But as for you, you are an alien in this world and a citizen of Jerusalem, the city above ...'[573].

In all this, important elements of a doctrine of the two cities can be perceived. The Christian's state of being an alien is emphasized, along with his being a citizen of the heavenly Jerusalem. But is this world , which is opposed to it, also described as Babylon? This element does not occur literally in Tertullian's writings, but it is often more or less clearly understood. Sometimes Tertullian identified Rome with Babylon[574]. What is particularly important, though, is

---

565 *Saeculo renuntiare*, for example in *Ad mart.* 2, 5; *mundo renuntiare* in *Adv. Marc.* V, 4, 15.

566 *De bapt.* 9, 1: 'Liberantur de saeculo nationes, per aquam scilicet, et diabolum dominatorem pristinum in aqua obpressum derelinquunt'.

567 J.H. Waszink, 'Pompa diaboli', *VC* 1 (1947) 13-41.

568 E.g. *De spect.* 4, 1: 'Cum aquam ingressi Christianam fidem in legis suae verba profitemur, renuntiasse nos diabolo et pompae et angelis eius ore nostro contestamur'; *De an.* 35,3: '... pactus es enim renuntiasse ipsi [sc. diabolo] et pompae et angelis eius'; *De cor.* 3, 3: '... contestamur nos renuntiare diabolo et pompae et angelis eius'. Instead of *renuntiare* Tertullian sometimes used *eierare*, for example in *De spect.* 24, 2 and *De idol.* 18, 8.

569 See esp. *De idol.* 18; cf. *De idol.* 19.

570 *Apol.* 38, 3: '... nec ulla magis res aliena quam publica'.

571 *De praescr.* 7, 9: 'Quid ergo Athenis et Hierosolymis? quid academiae et ecclesiae?'

572 *De exh. cast.* 12, 1: '... non et nos peregrinantes—in isto saeculo—sumus'.

573 *De cor.* 13, 4: 'Sed tu, peregrinus mundi huius et civis civitatis supernae Hierusalem ...'. This is followed by a reference to *Phil.* 3:20. See also *De res. mort.* 43, 2 in which 2 *Cor.* 5:6 is quoted.

574 *Adv. Marc.* III, 13, 10: 'Sic et Babylon etiam apud Iohannem nostrum

his clear picture of the two antithetical camps (cf. Cyprian): the camp of light opposing that of darkness[575]. Pagan culture and society, the *imperium*, Rome, are contaminated with idolatry, which comes from the demons. The life of a Christian on earth is that of a soldier, a *miles Christi*[576]. 'Incompatible is the oath (sacramentum) to serve God with the oath to serve man, the standard of Christ with the standard of the devil, the camp of light with the camp of darkness. No one can serve two masters, God and Caesar'[577].

There is no explicit, detailed doctrine of two antithetical cities or kingdoms in the works of Tertullian as there is in Augustine's. He rarely used *civitas Dei* to designate the Church[578] and the expressions *civitas diaboli* and *terrena civitas* are not to be found in his work[579]. He also spoke seldom of a *regnum Dei*[580], and nowhere did he place it in direct opposition to a *regnum diaboli* or a *regnum terrenum*[581]. But he did speak clearly of this world (saeculum,

---

Romanae urbis figura est, proinde magnae et regno superbae et sanctorum dei debellatricis'. In the background is John's *Apoc.* (4:8; 17:5; 18:10). Cf. the almost identical passage in *Adv. Iud.* 9,15. For a plausible explanation of the similarity between this and other passages in *Adv. Iud.* and *Adv. Marc.*, see the 'Einleitung' by H. Tränkle to his text-edition *Q.S.F. Tertulliani Adversus Iudaeos*, Wiesbaden 1964, XI-LXXXVIII. Tränkle argues that *Adv. Iud.* was indeed by Tertullian and was written before *Adv. Marc.*. Although the names of Babylon and Rome are not mentioned in it, e.g. *De cultu fem.* II, 12, 2 is also important for the equating of Rome and Babylon.

575 *De idol.* 19, 2 (see n. 577) and *De cor.* 11, 4: 'Ipsum de castris lucis in castra tenebrarum nomen deferre transgressionis est'. Cf. e.g. *De pud.* 14,17 (castra ecclesiae) and *De spect.* 24, 4 (castra hostium).

576 E.g. *De exh. cast.* 12, 1: 'Non enim et nos milites sumus ...'; *Ad mart.* 3, 1: 'Vocati sumus ad militiam Dei vivi iam tunc, cum in sacramenti verba respondimus'.

577 *De idol.* 19, 2: 'Non convenit sacramento divino et humano, signo Christi et signo diaboli, castris lucis et castris tenebrarum; non potest una anima duobus deberi, deo et Caesari'.

578 *Adv. Marc.* III,23, 2: '... spiritum scilicet sanctum, qui aedificat ecclesiam, templum scilicet et domum et civitatem dei'. Cf. *Adv. Iud.* 13, 25.

579 Cf. G. Claesson, *Index Tertullianeus*, I-III, Paris 1974-'75.

580 E.g. *De res. mort.* 26, 7; 33, 8; 49, 10 ff. In this connection it should be observed that the phrase *regnum Dei* generally occurs when quotations from the Bible give rise to its use, as in *Adv. Marc.* IV, 14, 1 (*Luke* 6:20; *Matt.* 5:3); *Adv. Marc.* IV, 26, 10 (*Luke* 11:20); *Adv. Marc.* V, 14, 4 (1 *Cor.* 15:50); *De iei.* 15,5 (*Rom.* 14:17). *Regnum caelorum* is to be found, for example, in *De carne Christi* 4, 5.

581 The concepts just mentioned do not occur literally in Tertullian. In *Adv. Marc.* III, 13, 10 and *Adv. Iud.* 9, 15 Babylon/Rome is the city proud of its supremacy (regno superbae). *De res. mort.* 47, 13 mentions the *regnum mortis*. *De spect.* 25, 5 places the *ecclesia Dei* and the *ecclesia diaboli* opposite each other; cf. *De spect.* 27, 3. Sometimes the Church appears as *corpus* (*Apol.* 39, 1; *De virg. vel.* 2, 2; *De bapt.* 6, 2), but there is no mention of a *corpus diaboli*.

mundus) as being under the rule of the demons, of the Christian's state of being an alien in this world, and especially of the two camps opposing each other.

In all these essential features, Tertullian's theology shows a close affinity with Augustine's doctrine of the two cities. That Tertullian did not elaborate on these elements systematically is probably related to his style of presentation. He was above all a pamphleteer, a shrewd and incisive journalist who preferred to write articles of 2000 to 4000 words, commenting on the 'topics of the day'. But the essence of his theology is clear. What do the Church and the world have in common? They are two absolutely antithetical societies, one of God, the other ruled by Satan. Caesars belong to this world (saeculum); Christians cannot be emperors[582]. We are a separate *corpus*[583]. 'What a city, the new Jerusalem!'[584]

It is this apocalyptic atmosphere of antithesis to the surrounding world, the heathen culture and pagan Rome in particular, that is constantly found in the West in the centuries preceding and following Constantine. This antithesis is characteristic of a theology of the two cities. It is encountered especially in the writings of Tertullian and Cyprian; furthermore to a greater or lesser degree in various other authors belonging to the tradition of Western Christianity prior to Augustine. With reason, therefore, it has been observed: 'The theology of the Two Cities, Jerusalem and Babylon, was never to die out completely in western Christian thought'[585].

This remark, however, needs some explanation. For it has not

---

[582] *Apol.* 21, 24: 'Sed et Caesares credidissent super Christo, si aut Caesares non essent necessarii saeculo, aut si et Christiani potuissent esse Caesares'. A reconciliation between Church and Roman state is out of the question. However, various positive observations on the Roman state can be found in Tertullian's works—see esp. R. Klein, *Tertullian und das römische Reich*, Heidelberg 1968—, but they should not be given a one-sided interpretation as is done by Klein. For a discussion of Klein's study, see esp. R. Braun in *Latomus* 29 (1970) 203-204. For Tertullian's dual attitude (on the one hand his apology addressed to outsiders and his speaking as a Roman citizen, on the other hand his statements intended for Christians), see D'Alès, *Tertullien*, 303; T. D. Barnes, *Tertullian. A Historical and Literary Study*, Oxford 1971 (1985[2]), 118; J.-C. Fredouille, *Tertullien et la conversion de la culture antique*, Paris 1972, 249 ff. But even in his apologetic work Tertullian does not conceal his sharp rejection of Rome.

[583] *Apol.* 39, 1: 'Corpus sumus de conscientia religionis et disciplinae unitate et spei foedere'.

[584] *De spect.* 30, 1: 'Qualis civitas nova Hierusalem!'

[585] Frend, *Martyrdom*, 550.

been clearly demonstrated that in Western Christianity preceding Augustine a comprehensive doctrine of the two cities was developed as was drawn up by this church father. Only Tyconius might be an exception in this respect[586]. One can at most point out some significant elements of the concept that appeared in a fully elaborated form in the writings of Augustine.

But these elements were certainly important. There is every reason to believe that Augustine learned extensively from predecessors like Tertullian, Cyprian and Tyconius. The spirit found in their theology is the same one that occurs, for example, in that of the Roman presbyter Hippolytus (died 235)[587]. He fiercely denounced the idolatrous and persecuting *imperium*[588]. Like his contemporary Tertullian, he saw it as the harlot of the *Apocalypse of John*[589]. For Hippolytus even the whole world was Babylon[590]. Another of Tertullian's contemporaries, the Africa-born apologist Minucius Felix, directed in his dialogue *Octavius* some scathing remarks at Rome, the city which had become great through wars and crime[591]. And in particular one finds the clear-cut antithesis to the Roman Empire—even to the Rome of the Christian emperors—in the influential popular movement of Donatism in Africa. Here especially Tertullian's and Cyprian's theologies had been preserved[592]. The Christian emperor Constans was characterized as a tyrant, a forerunner of the Antichrist[593]. For Donatus and his followers, the Empire

586 See pp. 254-274, esp. pp. 272-274.

587 There is no evidence available that A. was acquainted with him. But this theologian, who wrote in Greek, was known to contemporaries such as Ambrose and Jerome; cf. Harnack, *Literatur*, I/2, 611.

588 E.g. *In Dan.* IV, 9, 2-3: the Roman Empire has received its power from the devil; *De Antichr.* 50: behind the number 666 of the beast from the abyss (*Apoc.* 13: 18) the word *lateinos* is hidden; the beast is Rome.

589 *De Antichr.* 29: *pornè*; cf. Tertullian, *De cultu fem.* II, 12, 2.

590 See esp. *In Dan.* III, 31, 2 f.; cf. *In Dan.* I, 4, 5 and II, 27, 9.

591 Esp. *Oct.* 25. It is not certain that A. was acquainted with the dialogue. But the idea is not far-fetched: Minucius Felix was known to a number of predecessors and contemporaries. See J. Beaujeu, *Minucius Felix, Octavius*, Paris 1964, XIV ff. and CX-CXI; also Harnack, *Literatur*, I/2, 647.—For *Oct.* 25, see E. Heck, 'Minucius Felix und der römische Staat. Ein Hinweis zum 25. Kapitel des «Octavius»', *VC* 38 (1984) 154-164.

592 Tertullian anticipated the Donatist viewpoint particularly in regard to baptism, ecclesiology and martyrdom; see e.g. Frend, *Donatist Church*, 118-124. In the main this holds for Cyprian too; cf. Frend, *Donatist Church*, esp. 131 and 136-137.

593 *Passio Marculi* (*MPL* 8, 761A); cf. Frend, *Martyrdom*, 554 n. 101. See also Frend, *Donatist Church*, 159 f. for the *Passio Donati*.

during and after the reign of Constantine was still generally the persecutor Babylon, which was causing suffering to the Christian congregation. Donatist acts of the martyrs describe the struggle of the saints against the devil, who works through the Roman authorities[594].

All this gives evidence of a theology of the two cities. The Christian congregation sojourns in this world as an alien: enduring, suffering, bearing; world and Church confront each other as two separate societies. But no explicit antithesis of two cities (civitates, poleis) can be found in the works of the above-mentioned writers. Nor is it present in what has been handed down from Donatism, with which Augustine was so thoroughly familiar. Here, again, only Tyconius might be a clear exception. What one does find, however, in the Western tradition prior to Augustine, and particularly in authors from Africa, is a way of thinking closely related to his. Were the constituent elements of it passed on from there and combined by Augustine into an impressive whole?

The foregoing enables us to answer this question in the affirmative. For his doctrine of the two cities Augustine was able to learn a great deal from predecessors in the Western Christian tradition, in particular from the Christian tradition in Africa. The extent to which a special form of Christianity, originally closely related to Judaism, may also have played a part will be discussed later[595]. First, however, other possible sources require attention.

4. *The Shepherd of Hermas*

One work that is important in this context has not yet been discussed. There is a reason for this. In the Western Christian tradition prior to Augustine at least one very distinct reference to two antithetical cities occurs. But the interpretation of the relevant passage presents a number of considerable problems and therefore it should be dealt with separately. The reference is to the first Similitude from the *Shepherd of Hermas*[596].

---

594 Such as the *Passio Marculi*, written in or shortly after 347. For the Donatist bishop Marculus, see Frend, *Donatist Church*, esp. 179. The *Passio Maximiani et Isaaci*, which dates from the same time, speaks of the struggle 'inter militem Christi et milites Diaboli' (*MPL* 8, 769C).

595 See p. 365 ff.

596 This is not the first reference to *Sim.* I; cf. p. 12 for the views of Scholz, Salin, Frick, Lietzmann, Quispel, Ladner, et al. Further argumentation and an explanation of the parable are lacking, though.

As to the work itself a few introductory remarks will suffice[597]. The *Pastor Hermae* is a rather lengthy work in which a certain Hermas communicates revelations that have been given to him. It consists of five Visions, twelve Commandments or Mandates and ten Similitudes (Parables). It is generally believed to have been composed by one author, but one who incorporated various traditions into his work[598]. There is no doubt that it originated in Rome, almost certainly in the first half of the second century and probably before 140[599].

Hermas is usually numbered among the writings of the so-called Apostolic Fathers. But it occupies a special place among them, because it is part of apocalyptic literature. In the Early Church it was widely circulated and exerted considerable influence[600]. Part of it was included in the famous Codex Sinaiticus of the fourth century, among the writings of the New Testament. This in itself says much about its authority. Elsewhere, too, there was no unanimity for a long time as to whether or not it had canonical status. In Alexandria and also in the Western Church, Hermas was read for hundreds of years. Irenaeus was familiar with the work, the well-known Canon Muratori mentioned it and, among others, Tertullian was well-acquainted with its contents. In Alexandria

---

597 For more details see Altaner and Stuiber, *Patrologie*, 55-58 and Quasten, *Patrology*, I, 92-105; also the introductions to the studies and translations named below.

598 This is the opinion of, e.g., M. Dibelius, *Der Hirt des Hermas*, Tübingen 1923 (*HNT*, Erg.-Band), esp. 419 ff. and 424; R. Joly, *Hermas, Le Pasteur*, Paris 1958 (*SC* 53), 46-54; G.F. Snyder, *The Shepherd of Hermas*, London-Toronto 1968 (*The Apost. Fathers*, Vol. 6), 13-18. They are all more or less certain that it was the work of a single author. The view of S. Giet, *Hermas et les pasteurs*, Paris 1963, that three writers were involved, has not found many adherents; neither has the opinion of W. Coleborne, '*The Shepherd* of Hermas, A Case for Multiple Authorship and Some Implications', *SP* 10 (*TU* 107), Berlin 1970, 65-70, who supposes there were six. For the view that there was very likely one author who used material from different sources, see also J. Reiling, *Hermas and Christian Prophecy. A Study of the Eleventh Mandate*, Leiden 1973, 22-24 and 25-26; A. Hilhorst, *Sémitismes et latinismes dans le Pasteur d'Hermas*, Nijmegen 1976, 19-31.

599 E.g. Dibelius, *Hirt*, 422 ('Es deuten also alle inneren Kriterien auf das dritte, allenfalls das vierte Jahrzehnt des zweiten Jahrhunderts'); Joly, *Hermas*, 13 ff.; Snyder, *Shepherd*, 24 ('I would prefer before 140 ...'); Reiling, *Hermas*, 24; Hilhorst, *Sémitismes*, 32-35. Giet, *Hermas*, 300 ff., arrives at a later date for what he sees as the last sections of the work: 160-170 or even later.

600 Cf. Harnack in the 'Prolegomena' to O. de Gebhardt – A. Harnack, *Hermae Pastor Graece, addita versione Latina recentiore e codice palatino*, Lipsiae 1877 (O. de Gebhardt – A. Harnack – Th. Zahn, *Patrum Apostolicorum Opera*, fasc. III), XLIV-LXXI and Harnack, *Literatur*, I/1, 49-58.

Hermas had a special importance for Clement, Origen and Athanasius. Here and there in the Western Church, even as late as the fifteenth century, the *Pastor Hermae* was included in Latin Bibles among the Apocrypha of the Old Testament.

Whether Augustine was acquainted with the work is a separate question. He did not mention Hermas anywhere and to the best of my knowledge there is no indication of a clear quotation either[601]. But a total unfamiliarity with the work would actually be more surprising than some familiarity. For not only was it translated from the original Greek into Latin at an early date[602] and possibly already in Tertullian's time read in the Church at Carthage[603], but contemporaries of Augustine were acquainted with it, too. These certainly included Jerome and John Cassian[604]; possibly Ambrose as well[605]. Moreover, Augustine may have come to know Hermas when he was among the Manichaeans[606].

The *Pastor Hermae* provides abundant evidence of an archaic Christianity that was closely related to Jewish traditions. True, one need not go so far as to regard the author as a converted Jew[607], or even as a direct descendant of the Essenes who fled from Palestine

---

601 One phrase from *DCD* VII, 1 ('Eliguntur in aedificio lapides angulares, non reprobatis ceteris, qui structurae partibus aliis deputantur') may seem to come from Hermas but does not; it is more reminiscent of *Ps.* 117 (118):22 than of *Vis.* III, 2, 4 ff. or *Sim.* IX, 3, 3-4. The parallels enumerated by M. Marin, 'Sulla fortuna della Similutidini III e IV di Erma', *VetChr* 19 (1982) 331-340, esp. 336 ff., offer no proof of borrowing, but at most of similarity.

602 The earliest version, the so-called Vulgate (lt[1]) possibly dates back to the second century; the so-called Palatine (lt[2]) possibly to the fifth. See Harnack, 'Prolegomena', LXV-LXVII and Harnack, *Literatur*, I/1, 50-51. Lt[1] has been consulted in the edition of A. Hilgenfeld, *Hermae Pastor. Veterem latinam interpretationem e codicibus*, Lipsiae 1873; lt[2] in the above-mentioned one of Gebhardt and Harnack. Although work is in progress, esp. by R.A.B. Mynors (Oxford), no better editions have appeared to date.

603 Harnack, 'Prolegomena', XLVIII; Harnack, *Literatur*, I/1, 52.

604 Harnack, 'Prolegomena', LXIII-LXV and Harnack, *Literatur*, I/1, 56-57.

605 Harnack, *Literatur*, I/1, 56, compares *Hexaëm.* III, 12, 50 with *Sim.* V, 2, 5. Ambrose may (also?) very well have become acquainted with Hermas via Origen.

606 F.W.K. Müller, 'Eine Hermas-Stelle in manichäischer Version', *SPAW*, Berlin 1905, 1077-1083. This is a text from Turfan. But elsewhere Hermas was also highly respected by the Manichaeans. One should not rule out the possibility that signs of familiarity with *Hermas* can be detected in the work of the Western Manichaean Secundinus: in his *Ep. ad Aug.* 2 he refers in a remarkable way to the struggle of the two spirits (the *spiritus virtutum* and the *spiritus vitiorum*) for the soul of man *and* to the necessity of penance.

607 E.g. Th. Zahn, *Der Hirt des Hermas untersucht*, Gotha 1868, 495-496.

in and after AD 70[608]. Nor does one have to regard his writing as a Jewish work with only Christian interpolations[609]. But the presence of Jewish elements is unmistakable[610]. That this need not rule out the influence of Hellenistic ideas has been demonstrated by J. Reiling in respect to Hermas' statements on Christian prophecy[611]. But above all the *Shepherd* provides irrefutable evidence for the fact that, towards the middle of the second century, ideas that were originally Jewish still had a prominent position in the Christian congregation of Rome—or at any rate in part of it[612].

Whether this also applies to the first Similitude should be investigated. Hermas included several kinds of current traditions in his work and consequently various interpretations are possible. Before

---

608 J.-P. Audet, 'Affinités littéraires et doctrinales du *Manuel de Discipline*' (suite) (1), *RB* 60 (1953) 41-82, and, following in his footsteps, P. Lluis-Font, 'Sources de la doctrine d'Hermas sur les deux esprits', *RAM* 39 (1963) 83-98. See also A.T. Hanson, '*Hodayoth* VI and VIII and Hermas *Sim.* VIII', *SP* 10 (*TU* 107), Berlin 1970, 105-108, who sees no direct influence but is of the opinion, 'that the author of the Shepherd of Hermas had access to the Qumran tradition, and even that he was acquainted with the *Hodayoth* material in some form or other' (108).

609 E.g. F. Spitta, H.A. van Bakel, D. Völter, G. Schläger; cf. Hilhorst, *Sémitismes*, 20.

610 This can be seen in Hermas' repeated references to the two ways and the two spirits or angels, although here, too, influence from another source should not to be ruled out. In this respect he demonstrates a similarity with Jewish writers and with early-Christian writers who remained closely associated with Judaism; see p. 322 ff. In the whole discussion on the Jewish and 'Jewish-Christian' element in *Hermas*, the opinion of L. Pernveden, *The Concept of the Church in the Shepherd of Hermas*, Lund 1966, 283, seems well-balanced and correct: '... we suppose that the Shepherd is to be regarded as a branch of the stream of tradition that contains both Jewish and Christian elements at the same time, the Jewish elements being used in such a way that their original meaning has often been obscured or replaced by contents that were included in a Christian concept of faith more or less without friction'.

611 Reiling, *Hermas*, passim.

612 The diversity in the earliest Christianity in Rome on the one hand and the often far-reaching Jewish influence on the other have been pointed out by e.g. Raymond Brown. See R.E. Brown – J.P. Meier, *Antioch and Rome. New Testament Cradles of Catholic Christianity*, London 1983, 87-210. The existence of different congregations in Rome may possibly be concluded from the heading of Ignatius' letter to the Romans ('... prokathèmenè en topōi chōriou Rōmaiōn ...'; ... prokathèmenè tès agapès ...'); cf. Snyder, *Shepherd*, 20. That the Jewish element in Rome was strong in the early period was reported centuries later by the so-called Ambrosiaster; see the beginning of his commentary on *Rom.*, where he states that the Romans 'received the faith in Christ *ritu licet Iudaico*' (*Ad Rom., arg.* 4, ed. Vogels, p. 6).

considering some possibilities of interpretation, let us look at a translation[613]:

1. He said to me: 'You know,' said he, 'that you, the servants of God, dwell in a foreign country. For your city (polis) is far from this city. If then,' said he, 'you know your city in which you are going to live, why do you prepare here fields, expensive possessions, houses and superfluous buildings? 2. He, therefore, who prepares these in[614] this city does not expect (or: is not able) to return to his own city. 3. Foolish and double-minded and miserable man, do you not understand that all these things are foreign and are under the power of another? For the lord of this city will say: I do not want you to live in my city, but go out from this city because you do not live in accordance with my law. 4. You, then, who have fields, houses and many other possessions, what will you do with your field, your house and all the rest that you have prepared for yourself, when you are cast out by him? For the lord of this country justly says to you: Either live in accordance with my laws or depart from my country. 5. You then, what are you going to do, seeing that you have a law in your own city? Will you renounce your law entirely for the sake of your field and the other possessions, and live in accordance with the law of this city? Beware, lest it be harmful to renounce your law. For if you wish to return to your city, you will not be received, because you have renounced the law of your city, and you will be excluded from it. 6. Therefore, you, beware: as one who lives in a foreign country, do not prepare for yourself more than is strictly necessary and be ready so that, whenever the ruler of this city wishes to throw you out for resisting his law, you can leave his city and go to your city and live in accordance with your own law, rejoicing without presumption. 7. Beware then, you who serve the Lord and have Him in your hearts. Do the deeds of God, remembering His commandments and the promises which He made, and believe Him, for He will keep them if His commandments are observed. 8. Therefore instead of fields purchase afflicted souls[615], each according to his ability, and visit the widows and orphans and do not overlook them, and spend your wealth and all your possessions which you have received from God[616] on such fields and houses. 9. For to this end the Lord made you rich, that you should fulfil these ministries for Him. It is far better to purchase such fields and possessions and houses that you will find in your own city when you go home to it. 10. Such rich-

---

[613] M. Whittaker, *Der Hirt des Hermas* (*Die Apostolischen Väter*, I) Berlin 1967[2] (*GCS* 48[2]) and Joly, *Hermas*, have provided critical editions of the Greek text. The two editions differ little, and as far as the first parable is concerned in only one detail: in *Sim.* I, 2 *prosdokai* (Joly) instead of *dynatai*. A new edition is being prepared by K. Wengst.

[614] For *eis* as *en*: Hilhorst, *Sémitismes*, 25, 27 and 32; likewise lt[1] and lt[2]: *in*.

[615] Cf. *Mand.* VIII, 10: comforting those who are oppressed in spirit, etc.

[616] Cf. lt[2]: ... quia propterea haec accepistis a deo'.

ness is good and holy, it brings neither grief nor fear, but brings joy. So do not strive for the wealth of the heathen, for it has no advantage to you, the servants of God. 11. Strive for your own wealth in which you can rejoice, and do not counterfeit or touch what belongs to another or desire it. For it is wicked to desire the goods of others. Do your own work and you will be saved.'

The interpretation of this Similitude is complicated by some problems, of which only the most important one for this context will be discussed. It is, at the same time, the central theme of *Sim.* I: the antithesis between the two cities (poleis) and, closely connected with it, the Christian status of being an alien.

What did Hermas mean by the two antithetical cities? One could think of Rome on the one hand and the Church on the other. One could also consider whether Rome in this context was the antithesis of Jerusalem. In a more general sense one could think of a contradistinction between what is worldly and what is heavenly, the present age and the age to come, the earthly city and the heavenly one.

If one weighs the various possibilities, one realizes that mutually exclusive alternatives are virtually out of the question. Various themes are intertwined and appear to be related. 'This city' is possibly a reference to Rome, in which some of the Christians are preoccupied with such earthly matters as wealth and the acquisition of property. This defection is also evident in numerous other passages in *Hermas*, and it is perhaps not without reason that the first Similitude is linked to a preceding Commandment (*Mand.* XII), which contains a warning against evil desire. Due to wealth, honour and a craving for glory, it is stated elsewhere, some have become apostates[617].

But 'this city' need not only be Rome[618] nor its lord the emperor. Behind the Roman emperor the image of the devil emerges as the real adversary of the Christians. In the preceding Commandments and especially in *Mand.* XII it is he who is pictured as the opponent of God. Therefore the law of this city is not necessarily the law of the State which makes it impossible for the Christians to stay in Rome. This is not to be ruled out, for persecution was not unknown to Hermas[619] and, furthermore, he repeatedly drew attention to

617 *Sim.* VIII, 9, 1-4.
618 'This city' in *Vis.* II, 4, 3 certainly denotes Rome.
619 E.g. *Vis.* III, 1, 9; *Vis.* III, 2, 1; *Sim.* IX, 28, 1-8.

future distress and oppression[620]. But it is much more likely that the law of this city denotes the life-style of this world. As in the following Similitudes and in the preceding Mandates, the principal danger now is becoming engrossed in the things of this world.

Closely connected with this problem is the question: What is meant by 'his [i.e. the Christian's] own city', 'your city'? One might think first of the Church, which is in opposition to the earthly city of Rome. But even the acquisition of fields, houses and possessions which, by doing good deeds, one will find in one's own city (8 ff.) creates a difficulty. In the Church such goods are not acquired, whereas they are in the heavenly city. Or was the author referring to a materialistic eschatology, an acquisition of goods in the eschatological, earthly Jerusalem? The one does not necessarily preclude the other. The most logical course, however, is to compare the pronouncements of Hermas with e.g. *Matt.* 6:20 and *Luke* 12:33: a Christian lays up for himself treasures in heaven[621]. The reference, then, is to the heavenly city.

Hermas most likely used the antithesis between the two cities to indicate the difference between the earthly city, the world, and the heavenly city. One might object to this interpretation on the basis of the word *epanakamptō*, which occurs twice in our Similitude (2 and 5); it is rendered in the Latin translations as *redeo* and *revertor*, and it has been translated here as 'return'. But surely the believers do not literally return to heaven, and Hermas did not teach them that they had a pre-existence in heaven[622]. Besides the possible rendering of *epanakamptō* as 'to direct oneself again (or: upward)', a much better explanation can be given—certainly if the authority of the Latin translations is also recognized. For Hermas the Church is represented by a tower of cosmic dimensions, the heavenly city or

620 E.g. *Vis.* II, 2, 7; *Vis.* II, 3, 4; *Vis.* IV. However, one should ask whether the coming *thlipsis* does not rather signify eschatological oppression.

621 Cf. *Luke* 16:9.

622 That he does speak of the pre-existence of the Church is another matter. For an explanation of *Vis.* II, 4, 2, see, besides Dibelius, *Hirt*, 452, and Snyder, *Shepherd*, 39, esp. Pernveden, *Concept*, 17-37: 'The Church as the first thing in creation'. Pernveden presents a number of Jewish and Christian parallels, but these texts do not necessarily imply a pre-existence of the individual believer.—Philo did teach a pre-existence of the soul, and connected with this view is his emphasis on the believer's being an alien and sojourner in the world; man literally returns to heaven, for that is the true native city. Cf. e.g. *De conf. ling.* 76-78; *De agric.* 65; *De cher.* 120. There is no possible reason, however, why Hermas should resemble Philo here. Moreover, *epanakamptō* does not occur in Philo.

heavenly mountain[623]. One can be removed from that tower which is under construction; one may also return to it. For the second time one can be used in the building of the tower after one has done penance a second time. It is in this connection that *epanakamptō* occurs one more time[624].

Consequently, to return to one's own city means to return to the Church, which is at the same time the heavenly city. Here again one notices how extensively in Hermas the images are interwoven and related to each other. The Jewish and Christian notion of the heavenly city (as in 4 *Ezra* 10:27; *Heb.* 11:10; 12:22; 13:14; *Apoc.* 21) is linked to the concept of the Church as the spiritual city of God. Moreover, in this Similitude, which—as is so often the case in apocalyptic literature—includes material of different origins, one can also find clear evidence of traditions borrowed from Jewish-Hellenistic sources and from the Stoa. Philo already saw this world as a large, alien city, and heaven as the real native city[625]. In the Stoa emphasis was given to the distinction between what is one's own (idion) and what is alien (allotrion)[626]. Particularly *Sim.* I, 6 contains in all probability an element of Cynic-Stoic ethics: the virtue of *autarkeia*[627]. And in the writings of Philo as well as in the Stoa the state of being an alien plays an important role.

But one finds above all a Jewish and Christian legacy in *Sim.* I[628]. In the first place there is the alienation and peregrination of the servants of God. This is in accordance with the intense awareness in Judaism, and certainly in earliest Christianity as well, of sojourning in this world in diaspora and exile (e.g. 1 *Peter* 1:1 and 2:11; *James* 1:1; *Heb.* 11:13). One's true city is in heaven (*Gal.* 4:26; *Phil.* 3:20); the believers have no lasting city here, but seek the city which is to come (*Heb.* 13:14). Therefore the believer's state of being an alien was repeatedly emphasized in many early-Christian

623 Cf. *Vis.* III and *Sim.* IX.

624 *Sim.* IX, 14, 1. Also 'being used' and 'being removed' (*Sim.* I, 5) probably refer to the image of the tower and its gate(s); for *ekkleiō*, see *Vis.* III, 9, 6.

625 See *supra* n. 622 and esp. pp. 250-251.

626 E.g. Epictetus, *Diss.* 22, 38.

627 But see also *Prov.* 30:8; in addition, as a parallel, 1 *Tim.* 6:6. The verses of 1 *Tim.* that follow this show great affinity to *Sim.* I; see the commentaries, e.g. Dibelius' in *HNT*.

628 Which, of course, does not rule out the possibility of other traditions (Philonic-Hellenistic, Stoic) continuing to exert their influence.

writings[629]. Indeed, his city (polis) is 'far from this city'.

This city is under the dominion of a lord (kyrios). The devil as the prince of this world was a frequent theme in Judaism and Christianity[630]. That this dominion manifested itself extensively in the Roman Empire, its emperor and magistrates, was already apparent in Jewish writings[631], and it occurred frequently in Christian writings as well[632]. The view probably played a role in this Similitude, too. But the fact that in this case a pre-eminent role should especially be ascribed to the general idea of world dominion by Satan and his henchmen[633] can be substantiated through information from other sources.

First of all, in the *Gospel according to Thomas* there is a striking parallel with the idea Hermas conveyed in his Similitude[634]. In *logion* 21 we read:

> 'Mary said to Jesus: Whom are your disciples like? He said: They are like little children who have installed themselves in a field which is not theirs. When the owners of the field come, they will say: «Release our field to us!» They take off their clothes before them to release it [the field] to them and to give back their field to them'[635].

---

629 We shall return to this a few times; for the NT texts and the earliest data outside the NT, reference can be made in particular to G. Stählin, 'Xenos ...', *TWNT*, V, esp. 27 ff.; K.L. and M.A. Schmidt, 'Paroikos ...', *ibid.*, 849-852; K.L. Schmidt, 'Diaspora', *TWNT*, II, 102-104. See also—esp. for data from later years—J. Roldanus, *Vreemdeling zonder vaste woonplaats. Vroegchristelijke gedachten over geloof en vreemdelingschap*, Leiden 1980, and Roldanus, 'Tweeërlei burgerschap van de christen', *K&T* 36 (1985) 265-283.

630 E.g. *Mart. Isa.* 2:4; *John* 12:31; 14:30; 16:11. Cf. the commentaries, such as R. Bultmann on *John* 12:31 in Meyer's *KEK*; also Billerbeck, I, 153 and II, 552, who refers to (later) rabbinical parallels. See also Bousset and Gressmann, *Religion*, 254, and the rather comprehensive exposition by H. Bietenhard, *Die himmlische Welt im Urchristentum und Spätjudentum*, Tübingen 1951, 113 ff.

631 Edom (= Rome) is under the dominion of Sammael (= Satan); see e.g. Bietenhard, *Himmlische Welt*, 113. For the negative attitude towards Rome, see also Fuchs, *Widerstand*, 21 and 62-73.

632 It should be recalled that Babylon was the oft-recurring apocalyptic denotation for Rome as the city of the devil and of all power directed against God. See e.g. Fuchs, *Widerstand*, 21 f. and 74 ff.; cf. pp. 300-301. In this connection the acts of the martyrs should also be named. In the Donatist *Acta Saturnini*—dating from 304 or very soon thereafter—the power of Rome and of its magistrates is still that of the devil: 'Quid agis hoc in loco, diabole?' (c. 6).

633 Satan is not the only ruler, there are also the *archontes*; cf. e.g. 1 *Cor.* 2:6.

634 Cf. G. Quispel, *Makarius, das Thomasevangelium und das Lied von der Perle*, Leiden 1967, 54.

635 Translation in accordance with G. Quispel's in: A. Guillaumont et al., *The Gospel according to Thomas*, Leiden 1959, 15.

The notion that Christians are aliens in the land of another ruler who wields authority here with his followers is evident in this gospel, in which a tradition emerges that is independent of the canonical gospels, very probably Jewish-Christian and linked to Encratitic ideas. One has to put aside earthly desires; true disciples of Jesus do that and are aliens in this world.

Another important parallel is to be found in the *Pseudo-Clementines*[636]. Christians are compared to intruders (literally *parhoristai*, transgressors), who are in the kingdom of a foreign king. There are two kingdoms, a kingdom of the good and a kingdom of the evil, the kingdom of the present world (kosmos) and the kingdom of the future eternal age (aiōn). Those who choose the present are rich, they revel in luxury and indulge in pleasures. But those who prefer the things of the future kingdom content themselves with the barest necessities: water, bread, a single garment. For they have no right to regard as their own (idia) the things of a foreign king (allotrios basileus). They are aliens here, in a foreign country.

When these details, which in essence very likely reflect archaic Jewish-Christian ideas, are compared with Hermas' first Similitude, important similarities stand out. The idea of the believer's alienation is often found in early-Christian literature. But probably nowhere else do imagery and a coherent way of thinking agree to such an extent with Hermas as they do in these passages from the *Gospel according to Thomas* and the *Pseudo-Clementines*. This might be another confirmation of the presence of archaic, Jewish-Christian elements in Hermas.

The antithesis between the two cities in Hermas' first Similitude can best be seen as the contradistinction between what is of the earth and what is heavenly, between this age or world and the one to come, between the earthly and the heavenly city. The fact that Rome on the one hand and the (or: a) Church in Rome on the other were the first realizations of this metaphor does not invalidate this

---

636 *Hom.* XV, 7. In this passage the Jewish-Christian tradition almost certainly resounds. According to O. Cullmann, *Le problème littéraire et historique du roman pseudo-clémentin*, Paris 1930, 86, the passage may originally have been part of the *Kerygmata Petrou*, a Jewish-Christian source of the *Ps. Clem.*; Schoeps, *Judenchristentum*, 52 (cf. 197), is sure of this. G. Strecker, *Das Judenchristentum in den Pseudoklementinen*, Berlin 1958, 80 et al., thinks that in *Hom.* XV, 7 the theme of the two kingdoms in any case belonged to the so-called *Grundschrift* of the *Ps. Clem.*; this contained Jewish-Christian elements (cf. also Strecker in: Hennecke and Schneemelcher, *NTAp*, II, 65).

interpretation. Hermas explicitly mentions the two antithetical cities and he could assume that his audience and readers were familiar with this doctrine, as can be seen, among other places, in the first lines of his parable[637]. Already here on earth the believer is a citizen of the heavenly city; he has to live in accordance with her laws and therefore knows that he is an alien in foreign territory. It is important to note in this connection that in the earliest Latin translation, the Vulgate, *polis* is rendered as *civitas*[638].

Through Hermas the metaphor of the two *civitates* and the appeal to live as an alien were widely used for hundreds of years. When Augustine speaks of the *civitas Dei* as being opposed to the *terrena civitas* (which is basically a *civitas diaboli*) and of the *peregrinatio* as being inextricably tied up with it, he expresses himself in the same way as Hermas.

Concerning the other 'Apostolic Fathers' some brief remarks will suffice. In contrast to Hermas, they do not make use of the metaphor of the two cities, nor do they refer explicitly to the two antithetical kingdoms. There is no evidence that Augustine was acquainted with them[639]. One can find ideas in their writings that show some relationship with the doctrine of the two cities. After all, the alienation and peregrination of the Church and the individual believer is an important theme in these early-Christian texts[640]. But *polis* in the sense that relates to this study does not occur. Moreover, the word *politeuomai*, which in the New Testament (*Phil.* 1:27) may still have been related to *polis* and can be translated as 'to have one's citizenship' (viz. of the heavenly city)[641], is used in every or nearly every instance in the muted meaning of 'to live', conduct oneself, 'walk'[642]. In general, ethical behaviour is stressed rather than eschatological citizenship.

---

[637] *Sim.* I, 1: 'You know ... For ... If you know your city now, (...) why ...'.

[638] Cf. ed. Hilgenfeld, 69-71. In lt^2 *civitas* and *urbs* alternate.

[639] For *Did./Doctr. apost.* see also p. 343 ff.

[640] E.g. 1 *Clem., praescr.*; Polyc., *Ad Phil. praescr.; Mart. Pol., praescr.*; 2 *Clem.* 5. These passages deal with *paroikeō*, sojourning somewhere as an alien for some time (and with certain rights, but without the rights of a citizen); the Christian congregation is *paroikia*, parish.

[641] Cf. Schmidt, *Polis*, 15 ff. and 27; Bieder, *Ekklesia*, 19 ff.

[642] 1 *Clem.* 3, 4; 6, 1; 44, 6; 51, 2; 54, 4; Polyc., *Ad Phil.* 5, 2. An exception to these might be 1 *Clem.* 54, 4: *politeuomai* possibly indicates the connection with the heavenly city. The translation by R. Knopf, *Die Lehre der Zwölf Apostel, Die zwei Clemensbriefe*, Tübingen 1920 (*HNT*, Erg.-Band), 132, is characteristic: 'So haben jene, die als Bürger des göttlichen Reiches leben ...' (hoi politeuomenoi tèn ... politeian tou theou); likewise J.A. Kleist, *The Epistles of St. Clement of Rome and of*

On the whole, the same can be said and even more emphatically of the early-Christian apologists. In their writings the eschatological antithesis of the two cities or kingdoms played no part either. Even the awareness of being an alien and sojourner in this world was no more than peripheral[643]. In respect to this last observation only the anonymous *Epistle to Diognetus* appears to be something of an exception[644].

Of all the Christian writings from the second century, it is only in the *Shepherd of Hermas* that the idea of two antithetical cities, linked to the admonition to live as an alien, is unmistakably present. Again the question arises as to whether there is in this work a special tradition with which other writers were not acquainted.

5. New Testament, Old Testament, Apocrypha and Pseudepigrapha

Before we go further back in history and examine the writings of the New Testament to see whether they may provide the source of Augustine's concept of the two cities, we should make some prefatory remarks. First, it is incorrect to study these writings without taking their background and context fully into account. A principal factor is the close relationship between the New and the Old Testament, and we should realize that when Augustine referred to biblical passages in the framework of his concept of the two cities, he took them indiscriminately from the New and the Old Testament, but much more often from the latter. Furthermore, it is necessary to see what can be found in non-canonical literature; does it contain—and possibly in a more explicit way—a doctrine of two cities or kingdoms? Of this literature, i.e. works that were not incorporated into the Hebrew canon, it is especially Jewish writings from the time of the

---

St. Ignatius of Antioch, Westminster, Md. 1946 (*ACW* 1), 42: 'Those who live as citizens of Gods Kingdom ...'. For *politeia* see also 1 *Clem.* 2, 8. *Politeuma*—whose presence in *Phil.* 3:20 is significant—does not occur in the writings of the Apostolic Fathers.

643 *Paroikeō, paroikia, paroikos* do not occur, nor is there any mention of the Christian *xeniteia*; *diaspora*, occurring 5 x in Justin's *Dialogue*, refers only to the Jewish diaspora; *parepidèmos*, which occurs once in Justin's *Apology* (67, 6), does not refer to the Christian's being a sojourner in this world; *politeuma*, occurring once in Tatianus' writings (*Oratio* 19, 2), has only the weakened meaning 'behaviour, way of living'.

644 *Ad Diogn.*, esp. 5. But here, too, philosophical influence is apparent, as a result of which the sharp eschatological antithesis is mitigated. Cf. K. Wengst, *Didache (Apostellehre), Barnabasbrief, Zweiter Klemensbrief, Schrift an Diognet*, Darmstadt 1984 (*Schriften des Urchristentums*, II), 299 ff. and 345.

Second Temple that are meant (particularly the Apocrypha and Pseudepigrapha of the Old Testament; Philo has already been discussed, and the writings from Qumran will be treated separately). Moreover, the so-called Apocrypha of the New Testament are important.

Time and again Augustine indicates in his works that he has read in Scripture that there is a city of God. In doing so he refers above all to texts from the *Psalms*. In Book XI of the *City of God*, when he is about to discuss the origin of the two cities, Augustine states that 'we call city of God that city to which Scripture bears witness'[645]. He quotes *Ps.* 86 (Heb. 87):3; *Ps.* 47:2-3.9 (48:1-2.8) and *Ps.* 45:5-6 (46:4-5). 'From these and similar testimonies, which are too numerous for all to be mentioned, we have learnt that there is a city of God'[646].

It is not exactly clear to which texts Augustine is alluding in this quotation. In his explanations of the psalms he repeatedly points to texts that refer to the city of God[647]; in other writings his use of *Gal.* 4:21 ff. is also noteworthy[648]. Over and over Augustine sees evidence in Scripture of the existence of God's city, 'the eternal city which in our sacred books is called the city of God'[649].

Thus for Augustine the existence of the *civitas Dei* emerges from his exegesis of Scripture. He refers to Scripture as his source, and when he wants to show that there is a city of God he generally uses the language of the *Psalms*. At the beginning of Book XI, and elsewhere too, he mentions the earthly city in direct connection with this city of God. It should be noted, however, that the above-cited Bible texts do not speak of it. On the other hand, Augustine repeatedly quotes texts in which the name Babylon occurs. But biblical passages in which Babylon is explicitly placed in opposition to Jerusalem, the earthly city in opposition to the heavenly one, do not play a central role as evidence of the existence of the two cities.

Was the Bible the source of Augustine's doctrine of the two cities? After a first reading of a central passage like XI,1 it would seem so.

---

645 *DCD* XI, 1: 'Civitatem Dei dicimus, cuius ea scriptura testis est ...'.

646 *DCD* XI, 1: 'His atque huius modi testimoniis, quae omnia commemorare nimis longum est, didicimus esse quandam civitatem Dei ...'.

647 Such as *Ps.* 86 (87):3 in *En. in Ps.* 44, 33; 61, 7; 142, 3. None of the other texts just named occupy an important place like this; but passages in the *Psalms* in which the name of Jerusalem/Zion occurs do.

648 In *DCD* for the first time in XV, 2; after that repeatedly in Books XV, XVI and XVII. *Gal.* 4:21 ff. is often quoted in the *En. in Ps.*

649 *DCD* V, 19: '... civitatis aeternae, quae in sacris litteris nostris dicitur civitas Dei ...'.

Augustine alludes to Scripture for his statements about God's city. Its opposite appears to be the earthly city, often referred to elsewhere as Babylon.

One can agree with scholars like Kamlah, Bardy, Lauras-Rondet and Ratzinger when they stress the importance of Scripture in Augustine's statements about the city of God[650]. But not when they maintain at the same time that this proves that Scripture was clearly the real source of Augustine's concept of the two cities. The term *civitas Dei* in Augustine's writings is a metaphor from the language of Scripture, particularly of the *Psalms*. But whether this can also be said of the comprehensive doctrine of the two antithetical cities is debatable. It should be noted, though, that in XIV, 1 Augustine speaks of two kinds of human society, 'which according to our Scriptures we can justly call two cities'[651]. Apparently he found not only the city of God clearly present in Scripture, but also, connected with it, its antithesis. 'For the one is the city of the people who wish to live according to the flesh, the other the city of the people who wish to live according to the Spirit—each in its own kind of peace'[652].

These two statements unquestionably call to mind biblical themes. For it is clear that, especially in the New Testament and most explicitly in the writings of Paul, two kinds of people are spoken of. There are those who live according to the flesh and those who live according to the Spirit, the earthly people and the heavenly ones, those of the flesh and those of the Spirit, mankind in Adam and mankind in Christ[653]; there are also two kingdoms[654].

---

650 Kamlah, *Christentum*, 157 ff.; Bardy, 'Formation' and *BA* 33, 59-62; Lauras and Rondet, 'Thème', 152; Ratzinger, 'Herkunft'.

651 *DCD* XIV, 1: '... duo quaedam genera humanae societatis existerent, quas civitates duas secundum scripturas nostras merito appellare possemus (possimus)'.

652 *DCD* XIV, 1: 'Una quippe est hominum secundum carnem, altera secundum spiritum vivere in sui cuiusque generis pace volentium ...'.

653 Of course we have in mind biblical passages like *Rom.* 5-8 and 1 *Cor.* 15. Instead of citing many texts we refer to the expositions of E. Brandenburger, *Fleisch und Geist. Paulus und die dualistische Weisheit*, Neukirchen 1968. Not only does Brandenburger discuss the two kinds of people as they occur in the writings of Paul (46 ff. et al.), but he also indicates the connections with, for example, the Jewish apocalyptic writings (65 ff.) and with Philo (esp. 145 and 188-196).

654 The synoptics, for example, refer not only to Jesus' teaching of the kingdom of God, but also clearly to the kingdom (basileia) of Satan (as in *Mark* 3:24 and parallels). For more on this and other biblical passages, see W. Foerster, 'Diabolos', *TWNT*, II, 78-80, who observes: 'Somit finden wir alle Funktionen, die das Spätjudentum Satan geben kann, auch im NT wieder, nur durchgeführt zu dem Gedanken der einheitlichen, übermenschlichen Macht Satans, eines einheitlichen Reiches Satans, dem grundsätzlich auch die Dämonen und dieser ganze Aeon zu Dienst steht' (79); cf. K.L. Schmidt, 'Basileia', *TWNT*, I, 581.

Augustine showed repeatedly that he recognized this duality. In a number of passages he described the two kinds of people (duo genera hominum) as two peoples (populi), societies (societates), bodies (corpora) or kingdoms (regna) and, moreover, he identified them with the two *civitates*[655]. But this does not yet explain the true origin and central position of his metaphor of the two cities.

After all, does the antithesis of the two cities as Augustine described it occur in the biblical texts? We have already seen that in the scriptural passages to which he referred explicitly, or to which he repeatedly gave a prominent place in his argument, only the city of God is mentioned. This is the case in the just-cited texts from the Psalms. Moreover, the reference in these passages is never to Jerusalem as the *heavenly* city (civitas caelestis). But Augustine interpreted these texts from a New Testament perspective. For example, he referred to the 'Jerusalem which is above, our eternal mother in heaven' (*Gal.* 4:26)[656], and to Paul's speaking of our *politeuma* in heaven (*Phil.* 3:20)[657]. Furthermore, he repeatedly quoted *2 Cor.* 5:6 ff., in which the *peregrinatio* of the believer is emphasized (*ekdèmoumen* is rendered as *peregrinamur*!), and connected this passage with the peregrination on earth of the citizens of the heavenly city[658].

These texts, however, make no mention of the existence of two antithetical cities. It is only on the basis of the *Apocalypse of John* that Augustine's antithesis of the two cities could acquire a clearly exegetical foundation. In this book Babylon stands as the city of this world and of the ungodly power against Jerusalem as the city of God (*Apoc.* 14:8; 16:17-21; 17; 18; 21:2.9-27)[659]. But it is remarkable

---

655 From the many examples only a few will be named: *DCD* XII, 1 (two societates as civitates); *DCD* XV, 1 (two genera, regna, corpora, civitates); *En. in Ps.* 61,6 (two populi, corpora, civitates).

656 See n. 648; also *En. in Ps.* 67, 38; 86, 2; 121, 3; et al.

657 E.g. *En. in Ps.* 38, 10; 48, *s.* 2, 2; 52, 5; 64, 3; et al.

658 E.g. *En. in Ps.* 26 *en.* II, 10; 37, 15; 41, 6. 10; et al. We should note that *Heb.* 11:10; 12:22 and 13:14 do not have a prominent position. This fact is probably related to the minor position this epistle occupied in the works of A. and his contemporaries; see A.-M. La Bonnardière, 'L'épître aux Hébreux dans l'oeuvre de saint Augustin', *REA* (1957) 137-162.

659 As in the case of the other texts from the OT and the NT, no detailed exegesis is given here, but only references to the commentaries, e.g. Bousset, *Offenbarung*, particularly his interpretations of *Apoc.* 14:8; 16:17-21; 17 ff. and 21. G. Harder, 'Eschatologische Schemata in der Johannes-Apokalypse', *Theologia Viatorum 9, Jahrbuch der kirchlichen Hochschule Berlin 1963*, Berlin 1964, 70-87, esp. 85, names the scheme of the two cities as one of the separate schemes that occur in the *Apoc.* See also O. Böcher, 'Die heilige Stadt im Völkerkrieg. Wandlungen eines apokalyptischen Schemas', in: *Josephus-Studien* (FS O. Michel), Berlin 1974, 55-76, who

that Augustine only rarely cited passages from the *Apocalypse* about Jerusalem and Babylon when he discussed the two antithetical cities. Not once did he quote a text from the last book of the Bible in which Babylon is actually named, and only once a text in which Jerusalem is named[660]. Yet it should be noted that in Book XX of *De civitate Dei*, in the course of his interpretation of *Apoc.* 20, Augustine spoke on the one hand of 'the wicked city', 'the whole city of the devil', 'the hostile city', and on the other of 'the city of God', 'the most glorious city of Christ', 'the whole city of God', 'God's beloved city'[661].

It may be possible, therefore, to find in the *Apocalypse* an explanation for Augustine's metaphor. When he wrote that the two kinds of human society 'according to our Scriptures can rightly be called two cities', he could well have had the *Apocalypse* in mind. It may be recalled in this context how Tyconius in his commentary on this book of the Bible most probably spoke of the two antithetical *civitates*[662]. This mode of expression may have influenced Augustine so strongly that he was led to develop his doctrine of the two cities. But it should also be deemed possible that Augustine arrived at his metaphor through his own independent exegesis of the last book of the Bible.

Augustine himself, however, did not provide decisive proof for this. Nor does Tyconius' commentary provide compelling evidence because of the very complex situation surrounding it. Besides, the possibility should also be considered that Augustine had been influenced by someone like Origen for his metaphor of the two antithetical cities Jerusalem and Babylon[663]. At any rate it is certain that he was familiar with the concept, and that time and again he pointed it out in scriptural passages. In the Psalms he repeatedly found Jerusalem as the heavenly city confronting Babylon as the earthly city[664]; in the history of Israel and particularly in the bibli-

---

speaks of the 'Zionsschema' in the *Apoc.* and examines the essential elements of it elsewhere too (e.g. in *Ps.* 46; 48 and 76). One of the results of dualistic influence on the 'Zionsschema', according to Böcher (74), is the antithesis between Jerusalem and Babylon.

660 *DCD* XX, 17. This is stated on the basis of an analysis of unpublished material made available by Prof. C.P. Mayer and his collaborators on the *Augustinus-Lexikon*.

661 *DCD* XX, 9. 11 and 14 resp.

662 See p. 272 ff.

663 See p. 120 f.

664 E.g. *En. in Ps.* 26 *en.* 2, 18; *En. in Ps.* 51, 6; 61, 6; et al. As to be expected,

cal account of the Babylonian captivity he saw Jerusalem opposed to Babylon[665]; in the very early history of Israel he read about Babylon and he described this city as the *terrena civitas* opposing the city of God[666]. In Abel and Cain the beginning of Jerusalem and Babylon can already be discerned[667], and even the light created on the first day may be a designation for the heavenly Jerusalem[668].

Thus world history and the history of salvation are described in the figurative language of the two cities. This metaphor may very well have been derived from the *Apocalypse of John*, perhaps through the influential Tyconius. Well-known biblical themes, to a large extent occurring in the Pauline writings, such as the theme of the two kinds of people, the earthly and the heavenly, of the society of those who live according to the flesh and the society of those who live according to the Spirit, and of the two kingdoms, are related to this image. The same can be said of the notion of alienation and peregrination, which occurs frequently in the Old and the New Testament. For Augustine, as we have seen, the state of being an alien was an essential characteristic of the city of God and her inhabitants, and he was able to substantiate this idea each time with passages from Scripture[669]. For the presence of humans and angels in the *civitas Dei* he found evidence, for example, in *Heb.* 12:22[670].

Thus biblical themes resound in Augustine's doctrine of the two cities. The metaphor of the two cities itself can also be found in Scripture[671]. Moreover, in pre-Augustinian Christian tradition—besides Tyconius—the city of God of the Psalms and the Jerusalem of, for example, *Galatians, Hebrews* and the *Apocalypse of John* had

---

A. found the antithesis particularly in those Psalms in which Babylon is explicitly named; see his interpretation of *Ps.* 86 (87) and esp. of *Ps.* 136 (137). But there is certainly no antithesis in the text as it stands, at least not in the same degree as A. assumed. As he did with many other texts, such as those of the prophets, the church father interprets here on the basis of his fixed scheme.

665 For example, repeatedly in *DCD* XVII and XVIII; cf., in a condensed form, *De cat. rud.* 37.

666 E.g. *DCD* XVI, 3 ff.

667 E.g. *En. in Ps.* 61, 6: 'Illa [civitas Babylonia] incoepit a Cain; haec ab Abel'; *En. in Ps.* 64, 2: 'Ierusalem accepit exordium per Abel; Babylon per Cain ...'. Cf. *DCD* XV, 1.

668 *DCD* XI, 7.

669 See pp. 131-142.

670 *Quaest. in Hept.* I, 158.

671 There is no evidence that, besides the *Apoc.*, the prophecies of *Isa.* 24-27 or a text like *Zech.* 2:7 played a part in his idea of the two cities.

repeatedly been interpreted allegorically as the congregation of Christ, whereas Babylon had often been a designation for this depraved world[672]. Important elements of the Augustinian concept prove to be present both in Scripture and in the writings of previous Christian authors.

Yet Augustine was the only one to present a comprehensive doctrine of two antithetical *civitates*. Only he described the entire history of the world as the history of the two cities. It was Augustine who emphasized that each of the two cities contains angels and people and that these two societies are engaged in a gigantic struggle. Before conclusions can be drawn on the basis of the foregoing, further inquiry will have to be made in order to determine whether essential elements of Augustine's comprehensive doctrine of the two cities occurred elsewhere.

As regards the various writings not included in the Hebrew or New Testament canon, a few remarks will suffice. Along with the writings of Philo and from Qumran, these works can serve as a background to and illustration for the biblical material. In the Apocrypha and Pseudepigrapha of the Old Testament one discerns a growing tendency towards dualism, manifesting itself especially in the first century of the Christian era and more particularly after the fall of Jerusalem in AD 70. Increasingly there was a separation between 'Diesseits' and 'Jenseits', immanence and transcendence, this world or age (ᶜolām, aiōn, saeculum, mundus; sometimes also: tempus) and the one to come[673]. The present world was regarded as being under God's judgement (e.g. *4 Ezra* 7:11), fallen into the power of demons and devil (e.g. *Jub.* 10:8: Mastema; elsewhere referred to as Beliar, Belial and Satan), as the kingdom of the Evil One which in the course of time continues in its satanic hatred towards God, towards those who are good and towards what is good (e.g. *Test. Dan.* 6: 2. 4; *2 Bar.* 53 ff.; *4 Ezra* 4:27 ff.). Its antithesis is the

672 For various early-Christian writers see pp. 118-123; in addition, for Ambrose, esp. p. 277 ff.; for Origen, p. 281 ff.; for Commodian, p. 292 f.; for Tertullian, p. 297 ff.

673 For the different meanings of *ᶜolām* etc., see H. Sasse, 'Aiōn', *TWNT*, I, 197-209; P. Volz, *Die Eschatologie der jüdischen Gemeinde im neutestamentlichen Zeitalter*, Tübingen 1934, esp. 63 ff., and Billerbeck, *Kommentar*, IV, 799-976 in particular. A. Nygren, 'Luthers Lehre von den zwei Reichen' (1949), reprinted in: Schrey (Hrsg.), *Reich Gottes und Welt*, 277-289, points out the significance for Luther of the scheme of the two aeons, which is influential in the NT. However, one source at most of Luther's doctrine of the two kingdoms has thus been pointed out.

transcendental, heavenly, divine world, the kingdom of God, paradise, the heavenly city, Jerusalem.

There is no need to go into detail about the diversity of these writings. They vary considerably in their statements on the future of the earthly Jerusalem/Zion, on salvation in a heavenly Jerusalem which may or may not be pre-existent and which descends to earth, and on paradise[674]. What is clear, though, is the ever-present distance between earthly and heavenly things, this world and the one to come, present misery and future salvation. In these writings reference is made to two kingdoms, the kingdom of God and the reign of Satan[675], to two kinds of people[676], and in some instances also to two antithetical cities, Babylon and Jerusalem. It is not surprising that these two names occur frequently in Jewish writings of that time[677]. They denote on the one hand the earthly empire that is estranged from God and hostile to Him, and on the other the city of God on earth or in heaven. Especially in *4 Ezra* (3:1. 2. 31) and in the *Sibylline Oracles* (V, 418 ff.) there is an antithesis between Jerusalem/Zion and Babylon (Rome) as the wicked city. In this way, besides the names Jerusalem and Babylon, the metaphor of the two antithetical cities was also present in Jewish circles. No wonder that it was given prominence in a work like the *Apocalypse of John*, which was shaped to an important degree by Jewish apocalyptic traditions.

In the many and varied writings which can be designated as the Apocrypha of the New Testament one finds again the ideas and images that have been described briefly in the foregoing. These writings speak of the kingdom of God and the reign of Satan, of the world that is alienated from God, of the believer's state of being an alien, and frequently of Jerusalem and Babylon as well[678]. In the

---

674 See, e.g., the tables in Volz, *Eschatologie*, 420-421.

675 The kingdom of this world is increasingly regarded as being under the dominion of the demons and Satan; see Volz, *Eschatologie*, 83-89, esp. 87 ff. It is true that explicit mention of a kingdom of Satan is made only in *Test. Dan.* 6, 2. 4: 'hè basileia tou echthrou'.—Along with most recent scholars, we consider the *Testaments of the Twelve Patriarchs* to be Jewish documents with Christian interpolations; see e.g. H.C. Kee, 'Testaments of the Twelve Patriarchs', in: Charlesworth (ed.), *OTP*, I, esp. 777, and J.J. Collins, 'Testaments', in: M.E. Stone (ed.), *Jewish Writings of the Second Temple Period*, Assen-Philadelphia 1984, 331-344. Here and elsewhere we quote from the text-edition of M. de Jonge et al., *The Testaments of the Twelve Patriarchs*, Leiden 1978.

676 E.g. Volz, *Eschatologie*, 85 f.

677 E.g. Charles (ed.), *APOT*, II, 840 and 854.

678 See e.g. the indices in Hennecke and Schneemelcher, *NTAp*, II, s. v. Reich, Satan, Teufel, Fürst, Fremdlingschaft, Babel/Babylon, Jerusalem, etc.

Apocalypse of Paul there is a rather extensive account of the city of Christ[679], and in the Greek version of the *Acts of Thomas* reference is made to two *mètropoleis*[680]. But a clear antithesis between two cities is not to be found in these works.

Yet one depiction of two cities can be mentioned. It occurs in the *Acts of Peter and the Twelve Apostles*, the first writing from Codex VI of the Coptic library discovered near Nag Hammadi (Egypt) in 1945. In this work this world on the one hand and the heavenly kingdom on the other are described as cities.

Briefly these *Acts* present the following narrative[681]. The apostles set out by boat to carry out missionary work and arrive at a city situated in the middle of the sea. There Peter meets a foreigner named Lithargoel, who calls out 'Pearls, pearls'. He invites the poor of the city to come to his city to receive a pearl. Peter and his companions travel the difficult and dangerous way to the city of Lithargoel; meanwhile they fast and renounce all goods. Upon their arrival at the city they meet a physician; it is Lithargoel, who now reveals himself as Jesus Christ. He charges the disciples to go back to the city from which they have come and to care for the sick and the poor.

The narrative of these *Acts* is full of symbolism. For example, the pearl that Lithargoel gives without cost to those who believe in him is salvation. The difficult and dangerous way on which they have to journey is the way to salvation. The wild animals and the robbers on the way are the demons. And, most significant, the two cities symbolize on the one hand this world as the *terrena civitas* and on the other the heavenly kingdom as the *civitas caelestis*.

---

679 Hennecke and Schneemelcher, *NTAp*, II, 550 ff.

680 *Acta Thomae*, c. 84-85 (ed. Bonnet, pp. 200-201: 'estin gar hautè [sc. the impurity] hè mètropolis tōn kakōn hapantōn ...; hautè [the holiness] gar mètropolis estin para tōi theōi tōn agathōn hapantōn'.

681 See the edition and translation of M. Krause – P. Labib, *Gnostische und hermetische Schriften aus Codex II und Codex VI*, Glückstadt 1971 (*ADAIK*, Bd. II), 107-121; of R. Mcl. Wilson and D.M. Parrott in: D.M. Parrott (ed.), *Nag Hammadi Codices V, 2-5 and VI with Papyrus Berolinensis 8502, 1 and 4*, Leiden 1979, 197-229; a German translation with introduction by H.M. Schenke, 'Die Taten des Petrus und der zwölf Apostel', *TLZ* 98 (1973) 13-19; an English one with a short introduction by Parrott and Wilson in: J.M. Robinson (ed.), *The Nag Hammadi Library in English*, Leiden 1977, 265-270. Also important are M. Krause, 'Die Petrusakten in Codex VI von Nag Hammadi', in: M. Krause (ed.), *Essays on the Nag Hammadi Texts in Honour of Alexander Böhlig*, Leiden 1972, 36-58 and esp. A. Guillaumont, 'De nouveaux Actes apocryphes: Les Actes de Pierre et des Douze Apôtres', *RHR* 4 (1979) 141-152.

The precise meaning of the name Lithargoel is disputed[682]. It is certain, however, that El is a divine name discernible in the names of angels: Michael, Raphael, Gabriel, etc.[683]. Christ appears here as an angel[684]. This points to an archaic Jewish-Christian milieu[685]. The same is true for the special attention given to the poor and the severe judgement that is passed upon the rich[686]. Certain characteristics of the narrative may point more specifically to a Syriac Jewish-Christian milieu: the symbolism of the pearl, the wandering apostles, Lithargoel as an itinerant merchant, the emphatically mentioned state of being aliens of both Lithargoel and the apostles[687].

Of course more could be said and asked about these remarkable *Acts*. Do they form an integrated whole or consist of separate parts?[688] Were the Manichaeans also familiar with these *Acts* and was perhaps even Augustine acquainted with them?[689] Further research may reveal the answers to these and similar questions. What is most important here is that this writing, whose original version can be dated to the second or the third century, contains the imagery of two cities. This world is described as a city in which the believer sojourns as an alien; heaven is also described as a city, one for which the believer sets out as to his true habitation.

Until now the clearest presentation of the idea of two antithetical

---

682 Krause, 'Petrusakten', 51: 'der Gott (El) des hellglänzenden (argos) Steines (lithos)'; Schenke, 'Taten', 15: 'Lith-Raguel'; Parrott and Wilson in: Robinson (ed.), *Library*, 265: 'the god of the glistening stone, the god of the pearl'; Guillaumont, 'Actes', 147: 'lithos argos, la pierre brillante; ou bien, plus simplement, lithargyros, la litharge, le protoxyde de plomb'.

683 Cf. J. Michl, 'Engel V (Engelnamen)', *RAC* V (1962) 200-239.

684 For Lithargoel's being clothed in a linen robe with a gold belt (2, 11-13), cf. the angel in *Dan.* 10:5, the Son of Man as an angel in *Apoc.* 1:13 and the seven angels in *Apoc.* 15:6.

685 For angelomorphic christology, see J. Daniélou, 'Trinité et angélologie dans la théologie judéo-chrétienne', *RSR* 45 (1957) 5-41.

686 E.g. 10, 8 ff. and 11, 27 ff.

687 For the symbolism of the pearl, see esp. A.F.J. Klijn, *The Acts of Thomas*, Leiden 1962, 272 ff.; for the Syriac Christian as a wanderer and an alien, see also Quispel, *Makarius*, passim.

688 Krause, 'Petrusakten', 46 ff., is of the opinion that they consist of two (or three) separate books; Guillaumont, 'Actes', 142 and 150-152, maintains that it is one book. Cf. also Wilson and Parrott in: Parrott (ed.), *Codices*, 200-202.

689 Cf. K. Schäferdiek and W. Schneemelcher in: Hennecke and Schneemelcher, *NTAp*, II, 117 ff. and 181-182 resp. For the role of *Acts of Peter* in the writings of the Manichaeans and of A., see Altaner, 'Apokryphen', 205-207.

cities has been encountered in writings in which the archaic Jewish-Christian element occupies an important place: the *Apocalypse of John*, the *Shepherd of Hermas*, the *Acts of Peter and the Twelve Apostles*.

6. *A catechetical tradition?*

In the preceding section Christian and Jewish writings prior to Augustine were examined to determine where the metaphor of the two cities or the idea of two kingdoms occurred in a distinctive way. Attention has been focussed on the metaphor of the two cities because it is the most characteristic element of Augustine's concept. Conclusions based on this investigation will be drawn at the end of this book.

But first one more facet must be examined. Augustine presented his doctrine of the two *civitates* especially in a catechetical context. This can be seen most clearly in the long model catechesis for Deogratias, in some letters, and in the *City of God*[690]. Moreover, it is striking that Manichaean writings speak of the two kingdoms and the three times as a fundamental doctrine and even as a kind of catechesis[691]. It can be asked whether the two cities or kingdoms are discussed in a catechetical context in other writings as well.

This is indeed the case. First of all the so-called *Manual of Discipline* (1 *QS*), discovered at Qumran in 1947, should be considered[692]. Although it contains—just as other writings and fragments found at Qumran—no explicit reference to an antithesis between two cities or kingdoms, it does contain some elements that are important in this framework. This applies especially to 1 *QS* 3,13 – 4,26, which is regarded by many scholars as a separate part[693] and by some of

---

[690] See pp. 175-198.

[691] See pp. 212-222, esp. 213-217.

[692] Of the many editions, translations and commentaries, see e.g.: W.H. Brownlee, *The Dead Sea Manual of Discipline*, New Haven 1951 (*BASOR*, Suppl. Series 10-12); P. Wernberg-Møller, *The Manual of Discipline*, Leiden 1957; H.A. Brongers, *De gedragsregels der Qoemraan-gemeente*, Amsterdam 1958; J. Carmignac – P. Guilbert, *Les textes de Qumran*, I, Paris 1961; A.R.C. Leany, *The Rule of Qumran and its Meaning*, London 1966; E. Lohse, *Die Texte aus Qumran*, Darmstadt 1971^2.

[693] See e.g. A. Dupont-Sommer, 'L'instruction sur les deux Esprits dans le *Manuel de Discipline*', *RHR* 72 (1952) 5-35, esp. 5; J. Licht, 'An Analysis of the Treatise on the Two Spirits in DSD', *ScrHier* 4 (1958) 88-100; Leany, *Rule*, 112 ff.; J. Murphy-O'Connor, 'La génèse littéraire de la Règle de la Communauté, *RB* 76 (1969) 528-549, esp. 541-542; P. von der Osten-Sacken, *Gott und Belial. Traditions-*

them even attributed (for the greater part) to the central and at the same time mysterious figure in this community, the Teacher of Righteousness[694]. It is a catechesis, to be used by the *maskīl*[695] in his teaching.

Its contents can be summarized as follows. The *maskīl* has to instruct and teach all the sons of light about the natures (*tōledōth*)[696] of the sons of man, the spirits who exert their influence on them, their works in their societies (*dōrōth*)[697] and their final punishment or reward (1 *QS* 3, 13-15). God is the author of all that is or will be and everything has been determined by Him (3, 15-16). He created man and allotted two spirits for him in which to walk: the spirit of truth and the spirit of perversity (3, 17-19). The prince of lights rules over the righteous; they walk in the ways of light. Conversely, the angel of darkness rules over the wicked; they walk in the ways of darkness

---

geschichtliche Untersuchungen zum Dualismus in den Texten aus Qumran, Göttingen 1969, 17-27. Like Murphy-O'Connor and Von der Osten-Sacken, J.L. Duhaime, 'L'instruction sur les deux esprits et les interpolations dualistes à Qumrân (1 QS III, 13 – IV, 26)', *RB* 84 (1977) 566-594 and D.C. Allison Jr., 'The Authorship of 1 QS III, 13 - IV, 14', *RdQ* 10 (1980) 257-268 discuss various phases of the composition of 1 *QS* as a whole, and interpolations in and additions to 1 *QS* 3, 13 – 4, 14 (+ 15-26). Here we can consider 1 *QS* 3, 13 – 4, 26 as a separate entity.

694 See esp. Allison, 'Authorship'.

695 The *maskīl* is not just a 'sage', but very probably a special office-holder, the teacher who has to instruct and judge whether a person may be admitted into the community. See e.g. F. Nötscher, 'Vorchristliche Typen urchristlicher Ämter? Episkopos und Mebaqqer' (1960), and F. Nötscher, *Vom Alten zum Neuen Testament*, Bonn 1962, 118-220, esp. 212-214.

696 There is no unanimity of opinion concerning the meaning of *tōledōth*. Brownlee (*Manual*, 12) translates it as '(succeeding) generations'; Dupont-Sommer ('Instruction', 7) as 'générations'; J.-P. Audet ('Affinités littéraires et doctrinales du *Manuel de Discipline*', I, *RB* 59 (1952) 227) as 'lignages'; Wernberg-Møller (*Manual*, 25) as 'genealogies'; Brongers (*Gedragsregels*, 67) as 'naturen'; Carmignac and Guilbert (*Textes*, I, 32) as 'histoire'; Leany (*Rule*, 143) as 'history'; Lohse (*Texte*, 11) as 'Ursprung'. It is difficult to make a choice—cf. *tōledōth* in 1 *QS* 3, 19 and 4, 15—and most scholars make this clear in their commentary. The most suitable translation seems to be 'natures', indicating the different dispositions of people in accordance with the spirits within them; cf. G. Scholem in his edition of the early-medieval physiognomic work *Hakarath Panim* in: *Sefer Asaf*, Jerusalem 1954, 477.

697 *Dōrōth* (cf. 1 *QS* 4, 15) is usually rendered as 'generations'. But it is also possible to translate it as 'societies', 'kinds', or 'classes', and these translations are probably even to be preferred; cf. *dōr* in *Deut.* 32:5 and 20; *Ps.* 14:5; 24:6; 112:2. F.J. Neuberg, 'An unrecognized meaning of Hebrew Dōr', *JNES* 9 (1950) 215-217, on the basis of Ugaritic parallels, points out the possibility of translating *dōr* as 'assembly, council, congregation'. Brownlee, *Manual*, 12 and 13 n. 24, prefers 'societies'; E. Kamlah, *Die Form der katalogischen Paränese im Neuen Testament*, Tübingen 1964, 40, translates *dōrōth* as 'Gattungen'.

(3, 20-21). The angel of darkness also exerts influence on the sons of light, but God and the angel of His truth help them (3, 21-25). God created both spirits; His love for the one and His hatred for the other are eternal (3,25 – 4,1). The ways of the spirit of light and the reward of those who walk in it (4, 2-8) are antithetical to the ways of the spirit of darkness and those who walk in it (4, 9-14). The two spirits exist simultaneously in the sons of man and they are engaged in a struggle with each other (4, 15-18). In the end evil will be destroyed and good will triumph (4, 19-23). Until then the two spirits will continue to struggle in the heart of man (4, 23-25). God is the author of everything (4, 25-26).

The passage 1 *QS* 3,13 – 4,26 is not only a separate part, but to a certain extent—and notwithstanding various repetitions[698]—also a logical unit. Although it is difficult to demonstrate what makes it a logical unit[699], most investigators agree that the doctrine of the two spirits is the central and binding element of this exposition. The two spirits exist both in the cosmos and in the soul of man and are engaged in a struggle with each other. Origin, history and final destination of mankind and the individual are very closely interwoven with these two spirits and their struggle.

In connection with this dualism of the two spirits 1 *QS* 3, 13 – 4,26 describes the two kinds of ways. On the one hand there are the ways of light in which the sons of justice walk (3, 20); on the other the ways of darkness in which the sons of deceit walk (3, 21). The ways of the two spirits are described in more detail in catalogues of virtues (4, 2-6) and vices (4, 9-11). All men walk in the ways of the two spirits (4,15); there are the ways of truth (4,17) and of wickedness (4,19).

Thus the members of the Qumran community were taught that there are two spirits—also referred to as angels of light and of darkness—and two kinds of ways. This doctrine of two spirits or angels and of two (kinds of) ways deserves further attention, for it also occurs elsewhere in a distinctive manner. First, however, we will look at the question of whether the teacher also spoke about two kingdoms.

---

698 Cf. 1 *QS* 3, 15-16 with 4, 25b-26; 4, 15-16a with 4, 24-25a; 4, 16b-18a with 4, 23c; 4, 18b-19a with 4, 23b.

699 See e.g. Licht, 'Analysis', and—although reasoning from another point of view—P. Guilbert, 'Le plan de la Règle de la Communauté', *RdQ* 1 (1958-'59) 323-344. Moreover the various commentators, in spite of the fact that they all see a certain structure, give different divisions.

The idea of two antithetical kingdoms is not named explicitly in 1 *QS* 3,13 – 4,26[700]. But it is clear that, connected with the dualistic doctrine of the two spirits and the two kinds of ways, a continual distinction is made between two societies. The children of light oppose the children of darkness[701]; there are two different divisions, groups and classes of men[702]. In another passage of the *Manual* it is stated that the chosen are connected with the sons of heaven in one 'council of community'[703]. Thus people and angels form one whole and this society is the opposite of 'wicked mankind, the assembly (or: council, *sōd*) of erring flesh'[704].

In this Qumran text the two antithetical spirits, the two kinds of ways and the two different societies of good and evil are closely connected with each other. The prince of light has dominion over the righteous and they walk in the ways of light; the angel of darkness has dominion over the evil and they walk in the ways of darkness (3,20-21). God made for man two spirits in which to walk until the appointed time of His visitation (3, 18). These two spirits are determinant for the natures, origin, history (tōledōth) of all people; all are part of one or the other of the two divisions, classes, ranks, categories (miphlagōth) and in their ways they walk (4, 15-16).

Not only the fact that these spirits, ways and societies are connected with each other deserves attention, but also that this part of the *Manual* is a catechesis. The teacher (maskīl) instructs the children of light in accordance with *this* catechetical scheme; origin, history and final destination of mankind are expounded in this way. It is not entirely clear whether this was a first lesson which was meant to give information on the views of the community, or a review of material

---

700 The notion *malkuth*, for example, occurs neither here nor elsewhere in 1 *QS*, but it does, for example, in 1 *QM* 12, 7. 15. 16. *Memsjālāh* in 1 *QS* 4, 19 is translated by Brongers (*Gedragsregels*, 70) as 'rijk' (kingdom), but here it refers to 'dominion' (Herrschaft, rule, pouvoir, empire); cf. 1 *QS* 3, 17. 20. 21. 22. 23 and, among others, 1, 18 and 23.

701 This contrast—probably under the influence of 1 *QS* 3, 13 – 4, 14 (+ 15-26)—is discussed in detail in 1 *QM*: the Scroll of the war of the sons of light against the sons of darkness.

702 Besides *dōrōth* in 3, 24 and 4, 15: *gōrāl*, portion (Los, partage, lot, part) in 3,24 and 4, 24; *sōd*, council (Rat, assembly, conseil) in 4, 1; *miphlagōth*, divisions (Klassen, classes, catégories, classes) in 4, 15. 16. 17. In 1 *QS* 2, 2. 5 a distinction is made between the *gōrāl* of God and the *gōrāl* of Belial; 1 *QS* 11, 7 speaks of the *gōrāl* of the saints, 1 *QM* 1, 1 of the *gōrāl* of the sons of darkness. Cf. 1 *QM* 1, 5 and 1 *QH* 3, 25 and 6, 13.

703 1 *QS* 11, 7 f.

704 1 *QS* 11, 9.

that was already familiar. Probably the one does not rule out the other, for it was the duty of the *maskīl* to form an opinion about his fellow-members, to recommend them for (further) acceptance in the community or to prepare them for it[705]. In any case it is certain that in 1 *QS* 3, 13-4, 26 the central tenets of the Qumran community are expounded[706].

Essential elements of this instruction given in Qumran are also to be found in other Jewish and Christian writings. Mention is made of two spirits (angels, kings), two ways and two societies or kingdoms, and often they are clearly connected with each other.

The idea of two spirits or angels will be considered first. In 1 *QS* 3, 13 – 4, 26 this idea occurs mainly in a macrocosmic context. World and humanity are divided into two parts, a good one and an evil one, under the dominion of the prince of light and the angel of darkness respectively. Besides this cosmic dualism[707]—and directly connected with it—there is a psychological dualism: in the heart of man the two spirits are at war with each other (1 *QS* 4, 23 – 25). A similar idea is found—though it comes from a broader dualistic antithesis, that between God and Beliar—in the *Testaments of the Twelve Patriarchs*, for instance in the *Testament of Judah* (20:1): 'Know then, my children, that two spirits (pneumata) wait upon man, the spirit of truth and the spirit of error'[708]. This idea was expressed by Her-

---

[705] 1 *QS* 9, 12 ff., esp. 15 f.

[706] Cf. Allison, 'Authorship', 258 f. and 262 ff. for his opinion and that of others concerning the considerable influence of 1 *QS* 3, 13 ff. on other Qumran writings.

[707] A subordinate dualism, not an absolute dualism of two entirely independent powers as in Manichaeism and probably (partly) in Iran. It is not necessary here to go into the possible influence of Iran on the religious history of Israel. For Judaism around the beginning of the Christian era—mainly apocalyptic Judaism—see Bousset and Gressmann, *Religion*, esp. 513 ff. concerning Iranian and Jewish dualism; for Qumran, see Dupont-Sommer, 'Instruction', 16-17, 22, 28 and esp. K.G. Kuhn, 'Die Sektenschrift und die iranische Religion', *ZThK* 49 (1952) 296-316. Attention should also be given to the circumspect remarks of F. Nötscher, *Zur theologischen Terminologie der Qumran-Texte*, Bonn 1956, 79-92. M. Hengel, *Judentum und Hellenismus*, Tübingen 1969, 418-420—like Kuhn—is convinced that there is Iranian influence in the dualism of Qumran; he suggests the possibility that mediation took place through 'eine alexandrinisch-jüdische Quelle (...), zumal anscheinend auch das alexandrinische Judentum die hellenistische Zarathustraüberlieferung gekannt hat' (419). However this may be, mention should be made in this context of the fact that the Gathas speak frequently not only of two antithetical spirits, but of two ways and two 'societies' as well (*Yasna* 31, 2). Parallelism, however, does not necessarily imply influence.

[708] Cf. *Test. Benj.* 6, 1-4 and *Test. Asher* 1, 3-9; the concept of the two ways is also present in the latter pericope.

mas in a similar way, for example in *Mand.* VI, 2,1: 'There are two angels with man, one of righteousness and one of evil'[709].

Often linked to this duality of two spirits or angels[710] is the idea of two ways. The catechesis 1 *QS* 3, 13 – 4, 26 makes a direct connection between the two spirits and the two (kinds of) ways. In the *Shepherd of Hermas* (particularly *Mand.* VI,1-2) there are similar images of two ways and two angels. But most important in this context are the *Didache, Barnabas* and the Latin *Doctrina apostolorum*.

For it is in these writings that an elaborate doctrine of two ways has a prominent place. The *Didache* or *Teaching of the Twelve Apostles*[711] states: 'There are two ways, one of life and one of death. And there is a great difference between the two ways' (*Did.* 1:1). Subsequently the way of life is expounded in a number of commandments, prohibitions, vices to be shunned and virtues to be pursued (*Did.* 1:2-3a and 2:2 – 4:14)[712]. Then there is a description of the way of death through the enumeration of a number of vices (*Did.* 5) and after that a—possibly tentative[713]—conclusion (*Did.* 6:1)[714]. In the *Epistle of Barnabas*[715] we read: 'There are two ways of teaching

---

709 The concept of two angels or spirits occurs frequently in *Hermas*; for a survey, see Lluis-Font, 'Sources', 84 ff.

710 For the question as to whether there are connections with Jewish concepts of *yeṣer* and with the later rabbinical idea of the two *y^eṣārīm*, see G.H. Cohen Stuart, *The struggle in man between good and evil. An inquiry into the origin of the Rabbinic concept of Yeṣer Haraᵓ*, Kampen 1984, esp. 94-95 and 208-209 with respect to 1 *QS*; for *Hermas* and the *Test.*, see 146-159 and 210-212.

711 For introductions to this highly interesting work, which probably dates from c. 100, see Altaner and Stuiber, *Patrologie*, 79-82, and A. Tuilier, 'Didache', *TRE* 8 (1981) 731-736; they also give (as do Altaner and Stuiber, 557) a selection of the most important text-editions and studies. Of these the following should be named: J.-P. Audet, *La Didachè. Instructions des apôtres*, Paris 1958 (*ÉtBibl*) and W. Rordorf – A. Tuilier, *La Doctrine des douze apôtres (Didachè)*, Paris 1978 (*SC* 248); furthermore, the most recent edition by Wengst, *Schriften*, 1-100.

712 *Did.* 1, 3^b – 2, 1 is generally considered to have been added by the writer (or writers, editors) to the original work.

713 There are arguments to support the theory that important parts of the eschatological chapter *Did.* 16 originally formed the end of the exposition of the two ways as it occurs in the *Did.* Cf. *Barn.* 21, 2 ff. and *Doctr.* 6, 1 ff.; possibly 1 *QS* 4, 6^b f. also.

714 Or *Did.* 6, 1-3?

715 An introduction to the most important studies on this work—which was probably written shortly after 130 by a gentile Christian (not Paul's companion Barnabas)—is given by Altaner and Stuiber, *Patrologie*, 53-55 (+ 552-553) and K. Wengst, 'Barnabasbrief', *TRE* 5 (1980) 238-241. Important text-editions with annotations: P. Prigent – R.A. Kraft, *Épître de Barnabé*, Paris 1971 (*SC* 172); Wengst, *Schriften*, 101-202.

and power[716]: that of light and that of darkness. And there is a great difference between the two ways. For over the one are set light-bearing angels of God, but over the other angels of Satan. And the one is Lord from eternity and to eternity, but the other is the ruler of the present time of lawlessness' (*Barn.* 18:1b - 2). Next a description is given of the way of light (*Barn.* 19) and of the way of the Black One (= Satan) (*Barn.* 20). Finally the doctrine of the two ways is ended, as well as the letter itself (*Barn.* 21). The *Doctrina apostolorum*[717], a Latin version of the two ways, begins as follows: 'There are two ways in the world, of life and of death, of light and of darkness. Two angels are set over them, one of righteousness, the other of iniquity. The difference between the two ways, however, is great' (*Doctr.* 1:1). Then there is a description of the way of life (*Doctr.* 1:2 – 4:14), followed by one of the way of death (*Doctr.* 5). The end consists of a brief admonition, some eschatological statements and a Christian closing formula (*Doctr.* 6).

Even from this brief summary one can gain an impression of the doctrine of the two ways as it occurs in these writings in a detailed form. One perceives the similarities and also a few differences. Each of these points needs further comment.

First the similarities. The common elements in these writings are the two ways and the presentation of their contents in the form of commandments and prohibitions, catalogues of virtues and vices.

---

716 'Hodoi duo eisin didachès kai exousias'. For a plausible explanation of *exousia*, see H. Windisch, *Der Barnabasbrief*, Tübingen 1920 (*HNT*, Erg.-Band), 397, and R.A. Kraft, *Barnabas and the Didache*, Toronto et al. 1965 (*The Apostolic Fathers*, 3), 135-136: *exousia* indicates that the ruler has dominion over those who walk on his way. Kamlah, *Form*, 211 n. 2, and Wengst, *Schriften*, 187 n. 256, give a similar interpretation.

717 In a codex in Munich, which originated at Freising (*Cod. Lat. Monac.* 6264, olim *Frising.* 64) and dates from the eleventh century, a complete text was discovered by J. Schlecht; see his *Doctrina XII Apostolorum. Die Apostellehre in der Liturgie der katholischen Kirche*, Freiburg i. Br. 1901. Earlier, in 1723, a fragment of a codex from Melk was published by the Benedictine scholar B. Pez; it was forgotten, but after the discovery of the *Did.* attention was drawn to it by O. von Gebhardt, 'Fragment' (1886). Funk, *Doctrina*, 102-104, published it anew in 1887 and recently a new critical edition was given by K. Niederwimmer, 'Doctrina apostolorum (Cod. Mellic. 597)', in: H.C. Schmidt-Lauber (Hrsg.), *Theologia scientia eminens practica* (FS Fritz Herbst), Wien et al. 1979, 266-272 (text 270). A recension of the two texts (*Monac.* and *Mellic.*) was given by H. Lietzmann, *Die Didache. Mit kritischem Apparat*, Bonn 1923^3 (*KlT* 6) and by Rordorf and Tuilier, *Doctrine*, 207-210.—It should be noted that the *Doctrina* is not a translation of *Did.* 1-6 (or *Barn.* 18-21), but an independent version of an originally Jewish work on the two ways. The very important influence of this work in the Western Church has still, for the most part, to be examined.

An example of this phenomenon can be seen in the Jewish document 1 *QS* 3, 13 – 4, 26. However, long before the finds at Qumran and even a considerable time before the discovery of the *Didache* and the attendant rediscovery of the Latin *Doctrina apostolorum*, scholars had postulated the existence of a separate work on the two ways, mainly on the basis of *Barnabas*, the expositions on the two ways in the *Constitutiones Apostolorum* and the so-called *Apostolic Church Order*[718]. The discovery and subsequent publication of the *Didache* (editio princeps by Philotheos Bryennios, Constantinople 1883) provided important new information. C. Taylor pointed out the numerous links between the statements on the two ways in Christian writings—especially the *Didache*—and in Jewish ones[719]. It was commonly assumed that there must have been an originally Jewish document concerning the two ways that served as a common source. The discovery of the *Manual of Discipline* substantiated this.

This brief, general survey might create the impression that a universally accepted solution has been found to the many problems surrounding the contents of and the relationship between *Didache, Barnabas, Doctrina* and other works similar to them in respect to the doctrine of the two ways. This, however, is not the case. But concerning its origin there is almost complete agreement. It stems from a Jewish source. Around the beginning of the Christian era ethical instruction was given in Jewish circles following the scheme of the two ways. It was in accordance with this model (of which an early elaboration can be found in 1 *QS* 3,13 – 4,26) that, directly or indirectly, the later Christian versions of the doctrine of the two ways were made: the Latin *Doctrina apostolorum*, the two ways in *Barnabas*, the *Didache* and also in later works such as the *Apostolic Church Order*, the *Didascalia* and the *Apostolic Constitutions*[720].

---

718 See e.g. A. Harnack, *Die Apostellehre und die jüdischen beiden Wege*, Leipzig 1896², 26 f.

719 C. Taylor, *The Teaching of the Twelve Apostles with illustrations from the Talmud*, Cambridge 1886. (In spite of several attempts I have been unable to consult this study.)

720 Cf. Harnack, *Apostellehre*, 27 ff.; Harnack, *Literatur*, I/1, 86 f.; Audet, 'Affinités', 219-238; Audet, *Didachè*, 131 ff. (Audet frequently asserts that the Latin *Doctr.* is the closest to the Jewish source of all the versions that were current in Christian circles); Kraft, *Barnabas and the Didache*, 4-11; L.W. Barnard, *Studies in the Apostolic Fathers and their Background*, Oxford 1966, 87-107, esp. 97 f. (cf. the scheme on p. 107); Prigent and Kraft, *Barnabé*, 12-20; M.J. Suggs, 'The Christian Two Ways Tradition: its Antiquity, Form and Function', in: *Studies in the New Testament and Early Christian Literature* (FS A.P. Wilken), Leiden 1972, 60-74, esp. 62 f.;

In addition to these similarities in the main points—the idea of the two ways, elaborated further in enumerations of commandments and prohibitions, virtues and vices[721]—there are also differences. The *Didache* only refers to the two ways as those of life and death; *Barnabas* calls them the way of light and the way of darkness and mentions the angels of God and of Satan, too; the *Doctrina apostolorum* describes them as the way of life and the way of death, of light and of darkness, and also names the two angels. Ehrhard Kamlah[722] claims to see some development on the basis of these differences: from a mythological reference to two spirits or angels (as in 1 *QS* 3,13 – 4,26; *Doctr.*; *Barn.*) to a 'Spiritualisierung des mythischen Stoffes' whereby only the two ways remain (as in *Test. Aser* 1:3-9; *Did.*). This, however, may be questioned. Is it not more likely that a development, if there was one, took the opposite course: from a contradistinction between two ways which already occurred more or less clearly in the Old Testament[723] to a doctrine of two antithetical ways and spirits developed extensively under dualistic influence? At any rate it is certain that the sharp antithesis between two ways and two spirits found a wide response in the Christian Church, not only in the first centuries of the Christian era, but long after. Presently we will find this antithesis as it occurs in the *Pseudo-Clementines*.

But first the framework in which the two ways (and spirits) appear in the previously-mentioned works should be considered. In Qumran the context is catechetical. This is also the case in the *Didache*: the candidate is first instructed in the two ways and then baptized. For after the passage on the two ways (*Did.* 1-6) it reads (*Did.* 7:1): 'Having first rehearsed all these things, baptize in the name of the Father and of the Son and of the Holy Spirit in running water'. To be sure, Jean-Paul Audet in his commentary regards the phrase 'having first rehearsed all these things' (tauta panta proeipontes) as a later addition[724]. By doing so he ignores the fact that in the time

---

W. Rordorf, 'Un chapitre d'éthique judéo-chrétienne: les deux voies', *RSR* 60 (1972) 109-128 (= *Judéo-christianisme*, FS J. Daniélou, Paris 1972); Rordorf and Tuilier, *Doctrine*, 22-34; Wengst, *Schriften*, 20.

[721] Besides many concurrences, these catalogues show various differences. This is probably a result of oral tradition, adaptations, etc.

[722] Kamlah, *Form*, 172 ff.; cf. 210-214.

[723] E.g. *Ps.* 1:6; *Prov.* 4:18-19 and the like; cf. W. Michaelis, 'Hodos', *TWNT*, V, 54 f. But it should be noted that Michaelis—in contrast to many scholars—is very reserved concerning the existence of a metaphor of the two ways.

[724] Audet, *Didachè*, 58-62 and 358 f.

and milieu in which the *Didache* originated the doctrine of the two ways functioned as instruction prior to baptism. But other commentators did not follow his example and Audet's predecessors, too, had correctly seen the two ways in the *Didache* as being part of the instruction leading to baptism[725]. One might well ask whether this was already the case in Judaism, for opinions differ widely concerning the possible existence of a Jewish catechism for proselytes according to the scheme of the two ways[726]. It is certain, though, that in Jewish circles ethical instruction was given according to this scheme[727]. The *Didache* connects the doctrine of the two ways with baptism, in the form of a catechesis prior to it[728]. *Barnabas* also shows this connection with baptism, but primarily as post-baptismal instruction: its author addresses those who are already baptized[729] and reminds them of the instruction they received earlier[730]. The *Doctrina apostolorum* and related versions of the *Duae viae* were used in the Western Church to recapitulate the instruction given at baptism[731]. Here, too, it appears that prior to baptism the candidates were instructed in the two ways. Athanasius indicated that

---

[725] Cf. Rordorf and Tuilier, *Doctrine*, 31 and 170 n. 3; Wengst, *Schriften*, 16 n. 54, and of the earlier commentators: Harnack, *Lehre*, 22; Funk, *Doctrina*, XLIV and 21; Knopf, *Lehre*, 21. An important argument is the phrase in *Did.* 11, 1 which is almost parallel to *Did.* 7, 1; also the fact that the text of *Did.* in *CA* VII is considerably adapted. That in *CA* VII, 1-21 the doctrine of the two ways functions as an 'exhortation aux fidèles' (Audet, *Didachè*, 58) is not a strange phenonomen; cf. its use in *Barn.* and in the sermons under the name of Boniface.

[726] The question need not be examined here in detail; it should probably be the subject of a separate investigation. Some of the scholars who have thought that such a catechism for proselytes existed are Harnack, *Apostellehre*, 27 ff. (who also pointed to Taylor and George Salmon) and—though taking a more moderate position—A. Seeberg in various publications, esp. *Der Katechismus der Urchristenheit*, Leipzig 1903 (repr. München 1966), 44; *Die beiden Wege und das Aposteldekret*, Leipzig 1906, 1 ff.; *Die Didache des Judentums und der Urchristenheit*, Leipzig 1908, 1 ff. See also Knopf, *Lehre*, 2 and 4; Moore, *Judaism*, I, 188. Objections have been raised by Michaelis, 'Hodos', 58 and 99; Rordorf and Tuilier, *Doctrine*, 31 n. 5.

[727] Besides the texts mentioned so far, see e.g. 1 *En.* 91, 18-19 and 2 *En.* 30, 15.

[728] Whether this instruction immediately preceded baptism, or there was a certain preparatory period in which the candidates demonstrated they were living according to the given rules (which were possibly repeated at baptism), is not clear.

[729] This is specifically discussed by Schille, 'Zur urchristlichen Tauflehre. Stilistische Beobachtungen am Barnabasbrief', *ZNW* 49 (1958) 31-52. Schille sees in the entire letter the 'katechetische Stil des Lehrers' who is giving post-baptismal instruction.

[730] Is it also possible to see the two ways in Hermas, *Mand.* VI, 1, 2-5—though intermingled with Hellenistic elements—in this framework?

[731] Cf. Schlecht, *Doctrina*, 75 ff.

in his day 'the so-called Teaching of the apostles'[732]—he was probably only referring to the section concerning the two ways[733]— had a place in the instruction of the (prospective?) catechumens[734]. It will be seen that the *Pseudo-Clementines* also testify to the fact that in catechetical instruction the two ways were mentioned.

Thus in the early Christian Church the doctrine of the two ways—with or without specific mention of the two spirits or angels—had its 'Sitz im Leben' first of all in the baptismal catechesis. Originally given as instruction prior to baptism, this doctrine could also function as a recapitulation of baptismal instruction[735]. But its primary function was to prepare the candidate for baptism. It cannot be ruled out that the so-called *abrenuntiatio diaboli*[736], which also preceded baptism, was closely connected with this doctrine. For in this *abrenuntiatio* the devil (Satan), his *pompa(e)*, angels, works etc. were renounced by the person to be baptized[737]. Do the formulas used in this ceremony—in which the various sins are sometimes listed in catalogues—point to previous instruction on the two ways and the two spirits? It does not seem advisable to attach too much weight to the fact that in one of these formulas not only Satan is mentioned, but also his evil ways and angels[738]. Of more consequence seems to be the fact that in the *Pastor of Hermas* (*Mand.* VI) mention is made of the two ways and the two angels, and that towards the end of this exposition we read: 'You see that it is good

---

[732] In *Ep.* 39, the well-known festal letter: '... kai Didachè kaloumenè tōn apostolōn ...'; see Zahn, *Geschichte*, II, 212.

[733] It is sometimes impossible to deduce from the references in early-Christian writings whether the entire *Did.* is meant or only the first part; cf. Rordorf and Tuilier, *Doctrine*, 107 ff.

[734] *Ep.* 39: '... tois arti proserchomenois kai boulomenois katècheisthai ton tès eusebeias logon ...'.

[735] Later the doctrine of the two ways was also given a place in monastic rules, e.g. in the famous *Regula Benedicti*, Ch. 4. For this and other (possible) forms of influence—perhaps even as far as the catechisms of the Waldenses, the Bohemian Brethren and Luther—see Schlecht, *Doctrina*, 86-97; Rordorf, 'Deus voies', 122-128.

[736] H. Kirsten, *Die Taufabsage. Eine Untersuchung zu Gestalt und Geschichte der Taufe nach den altkirchlichen Taufliturgien*, Berlin 1960. Cf. M. Rothenhaeusler – Ph. Oppenheim, 'Apotaxis', *RAC*, I, 558-564.

[737] An enumeration of 62 *formulae abrenuntiationis* is given by Kirsten, *Taufabsage*, 39-51.

[738] Cf. Kirsten, *Taufabsage*, 48, for an Armenian rite, in the translation of F.C. Conybeare: '... thee, Satan, and all thy deceitfulness and thy wiles and thy service and thy paths and thine angels...'.

to follow (akolouthein) the angel of righteousness and to renounce (apotaxasthai) the angel of wickedness' (*Mand.* VI, 2, 9). This is reminiscent of the later *formulae abrenuntiationis*, and it perhaps also shows the connection with the two ways and the two spirits. As is indicated most clearly in later texts: at baptism not only is Satan renounced (apotagè tou Satana; abrenuntiatio diaboli), but also the covenant with Christ is concluded (syntagè tōi Christōi; pactum cum Christo). This calls to mind the concept of the two kingdoms, too. Through baptism a person goes over from one dominion to the other. Before he was under the rule of Satan[739]; now he belongs to Christ and His kingdom[740]. When the sacrament of baptism has especially this meaning, it can be expected that the two kingdoms are referred to in the instruction preceding the ceremony.

Prior to a discussion of some texts in which this actually happens, a few more comments should be made on the doctrine of the two ways and the two spirits. For is the concept of the two kingdoms not already implicitly present in this doctrine? In the catechesis of 1 *QS* 3, 13 – 4, 26 the two concepts appear jointly: the two spirits and their ways are accompanied by the two societies of the good and the evil. The same occurs in other texts, for instance in the *Didache*, the *Doctrina* and *Barnabas*. To the two ways (and the two spirits) belong two antithetical groups of people, the good and the evil, the righteous and the wicked. In *Barnabas* we read: 'Thou shalt not join thyself to those who walk in the way of death' (*Barn.* 19:2). The doctrine of the two ways functions as 'an instrument of group identity'[741]. *Barnabas* also says that the way leads to an appointed place (*Barn.* 19:1: 'hōrismenon topon'). The ways are described in terms of the deeds of the people walking in them and as leading to a certain desti-

---

739 See e.g. a formula of abjuration used by Ambrose: '... tibi, diabole ... et imperiis tuis ...' (*Hexaem.* I, 4, 14); likewise Ildephonse of Toledo (*Liber de cognitione baptismi*, Ch. 3). Ambrose called the devil (Pharaoh) 'princeps huius mundi' (*ibid.*). For the devil as the master of this world, cf. p. 309 f. The repeated abjuration of 'the world' in the *formulae abrenuntiationis* can be understood against this background. For the *saeculo/mundo renuntiare* in the writings of Cyprian and Tertullian, see p. 294 ff.; for the *pompa diaboli*, Waszink, 'Pompa diaboli', passim.

740 See *Col.* 1:13, a text that—like *Acts* 26:18—should very probably be understood in the context of baptism. See esp. E. Käsemann, 'Eine urchristliche Taufliturgie' (1949), repr. in *Exegetische Versuche und Besinnungen*, I, Göttingen 1960, 43-47. For the idea that outside Christ's kingdom Satan rules, see also 2 *Cor.* 4:4 or *Eph.* 2:2. One becomes a child of God through baptism, which endows one with the Spirit of God instead of the spirit of the devil (e.g. 1 *John* 3:8 ff.; 4:13).

741 Suggs, 'Two ways', 71.

nation. This last idea was already present in *Matt.* 7:13-14: one way leads to life, i.e. to the kingdom of God; the other to destruction[742].

It is in the so-called *Pseudo-Clementines* that a clear connection between two ways, two spirits (kings) and two kingdoms can finally be perceived. Here the acts of the itinerant apostle Peter are described. In one of his discourses (*Hom.* XX, 2) Peter says not only that God has instituted two kingdoms (basileiai), but also that there are two ways (hodoi) and two kings (basileis). The same idea of two ways, two kings and/or two kingdoms can be found in many other passages of the *Pseudo-Clementines*. But before discussing some of them, we need to make a few general comments on these remarkable and—particularly as regards their sources—still mysterious writings.

The *Pseudo-Clementines* have, for the most part, come down to us in two forms: 20 Greek *Homiliae* (H) and 10 books of *Recognitiones* (R) in the Latin version of Rufinus, a contemporary of Jerome. They describe Peter's wanderings in Palestine and Syria and his struggle with Simon Magus. Connected with this is an account of the life of Clement of Rome, who has gone on a journey in search of truth and meets Peter. It has been established that earlier writings were incorporated into these, but there is a great deal of disagreement regarding their size and dates[743]. Probably both H and R were based independently of each other on a common *Grundschrift* (G), which may have originated in Syria or Transjordan in the first half of the third century[744]. It is generally assumed that the author of this *Grundschrift* was of Jewish-Christian descent or was at least influenced by his Jewish-Christian environment[745]. This author, for his part, also made use of earlier material, of which the *Kerygmata Petrou* (KP) are particularly important. Oscar Cullmann, Hans Joachim Schoeps

---

742 See the commentaries, e.g. E. Klostermann, *Das Matthäusevangelium*, Tübingen 1927[2] (*HNT* 4), 68-69; for the 'Zielgedanke' in the metaphor of the way, see esp. E. Repo, *Der 'Weg' als Selbstbezeichnung des Urchristentums*, Helsinki 1964, 189 ff.

743 A clear survey is given by F.S. Jones, 'The Pseudo-Clementines. A History of Research', *The Second Century* 2 (1982) 1-33 and 63-96.

744 This is the view of, among others, H. Waitz (who situated G in Rome, however), O. Cullmann, H.J. Schoeps, G. Strecker. Others (such as C. Schmidt, B. Rehm, J. Irmscher) also recognize the existence of a *Grundschrift*, but are of the opinion that R is based on G and H. Rather recently J. Rius-Camps went back to the other possibility: H is based on R and G. Cf. Jones, 'Pseudo-Clementines', esp. 8-14.

745 E.g. Cullmann, *Problème*, 150-157; Schoeps, *Judenchristentum*, 37-45; cf. Strecker, *Pseudoklementinen*, esp. 259.

and Georg Strecker have shown that these *Kerygmata* go back to a very considerable degree to Jewish-Christian tradition[746]. It is possibly in these sermons by Peter, dating from the second century and also originating in the Syrian-Palestinian milieu[747], that the idea of the two antithetical kingdoms is unfolded[748].

This is not the occasion to go further into the various sources of the *Pseudo-Clementines* (there are a few more in addition to those mentioned), their possible size or dates. The foregoing summarizes the research that has been carried out in the course of many years, and presents a few views that can claim a broad consensus. However, these views have not been corroborated and, for example, on the question of which parts of the *Homiliae* or the *Recognitiones* can be attributed to the *Grundschrift* or the *Kerygmata* the opinions are divergent. To a certain extent scholars agree that the *Kerygmata Petrou*, or at any rate the *Grundschrift*, contained the idea of the two kingdoms. Thus it is supposed that this idea came into existence very early and belonged to Jewish-Christian tradition.

However, these opinions need not be the basis of this study. Rather than the uncertain road of source analysis, preference is given to an examination of the texts in their present state[749].

---

746 Cullmann, *Problème*, 98 et al.; Schoeps, *Judenchristenum*, 45 ff. et al.; Strecker, *Pseudoklementinen*, esp. 213-220.

747 Cullmann, *Problème*, 98 (early 2nd cent., Trans-Jordan); Schoeps, *Judenchristentum*, 53-56 (c. 160-190, border region Palestine and Syria); Strecker, *Pseudoklementinen*, 219 (c. 200; Syria, possibly near Beroea); cf. Strecker, 'Die Kerygmata Petrou', in: Hennecke and Schneemelcher, *NTAp*, II, 68-69.

748 Cullmann, *Problème*, 86; Schoeps, *Frühchr. Zeit*, 48: 'Diese Lehre von den beiden Reichen hat zweifellos in G. gestanden'; 48 n. 2: 'Sie dürfte dem 6. Buch K.P. entstammen'; likewise Schoeps, 'Der Ursprung des Bösen und das Problem der Theodizee im pseudoklementinischen Roman', *RSR* 60 (1972) 133: 'Diese Lehre von den beiden Reichen dürfte einer ebionitischen Quelle der Grundschrift entstammen ...'. Cf. Strecker, *Pseudoklementinen*, 159: 'Die Ähnlichkeit zwischen der Zweiäonenlehre der *KP* und der Theorie von den beiden Reichen, wie sie in der Grundschrift nachzuweisen ist (...), könnte die Vermutung nahelegen, dass beides schon in den Kerygmen miteinander verbunden war.' Opposing Strecker's attempt (*Pseudoklementinen*, 159-160) to differentiate between the doctrine of the two kingdoms and the doctrine of the two aeons is Schoeps, 'Ursprung des Bösen', 133 n. 7: 'Das scheint mir weder sachlich möglich noch terminologisch durchführbar. Die Vorstellungen schillern zu sehr und gehen, wie auch die Qumranschriften zeigen, oft in einander über. Allzu grosser Scharfsinn ist dieser ganzen Gedankenwelt gegenüber unangebracht'. For criticism of Strecker's view, see also H. Braun, *Qumran und das Neue Testament*, II, Tübingen 1966, 216.

749 It is almost generally assumed that H and R in their present form were composed in the course of the 4th cent., at any rate before 381. H is quoted according

Similarity with the Jewish and Christian writings that were discussed earlier will appear in more than one respect and also in a wider context than has been seen until now by the various investigators.

In *Hom.* XX, 2 Peter gives an exposition. He teaches 'the truth concerning the harmony of evil'. God established two kingdoms (basileiai) and two ages (aiōnes). He gave the present world (kosmos) to the Evil One because it is small and of short duration; the age (aiōn) to come is for the Good One because it is great and eternal. After discussing free will and the fact that man consists of two kinds of 'dough' (phyrama), female and male, Peter mentions the two ways: there is the way of the law (nomos) and that of lawlessness (anomia)[750]. Moreover, two kingdoms (basileiai) have been established, the kingdom of heaven and the kingdom of those who now rule over the earth. There are also two kings (basileis), one who rules according to the law of the present transitory world, the other the king of the future age. The rest of the homily contains, among other things, a description of the work of the good king and that of the evil one; they were both appointed by God, 'the swift hands of God' (*Hom.* XX, 3).

There is a direct connection in this exposition between the two kingdoms, the two ways and the two kings. Nowhere else in the *Pseudo-Clementines* does this happen as explicitly as in *Hom.* XX, 2. But the idea of the two ways connected with the two kings is also found (e.g. in *Rec.* VIII, 54; *Hom.* VII, 3 and 7), and one often reads about the two kingdoms and/or the two kings (e.g. in *Hom.* III, 19; VIII, 21-22; XV, 6-7 and 9; *Rec.* I, 24; II, 24; III, 52; V, 9; VIII, 52-55; IX, 4). It goes without saying that the idea of two kings implies at the same time the existence of two kingdoms (and the concept of the two kingdoms that of the two kings). But special attention should be given to the framework in which the *Pseudo-Clementines* generally refer to the two kingdoms, kings and ways.

Let us first consider *Hom.* VII, 1-5. Peter addresses the inhabitants of Tyre. He gives an exposition about the two kings (rulers)

---

to the edition of B. Rehm – J. Irmscher – F. Paschke, *Die Pseudoklementinen, I, Homilien*, Berlin 1969 (*GCS* 42²); R according to the edition of B. Rehm – F. Paschke, *Die Pseudoklementinen, II, Rekognitionen in Rufins Übersetzung*, Berlin 1965 (*GCS* 51).

750 Braun, *Qumran*, II, 216, points to the parallelism with, on the one hand, 1 *QS* 5, 7 and 1 *QS* 8, 14 f., and on the other hand 1 *QS* 4, 9-11.

who have been appointed by God, the Creator of everything (VII, 3). Then he mentions a number of precepts and commandments, which concur by and large with the decisions of the apostolic council in *Acts* 15[751] (VII, 4). After baptism has been administered (VII, 5) Peter goes to Sidon (VII, 6). Here he teaches according to the scheme of the two ways: the wide and the narrow way over which unbelief (apistia) and belief (pistis) have dominion (VII, 7). After that he gives, again parallel to *Acts* 15, a series of precepts (VII, 8).

This framework containing on the one hand the two rulers (and thus by implication their two kingdoms) and on the other the two ways is without a doubt catechetical. After Peter's exposition the inhabitants of Tyre are baptized and—although it is not said in so many words—this also happens at Sidon, for people become believers there and Peter is able to establish a congregation in that town (VII, 8). It should be noted that instruction according to the scheme of the two ways and instruction about the two kings (and their kingdoms) are apparently equivalent: they function in the same way in the catechesis.

It is this catechetical framework that stands out each time the two ways, the two kings and/or the two kingdoms are discussed in the *Pseudo-Clementines*. In the aforementioned *Hom.* XX, 2 and *Hom.* VII, 1-8 this catechetical framework is apparent. The same is true of *Rec.* I, 24; III, 52; V, 9. Peter teaches about the two kingdoms, the two kings and/or the two ways, either in the form of initial instruction or as further teaching for people in the circle around him. Moreover, in *Rec.* VIII, 54-55 it is Aquila who acquits himself of this task and in *Rec.* IX, 4 Clement himself does so. In both instances it involves individual instruction for an old man, Clement's father, and in the end his baptism can also be reported (*Rec.* X, 72).

Thus the doctrine of the two kingdoms occurs in the *Pseudo-Clementines* in a special way. On the one hand there is the connection with the two ways, on the other the catechetical framework. It is true that the two kingdoms are not always mentioned in a clearly catechetical context, for the instruction rather often assumes the character of a more theoretical and philosophical treatise (as in *Hom.* III, 19 and VIII, 21-22 on the two kings; *Hom.* XV, 6 ff. on the two

---

[751] Cf. E. Molland, 'La circoncision, le baptême et l'autorité du décret apostolique (Actes XV, 28 sq.) dans les milieux judéo-chrétiens des Pseudo-Clémentines', *ST* 9 (1955) 1-39, esp. 27-29.

kings and the two kingdoms; *Rec.* II, 52 on the two kinds of people, each under its king). But in some instances the role of the doctrine of the two kingdoms as a central element in the catechesis is clear. One may wonder to what extent this was already the case in the earliest sources, the *Grundschrift* or even the *Kerygmata Petrou*. A text that may be important in this respect is *Hom.* XVII, 7, which, according to Cullmann and Schoeps, is part of the *Kerygmata Petrou*[752]. It states that the apostles were sent to the uninstructed heathens to baptize them after they had first taught them (proteron didaxai autous). On the basis of the assertion by Cullmann and Schoeps that perhaps in these *Kerygmata*, or at any rate in the *Grundschrift*, the idea of the two kingdoms was expounded[753], it may be concluded that in the *Kerygmata* or even the *Grundschrift* the doctrine of the two kingdoms had a function in the catechesis.

This, however, is not absolutely certain. The sources of the *Pseudo-Clementines* are 'potenziert verschollen', and an exact analysis of them is—at least in the present circumstances—'hoffnungslos'[754]. We read these writings in the form in which they are now available. We then ascertain that the doctrine of the two kingdoms functions as a central element in the catechetical instruction, and we also see a wider context. This is clearly the case in *Rec.* I, 24, in which the exposition of the two kingdoms is situated within the framework of a catechesis on the history of salvation. This instruction is also called *narratio* and there is a certain order in the historical narrative, an *ordo narrandi*[755]. Clement was first taught by Peter about history, from the beginning of creation until the time that he came to Peter at Caesarea (I, 22: '... ab initio creaturae usque ad id temporis, quo ad eum Caesaream devolutus sum'). Then Clement reproduces the main points of this catechesis in accordance with the sequence of Peter's exposition (ordo disputationis tuae; I, 23). First he discusses eternity; then the creation of the world and mankind. Next God's law and God's institution of the two kingdoms (regna), the kingdom of the present age and that of the age to

---

[752] Cullmann, *Problème*, 85, following Waitz; Schoeps, *Judenchristentum*, 51, 53 et al.

[753] Cf. p. 335, also for Strecker's view.

[754] This was Schoeps' opinion later, given in his review of Strecker's book 'Das Judenchristentum in den Pseudoklementinen', *ZRGG* 11 (1959) 72-77 (quotations 73).

[755] *Rec.* I, 22 (narratio) and I, 25 (narrandi ordo); cf. *Rec.* I, 23; III, 51; IX, 37 et al.

come, are dealt with. For each of the kingdoms the time is fixed. In the end judgement will be pronounced: the wicked will go to the eternal fire; those who have lived in accordance with God's will are to be ushered into eternal life.

In summary, this catechesis deals with eternity and creation, the existence of the two kingdoms, the judgement. All this brings to mind the main features of Augustine's model catechesis and of the *City of God* as well. This similarity appears more remarkable when it is observed that shortly after giving his instruction, Peter repeated it himself (I, 26: '... repetamus quae dicta sunt, et confirmemus ea in corde tuo') by means of a detailed presentation of the *Heilsgeschichte* from the creation until his own day (I, 27-74)[756]. Apparently this was all part of the instruction necessary for an interested pagan like Clement.

In many respects the catechetical expositions in the *Pseudo-Clementines* are similar to the instruction given in Qumran, the *Didache, Barnabas* and the *Doctrina apostolorum*. But is there an even closer kinship between these and other catecheses of the Early Church, particularly those of Augustine? And if these catecheses discuss the concept of the two kingdoms or cities, in what way?

A full exposition of the early-Christian catechesis need not be given here[757]. Only a few main features deserve attention. A clear distinction should be made between the teaching just described and the catechetical instruction in the works of e.g. Cyril of Jerusalem, Theodore of Mopsuestia, Chrysostom and Ambrose. Cyril provided special catecheses for those who were already catechumens and had now applied for baptism: a procatechesis to introduce the subsequent eighteen discourses addressed to the candidates for baptism (of which the last thirteen give an exposition of the Creed) and then, after baptism, five mystagogical catecheses to initiate the neophytes into the significance of the sacraments and the liturgy of mass. The catecheses of Theodore of Mopsuestia are similar: ten explain the

---

[756] According to Cullmann, *Problème*, e.g. 82 n. 3 and 90, and Schoeps, *Judenchristentum*, esp. 51-52, almost the whole passage belongs to the *KP*. A. Hilgenfeld, too, seems to have attributed nearly the entire passage to an earlier source (Kerygma Petrou). Strecker, *Pseudoklementinen*, esp. 221-254, traces *Rec.* I, 33-71 largely to the 'AJ II-Quelle' (Anabathmoi Jakobou), a source from the 2nd half of the 2nd cent. which contained 'ein ursprünglicheres Judenchristentum als die *KP*' (254 n. 1).

[757] For various data, see p. 175 ff. (p. 176 n. 71 for the most important bibliographical data). Some of those facts will reappear here.

Creed, one concerns the Lord's Prayer, while five mystagogical catecheses expound the significance of baptism, anointment and the eucharist. The catecheses of John Chrysostom are also discourses delivered immediately before and after baptism; in the same way Ambrose's catechetical writings discuss the significance of baptism, anointment, the eucharist and the Creed. A considerable number of such discourses by Augustine have also come down to us.

Thus form and content of this genre of baptismal catechesis are sufficiently known. But it is not this instruction for baptismal candidates and the newly-baptized that requires further attention now. The early-Christian catechumenate—certainly in the fourth and fifth centuries—consisted of various stages. Besides the *competentes*, those who had applied for baptism at the beginning of Lent and who from that time onwards had received separate instruction (after baptism, which usually took place at Easter, they were called *infantes* or *neophyti*, 'newborn children'), there were the ordinary catechumens. It cannot be said with certainty whether the latter received separate and regular instruction[758]. In the fourth and the fifth centuries the adult catechumens attended the first part of the church service, hearing the lessons and the sermon and praying with the others, but they were sent away at the end of the *missa catechumenorum*[759]; small children received their instruction at home[760]. So it was only at the beginning of the catechumenate—as well as immediately before and after baptism—that special instruction took place. It was given to the *accedentes* or *rudes*, the newcomers.

This introductory catechesis is best known from Augustine's *The Catechizing of the Uninstructed*, whose contents have already been discussed in detail[761]. The central elements of this catechesis are the *narratio* of the *Heilsgeschichte* as the history of the two cities, the exhortations and the precepts (praecepta). Are these and other elements found elsewhere, too? To answer this question, a comparison with the previously discussed catechetical expositions is most important.

---

758 Mayer, *Katechumenat*, 289, states this, but on the basis of an incorrect interpretation of *De cat. rud.* 16. Reference can be made, on the other hand, to Hippolytus, *Trad. Ap.*, 16-19: *doctores* regularly gave catechetical instruction. Cf. also Cyprian, *Ep.* 29: *doctores audientium*.

759 Cf. Busch, 'Initiatio', 425-426.

760 For A. see pp. 25-30. That this home tuition—particularly by women—had a great influence, can also be seen in the lives of Basil the Great, Gregory of Nyssa, John Chrysostom, Ambrose.

761 See pp. 180-186.

For it should be clear that these catechetical expositions are to be regarded as instructions to 'newcomers' rather than catecheses for *competentes* and *neophyti*[762]. In the Qumran texts, the *Didache*, the *Doctrina apostolorum* and the *Pseudo-Clementines* the purpose was to provide an introduction to the doctrine and morals of the Jewish or Christian community; *Barnabas* is reminiscent of this instruction. These writings do not give an explanation of the Creed, the Lords' Prayer or the meaning of the sacraments.

Let us first look at the *narratio*. Elements of it are to be found in Qumran: 1 *QS* 3, 13 – 4, 26 speaks of the creation, history and struggle, and eschatology. It is more clearly present in the *Pseudo-Clementines* (*Rec.* I, 24 ff.), where the *narratio* also refers more explicitly to the existence of the two kingdoms. That the *narratio* of the *Heilsgeschichte* is part of the introductory catechesis is evident from the precepts in the *Apostolic Constitutions*[763]. But the clearest occurence of the *narratio*, the one most similar to Augustine's, is the *narratio* in Irenaeus' *Epideixis* or *Demonstratio praedicationis apostolicae*.

This work requires some special attention. Until 1904 no more was known about Irenaeus' *Demonstratio* than its title (Eusebius, *HE* V, 26); in 1904 the entire text was discovered in an Armenian version[764]. It is addressed to a certain Marcianus and reminds him of the instruction he has received[765]. As he states in his introduction, Irenaeus wants first of all to give an exposition of the truth; after that he will provide evidence to substantiate it. The first part of his work tells about God and the creation of the world; paradise with Adam and Eve; the Fall; the dominion of evil in the world; the

[762] Of course one may question whether the last-mentioned types of catechesis were known at the time *Did.*, *Barn.* and *Doctr.* were composed. It is not likely. However, separate catecheses for *competentes* are spoken of in the *Ps. Clem.*, *Rec.* III, 67.

[763] *CA* VII, 39. What is prescribed here applied first of all to the 'novices', the *accedentes*; see esp. VII, 39, 4: 'Tauta kai ta toutois akoloutha manthanetō en tèi katèchèsei ho prosiōn', correctly translated by F.X. Funk, *Didascalia et Constitutiones apostolorum*, I, Paderbornae 1905, 443 as: 'Haec et his consentanea discat in catechesi, qui *accedit*'. This is followed by a new passage dealing with the catechesis immediately prior to baptism. Cf. also Holzmann, 'Katechese', 106.

[764] We will follow the French translation with introduction and notes by L.M. Froidevaux, *Irénée de Lyon, Démonstration de la Prédication apostolique*, Paris 1959 (*SC* 62).

[765] *Dem.* 1: '... et, par le moyen d'un abrégé, t'exposer la prédication de la vérité, afin d'affermir ta foi.' Etc. Several statements in *Dem.* 1 and 3 bear witness to the fact that Marcianus was a baptized Christian.

Flood; Noah and his sons; the building of the tower and the confusion of tongues; Abraham and his descendants; Egypt and the exodus; Moses and the giving of the law; the entry into the promised land; the era of the kings and the prophets; the incarnation, the suffering, the resurrection of Christ; the descent of the Holy Spirit and the spreading of the gospel (*Dem.* 2-41). The second part gives in particular evidence for the truth of the Christian revelation from the prophecies of the Old Testament and presents Jesus as the Son of David and the Messiah (*Dem.* 42-97). The author closes with an exhortation to live in accordance with this preaching and he warns against heresy (*Dem.* 98-100).

Paul Drews was correct when, already in 1907, he pointed out that this work is a catechesis[766]. Irenaeus repeats for his pupil Marcianus the instruction he gave earlier. Moreover, his catechetical scheme is in accordance with the precepts for giving catechesis in the *Constitutiones apostolorum* (VIII, 39) as well as with the structure of the longer model catechesis in *The Catechizing of the Uninstructed*[767]. True, Augustine emphasizes slightly different aspects in his *narratio*. For the fact that Irenaeus makes direct connections between the various typological explanations and the *narratio* we can only admire his deeper pedagogical insights[768].

Thus the *narratio* is a basic element of the early-Christian introductory catechesis. The narrative expounds the history of salvation and the purpose of this exposition is to arouse faith. Granted, the term *narratio* is not a specifically Christian one, but borrowed from classical rhetoric[769]. Not only Augustine and Deogratias[770] were familiar with it; Rufinus also used it in his version of the *Pseudo-Clementines* in a catechetical meaning[771]. The word *narratio* accurate-

---

766 P. Drews, 'Der literarische Charakter der neuentdeckten Schrift des Irenäus *Zum Erweise der apostolischen Verkündigung*', *ZNW* 8 (1907) 226-233.

767 For the *CA*, cf. Drews, 'Charakter', 226-230; 230-231 esp. for *De cat. rud.*.

768 Cf. J. Daniélou, 'L'histoire du salut dans la catéchèse', *MD* 30 (1952) 24.

769 Broadly speaking, the order of the *partes orationis* was: *exordium, narratio, probatio, refutatio, peroratio*. Cf. H. Hommel, 'Rhetorik', *Lexikon der Antike* 4, München 1975², 127-143, esp. 140-141.

770 *De cat. rud.* 1 and 4. Deogratias was familiar with the concept *narratio*, but his problem was the *modus narrationis*: in what way should the story be told and should it be followed by an exhortation, or does it suffice to lay down the precepts (praecepta)?

771 Cf. p. 338 f.

ly indicates the essence of the introductory catechesis. The Christian faith is a historical faith and the facts and events of the *Heilsgeschichte* must be expounded. There is a history with God and one without God, a history of salvation and one of sin. Both the *Pseudo-Clementines* and Augustine demonstrate how the idea of the two kingdoms or cities can have its natural place in the *narratio*.

Besides the *narratio*, Augustine's catechesis contains the *exhortatio* and the precepts as its practical applications. Were these elements also present in earlier catecheses and can they, too, be connected with the idea of the two *civitates*? It is noteworthy that various scholars have mentioned the *Didache* or the idea of the two ways in general as a possible source of *The Catechizing of the Uninstructed*[772]. But they have never provided any evidence to support this. They apparently assumed that prior to Augustine the doctrine of the two ways had functioned as an introductory catechesis and that therefore he was probably influenced by it. Christopher supposed that when Deogratias referred to the precepts (praecepta) he may have meant the two ways[773], but he did not believe they played a part in Augustine's catechesis itself. Following Paul Rentschka, Christopher stated that for Augustine the Decalogue was the only valid standard for Christian ethics[774]. And this could be seen in the models he wrote for Deogratias.

Rentschka's view that Augustine composed special Decalogue-catecheses has been sharply criticized, and rightly so[775]. There is no reason to presume that the precepts in Augustine's model catecheses were especially given according to the Decalogue. On the contrary, it can be demonstrated—without denying that Augustine recognized the importance of the Decalogue as a standard for the Christian[776]—that precisely in his introductory catechesis elements of the doctrine of the two ways are *probably* present.

What can be noted first in *De catechizandis rudibus* are the refer-

---

772 Combès and Farges, *BA* 11, 10, and also Christopher, *Cat. Instruction*, 7. Cf. the similarly superficial assertions of Cordovani, 'Due città', 444.

773 Christopher, *Cat. Instruction*, 95 n. 10.

774 Christopher, *Cat. Instruction*, 5-6; P. Rentschka, *Die Dekalogkatechese des hl. Augustinus. Ein Beitrag zur Geschichte des Dekalogs*, Kempten 1905, esp. 108.

775 Already by F.X. Eggersdorfer, *Der heilige Augustinus als Pädagoge und seine Bedeutung für die Geschichte der Bildung*, Freiburg i. Br. 1907, esp. 168; Busch, 'Initiatio', 446 and 471.

776 E.g. *C. Faust.* XII, 14; *De fide et op.* XI, 17 and esp. *s.* 9, A.'s most comprehensive exposition of the Decalogue.

ences to 'the way' (via). Augustine states that it is our task to see that the one who hears us 'enters upon the way of Christ with eagerness' (*De cat. rud.* 11: '... et viam Christi alacriter ingredi ...'); we as catechetes point out the way and lead along the paths of peace (17: '... demonstramus viam ... per itinera pacis ... deducimus'); Christ wanted to show the way of humility and He made himself the way to heaven for us (40: '... humilitatis ostendebat viam, qui se ipsum nobis viam fecit in coelum ...'); there are those who already walk the straight way (48: '... qui iam rectam viam tenent ...'); the pupil must not deviate from the right way (49: '... nec a bona via deviaveris ...'). These examples are not striking in themselves. But they take on a new perspective, at least to a certain degree, when they are examined more closely. In his *Demonstratio* Irenaeus also referred several times to 'the way'[777], and this may very possibly be reminiscent of the image of the two ways at the beginning of his work[778]. In the *Pseudo-Clementines* this happens too: besides the passages about the two ways that have been named, other passages in these writings mention 'the way' distinctly[779]. Thus reminiscences of the doctrine of the two ways may also be seen in *The Catechizing of the Uninstructed*.

But there is more. Augustine counselled Deogratias to warn the

---

[777] E.g. *Dem.* 6: 'la voie de la justice'; *Dem.* 41: the apostles show the pagans 'le chemin de la vie, pour les détourner des idoles, de la fornication et de l'avarice ...'; *Dem.* 89: '... le Verbe qui a préparé la voie nouvelle, la voie de la piété et de la justice ...'; *Dem.* 98: '... tel est le chemin de la vie ...'.

[778] *Dem.* 1 : 'Car, pour tous ceux qui voient, il n'y a qu'un chemin—et ascendant—qu'illumine la lumière céleste; mais, pour ceux qui ne voient pas, il y a beaucoup de chemins enténébrés et qui vont en sens opposé. Celui-là conduit au royaume des cieux en unissant l'homme à Dieu, mais ceux-ci font descendre à la mort, en séparant l'homme de Dieu'. Etc. Cf. Froidevaux's remark, 28 n. 7. In this context the first sentence of the work might become especially significant if—by analogy with *Dem.* 89—the word 'chose' is replaced by 'voie': 'Connaissant, mon cher Marcianus, ton empressement à marcher dans la piété—la seule [voie?] qui conduise l'homme à la vie éternelle—...'.

[779] See e.g. Peter's address before a large crowd in *Rec.* II, 20 ff. (which, according to Schoeps, *Judenchristentum*, 52, belonged to the *KP*; cf. Cullmann, *Problème*, 91). Here the true way to the kingdom of God is an important theme. Through good works one can reach the kingdom of God, a very large city (*Rec.* II, 21: '... bonis operibus ... ad regnum dei tanquam ad urbem maximam pervenire'). The way to this city is our course of life, the travellers are those who do good works, the gate to this city is the true prophet, the city is the kingdom (II, 22: '... viam esse hunc vitae nostrum cursum, viatores eos, qui bona opera gerunt, portam verum prophetam, de quo dicimus, urbem regnum esse ...'). This way is also called the way of God and the way of peace (II, 25), the way of salvation (II, 31), etc.

pupil against the wicked men outside the Church and especially against the hypocrites within it. Then he should give the precepts (praecepta) for a Christian and upright manner of life (conversatio). Following this the pupil ought to be urged to associate with those who are good: 'The prospect should be held out to him that he will find many good Christians in the Church, most true citizens of the heavenly Jerusalem ...'. This will all result in the pupil's making progress and walking the way of Christ with eagerness (*De cat. rud.* 11). In the practical example these main elements are repeated: beware of the wicked people outside the Church and particularly of the hypocrites within it; those who take the straight way are put to the test; observe the precepts (praecepta); associate with those who are good; one who does not stray from the right way will receive a greater reward (*De cat. rud.* 48-49).

A comparison of the content and sequence of this work with the content and sequence of the *Didache* and especially with the *Doctrina apostolorum*[780] brings important similarities to light: the pupil is warned of wicked people and hypocrites[781]; he is given precepts that apply to the way of life[782]; he is admonished to associate with those who are good[783]. Particularly in the catalogue of precepts a relationship can be discerned with the doctrine of the two ways. For it is not in accordance with the Decalogue[784], but rather with the mutually differing catalogues of the doctrine of the two ways that Augustine gives his enumeration[785]. There is perhaps substantiation for this in a sermon for newly baptized Christians, in which Augustine also gives an admonition to avoid those who are wicked, to associate with those who are good, and to take the straight and

---

780 Especially the Latin *Doctr.* in view of its origin (Africa?) and dissemination.

781 *Doctr.* 3, 1: 'Fili, fuge ab homine malo et homine simulatore'.

782 *Doctr.* 3, 2 ff.

783 *Doctr.* 3, 9: '... sed cum iustis humilibusque conversaberis'; 4, 2: 'Require autem facies sanctorum, ut te reficias verbis illorum.'

784 Cf. Rentschka, *Dekalogkatechese*, 111: 'So hat Augustin dem Dekalog schon bei der Aufnahmskatechese die zentrale Stellung in der Sittenunterweisung gegeben'; 'In der exhortatio bringt dann der hl. Kirchenlehrer die zehn Gebote mehr unauffällig [NB!] zur Geltung.'

785 *De cat. rud.* 11: '... simul etiam praecepta breviter et decenter commemorentur christianae atque honestae conversationis, ne ab ebriosis, avaris, fraudatoribus, aleatoribus, adulteris, fornicatoribus, spectaculorum amatoribus, remediorum sacrilegorum alligatoribus, praecantatoribus, mathematicis, vel quarumlibet artium vanarum et malarum divinatoribus, atque huiusmodi caeteris ita facile seducatur ...'; cf. 48. This is not the only instance of only one of the two ways being described; cf. Rordorf and Tuilier, *Doctrine*, 26 and 119.

narrow way[786]. Given all these similarities it certainly cannot be ruled out that Augustine was acquainted with the *Doctrina apostolorum* or another version of the doctrine of the two ways. Possible traces of the *Doctrina* and/or *Didache* in the work of predecessors of Augustine in Africa have already been pointed out by other investigators[787].

Thus in its essential elements Augustine's catechesis shows agreement with earlier catecheses. So far we have discerned the idea of the two kingdoms (more or less clearly in 1 *QS*; explicitly in the *Pseudo-Clementines*) and the *narratio* of the *Heilsgeschichte* (in a rudimentary form in 1 *QS*; fully developed in Irenaeus and in the *Pseudo-Clementines*; as a precept in the *Constitutiones apostolorum*). Moreover, in the catechetical tradition prior to Augustine instruction was given about the two ways (in a basic outline in 1 *QS*; most clearly in *Didache*, *Barnabas* and *Doctrina apostolorum*). We have also seen that this doctrine of the two ways is connected with the concept of the two spirits, angels or kings (1 *QS, Barnabas, Doctrina* and *Pseudo-Clementines*) and thus with the existence of the two societies or kingdoms (the latter most explicitly in 1 *QS* and the *Pseudo-Clementines*). Associated with the antithetical spirits, angels and kings are the two absolutely different groups of people who walk on the opposite ways. The ways of these groups of people and their leaders are described in terms of ethical behaviour. Already in the writings from Qumran it appears that the signs by which each person's spirit can be recognized are his works (1 *QS* 3, 14); the ways of the spirits and their followers are presented in the form of catalogues of virtues (1 *QS* 4, 26) and vices (1 *QS* 4, 9-11).

Considering that in the earlier tradition—particularly in the

---

[786] *S.* 224, 1: 'Quia ergo membra Christi facti estis, admoneo vos: timeo vobis, non tantum a Paganis, non tantum a Judaeis, non tantum ab haereticis, quantum a malis Catholicis. Eligite vobis in populo Dei quos imitemini. Nam si turbam imitari volueritis, inter paucos angustam viam ambulantes non eritis. Abstinete vos a fornicatione, a rapinis, a fraudibus, a perjuriis, ab illicitis rebus, a jurgiis: ebrietas repellatur a vobis: adulterium sic timete quomodo mortem ...'. Even in the small details (the naming of pagans, Jews, heretics, resp.; the reference to the mass) this passage concurs with *De cat. rud.* 11 and 48.

[787] Cf. the various—partly contradictory—remarks of Gebhardt, 'Fragment', 282-286; F.X. Funk, 'Die Didache in der afrikanischen Kirche', *ThQ* 76 (1894) 601-604; Schlecht, *Doctrina*, 10, 67-68; H. Koch, 'Die Didache bei Cyprian?', *ZNW* 8 (1907) 69-70; B. Altaner, 'Die lateinische Doctrina Apostolorum und die griechische Grundschrift der Didache', *Schriften*, 335-342; Rordorf and Tuilier, *Doctrine*, esp. 15 n. 1, 33, 80.

catechesis—the two ways, the two spirits (angels, kings) and the two kingdoms were so closely connected, one may logically ask whether this is not the case in the works of Augustine too. From the expositions we have already given[788], it is clear that the two antithetical cities, the earthly and the heavenly *civitas*, are connected with God and the devil as their rulers. It should be recalled that by the two cities Augustine means already existing societies of good and evil angels respectively. The two *civitates* are ethically defined: two kinds of love founded two cities[789]; the love of God founds Jerusalem, the love of the world Babylon[790]. In other passages the virtues and vices of the people belonging to the two different cities and their kings are also recorded in detail[791]. One is reminded of the catalogues of virtues and vices of the people who walk on the two different ways.

But it should be observed that Augustine himself did not explicitly connect the existence of the two *civitates* with that of the two ways[792]. He did mention, in *The Catechizing of the Uninstructed* and elsewhere, the theme of the way and the two ways remarkably often. Here, too, one gets the impression that these words in many cases have a wider meaning than they do in *Matt.* 7:13-14 or in other scrip-

---

788 Cf., for example, p. 115 ff.

789 *DCD* XIV, 28 (see p. 68-69); *De Gen. ad litt.* XI, 15, 20: 'Hi duo amores—quorum alter sanctus est, alter inmundus, alter socialis, alter privatus, alter communi utilitati consulens propter supernam societatem, alter etiam rem cummunem in potestatem propriam redigens propter adrogantem dominationem, alter subditus, alter aemulus Deo, alter tranquillus, alter turbulentus, alter pacificus, alter seditiosus, alter veritatem laudibus errantium praeferens, alter quoquo modo laudis avidus, alter amicalis, alter invidus, alter hoc volens proximo quod sibi, alter subicere proximum sibi, alter propter proximi utilitatem regens proximum, alter propter suam—praecesserunt in angelis, alter in bonis, alter in malis, et distinxerunt conditas in genere humano civitates duas (...) alteram iustorum, alteram iniquorum.'

790 *En. in Ps.* 64,2: 'Duas istas civitates faciunt duo amores; Ierusalem facit amor Dei; Babyloniąm facit amor saeculi.'

791 E.g. *En. in Ps.* 61, 6: 'Omnes qui terrena sapiunt, omnes qui felicitatem terenam Deo praeferunt, omnes qui sua quaerunt, non quae Iesu Christi, ad unam illam civitatem pertinent, quae dicitur Babylonia mystice, et habet regem diabolum. Omnes autem qui ea quae sursum sunt sapiunt, qui caelestia meditantur, qui cum sollicitudine in saeculo vivunt ne Deum offendant, qui cavent peccare, quos peccantes non pudet confiteri, humiles, mites, sancti, iusti, pii, boni; omnes ad unam civitatem pertinent, quae regem habet Christum.'

792 That the (good) way leads to the city of God or the homeland (patria) is in this context certainly important. See e.g. *En. in Ps.* 106, 4. 9 and 14; 125, 2 and 4; 134, 26. But the more comprehensive doctrine of the two cities that already exist and are ethically determined is not explicitly spoken of, nor is there a clear reference to *two* ways and *two* cities.

tural passages[793]. It is almost certain that Augustine was aware of a more comprehensive doctrine of the two ways, but, in contrast to his predecessors, did not explicitly connect it in his catechesis or elsewhere with the idea of the two spirits, kings or kingdoms. Only the two *civitates*, composed of the two antithetical kings and the two antithetical kinds of people with their virtues or vices, are prominent in his work.

Yet it is not only in the catechetical tradition prior to Augustine that the two ways, spirits and kingdoms are connected with each other. This is also the case with authors of a later period who were more or less akin to Augustine and inspired by him. One of these is Caesarius, bishop of Arles from 502 to 504, and so much influenced by Augustine that for centuries many of his sermons were passed on under Augustine's name[794]. Caesarius' sermons 149 and 150[795] confirm that he used the image of the two ways in a broader sense than he could have found in Scripture (e.g. *Matt.* 7:13-14; *Deut.* 30:19). Caesarius says that Christ is at the head of the narrow way, the devil at the head of the broad way. Christ invites us to go to heaven (the kingdom, paradise, our native country); the devil leads one to hell[796]. Belonging to the two ways and their 'spirits' are the people who go on these ways; their virtues and vices are listed in catalogues[797]. In another sermon delivered by Caesarius while

---

[793] E.g. *s.* 224, 1: 'Nam si turbam imitari volueritis, inter paucos angustam viam ambulantes non eritis. Abstinete vos a fornicatione, a rapinis, a fraudibus, a perjuriis, ab illicitis rebus, a jurgiis ...'; *En. in Ps.* 48, *s.* II, 4: 'Sed qui male agunt, et viam saeculi eligunt, mors pastor est eius; qui autem eligunt viam Dei, vita pastor est eius.' A little further on it appears that these two *pastores* are identified as the devil and Christ.

[794] Only rather recently Caesarius' sermons, to a considerable degree from the *sermones dubii* and *suppositii* of A., were collected and published by G. Morin (Maredsous 1937). We quote the reprint of this edition in *CCL* 103-104.

[795] Handed down earlier as *sermones suppositii* of A.; cf. *MPL* 39, 1873-1877.

[796] E.g. *s.* 149, 2: 'Viae enim artae et angustae praesidet Christus, viae latae et spatiosae praeest diabolus: ille invitat ad regnum, ille sollicitat ad infernum: ille elevat in altum, ille deprimit in profundum'.

[797] *S.* 150, 3: 'Sed forte aliquis dicit: Vellem scire qui sint illi qui cum periculoso gaudio per latam descendunt, qui autem sint illi qui per artam et angustam cum labore conscendunt. Omnes enim amatores mundi, superbi, avari, raptores, invidi, ebriosi, et adulteria committentes, stateras dolosas et mensuras duplices habentes, odium in corde servantes, malum pro malo reddentes, spectacula vel cruenta vel furiosa vel turpia diligentes, per latam et spatiosam descendere conprobantur; casti vero et sobrii, misericordes, iustitiam tenentes, secundum vires suas elymosinas prompto et hilari animo facientes, contra nullum hominem odium in corde servantes, per artam at angustam viam ad superna conscendunt.'

travelling around in his diocese (to remind his congregation of the ethical instruction preceding baptism?), he not only mentions the two ways and their 'spirits', but also discusses in detail the two *civitates* and the Christian's peregrination[798].

Several sermons attributed to Boniface are also important[799]. In both of the earlier-mentioned codices in which the *Doctrina apostolorum* occurs, the manuscript from Munich (olim Freising) and that from the renowned Melk monastery[800], the treatise on the two ways is preceded by a sermon by Boniface[801]. This sermon—with some variation[802]—is entitled: 'Admonitio (sancti Petri) sive praedicatio Bonifacii episcopi de abrenuntiatione in baptismate'. It is a discourse delivered during the weeks of Advent, in which Germanic tribes which have recently been converted to Christianity are reminded of their baptismal vows and called upon to lead a pious life. Both the context of the sermon and its content point to a direct relationship with the two ways. A list of sins is given which shows a significant degree of kinship to the *Didache* and the *Doctrina*[803]; just as in those works there is shortly thereafter a reference to the commandment that one should love God and one's neighbour and to the

---

798 *S.* 151, esp. 1, 4 and 5 on the two ways (and their 'spirits', Christ and the devil); 151, 2 on the two cities: 'Duae sunt civitates, fratres carissimi: una est civitas mundi, alia est civitas paradisi. In civitate mundi bonus christianus semper peregrinatur; in civitate paradisi civis esse cognoscitur. Ista est civitas laboriosa, illa quieta; ista misera, illa beata: in ista laboratur, in illa requiescitur: qui in ista male vivit, ad illam pervenire non poterit. Peregrini esse debemus in hoc saeculo, ut cives esse mereamur in caelo'. Etc. Belonging to one city or the other, as well as going on one way or the other, represents ethical behaviour; see also 151, 8. This sermon, too, was handed down as one of the *sermones suppositii* of A.; cf. *MPL* 39, 1877-1879.

799 For an inquiry into their authenticity, see R. Rau (Hrsg.), *Die Briefe des Bonifatius; Willibalds Leben des Bonifatius*, Darmstadt 1968, 373 f.. Bouhot, 'Alcuin', 185-191 rejects their authenticity almost completely; he is of the opinion that the collection of sermons, the work of a compiler, dates from c. 850.

800 Cf. p. 328 n. 717.

801 Re-edited by Schlecht and based on the mss. mentioned and on an ms. from the Vatican (olim Lorsch); see Schlecht, *Doctrina*, 124-126. In *Monac.* 6264 the sermon precedes *Doctr.* directly; in the codex from Melk there are short fragments from A.'s works between the two. Cf. Schlecht, 37 f. and Niederwimmer, 'Doctrina', 269.

802 Schlecht, *Doctrina*, 124; Niederwimmer, 'Doctrina', 269.

803 Schlecht, *Doctrina*, 76 ff., and earlier J. Rendel Harris, *The Teaching of the Apostles*, London-Baltimore 1887, 59-60. Bouhot, 'Alcuin', 186, denies there is such a relationship but offers only one example, to which he makes a well-founded objection.

so-called golden rule[804]. In the other sermons under the name of Boniface too, one is repeatedly reminded of the doctrine of the two ways[805]. There is every reason to believe—and the enumeration of catechetical subjects supports this[806]—that possibly in the days of Boniface, and in any case not much later, the doctrine of the two ways had an important place in the catechesis preceding baptism. In these sermons there are indications of this being so, and precepts are given in accordance with this model. And most significant is the fact that in the eleventh sermon, handed down under the name of Boniface, the two kingdoms are spoken of and again the old ethical truths are enumerated in connection with them[807].

Thus once more the idea of the two kingdoms was connected with the doctrine of the two ways. It is quite possible that in the eighth or ninth century too, in the catechesis that *preceded* baptism, mention was made not only of the two ways and their ethical implications but—whether or not in direct connection with the renunciation of the devil and his evil works and the concluding of the covenant with Christ—also of the two kingdoms. A few centuries later a writer from the abbey of St. Victor in Paris provided more evidence for the fact that the idea of the two *civitates* (referred to as Jerusalem and Babylon), of the two peoples (populi) and of the two kings (reges), was connected with the concept of the two ways (viae)[808]. Furthermore, a certain Werner, abbot of St. Blaise in the Black Forest, mentioned the two *civitates*, Jerusalem and Babylon, the two peoples (populi), the two kings, Christ and the devil, and their ruling the narrow and the broad way[809]. And although examples of such a connection between the ethical doctrine of the two ways and the two cities in the writings of other medieval authors who all were directly or indirectly influenced by Augustine are not numerous[810], men-

---

804 Schlecht, *Doctrina*, 125; *MPL* 89, 870C-D.

805 Cf. Schlecht, *Doctrina*, 79-81.

806 In both codices typically catechetical subjects are dealt with: essentials of ecclesiology, the resurrection, faith, the *abrenuntiatio*, the two ways. Cf. Schlecht, *Doctrina*, 37 f., 40 and 75; Niederwimmer, 'Doctrina', 269.

807 *MPL* 89, 863-864: 'De duobus regnis a Deo statutis'.

808 *Miscellanea* (Appendix ad Hugonis opera dogmatica), *lib.* I, *tit.* 48; *MPL* 177, 496-497A. For the two ways, the two peoples and the two kings, see also *Misc.* I, *tit.* 56; *MPL* 177, 502C.

809 *Deflorationes*, II: 'De duobus dominis, et duabus civitatibus, et diversis aliis rebus', *MPL* 157, 1144 f. For his anthology Werner drew also—and not least—from A.'s writings.

810 Cf. also Hugo of St. Victor, *De fructibus carnis et spiritus*; *MPL* 176, 997-1010.

tion should be made, finally, of the description of the two *civitates* given specifically in terms of ethical behaviour. A sermon handed down under the name of Hildebert of Lavardin describes the two cities in the *mores* of their citizens[811]; and a pupil of the school of St. Bernard saw the spiritual struggle, the conflict between the virtues and the vices, as the struggle between Jerusalem and Babylon[812].

E. Conclusions

The foregoing makes one fact very clear: it is incorrect to follow the example of a number of scholars who have pointed to *one* source as the origin of Augustine's doctrine of the two *civitates*, sometimes to the exclusion of other possibilities. On the contrary, the origin of Augustine's concept turns out to be a complex matter.

Augustine was thoroughly familiar with the Manichaean doctrine of the two kingdoms and, what is more significant, his writings contain many similarities with it. The Manichaeans often referred to the heavenly kingdom and the heavenly city, whose antithesis is the internally divided kingdom of darkness as the kingdom of this world (kosmos), while there is even mention of a city of demons. The heavenly city is a city of angels and people; the believers are on their way to this city and are added to the number of the angels. Moreover, this heavenly city is referred to once as Jerusalem, and its counterpart is possibly Babylon (cf. *Hom.* 14, 9 ff.). In combination with the idea of the two kingdoms, Mani's followers strongly emphasized the believer's state of exile. It should be noted that both for the Manichaeans and for Augustine a doctrine of two kingdoms or *civitates* was connected with a division of history into three times (initium, medium, finis; exortus, excursus, debiti fines). This central doctrine, occurring for instance in Mani's own *Epistula fundamenti* with which Augustine was thoroughly familiar, was even used by the Manichaeans as a catechesis.

The similarities with Augustine are evident. It is true that the church father did not recognize an absolute dualism of two entirely independent and, in respect to substance, entirely different kingdoms which have confronted each other from eternity and which will confront each other again for all eternity. This Manichaean princi-

---

811 *S.* 113; *MPL* 171, 864 ff.
812 *Parabolae* II-III; *MPL* 183, 761-767.

ple was fundamentally at variance with his Catholic Christian belief. On the other hand, the rather strong emphasis Augustine laid on a subordinated dualism most likely indicates that Manichaeism had continued to influence his theology significantly.

It is not without reason that, despite a paucity of textual evidence, some investigators have argued forcefully in favour of Manichaeism as the source of Augustine's doctrine of the two *civitates*. The discovery of the *Cologne Mani-Codex*, however, placed the matter in a new perspective. It does not suffice to point out similarities between Manichaeism and Augustine; there should also be an inquiry into the sources of Mani's religion itself. The recently found codex points clearly to Jewish-Christian influence. This means that various views of Mani and his followers can better be accounted for. It also means that their doctrine of the two kingdoms can be seen in a new light, for it was precisely in Jewish-Christian circles that the idea of two kingdoms was present. The *Pseudo-Clementines* attest to this and Epiphanius, among others, reported that the Ebionites taught that Christ and the devil are kings of two kingdoms (*Pan.* 30, 16, 2). Therefore we ended this part of our inquiry with the provisional conclusion that the large degree of similarity between Augustine and Manichaeism need not be accounted for on the basis of Augustine subconsciously or (and this is very improbable) consciously acquiring Manichaean views. Mani and Augustine may have been influenced by a similar Jewish-Christian source.

As he was with Manichaeism, Augustine was thoroughly familiar with (Neo)Platonism. Little similarity, however, could be discerned between Augustine's concept of two worlds, kingdoms or cities and those in (Neo)Platonism, the Stoa or Philo. In fact, closer examination has brought a number of fundamental differences to light. While Platonists saw a distinction between two worlds, whereby the material world is a representation of the immaterial one and the two are thus related to each other in a positive way, for Augustine the central issue was the absolute antithesis between two *civitates*. The earthly city is not an adumbration of the heavenly one. Nor did Augustine agree in essence with the views about two cities in the Stoa or Philo. His emphasis on the antithesis of the two *civitates* (each of which, moreover, has its own ruler), and his exposition of their origin, progress in history and definitive separation testified to profound differences.

Of the Christian writers prior to Augustine, the first to be examined was the Donatist Tyconius. Many investigators have referred to him as the actual source of Augustine's idea of the two cities. However, due to the very complicated problems surrounding Tyconius' commentary on the *Apocalypse*, great caution must be exercised. At any rate one cannot simply refer to the *Liber regularum*. Yet the conclusion was reached—though partly on other grounds than those of earlier investigators—that it is quite possible and even probable that, in his commentary on the last book of the Bible, Tyconius already spoke of two antithetical *civitates*, Jerusalem and Babylon. Besides, Augustine's use of the words *corpus* and *civitas* turned out to be akin to Tyconius'.

However, to see Tyconius on this basis as the only source is going too far. First it is necessary to ask whether Tyconius himself was not part of some tradition. Nowhere did Augustine say that the doctrine of the two antithetical cities was a speciality of Tyconius. Nor do any relevant passages from the *Apocalypse of John* have a prominent place in Augustine's exposition of the doctrine of the two cities, whereas they probably did in Tyconius' lost commentary and certainly did in the writings of later commentators of the *Apocalypse*. Moreover, Augustine set forth a fully-developed doctrine of the two *civitates*, he described world history as the history of two absolutely antithetical cities, and he stressed that the two societies consist of two kinds of people, angels and kings. One does not find this in the work of Tyconius.

In the Christian, Jewish and Jewish-Christian tradition prior to Augustine, many authors besides Tyconius were found whose writings can be considered important for the church father's doctrine of the two cities. Going back in time we first encountered Ambrose, whose works contain significant parallels. A contradistinction between two *civitates* in a letter to the Christians at Vercellae turned out to be particularly relevant. Moreover, Ambrose spoke of the *terrena civitas* and it may be that this terminology, which Augustine frequently used, can be clearly defined through his writings: *terrenus* denotes belonging to the devil. Yet for Ambrose the idea of two antithetical cities had nowhere near the central position it had for Augustine. Ambrose saw the antithesis above all in man's soul; he spiritualized and individualized. The contradistinction between Jerusalem and Babylon was for him hardly ever a macrocosmic one. Therefore Ambrose, in contrast to Augustine, seldom referred to a historical development. To be sure, the antithesis between the two cities is present in his writings, but it is restricted chiefly to the microcosmic area of individual ethics and is not a constituent element of world history.

Broadly speaking, these summary remarks regarding Ambrose can also be applied to Origen. He, too, referred to a contradistinction between two cities, but he stressed the microcosmic aspect: Jerusalem and Babylon confront each other in man's soul. Neither in the works of Origen, nor in the works of writers who show kinship to him such as Clement of Alexandria, Basil the Great, Gregory of Nazianzus or Gregory of Nyssa, could an elaborate doctrine of two antithetical cities which determine the course of history be found. Apparently no such doctrine occurred in the Greek theology which was influenced strongly by Origen and closely related to Platonism.

An examination of Augustine's predecessor Lactantius brings us to quite a different world. He was moulded to a considerable degree by his rhetorical training and by gnostic-theosophic speculation, but his 'theology' is also characterized by a number of traits that point to authentic Christian sources and even to Jewish heritage. Although Lactantius does not set forth a comprehensive doctrine of two *civitates*, he nevertheless gives a fully-detailed dualistic contradistinction between good and evil, light and darkness, God and devil (each of them with their good angels and evil demons), the two ways, and the two spirits struggling with each other. This antithesis may very well have influenced Augustine. Moreover, Lactantius' major work, the *Divinae institutiones*, shows in both aim and structure a more than superficial likeness to the *City of God*: Lactantius wanted to defend and instruct.

In the works of Lactantius' teacher Arnobius, of Victorinus of Pettau and of Commodian, no explicit reference to an antithesis between two cities or kingdoms was found. Arnobius made much use of rhetoric, but there is in his writing little evidence of profound insight into Christianity. In his interpretation of the *Apocalypse* Victorinus speaks of Jerusalem and Babylon, but he does not give a doctrine of two antithetical cities in the way that Augustine does. Commodian was included in this context because he may provide evidence of archaic elements in African Christianity; he mentioned the idea of two ways, referred to this world as a *civitas* and used the names Jerusalem and Babylon (= Rome).

In the work of Cyprian and Tertullian considerably more similarity with Augustine could be found. Although these predecessors also did not give a detailed exposition of a doctrine of two cities as Augustine did, each of them presented a theology containing some important elements of it. Cyprian's manner of speaking about the world and secular matters was nearly always negative. At baptism the Christian renounced the devil and the world and he was called upon to continue doing so. The believer's peregrination was stressed. Especially when Cyprian discussed the two antithetical army camps, an analogy with Augustine's doctrine of the two *civitates* was discernible: there is the camp of God (castra Dei) and the camp of the devil (castra diaboli).

Generally speaking, the same can be said of the writing of Cyprian's great precursor Tertullian. Here again one finds a negative attitude towards the world and what is worldly, the renunciation at baptism, emphasis on the Christian's peregrination, and the image of the two army camps. Tertullian did not specifically mention an antithesis between two cities or kingdoms, but his theology as a whole demonstrated a close affinity with Augustine's doctrine. It was characterized by the same apocalyptic atmosphere of opposition towards the surrounding world, pagan culture and pagan Rome in particular that existed elsewhere in the West, for instance in the theology of Hippolytus. A long time later the Donatists still spoke in this way. From this it was possible to conclude that in Western tradition—particularly in Africa—a way of thinking existed that showed great affinity with Augustine's. Although the exact terminology and also the historiography connected with Augustine's doctrine of the two *civitates* were lacking, there certainly was a theology of the two cities.

This was corroborated in the first parable of the *Shepherd of Hermas*, the earliest work in which the metaphor of the two cities was prominent. There the antithesis between the two cities symbolized the contradistinction between this aeon and the one to come, between earthly things and heavenly ones, this world and the future world. The city of Rome on the one hand and the Christian congregation living there on the other hand were the earliest concrete representations of this image. Hermas stressed the idea that the believer must sojourn as an alien in the territory now ruled by the devil; passages from the *Gospel according to Thomas* and the *Pseudo-Clementines* served as striking parallels to it. The wide diffusion of Hermas' writing and the great influence it exerted in the first centuries of the Christian era warranted the conclusion that many people must have been familiar with the metaphor of the two cities. The idea inherent in it of the Christian being an alien also turned out to be present in other writings of the so-called Apostolic Fathers, including the anonymous *Letter to Diognetus*.

The study of evidence that could be found in the Old and in the New Testament revealed a remarkable fact. Augustine referred to passages in the *Psalms* to prove the existence of the city of God, but he read them in the light of what the New Testament says about the heavenly city (e.g. *Gal.* 4:26). As its counterpart he named Babylon, but he did not provide any explicit evidence through scriptural passages that show Babylon confronting Jerusalem, the earthly city confronting the heavenly one. Although he connected his idea of the two cities to biblical discussions of the two kinds of people and the two kingdoms, he made no specific reference to scriptural texts, whereas he might have referred to the *Apocalypse of John*. Only in Book XX of the *City of God*, when dealing with eschatology, did Augustine clearly mention the two cities of the *Apocalypse*.

On the basis of these facts it can only be concluded that Augustine, rather than obtaining his concept of the two antithetical cities through an independent exegesis of the Bible, actually read into the Scriptures his already existing concept by means of 'eisegesis'. It is possible that Tyconius' commentary on the *Apocalypse* exerted some influence; Origen and Ambrose may have too. At any rate it is certain that Augustine was acquainted with the metaphor of the two antithetical cities, Jerusalem and Babylon, and that he saw it repeatedly in the Scriptures. Well-known biblical themes, such as that of the Christian sojourning as an alien, were connected with this antithesis.

Thus scriptural data have an important place in Augustine's doctrine of the two *civitates*, but they did not prove to be the actual source. Less important but also significant were the Jewish apocalyptic writings dating from around the beginning of the Christian era. They revealed a growing tendency towards dualism: an antithesis between present and future, 'Diesseits' and 'Jenseits', immanence and transcendance, this world or age (ᶜolām, aiōn, saeculum, mundus; sometimes also: tempus) and the one to come. Mention was made of two antithetical kingdoms, two kinds of people, even of two antithetical cities. Direct influence of these writings might be possible, but there was no evidence for it. Nor was there evidence for any direct influence by the *Acts of Peter and the Twelve*

Apostles. These *Acts*, whose original version dates back to the second or the third century, were notable for the way they discuss two antithetical cities: on the one hand this world as the city in which the believer sojourns as an alien, on the other hand heaven as the city for which he sets out as for his true residence.

From these data it can be concluded that essential elements of Augustine's doctrine of the two cities were often present in works of Christian writers preceding him. These writers spoke of an antithesis between this world or age and the world or age to come, of two kinds of people and of two realms of influence, that of God and that of Satan, which were sometimes described as two antithetical kingdoms or, for example, army camps. Moreover, they repeatedly mentioned the related notion of the believer's being an alien. Furthermore, the idea of two antithetical cities was explicitly stated most clearly in writings in which archaic Christian concepts closely related to Judaism had an important place: the *Apocalypse of John*, the *Shepherd of Hermas*, and the *Acts of Peter and the Twelve Apostles*.

In view of the fact that the two antithetical realms of influence of God and Satan, sometimes even referred to as two cities, had in this way an important place in many early-Christian and Jewish writings, a conclusion is obvious in a wider context also. *Augustine's concept of the two civitates concurs with preceding Christian and Jewish tradition. There is no essential influence of (Neo)Platonism, the Stoa or Philo. Nor can Tyconius be pointed to as the pre-eminent source. The considerable similarity between Augustine and Manichaeism is to be attributed to their common Jewish-Christian background. The actual source, therefore, is rather the pre-Augustinian Christian, the Jewish and in particular the archaic Jewish-Christian tradition.*

Further substantiation for this view was found by investigating the question of whether one can even speak of a catechetical tradition. Such an important idea as that of the two cities was not only part of Augustine's catechesis and of Manichaean teaching, but earlier and elsewhere it played an important role in preliminary instruction. In the Dead Sea Scrolls (1 *QS* 3,13 – 4,26) there was already a catechesis containing a description of two antithetical spirits, two antithetical (kinds of) ways, and two antithetical societies of people who are good or evil. The prince of light has dominion over the righteous and they walk on the ways of light; the angel of darkness has dominion over the evil and they walk on the ways of darkness. Essential elements of this instruction given at Qumran also occurred elsewhere. The originally Jewish doctrine of the two ways stands out particularly in the *Didache* and the Latin *Doctrina apostolorum* as a catechesis prior to baptism; in *Barnabas* it appears as a recapitulation of the baptismal instruction. The two ways are described in the virtues or vices of those who walk on them. Connected with the two ways (and the two spirits) are the two antithetical societies of people, good and evil, righteous and wicked. It is quite possible that the later formulas for the renunciation of the devil at baptism (the so-called *abrenuntiatio diaboli*, with the covenant with Christ as its counterpart) derive ultimately from an earlier catechesis dealing with the two ways and the two spirits. Through baptism one is translated from the one dominion to the other, from Satan's rule to Christ's kingdom. The idea of the two kingdoms is present here, at least in the background. It is in the context of his reference to the baptismal renunciation that Augustine mentions the two cities, Jerusalem and Babylon[813].

The investigation of the *Pseudo-Clementines*, in which the archaic Jewish-Christian element occupies a prominent place, showed that instruction was given not only on the two ways but, clearly connected to it, also concerning the two kings and their two kingdoms. In these writings—with which Augustine may have been familiar, although this is not certain—it also appeared that instruction based on the two ways was equivalent to instruction concerning the two kings and their kingdoms. Moreover, the concept of the two kingdoms functioned by itself as a central element of the catechesis. The doctrine of the two kingdoms was even expounded here in the framework of a *narratio* of the *Heilsgeschichte*. So the catechetical expositions in the *Pseudo-Clementines* show similarity not only with the instruction found in the Qumran Scrolls, the *Didache*, *Barnabas*, and the *Doctrina apostolorum*, but also with Augustine's long model catechesis, and consequently with the *City of God* as well.

Thus it was found that in the tradition preceding Augustine, especially in the introductory catechesis, a combination existed of the two ways, the two spirits (angels, kings) and the two societies or

---

[813] *S.* 216, 4: 'Babylonicae captivitatis vos aliquando jam taedeat. Ecce Jerusalem mater illa coelestis, in viis hilariter invitans occurrit ...'. Cf. *En. in Ps.* 26, *en.* II, 18, where renunciation at baptism is very probably being recalled: 'Cognovimus alium patrem, Deum; reliquimus diabolum. (...) Cognovimus aliam matrem, Ierusalem caelestem, quae est sancta ecclesia, cuius portio peregrinatur in terra; reliquimus Babyloniam'. The guideline here is the text from *Ps.* 26 (27):10.

kingdoms. Another important element of this kind of catechesis turned out to be the *narratio* of the *Heilsgeschichte*. It was found in a rudimentary form in the Qumran Scrolls, in greater detail in the *Constitutiones apostolorum* (VII, 39), and fully developed in the *Pseudo-Clementines*, Irenaeus' *Demonstratio* and Augustine's *De catechizandis rudibus*. The last two works also showed a marked similarity in structure. Further analysis of *De catechizandis rudibus* also revealed that it contains not only the *narratio* of the *Heilsgeschichte* and the idea of the two cities, but probably also elements of the doctrine of the two ways. Augustine may have been acquainted with the Latin *Doctrina apostolorum* or another account of the two ways. Although his works present no explicit connection between two ways and two rulers with their kingdoms or cities as was found in the writings of predecessors, this connection reappeared in the works of his immediate followers. In sermons by Caesarius there is the combination of two ways, two 'spirits' and their two *civitates*. In sermons under the name of Boniface a similar view was found. Medieval authors who were directly or indirectly influenced by Augustine made use of the ethical doctrine of the two ways, the two kings and the two cities.

These facts warrant the conclusion that it is not only in a general sense that the preceding Christian, the Jewish and particularly the archaic Jewish-Christian tradition can be seen as the most likely source of Augustine's doctrine of the two *civitates*. In a more specific sense one may almost certainly point to a prior catechetical tradition in the Early Church. In this tradition, too, the originally Jewish element occupied an important place.

CHAPTER FIVE

SUMMARY AND FINAL REMARKS

At the end of this investigation we shall give a résumé of the most important results and close with a few more general comments.

The introductory chapter presents a survey of the research carried out so far on aim, structure and central theme of the *City of God*. We concluded that particularly in respect to the inquiry into the origins of the concept of the two cities the results diverge.

Chapter II opens with a biographical sketch of Augustine. The author of one of the most influential works of world literature is portrayed first of all as a man from the Roman province of Africa. Although nothing can be said with certainty of a possible Berber extraction, his African descent does merit special attention. It may partly account for the fact that Augustine, in his *magnum opus* and elsewhere, often spoke in such negative terms about Rome, the earthly city. Augustine's thorough training in rhetoric explains his ability to quote extensively from Latin classical authors. His knowledge of Greek, however, was limited, not only in his early years, but later on as well. This, too, is ultimately important for the inquiry into the origin of his concept of the two cities: Augustine was only slightly influenced by Greek theological thinking. Of much more importance was his education as a catechumen in the tradition of the African Church. This education made a profound impression on him. The same can be said of his subsequent stay among the Manichaeans. For a number of years, at first in the spirit of total surrender, the later church father lived the life of a Manichaean *auditor*. After that a Neoplatonic form of Christendom was a veritable revelation to him. The high esteem in which he held the Platonists remained in later years. But in addition, the influence of the Bible and previous theological thinking became increasingly important, especially Latin theology and more specifically the theology of his African predecessors.

The account of Augustine's development provided substantial data in itself for an interpretation of the *City of God* and especially of his doctrine of the two cities. Augustine emerged as the man from Africa who was brought up as a catechumen of the Catholic Christian Church, received a thorough training in rhetoric, associated with the Manichaeans from his 19th till after his 29th year, was greatly influenced by Neoplatonism and ended up as one of the leading bishops of the Catholic Church in Africa.

Chapter II continues with a description of a few basic facts concerning the *City of God*. The sacking of Rome in 410 and the tremendous reaction this catastrophe provoked were an immediate cause but not the actual reason for the inception of the work. Earlier Augustine had already promised an exposition on the two cities. Despite its impressive scope and numerous digressions, the work testifies to a carefully planned design. The reason for its division into twenty-two books, however, is not easy to give. In any case the *City of God* is a compendium of Augustine's theology, his *magnum opus* in which previous thinking attains its maturity and serenity, the later guide for both pope and emperor, the bible of the Middle Ages.

Next the origin and the history of the two cities, especially as they are expounded by Augustine in the *City of God*, are considered. His periodization of history was to exert an important influence on later historiography. In his view of *Heilsgeschichte* Augustine shows a similarity with Old Testament historiography. There is a certain progression in the different stages of the *Heilsgeschichte*; its ultimate goal is the completion of the city of God.

An inquiry into the concept *civitas* revealed that it corresponds most to the Greek concept *polis*. *Civitas* can best be rendered as 'city', provided that we bear in mind that both cities are ruled by a prince. In the development of Augustine's doctrine of the two cities the influence of previous philosophical traditions can be seen. This fact, however, does not explain the actual sources of his doctrine. Even though the two cities are interwoven in this *saeculum*, they are radically different. This antithesis is described especially by Augustine as the antithesis between Jerusalem and Babylon.

Chapter II gives some other aspects of the doctrine of the two cities as well. The city of God and the Church were virtually identical for Augustine, for they are both first and foremost eschatological entities. The antitype of the city of God is the earthly city; it encompasses all those who live according to man, 'according to the flesh'. The Roman Empire is *terrena civitas*, but the earthly city does not coincide with it. A fundamental characteristic of the city of God in this world is its state of being an alien. An enumeration of all the passages in the *City of God* in which *peregrinari*, *peregrinatio* and *peregrinus* occur demonstrated this and in other writings it is also apparent. In the light of this emphasis on peregrination, the significance of Augustine's distinction between use (uti) and enjoyment (frui) becomes clear, as does his evaluation of earthly peace (pax terrena). Although Augustine emphasized that the two antithetical cities are intermingled now, it cannot be said that he recognized a third city as a neutral and independent territory. On the basis of his doctrine of the two cities Augustine also arrived at an evaluation of the Roman Empire, now Christian and with Christian emperors, that differs in many respects from that of predecessors (e.g. Eusebius of Caesarea), contemporaries, and a pupil like Orosius.

Chapter III describes the *City of God* as an apology and a catechetical work. Many scholars have pointed out that the work is to be regarded as an apology, the terminus and climax of a long series. Early Christian apologetics, however, did not confine themselves to polemics, but also provided a positive exposition of the author's own point of view. This thetic element is certainly characteristic of the *City of God* too. In the work itself Augustine emphasizes it frequently. This element is particularly evident in the recently discovered letter to Firmus (*Ep.* 2*). A close comparison of structure and content of the *City of God* with structure and content of the introductory catechesis in *The Catechizing of the Uninstructed* (particularly the first, detailed model) revealed quite a remarkable similarity. This provided the justification for characterizing Augustine's *magnum opus* as a type of catechesis. He evidently considered instruction to be the best form of apologetics. In both *The Catechizing of the Uninstructed* and the *City of God* he uses the questions of those who are to receive instruction as his point of departure. Then he gives the *narratio* of the *Heilsgeschichte* and, finally, the *exhortatio*. It is noteworthy that Augustine often presented his doctrine of the two cities in a catechetical context.

Chapter IV presents an investigation into the possible sources of Augustine's doctrine of the two cities in Manichaeism, in (Neo) Platonism, the Stoa and Philo, and in the works of the Donatist Tyconius. In each case first a short sketch is given of the religion, philosophical movement or person concerned in relation to Augustine. Then the reasons given by others for considering them to be (possible) sources are mentioned. Subsequently these possible sources are examined in detail. Each section closes with an exposition of the similarities and differences. Finally, in a separate section, the Christian, Jewish and Jewish-Christian traditions that preceded Augustine are discussed.

Only the main points of the detailed conclusions at the end of Chapter IV will be given here. Augustine's doctrine of the two cities bears a striking resemblance to the Manichaean doctrine of the two kingdoms. The recently discovered *Cologne Mani-Codex*, however, places this fact in a different perspective. Mani, the founder of a syncretistic world religion, grew up in a Jewish-Christian environment and it was precisely in Jewish-Christian circles that the idea of two kingdoms was present. Might it be, it was tentatively suggested at that stage of the inquiry, that Mani and Augustine were ultimately influenced by the same Jewish-Christian tradition? As he was with Manichaeism, Augustine was thoroughly acquainted with (Neo) Platonism, but his concept showed little similarity with ideas of two worlds, kingdoms or cities as they occurred in (Neo)Platonism, the Stoa or Philo. The highly complicated problems surrounding Tyconius' commentary on the *Apocalypse* necessitated the exercise of great caution. Yet it could be concluded that in his commentary Tyconius probably did speak of two antithetical *civitates*. Nowhere, however, did Augustine name the learned Donatist as his source. Moreover, there were many other authors who could be considered of importance for Augustine's doctrine. The closest in time, Ambrose was the first to be mentioned. He referred to a contradistinction between two *civitates* and, furthermore, spoke about a *terrena civitas*. These references, however, turned out to be generally quite different from Augustine's, for Ambrose spiritualized and individualized. Origen, too, emphasized the microcosmic aspect. No detailed doctrine of two antithetical cities which determine the course of history could be found anywhere else in Greek theology. Lactantius, who came from the Roman West (Africa), differed in many respects. He set forth a comprehensive, dualistic contradistinction between good and evil, light and darkness, God and devil, the two ways and the two warring spirits. This contradistinction might well have influenced Augustine. The writings of Cyprian and Tertullian did not contain an elaborated doctrine of two cities like Augustine's either, though important elements of it proved to be present. Essential elements of a theology of the two cities were also found in other writings emanating from the West. The metaphor of the two cities was clearly present in the influential *Shepherd of Hermas*; inherent to the antithesis between the two *poleis* was an emphasis on the believer's state of being an alien. This emphasis on peregrination also occurred in works of other 'Apostolic Fathers'. Augustine did not use specific passages from the Old or New Testament to prove the existence of the two antithetical cities. He might have referred to the *Apocalypse of John*, but he did not put forward any of its statements on Jerusalem and Babylon as explicit substantiation. On the other hand, he did refer to passages on the city of God in the *Psalms*, but he read them in the light of what the New Testament says about the heavenly city. In this way details from Scripture played an important role in Augustine's doctrine of the two cities, but they were not the actual source. Nor were Jewish writings like 4 *Ezra* or the *Sibylline Oracles*. In the *Acts of Peter and the Twelve Apostles*, one of the New Testament apocrypha, an apparent antithesis was found between this world as the city in which the believer sojourns as an alien and heaven as the city of his true residence to which he is travelling.

On the basis of all these facts it was concluded that in the Christian and Jewish traditions prior to Augustine essential elements of his doctrine of the two cities were often present. The idea of two antithetical cities proved to be present most clearly in writings in which, closely related to Jewish thinking, archaic Christian concepts occupy an important place: the *Apocalypse of John*, the *Shepherd of Hermas*, the *Acts of Peter and the Twelve Apostles*. Furthermore, as there was no proof of any significant influence deriving from (Neo)Platonism, the Stoa or Philo, and because neither Tyconius nor Manichaeism could be pointed to as a major source, the following provisional inference could be made: the actual source is most likely the pre-Augustinian Christian, the Jewish and particularly the archaic Jewish-Christian tradition.

This was corroborated by the exploration of a catechetical tradition that preceded Augustine and already existed in Judaism. In the Qumran texts (1 *QS* 3, 13 – 4, 26) the earliest example of a catechesis was discovered in which mention was made of two antithetical spirits (princes, angels), two antithetical (kinds of) ways and two antithetical societies of good and evil people. Essential elements of this instruction were found particularly in the *Didache, Barnabas* and the Latin *Doctrina apostolorum*. The two antithetical ways were described in terms of the virtues and vices of those walking on them; connected with the two ways (and spirits) were the two antithetical societies. From the *Pseudo-Clementines* it became clear that instruction on the two ways and instruction on the two kings and their two kingdoms could be synonymous. Moreover, the idea of the two kingdoms by themselves functioned here as a central element of the catechesis. In these writings, in which the archaic Jewish-Christian element was prominent, the doctrine of the two kingdoms was even expounded in the framework of a *narratio* of the *Heilsgeschichte*.

In this way the connection between two ways, two spirits (angels, kings) and two kingdoms occurred prior to Augustine, particularly in a catechetical context. Although Augustine himself did not explicitly combine the two ways, the two rulers, and their kingdoms or cities, this connection reappeared later: in the writings of an immediate follower like Caesarius, in sermons attributed to Boniface and in subsequent medieval authors.

We concluded that it is not merely in a general sense that the preceding Christian, the Jewish and especially the archaic Jewish-Christian tradition should be considered as the most likely source of Augustine's doctrine of the two *civitates*. More explicitly, previous catechetical tradition in the Early Church could be pointed to as a highly probable source. In this tradition, too, the originally Jewish element occupied a prominent place.

* *
*

Some final remarks are in order. Now that it has been established that the concepts of two antithetical cities (kingdoms, societies) and of two antithetical ways were explicitly present in the archaic Jewish-Christian tradition, it may be asked whether this tradition continued down to the time of Augustine. Are there any indications that Jewish and Jewish-Christian influences may have been present in the preceding Christianity in Africa?

Recent research has indeed given increasing attention to this question. Although much of the origin of Christianity in Roman Africa is still shrouded in mystery, a few facts are becoming clear. There is irrefutable evidence that in Africa, and particularly in Carthage, there was an influential Jewish community in the early centuries of the Christian era. Jesus must have been proclaimed very early among these Jews to be the promised Messiah (as early the first century?), and from the influence of their community various characteristics of later Christianity in Africa can be accounted for. Some of the main facts will be considered.

Already at the beginning of this century Paul Monceaux called attention to the wide diffusion of Jewish communities in Africa[1]. Moreover, he indicated how much evidence there is for the assumption that the earliest Christian congregations originated from the synagogues[2]. Monceaux was uncertain about the place of origin of the first evangelists (Jerusalem, Antioch, Alexandria, Asia Minor?)[3], but in any case he considered it most likely that the earliest Christian influence stemmed from the East[4]. For Monceaux the main substantiation for the idea that the cradle of the Church in Africa and in Carthage in particular was the synagogue was the evidence found in the large Jewish Gamart necropolis, north of Carthage. In this cemetery, as Delattre et al. had reported shortly before[5], Christians had been buried among the Jews. This was apparently possible in a period before Christians and Jews confronted each other as 'frères ennemis'.

The scholarly work of Monceaux and others has not been spared criticism. Objections have been raised to the assertion that the evidence found at Gamart was specifically Christian and these objections are apparently valid[6]. But in another place close to Carthage evidence did turn up that most likely indicates a peaceable interment of Jews and Christians together[7]. And, moreover, there are many other indications that Jewish influence on Christianity in Africa was important not only in the earliest period but in the centuries following as well.

These are, briefly, some of the most important facts. In the first century AD Jews were already living in several locations in North

---

[1] P. Monceaux, 'Les colonies juives dans l'Afrique romaine', *REJ* 44 (1902) 1-28.

[2] Monceaux, *Histoire*, I, 5 ff.

[3] Monceaux, *Histoire*, I, 5.

[4] Monceaux, *Histoire*, I, 7: '... il semble bien résulter que le christianisme avait été apporté d'Orient en Afrique avant l'intervention des premières missions romaines'.

[5] A.L. Delattre, *Gamart ou la nécropole juive de Carthage*, Lyon 1895.

[6] E.g. Barnes, *Tertullian*, 274 (who bases his argument mainly on J. Ferron); W.H.C. Frend, 'Jews and Christians in Third Century Carthage', in: *Paganisme, Judaïsme, Christianisme. Influences et affrontements dans le monde antique. Mélanges offerts à Marcel Simon*, Paris 1978, 185-194 (= Frend, *Town and Country*, Ch. XVII), 185; W.H.C. Frend, *The Rise of Christianity*, London 1984, 347: 'It was believed that Christians were also buried there, but the evidence comes from a period of excavations when such results could not be checked'.

[7] E.g. Frend, 'Jews and Christians', 189-190; Frend, *Rise*, 347.

Africa, mainly along the coast[8]. Especially after the fall of Jerusalem in 70, and certainly after the revolt of the Jews in Egypt and Cyrene under Trajan (115), their numbers in Africa increased considerably[9]. Tertullian named the Jews repeatedly in his works, Cyprian directed the entire first book of his *Testimonia* against them, Lactantius planned to attack the Jews in a separate work and Augustine, too, demonstrated time and again that he was in touch with an active Jewish community[10]. Mention has already been made of the rather mysterious figure of Commodian, who probably entered the Church via the synagogue[11].

Not only is the testimony provided by the aforementioned writers important—we shall return to part of it shortly—but other facts as well. Much evidence points to the circumstance that in Africa, particularly in Carthage, the Christian Church was born in the synagogue. In an appendix to his article 'The Discussion of Judaic Christianity' (1968)[12], G. Quispel gave a number of characteristics of the earliest Christianity in Africa, and later research by, among others, Frend, Daniélou and Quispel himself has largely confirmed these findings[13]. The earliest Bible translation in Africa testifies to the influence of Hebrew[14]; Tertullian was much indebted to the Jewish Haggadah[15]; the African Minucius Felix made mention of a ritualistic interpretation of the Apostolic Decree (*Acts* 15:29)[16]; Tertul-

---

8 Monceaux, 'Colonies', passim and H.Z. (J.W.) Hirschberg, *A history of the Jews in North Africa*, I, Leiden 1974, 10 f., 21 ff., 27 ff., et al.

9 E.g. Hirschberg, *History*, I, 26 ff.

10 Cyprian, *Ad Quirinum* I; Lactantius, *Div. inst.* VII, 1, 26: 'Sed erit nobis contra Iudaeos separata materia, in qua illos erroris et sceleris revincemus'. For Tertullian and A., see below.

11 See pp. 292-293.

12 Re-issued in *GS*, I, 146-157; 'Additional Note': 157-158.

13 See e.g. Frend's 'Jews and Christians' and several passages in his opus magnum *The Rise of Christianity*, esp. 339 f.; Daniélou's *The Origins of Latin Christianity*, which appeared posthumously in 1977. Quispel summarized his research in 'African Christianity before Minucius Felix and Tertullian', in: Den Boeft and Kessels (eds.), *Actus*, 257-335. See also the earlier fundamental considerations by Marcel Simon, such as 'Judaïsme berbère' (1946), re-issued in Simon, *Recherches*, esp. 31 ff., and 'Punique ou Berbère' (1955), *Recherches*, 98 ff.

14 E.g. Quispel, 'Discussion', 157; Daniélou, *Origins*, 6 f.; Frend, 'Jews and Christians', 186 and 188-189; Frend, *Rise*, 347; Quispel, 'African Christianity', 260-265.

15 E.g. Quispel, 'Discussion', 157; 'African Christianity', 266-269.

16 E.g. Quispel, 'Discussion', 157; Frend, 'Jews and Christians', 186; Quispel, 'African Christianity', 285-287.

lian reported that the Jews in Carthage called the Christians 'Nazarenes'[17]; there were lay elders, the *seniores laici*[18]; the number 70 played an important part in the initial period of the Church of Africa[19]; the offertory box in the church of Carthage was still called 'corban'[20]; etc.[21]. Moreover, René Braun showed convincingly that theological terms like *revelatio, surgere, deus vivus, omnipotens, altissimus* and *salus* were current in Jewish circles before they came into Christian usage[22]. Claude Aziza devoted a separate study to Tertullian's relationship with the Jews[23]. One can agree with Theodor Mommsen's well-known remark that in Africa Christianity, once a Jewish sect, became a world religion.

But there is more. Not only should the close tie that initially existed between the Christian Church and the large, influential Jewish community be recognized, but the later connections as well. It is known that Jews were living in many places in Africa[24]. Augustine mentioned their presence in Carthage, Hippo Regius and also in Uzali, Simittu, Oea et al.[25]. He also referred in his works to

---

[17] E.g. Quispel, 'Discussion', 157; W.H.C. Frend, 'The Early Christian Church in Carthage', in: *Excavations at Carthage in 1976, conducted by the University of Michigan*, Ann Arbor, Mich. 1977, 21-40 (reprinted in Frend, *Town and Country*, Ch. XVI), 21; Frend, *Rise*, 347. Reference is made to *Adv. Marc.* IV, 8: 'nos Iudaei Nazarenos (Nazaraeos, Nazoraeos?) appellant'.

[18] E.g. W.H.C. Frend, 'The *Seniores Laici* and the Origins of the Church in North Africa', *JTS* 12 (1961) 280-284; Frend, 'Church in Carthage', 30. He is of the opinion that the institution of lay-elders had been taken over from the local synagogue; see also Ambrosiaster, *Ad Tim.* I, 5, 2: 'Unde et synagoga, et postea ecclesia seniores habuit, quorum sine consilio nihil agebatur in ecclesia'. Quispel, 'African Christianity', 275-277, wonders whether this institution of *seniores laici* may provide evidence for the idea that there was direct influence from Palestinian Christians.

[19] Frend, e.g. 'Jews and Christians', 190-191.

[20] E.g. Quispel, 'Discussion', 157; Frend, 'Jews and Christians', 189; Quispel, 'African Christianity', 289-290. Reference is made to Cyprian, *De op. et el.* 15. However, it might be worth looking into the possibility that the word *corban* came from Punic.

[21] See e.g. Quispel, 'African Christianity', 290 ff. for *cena pura*, the fact that the spelling of some biblical names is closely related to Hebrew, the role of the *lector*, etc.

[22] R. Braun, *'Deus Christianorum'. Recherches sur le vocabulaire doctrinal de Tertullien*, Paris 1962 (1977^2) 555 ff. et al.

[23] C. Aziza, *Tertullien et le judaïsme*, Nice 1977.

[24] Enumerations have been given by Monceaux, 'Colonies', 10 and B. Blumenkranz, *Die Judenpredigt Augustins. Ein Beitrag zur Geschichte der jüdisch-christlichen Beziehungen in den ersten Jahrhunderten*, Basel 1946 (repr. Paris 1973), 59-60. Cf., among others, Hirschberg, *History*, I, esp. 50 ff. and the map on p. 22.

[25] Evidence is given by Blumenkranz, *Judenpredigt*, 60; B. Blumenkranz, 'Augustin et les juifs. Augustin et le judaïsme', *RA* 1 (1958) 225-241 (repr. in B.

his own personal contacts with Jews[26]. Moreover, it should be recalled that in the first century AD Jewish teachings already began to exert a powerful influence among the original inhabitants of the country, the Berbers, so that Marcel Simon could speak of a 'judaïsme berbère'[27]. Jewish influence in North Africa not only preceded Christianity, but spread and in the end outlasted the Christian Church there. Blumenkranz noted that at the time of the Moslim conquest (698) the city fathers of Hippo were Jewish[28]. As a result of this Muslim invasion the greater part of the Christian Church soon disappeared, and after the eleventh century nothing more was heard of it[29]. Monceaux gave the following figures for the Jewish population at the beginning of the twentieth century: Tunesia 18,000, Algeria 60,000, and Morocco 80,000[30].

What is the significance of all this for the origin and history of the Church of Africa, and for this investigation in particular? First of all that there was, as recent research clearly shows, a Jewish and a Jewish-Christian[31] element in the early stages of Christianity in

---

Blumenkranz, *Juifs et Chrétiens. Patristique et Moyen Age*, London 1977, Ch. III), 226. Cf. Hirschberg, *History*, I, 80-81.

[26] In *De serm. Dom.* I, 9, 23, for example, A. states that he was taught the meaning of the Hebrew word *racha* by a Jew. For this and other data (and also for *iudaizantes* in A.'s environment), see Blumenkranz, *Judenpredigt*, 61 ff.; Blumenkranz, 'Augustin et les juifs', esp. 226 ff. and 236 ff. Cf. M. Simon, *Verus Israel. Étude sur les relations entre Chrétiens et Juifs dans l'Empire Romain (135-425)*, Paris 1948 (réimpr. Paris 1964, avec 'Post-scriptum'), 386-387.

[27] Simon, 'Judaïsme berbère', *Recherches*, 30-87.

[28] Blumenkranz, *Judenpredigt*, 62. In my view Blumenkranz's subsequent conclusion that there must have been more Jews at Hippo at the time of A. than one would gather from his writings is incorrect.

[29] J. Ferron - G. Lapeyre, 'Carthage', *DHGE* 11 (1949) 1149-1233, esp. 1210-1212.

[30] Monceaux, 'Colonies', 1.

[31] Reference has already been made to the use of the term 'Jewish-Christian' which has led to confusion in scholarly discussions; see p. 228 n. 144. The term is used here in the meaning that is given by Simon, 'Réflexions'; for a discussion of the terminology see also Simon, *Verus Israel*, 503-512 ('Post-scriptum') and M. Simon, 'Problèmes du judéo-christianisme', in: *Aspects du judéo-christianisme. Colloque de Strasbourg 23-25 avril 1964*, Paris 1965, 1-16.—Quispel has repeatedly indicated that he considers the geographical component important in the description of Jewish Christianity since it was, in his view, the Christianity that emanated from Palestine. See e.g. his contribution to the discussion following Simon's exposition in *Aspects*, 17, and his 'African Christianity', 272, 277, 290. It does indeed seem possible that the earliest Christian Church with its centre at Carthage was directly descended from Jerusalem/Palestine, but this has not (yet) been proved by means of convincing arguments (cf. below, n. 32).—A.F.J. Klijn, 'The Study of Jewish Christianity', *NTS* 20 (1974) 419-431, is certainly also important for the defining

Africa. Conjectures by earlier investigators—and possibly statements by ancient witnesses as they are perhaps still to be found in Augustine's writings[32]—have in this way been confirmed. All this explains why the character of African Christianity was dissenting in many ways. Jewish exclusiveness joined with Semitic-Punic and Berber particularism, and thus a movement like Donatism, constantly in protest against Rome and its empire, can be more clearly understood. In this way fundamental characteristics of the African Church, and of the Western Church in general, can also be accounted for, such as its legalism. Hansen referred to Tertullian's Christianity as a 'baptized Judaism'[33].

Finally, it is also against the backdrop of this Jewish and Jewish-

---

of Jewish Christianity. Klijn gives a clear survey of the use and misuse of the term and emphasizes that the study of this form of Christianity involves 'such Jewish elements in the primitive Church as are not available in the New Testament and were either neglected or adapted by a developing orthodoxy' (431; cf. esp. 426). Following him, but trying to formulate it more sharply, we describe Jewish-Christian as applying to those elements in the Christianity of the first centuries which—although sometimes in principle present in the New Testament—clearly came to the fore under Jewish influence. *Described in this way, both the notion of the two ways and the notion of the two cities are Jewish-Christian.*—As far as the doctrine of the two ways is concerned it may be observed that an originally Jewish document like the *Duae viae* could very possibly have been translated into Latin at Carthage and from there as *Doctrina apostolorum* exerted its influence in the Western Church. Schlecht, *Doctrina*, 67-68, has already pointed to the possibility of such an origin; for a discussion on so-called 'Africanisms' in the *Doctrina*, see Wohleb, *Didache*, 86 f.

[32] A. states that the Donatists 'had cut themselves off from the root of the Eastern Churches from which the Gospel had come to Africa; but if someone brings them soil from there, they worship it ...'. See *Ep.* 52, 2: '... ab illa radice orientalium ecclesiarum se esse praecisam, unde evangelium in Africam venit, unde terra si eis adferatur, adorant ...'. If we compare this statement with a passage from *DCD* XXII, 8, in which we find that soil *from Jerusalem* was being worshipped, we might perhaps be able to conclude that, according to A., the Gospel was brought to Africa directly from Jerusalem. However, he refers to the *ecclesiae orientales*. Elsewhere, too, A. speaks of the Eastern church*es* and then he means the churches of Corinth, Galatia, Ephesus, Colossae, Philippi and Thessalonica; see *Ep.* 51, 5 and also *Ep.* 43, 7. That the Gospel spread from Jerusalem and thus (eventually) reached Africa is apparently a manner of speaking; see e.g. *En. in Ps.* 147, 18 (in fine).—One may wonder whether any convincing evidence is to be derived from the mention of the *regiones Africae* in the Latin text of *Acts* 2:9-11, quoted by Tertullian (*Adv. Iud.* 7, 4; cf. Quispel, 'African Christianity', 271-272). For various traditions concerning founders of the Church of Africa (Peter, his disciple Crescens, Barnaba(s?), Juda(s?), Simon Cananeus, Juda(s?) the Zealot, Mark) see Monceaux, *Histoire*, I, 5 f. Research should be carried out to determine whether, for each of these, it is a question of legendary tradition, as Monceaux believes.

[33] R.P.C. Hanson, 'Notes on Tertullian's Interpretation of Scripture', *JTS* 12 (1961) 273-279; quotation on 279.

Christian ferment that Augustine's doctrine and imagery of the two cities can be understood. As we have seen, it was precisely in Jewish and Jewish-Christian circles that the concept of the two kingdoms occurred and was depicted in the metaphor of the two cities. When Augustine sets forth his doctrine he uses basically the same terminology. Moreover, his statements concur almost completely with those of his predecessors in the Western and particularly in the African Christian tradition. He emphasizes the antithesis between the city of God and the earthly city, the Christian's state of being an alien, the ultimately negative valuation of this world and Rome as the city of the devil. Two antithetical societies confront each other throughout history, from creation to eschaton. And they are referred to by names ultimately deriving of Jewish origin: Jerusalem and Babylon.

LIST OF ABBREVIATIONS

ACF	Annuaire du Collège de France
ACW	Ancient Christian Writers
ADAIK	Abhandlungen des Deutschen Archäologischen Instituts, Kairo
AFP	Archivum Fratrum Praedicatorum
AKG	Arbeiten zur Kirchengeschichte
AM	Augustinus Magister, I-III, Paris 1954-'55
APAW	Abhandlungen der Preussischen Akademie der Wissenschaften, Phil. - Hist. Klasse
AS	Augustinian Studies, Villanova
ATA	L'Année Théologique Augustinienne, Paris
AThijm	Annalen van het Thijmgenootschap
Aug	Augustinianum, Rome
Aug(L)	Augustiniana, Leuven
BA	Bibliothèque Augustinienne, Oeuvres de Saint Augustin, Paris
BKV	Bibliothek der Kirchenväter
BLE	Bulletin de Littérature Ecclésiastique
BSOAS	Bulletin of the School of Oriental and African Studies
CCCM	Corpus Christianorum, Continuatio Mediaevalis
CCL	Corpus Christianorum, Series Latina
Ciudad	La Ciudad de Dios. Numero extraordinario de homenaje a San Agustin ..., Estudios sobre la 'Ciudad de Dios', I - II, El Escorial 1955-'56
CSEL	Corpus Scriptorum Ecclesiasticorum Latinorum
DACL	Dictionnaire d'Archéologie Chrétienne et de Liturgie
DS	Dictionnaire de Spiritualité, ascétique et mystique
DThC	Dictionnaire de Théologie Catholique
EA	Études Augustiniennes
EPh	Les Études Philosophiques
EphLit	Ephemerides Liturgicae
ÉtBibl	Études Bibliques
EvTh	Evangelische Theologie
GCS	Die Griechischen Christlichen Schriftsteller der ersten (drei) Jahrhunderte
HJ	Historisches Jahrbuch der Görres-Gesellschaft
HNT	Handbuch zum Neuen Testament
HSCP	Harvard Studies in Classical Philology
HTR	Harvard Theological Review
ICC	The International Critical Commentary
ICS	Illinois Classical Studies
IDB	The Interpreter's Dictionary of the Bible
IdF	Impulse der Forschung
JA	Journal Asiatique
JbAC	Jahrbuch für Antike und Christentum
JEH	The Journal of Ecclesiastical History
JNES	Journal of Near Eastern Studies
JQS	The Jewish Quarterly Review
JTS	The Journal of Theological Studies
KEK	Kritisch-Exegetischer Kommentar über das Neue Testament

KlT	Kleine Texte für Vorlesungen und Übungen
KP	Der Kleine Pauly. Lexikon der Antike
K&T	Kerk en Theologie
LCL	The Loeb Classical Library
LThK	Lexikon für Theologie und Kirche
LuJ	Luther-Jahrbuch
MA	Miscellanea Augustiniana, s.l. 1930
MAg	Miscellanea Agostiniana, Testi e studi, I - II, Roma 1930-'31
MD	La Maison-Dieu. Revue de pastorale liturgique
MPL	Patrologiae Cursus Completus, Series Latina, accurante J.-P. Migne
MPL,S	MPL, Supplementum, accurante A. Hamman
MSR	Mélanges de Science Religieuse
MThZ	Münchener Theologische Zeitschrift
NTS	New Testament Studies
NTT	Nederlands Theologisch Tijdschrift
OLZ	Orientalistische Literaturzeitung
OrChr	Oriens Christianus
PRE	Pauly's Real-Encyclopädie der classischen Altertumswissenschaft
RA	Recherches Augustiniennes
RAC	Reallexikon für Antike und Christentum
RAfr	Revue Africaine
RAM	Revue d'Ascétique et de Mystique
RB	Revue Biblique
RBén	Revue Bénédictine
RdQ	Revue de Qumrân
RE	Realencyclopädie für protestantische Theologie und Kirche, Dritte Auflage
REA	Revue des Études Augustiniennes
REAn	Revue des Études Anciennes
REJ	Revue des Études Juives
REL	Revue des Études Latines
RGG	Die Religion in Geschichte und Gegenwart, Dritte Auflage
RHLR	Revue d'Histoire et de Littérature Religieuses
RHR	Revue de l'Histoire des Religions
RicRel	Ricerche Religiose
RMAL	Revue du Moyen-Âge Latin
RQ	Römische Quartalschrift
RSPT	Revue des Sciences Philosophiques et Théologiques
RSR	Recherches de Science Religieuse
RTAM	Recherches de Théologie Ancienne et Médiévale
SBEc	Studia Biblica et Ecclesiastica
SC	Sources Chrétiennes
ScrHier	Scripta Hierosolymitana
SE	Sacris Erudiri
SMSR	Studi e Materiali di Storia delle Religioni
SP	Studia Patristica
SPAW	Sitzungsberichte der Preussischen Akademie der Wissenschaften, Phil.-Hist. Klasse
Spec.	Speculum. A Journal of Mediaeval Studies
ST	Studia Theologica, Lund
StC	Studia Catholica

SVF	Stoicorum Veterum Fragmenta, ed. I. ab Arnim
ThPh	Theologie und Philosophie
ThQ	Theologische Quartalschrift
ThR	Theologische Revue
TKTG	Texte zur Kirchen- und Theologiegeschichte
TLL	Thesaurus Linguae Latinae
TLZ	Theologische Literaturzeitung
TR	Theologische Rundschau
TRE	Theologische Realenzyklopädie
TRef	Theologia Reformata
TS	Theological Studies, Woodstock
T&S	Texts and Studies, Cambridge
TU	Texte und Untersuchungen zur Geschichte der altchristlichen Literatur
TvT	Tijdschrift voor Theologie
TWNT	Theologisches Wörterbuch zum Neuen Testament
VC	Vigiliae Christianae
VetChr	Vetera Christianorum
WdF	Wege der Forschung
WSt	Wiener Studien
ZKG	Zeitschrift für Kirchengeschichte
ZKTh	Zeitschrift für Katholische Theologie
ZKWL	Zeitschrift für kirchliche Wissenschaft und kirchliches Leben
ZNW	Zeitschrift für die Neutestamentliche Wissenschaft und die Kunde der älteren Kirche
ZPE	Zeitschrift für Papyrologie und Epigraphik
ZRGG	Zeitschrift für Religions- und Geistesgeschichte
ZThK	Zeitschrift für Theologie und Kirche

BIBLIOGRAPHY

Primary sources are given first, then secondary sources (bibliographies, dictionaries, other reference works, studies, translations). General articles in lexicons like *DS, LThK, PRE, RAC, RE, RGG, TRE, TWNT* and the 'Notes complémentaires' in *BA* are only listed in special cases.

A. Primary sources

1. Augustine

		CCL	CSEL	BA	MPL
Brev. coll.	Breviculus collationis cum Donatistis	149A	53	32	43
C. acad.	Contra academicos	29	63	4	32
C. Adim.	Contra Adimantum	—	25,1	17	42
C. adv. leg.	Contra adversarium legis et prophetarum	49	—	—	42
C. Cresc.	Contra Cresconium	—	52	31	43
C. ep. fund.	Contra epistulam quam vocant fundamenti	—	25,1	17	42
C. ep. Parm.	Contra epistulam Parmeniani	—	51	28	43
C. Faust.	Contra Faustum	—	25,1	—	42
C. Fel.	Contra Felicem	—	25,2	17	42
C. Fort.	Contra Fortunatum	—	25,1	17	42
C. Iul.	Contra Iulianum	—	—	—	44
Conf.	Confessiones	27	33	13-14	32
C. litt. Petil.	Contra litteras Petiliani	51	52	30	43
DCD	De civitate Dei	47-48	40,1-2	33-37	41
De agone	De agone christiano	—	41	1	40
De an.	De natura et origine animae	—	60	22	44
De bono vid.	De bono viduitatis	—	41	3	40
De b. vita	De beata vita	29	63	4	32
De cat. rud.	De catechizandis rudibus	46	—	11	40
De cons. ev.	De consensu evangelistarum	—	43	—	34
De div. quaest. 83	De diversis quaestionibus LXXXIII	44A	—	10	40
De doctr. chr.	De doctrina christiana	32	80	11	34
De duab. an.	De duabus animabus	—	25,1	17	42
De Gen. ad litt.	De Genesi ad litteram	—	28,1	48-49	34
De Gen. c. Man.	De Genesi contra Manichaeos	—	—	—	34
De gratia Christi et de pecc. orig.	De gratia Christi et de peccato originali	—	42	22	44
De haer.	De haeresibus	46	—	—	42
De lib. arb.	De libero arbitrio	29	74	6	32
De mor.	De moribus ecclesiae catholicae et de moribus Manichaeorum	—	—	1	32

De mus.	De musica	—	—	7	32
De nat. et gr.	De natura et gratia	60	—	21	44
De ord.	De ordine	29	63	4	32
De trin.	De trinitate	50-50A	—	15-16	42
De ut. cred.	De utilitate credendi	—	25,1	8	42
De vera rel.	De vera religione	32	77	8	34
Ench.	Enchiridion	46	—	9	40
En. in Ps.	Enarrationes in Psalmos	38-40	—	—	36-37
Ep.	Epistulae	—	34,1-2; 44; 57-58	—	33
Ep.*	Epistolae (ed. Divjak)	—	88	—	—
Opus imp. c. Iul.	Opus imperfectum contra Iulianum	—	85,1(1)	—	45
Psalmus	Psalmus contra partem Donati	—	51	28	43
Quaest. in Hept.	Quaestiones in Heptateuchum	33	28,3	—	34
Retract	Retractationes	57	36	12	32
s.	Sermones	41(2)	—	—	38-39(3)
Sol.	Soliloquia	—	—	5	32
Tract. in Ep. Ioh.	Tractatus in Epistulam Iohannis ad Parthos	37	—	—	35(4)
Tract. in Ioh. Ev.	Tractatus in Iohannis Evangelium	36	—	71-72(5)	35

(1) Books I-III, ed. M. Zelzer, 1974.
(2) *Sermones de vetere testamento (1-50)*, ed. C. Lambot.
(3) For 'Sermones post Maurinos reperti', see the critical edition by G. Morin in *MAg* I. Most of the texts that were discovered later appeared in *RBén*; see e.g. P.-P. Verbraken, *Études critiques sur les sermons authentiques de saint Augustin*, Steenbrugge – 's-Gravenhage 1976 and the annual 'Bulletin' in *REA*. The critical editions by C. Lambot, *Sancti Aurelii Augustini sermones selecti duodeviginti*, Ultraiecti – Bruxellis 1950 and S. Poque, *Augustin d'Hippone, Sermons pour la Pâque*, Paris 1966 (*SC* 116) are also quoted.
(4) Revised edition by P. Agaësse, *SC* 75.
(5) *Tract.* I-XVI and XVII-XXXIII respectively.

2. *Other early Christian and Medieval writers*

Acta Petri — Acts of Peter and the Twelve Apostles, ed. M. Krause – P. Labib, *Gnostische und hermetische Schriften aus Codex II und Codex VI*, Glückstadt 1971 (*ADAIK*, II), 107-121; R. Mcl. Wilson – D.M. Parrott in: Parrott (ed.), *Nag Hammadi Codices V, 2-5 and VI with Papyrus Berolinensis 8502, 1 and 4*, Leiden 1979, 197-229.

Acta Saturnini — *MPL* 8, 690-703.

Acta Thomae — M. Bonnet, *Acta Apostolorum apocrypha*, II, 2, Leipzig 1903 (repr. Hildesheim 1959), 99-288.

Ambrosiaster,	
Ad Rom.	Ambrosiastri qui dicitur Commentarius in Epistulas Paulinas, Pars I: In Epistulam ad Romanos, ed. H.J. Vogels, CSEL 81,1.
Ambrose,	
De Abr.	De Abraham, ed. C. Schenkl, CSEL 32,1.
De apol. proph. David	De apologia prophetae David, ed. Schenkl, CSEL 32,2.
De Cain et Abel	De Cain et Abel, ed. Schenkl, CSEL 32,1.
De exc. fratris	De excessu fratris, ed. O. Faller, CSEL 73.
De fide	De fide, MPL 16.
De fuga saeculi	De fuga saeculi, ed. Schenkl, CSEL 32,2.
De interp. Iob et David	De interpellatione Iob et David, ed. Schenkl, CSEL 32,1.
De Isaac vel anima	De Isaac vel anima, ed. Schenkl, CSEL 32,1.
De ob. Theodosii	De obitu Theodosii, ed. Faller, CSEL 73.
De ob. Valentiniani	De obitu Valentiniani, ed. Faller, CSEL 73.
De paen.	De paenitentia, ed. Faller, CSEL 73.
De paradiso	De paradiso, ed. Schenkl, CSEL 32,1.
De sp. sancto	De Spiritu Sancto, ed. Faller, CSEL 79.
De virg.	De virginitate, MPL 16.
Ep.	Epistulae, ed. Faller, CSEL 82 (incomplete ed.); MPL 16.
Exh. virg.	Exhortatio virginitatis, MPL 16.
Exp. Luc.	Expositio evangelii secundum Lucam, ed. M. Adriaen, CCL 14.
Exp. Ps. CXVIII	Expositio super psalmo CXVIII, ed. M. Petschenig, CSEL 72.
Expl. Ps.	Explanatio super psalmos XII, ed. Petschenig, CSEL 74.
Ambrosius Autpertus,	
Exp.	Expositio in Apocalypsim, ed. R. Weber, CCCM 27-27A.
Athanasius,	
Ep.	Epistolae festales, MPG 26.
Barn.	Letter of Barnabas, ed. O. de Gebhardt – A. Harnack – Th. Zahn, *Patrum Apostolicorum Opera*, Fasc. I, Part. II, Ed. II, Lipsiae 1878, 2-83; F.X. Funk, *Patres Apostolici*, I, Tubingue 1901, 38-96; F.X. Funk – K. Bihlmeyer, *Die Apostolischen Väter*, I, Tübingen 1924[2] (repr. 1970), 10-34; P. Prigent – R.A. Kraft, *Épître de Barnabé*, Paris 1971 (*SC* 172); K. Wengst, *Schriften des Urchristentums*, II, Darmstadt 1984, 138-194.
Beatus,	
In Apoc.	*Beati in Apocalypsin libri XII*, ed. H.A. Sanders, Roma 1930.

Beda
Expl. — Explanatio Apocalypsis, MPL 93.

CA — Constitutiones apostolorum, ed. F.X. Funk, *Didascalia et Constitutiones apostolorum*, I-II, Paderbornae 1905.

Caesarius
Exp. — Expositio in Apocalypsim, ed. G. Morin, *Sancti Caesarii Opera Varia* ..., Maretioli 1942, 209-277.
s. — Sermones, ed. G. Morin, CCL 103-104.

Cassiodorus
Inst. — Institutiones, ed. R.A.B. Mynors, Oxford 1961[2].

1/2 Clem. — 1/2 Clement, ed. Gebhardt, Harnack and Zahn, *Patr. Ap. Op.*, I/I, 2-143; Funk, *Patr. Ap.*, I, 98-210; Funk and Bihlmeyer, *Ap. Väter*, I, 35-81; Wengst, *Schriften*, 238-268 (= 2 *Clem.*); in addition, for 1 *Clem.*: J.A. Fischer, *Schriften des Urchristentums*, I, München 1956 (repr. Darmstadt 1976[7]), 24-106; A. Jaubert, *Clément de Rome, Épître aux Corinthiens*, Paris 1971 (*SC* 167).

For Ps. Clem., *Hom.* and *Rec.*, see below.

Commodian,
Carmen — Carmen apologeticum, ed. J. Martin, CCL 128.
Instr. — Instructiones, ed. Martin, CCL 127.

Cyprian,
Ad Demetr. — Ad Demetrianum, ed. M. Simonetti, CCL 3A.
Ad Don. — Ad Donatum, ed. Simonetti, CCL 3A.
Ad Fort. — Ad Fortunatum, ed. R. Weber, CCL 3.
De bono pat. — De bono patientiae, ed. C. Moreschini, CCL 3A.
De lapsis — De lapsis, ed. M. Bévenot, CCL 3.
De mort. — De mortalitate, ed. Simonetti, CCL 3A.
Ep. — Epistulae, ed. L. Bayard, *Saint Cyprien, Correspondance*, I-II, Paris 1925.

For Ps. Cypr., *De cent.* and *De mont.*, see below.

Cyril,
Cat. — A. Piédagnel - P. Paris, *Cyrille de Jérusalem, Catéchèses mystagogiques*, Paris 1966 (*SC* 126).

De cent. — De centesima, sexagesima, tricesima, ed. R. Reitzenstein, *ZNW* 15 (1914) 74-90 (= *MPL,S.* I, 53-67).

De mont. — De montibus Sina et Sion, ed. G. Hartel, CSEL 3,3.

Did./Doctr. — Didachè/Doctrina apostolorum, ed. J. Rendel Harris, *The Teaching of the Apostles*, London-Baltimore 1887 (Did.); Funk, *Patr. Ap.*, I, 2-37 (Did.); Funk and Bihlmeyer, *Ap. Väter*, I, 1-9 (Did.); H. Lietzmann, *Die Didachè*, Bonn 1923[3] (*KlT* 6; Did./Doctr.); J.-P. Audet, *La Didachè. Instructions des apôtres*, Paris 1958 (Did.); W. Rordorf – A. Tuilier, *La Doctrine des douze apôtres (Didachè)*, Paris 1978 (*SC* 248; Did./Doctr.); Wengst, *Schriften*, 66-90 (Did.). Other editions of the *Doctr.* referred to: F.X. Funk, *Doctrina duodecim apostolorum*, Tubingue 1887, 102-104 (ed. Mellic. 597); J. Schlecht, *Doctrina XII Apostolorum. Die Apostellehre in der Liturgie der katholischen Kirche*, Freiburg i. Br. 1901, 101-104 (ed. Monac. 6264); K. Niederwimmer, 'Doctrina apostolorum (Cod. Mellic. 597)' in: H.C. Schmidt-Lauber (Hrsg.), *Theologia scientia practica* (FS Fritz Herbst), Wien et al. 1979, 270.

Diogn. — Epistle to Diognetus, ed. Gebhardt, Harnack and Zahn, *Patr. Ap. Op.*, I/II, 154-164; Funk, *Patr. Ap.*, I, 390-412; Funk and Bihlmeyer, *Ap. Väter*, I, 141-149; H.-I. Marrou, *A Diognète*, Paris 1965[2] (*SC* 33bis); Wengst, *Schriften*, 312-340.

Epiphanius,
Pan. — Panarion (Haer. 1-33), ed. K. Holl, GCS 25.
De mens. et pond. — De mensuris et ponderibus, MPG 43.

Eusebius,
HE — Historia Ecclesiastica, ed. E. Schwartz, GCS 9, 1/2.

Gennadius,
De viris inl. — Liber de viris inlustribus, ed. E.C. Richardson, Leipzig 1896 (*TU* 14).

Gospel of Thomas — The Gospel according to Thomas, ed. A. Guillaumont – H.-Ch. Puech – G. Quispel – W. Till – Yassah 'Abd Al Masīḥ, Leiden 1976[2].

Hermas,
Vis. Mand. Sim. — The Shepherd of Hermas, ed. A. Hilgenfeld, *Hermae Pastor. Veterem latinam interpretationem e codicibus*, Lipsiae 1873; O. de Gebhardt – A. Harnack, *Hermae Pastor Graece, addita versione latina recentiore e codice Palatino*, Lipsiae 1877 (= Gebhardt, Harnack and Zahn, *Patr. Ap. Op.*, III); Funk, *Patr. Ap.*, I, 414-639; R. Joly, *Hermas, Le Pasteur*, Paris 1958 (*SC* 53); M. Whittaker, *Der Hirt des Hermas (Die apostolischen Väter*, I), Berlin 1967[2] (*GCS* 48[2]).

Hilarius,
In Ps. Tractatus super Psalmos, ed. A. Zingerle, CSEL 22.

Hippolytus,
De Antichr. De Christo et Antichristo, ed. H. Achelis, GCS 1.
In Dan. Commentarii in Danielem, ed. G.N. Bonwetsch, GCS 1.

Irenaeus,
Dem. Demonstratio, trad. de l'arménien par L.M. Froidevaux, *Irénée de Lyon, Démonstration de la Prédication apostolique*, Paris 1959, 1971² (*SC* 62).

Jerome,
De vir. inl. De viris inlustribus, ed. E.C. Richardson, Leipzig 1896 (*TU* 14).
Ep. Epistulae, ed. J. Hilberg, CSEL 44-46.
In Hier. In Hieremiam prophetam, ed. S. Reiter, CSEL 49.
In Ps. Tractatus LIX in Psalmos, ed. G. Morin, CCL 78.

Justin,
Apol. Apologia, ed. E.J. Goodspeed, *Die ältesten Apologeten*, Göttingen 1915 (repr. New York 1950), 26-89.
Dial. Dialogus cum Tryphone Iudaeo, ed. Goodspeed, *Apologeten*, 90-265.

Lactantius,
De ira De ira Dei, ed. H. Kraft – A. Wlosok, *Laktanz, Vom Zorne Gottes*, Darmstadt 1983⁴.
De opif. *De opificio Dei*, ed. M. Perrin, *Lactance, L'ouvrage du Dieu créateur*, Paris 1974 (*SC* 213-214).
Div.inst. Divinae institutiones, ed. S. Brandt, 1890, CSEL 19; P. Monat, *Lactance, Institutions divines, Livre V*, Paris 1973 (*SC* 204-205).
Epit. Epitome divinarum institutionum, ed. Brandt, CSEL 19.

Mart. Polyc. Martyrium Polycarpi, ed. Gebhardt, Harnack and Zahn, *Patr. Ap. Op.*, II, 132-168; Funk, *Patr. Ap.*, I, 314-344; Funk and Bihlmeyer, *Ap. Väter*, I, 120-132; H. Musorillo, *The Acts of the Christian Martyrs*, Oxford 1972, 2-20.

Minucius Felix,
Oct. Octavius, ed. J. Beaujeu, *Minucius Felix, Octavius*, Paris 1964, 1974².

Origen,
C. Celsum — Contra Celsum, ed. M. Borret, *Origène, Contra Celse*, Paris 1967-'76 (*SC* 132, 136, 147, 150, 227).
Comm. in Cant. — Libri X in Canticum canticorum, ed. W.A. Baehrens, GCS 33.
Comm. in Ioh. — Commentarii in Iohannem, ed. E. Preuschen, GCS 10.
De oratione — De oratione, ed. P. Koetschau, GCS 3.
De princ. — De principiis, ed. Koetschau, GCS 22; H. Görgemanns - H. Karpp, *Origenes, Vier Bücher von den Prinzipien*, Darmstadt 1976.
In Ez. hom. — In Ezechielem homiliae XIV, ed. W.A. Baehrens, GCS 33.
In Gen. hom. — In Genesim homiliae XVI, ed. W.A. Baehrens, GCS 29.
In Ier. hom. — Homiliae XX in Ieremiam graecae; Fragmenta graeca, ed. E. Klostermann, GCS 6.
In Iesu Nave hom. — In Iesu Nave homiliae XXVI, ed. W.A. Baehrens, GCS 30.
In Luc. hom. — In Lucam homiliae XXXIX, ed. M. Rauer, GCS 49.
In Num. hom. — In Numeros homiliae XXVIII, ed. W.A. Baehrens, GCS 30.

Orosius,
Hist. — Historiarum adversus paganos libri septem, ed. C. Zangemeister, CSEL 5.

Polycarp,
Ad Phil. — Epistula ad Philippenses, ed. Gebhardt, Harnack and Zahn, *Patr. Ap. Op.*, II, 110-132; Funk, *Patr. Ap.*, I, 296-312; Funk and Bihlmeyer, *Ap. Väter*, I, 114-120; Fischer, *Schriften*, 246-264.

For *Mart. Polyc.*, see above.

Possidius,
Elenchus — Operum S. Augustini elenchus, ed. A. Wilmart, *MAg*, II, 149-233.
Vita — Vita S. Augustini, ed. M. Pellegrino, Alba 1955.

Primasius
Comm. — Commentarius in Apocalypsin, ed. W. Adams, CCL 92.

Ps. Clem., — Pseudo-Clementines,
Hom. — Homiliae, ed. B. Rehm - J. Irmscher - F. Paschke, GCS 42².
Rec. — Recognitiones, ed. Rehm and Paschke, GCS 51.

Tatian,
Or. — Oratio ad Graecos, ed. M. Whittaker, *Tatian, Oratio ad Graecos and Fragments*, Oxford 1982.

Tertullian,
Apol. — Apologeticum, ed. E. Dekkers, CCL 1.
Ad mart. — Ad martyras, ed. Dekkers, CCL 1.
Adv. Iud. — Adversus Iudaeos, ed. A. Kroymann, CCL 2; H. Tränkle, *Q.S.F. Tertulliani Adversus Iudaeos*, Wiesbaden 1964.
Adv. Marc. — Adversus Marcionem, ed. Kroymann, CCL 1.
Adv. Prax. — Adversus Praxean, ed. A. Kroymann - E. Evans, CCL 2.
De an. — De anima, ed. J.H. Waszink, CCL 2; J.H. Waszink, *Q.S.F. Tertulliani De anima, edited with introduction and commentary*, Amsterdam 1947.
De bapt. — De baptismo, ed. J.G.Ph. Borleffs, CCL 1.
De carne Christi — De carne Christi, ed. Kroymann, CCL 2,.
De cor. — De corona, ed. Kroymann, CCL 2.
De exh. cast. — De exhortatione castitatis, ed. Kroymann, CCL 2.
De idol. — De idololatria, ed. A. Reifferscheid - G. Wissowa, CCL 2.
De iei. — De ieiunio, ed. Reifferscheid and Wissowa, CCL 2.
De praescr. — De praescriptione haereticorum, ed. R.F. Refoulé, CCL 1.
De pud. — De pudicitia, ed. Dekkers, CCL 2.
De res. mort. — De resurrectione mortuorum, ed. Borleffs, CCL 2.
De spect. — De spectaculis, ed. Dekkers, CCL 1.
De virg. vel. — De virginibus velandis, ed. Dekkers, CCL 2.

Tyconius,
Lib. reg. — Liber regularum, ed. F.C. Burkitt, *The Book of Rules of Tyconius*, Cambridge 1894 (*T&S* III,1).
Turin Fragments — ed. F. Lo Bue, *The Turin Fragments of Tyconius' Commentary on Revelation*, Cambridge 1963 (*T&S, NS* VII, prepared for the press by G.G. Willis).

Victorinus of Pettau,
Comm. in Apoc. — Commentarii in Apocalypsim Ioannis, ed. J. Haussleiter, CSEL 49.

3. *Jewish sources*

I mainly used the following translations of Jewish writings of the last centuries before Christ and the first centuries of the Christian era which are not part of the Hebrew canon: Charles (ed.), *APOT*, I - II; Charlesworth (ed.), *OTP*, I - II and Kautzsch (Hrsg.), *APAT*, I - II.—Philo is quoted from the edition of F.H. Colson and G.H. Whitaker in *LCL* (Suppl. I - II, ed. by R. Marcus); the writings of Josephus were also consulted in *LCL*.—For the Qumran texts use is made of the

edition of E. Lohse, *Die Texte aus Qumran*, Darmstadt 1971^{2}; for the *Testaments of the Twelve Patriarchs* of M. de Jonge et al., *The Testaments of the Twelve Patriarchs*, Leiden 1978.
For editions of translated texts, see also under section B: Secondary Sources.

4. Manichaica

Adam, Texte
A. Adam, *Texte zum Manichäismus*, Berlin 1969^{2} (*KlT* 175).

Arabian:

Ibn al-Nadīm, Fihrist
B. Dodge, *The Fihrist of al-Nadīm*, New York-London 1970.

Chinese:

Haloun and Henning, 'Compendium'
G. Haloun - W.B. Henning, 'The Compendium of the Doctrines and Styles of the Teaching of Mani, the Buddha of Light', *Asia Major* 3 (1952) 184-212.

Chavannes and Pelliot, 'Traité'
É. Chavannes - P. Pelliot, 'Un traité manichéen retrouvé en Chine', *JA* 10e série, XVIII (1911) 499-617; *JA* 11e série, I (1913) 99-199; 261-394.

Tsui Chi, 'Hymns'
Tsui Chi, 'Mo Ni Chiao Hsia Pu Tsan. The Lower (Second?) Section of the Manichaean Hymns', BSOAS 11 (1943) 174-219.

Waldschmidt and Lentz, 'Dogmatik'
E. Waldschmidt - W. Lentz, 'Manichäische Dogmatik aus chinesischen und iranischen Texten', *SPAW* 13 (1933) 480-607.

Waldschmidt and Lentz, Stellung Jesu
E. Waldschmidt - W. Lentz, *Die Stellung Jesu im Manichäismus*, Berlin 1926 (*APAW* 4).

Coptic:

Hom.
H.J. Polotsky, *Manichäische Homilien*, Bd. I, *Manichäische Handschriften der Sammlung A. Chester Beatty*, Stuttgart 1934.

Keph.
H.J. Polotsky - A. Böhlig, *Kephalaia*. Bd. I, 1. Hälfte, *Manichäische Handschriften der Staatlichen Museen Berlin*, Stuttgart 1940; A. Böhlig, *Kephalaia*, Bd. I, 2. Hälfte, Stuttgart 1966.

Psalm-Book — C.R.C. Allberry, *A Manichaean Psalm-Book*, Part II, *Manichaean Manuscripts in the Chester Beatty Collection*, Vol. II, Stuttgart 1938.

East Turkish: See section B: Asmussen, *X^uāstvānīft*.

Bang,
'Beichtspiegel' — W. Bang, 'Manichäische Laien-Beichtspiegel', *Le Muséon* 36 (1923) 137-242.

Greek:
CMC — A. Henrichs – L. Koenen, 'Ein griechischer Mani-Codex (P. Colon. inv. nr. 4780)', *ZPE* 5 (1970) 97-216; *ZPE* 19 (1975) 1-85; *ZPE* 32 (1978) 87-199; *ZPE* 44 (1981) 201-318; *ZPE* 48 (1982) 1-59.

Iranian:
Andreas-Henning,
'Mir. Man.', I — F.C. Andreas – W.B. Henning, 'Mitteliranische Manichaica aus Chinesisch-Turkestan', I, *SPAW* 1932, 175-222.
'Mir. Man.', II — *idem*, II, *SPAW* 1933, 294-363.
'Mir. Man.', III — *idem*, III, *SPAW* 1934, 848-912.

Boyce,
Reader — M. Boyce, *A Reader in Manichaean Middle Persian and Parthian*, Leiden 1975.

Henning,
Bet- und Beichtbuch — W.B. Henning, *Ein manichäisches Bet- und Beichtbuch, APAW* 10, 1936, Berlin 1937.

Müller,
'Hermas-Stelle' — F.W.K. Müller, 'Eine Hermasstelle in manichäischer Version', *SPAW* 1905, 1077- 1083.

Sundermann,
Texte — W. Sundermann, *Mitteliranische manichäischen Texte kirchengeschichtlichen Inhalts*, Berlin 1981.

Latin: See Augustine, esp. *C. Adim., C. ep. fund., C. Faust., C. Fel., C. Fort., De mor., De haer.*

5. Other sources

Diehl,
Inscr. — E. Diehl, *Inscriptiones Latinae Christianae Veteres*, I-III, Dublin-Zürich 1970[3]; Vol. IV, ed. J. Moreau – H.-I. Marrou, Dublin-Zürich 1967.

Ginzā — M. Lidzbarski, *Ginzā. Der Schatz oder das Grosse Buch der Mandäer*, Göttingen-Leipzig 1925.

Plotinus, *Enn.* — Enneaden, ed. P. Henry – H.-R. Schwyzer, *Plotini Opera*, I-III, Paris-Bruxelles/Leiden 1951-'73.

SVF, frg. — *Stoicorum veterum fragmenta*, I-IV, ed. I. ab Arnim, Lipsiae 1903-'24.

For non-Christian classical writers such as Plato, Cicero and Seneca, use is made of the *LCL* editions.

B. Secondary sources

A. Adam, 'Der manichäische Ursprung der Lehre von den zwei Reichen bei Augustin' (1952), in: Adam, *Sprache und Dogma*, 133-140.

——, 'Das Fortwirken des Manichäismus bei Augustin' (1958), in: Adam, *Sprache und Dogma*, 141-166.

——, 'Manichäismus', in: B. Spuler et al. (Hrsg.), *Handbuch der Orientalistik*, Erste Abteilung, Band VIII, 2, Leiden-Köln 1961, 102-119.

——, 'Die Herkunft des Lutherwortes vom menschlichen Willen als Reittier Gottes', *LuJ* 29 (1962) 25-34.

——, *Sprache und Dogma. Untersuchungen zu Grundproblemen der Kirchengeschichte*, hrsg. von G. Ruhbach, Gütersloh 1969.

——, *Lehrbuch der Dogmengeschichte*, I, *Die Zeit der Alten Kirche*, Gütersloh 1970[2].

B. Aland(-Ehlers), 'Bardesanes von Edessa—ein syrischer Gnostiker', *ZKG* 81 (1970) 334-351.

——, 'Mani und Bardesanes. Zur Entstehung des manichäischen Systems', in: Dietrich (Hrsg.), *Synkretismus*, 123-143.

—— et alii (Hrsg.), *Gnosis. Festschrift für Hans Jonas*, Göttingen 1978.

A. d'Alès, *La théologie de Tertullien*, Paris 1905.

P. Alfaric, *L'Évolution intellectuelle de saint Augustin*, I, *Du Manichéisme au Néoplatonisme*, Paris 1918.

——, *Les écritures manichéennes*, I, *Vue générale*, Paris 1918; II, *Étude analytique*, Paris 1919.

G.H. Allard, 'Pour une nouvelle interprétation de la *Civitas Dei', SP* IX (*TU* 94), Berlin 1966, 329-339.

A. Allgeier, 'Der Einfluss des Manichäismus auf die exegetische Fragestellung bei Augustin. Ein Beitrag zur Geschichte von Augustins theologischer Entwicklung', in: M. Grabmann – J. Mausbach (Hrsg.), *Aurelius Augustinus. Die Festschrift der Görres-Gesellschaft zum 1500. Todestage des heiligen Augustinus*, Köln 1930, 1-13.

D.C. Allison Jr., The Authorship of 1 QS III,13-IV,14', *RdQ* 10 (1980) 257-286.

B. Altaner, 'Augustin und die griechische Sprache' (1939), in: Altaner, *Schriften*, 129-153.

——, 'Augustinus und Philo von Alexandrien' (1941), in: Altaner, *Schriften*, 181-193.

——, 'Die Benützung von original griechischen Vätertexten durch Augustinus' (1948), in: Altaner, *Schriften*, 154-163.

——, 'Augustinus und Irenäus' (1949), in: Altaner, *Schriften*, 194-203.
——, 'Augustinus und die neutestamentlichen Apokryphen, Sibyllinen und Sextussprüche' (1949), in: Altaner, *Schriften*, 204-215.
——, 'Babylon' (Israelitisch, Christlich), *RAC* 1 (1950) 1128-1134.
——, 'Augustinus und Basilius der Grosse' (1950), in: Altaner, *Schriften*, 269-276.
——, 'Beiträge zur Kenntnis des Schriftstellerischen Schaffens Augustins' (1950), in: Altaner, *Schriften*, 3-56.
——, 'Augustinus und Origenes' (1951), in: Altaner, *Schriften*, 224-252.
——, 'Augustinus und Gregor von Nazianz, Gregor von Nyssa' (1951), in: Altaner, *Schriften*, 277-285.
——, 'Augustinus und die griechische Patristik. Eine Zusammenfassung und Nachlese zu den quellenkritischen Untersuchungen' (1952), in Altaner, *Schriften*, 316-331.
——, 'Die lateinische Doctrina Apostolorum und die griechische Grundschrift der Didache' (1952), in: Altaner: *Schriften*, 335-342.
——, *Kleine patristische Schriften*, hrsg. von G. Glockmann, Berlin 1967*.
B. Altaner – A. Stuiber, *Patrologie. Leben, Schriften und Lehre der Kirchenväter*, Freiburg-Basel-Wien 1978[8].
U. Álvarez Díez, 'La «Ciudad de Dios» y su arquitectura interna', *Ciudad*, I, 65-116.
C. Andresen, 'Apologetik, II', *RGG* I (1957) 480-485.
——, 'Erlösung', *RAC* 6 (1966) 54-219.
——, *Bibliographia Augustiniana*, Darmstadt 1973[2].
—— (Hrsg.), *Zum Augustingespräch der Gegenwart*, I, Darmstadt 1975[2].
——, 'Einführung' und 'Anmerkungen', in: Thimme, *Augustinus, Vom Gottesstaat*, I-II, V-XXXII and 533-621; V-XXXII and 837-1018.
—— (Hrsg.), *Zum Augustin-Gespräch der Gegenwart*, II, Darmstadt 1981.
P. Archambault, 'The Ages of Man and the Ages of the World. A Study of two Traditions', *REA* 12 (1966) 193-228.
A.H. Armstrong – R.A. Markus, *Christian Faith and Greek Philosophy*, London 1960.
A.H. Armstrong, 'Plotinus', in: A.H. Armstrong (ed.), *The Cambridge History of Later Greek and Early Medieval Philosophy*, Cambridge 1967, 193-268.
——, *St. Augustine and Christian Platonism*, Villanova 1967 (= A.H. Armstrong, *Plotinian and Christian Studies*, London 1979, Ch. XI).
H.-X. Arquillière, 'Réflexions sur l'essence de l'augustinisme politique', in: *AM*, II, 991-1001.
——, *L'Augustinisme politique. Essai sur la formation des théories politiques du Moyen Age*, Paris 1955[2].
J.P. Asmussen, *Xᵘāstvānīft. Studies in Manichaeism*, Copenhagen 1965.
——, 'Manichaeism', in: C.J. Bleeker and G. Widengren (eds.), *Historia Religionum. Handbook for the History of Religion*, I, Leiden 1969, 580-610.
Aspects du judéo-christianisme. Colloque de Strasbourg 23-25 avril 1964, Paris 1965.
J.-P. Audet, 'Affinités littéraires et doctrinales du *Manuel de Discipline*', *RB* 59 (1952) 219-238 and *RB* 60 (1953) 41-82.
H.J. Auf der Maur, *Das Psalmenverständnis des Ambrosius von Mailand. Ein Beitrag zum Deutungshintergrund der Psalmenverwendung im Gottesdienst der Alten Kirche*, Leiden 1977.
C. Aziza, *Tertullien et le judaïsme*, Nice 1977.
T. Baarda, 'Jezus zeide: «Weest passanten». Over betekenis en oorsprong van logion 42 in het Evangelie van Thomas', in: *Ad Interim. Opstellen over Eschatologie,*

* The various articles—a number of which were revised (this applies to the titles as well) by Altaner himself—have been quoted as they appear in this edition.

Apocalyptiek en Ethiek aangeboden aan Prof. Dr. R. Schippers ..., Kampen 1975, 113-140.

Ch. Baguette, 'Une période stoïcienne dans l'évolution de saint Augustin', *REA* 16 (1970) 47-77.

H.A. van Bakel, 'Tyconius, Augustinus ante Augustinum' (1930), in: H.A. van Bakel, *Circa Sacra. Historische Studiën*, Haarlem 1935, 114-135.

J.N. Bakhuizen van den Brink, 'Geschiedenis van het christendom tot het grote schisma van 1054', in: G. van der Leeuw (ed.), *De godsdiensten der wereld*, II, Amsterdam 1941[2], 213-267.

——, *Handboek der Kerkgeschiedenis*, I, Den Haag 1965.

——, *Constantijn de Grote*, Amsterdam-Oxford 1975.

——, *De Nederlandse belijdenisgeschriften*, Amsterdam 1976[2].

G. Bardy, *Saint Augustin. L'homme et l'oeuvre*, Paris 1946.

——, 'Tyconius', *DThC* 15 (1950) 1932-1934.

——, 'Apologetik', *RAC* 1 (1950) 533-543.

——, 'Post Apostolos Ecclesiarum Magister', *RMAL* 6 (1950) 313-316.

——, 'La formation du concept de «Cité de Dieu» dans l'oeuvre de Saint Augustin', *ATA* 12 (1952) 5-19.

——, 'Définition de la Cité de Dieu', *ATA* 12 (1952) 113-129.

——, 'Saint Augustin et Tertullien', *ATA* 13 (1954) 145-150.

——, 'Introduction générale à La Cité de Dieu', 'Introductions' et 'Notes', *BA* 33-37, Paris 1959-1960.

L.W. Barnard, *Studies in the Apostolic Fathers and their Background*, Oxford 1966.

——, 'Apologetik I', *TRE* 3 (1978) 371-411.

T.D. Barnes, *Tertullian. A historical and literary study*, Oxford 1971 (1985[2]).

——, *Constantine and Eusebius*, Cambridge, Mass.-London 1981.

R.H. Barrow, *Introduction to St.Augustine 'The City of God', being selections from the De Civitate Dei including most of the XIXth book* ..., London 1950.

——, 'Remota ... iustitia', *VC* 15 (1961) 116.

W. Bauer, *Griechisch-Deutsches Wörterbuch zu den Schriften des Neuen Testaments und der übrigen urchristlichen Literatur*, Berlin-New York 1971[5].

F.Chr. Baur, *Das manichäische Religionssystem nach den Quellen neu untersucht und entwickelt*, Tübingen 1831 (repr. Göttingen 1928).

T.J. van Bavel (avec la collaboration de F. van der Zande), *Répertoire bibliographique de saint Augustin 1950-1960*, Steenbrugge-Den Haag 1963.

——, *Augustinus. Van liefde en vriendschap*, Baarn 1970.

——, 'Wat voor kerk kies je? De ruimheid van Augustinus' ecclesiologie', *TvT* 16 (1976) 355-375.

N.H. Baynes, *The Political Ideas of St. Augustine's De Civitate Dei*, London 1936 reprinted in: R.A. Humphreys and A.D. Momigliano (eds.), *Byzantine Studies and other Essays*, London 1955, 288-306.

A. Becker, *De l'instinct du bonheur à l'extase de la béatitude. Théologie et pédagogie du bonheur dans la prédication de Saint Augustin*, Paris 1967.

H. Berkhof, *Die Theologie des Eusebius von Caesarea*, Amsterdam 1939.

——, *De kerk en de keizer. Een studie over het ontstaan van de byzantinistische en de theocratische staatsgedachte in de vierde eeuw*, Amsterdam 1946.

L. Berkowitz, *Index Arnobianus*, Hildesheim 1967.

H. Bettenson, *Augustine, Concerning the City of God against the Pagans*, Penguin Books 1972.

M. Bévenot, 'Cyprian von Karthago', *TRE* 8 (1981) 246-254.

U. Bianchi, *Antropologia e dottrina della salvezza nella religione dei manichei*, Roma 1983.

J. Bidez, *La Cité du Monde et la Cité du Soleil chez les Stoïciens*, Paris 1932.

W. Bieder, *Ekklesia und Polis im Neuen Testament und in der Alten Kirche*, Zürich 1941.

J. Biegler, *Die Civitas Dei des heiligen Augustinus*, Paderborn 1894.

H. Bietenhard, *Die himmlische Welt im Urchristentum und Spätjudentum*, Tübingen 1951.

A. Blaise, *Dictionnaire Latin-Français des Auteurs Chrétiens*, Turnhout s.a..

H. Bloch, 'The Pagan Revival in the West at the End of the Fourth Century', in: A. Momigliano (ed.), *The Conflict between Paganism and Christianity in the Fourth Century*, Oxford 1963, 193-218.

J.-M. Le Blond, *Les conversions de saint Augustin*, Paris 1950.

B. Blumenkranz, *Die Judenpredigt Augustins. Ein Beitrag zur Geschichte der jüdisch-christlichen Beziehungen in den ersten Jahrhunderten*, Basel 1946 (repr. Paris 1973).

——, 'Augustin et les juifs. Augustin et le judaïsme', *RA* I (1958) 225-241 (= B. Blumenkranz, *Juifs et Chrétiens. Patristique et Moyen Age*, London 1977, Ch. III).

O. Böcher, 'Die heilige Stadt im Völkerkrieg. Wandlungen eines apokalyptischen Schemas', in: *Josephus-Studien* (FS O.Michel), Berlin 1974, 55-76.

J. den Boeft and A.H.M.Kessels (eds.), *Actus. Studies in Honour of H.L.W. Nelson*, Utrecht 1982.

A. Böhlig, 'Eine Bemerkung zur Beurteilung der Kephalaia' (1938), in: Böhlig, *Mysterion und Wahrheit*, 245-251.

——, *Die Bibel bei den Manichäern*, Diss. Münster 1947.

——, 'Probleme des manichäischen Lehrvortrages' (1953), in: Böhlig, *Mysterion und Wahrheit*, 228-244.

——, 'Christliche Wurzeln im Manichäismus' (1957/1960), in: Böhlig, *Mysterion und Wahrheit*, 202-221.

——, 'Die Arbeit an den koptischen Manichaica' (1961/1962), in: Böhlig, *Mysterion und Wahrheit*, 177-187.

——, 'Zu den Synaxeis des Lebendigen Evangeliums', in: Böhlig, *Mysterion und Wahrheit*, 222-227.

——, *Mysterion und Wahrheit. Gesammelte Beiträge zur spätantiken Religionsgeschichte*, Leiden 1968.

——, 'Zu gnostischen Grundlagen der Civitas-Dei-Vorstellung bei Augustin', *ZNW* 60 (1969) 291-295.

——, 'Der Synkretismus des Mani', in: Dietrich (Hrsg.), *Synkretismus*, 144-169.

——, *Die Gnosis*, III, *Der Manichäismus*, Zürich-München 1980.

——, 'Der Manichäismus', in: M.J. Vermaseren (Hrsg.) *Die orientalischen Religionen im Römerreich*, Leiden 1981, 436-458.

——, 'The New Testament and the Concept of the Manichean Myth', in: Logan and Wedderburn (eds.), *The New Testament and Gnosis*, 90-104.

G. Boissier, 'La conversion de saint Augustin' (1888), in: G.Boissier, *La fin du paganisme. Étude sur les dernières luttes religieuses en Occident au quatrième siècle*, Paris 1891^1, 339-379.

G. Bonner, *St.Augustine of Hippo. Life and Controversies*, London 1963.

——, *Saint Bede in the Tradition of Western Apocalyptic Commentary* (Jarrow Lecture 1966), Newcastle-upon-Tyne 1967.

——, 'Towards a Text of Tyconius', *SP* X (*TU* 107), Berlin 1970, 9-13.

G. Bornkamm, 'Thomasakten', in: Hennecke and Schneemelcher (Hrsg.), *NTAp*, II, 297-372.

J.-P. Bouhot, 'Alcuin et le *De catechizandis rudibus* de Saint Augustin', *RA* 15 (1980) 176-240.

É. Boularand, 'Le thème des deux cités chez saint Augustin', *EPh* 17 (1962) 213-231.

W. Bousset, *Die Offenbarung Johannis*, Göttingen 1906 (repr. 1966).

W. Bousset - H. Gressmann, *Die Religion des Judentums im späthellenistischen Zeitalter*, Tübingen 1926^3 (repr. 1966^4, mit einem Vorwort von E. Lohse).

M. Boyce, *A Word-List of Manichaean Middle Persian and Parthian (with a Reverse Index by R. Zwanziger)*, Leiden 1977.

E. Brandenburger, *Fleisch und Geist. Paulus und die dualistische Weisheit*, Neukirchen 1968.
H. Braun, *Qumran und das Neue Testament*, I – II, Tübingen 1966.
R. Braun, '*Deus Christianorum'. Recherches sur le vocabulaire doctrinal de Tertullien*, Paris 1962.
R. van den Broek, *Apollo in Asia. De orakels van Clarus en Didyma in de tweede en derde eeuw na Chr.*, Leiden 1981.
R. van den Broek and M.J.Vermaseren (eds.), *Studies in Gnosticism and Hellenistic Religions presented to Gilles Quispel* ..., Leiden 1981.
H.A. Brongers, *De gedragsregels der Qoemraan-gemeente*, Amsterdam 1958.
P. Brown, 'Saint Augustine' (1963), in: Brown, *Religion and Society*, 25-45.
——, *Augustine of Hippo. A biography*, London 1967.
——, 'Christianity and Local Culture in Late Roman Africa' (1968), in: Brown, *Religion and Society*, 279-300.
——, 'The Diffusion of Manichaeism in the Roman Empire' (1969), in: Brown, *Religion and Society*, 94-118.
——, *Religion and Society in the Age of Saint Augustine*, London 1972.
R.E. Brown – J.P.Meier, *Antioch and Rome. New Testament Cradles of Catholic Christianity*, London 1983.
W.H. Brownlee, *The Dead Sea Manual of Discipline*, New Haven 1951.
R. Bultmann, *Das Evangelium des Johannes*, Göttingen 1941 (repr. 1964).
——, *Theologie des Neuen Testaments*, Tübingen 1965[5].
E. Buonaiuti, 'Manichaeism and Augustine's Idea of «massa perditionis»', *HTR* 20 (1927) 117-127.
——, *Geschichte des Christentums*, I, Bern 1948.
F.C. Burkitt, *The Religion of the Manichees*, Cambridge 1925.
J.H.S. Burleigh, *The City of God. A Study of St. Augustine's Philosophy*, London 1949.
B. Busch, 'De initiatione christiana secundum sanctum Augustinum' et 'De modo quo s. Augustinus descripserit initiationem christianam', *Eph. Lit.* 52 (1938) 159-178; 385-483.
F.W. Bussell, 'The purpose of the world-process and the problem of evil as explained in the Clementine and Lactantian writings in a system of subordinate dualism', *SBEc* 4 (1896) 133-188.
R. Cameron – A.J. Dewey, *The Cologne Mani Codex (P. Colon. inv. nr. 4780) 'Concerning the Origin of his Body'*, Missoula, Mont. 1979.
H. von Campenhausen, *Ambrosius von Mailand als Kirchenpolitiker*, Berlin-Leipzig 1929.
——, 'Augustin und der Fall von Rom' (1947), in: H. von Campenhausen, *Tradition und Leben. Kräfte der Kirchengeschichte. Aufsätze und Vorträge*, Tübingen 1960, 253-271.
——, *Lateinische Kirchenväter*, Stuttgart 1978[4].
R. Canning, 'The Augustinian uti/frui Distinction in the Relation between Love for Neighbour and Love for God', *Aug(L)* 33 (1983) 165-231.
B. Capelle, 'L'introduction du catéchuménat à Rome', *RTAM* 5 (1933) 129-154.
J. Carmignac – P. Guilbert, *Les textes de Qumran*, I, Paris 1961.
C. Cary-Elwes, 'Peace in the City of God', *Ciudad*, I, 417-430.
Catalogus verborum quae in operibus Sancti Augustini inveniuntur. II, *Enarrationes in Psalmos 1-50, Corpus Christianorum 38*, Eindhoven 1978; III, *Enarrationes in Psalmos 51-100, Corpus Christianorum 39*, Eindhoven 1980; IV, *Enarrationes in Psalmos 101-150, Corpus Christianorum 40*, Eindhoven 1981; VI, *Confessionum libri XIII, Corpus Christianorum 27*, Eindhoven 1982; VII, *De civitate Dei, Corpus Christianorum 47-48*, Eindhoven 1984.
F. Cavallera, 'Les «Quaestiones hebraicae in Genesim» de Saint Jerôme et les «Quaestiones in Genesim» de Saint Augustin', *MAg*, II, 359-372.

H. Chadwick, 'Philo and the beginnings of Christian thought', in: Armstrong (ed.), *Philosophy*, 133-192.
R.H. Charles (ed.), *The Apocrypha and Pseudepigrapha of the Old Testament in English*, I-II, Oxford 1913 (repr. 1976-1977) (= Charles (ed.), *APOT*, I-II).
J.H. Charlesworth (ed.), *The Old Testament Pseudepigrapha*, I-II, London 1983-'85 (= Charlesworth (ed.), *OTP*, I-II).
A. Chastagnol, 'Le sénateur Volusien et la conversion d'une famille de l'aristocratie romaine au Bas-Empire', *REAn* 58 (1956) 241-253.
J.P. Christopher, *St. Augustine, The First Catechetical Instruction*, Westminster, Md. - London 1955[2] (*ACW* 2).
L. Cilleruelo, 'La oculta presencia del maniqueísmo en la «Ciudad de Dios»', *Ciudad*, I, 475-509.
G. Claesson, *Index Tertullianeus*, I-III, Paris 1974-1975.
T.E. Clarke, *The Eschatological Transformation of the Material World according to Saint Augustine*, Woodstock, Md. 1956.
——, 'St. Augustine and Cosmic Redemption', *TS* 19 (1958) 133-164.
G.H. Cohen Stuart, *The struggle in man between good and evil. An inquiry into the origin of the Rabbinic concept of Yeṣer Haraᵓ*, Kampen 1984.
W. Coleborne, '*The Shepherd* of Hermas. A Case for Multiple Authorship and Some Implications', *SP* 10 (*TU* 107), Berlin 1970, 65-70.
J.J. Collins, 'Testaments', in: M.E. Stone (ed.), *Jewish Writings of the Second Temple Period*, Assen-Philadelphia 1984, 325-355.
C. Colpe, 'Manichäismus', *RGG* IV (1960) 714-722.
——, 'Philo', *RGG* V (1961) 341-346.
——, 'Gnosis II (Gnostizismus)', *RAC* 11 (1981) 538-659.
G. Combès, *La doctrine politique de Saint Augustin*, Paris 1927.
R. Cordovani, 'Le due città nel «De catechizandis rudibus» di S. Agostino', *Aug* 7 (1967) 419-447.
P. Courcelle, *Les lettres grecques en Occident. De Macrobe à Cassiodore*, Paris 1948[2].
——, 'A propos du titre «Augustinus Magister». Le «maître Augustin»', *AM*, III, 9-11.
——, 'Propos antichrétiens rapportés par saint Augustin', *RA* 1 (1958) 149-184.
——, 'Saint Augustin a-t-il lu Philon d'Alexandrie?', *REAn* 63 (1961) 78-85.
——, *Les 'Confessions' de saint Augustin dans la tradition littéraire. Antécédents et postérité*, Paris 1963.
——, *Histoire littéraire des grandes invasions germaniques*. Paris 1964[3].
——, *Recherches sur les Confessions de saint Augustin*, Paris 1968[2].
Ch. Courtois, 'Saint Augustin et le problème de la survivance du punique', *RAfr* 94 (1950) 259-282.
F.E. Cranz, '*De Civitate Dei* XV, 2, et l'idée augustinienne de la société chrétienne', *REA* 3 (1957) 15-27 (= '*De Civitate Dei* XV, 2 and Augustine's Idea of the Christian Society', *Spec.* 25 (1950) 215-225; repr. in Markus (ed.), *Augustine*, 404-421).
H. Crouzel, 'Geist (Heiliger Geist)', *RAC* 9 (1976) 490-545.
O. Cullmann, *Le problème littéraire et historique du roman pseudo-clémentin. Étude sur le rapport entre le gnosticisme et le judéo-christianisme*, Paris 1930.
——, *Heil als Geschichte. Heilsgeschichtliche Existenz im Neuen Testament*, Tübingen 1965[1].
——, 'Die Schöpfung im Neuen Testament', in: *Ex auditu verbi. Theologische opstellen aangeboden aan Prof. Dr. G.C. Berkouwer*..., Kampen 1965, 56-72.
H. Dahlmann, 'M. Terentius Varro', *PRE, Suppl.* 6 (1935) 1172-1177.
J. Daniélou, 'La typologie millénariste de la semaine dans le christianisme primitif', *VC* 2 (1948) 1-16.

——, 'L'histoire du salut dans la catéchèse', *MD* 30 (1952) 19-35.
——, 'Trinité et angélologie dans la théologie judéo-chrétienne', *RSR* 45 (1957) 5-41.
——, *Das Judenchristentum und die Anfänge der Kirche*, Köln-Opladen 1964.
——, *The Theology of Jewish Christianity*, London-Philadelphia 1964.
——, *Gospel Message and Hellenistic Culture*, London-Philadelphia 1973.
——, *The Origins of Latin Christianity*, London-Philadelphia 1977.
—— -R. du Charlat, *La catéchèse aux premiers siècles*, Paris 1968.
E. Dassmann, 'Ecclesia vel anima. Die Kirche und ihre Glieder in der Hoheliederklärung bei Hippolyt, Origenes und Ambrosius von Mailand', *RQ* 61 (1966) 121-144.
——, 'Ambrosius', *TRE* 2 (1978) 362-386.
J.A. Davids, 'Sint Augustinus en Sint Ambrosius', *MA*, 242-255.
Ch. Dawson, 'St. Augustine and his Age', in: M.C. d'Arcy et al., *Saint Augustine*, New York-London 1957[3], 11-77.
F. Decret, *Aspects du manichéisme dans l'Afrique romaine. Les controverses de Fortunatus, Faustus et Felix avec saint Augustin*, Paris 1970.
——, *Mani et la tradition manichéenne*, Paris 1974.
——, *L'Afrique manichéenne (IVe-Ve siècles). Étude historique et doctrinale*, I-II, Paris 1978.
A.-L. Delattre, *Gamart ou la nécropole juive de Carthage*, Lyon 1885.
P. Delhaye, 'S. Augustin et les valeurs humaines', *MSR* 12 (1955) 121-138.
E. Dhanens, *Hubert en Jan van Eyck*, Antwerpen 1980.
M. Dibelius, *Der Hirt des Hermas*, Tübingen 1923 (*HNT*, Erg.-Band).
Sr. Agnes (Dicker), 'De eenheid van S. Augustinus' De Civitate Dei', *StC* 6 (1929-1930) 110-126; 164-181.
A. Dietrich (Hrsg.), *Synkretismus im syrisch-persischen Kulturgebiet*, Göttingen 1975.
E. Dinkler, 'Ticonius', *PRE Suppl.* 6 (1935) 849-856.
——, 'Friede', *RAC* 8 (1972) 434-493.
J. Divjak, 'Augustins erster Brief an Firmus und die revidierte Ausgabe der Civitas Dei', in: *Latinität und Alte Kirche. Festschrift für Rudolph Hanslik* ..., Wien-Köln-Graz 1977, 56-70.
F.J. Dölger, 'Zur Symbolik des altchristlichen Taufhauses. Das Oktogon und die Symbolik der Achtzahl', in: F.J. Dölger, *Antike und Christentum*, 4, Münster 1934 (repr. 1975), 153-187.
——, 'Beiträge zur Geschichte des Kreuzzeichens VIII', *JbAC* 8/9 (1965-1966) 7-52.
——, *Die Sonne der Gerechtigkeit und der Schwarze*, Münster 1971[2].
H. Dörrie, 'Das fünffach gestufte Mysterium. Der Aufstieg der Seele bei Porphyrios und Ambrosius', in: *Mullus. Festschrift für Theodor Klauser*, (*JbAC*, Erg. Bd. 1), Münster 1964, 79-92.
——, 'Akademeia', *KP* 1 (1979) 211-213.
——, 'Die Andere Theologie. Wie stellten die frühchristlichen Theologen des 2.-4. Jahrhunderts ihren Lesern die «Griechische Weisheit» (= den Platonismus) dar?', *ThPh* 56 (1981) 1-46.
H. Dörries, 'Fünfzehn Jahre Augustin-Forschung', *ThR* 1 (1929) 217-240.
J. Doignon, 'Le retentissement d'un exemple de la survie de Lactance', in: J. Fontaine – M. Perrin (éds.), *Lactance et son temps*, Paris 1978, 297-306.
U. Domínguez del Val, 'El martirio, argumento apologético en la «Ciudad de Dios»', *Ciudad*, I, 527-542.
J. Dougherty, *The Fivesquare City. The City in the Religious Imagination*, Notre Dame – London 1980.
P. Drews, 'Der literarische Charakter der neuentdeckten Schrift des Irenäus «Zum Erweise der apostolischen Verkündigung»', *ZNW* 8 (1907) 226-233.

H.J.W. Drijvers, *Bardaiṣan of Edessa*, Assen 1966.
——, 'Edessa und das jüdische Christentum', *VC* 24 (1970) 4-33.
——, 'Mani und Bardaiṣan. Ein Beitrag zur Vorgeschichte des Manichäismus', in: *Mélanges d'histoire des réligions offerts à Henri-Charles Puech*, Paris 1974, 459-469.
——, 'Bardaiṣan von Edessa als Repräsentant des syrischen Synkretismus', in: Dietrich (Hrsg.), *Synkretismus*, 109-122.
——, 'Bardesanes', *TRE* 5 (1980) 206-212.
——, 'Odes of Solomon and Psalms of Mani. Christians and Manichaeans in Third-Century Syria', in: Van den Broek and Vermaseren (eds.), *Studies in Gnosticism and Hellenistic Religions*, 117-130.
U. Duchrow, *Christenheit und Weltverantwortung. Traditionsgeschichte und systematische Struktur der Zweireichelehre*, Stuttgart 1970.
H. Duensing, 'Apokalypse des Paulus', in: Hennecke and Schneemelcher, *NTAp*, II, 536-567.
J.L. Duhaime, 'L'instruction sur les deux esprits et les interpolations dualistes à Qumran (1 QS III, 13 – IV, 26)', *RB* 84 (1977) 566-594.
A. Dupont-Sommer, 'L'instruction sur les deux Esprits dans le «Manuel de Discipline»', *RHR* 72 (1952) 5-35.
F. Dvornik, *Early Christian and Byzantine Political Philosophy. Origins and Background*, Washington-New York 1966.
H. Eger, *Die Eschatologie Augustins*, Greifswald 1933.
F.X. Eggersdorfer, *Der heilige Augustinus als Pädagoge und seine Bedeutung für die Geschichte der Bildung*, Freiburg i. Br. 1907.
A.A.T. Ehrhardt, *Politische Metaphysik von Solon bis Augustin*, I-III, Tübingen 1959-1969.
E. Elorduy, *Die Sozialphilosophie der Stoa*, Leipzig 1936.
G. del Estal – J.J. Rosado, 'Equivalencia de «civitas» en el De Civitate Dei', *Ciudad*, II, 367-454.
J.M. del Estal, 'Historiographía de la «Ciudad de Dios». De 1928 a 1954', *Ciudad*, II, 647-774.
V. Fàbrega, 'Die chiliastische Lehre des Laktanz', *JbAC* 17 (1974) 126-146.
E. Feldmann, *Der Einfluss des Hortensius und des Manichäismus auf das Denken des jungen Augustinus von 373*, Diss. Münster 1975.
——, 'Christus-Frömmigkeit der Mani-Jünger. Der suchende Student Augustinus in ihrem «Netz»?', in: E. Dassmann – K.S. Frank (Hrsg.), *Pietas. Festschrift für Bernhard Kötting* (*JbAC*, Erg. Bd. 8), Münster 1980, 198-216.
K.G. Fellerer, 'Die Musica in den Artes Liberales', in: J. Koch (Hrsg.), *Artes Liberales. Von der Antiken Bildung zur Wissenschaft des Mittelalters*, Leiden 1976², 33-49.
L.C. Ferrari, 'Background to Augustine's «City of God»', *CJ* 67 (1972) 198-208.
——, 'Augustine's «Nine Years» as a Manichee', *Aug(L)* 25 (1975) 210-216.
J. Ferron – G. Lapeyre, 'Carthage', *DHGE* 11 (1949) 1149-1233.
J.N. Figgis, *The Political Aspects of St. Augustine's «City of God»*, London 1921 (repr. Gloucester, Mass. 1963).
G. Flügel, *Mani, seine Lehre und seine Schriften*, Leipzig 1862 (repr. Osnabrück 1969).
W. Foerster, 'Diabolos', *TWNT* II (1935) 74-80.
G. Folliet, 'Pour le dossier «Augustinus Magister»', *REA* 3 (1957) 67-68.
K. Forster, 'Die ekklesiologische Bedeutung des corpus-Begriffes im Liber Regularum des Tyconius', *MThZ* 7 (1956) 173-183.
P. Frederiksen Landes, 'Tyconius and the End of the World', *REA* 18 (1982) 59-75.
J.-C. Fredouille, *Tertullien et la conversion de la culture antique*, Paris 1972.
W.H.C. Frend, 'A Note on the Berber Background in the Life of Augustine', *JTS* 43 (1942) 188-191 (= Frend, *Religion*, Ch. XIV).

——, *The Donatist Church. A Movement of Protest in Roman North Africa*, Oxford 1952.
——, 'The Gnostic-Manichaean Tradition in Roman North Africa', *JEH* 4 (1953) 13-26 (= Frend, *Religion*, Ch. XII).
——, 'Manichaeism in the Struggle between Saint Augustine and Petilian of Constantine', *AM*, II, 859-866 (= Frend, *Religion*, Ch. XIII).
——, 'The *Seniores Laici* and the Origins of the Church in North Africa', *JTS* 12 (1961) 280-284.
——, *Martyrdom and Persecution in the Early Church*, Oxford 1965.
——, *Religion Popular and Unpopular in the Early Christian Centuries*, London 1976.
——, 'The Early Christian Church in Carthage', in: *Excavations at Carthage in 1976, conducted by the University of Michigan*, Ann Arbor, Mich. 1977, 21-40 (= Frend, *Town and Country*, Ch. XIV).
——, 'Jews and Christians in Third Century Carthage', in: *Paganisme, Judaïsme, Christianisme. Influences et affrontements dans le monde antique. Mélanges offerts à Marcel Simon*, Paris 1978, 185-194 (= Frend, *Town and Country*, Ch. XVII).
——, *Town and Country in the Early Christian Centuries*, London 1980.
——, *The Rise of Christianity*, London 1984.
R. Frick, *Die Geschichte des Reich-Gottes-Gedankens in der alten Kirche bis zu Origenes und Augustin*, Giessen 1928.
J. Friedrich – W. Röllig, *Phönizisch-Punische Grammatik*, Roma 1970².
J.M. Froidevaux, *Irénée de Lyon, Démonstration de la Prédication apostolique*, Paris 1959 (*SC* 62).
R.N. Frye, 'The Cologne Greek Codex about Mani', in: *Ex orbe religionum. Studia Geo Widengren ... oblata ...*, I, Leiden 1972, 424-429.
H. Fuchs, *Augustin und der antike Friedensgedanke. Untersuchungen zum neunzehnten Buch der Civitas Dei*, Berlin 1926.
——, *Der geistige Widerstand gegen Rom in der antiken Welt*, Berlin 1938.
F.X. Funk, 'Die Didache in der afrikanischen Kirche', *ThQ* 76 (1894) 601-604.
A. Gabillon, 'Romanianus, alias Cornelius. Du nouveau sur le bienfaiteur et l'ami de Saint Augustin', *REA* 24 (1978) 58-70.
J. Gagé, 'Felicitas', *RAC* 7 (1969) 711-723.
O. von Gebhardt, 'Ein übersehenes Fragment der *Didachè* in alter lateinischer Übersetzung', in: Harnack, *Lehre*, 275-286.
W. Geerlings, 'Zur Frage des Nachwirkens des Manichäismus in der Theologie Augustins', *ZKTh* 93 (1971) 45-60.
——, 'Der manichäische «Jesus patibilis» in der Theologie Augustins', *ThQ* 152 (1972) 124-131.
J. Geffcken, *Zwei griechische Apologeten*, Leipzig-Berlin 1907.
S. Giet, *Hermas et les pasteurs*, Paris 1963.
O. Gigon, *Die antike Kultur und das Christentum*, Gütersloh 1966.
É. Gilson, *Introduction à l'étude de saint Augustin*, Paris 1929¹.
——, *Les metamorphoses de la Cité de Dieu*, Louvain-Paris 1952.
F. Glorie, 'Das «zweite Aenigma» in Augustins *Opusculorum Indiculus* cap. X⁴, 1-4: *«Tractatus Psalmorum»*', in: *Corona gratiarum. Miscellanea ... Eligio Dekkers ... oblata*, I, Brugge-'s-Gravenhage 1975, 289-309.
F.C.J. van Goens, *De Aurelio Augustino Apologeta secundum libros De Civitate Dei*, Amstelodami-Lugduni Batavorum 1838.
H.-W. Goetz, *Die Geschichtstheologie des Orosius*, Darmstadt 1980.
I.M. Gómez, 'El perdido comentario de Ticonio al Apocalipsis. Principios de crítica literaria textual para su reconstrucción', in: *Miscellanea biblica B. Ubach*, Montisserrati 1953, 387-411.
L. González, 'Valor apologético del milagro en la «Ciudad de Dios»', *Ciudad*, I, 543-570.

M.M. Gorman, 'Aurelius Augustinus: The Testimony of the Oldest Manuscripts of Saint Augustine's Works', *JTS* 35 (1984) 475-480.

L.H. Grondijs, 'Numidian Manicheism in Augustinus' Time', *NTT* 9 (1954-1955) 21-42.

——, 'Analyse du manichéisme numidien au IVe siècle', *AM*, III, 391-410.

H. Grundmann, *Ketzergeschichte des Mittelalters*, Göttingen 1967^2.

P. Guilbert, 'Le plan de la Règle de la Communauté', *RdQ* 1 (1958-1959) 323-344.

A. Guillaumont, 'De nouveaux Actes apocryphes: Les Actes de Pierre et des Douze Apôtres', *RHR* 4 (1979) 141-152.

J.-C. Guy, *Unité et structure logique de la 'Cité de Dieu' de saint Augustin*, Paris 1961.

R. Haardt, *Die Gnosis. Wesen und Zeugnisse*, Salzburg 1967.

A.C.J. Habets, *Geschiedenis van de indeling van de filosofie in de Oudheid*, Diss. Utrecht 1983.

P. Hadot – U. Brenke, *Christlicher Platonismus. Die theologische Schriften des Marius Victorinus*, Zürich-Stuttgart 1967.

P. Hadot, 'La Présentation du Platonisme par Augustin', in: A.M. Ritter (Hrsg.), *Kerygma und Logos. Beiträge zu den geistesgeschichtlichen Beziehungen zwischen Antike und Christentum. Festschrift für Carl Andresen* ..., Göttingen 1979, 273-279.

——, 'Fürstenspiegel', *RAC* 8 (1972) 555-632.

H. Hagendahl, *Augustine and the Latin Classics*, Göteborg 1967.

——, 'Die Bedeutung der Stenographie für die spätlateinische christliche Literatur', *JbAC* 14 (1971) 24-38.

T. Hahn, *Tyconius-Studien. Ein Beitrag zur Kirchen- und Dogmengeschichte des vierten Jahrhunderts*, Leipzig 1900 (repr. Aalen 1971).

G. Haloun – W.B.Henning, 'The Compendium of the Doctrines and Styles of the Teaching of Mani, the Buddha of Light', *Asia Major* 3 (1952) 184-212.

E. Hammerschmidt, 'Das Thomasevangelium und die Manichäer', *OrChr* 46 (1962) 120-123.

M. Hammond, *City-State and World State in Greek and Roman Political Theory until Augustus*, Cambridge, Mass. 1951.

A.T. Hanson, '*Hodayoth* VI and Hermas *Sim.* VIII', *SP* 10 (*TU* 107), Berlin 1970, 105-108.

R.P.C. Hanson, 'Notes on Tertullian's Interpretation of Scripture', *JTS* 12 (1961) 273-279.

G. Harder, 'Eschatologische Schemata in der Johannes-Apokalypse', *Theologia viatorum 9, Jahrbuch der kirchlichen Hochschule Berlin 1963*, Berlin 1964, 70-87.

A. (von) Harnack, *Die Lehre der zwölf Apostel*, Leipzig 1884 (*TU* II,1).

——, *Augustins Konfessionen*, Giessen 1888, in: A. Harnack, *Reden und Aufsätze*, I, Giessen 1906^2, 49-79.

——, *Die Apostellehre und die jüdischen beiden Wege*, Leipzig 1896^2.

——, *Lehrbuch der Dogmengeschichte*, I – III, Tübingen $1909\text{-}1910^4$ (repr. Darmstadt 1964).

——, *Geschichte der altchristlichen Literatur bis Eusebius*, I, 1/2, hrsg. von K. Aland, Leipzig 1958^2.

J. Haussleiter, 'Die Kommentare des Victorinus, Tichonius und Hieronymus zur Apokalypse', *ZKWL* 7 (1886) 239-257.

——, 'Ticonius', RE^3 20 (1908) 851-855.

E. Heck, *Die dualistischen Zusätze und die Kaiseranreden bei Lactantius. Untersuchungen zur Textgeschichte der 'Divinae institutiones' und der Schrift 'De opificio dei'*, Heidelberg 1972.

——, 'Minucius Felix und der römische Staat. Ein Hinweis zum 25. Kapitel des «Octavius»', *VC* 38 (1984) 154-164.

G.J. v.d.Heide, *Christendom en politiek in de tijd van Constantijn de Grote*, Kampen 1979.

E. Hendrikx, 'Augustinus en het Imperium Romanum', *AThijm* 44 (1956) 95-110.

M. Hengel, *Judentum und Hellenismus. Studien zu ihrer Begegnung unter besonderer Berücksichtigung Palästinas bis zur Mitte des 2. Jh. v. Chr.*, Tübingen 1969.
E. Hennecke (Hrsg.), *Neutestamentliche Apokryphen*, Tübingen 1924².
E. Hennecke – W.Schneemelcher (Hrsg.), *Neutestamentliche Apokryphen in deutscher Übersetzung*, I – II, Tübingen 1953³-1964³ (= Hennecke and Schneemelcher (Hrsg.), *NTAp*, I-II).
A. Henrichs, 'Mani and the Babylonian Baptists: A Historical Confrontation', *HSCP* 77 (1973) 23-59.
——, 'The Cologne Mani Codex Reconsidered', *HSCP* 83 (1979) 334-367.
P. Henry, *Plotin et l'Occident. Firmicus Maternus, Marius Victorinus, Saint Augustin et Macrobe*, Louvain 1934.
——, *La vision d'Ostie. Sa place dans la vie et l'oeuvre de saint Augustin*, Paris 1938.
L. Herrmann, 'Commodien et Saint Augustin', *Latomus* 20 (1961) 312-321.
A. Hilhorst, *Sémitismes et latinismes dans le Pasteur d'Hermas*, Nijmegen 1976.
H.Z. (J.W.) Hirschberg, *A history of the Jews in North Africa*, I, Leiden 1974.
F. Hofmann, *Der Kirchenbegriff des hl. Augustinus in seinen Grundlagen und in seiner Entwicklung*, München 1933.
K. Holl, 'Augustins innere Entwicklung' (1922), in: K. Holl, *Gesammelte Aufsätze zur Kirchengeschichte*, III, Tübingen 1928, 54-116.
R. Holte, *Béatitude et Sagesse. Saint Augustin et le problème de la fin de l'homme dans la philosophie ancienne*, Paris 1962.
——, 'Glück (Glückseligkeit)', *RAC* 11 (1981) 246-270.
H.J. Holtzmann, 'Die Katechese der alten Kirche', in: *Theologische Abhandlungen Carl von Weizsäcker ... gewidmet*, Freiburg 1892, 61-110.
H. Hommel, 'Rhetorik', *Lexikon der Antike*, 4, München 1975², 127-143.
H.A.M. Hoppenbrouwers, *Recherches sur la terminologie du martyre de Tertullien à Lactance*, Nijmegen 1961.
H. Huisman, *Augustinus' briefwisseling met Nectarius. Inleiding, tekst, vertaling, commentaar*, Amsterdam 1956.
E. von Ivánka, *Plato Christianus. Übernahme und Umgestaltung des Platonismus durch die Väter*, Einsiedeln 1964.
F.S. Jones, 'The Pseudo-Clementines. A History of Research', *The Second Century* 2 (1982) 1-33, 63-96.
O.J. de Jong, *Geschiedenis der kerk*, Nijkerk 1980¹⁰.
Ch. Journet, *L'Église du Verbe incarné*, II, Paris 1951.
——, 'Les trois cités: celle de Dieu, celle de l'homme, celle du diable', *Nova et vetera* 33 (1958) 25-48.
Judéo-christianisme. Recherches historiques et théologiques offertes en hommage au Cardinal Jean Daniélou, Paris 1972 (= *RSR* 60 (1972) 1-320).
E.H. Kaden, 'Die Edikte gegen die Manichäer von Diokletian bis Justinian', in: *Festschrift für Hans Lewald*, Basel 1953, 55-68.
E. Käsemann, 'Eine urchristliche Taufliturgie' (1949) in: *Exegetische Versuche und Besinnungen*, I, Göttingen 1960, 43-47.
J.-D. Kaestli, 'L'utilisation des Actes apocryphes des apôtres dans le manichéisme', in: M. Krause (ed.), *Gnosis and Gnosticism*, Leiden 1977, 107-116.
E. Kamlah, *Die Form der katalogischen Paränese im Neuen Testament*, Tübingen 1964.
W. Kamlah, *Christentum und Geschichtlichkeit. Untersuchungen des Christentums und zu Augustins 'Bürgerschaft Gottes'*, Stuttgart-Köln 1951².
C. Kannengiesser, 'Enarratio in psalmum CXVIII: Science de la révélation et progrès spirituel', *RA* 2 (1962) 359-381.
H. Karpp, 'Christennamen', *RAC* 2 (1954) 1114-1138.
H.T. Karsten, *Augustinus over het Godsrijk. Beschrijving van den inhoud der twee en twintig boeken. Met inleiding en aantekeningen*, Haarlem 1914.

A.F. van Katwijk, *Lexicon Commodianeum*, Amstelodami 1934.

E. Kautsch (Hrsg.), *Die Apokryphen und Pseudepigraphen des Alten Testaments*, I – II, Tübingen 1900 (repr. Darmstadt 1975) (= Kautsch (Hrsg.), *APAT*, I – II).

P. Kawerau, *Geschichte der Alten Kirche*, Marburg 1967.

H.C. Kee, 'Testaments of the Twelve Patriarchs', in: Charlesworth (ed.), *OTP*, I, 775-828.

A. Kehl, 'Gewand (der Seele)', *RAC* 10 (1978) 945-1025.

P.M.A. van Kempen-van Dijk, *Monnica. Augustinus' visie op zijn moeder*, Amsterdam 1978.

K. Kessler, *Mani. Forschungen über die manichäische Religion*, I, *Voruntersuchungen und Quellen*, Berlin 1889.

H. Kirsten, *Die Taufabsage. Eine Untersuchung zu Gestalt und Geschichte der Taufe nach den altkirchlichen Taufliturgien*, Berlin 1960.

H.D.F. Kitto, *The Greeks*, Penguin Books 1951.

R. Klein, *Tertullian und das römische Reich*, Heidelberg 1968.

——, *Symmachus, eine tragische Gestalt des ausgehenden Heidentums*, Darmstadt 1971.

——, *Der Streit um den Victoriaaltar*, Darmstadt 1972.

J.A. Kleist, *The Epistles of St. Clement of Rome and of St. Ignatius of Antioch*, Westminster, Md. 1946 (*ACW* 1).

A.F.J. Klijn, *The Acts of Thomas*, Leiden 1962.

——, 'The Study of Jewish Christianity', *NTS* 20 (1974) 419-431.

A.F.J. Klijn – G.J.Reinink, 'Elchasai and Mani', *VC* 28 (1974) 277-289.

E. Klostermann, *Das Matthäusevangelium*, Tübingen 1927[2] (*HNT* 4).

R. Knopf, *Die Lehre der Zwölf Apostel, Die zwei Clemensbriefe*, Tübingen 1920 (*HNT*, Erg.-Band).

H. Koch, 'Die Didache bei Cyprian?', *ZNW* 8 (1907) 69-70.

L. Koenen, 'Augustine and Manichaeism in Light of the Cologne Mani Codex', *ICS* 3 (1978) 154-195.

B. Kötting, *Peregrinatio religiosa. Wallfahrten in der Antike und das Pilgerwesen in der alten Kirche*, Münster 1950.

J. Koopmans, *Het oudkerkelijk dogma in de reformatie, bepaaldelijk bij Calvijn*, Wageningen 1938 (repr. Amsterdam 1983).

H. Kraft, *Clavis patrum apostolicorum*, Darmstadt 1963.

—— (Hrsg.), *Konstantin der Grosse*, Darmstadt 1974.

R.A. Kraft, *Barnabas and the Didache*, Toronto et al. 1965.

G.H. Kramer, *Ambrosius van Milaan en de geschiedenis*, Amsterdam 1983.

M. Krause, 'Die Petrusakten in Codex VI von Nag Hammadi', in: M. Krause (ed.), *Essays on the Nag Hammadi Texts in Honour of Alexander Böhlig*, Leiden 1972, 36-58.

K.G. Kuhn, 'Die Sektenschrift und die iranische Religion', *ZThK* 49 (1952) 296-316.

A. Kunzelmann, 'Die Chronologie der Sermones des hl. Augustinus', *MAg*, II, 417-520.

A.-M. La Bonnardière, 'L'épître aux Hébreux dans l'oeuvre de saint Augustin', *REA* 3 (1957) 137-162.

——, *Biblia Augustiniana. A.T. Les douze petits prophètes*, Paris 1963.

——, '«Aurelius Augustinus» ou «Aurelius, Augustinus»?' *RBén* 91 (1981) 231-237.

P. de Labriolle, *Saint Augustin: La Cité de Dieu, I: livres I-V*, Paris 1941.

B. Lacroix, 'La date du XIe livre du De Civitate Dei', *VC* 5 (1951) 121-122.

G.B. Ladner, *The Idea of Reform. Its Impact on Christian Thought and Action in the Age of the Fathers*, Cambridge, Mass. 1959.

C. Lambot, 'Lettre inédite de saint Augustin relative au «De civitate Dei»', *RBén* 51 (1939) 109-121.

É. Lamirande, *Un siècle et demi d'études sur l'ecclesiologie de saint Augustin. Essai bibliographique*, Paris 1962.

——, *L'Église céleste selon saint Augustin*, Paris 1963.

——, 'Le thème de la Jérusalem céleste chez saint Ambrose', *REA* 29 (1983) 209-232.

J. Lamotte, 'Le Mythe de Rome «Ville Éternelle» et saint Augustin', *Aug(L)* 11 (1961) 225-260.

G.W.H. Lampe, *A Patristic Greek Lexicon*, Oxford 1976^4.

J. Laufs, *Der Friedensgedanke bei Augustinus. Untersuchungen zum XIX. Buch des Werkes 'De Civitate Dei'*, Wiesbaden 1973.

A. Lauras, 'Deux cités, Jérusalem et Babylone. Formation et évolution d'un thème central du «De Civitate Dei»', *Ciudad*, I, 117-150.

——, 'Saint Léon le Grand et le Manichéisme Romain', *SP* 11 (*TU* 108), Berlin 1972, 203-209.

A. Lauras – H. Rondet, 'Le thème des deux cités dans l'oeuvre de Saint Augustin', in: H. Rondet – M. Le Landais – A. Lauras – C. Couturier, *Études Augustiniennes*, Paris 1953, 97-160.

A.R.C. Leany, *The Rule of Qumran and its Meaning*, London 1966.

H. Leclercq, 'Catéchèse-Catéchisme-Catéchumène', *DACL* 2 (1935) 2530-2579.

——, 'Livres canoniques', *DACL* 9 (1930) 1791-1810.

B. Legewie, 'Die körperliche Konstitution und die Krankheiten Augustin's, *MAg*, II, 5-21.

H. Leisegang, 'Der Ursprung der Lehre Augustins von der civitas dei', *AKG* 16 (1926) 127-158.

Les lettres de Saint Augustin découvertes par Johannes Divjak. Communications présentées au Colloque des 20 et 21 Septembre 1982, Paris 1983.

G. Lewis, 'Augustinisme et cartésianisme', *AM*, II, 1087-1104.

J. Licht, 'An Analysis of the Treatise on the Two Spirits in DSD', *ScrHier* 2 (1958) 88-100.

M. Lidzbarski, *Ginzā. Der Schatz oder das Grosse Buch der Mandäer*, Göttingen-Leipzig 1925.

H. Lietzmann, *Geschichte der Alten Kirche*, I – IV, Berlin 1961^4-1961^3.

P. Lluis-Font, 'Sources de la doctrine d'Hermas sur les deux esprits', *RAM* 39 (1963) 83-98.

W. von Loewenich, *Augustin und das christliche Geschichtsdenken*, München 1947.

K. Löwith, *Weltgeschichte und Heilsgeschehen. Die theologischen Voraussetzungen der Geschichtsphilosophie*, Stuttgart et al. 1953.

L.J. van der Lof, 'The date of the De catechizandis rudibus', *VC* 16 (1962) 198-204.

——, 'Die Übersetzung von «civitas Dei» ins Deutsche und ins Niederländische', *Aug(L)* 13 (1963) 373-386.

——, 'Der numidische Manichäismus im vierten Jahrhundert', *SP* 8 (*TU* 93), Berlin 1966, 118-129.

A.H.B. Logan and A.J.M. Wedderburn (eds.), *The New Testament and Gnosis. Essays in honour of Robert McL. Wilson*, Edinburgh 1983.

B. Lohse, 'Augustins Wandlung in seiner Beurteilung des Staates', *SP* 6 (*TU* 81), Berlin 1962, 447-475.

F. Loofs, *Leitfaden zum Studium der Dogmengeschichte*, Tübingen 1968^7 (hrsg. von K. Aland).

R. Lorenz, 'Fruitio Dei bei Augustin', *ZKG* 63 (1950-1951) 75-132.

——, 'Die Herkunft des augustinischen «Frui Deo»', *ZKG* (1952-1953) 34-60.

——, 'Augustin', *RGG* I (1957) 738-748.

——, 'Augustinliteratur seit dem Jubiläum von 1954', *TR* 25 (1959) 1-75.

——, *Das vierte bis sechste Jahrhundert (Westen)*, Göttingen 1970.
——, 'Zwölf Jahre Augustinforschung (1959-1970)', *TR* 38 (1973) 293-333; 39 (1974) 95-138, 253-286, 331-364; 40 (1975) 1-41, 97-149, 227-261.
H. de Lubac, *Histoire et Esprit. L'intelligence de l'Écriture d'après Origène*, Paris 1950.
A. Luneau, *L'histoire du salut chez les Pères de l'Église. La doctrine des âges du monde*, Paris 1964.
G.P. Luttikhuizen, *The Revelation of Elchasai. Investigations into the Evidence for a Mesopotamian Jewish Apocalypse of the Second Century and its Reception by Judeo-Christian Propagandists*, Tübingen 1985.
J.A. McCallin, 'The Christological Unity of Saint Augustine's *De Civitate Dei*', *REA* 12 (1966) 85-109.
G.E. McCracken, *Arnobius of Sicca, The Case against the Pagans*, Westminster, Md. 1949 (*ACW* 7).
S. MacKenna – B.S.Page, *Plotinus, The Enneads*, London 1969[4].
G. Madec, 'Tempora christiana. Expression du triomphalisme chrétien ou récrimination païenne?', in C.P. Mayer – W. Eckermann (Hrsg.), *Scientia Augustiniana* (FS A. Zumkeller), Würzburg 1975, 112-136.
——, 'Si Plato viveret ... (Augustin, «De vera religione» 3,3)' in: *Néoplatonisme. Mélanges offerts à Jean Trouillard*, Fontenay-aux-Roses 1981, 231-247.
J.P. Maher, 'Saint Augustine and Manichaean Cosmogony', *AS* 10 (1979) 91-104.
F.G. Maier, *Augustin und das antike Rom*, Stuttgart-Köln 1955.
G. Maier, *Die Johannesoffenbarung und die Kirche*, Tübingen 1981.
A. Mandouze, *Saint Augustin. L'aventure de la raison et de la grâce*, Paris 1968.
——, 'Saint Augustin et la cité grecque', *REL* 47 (1969) 396-417.
—— et al., *Prosopographie de l'Afrique chrétienne (303-533)*, Paris 1982 (= *PAC*).
M. Marin, 'Sulla fortuna della Similitudini III e IV di Erma', *VetChr* 19 (1982) 331-340.
R.A. Markus, 'Marius Victorinus', in: Armstrong (ed.), *Cambridge History*, 331-340.
——, *Saeculum: History and Society in the Theology of St Augustine*, Cambridge 1970.
—— (ed.), *Augustine. A Collection of Critical Essays*, New York 1972.
H.-I. Marrou, *Histoire de l'éducation dans l'antiquité*, Paris 1948.
——, 'La technique de l'édition à l'époque patristique' (1949), in : Marrou, *Patristique et Humanisme*, 239-252.
——, 'La division en chapitres des livres de La Cité de Dieu' (1951), in: Marrou, *Patristique et Humanisme*, 253-265.
——, *St Augustin et l'augustinisme*, Paris 1955.
——, 'Civitas Dei, civitas terrena: num tertium quid?', *SP* 2 (*TU* 64), Berlin 1957, 342-350.
——, *Saint Augustin et la fin de la culture antique*, Paris 1958[4].
——, *Patristique et Humanisme. Mélanges*, Paris 1976.
——, 'Saint Augustin, Orose et l'augustinisme historique', in: *La storiografia altomedievale*, I, Spoleto 1970, 59-87.
R.T. Marshall, *Studies in the political and socio-religious terminology of the De Civitate Dei*, Washington 1952.
J. Mausbach, *Die Ethik des heiligen Augustinus*, I – II, Freiburg 1929[2].
J. Mayer, *Geschichte des Katechumenats und der Katechese in den ersten sechs Jahrhunderten*, Kempten 1868.
L.S. Mazzolani, *The Idea of the City in Roman Thought. From walled City to spiritual Commonwealth*, London-Sidney-Toronto 1970.
F. van der Meer, *Augustinus de zielzorger. Een studie over de praktijk van een kerkvader*, Utrecht-Brussel 1947.
J. Mehlmann, 'Tertulliani Liber De Carne Christi ab Augustino citatus', *SE* 13 (1966) 269-289.

E.P. Meijering, 'Wie platonisierten Christen? Zur Grenzziehung zwischen Platonismus, kirchlichem Credo und patristischer Theologie', *VC* 28 (1974) 15-28.

J.P. de Menasce, 'Augustin manichéen', in: *Freundesgabe für Ernst Robert Curtius*, Berlin 1956, 79-93.

H. Merkel, *Widersprüche zwischen den Evangelien. Ihre polemische und apologetische Behandlung in der Alten Kirche bis zu Augustin*, Tübingen 1971.

E. Meuthen, 'Der ethische Charakter der civitates bei Augustinus und ihre platonische Fehldeutung', in: J. Engel – H.M. Klinkenberg (Hrsg.), *Aus Mittelalter und Neuzeit. Gerhard Kallen zum 70. Geburtstag ...*, Bonn 1957, 43-62.

W. Michaelis, 'Hodos', *TWNT* V (1954) 42-118.

J. Michl, 'Engel V (Engelnamen)', *RAC* 5 (1962) 200-239.

Chr. Mohrmann, *Tertullianus. Apologeticum en andere geschriften uit Tertullianus' voormontanistischen tijd*, Utrecht-Brussel 1951.

——, 'Saint Jérôme et Saint Augustin sur Tertullien', *VC* 5 (1951) 111-112.

E. Molland, 'La circoncision, le baptême et l'autorité du décret apostolique (Actes XV, 28 sq.) dans les milieux judéo-chrétiens des Pseudo-Clémentines', *ST* 9 (1955) 1-39.

P. Monceaux, *Histoire littéraire de l'Afrique chrétienne*, I – VII, Paris 1901-1923.

——, 'Les colonies juives dans l'Afrique chrétien', *REJ* 44 (1902) 1-28.

——, *Le Manichéen Faustus of Milev. Restitution de ses capitula*, Paris 1924.

G.F. Moore, *Judaism in the First Centuries of the Christian Era. The Age of the Tannaim*, I, Cambridge, Mass. 1970[11].

M. Moreau, 'Le dossier Marcellinus dans la correspondance de saint Augustin', *RA* 9 (1973) 3-181.

G. Morin, 'Le commentaire homilétique de S. Césaire sur l'Apocalypse', *RBén* 45 (1933) 43-61.

J.A. Mourant, 'The «cogitos»: Augustinian and Cartesian', *AS* 10 (1979) 27-42.

J. Murphy-O'Connor, 'La génèse littéraire de la Règle de la Communauté', *RB* 76 (1969) 528-549.

P. Nagel, 'Die Psalmoi Sarakoton des manichäischen Psalmbuches', *OLZ* 62 (1957) 123-130.

——, 'Die apokryphen Apostelakten des 2. und 3. Jahrhunderts in der manichäischen Literatur', in: K.-W. Tröger (Hrsg.), *Gnosis und Neues Testament. Studien aus Religionswissenschaft und Theologie*, Berlin 1973, 149-182.

P. Nautin, *Origène. Sa vie et son oeuvre*, Paris 1977.

E. Nebreda, *Bibliographia Augustiniana*, Roma 1928.

F.J. Neuberg, 'An unrecognized meaning of Hebrew Dôr', *JNES* 9 (1950) 215-217.

J.E. Niederhuber, *Die Lehre des hl. Ambrosius vom Reiche Gottes auf Erden*, Mainz 1904.

F. Nötscher, *Zur theologischen Terminologie der Qumran-Texte*, Bonn 1956.

——, 'Vorchristliche Typen urchristlicher Ämter? Episkopos und Mebaqqer' (1960), in: F. Nötscher, *Vom Alten zum Neuen Testament. Gesammelte Aufsätze*, Bonn 1962, 118-220.

O. Noordmans, *Augustinus* (1933/1952[2]) in: Noordmans, *VW* 3, 32-198.

——, 'Augustinus' (1940), in: Noordmans, *VW* 3, 249-255.

——, *Verzamelde werken*, 3, Kampen 1981.

H.S. Nyberg, 'Forschungen über den Manichäismus' (1935), in: Widengren (Hrsg.), *Manichäismus*, 3-28.

A. Nygren, 'Luthers Lehre von den zwei Reichen' (1949), in: Schrey (Hrsg.), *Reich Gottes und Welt*, 277-289.

J. Obersteiner, 'Augustins «Civitas Dei» und die Geschichtstheologie der Bibel', *Ciudad*, I, 313-350.

R.M. Ogilvie, *The Library of Lactantius*, Oxford 1978.
J.J. O'Meara, 'Augustine and Neo-platonism', *RA* I (1958) 91-111.
——, *Porphyry's Philosophy from Oracles in Augustine*, Paris 1959.
——, *Charter of Christendom: The Significance of the «City of God»*, New York 1961.
——, *The Young Augustine. An introduction to the Confessions of St Augustine*, London-New York 1980.
J. van Oort, 'Augustinus Verbi Divini Minister', in: J. van Oort et al. (ed.), *Verbi Divini Minister*, Amsterdam 1983, 167-188.
A.P. Orbán, *Les dénominations du monde chez les premiers auteurs chrétiens*, Nijmegen 1970.
——, 'Die Benennungen der Welt in Augustins *De civitate Dei* : eine Untersuchung über Augustins Weltanschauung', in: Den Boeft and Kessels (eds.), *Actus*, 211-246.
L.J.R. Ort, *Mani. A religio-historical description of his personality*, Leiden 1967.
P. von der Osten-Sacken, *Gott und Belial. Traditionsgeschichtliche Untersuchungen zum Dualismus in den Texten aus Qumran*, Göttingen 1969.
C. Parma, 'Plotinische Motive in Augustins Begriff der Civitas Dei', *VC* 22 (1968) 45-48.
D.M. Parrott – R. McL.Wilson, 'The Acts of Peter and the Twelve Apostles', in: J.M. Robinson (ed.), *The Nag Hammadi Library in English*, Leiden 1977, 265-270.
O. Perler, 'Le «De unitate» (chap. IV-V) de saint Cyprien interprété par saint Augustin', *AM*, II, 835-858.
——, *Les voyages de saint Augustin*, Paris 1969.
L. Pernveden, *The Concept of the Church in the Shepherd of Hermas*, Lund 1966.
D. Pesce, *Città terrena e città celeste nel pensiero antico (Platone, Cicerone, S. Agostino)*, Firenze 1957.
C. Peters, *Das Diatessaron Tatians*, Rome 1939.
M. Peters, 'Augustins erste Bekehrung', in: *Harnack-Ehrung*, Leipzig 1921, 195-211.
E. Peterson, 'Kaiser Augustus im Urteil des antiken Christentums', *Hochland* 30 (1932-1933), 289-299.
——, *Der Monotheismus als politisches Problem. Ein Beitrag zur Geschichte der politischen Theologie im Imperium Romanum*, Leipzig 1935, in: E. Peterson, *Theologische Traktate*, München 1951, 45-147.
S. Pétrement, *Le dualisme chez Platon, les gnostiques et les manichéens*, Paris 1947.
G. Pfligersdorffer, 'Zu den Grundlagen des augustinischen Begriffspaares «uti-frui»', *WSt* 84 (1971) 195-224.
A. Pincherle, 'Da Ticonio a Sant'Agostino', *RicRel* 1 (1925) 443-466.
J.C. Plumpe, 'Mors secunda', in: *Mélanges de Ghellinck*, I, Gembloux 1951, 387-403.
H.J. Polotsky, 'Manichäismus' (1935), in: Widengren (Hrsg.), *Manichäismus*, 101-144.
M. Pontet, *L'Exégèse de S. Augustin prédicateur*, Paris s.a..
J.H.J. v.d. Pot, *De periodisering der geschiedenis. Een overzicht der theorieën*, 's-Gravenhage 1951.
R. Pottier, *Saint Augustin le Berbère*, Paris 1945.
H.-Ch. Puech, *Le Manichéisme. Son fondateur, sa doctrine*, Paris 1949.
——, 'Gnostische Evangelien und verwandte Dokumente', in: Hennecke and Schneemelcher (Hrsg.), *NTAp*, I, 158-271.
——, 'Liturgie et pratiques rituelles dans le Manichéisme (suite)', *ACF* 59 (1959) 264-269.
——, 'Musique et hymnologie manichéennes', *Encyclopédie des musiques sacrées*, I, Paris 1968, 353-386.

P. de Puniet, 'Catéchuménat', *DACL* 2 (1925) 2579-2621.
A. Quacquarelli, *La concezione della Storia nei Padri prima di S. Agostino*, I, Roma 1955.
J. Quasten, *Patrology*, I – III, Utrecht-Antwerp/Westminster, Md. 1962-1963.
G. Quispel, 'Der gnostische Anthropos und die jüdische Tradition' (1954), in: Quispel, *GS*, I, 173-195.
——, *Makarius, das Thomasevangelium und das Lied von der Perle*, Leiden 1967.
——, 'The Discussion of Judaic Christianity' (1968), in: Quispel, *GS*, II, 146-158.
——, 'Manicheans', *Man, Myth & Magic* 61 (1971) 1721-1724.
——, 'Mani et la tradition évangélique des judéo-chrétiens', in: *Judéo-christianisme*, 143-150.
——, 'Mani the Apostle of Jesus Christ' (1972), in: Quispel, *GS*, II, 230-237.
——, 'The Birth of the Child. Some Gnostic and Jewish Aspects' (1973), in: Quispel, *GS*, I, 221-239.
——, 'Saint Augustin et l'Évangile selon Thomas', in: *Mélanges d'histoire des réligions offerts à Henri-Charles Puech*, Paris 1974, 375-378.
——, *Gnostic Studies*, I – II, Istanbul 1974-1975 (= *GS*, I – II).
——, *Tatian and the Gospel of Thomas. Studies in the History of the Western Diatessaron*, Leiden 1975.
——, *The secret Book of Revelation*, New York 1979.
——, 'African Christianity before Minucius Felix and Tertullian', in: Den Boeft and Kessels (eds.), *Actus*, 257-335.
——, 'Judaism, Judaic Christianity and Gnosis', in: Logan and Wedderburn (eds.), *The New Testament and Gnosis*, 46-68.
G. von Rad, 'Das Wort Gottes und die Geschichte im Alten Testament' (1941), in: Von Rad, *Gottes Wirken*, 191-212.
——, 'Die deuteronomistische Geschichtstheologie in den Königsbüchern' (1947), in: G. von Rad, *Gesammelte Studien zum Alten Testament*, München 1958, 189-204.
——, 'Theologische Geschichtsschreibung im Alten Testament' (1948), in: Von Rad, *Gottes Wirken*, 175-190.
——, *Gottes Wirken in Israel. Vorträge zum Alten Testament*, Neukirchen 1974.
H.L. Ramsay, 'Le commentaire de l'apocalypse par Beatus de Liebana', *RHLR* 7 (1902) 419-447.
J. Ratzinger, *Volk und Haus Gottes in Augustins Lehre von der Kirche*, München 1954.
——, 'Herkunft und Sinn der Civitas-Lehre Augustins. Begegnung und Auseinandersetzung mit Wilhelm Kamlah', *AM*, II, 965-979.
——, 'Beobachtungen zum Kirchenbegriff des Tyconius im *Liber regularum*', *REA* 2 (1956) 173-185.
J. Reiling, *Hermas and Christian Prophecy. A Study of the Eleventh Mandate*, Leiden 1973.
J.H. Reinkens, *Die Geschichtsphilosophie des hl. Augustinus*, Schaffhausen 1866.
R. Reitzenstein, 'Augustin als antiker und als mittelalterlicher Mensch', *Vorträge der Bibliothek Warburg*, II, 1, Leipzig-Berlin 1924, 28-65.
P. Rentschka, *Die Dekalogkatechese des hl. Augustinus*, Kempten 1905.
E. Repo, *Der 'Weg' als Selbstbezeichnung des Urchristentums*, Helsinki 1964.
H. Reuter, *Augustinische Studien*, Gotha 1887 (repr. Aalen 1967).
J. Ries, 'Une version liturgique de l'*Epistola Fundamenti* de Mani réfutée par Saint Augustin', *SP* XI (*TU* 108), Berlin 1972, 341-349.
——, 'Commendements de la justice et vie missionaire dans l'église de Mani', in: M. Krause (ed.), *Gnosis and Gnosticism*, Leiden 1977, 93-106.
J.M. Robinson (ed.), *The Nag Hammadi Library in English*, Leiden 1977
J. Roldanus, *Vreemdeling zonder vaste woonplaats. Vroegchristelijke gedachten over geloof en vreemdelingschap*, Leiden 1980.
——, 'Tweeërlei burgerschap van de christen', *K&T* 36 (1985) 265-283.
H. Rondet, 'Pax tranquillitas ordinis', *Ciudad*, II, 343-364.

——, 'Essais sur la chronologie des *Enarrationes in Psalmos*', *BLE* 61 (1960) 111-127, 258-286.

H.W.A. van Rooijen-Dijkman, *De vita beata. Het zevende boek van de 'Divinae Institutiones' van Lactantius. Analyse en bronnenonderzoek*, Assen 1967.

W. Rordorf, 'Un chapitre d'éthique judéo-chrétienne: les deux voies', in: *Judéo-christianisme*, 109-128.

E. Rose, *Die manichäische Christologie*, Wiesbaden 1979.

M. Rothenhaeusler – Ph. Oppenheim, 'Apotaxis', *RAC* 1 (1950) 558-564.

F. de Rougemont, *Les deux cités. La philosophie de l'histoire aux différents âges de l'humanité*, I – II, Paris 1874.

O. Rousseau, 'Les Pères de l'Église et la théologie du temps', *MD* 30 (1952) 36-55.

K. Rudolph, 'Die Bedeutung des Kölner Mani-Codex für die Manichäismusforschung. Vorläufige Anmerkungen', in: *Mélanges d'histoire des réligions offerts à Henri-Charles Puech*, Paris 1974, 471-486.

——, *Die Gnosis. Wesen und Geschichte einer spätantiken Religion*, Göttingen 1978.

——, 'Der Mandäismus in der neueren Gnosisforschung' in: Aland et al. (Hrsg.), *Gnosis*, 244-277.

G. Ruhbach, 'Die politische Theologie Eusebs von Caesarea' (1974), in: G.Ruhbach (Hrsg.), *Die Kirche angesichts der konstantinischen Wende*, Darmstadt 1976, 236-258.

S. Runciman, *The Medieval Manichee. A Study of the Christian Dualist Heresy*, Cambridge 1955[2].

T. Säve-Söderbergh, *Studies in the Coptic Manichaean Psalm-Book. Prosody and Mandaean Parallels*, Uppsala et al. 1949.

E. Salin, *Civitas Dei*, Tübingen 1926.

K. Sallmann, 'Varro', *KP* 5 (1979) 1131-1140.

H. Sasse, 'Aiōn', *TWNT* I (1933) 197-209.

H.H. Schaeder, 'Urform und Fortbildungen des manichäischen Systems', *Vorträge der Bibliothek Warburg*, Leipzig 1927, 65-157.

H.M. Schenke, 'Die Taten des Petrus und der zwölf Apostel', *TLZ* 97 (1973) 13-19.

G. Schille, 'Zur urchristlichen Tauflehre. Stilistische Beobachtungen am Barnabasbrief', *ZNW* 49 (1958) 31-52.

O. Schilling, *Die Staats- und Soziallehre des hl. Augustin*, Freiburg 1910.

A. Schindler (Hrsg.), *Monotheismus als politisches Problem? Erik Peterson und die Kritik der politischen Theologie*, Gütersloh 1978.

——, 'Augustin/Augustinismus I', *TRE* 4 (1979) 645-698.

C. Schmidt – H.J. Polotsky – H. Ibscher, 'Ein Mani-Fund in Ägypten. Originalschriften des Mani und seiner Schüler', *SPAW* 1 (1933) 4-90.

E.G. Schmidt, 'Karneades', *KP* 3 (1979) 124-126.

F. Schmidt, 'Une source essénienne chez Commodien', in: M. Philonenko et al., *Pseudépigraphes de l'Ancien Testament et manuscripts de la Mer Morte*, I, Paris 1967, 11-25.

K.L. Schmidt, 'Basileia', *TWNT* I (1933) 579-595.

——, 'Diaspora', *TWNT* II (1935) 98-104.

——, *Die Polis in Kirche und Welt. Eine lexikographische und exegetische Untersuchung*, Zürich 1940.

K.L. Schmidt – M.A. Schmidt, 'Paroikos', *TWNT* V (1954) 840-852.

R. Schmidt, 'Aetates mundi. Die Weltalter als Gliederungsprinzip der Geschichte', *ZKG* 67 (1955-1956) 288-317.

W. Schneemelcher, *Bibliographia Patristica*, Berlin 1959 ff.

——, 'Petrusakten', in: Hennecke and Schneemelcher, *NTAp*, II, 177-221.

W. Schneemelcher – K. Schäferdiek, 'Apostelgeschichten des 2. und 3. Jahrhunderts. Einleitung', in: Hennecke and Schneemelcher, *NTAp*, II, 110-125.

K. Schneider, 'Achteck', *RAC* 1 (1950) 72-74.
E. Schneweis, *Angels and Demons according to Lactantius*, Washington 1944.
H.J. Schoeps, *Theologie und Geschichte des Judenchristentums*, Tübingen 1949.
——, *Aus frühchristlicher Zeit. Religionsgeschichtliche Untersuchungen*, Tübingen 1950.
——, 'Das Judenchristentum in den Pseudoklementinen', *ZRGG* 11 (1959) 72-77.
——, 'Der Ursprung des Bösen und das Problem der Theodizee im pseudoklementinischen Roman', in: *Judéo-christianisme*, 129-141.
H. Scholz, *Glaube und Unglaube in der Weltgeschichte. Ein Kommentar zu Augustins De civitate Dei*, Leipzig 1911 (repr. 1967).
H.-H. Schrey (Hrsg.), *Reich Gottes und Welt. Die Lehre Luthers von den zwei Reichen*, Darmstadt 1969.
A. Schröder, *Des heiligen Kirchenvaters Aurelius Augustinus zweiundzwanzig Bücher über den Gottesstaat*, I – III, Kempten-München 1911-1916.
E. Schürer, *Geschichte des jüdischen Volkes im Zeitalter Jesu Christi*, III, Leipzig 1909[4].
K.-H. Schwarte, *Die Vorgeschichte der augustinischen Weltalterlehre*, Bonn 1966.
A. Seeberg, *Der Katechismus der Urchristenheit*, Leipzig 1903 (repr. München 1966).
——, *Die beiden Wege und das Aposteldekret*, Leipzig 1906.
——, *Die Didache des Judentums und der Urchristenheit*, Leipzig 1908.
R. Seeberg, *Lehrbuch der Dogmengeschichte*, II, Leipzig 1923[3] (repr. Basel 1953[4]).
O. Seeck, *Geschichte des Untergangs der antiken Welt*, VI, Stuttgart 1920 (repr. Darmstadt 1966).
B. Seidel, *Die Lehre vom Staat beim hl. Augustinus*, Breslau 1909.
G.J. Seyrich, *Die Geschichtsphilosophie Augustins nach seiner Schrift 'De Civitate Dei'*, Chemnitz 1891.
F.H. Sihler, *From Augustus to Augustine*, Cambridge 1923.
M. Simon, 'Le Judaïsme berbère dans l'Afrique ancienne' (1946), in: Simon, *Recherches*, 30-87.
——, 'Punique ou Berbère? Note sur la situation linguistique dans l'Afrique Romaine' (1955), in: Simon, *Recherches*, 88-100.
——, *Recherches d'Histoire Judéo-Chrétienne*, Paris-La Haye 1962.
——, *Verus Israel. Étude sur les relations entre Chrétiens en Juifs dans l'Empire romain (135-425)*, Paris 1964[2].
——, 'Problèmes du judéo-christianisme', in: *Aspects du judéo-christianisme*, 1-16.
——, 'Réflexions sur le judéo-christianisme', in: J. Neusner (ed.), *Christianity, Judaism and other Greco-Roman cults. Studies for Morton Smith at sixty*, II, Leiden 1975, 53-76.
A. Sizoo, 'De geschiedbeschouwing van Augustinus', in: *De zin der geschiedenis*, Wageningen 1944, 58-78.
——, *Augustinus over den staat*, Kampen 1947.
——, 'Augustinus op de grens der oude en der nieuwe wereld', in: A. Sizoo – D. Nauta, *Augustinus. Redevoeringen ... 12 november 1954*, Kampen 1954, 5-21.
——, *Augustinus. Leven en werken*, Kampen 1957.
J.H. Sleeman – G. Pollet, *Lexicon Plotinianum*, Leiden-Louvain 1980.
B. Smalley, 'Thomas Waleys O.P.', *AFP* 25 (1954) 50-107.
H. Smitskamp, *Groen van Prinsterer als historicus*, Amsterdam 1940.
P. Smulders, 'De Pelgrim naar het Absolute. Eeuwigheidsverlangen en tijdelijke waarden bij Augustinus', *Bijdragen* 16 (1955) 136-155.
G.F. Snyder, *The Shepherd of Hermas*, London-Toronto 1968.
A. Solignac, 'Le cercle milanais', *BA* 14, 529-536.
——, 'Marius Victorinus', *DS* 10 (1978) 616-623.
M. Spanneut, *Permanence du stoïcisme. De Zénon à Malraux*, Gembloux 1973.
——, 'Le stoïcisme et saint Augustin', in: *Formula futuri. Studi in onore del Cardinale Michele Pellegrino*, Torino 1975, 896-914.

J. Spörl, 'Augustinus, Schöpfer einer Staatslehre?', *HJ* 74 (1955) 62-78.
G. Stählin, 'Xenos', *TWNT* V (1954) 1-36.
E. Stakemeier, *Civitas Dei. Die Geschichtstheologie des hl. Augustinus als Apologie der Kirche*, Paderborn 1955.
V. Stegemann, *Augustins Gottesstaat*, Tübingen 1928.
W. Steinmann – O. Wermelinger, *Aurelius Augustinus. Vom ersten katechetischen Unterricht*, München 1985.
(H.L. Strack-) P. Billerbeck, *Kommentar zum Neuen Testament aus Talmud und Midrasch*, I-IV, München 1926-1928.
H. Strathmann, 'Polis', *TWNT* VI (1959) 516-535.
J. Straub, 'Augustins Sorge um die regeneratio imperii. Das Imperium Romanum als civitas terrena', *HJ* 73 (1954) 36-60.
L. Straume-Zimmermann, *Ciceros Hortensius*, Bern-Frankfurt 1976.
G. Strecker, *Das Judenchristentum in den Pseudoklementinen*, Berlin 1958.
——, 'Die Kerygmata Petrou', in: Hennecke and Schneemelcher, *NTAp*, II, 63-80.
M.-B. von Stritzky, 'Beobachtungen zur Verbindung zwischen Gregor von Nyssa und Augustin', *VC* 28 (1974) 176-185.
M.J. Suggs, 'The Christian Two Ways Tradition: its Antiquity, Form and Function', in: *Studies in the New Testament and Early Christian Literature* (Essays in Honour of Allen P. Wikgren), Leiden 1972, 60-74.
M. Tardieu, *Le manichéisme*, Paris 1981.
E. TeSelle, *Augustine's Strategy as an Apologist*, Villanova 1974.
M. Testard, *Saint Augustin et Cicéron*, I – II, Paris 1958.
W. Theiler, *Porphyrius und Augustin*, Halle 1933.
——, 'Plotin zwischen Plato und Stoa', in: *Entretiens sur l'Antiquité classique*, V, *Les sources de Plotin*, Genève 1957, 63-86.
W. Thimme, *Aurelius Augustinus, Vom Gottesstaat (De civitate Dei)*, I – II, München 1977-1978.
F. Thomas, *St. Augustin, La Cité de Dieu*, Genève 1886.
K. Thraede, 'Beiträge zur Datierung Commodians', *JbAC* 2 (1959) 90-114.
——, 'Abecedarius', *JbAC* 3 (1960) 159.
——, 'Das antike Rom in Augustins De Civitate Dei. Recht und Grenzen eines verjährten Themas', *JbAC* 20 (1977) 90-148.
——, 'Gottesstaat (Civitas Dei)', *RAC* 12 (1983) 58-81.
G. Toscani, *Teologia della Chiesa in sant'Ambrogio*, Milano 1974.
E. Troeltsch, *Augustin, die christliche Antike und das Mittelalter. Im Anschluss an die Schrift 'De Civitate Dei'*, München-Berlin 1915 (repr. Aalen 1963).
A. Tuilier, 'Didache', *TRE* 8 (1981) 731-736.
A. Turck, *Evangélisation et Catéchèse aux deux premiers siècles*, Paris 1962.
——, 'Catéchein et Catéchèsis chez les premiers Pères', *RSPT* 47 (1963) 361-372.
——, 'Aux origines du catéchuménat', *RSPT* 48 (1964) 20-31.
H. Tur-Sinai (Torczyner), 'The Origin of the Alphabet', *JQS* 41 (1950) 277-301.
F. Vattioni, 'Sant'Agostino e la civiltà punica', *Aug* 8 (1968) 434-467.
A.C. de Veer, 'Rom. 14,23^b dans l'oeuvre de saint Augustin (Omne quod non est ex fide peccatum est)', *RA* 8 (1972) 149-185.
G. Verbeke, 'Augustin et le stoïcisme', *RA* 1 (1958) 67-89.
K. Vilhelmson, *Laktanz und die Kosmogonie des spätantiken Synkretismus*, Tartu 1940.
C.J. de Vogel, 'Plato in de latere en late oudheid, bij heidenen en christenen', *Lampas* 6 (1973) 230-254.
——, 'Platonism and Christianity: A mere antagonism or a profound common ground?', *VC* 39 (1985) 1-62.

P. Volz, *Die Eschatologie der jüdischen Gemeinde im neutestamentlichen Zeitalter*, Tübingen 1934.
M. Wacht, 'Güterlehre', *RAC* 13 (Lieferung 97, 1984) 59-150.
A. Wachtel, *Beiträge zur Geschichtstheologie des Aurelius Augustinus*, Bonn 1960.
Chr. Walter, *Der Ertrag der Auseinandersetzung mit den Manichäern für das hermeneutische Problem bei Augustin*, Diss. München 1972.
G. Wanke, 'Bibel, I', *TRE* 6 (1980) 1-8.
J.H. Waszink, *Q.S.F. Tertulliani De anima, edited with introduction and commentary*, Amsterdam 1947.
——, 'Pompa diaboli', *VC* 1 (1947) 13-41.
——, 'Der Platonismus und die altchristliche Gedankenwelt', in: *Entretiens sur l'Antiquité classique, III, Recherches sur la tradition platonicienne*, Genève 1955, 139-179.
H.B. Weijland, *Augustinus en de kerkelijke tucht*, Kampen 1965.
H.C. Weiland, *Het Oordeel der Kerkvaders over het Orakel*, Amsterdam 1935.
O. Weinreich, *Triskaidekadische Studien. Beiträge zur Geschichte der Zahlen*, Giessen 1916 (repr. Berlin 1967).
A.G. Weiss, *Die altkirchliche Pädagogik dargestellt in Katechumenat und Katechese der ersten sechs Jahrhunderten*, Freiburg 1869.
C. Wendel, *Die griechisch-römische Buchbeschreibung verglichen mit der des Vorderen Orients*, Halle 1949.
K. Wengst, 'Barnabasbrief', *TRE* 5 (1980) 238-241.
P. Wernberg-Møller, *The Manual of Discipline*, Leiden 1957.
G. Widengren, (Hrsg.) *Der Manichäismus*, Darmstadt 1977.
——, 'Der Manichäismus. Kurzgefasste Geschichte der Problemforschung', in: Aland et al. (Hrsg.), *Gnosis*, 278-315.
G. Wijdeveld, *De Belijdenissen van Aurelius Augustinus*, Utrecht-Merksem 1963.
——, *Aurelius Augustinus, Het eerste geloofsonderricht*, Baarn 1982.
——, *Aurelius Augustinus, De stad van God*, Baarn-Amsterdam 1983 (1984²).
A. Wilmart, 'La tradition des grands ouvrages de saint Augustin', *MAg*, II, 257-315.
W. Windelband, *Lehrbuch der Geschichte der Philosophie*, hrsg. von H. Heimsoeth, Tübingen 1957¹⁵.
J.C.M. van Winden, *'Idee' en 'Materie' in de vroeg-christelijke uitleg van de beginwoorden van Genesis. Een hoofdstuk uit de ontmoeting tussen Griekse filosofie en christelijk denken*, Amsterdam-Oxford-New York 1985.
H. Windisch, *Der Barnabasbrief*, Tübingen 1920 (*HNT*, Erg.-Band).
L. Wohleb, *Die lateinische Übersetzung der Didache kritisch und sprachlich untersucht*, Paderborn 1913.
J. Wytzes, *Der Streit um den Altar der Viktoria*, Amsterdam 1936.
——, *Augustinus: 'De Staat Gods'*, Kampen 1946.
——, 'Augustinus en Rome', *Hermeneus* 26 (1954) 41-50, 68-73.
Th. Zahn, *Der Hirt des Hermas untersucht*, Gotha 1868.
——, *Geschichte des neutestamentlichen Kanons*, I – II, Erlangen-Leipzig 1888-1892 (repr. Hildesheim-New York 1975).
O. Zwierlein, 'Der Fall Roms im Spiegel der Kirchenväter', *ZPE* 32 (1978) 45-80.

INDICES

I. INDEX AUGUSTINIANUS

II. INDEX OF NAMES